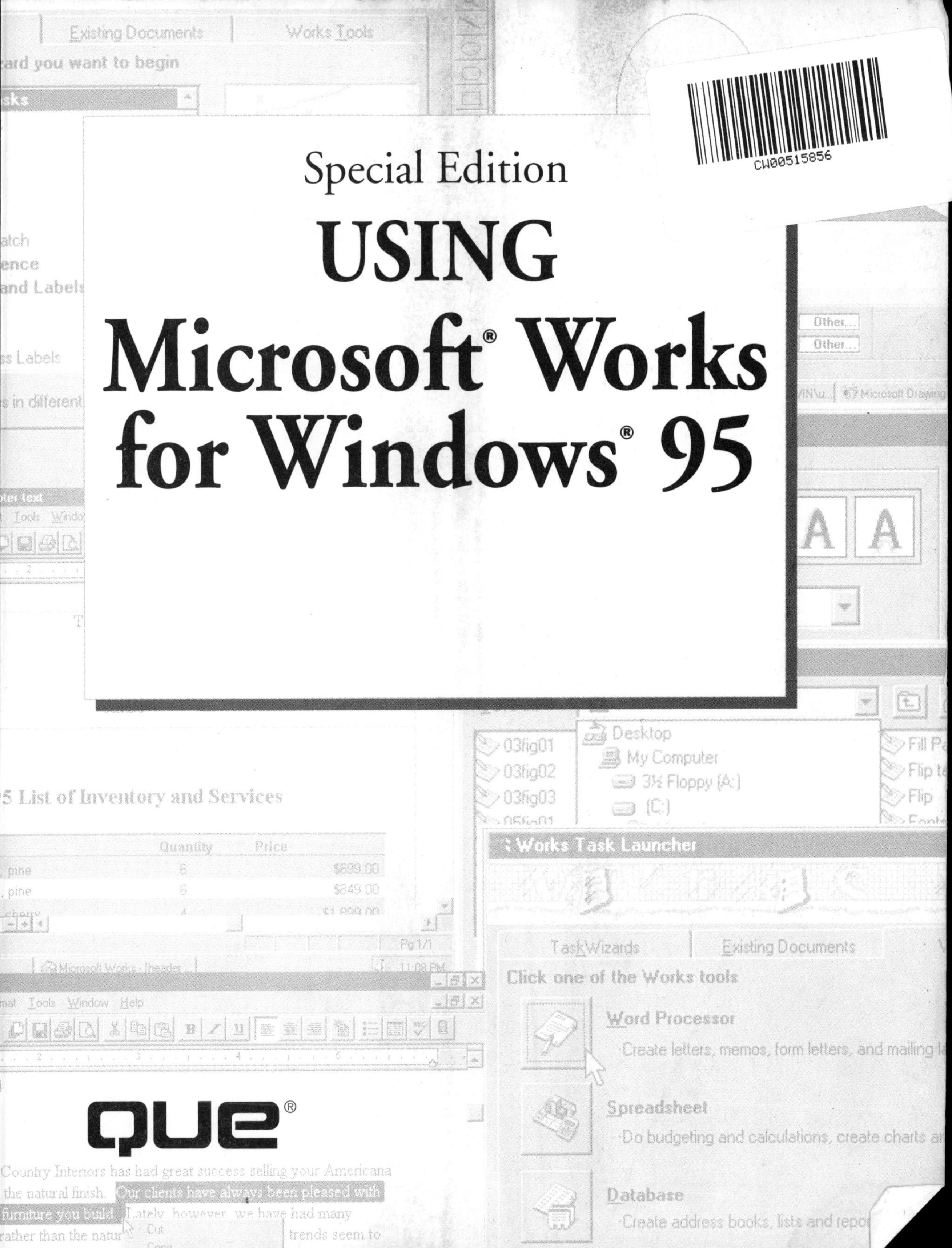

Special Edition
USING
Microsoft® Works
for Windows® 95
que®

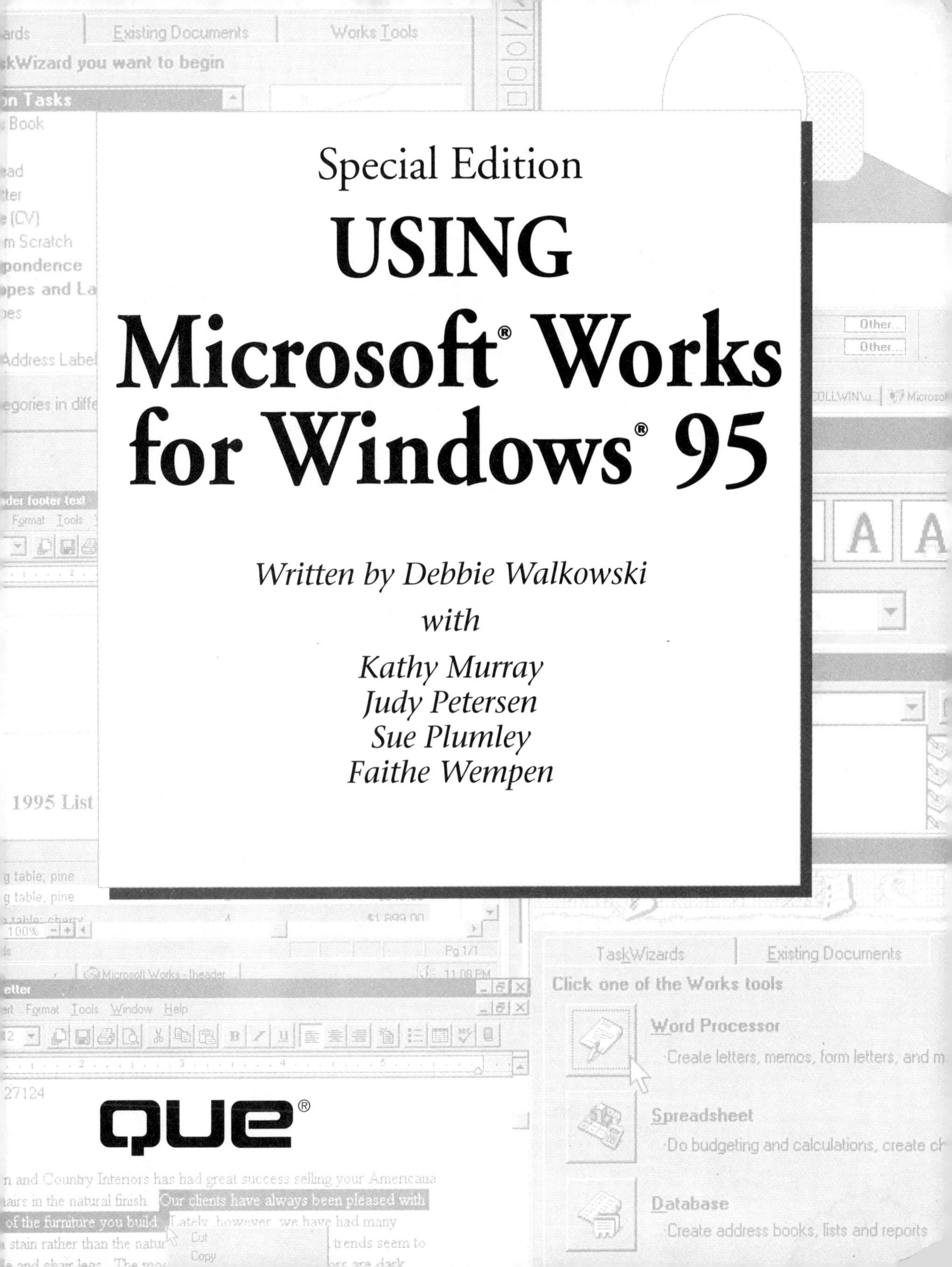
Special Edition
USING
Microsoft® Works
for Windows® 95
Written by Debbie Walkowski
with
Kathy Murray
Judy Petersen
Sue Plumley
Faithe Wempen
QUE®

Special Edition Using Microsoft Works for Windows 95

Library of Congress Catalog No.: 95-078883

ISBN: 0-7897-0462-5

97 96 95 6 5 4 3 2 1

Interpretation of the printing code: the rightmost double-digit number is the year of the book's printing; the rightmost single-digit number, the number of the book's printing. For example, a printing code of 95-1 shows that the first printing of the book occurred in 1995.

Screen reproductions in this book were created using Collage Plus from Inner Media, Inc., Hollis, NH.

Composed in *Stone Serif* and *MCPdigital* by Que Corporation

Credits

President
Roland Elgey

Vice President and Publisher
Marie Butler-Knight

Associate Publisher
Don Roche Jr.

Editorial Services Director
Elizabeth Keaffaber

Managing Editor
Michael Cunningham

Director of Marketing
Lynn E. Zingraf

Senior Series Editor
Chris Nelson

Acquisitions Editor
Deborah F. Abshier

Product Directors
Lorna Gentry
Rob Tidrow

Product Development Specialists
Lisa Bucki
Brian Underdahl
Keith Davenport

Production Editor
Theresa Mathias

Editors
Lisa Gebken
Lori Lyons
Christine Prakel

Assistant Product Marketing Manager
Kim Margolius

Technical Editors
Ron Holmes, M.B.A.
Greg Newman

Technical Specialist
Cari Skaggs

Acquisitions Coordinator
Tracy M. Williams

Operations Coordinator
Patty Brooks

Editorial Assistant
Jill Byus

Book Designer
Ruth Harvey

Cover Designer
Dan Armstrong

Production Team
Angela D. Bannan
Maxine Dillingham
Chad Dressler
Joan Evan
DiMonique Ford
Mike Henry
Daryl Kessler
Julie Quinn
Bobbi Satterfield
Jody York

Indexer
Ginny Bess

For my husband, Frank, my steadfast supporter, my biggest fan, and my voice of reason when things get a little too crazy.

About the Authors

Debbie Walkowski has worked in the computer industry since 1981 writing documentation, designing user interfaces, and teaching computer courses. Her company, The Writing Works, specializes in writing computer self-help books and providing writing services to companies such as Microsoft Corporation, Digital Equipment Corporation, and AT&T Wireless Services. Debbie has a bachelor's degree in scientific and technical communication and has authored and co-authored thirteen books on popular computer software, including WordPerfect, Microsoft Excel, Microsoft PowerPoint, Microsoft Office, Microsoft Works for DOS and Works for Windows, Microsoft Project, Lotus 1-2-3, Quicken, and Professional Write Plus.

Katherine Murray is the author of several computer books, including *Using Microsoft Money* and *Using PFS: First Choice*, 2nd Edition, and is the owner of reVisions Plus, Inc., a company specializing in publishing and training services.

Judy Petersen provides software training and support through a retail facility for the more popular word processing and spreadsheet programs. In her own business, Judy is a computer software consultant and trainer for businesses and individuals in the Tallahassee area and provides abstracts of titles for firms performing environmental audits of real estate property throughout the Southeastern U.S. She has been a contributing author of Que's *Using WordPerfect 6, Using WordPerfect 6 for Windows, Using WordPerfect 6.1 for Windows, Using PC Tools 8.0* and *Using PC Tools for Windows, Killer WordPerfect 6 Utilities, Killer Windows Utilities,* as well as the revision author for Que's *Computer User's Dictionary*, 5th Edition.

Sue Plumley owns and operates Humble Opinions, a consulting firm that offers training in popular software programs and network installation and maintenance. Sue's husband, Carlos, joined her company two years ago as a CNE. Sue is the author of twelve Que books, including *Crystal Clear DOS, Crystal Clear Word 6,* and *Microsoft Office Quick Reference* and co-author of sixteen additional books, including *Using WordPerfect 6 for DOS, Using OS/2 2.1,* and *Using Microsoft Office* for Que and its sister imprints.

Faithe Wempen is a freelance writer, editor, and computer software instructor from Indianapolis, Indiana. She has a Masters degree in English from Purdue University and has edited and/or written over 100 books for Macmillan Computer Publishing.

Acknowledgments

An author rarely writes a book completely alone. My appreciation and thanks to a terrific acquisitions editor, Debbie Abshier, for her thoroughness and professionalism, and to authors Kathy Murray, Judy Petersen, and Faithe Wempen for doing an excellent job of updating sections of this book for version 4.0 of Works. I'd also like to express a special thanks to Sue Plumley and Diane Koers, two professional women who work with or teach Works to students and business professionals. Thanks to both Sue and Diane for offering their expertise and unique ideas for using Works to accomplish real-world, down-to-earth, practical business tasks. My appreciation, also, to Carl von Papp, instructor at Bellevue Community College, Bellevue, Washington, for contributing his creative ideas for using Works. Finally, I'd like to thank Keith Davenport, Theresa Mathias, Ron Holmes, and Greg Newman for their expert editing and constructive comments and suggestions. These professionals and many others behind the scenes all contribute to the quality of this book.

We'd Like to Hear from You!

As part of our continuing effort to produce books of the highest possible quality, Que would like to hear your comments. To stay competitive, we *really* want you, as a computer book reader and user, to let us know what you like or dislike most about this book or other Que products.

You can mail comments, ideas, or suggestions for improving future editions to the address below, or send us a fax at (317) 581-4663. For the online inclined, Macmillan Computer Publishing has a forum on CompuServe (type **GO QUEBOOKS** at any prompt) through which our staff and authors are available for questions and comments. The address of our Internet site is **http://www.mcp.com** (World Wide Web).

In addition to exploring our forum, please feel free to contact me personally to discuss your opinions of this book: I'm at 76507,2715 on CompuServe and **karnoff@que.mcp.com** on the Internet.

Thanks in advance—your comments will help us to continue publishing the best books available on computer topics in today's market.

Kathie-Jo Arnoff
Title Manager
Que Corporation
201 W. 103rd Street
Indianapolis, Indiana 46290
USA

Contents at a Glance

Works Basics

Word Processing

Spreadsheets and Charting

Databases

Adding Visual Interest

Integration and Communications

Contents

25 Using WordArt and Note-It 515

VI Integration and Communications 531

26 Using the Works Tools Together 533

Introduction

If you're reading this page, it's probably because you're trying to decide whether or not to buy this book. "Do I really need it?" you're thinking. "What can it do for me?" "How is it different from other Works books?"

The answer to the first question is a decided "Yes!" You need this book because Microsoft Works 4.0 for Windows 95 doesn't include a manual anymore. Oh, sure, it comes with the Works Companion that, in less than 100 pages, gives you a high-level introduction to the many uses for Works. And, of course, there *is* new and improved online help. But will these be enough to answer all your questions or get you out of a jam when you're stuck? More importantly, will these resources help you get the most out of Works?

Don't count on it. Most software vendors want you to believe their programs are *so* intuitive, *so* easy to use, you'll never need a manual. Well, it simply isn't true. And it doesn't mean you're stupid, either. It just means that they're wrong.

So, what can this book do for you? And how is it different from other Works books? Well to begin with, it's far more than a reference manual. Usually arranged by function, a reference manual describes how to use a command. Period. It doesn't give you an overview of a situation, tell you how to approach a problem, or describe which method might best suit your needs. A reference manual simply tells you, "If you want to use this command, here's how." (And assumes that you know *which* command to use in the first place!)

In contrast to a reference manual, *Special Edition Using Works 4.0 for Windows 95* works the way you do; by recognizing that you don't just "use commands," you have *tasks* to accomplish. This book describes real-life tasks, gives you options for approaching tasks, and presents different ways to accomplish them. Along the way, you receive cautions where appropriate, tips for making tasks easier to accomplish, notes for additional information, and cross-references to related topics. This book even provides answers for those times when you get yourself into trouble. It doesn't leave anything out—it's a comprehensive book designed to teach you about everything you can do with Works.

Who Should Use This Book?

Special Edition Using Microsoft Works 4.0 for Windows 95 is for anyone who wants to learn how to use Works in a practical way. This book leads you through the basic steps involved in creating documents, spreadsheets, and databases—and builds on that foundation by teaching you more sophisticated features. You then learn how to use the additional tools Works provides such as Microsoft Draw, WordArt, ClipArt, and Note-It. You discover how to put pieces from various applications together and integrate them into a single document. Finally, you learn how to connect to other computers to read and gather information that you can use in the Works documents you create.

How To Use This Book

You can read selected chapters in *Special Edition Using Microsoft Works 4.0 for Windows 95;* or you can work through the book from beginning to end. If you choose not to read the chapters sequentially, begin with the first three chapters of the book before moving on to one of the specific sections.

This book opens with an introduction to the four components of Works and the basic steps for getting started with the program. The book then leads you through beginning and advanced chapters for the word processing, spreadsheet, and database programs. Next you learn how to use Microsoft Draw, WordArt, ClipArt, and Note-It. And finally, you learn about the communications application.

Following is a brief look at the contents of each chapter in *Special Edition Using Microsoft Works 4.0 for Windows 95*:

Chapter 1, "Introducing Microsoft Works 4.0 for Windows 95," describes the four basic Works applications as well as the Works accessories: Microsoft Draw, WordArt, ClipArt, and Note-It. This chapter also tells you how to integrate information from any of the four Works applications into a single document.

Chapter 2, "Getting Started with Works for Windows," tells you how to start and exit the program. You get a tour of the basic Works window, and instructions for using the mouse, keyboard, dialog boxes, and toolbars. In addition, you learn how to change your view of a document, wrap text within a document window, and get help when you need it.

In Chapter 3, "Working with Documents, TaskWizards, and Templates," you discover how to create, save, copy, and retrieve documents and how to use TaskWizards to help you create specific types of documents. You also learn how to create models, or *templates*, for documents that you use over and over again.

Chapter 4, "Creating, Saving, and Printing a Document," introduces you to the basic skills required to create a word processor document, move around in the document, correct minor errors, and then save and print the document when it's complete.

Chapter 5, "Editing a Document," teaches you how to select and change text by inserting, deleting, and typing over it. You also learn to move and copy text and undo changes that you make.

In Chapter 6, "Enhancing the Appearance of a Document," you learn all the tricks for making a document more attractive and readable, including changing the style and font of text, changing the alignment of paragraphs, indenting paragraphs and setting tab stops, and changing the line spacing in a document. You also learn about inserting page breaks in a document.

Chapter 7, "Working with Tables, Columns, and Inserted Objects," shows you how to create tables and format a document for multiple columns of text. You also learn how to move, size, and wrap text around inserted objects in a document.

Chapter 8, "Adding Headers, Footers, Footnotes, and Bookmarks to a Document," describes how to add repetitive text at the top and bottom of each page. You also learn how to cite references or add a comment to a document using footnotes, and how to find your place in a document using a bookmark.

In Chapter 9, "Checking Your Document," you learn how to view hidden characters in a document, how to search for text and replace text. To finish a document, you learn how to check for spelling errors and use the thesaurus.

Chapter 10, "Creating, Saving, and Printing a Spreadsheet," introduces you to the basic steps for creating a spreadsheet, moving around in the worksheet, and entering text and numbers in the cells. You also learn how to make changes to spreadsheet entries, enter simple formulas, save, and print a spreadsheet.

Chapter 11, "Working with Formulas and Functions," examines relative and absolute cell addressing, creating formulas using functions, and naming ranges of cells. You also learn the effects of moving, copying, and deleting formulas.

Chapter 12, "Enhancing the Appearance of a Spreadsheet," describes how to make a spreadsheet more attractive by applying number formats, changing the alignment of entries, choosing a font, size, color, and style for entries, and adjusting row height. You also learn how to add borders and patterns to cells. Finally, you see how to add repetitive text at the top and bottom of spreadsheet pages.

In Chapter 13, "Searching, Viewing, and Sorting a Spreadsheet," you discover how to find specific information in a spreadsheet and sort data in different ways. You also learn different viewing options, including zooming in and out, hiding rows or columns, freezing row and column headings, and displaying formulas in a spreadsheet rather than spreadsheet values.

Chapter 14, "Creating Charts," teaches you how to generate charts from spreadsheet data. You learn about the basic elements of a chart, and you learn how to create different chart types (for example, pie, bar, and XY). You also learn how to save, name, recall, and print a chart.

Chapter 15, "Editing and Enhancing a Chart," describes how to change the data plotted in a chart and how to enhance a chart with features such as titles, borders, grid lines, drop lines, legends, data markers, colors, and patterns.

Chapter 16, "Creating and Saving a Database File," introduces you to databases and database terminology. You learn basic skills for creating and saving a database file, using and customizing the Database toolbar, and switching between database views.

In Chapter 17, "Modifying a Database Form," you learn how to lay out a database form and create data entry fields.

Chapter 18, "Enhancing a Database Form," shows you how to spruce up your database forms with labels, fonts, rectangles, borders, colors, shading, drawings, pictures, Note-Its, and WordArt.

In Chapter 19, "Entering and Editing Data," you learn how to type data and save records. In addition, you learn to copy and move information and hide records.

Chapter 20, "Expanding Your Database Skills," teaches you how to sort and print records, use dates, times, math formulas and functions, protect your data, and format data in fields.

Chapter 21, "Retrieving Database Information," describes how to retrieve information from a database using specific criteria.

Chapter 22, "Creating a Database Report," tells you how to print database information in neatly formatted lists.

Chapter 23, "Customizing a Report," illustrates how to produce reports that require customized formatting and data selection and to print reports for use with other applications.

Chapter 24, "Using Microsoft Draw and ClipArt," introduces you to creating your own drawings by using Microsoft Draw or including prepared art in your files by choosing a file from the ClipArt gallery.

Chapter 25, "Using WordArt and Note-It," shows you how to create stylized text for your documents by choosing a unique font for your text, then bending, shaping, or curving it, and adding other effects such as borders, colors, and patterns. You also learn about Note-It, a tool that lets you add distinctive notes and annotations to your documents.

Chapter 26, "Using the Works Tools Together," teaches you how to copy information from one tool to another. You also learn how to *link* information, which causes data in one location to be updated automatically when the source data is changed.

Chapter 27, "Using Works with Non-Works Applications," explores how you can make use of other computer programs you own and use in combination with Works. You learn how to import and export files, copy text and objects between programs, size and scale objects in Works, and save and open files in other formats.

Chapter 28, "Creating Form Letters, Mail Labels, and Envelopes" describes how to merge database and word processor files to create and print form letters, mailing labels, and envelopes.

Chapter 29, "Communicating with Other Computers," first examines communications terms and then describes how to set up a new modem and specify all the required settings to establish communications with another computer or service. You learn how to save the settings in a file so you can use them again later. Also in this chapter are instructions for sending and receiving text and files.

Appendix, "Works for Windows Functions," lists all the functions included in Works, describes the arguments for each function, and provides an example of each. ❖

Part I

Works Basics

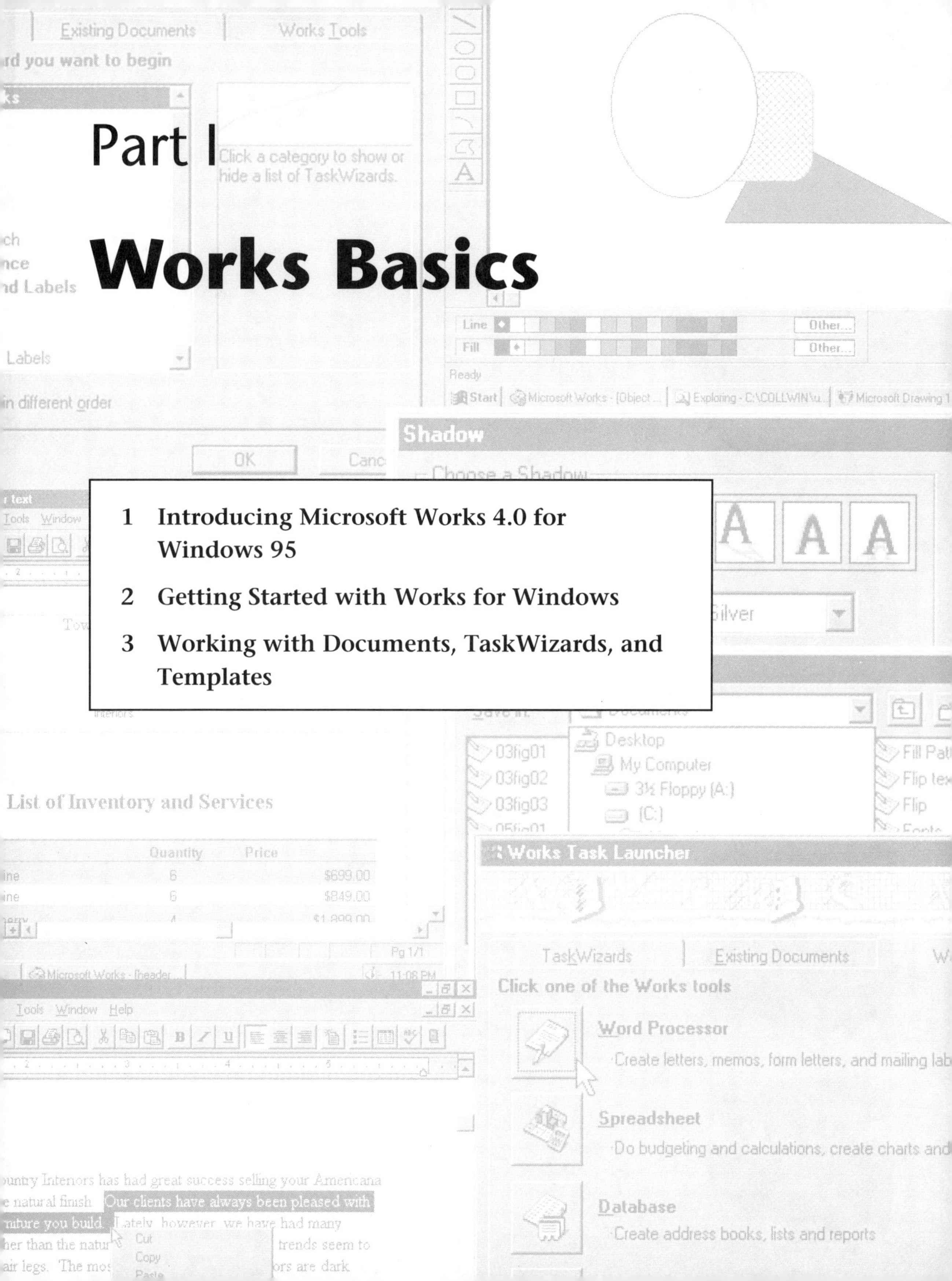

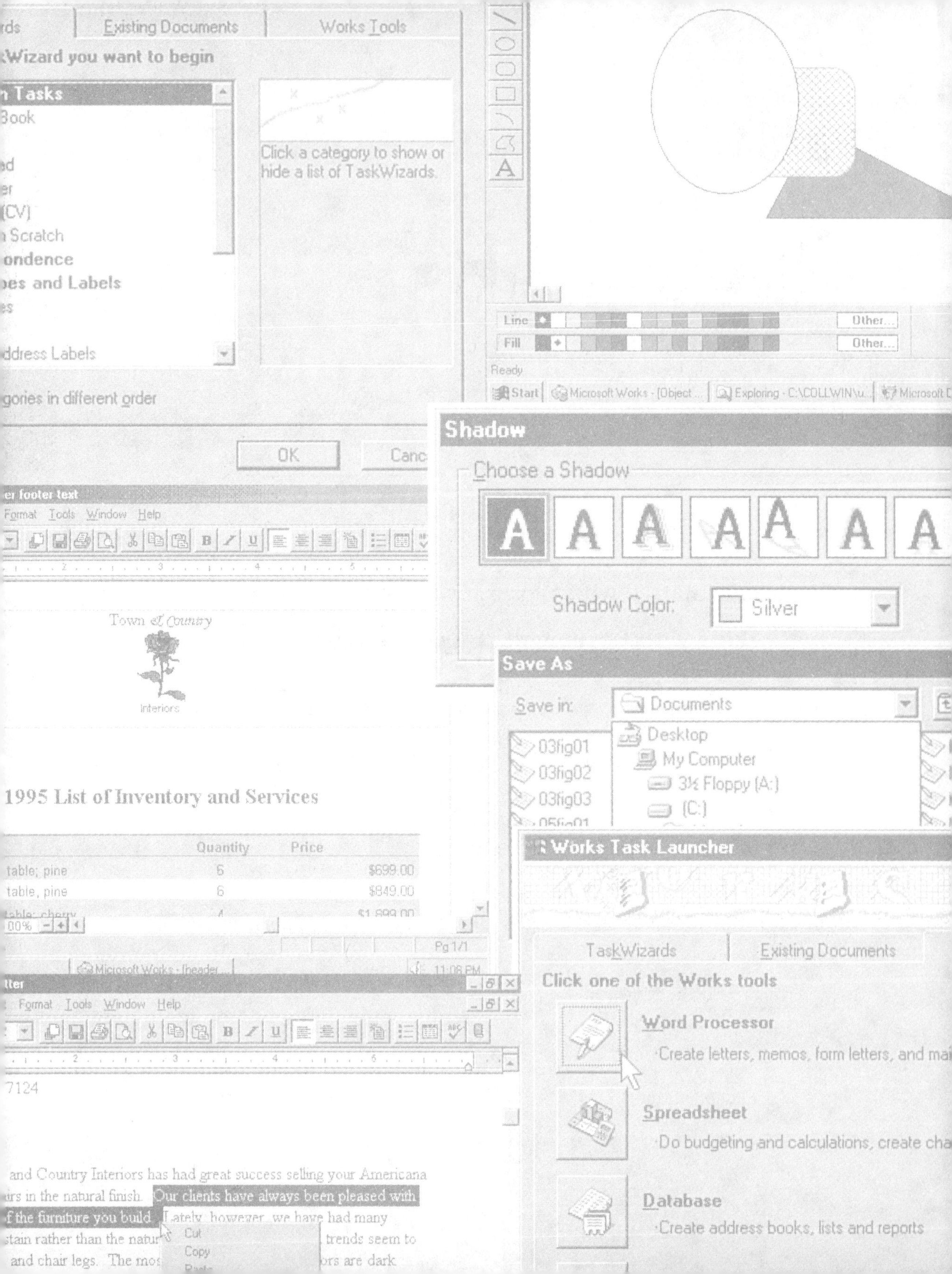
Existing Documents
Works Tools
Click a category to show or hide a list of TaskWizards.
Line
Fill
Other...
Ready
Start
OK
Shadow
Choose a Shadow
Shadow Color:
Silver
Save As
Save in:
Documents
Desktop
My Computer
3½ Floppy (A:)
(C:)
03fig01
03fig02
03fig03
Town & Country
Interiors
1995 List of Inventory and Services
Quantity
Price
Pg 1/1
Works Task Launcher
TaskWizards
Existing Documents
Click one of the Works tools
Word Processor
Create letters, memos, form letters, and mai
Spreadsheet
Do budgeting and calculations, create cha
Database
Create address books, lists and reports
Format Tools Window Help
Cut
Copy

Chapter 1

Introducing Microsoft Works 4.0 for Windows 95

Microsoft Works 4.0 for Windows 95 contains four software applications in one: a *word processor* with a drawing package, a *spreadsheet* with a charting package, a *database*, and a *communications* package. Each component is designed to help you create, present, illustrate, organize, sort, report on, and print information in the easiest possible way. Works is an *integrated* software program—all four applications are designed to work together.

Integrated software programs offer two distinct advantages over stand-alone programs. First, they offer *consistency*—you can use the same methods for performing basic tasks from application to application, such as saving a file or printing a document. Second, integrated programs also allow you to share data effortlessly among the applications. For example, you can easily include a spreadsheet, picture, or chart in a word processing document. Another benefit of Works 4.0 for Windows 95 (not necessarily true of other integrated programs) is that, because it is a Windows program, you can work with more than one document on the screen at the same time.

Aside from all this, Works offers one distinct advantage over other integrated programs: it's truly *easy to use*.

In this chapter, you learn about the following:

- Works applications: the word processor, spreadsheet, database, and communications
- Accessories: Microsoft Draw, ClipArt, and WordArt

- Time savers: TaskWizards and templates
- Integration of Works applications

The Word Processor

The easiest way to get started with Works is by using the word processor—an application that helps you create documents that primarily contain text. You can use a word processor to create a letter, a memo, a report, a legal document, a proposal, an article—even a book. One of the greatest advantages to using a word processor is that you can change what you have written before you print. If you make an error, you can erase and retype it; if you decide to rearrange paragraphs, you can move or copy them easily.

Another advantage of using a word processor is that you can create truly professional looking documents. You can choose from a wide variety of character styles and sizes and add features such as bold, underline, or italic. You can set margins and tabs anywhere you want; adjust line spacing; align text right, left, or center; or alter the size of a page. Other sophisticated features in the word processor enable you to do the following:

- Print in columns
- Insert footnotes in a document
- Add repetitive text at the top and bottom of each page
- Add tables or figures to a document
- Check your spelling
- Replace a word with a synonym
- Search a document for a word or phrase and replace it with other text

A sample word processing document is shown in figure 1.1. The logo was created by using a clip art illustration, described later in this chapter. You learn how to work the word processor in Part II, "Word Processing," and you learn how to create drawings by using Microsoft Draw in Part V, "Adding Visual Interest to Documents and Forms."

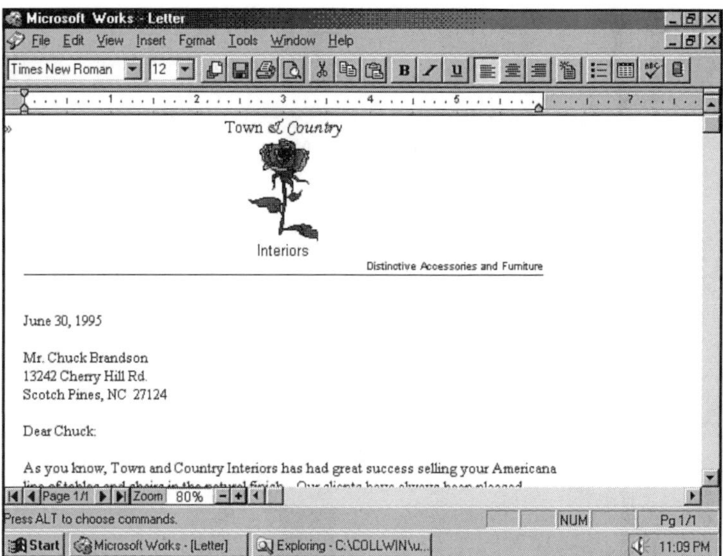

Fig. 1.1
This is a word processing document that uses a clip art logo.

The Spreadsheet

A *spreadsheet* is an electronic version of a paper worksheet used to perform numeric calculations. The advantage of the electronic spreadsheet over the paper one is that it calculates and updates figures automatically. Spreadsheets are generally used to calculate financial data, although you can use them to calculate and analyze mathematical and scientific data as well. Some of the most common uses for spreadsheets are for budgeting, creating balance sheets and income statements, and for sales forecasts. An example is shown in figure 1.2.

A spreadsheet is arranged in rows and columns, just like a paper worksheet. In each *cell* (the intersection of a row and column), you enter text, numbers, or formulas. *Text* describes the data in each row or column, *numbers* represent the raw data, and *formulas* perform calculations. When you change a number in a formula, the spreadsheet automatically recalculates the correct result. You can create your own formulas, or you can use special formulas called *functions*. Functions are designed to perform a specific type of calculation, such as computing the monthly payment amount of a loan.

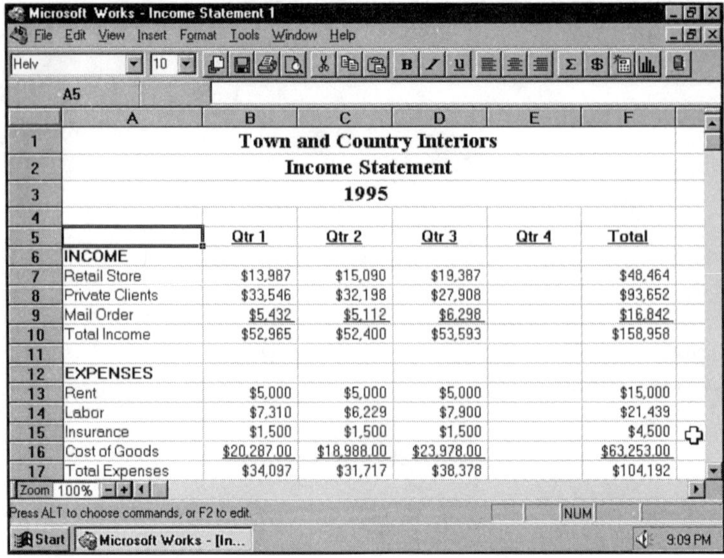

	A	B	C	D	E	F
1	Town and Country Interiors					
2	Income Statement					
3	1995					
4						
5		Qtr 1	Qtr 2	Qtr 3	Qtr 4	Total
6	INCOME					
7	Retail Store	$13,987	$15,090	$19,387		$48,464
8	Private Clients	$33,546	$32,198	$27,908		$93,652
9	Mail Order	$5,432	$5,112	$6,298		$16,842
10	Total Income	$52,965	$52,400	$53,593		$158,958
11						
12	EXPENSES					
13	Rent	$5,000	$5,000	$5,000		$15,000
14	Labor	$7,310	$6,229	$7,900		$21,439
15	Insurance	$1,500	$1,500	$1,500		$4,500
16	Cost of Goods	$20,287.00	$18,988.00	$23,978.00		$63,253.00
17	Total Expenses	$34,097	$31,717	$38,378		$104,192

Fig. 1.2
This is a sample income statement prepared with the Works spreadsheet program.

Like a word processing document, the electronic spreadsheet's advantage over its paper counterpart is that it allows you to change and rearrange data easily and all the calculations are done for you automatically. You can also enhance a worksheet by adding bold, underline, or italic to selected data, or by changing the size and style of the characters you use. Before printing, you can add a title or file name that appears at the top or bottom of each page, and you can add page numbers that appear at the bottom of each page.

Spreadsheet information can be difficult to interpret without the aid of a graph or chart, so the spreadsheet in Works includes a charting tool. You can choose from several chart styles, including variations of bar, line, and pie charts. After you create a chart, you can incorporate it into the spreadsheet or add it to a word processing document. A sample chart appears in figure 1.3. Chapters 10 through 15 discuss how to create spreadsheets and charts.

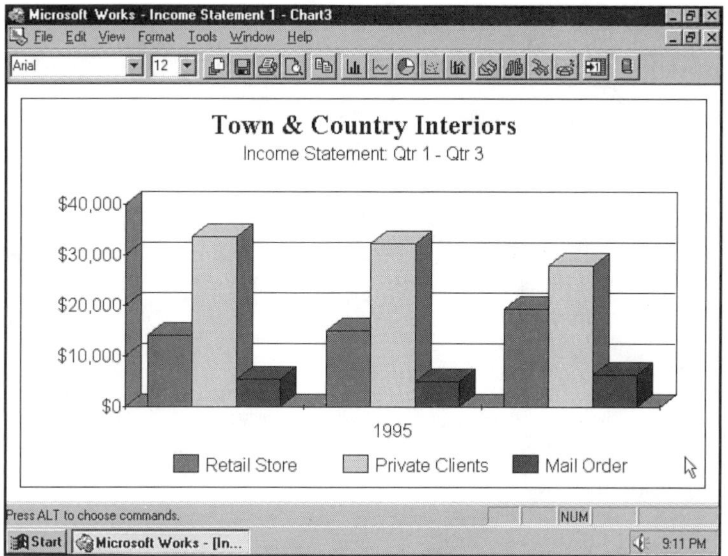

Fig. 1.3
This chart was drawn directly from the data in the spreadsheet shown in figure 1.2.

The Database

In the simplest terms, a *database* is nothing more than a collection of related information. You might think that you have never used a database, but you have. The telephone book—a common item that many people use every day—is an example of a database of names, addresses, and phone numbers. You can use the database in Works to create a database of client's or supplier's names, addresses, and phone numbers. Other examples of databases include a product list that contains item numbers, descriptions, and prices, or an inventory list that contains items and quantities.

Works lets you display a database in *List* view, *Form* view, or *Form Design* view. In List view, all the items in the database are displayed at once (see fig. 1.4). In Form view, each record in the database is displayed individually in an appealing format that's easy to work with (see fig. 1.5). In Form Design view, you can easily rearrange elements of the form exactly as you want them using drag-and-drop techniques.

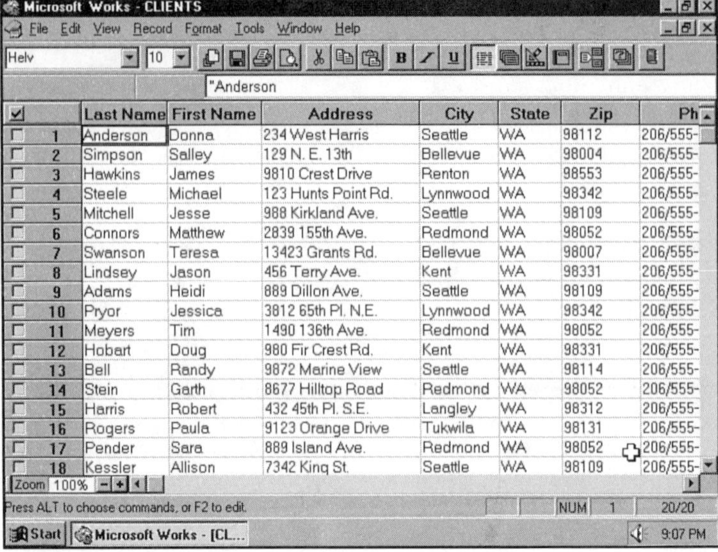

	Last Name	First Name	Address	City	State	Zip	Ph
1	Anderson	Donna	234 West Harris	Seattle	WA	98112	206/555-
2	Simpson	Salley	129 N. E. 13th	Bellevue	WA	98004	206/555-
3	Hawkins	James	9810 Crest Drive	Renton	WA	98553	206/555-
4	Steele	Michael	123 Hunts Point Rd.	Lynnwood	WA	98342	206/555-
5	Mitchell	Jesse	988 Kirkland Ave.	Seattle	WA	98109	206/555-
6	Connors	Matthew	2839 155th Ave.	Redmond	WA	98052	206/555-
7	Swanson	Teresa	13423 Grants Rd.	Bellevue	WA	98007	206/555-
8	Lindsey	Jason	456 Terry Ave.	Kent	WA	98331	206/555-
9	Adams	Heidi	889 Dillon Ave.	Seattle	WA	98109	206/555-
10	Pryor	Jessica	3812 65th Pl. N.E.	Lynnwood	WA	98342	206/555-
11	Meyers	Tim	1490 136th Ave.	Redmond	WA	98052	206/555-
12	Hobart	Doug	980 Fir Crest Rd.	Kent	WA	98331	206/555-
13	Bell	Randy	9872 Marine View	Seattle	WA	98114	206/555-
14	Stein	Garth	8677 Hilltop Road	Redmond	WA	98052	206/555-
15	Harris	Robert	432 45th Pl. S.E.	Langley	WA	98312	206/555-
16	Rogers	Paula	9123 Orange Drive	Tukwila	WA	98131	206/555-
17	Pender	Sara	889 Island Ave.	Redmond	WA	98052	206/555-
18	Kessler	Allison	7342 King St.	Seattle	WA	98109	206/555-

Fig. 1.4
This database is displayed in List view.

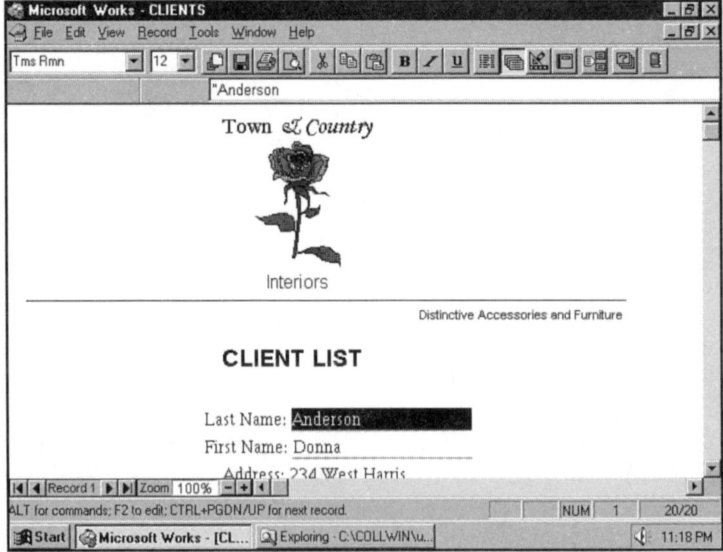

Fig. 1.5
This is record one of a database, displayed in Form view with a ClipArt logo.

Databases are not only handy for cataloging information, they can also be sorted by category and queried for specific information. For instance, records in a database are often entered at random, but you can put the records in alphabetical order by sorting the database. Or, if your database includes your clients' receivables, you can query the database to display all accounts that are 90 days past due.

Databases often contain a great deal of information, whether it's about clients, products, or inventory. Works allows you to print different types of database reports so that you have the information you need at your fingertips. You can select the data you want to include in (or exclude from) a report, summarize columns of figures, and give the report a polished appearance by adding a title and other special formatting. You learn how to create a database and work with database reports in Chapters 16 through 23.

Communications

As computers become more and more a part of everyday life, the capability to communicate from one computer to another computer (or to another *network* of computers) becomes critical. With a modem and communications software on your computer, you can use your personal computer to log on to your computer at the office, read your electronic mail, and send and receive files. Communications software also enables you to dial up to an information service such as CompuServe or a worldwide network such as the Internet and literally have a world of information at your fingertips—from current stock quotes to the Library of Congress to travel and shopping services. The communications software in Works provides the capability to perform all of these tasks.

You can incorporate any of the information you receive from other computers into your Works documents. For instance, you might want to collect a history of stock prices from an information service, copy the data into a spreadsheet, and create a chart that depicts the stock's performance over the previous year. Chapter 29, "Communicating with Other Computers," teaches you how to use the communications application in Works.

Integration

Integration is the real power of a package like Microsoft Works 4.0; it allows you to move or copy information effortlessly from one application to another. For example, using cut, paste, and copy commands, you can include text from a word processor document in a spreadsheet; or you can insert a spreadsheet table or a chart in a letter or report. Through a process called *linking*, information you include in one document is automatically updated when you change information in another document. These are extremely powerful tools that makes the task of producing documents as easy as it can possibly be.

The integration feature of Works also allows you to merge information from a database with a word processing document. For example, suppose you want to send collection letters to all of your clients whose accounts are 90 days past due. By including special codes in your collection letter, Works can automatically insert each client's name, address, and the dollar amount due in individual letters. The merge feature between the word processor and database also allows you to print mailing labels or envelopes for each letter. In Chapters 26 and 27, you learn how to integrate information from various Works applications into a single document.

Microsoft Works 4.0 for Windows 95 Accessories and Time Savers

Most documents have more visual appeal when they include illustrations. To help you enhance your word processor documents and database forms, Works provides four accessories:

- *Microsoft Draw* is a special drawing tool that lets you create your own color drawings. Using Draw, you can create illustrations, then insert them easily into your word processor files or database forms (see Chapter 24, "Using Microsoft Draw and ClipArt").

- *ClipArt* is a collection of prepared drawings included in Microsoft Works 4.0 for Windows 95. The collection includes illustrations across a wide variety of categories—from sports to animals to business. If you don't want to create your own drawing by using Microsoft Draw, you can include a prepared clip art drawing in your document (refer to fig. 1.5). For detailed information about using ClipArt, refer to Chapter 24, "Using Microsoft Draw and ClipArt."

- *WordArt* lets you dress up your documents with stylized text. Choose from a variety of font styles and sizes, then curve, slant, bend, or rotate the text and add shadows, borders, and shading. Use WordArt to create a professional-quality logo for your letterhead or an eye-catching banner for your monthly newsletter (refer to Chapter 25, "Using WordArt and Note-It").

- *Note-It* provides a distinctive and unique way for you to annotate your documents. An *icon* (a picture of a notepad, envelope, file folder, or other item) appears in your document indicating the location of a note. Double-click the icon to display the contents of the note, then click anywhere in the document to close the note. For information on using Note-It, refer to Chapter 25, "Using WordArt and Note-It."

If you have never used Microsoft Works 4.0 for Windows 95 and you're in a hurry to complete a task, you will appreciate TaskWizards and templates. For more information on using TaskWizards and templates, see Chapter 3, "Working with Documents, TaskWizards, and Templates."

- *TaskWizards* make it easy to complete a task, such as creating an address book, a resume, a newsletter, a brochure, or an invoice. You answer some simple on-screen questions related to the task you want to accomplish, then Works takes off and builds the document for you.

- A *template* is a model or guide for a document that you might want to use many times in different circumstances. When you create a document using a template, most of the work has already been done for you. Just add your unique text and save the document. You can use templates over and over again for different documents.

For Upgraders: What's New in Works 4.0 for Windows 95

If you are upgrading from Works 3.0 to Works 4.0, you'll be pleased with some of its new features. And although the new features are exciting, they don't change the familiar look and feel of Works—you'll still recognize it! Some of the new features are a result of Works now supporting Windows 95 and, therefore, supporting some of its new features. These features include:

- Support for long file names (no more eight-character files names with three-character extensions!)

- A new look and feel to online Help consistent with Windows 95
- Right mouse button support for common commands
- New tabbed dialog boxes
- Support for new writing and research tools like Microsoft Bookshelf and Encarta
- Revamping of Works' menus to be compatible with Microsoft Office

The remainder of the new features are specific to the applications in Works. The word processor has two new features called Easy Formats and Easy Text. Headers and footers are now in WYSIWYG (what-you-see-is-what-you-get) format, and you can now add shading and borders to paragraphs, or border an entire page. The word processor also supports Smart Quotes, has improved zoom and page view controls, and a newly designed ruler for the document window.

The spreadsheet boasts a new feature called Easy Calc, which lets you effortlessly include functions in a worksheet. The spreadsheet also has enhanced Fill Series and sorting commands, and has improved file compatibility with Microsoft Excel. You can also enter up to 256 characters in a cell. The charting tool in the spreadsheet application now features an expanded chart gallery, supports drag-and-drop of charts, and allows you to change the orientation of text in a chart.

The database features a new dialog box for creating a database, making it easier to set up the number and type of fields you want. You can enter more text (up to 2K) in a single field, mark records, and open a report in Preview.

The communications application features a new Easy Connect dialog box, making connections to all types of networks and services simpler. ❖

Chapter 2

Getting Started with Works for Windows

by Debbie Walkowski

Before you begin using the individual applications in Microsoft Works 4.0 for Windows 95, you need to learn the basics of using the program. To make the program as easy to use as possible, Microsoft provides consistency from application to application. For example, menus, commands, dialog boxes, and toolbars are elements that appear in each of the application windows. Although the choices among each of these elements vary, the method for working with them is the same from application to application. The goal of this chapter is to teach you about all the consistent elements so you can work comfortably with *any* of the applications in Works.

In this chapter, you learn how to:

- Start and close Works
- Use menus, commands, dialog boxes, and toolbars
- Open and arrange multiple document windows
- Get help when you need it

Using the Mouse

Works 4.0 for Windows 95 is designed to be used with a mouse. If your computer is not equipped with a mouse, you can use the keyboard to accomplish every action or command you might initiate using a mouse, but you don't have access to the toolbars.

The mouse is indicated on your screen by a mouse pointer that changes shape depending on its location (see Table 2.1). In a word processor or communications document, the mouse pointer is an I-beam. In a spreadsheet or database list document, the mouse pointer is a cross. In all of the Works applications, the mouse pointer changes to the shape of an arrow when you point to the toolbar, menu bar, or scroll bars. The arrow tracks your movement of the mouse on the mouse pad.

Table 2.1 Mouse Pointer Shapes

Shape	Description
(arrow)	The mouse pointer is an arrow when you point to a toolbar, menu, scroll bar, or anywhere in a database form.
I	The mouse pointer is an I-beam in a word processor document.
(cross)	The mouse pointer is a cross in a spreadsheet or database list document.

In general, you use the mouse to move, resize, or otherwise manipulate document windows or the Works window, and to select menu commands. Table 2.2 lists the terms used to describe mouse techniques.

Table 2.2 Mouse Techniques

Technique	Description
Point	Move the mouse pointer to a specific location on-screen.
Click	Press and release the left mouse button once.
Double-click	Press and release the left mouse button twice quickly.
Right-click	Press and release the right mouse button once.
Click and drag	Point to an object on-screen, press and hold the left mouse button, and then move the mouse to a new location before releasing the mouse button.

The left mouse button is used in Works for common tasks like selecting commands or text. Most of these actions are as simple as "point and click." To make an inactive window active, for example, you simply point anywhere in the window and click. The right mouse button, which was not implemented in previous versions of Works, displays shortcut menus. Each shortcut menu is different depending on the application you are using and the context in the application. Shortcut menus are noted where applicable throughout this book.

Starting Works

Works must be installed on your computer before you can start the program. During the installation process, Microsoft Works 4.0 is automatically added to the list of programs under the Windows Start menu (see fig. 2.1).

To start Works, follow these steps:

1. Turn your computer on and start Windows.
2. Click the Start button and choose Programs.
3. Choose the Microsoft Works 4.0 folder, then choose Microsoft Works 4.0.

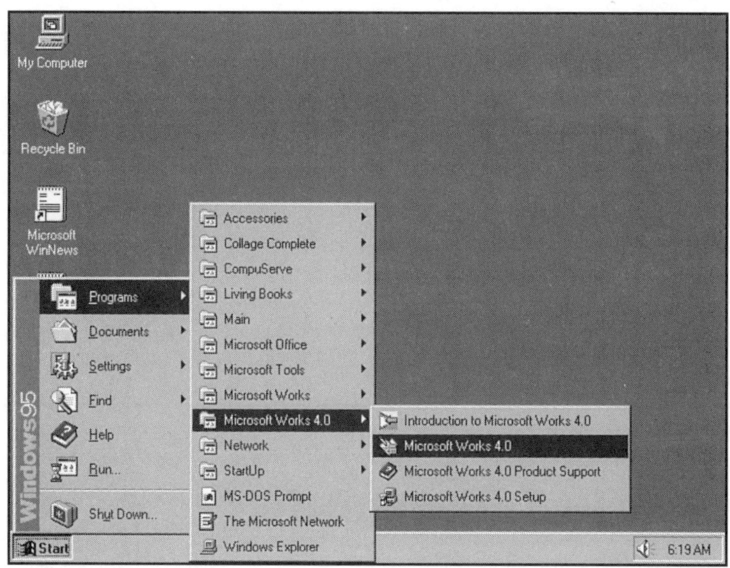

Fig. 2.1
Microsoft Works 4.0 is listed under Programs on the Start button.

When you install Works, you are given the option of creating a Shortcut to Microsoft Works 4.0 icon. If you use Works regularly, choose this option—it lets you open Works simply and quickly. Just double-click the shortcut icon that appears on your desktop (see fig. 2.2).

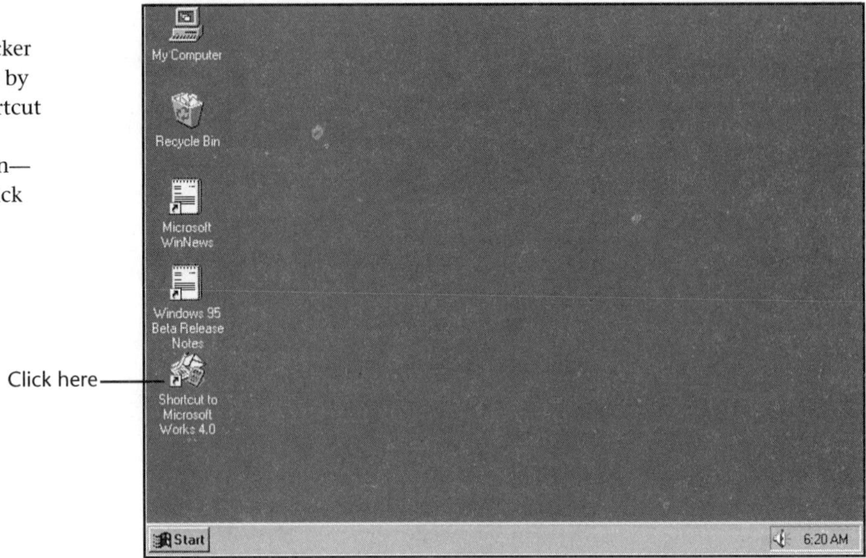

Fig. 2.2
It's much quicker to start Works by using the Shortcut to Microsoft Works 4.0 icon—just double-click your mouse.

The first time you start Microsoft Works 4.0 for Windows 95, a welcome screen appears asking if you want to see an introduction to Works. If you choose not to view the introduction now, you can view it later by selecting it from the Microsoft Works 4.0 folder (refer to fig. 2.1), or you can select it from the Help menu inside Works. You can skip the welcome screen the next time you start Works by clicking the Skip Welcome Screen option.

Troubleshooting

I can't find Microsoft Works 4.0 in the Start menu under Programs.

If you can't find Microsoft Works 4.0 in the Programs menu, the installation might not have been completed successfully. Try reinstalling Works and watch your screen to see that the installation is completed successfully. Microsoft Works 4.0 is automatically added to the Start menu under Programs.

The Works Task Launcher

After you close the welcome screen, you see the Works Task Launcher dialog box shown in figure 2.3. The Works Task Launcher is like "Command Central" in Works. It's your starting point for all of the tasks you do: writing letters, printing envelopes and labels, cataloging information, creating financial documents, and so on.

The Works Task Launcher dialog box contains three tabs: TaskWizards, Existing Documents, and Works Tools. You use these tabs to have Works help you create a document, to use an existing document, or to start a new document. These tabs in the Works Task Launcher are discussed briefly in the following section and in more detail in Chapter 3, "Working with Documents, TaskWizards, and Templates."

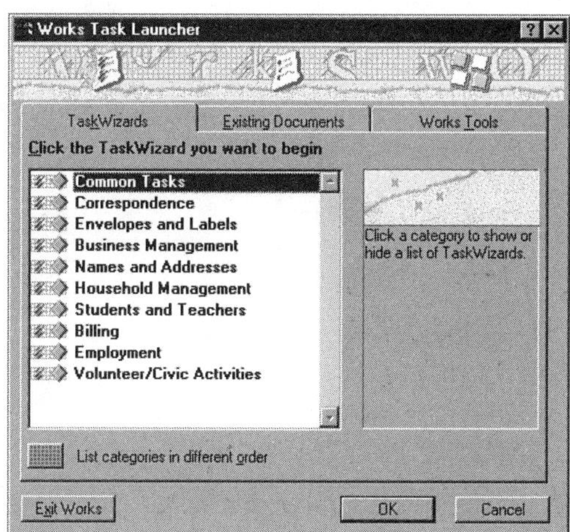

Fig. 2.3
From the Works Task Launcher, choose a TaskWizard, open an existing document, or start a Works tool.

Using TaskWizards

A *TaskWizard* is a tool that helps you build a particular type of document such as a business letter, a resume, an invoice, or a newsletter. TaskWizards are particularly useful for users who are new to Works, those who are not quite confident in their ability to create documents, or for users who are just in a hurry to get a job done!

The TaskWizards tab in the Works Task Launcher dialog box lists all TaskWizards by category. Specific types of documents are listed under each category (see fig. 2.4).

Note

Be sure to review the section "Using TaskWizards" in Chapter 3, "Working with Documents, TaskWizards, and Templates." TaskWizards are incredibly powerful tools that can save you a great deal of time and help you create a wide variety of documents.

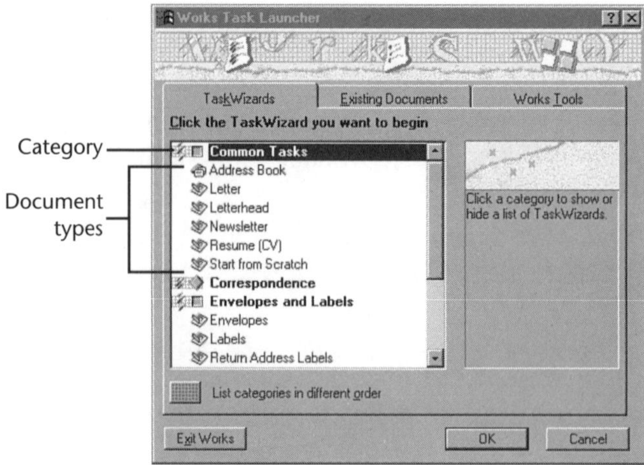

Fig. 2.4
Using TaskWizards, you can create specific types of documents.

Opening an Existing Document

When you click the Existing Documents tab, Works lists the documents you used most recently (see fig. 2.5). If the document you want to open is not shown, you can open a different document (select the Open a Document Not Listed Here button) or have Works help you find the document you want (select the Help Me Find a Document button).

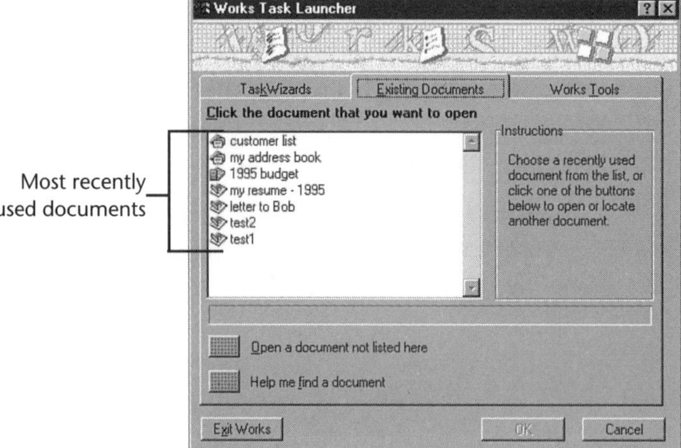

Fig. 2.5
Use the Existing Documents tab to open a saved document.

Opening a Works Application

The third tab in the Works Task Launcher, Works Tools, lets you go directly to a Works application and create a blank document (see fig. 2.6). Choose from Word Processor, Spreadsheet, Database, and Communications.

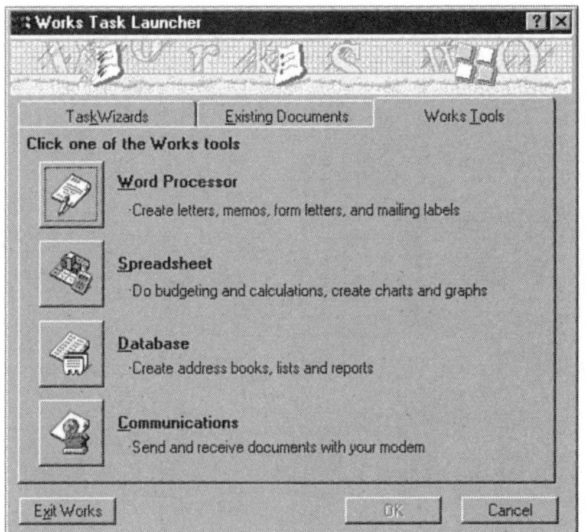

Fig. 2.6
Choose the Works Tools tab to create a new blank document.

The Standard Elements of a Works Window

The window Works displays is slightly different depending on the Works application you are using. For instance, a spreadsheet window contains a grid of rectangles for holding numbers or text, whereas a word processor window has a blank area for text. Some of the elements of the window, however, are the same regardless of the Works application you use. In this section, you learn about some of the standard window elements and how they work.

The Works window shown in figure 2.7 is a word processor window. It contains several typical window elements: title bar, menu bar, status bar, and scroll bars. It also contains buttons for controlling the window, such as the Minimize, Maximize, and Close buttons. The standard Windows taskbar appears at the bottom of the window.

When you look closely, you see that there are actually two windows: the *document* window (the word processor window where you type text) appears inside the Works window. Because there are two windows, there are actually two title bars and two sets of window control buttons (Minimize, Maximize, and Close). The title bar for the Works window says `Microsoft Works`, whereas the title bar of the document window says `Unsaved Document 1`.

You might be wondering, why two windows? It might seem unnecessary now, but when you learn how to work with more than one document at a time, it becomes quite clear why the Works window is separate from the document window. Think of the Works window as a container for one or more document windows. (For more information on sizing and shrinking windows, see the section "Arranging Multiple Document Windows.")

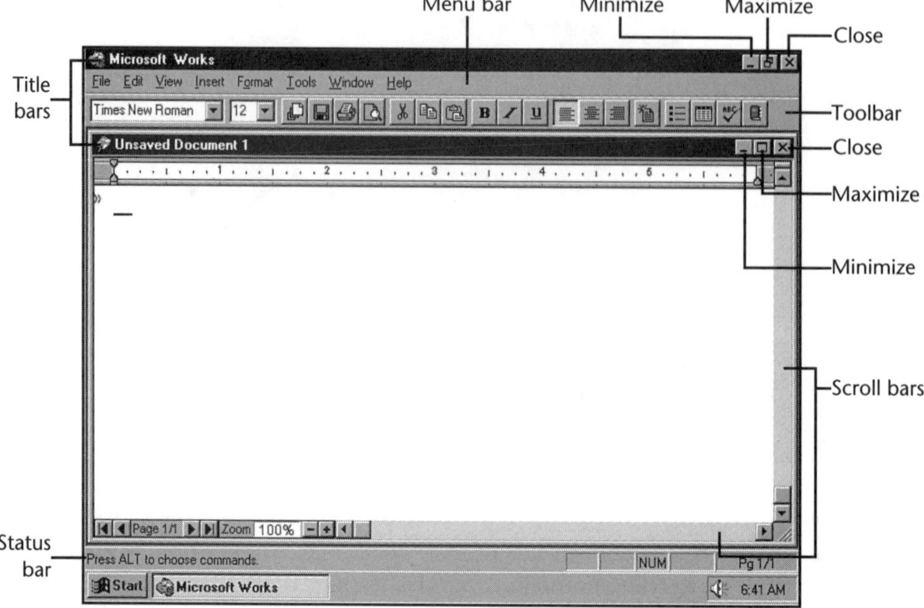

Fig. 2.7
Many window elements are common among all Works applications.

Initially, the document window is slightly smaller than the Works window. When you maximize the document window by clicking its Maximize button, the two windows blend together and share a title bar (see fig. 2.8). Notice that `Microsoft Works - Unsaved Document 1` now appears in the title bar. The window control buttons for the document window now appear at the far right end of the menu bar, just below the window control buttons for the Works window.

Moving Around in a Document Window

Regardless of the application you are using, all Works document windows contain vertical and horizontal scroll bars (refer to figs. 2.7 and 2.8). When a document is too long to be displayed completely in a window, use the vertical scroll bar to move the document up and down. When a document is too wide to be displayed in a window, use the horizontal scroll bar to move the document from side to side. The word processor and database document windows contain buttons on the horizontal scroll bar that allow you to move to a specific page (word processor) or record (database) in a document. (See Chapters 10 and 16 for more information about moving around in spreadsheet and database windows.)

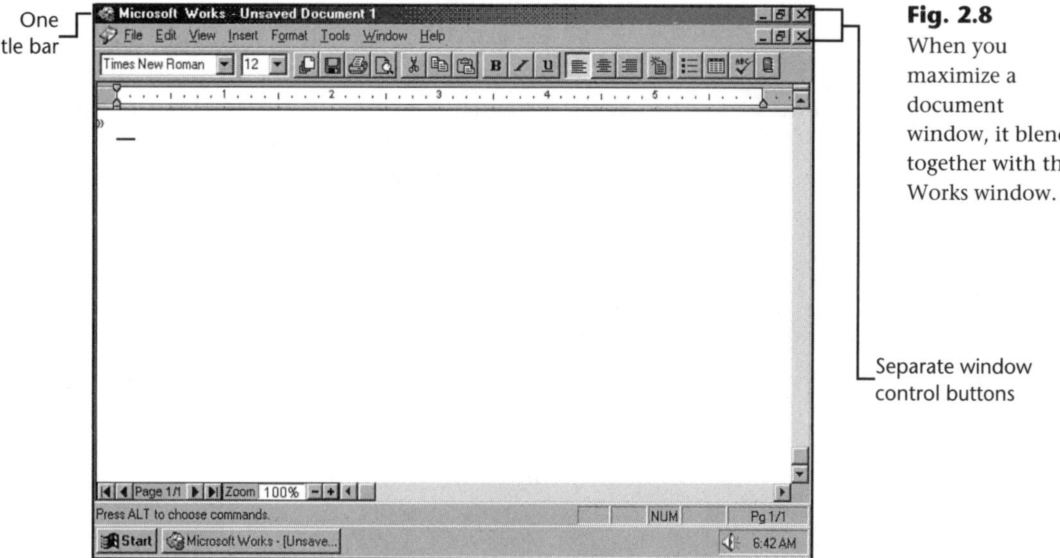

Fig. 2.8
When you maximize a document window, it blends together with the Works window.

Selecting Menus and Commands

When you're ready to tell Works what you want to do next, you select a *command*. Commands are grouped by categories and are listed on menus (see fig. 2.9). Commands that pertain to files appear on the File menu, those that pertain to editing are on the Edit menu, and so on. To select a command, click the menu name, and click the command name on the menu.

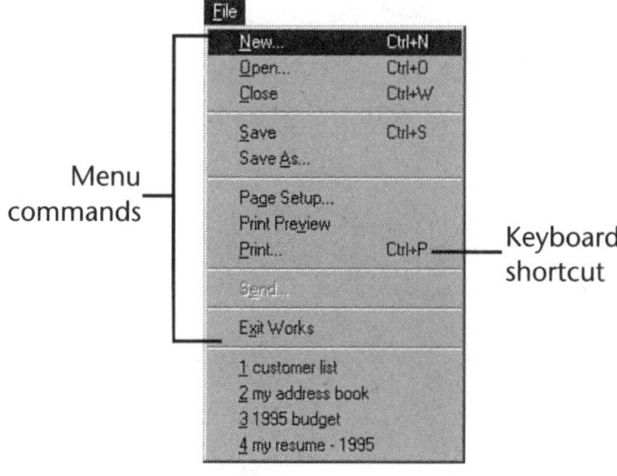

Fig. 2.9
When you choose a menu command with an ellipsis after the name (such as New...), a dialog box appears.

Some menu commands take immediate action, some toggle on and off, some open dialog boxes, and some appear grayed on the menu. When a toggle command is turned on, or *selected*, a check mark appears to the left of the command name on the menu. When a command doesn't apply to the task you are performing at the time, the command is shaded on the menu and you cannot select it.

The underlined letter in each menu name and menu command is called the *hotkey*. If you are using the keyboard, you open a menu by pressing Alt plus the hotkey in the menu name. To open the File menu, for example, press Alt+F. To select a command after you have opened a menu, simply type the hotkey of the command name (such as C for Close).

Some menu commands have keyboard shortcuts assigned to them. Keyboard shortcuts allow you to bypass the menu command, saving you the time of opening the menu and selecting the command. Keyboard shortcuts appear to the right of the command name on the menu. For example, the keyboard shortcut for the Save command on the File menu is Ctrl+S; you can activate the Save command just by pressing Ctrl+S.

Note

Throughout this book, when you are told to choose a menu command, the format for the command is the menu name followed by the command name. For example, File, New means choose the New command from the File menu.

Troubleshooting

I keep trying to select a menu command, and nothing happens.

The menu command might be grayed, meaning it isn't available at this time. Make sure you have completed the command you are currently using (such as entering information in a database form) before trying to select another. Or, check Help to see if you need to select text before using the command you want.

When I press Alt plus a hotkey to select a menu command, the menu disappears. What's wrong?

To select a command when a menu is already open, just type the hotkey; don't press Alt again.

Working with Dialog Boxes

A dialog box is a special window that appears on the screen when you select any menu command that is followed by an ellipsis (...), for example, the File, Print command. In a dialog box, you provide more information about the command you choose by typing an entry, making a selection, or specifying one or more options. The dialog box is displayed on top of the window in which you are working and remains on-screen until you close it.

Learning Dialog Box Elements

Because dialog boxes often contain many different choices, they are sometimes divided into tabbed sections (as in the Works Task Launcher dialog box you saw in fig. 2.2). On each tab, named sections of the dialog box contain different elements. The Save As dialog box shown in figure 2.10 illustrates command buttons as well as a check box, a drop-down list, and a list box (the Save In drop-down list is open). The Format Tabs dialog box shown in figure 2.11 illustrates text boxes and option buttons. The following are the most common dialog box elements:

- *Command buttons* such as OK and Cancel appear in every dialog box. To activate a command, click the button. Command buttons that are followed by an ellipsis open another dialog box with more choices.
- *List boxes* contain a list of items from which to choose. You can select only one item in a list box.
- *Check boxes* are options that you toggle on and off. To select an option, click the check box and an X will appear in the box; to cancel an option, click the check box to remove the X. When multiple check boxes appear in a dialog box, you can select more than one.
- *Drop-down lists* are similar to list boxes, but the list is hidden until you reveal it. To reveal the list, click the downward-pointing arrow at the right end of the box. Select one list item by clicking it. The list closes automatically.
- *Text boxes* allow you to enter specific information, such as a file name. Click the box, then type the information you are asked to supply.
- *Option buttons* represent either/or choices; you can choose only one option button when multiple option buttons are displayed. Clicking one cancels the option that is currently selected.

Making Selections in Dialog Boxes

Changing dialog box settings is as easy as clicking the option, command button, check box, or list item you want to select. For a text box, click in the box, and then type the appropriate text. A dotted rectangle, a highlight, or both indicate the option in the dialog box that is currently selected.

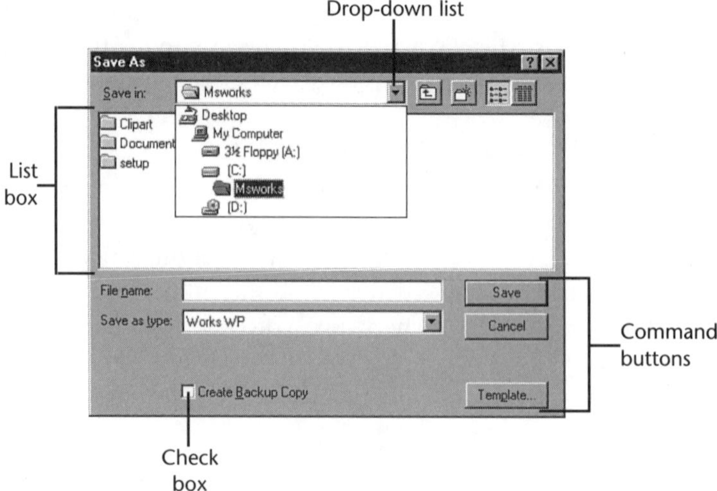

Fig. 2.10
Use command buttons, drop-down lists, check boxes, and list boxes to make selections in this dialog box.

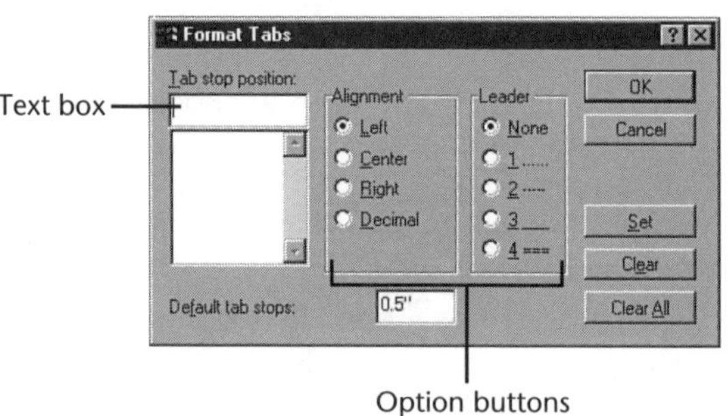

Fig. 2.11
Use option buttons and text boxes to make selections in this dialog box.

If you are using the keyboard, you can move forward through the sections of a dialog box by pressing the Tab key. Each time you press Tab, Works highlights an item in the current section of the dialog box. To highlight a different item in a section, use the up- and down-arrow keys. You can also press Shift+Tab to move backward through the sections of a dialog box.

Almost all dialog boxes have Cancel, OK, and Help buttons. Select OK to accept and carry out the changes you make and close the dialog box. Click Cancel to cancel all changes you made in the dialog box and use the previous settings. If you select a dialog box by mistake, close it without making changes by selecting Cancel.

Working with Tabbed Dialog Boxes

A tabbed dialog box looks similar to a regular dialog box but contains tabs along the top, similar to the tabs you might find in an index or recipe box. Each tab represents a category of choices in the dialog box.

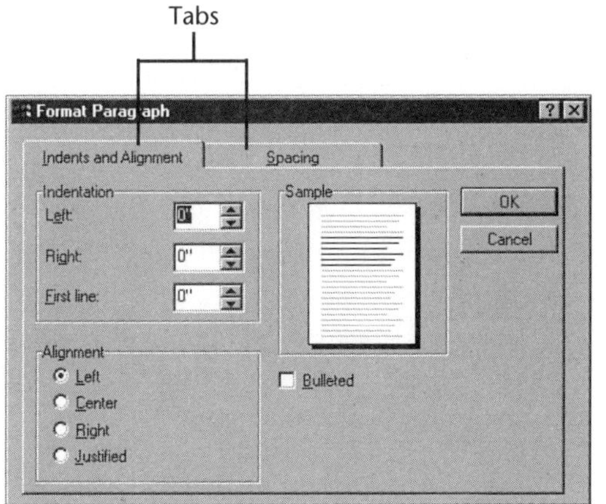

Fig. 2.12
Some dialog box options are organized under tabs.

To use a tabbed dialog box, click the tab you want to use to bring it to the foreground, and then choose options just like you would in any other dialog box. Click another tab to set more options, or click OK to close the dialog box. If you are using the keyboard, select a dialog box tab by pressing Alt plus the selection character for the tab.

Troubleshooting

I want to select two option buttons but can't.

The selections that option buttons represent (such as the Alignment group in figure 2.12) are usually in conflict with one another and, therefore, you can only select one at a time. For example, you can't choose both Left and Center alignment because the two options conflict with one another.

I want to select a shaded item in a dialog box but can't.

Just as menu commands are sometimes shaded when they don't apply to the task you are performing, dialog box items sometimes are shaded when they don't apply to the task you are performing.

Using Toolbars

A *toolbar* is a convenient feature of every Works application that allows you to initiate an action quickly. A toolbar contains *buttons*—small icons that represent menu commands. For example, to print a file, you can click the button that has a printer on it rather than choosing File, Print.

Each Works application uses a different toolbar with buttons that pertain to that particular application. The spreadsheet toolbar, for example, contains a button for formatting numbers with a dollar sign. This feature would be meaningless in the word processor window. Likewise, the database toolbar contains a button for creating database reports, a feature that has no meaning in either the word processor or spreadsheet applications. The toolbars for each of the four applications are shown in figure 2.13. The individual applications are described in the following chapters:

- Chapter 4, "Creating, Saving, and Printing a Document"
- Chapter 10, "Creating, Saving, and Printing a Spreadsheet"
- Chapter 16, "Creating and Saving a Database File"
- Chapter 29, "Communicating with Other Computers"

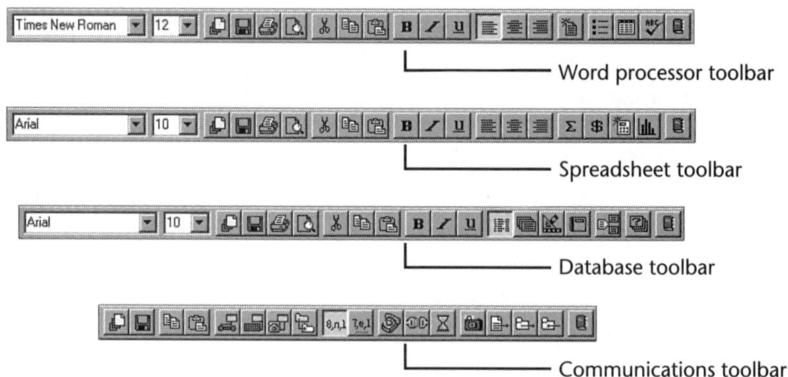

Fig. 2.13
The toolbars that appear in the word processor, spreadsheet, database, and communications applications.

Identifying Toolbar Buttons

Although the icons used on toolbar buttons are designed to reflect the commands they represent (such as a printer for the Print command), it can be difficult to remember what each toolbar button is for—especially if you've never used Works. When you're not sure which command a button represents, point to it with the mouse but don't click the mouse. The name of the button is displayed just below the button and disappears when you move the mouse pointer (see fig. 2.14). Windows and all Windows applications refer to this feature as ToolTips. If you don't want to use ToolTips, you can disable this feature by following the steps in the next section.

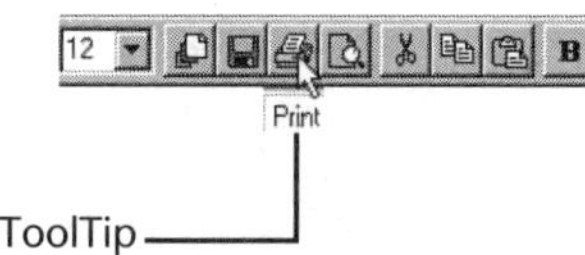

Fig. 2.14
Works displays a ToolTip when you point to a toolbar button without clicking the mouse.

Turning Off the Toolbar

Throughout this book, most of the figures that illustrate documents include the toolbar in the document window. You may have thought the toolbar was a permanent fixture of the document window, but it is not—you can remove the toolbar from the screen. Like maximizing the document window, removing the toolbar gives you the maximum working area on-screen. Often when you create a new document, you're more concerned about entering the text than about applying character styles, paragraph formats, or other enhancements—so you don't need the toolbar. Hiding the toolbar enables Works to display more lines of text in your document.

To control the toolbar, you use the Toolbar command on the View menu. When the toolbar is visible on-screen, a check mark appears next to the Toolbar command on the View menu. To hide the toolbar, choose View, Toolbar, removing the check mark. The command toggles on and off; choose the command again to make the toolbar visible on-screen.

Customizing the Toolbars

The toolbars in Works contain buttons that represent the most commonly used commands; they do not include a button for *every* Works command. As you become more familiar with Works 4.0, you will discover the commands you use most often; some of these commands will not be available on the standard toolbar. However, you can customize the toolbar for each of the Works applications. For example, if you need to insert the current date or time in all your word processor documents, you might want to add the Insert Current Date or Insert Current Time buttons to your word processor toolbar. These buttons do not appear on the standard word processor toolbar but are available if you want to add them. Use the Customize Works Toolbar dialog box to add buttons to a toolbar.

To customize a toolbar, follow these steps:

Tip
To display the Customize Works Toolbar dialog box, double-click in any blank area of the toolbar.

1. Open the Works application (word processor, spreadsheet, database, or communications) for which you want to customize the toolbar.

2. Choose Tools, Customize Toolbar. The Customize Works Toolbar dialog box appears (see fig. 2.15).

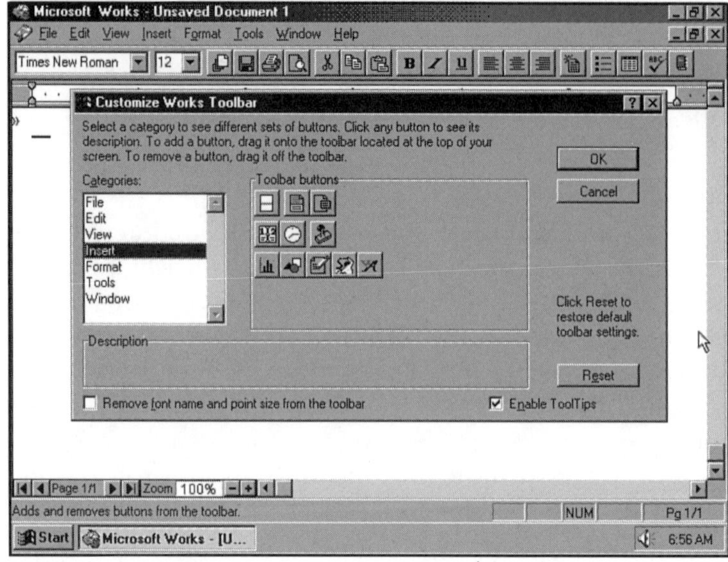

Fig. 2.15
Use the Customize Works Toolbar dialog box to add or remove toolbar buttons.

3. In the Categories box, choose a category from the list. The buttons displayed in the Toolbar Buttons area reflect the category you choose.

4. To see a description of a button, click the button once. The button's function is displayed in the Description box.

5. To add a button, drag and drop the button from the dialog box to the toolbar. You can place the button anywhere on the toolbar you choose, even between other buttons.

6. (Optional) You can Remove Font Name and Point Size from the Toolbar by selecting that check box, and you can disable ToolTips by deselecting the Enable ToolTips check box.

7. To remove a button from the toolbar, drag and drop the button from the toolbar to the Toolbar Buttons area of the dialog box.

8. Choose OK to accept the changes or choose Cancel to abandon the changes.

Troubleshooting

I have added and removed many toolbar buttons and now I don't remember the standard buttons. How can I restore them?

In the Customize Works Toolbar dialog box, click the Reset button, then click OK. When you restore the standard buttons, you lose your customized toolbar.

I want to rearrange the buttons on my toolbar. Is there a way to do this?

In the Customize Works Toolbar dialog box, drag the button on the toolbar that you want to move, move it, and then release the mouse button. Works moves the existing buttons aside and inserts the button you moved. Continue dragging other buttons to new locations to rearrange them. When you are finished rearranging buttons, click OK.

Working with Multiple Document Windows

You have already learned that the Works window contains Works document windows. You can open multiple documents of any type at one time; each document is displayed in a separate window and the windows can be different sizes. However, only one document at a time can be active. The menu and toolbar automatically reflect the active window (indicated by the highlighted title bar).

Opening Several Document Windows at Once

Earlier in this chapter, you were introduced to the Works Task Launcher dialog box (refer to fig. 2.2). When Works is running, you use the Works Task Launcher dialog box to start a new word processor, spreadsheet, database, or communications document. If you're already working on one document—for example, a database—you can create additional documents without closing the current one. When you create a new document, Works opens an additional document window on top of the window you are currently using; the new window becomes the active window. In figure 2.16, three document windows appear in the Works window.

To create a new document of any type when one is already open, follow these steps:

1. Click the Works Task Launcher button, or choose File, New.
2. Click the button for the type of document you want to create. A new document window appears inside the Works window.

Switching Among Document Windows

When several document windows are open at once, you can switch the active window simply by clicking another visible window. In figure 2.16, for example, the spreadsheet window is active—but the title bars for all other open windows are visible. Depending on how you arrange the windows, however, the window you want might not be visible. When a window is completely obscured by other windows, you can restore it by using the Window menu. At the bottom of the Window menu, the names of all open documents are listed. Click a document name, or press the number next to the file you want. The window immediately becomes the active window and appears on top of all other open windows.

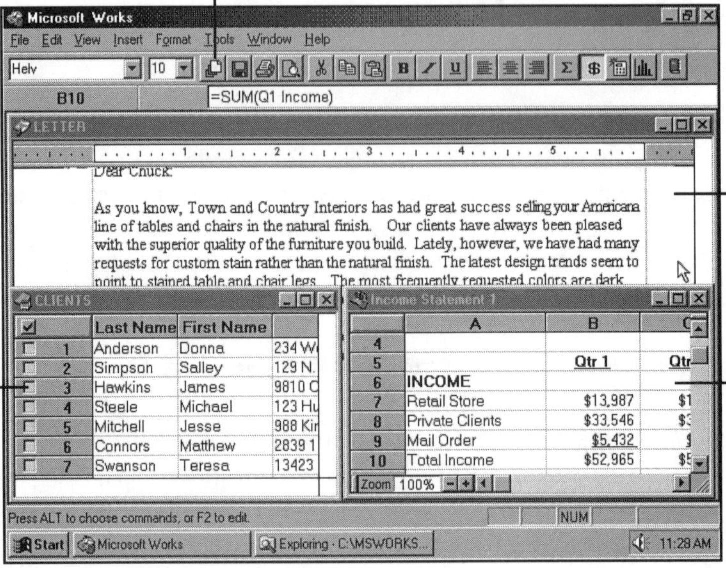

Fig. 2.16 Three separate document windows are open at once.

> **Note**
>
> Another way to activate a lost window is by pressing Ctrl+F6, which activates the next open document window. Press Ctrl+F6 repeatedly until the document window you want is active, or press Shift+Ctrl+F6 to move backwards through open windows.

Arranging Multiple Document Windows

When you have several document windows open on-screen at once, Works gives you two different arrangement styles. You can choose to *cascade* all open windows, which stacks the windows and leaves the title bar of each window visible (see fig. 2.17). Or you can *tile* all open windows, which varies depending on the number of document windows that are open at once (see fig. 2.18). To choose an arrangement select Window, Cascade or Window, Tile.

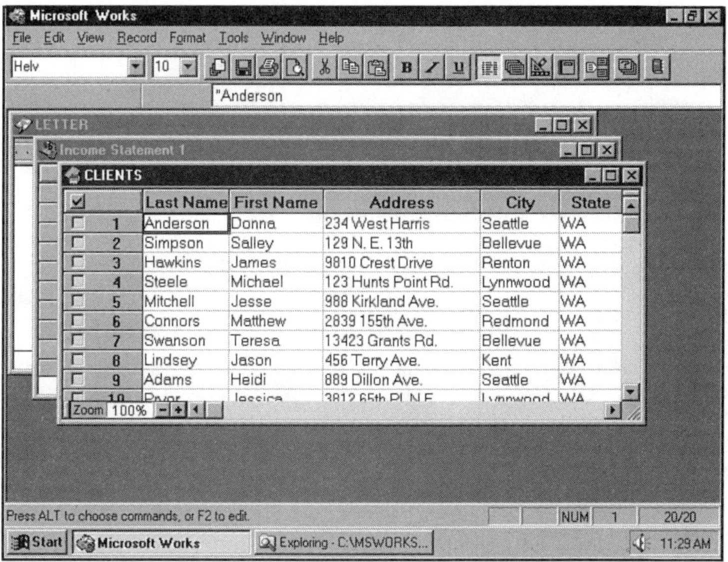

Fig. 2.17
All open document windows are cascaded.

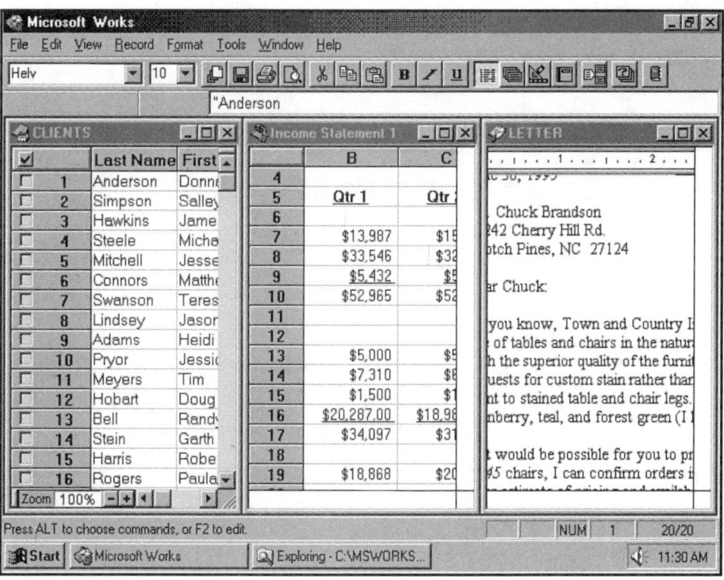

Fig. 2.18
All open document windows are tiled.

You can also arrange open windows by resizing and moving them to new locations on-screen. To resize a window, drag and drop any of the window borders. To resize in two dimensions at once and maintain the height-to-width proportions of the window, drag and drop any of the window corners. To move a window, drag and drop the title bar to a new location.

Another way to arrange open windows on-screen is to minimize them. Minimizing a window shrinks it to an icon but leaves the document open. Minimizing a window gets it out of your way but leaves it quickly accessible when you need it. In figure 2.19, the word processor window is active, and the database and spreadsheet windows are minimized.

Fig. 2.19
Minimized document windows appear as icons at the bottom of the Works window.

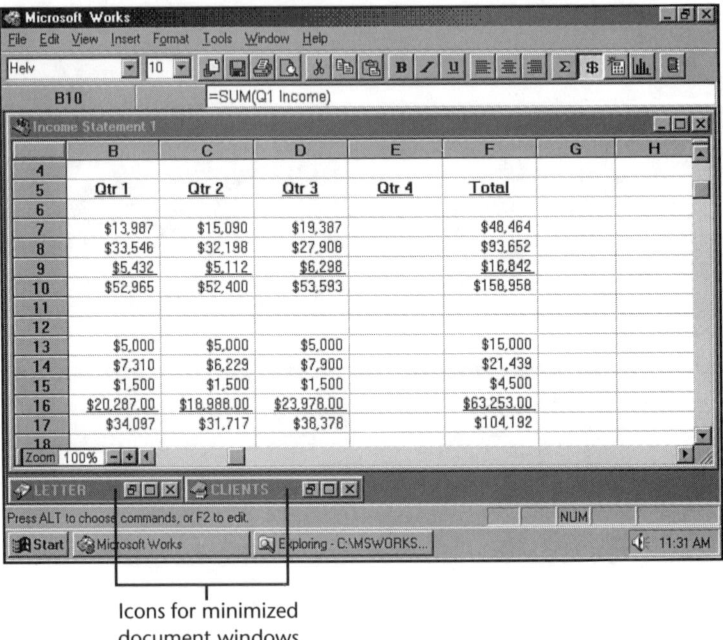

To minimize a window, click the document window's minimize button. To make a minimized window active again, click the program icon. The window is restored to its previous size and position on-screen.

Caution

Don't confuse the document window's Minimize button with the Works program window's Minimize button. If you do, you will shrink the Works window instead of just the document window. When a document window is maximized, its Minimize button appears at the far-right end of the menu bar.

Closing a Document Window

There are several ways to close a document window. First, click the window to make sure the window is active. The fastest way to close a window is to click the Close button in the upper-right corner of the window. You can also choose File, Close, or double-click the document window's control menu button. (If you single-click instead of double-click, the Control menu appears, from which you choose the Close command.) You can also press Ctrl+F4, the keyboard shortcut for closing a window.

Regardless of the method you choose, if you haven't saved recent changes to your file, a reminder message appears. Click Yes to save changes, No to abandon the changes, or Cancel to return to the document without saving changes. See Chapter 3, "Working with Documents, TaskWizards, and Templates," for more information on saving documents.

Changing Your View of a Document

A *view* defines the way Works displays a document on-screen. In the word processor, Works offers two different views: Normal and Page Layout, both described below. Each view has its advantages and unique characteristics.

- *Normal view.* Works uses this view by default; unless you choose another view, Works displays all documents in Normal view. Normal view reflects most aspects of your document as they will appear when printed. That is, Works displays accurate font and point sizes, text alignment and paragraph formats, and any inserted pictures or drawings. Missing from Normal view are margins, headers, footers, footnotes, and columns in their proper locations.

- *Page Layout view.* To view headers, footers, footnotes, and columns on-screen, use Page Layout view. This view presents all aspects of your document on-screen as they will appear when printed. The top, bottom, right, and left page margins are presented accurately on-screen. Headers and footers appear at the top and bottom of every page, footnotes appear at the bottom of the appropriate pages, and if you use multiple columns in a document, they appear on-screen as well.

The more document enhancements, features, and special effects you choose to display on-screen, the more computer resources Works requires. Page Layout view requires the most computer resources and may cause slow response on a computer lacking adequate memory. Normal view, on the other hand, requires fewer computer resources and is often the best view to use on a slow or low-memory computer. Typically you enter and edit a document in Normal view. An example of Page Layout view is shown in figure 2.20.

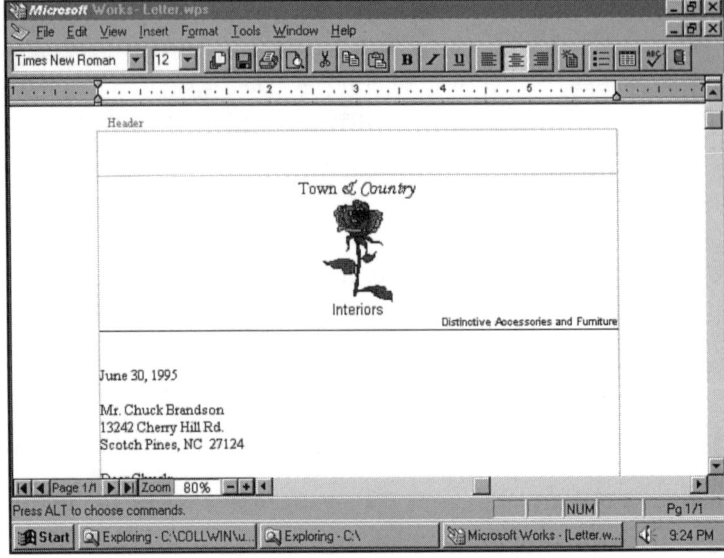

Fig. 2.20
Use Page Layout view when you're doing final editing of a document and you want to view all document elements in their proper locations.

To change your view of a document, follow these steps:

1. Choose the View menu. A check mark appears to the left of the view you currently are using.

2. To select another view, choose Normal or Page Layout. Works places a check mark next to the view you select and immediately switches your document to that view.

Using Zoom

Another feature Works offers that changes your view of a document is *Zoom.* Often, you might find Zoom helpful to magnify a particular area of a document. Zoom can also reduce the displayed size of a document. The Zoom dialog box (displayed by choosing View, Zoom) contains five preset magnification/reduction levels (see fig. 2.21). You can also display the Zoom dialog box by clicking the Zoom button at the bottom of the window.

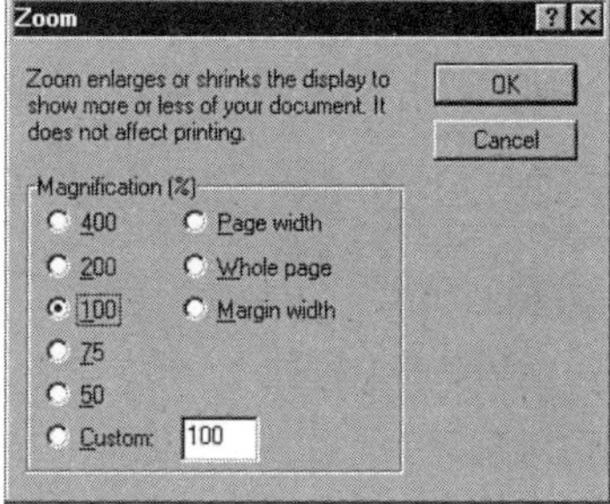

Fig. 2.21
Preset magnification/reduction levels include 400%, 200%, 100%, 75%, and 50%.

To use the Zoom feature in Works, follow these steps.

1. Choose View, Zoom. Works displays the Zoom dialog box shown in figure 2.21.

2. Select a magnification level or enter a number from 25 to 1,000 in the Custom text box.

3. Choose OK. Works displays the current document at the magnification level you choose.

An example of a magnified document is shown in figure 2.22. To return to 100 percent magnification (a normal view), use the preceding steps, choosing the 100 percent option.

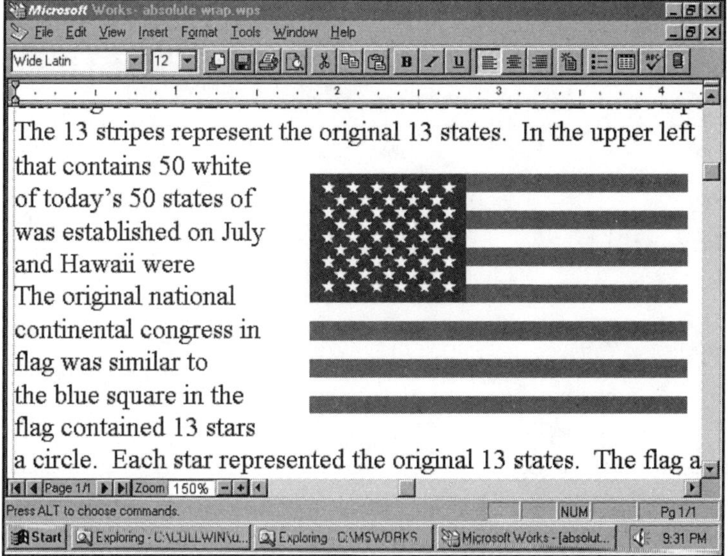

Fig. 2.22
At 150 percent, text is more readable and the detail of the figure is visible.

The Zoom dialog box also lets you change how text is displayed in the window. Following is a description of the three zoom/display options:

- *Page Width.* Choose this option when you want to display your document from left to right margins, regardless of the window size. For example, if your document window size is reduced, the entire page width of the document is still visible.
- *Whole Page.* Choose this option when you want your document to fit in the width of the document window. This is useful when using Landscape orientation; you don't have to scroll horizontally to see all the text.
- *Margin Width.* Choose this option when you want to maximize the amount of available typing space within the window.

Getting Help

When you first begin using Works or you're learning a new feature, there will be times when you wish you had the answer to a quick question or simple step-by-step instructions right at your fingertips. With online help, you do. Just press F1 or click the Help menu to reveal the list of help commands.

The help commands on the Help menu are shown in Table 2.3.

Table 2.3 Help Menu Commands and Their Functions

Help Command	Description
Contents	Displays a table of contents listing all help topics in the help file, categorized by the four Works applications. Use for browsing through all topics in the Help file, just like you would in the Table of Contents of a printed book.
Index	Displays an extensive alphabetical list of topics, similar to an index in the back of a printed book.
Introduction to Works	Introduces the Works Task Launcher, TaskWizards, and each of the applications in Works, and the type of work you can do with them.
How to Use Help	Gives brief instructions on using Help.
Hide/Show Help	Hides or shows the Help window on-screen when Help is running.
Launch Works Forum	If you are a subscriber of Microsoft Network, this connects you directly to the Works Forum, a bulletin board.

Help Command	Description
About Microsoft Works	Displays Microsoft Works 4.0 for Windows 95 copyright and version information.

When you choose a Help menu command, a Help window like the one shown in figure 2.23 appears. (The Works document window shrinks to make room for the Help window.) The Help window has two tabs. The Step-by-Step tab provides step-by-step instructions for accomplishing a particular task. Click the More Info tab if you want an overview of the topic you chose or troubleshooting information.

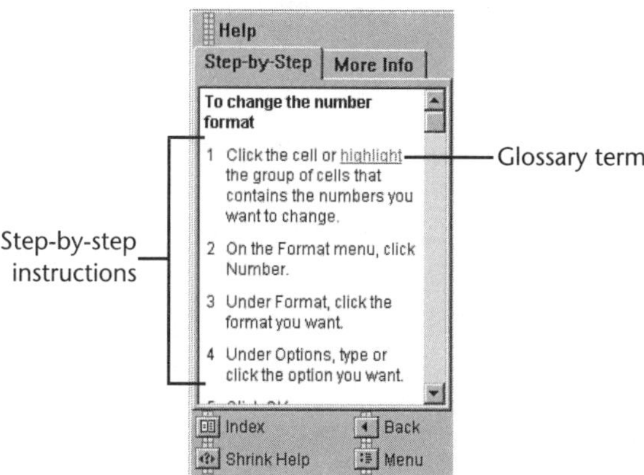

Fig. 2.23
A typical Help topic in Works.

> **Note**
>
> The Help button that appeared in dialog boxes in previous versions of Works has been replaced in Works 4.0 by the Help button, located in the upper-right corner of the dialog box. You can identify this icon by its question mark icon. Click the Help button to get help on a specific dialog box option. Or, select the dialog box option and right-click the mouse.

Help topics sometimes include *glossary terms* that appear in underlined characters. Click a glossary term to display a definition in a pop-up window. When you're finished reading the definition, click anywhere on the Help window or press any key on the keyboard.

Use the scroll bar on the right side of the Help window to scroll through long topics. At the bottom of the Help window are four buttons for navigating and controlling Help. These buttons are described in Table 2.4.

Table 2.4 Command Buttons Available in Help Windows

Command Button	Use
Index	Click to see the Index or Contents to Help and choose a topic.
Back	Retrace your steps through the Help pages when you have viewed many topics and you want to go back to a previous topic.
Shrink Help	Shrinks the Help window to a vertical bar, displayed to the right of the document window. To bring the Help window back, click the Shrink Help button or the Index button at the bottom of the vertical bar.
Menu	Displays a list of Help topics for the application that is currently active (such as the word processor).

When you select Contents or Index from the Help menu, a dialog box is displayed in addition to the Help window shown in figure 2.20. The Help Topics: Microsoft Works dialog box contains two tabs: Index and Contents. To display a detailed index of topics, click the Index tab (see fig. 2.24). In number 1, type the topic you're looking for. Number 2 lists all index entries for that topic.

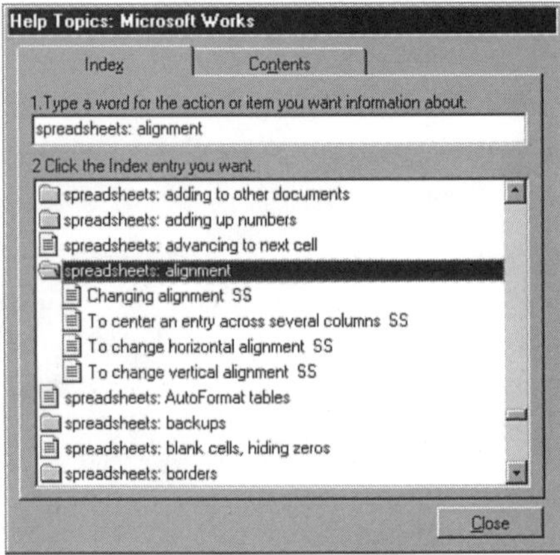

Fig. 2.24
The Index page displays a detailed index of Help topics.

In the Help Topics: Microsoft Works dialog box, Help topics are arranged hierarchically, just like they are in a printed book. This hierarchy is represented graphically in the Help window by book, folder, and page icons (see fig. 2.25). To display a Help topic, click the book you want, then the folder, then the page. (There might be several levels of folders inside folders.)

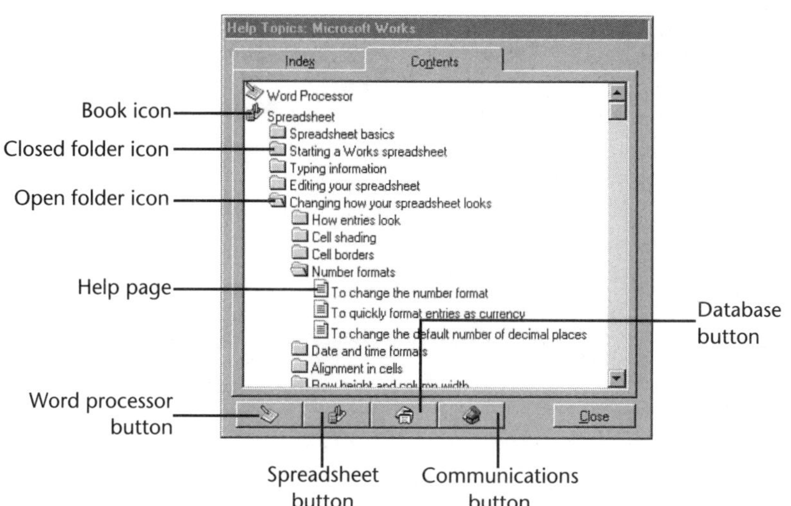

Fig. 2.25
Index and Contents topics are arranged hierarchically in books, folders, and pages.

At the bottom of the Help Topics: Microsoft Works dialog box are four icon buttons, one for each book (word processor, spreadsheet, database, and communications.) Click these buttons to move quickly to the topic you want. When you're finished using the Index or Contents tabs, click the Close button.

Note

Each time you start Works, Help appears automatically on the screen. If you don't want to display Help each time Works starts, choose Tools, Options, then click the View tab. Click the Show Help at Startup button to remove the check mark from the box, then choose OK.

Tip
To exit Works quickly, press Alt+F4. If open documents have not been saved, Works displays a reminder message asking if you want to save changes.

Exiting Works 4.0 for Windows 95

When you're finished using Works, choose File, Exit Works to close the program. If you have open document files that have not yet been saved, Works displays a dialog box for each file asking if you want to save the changes. Click Yes to save the most recent changes, click No to abandon the most recent changes, or click Cancel to return to Works. ❖

Chapter 3

Working with Documents, TaskWizards, and Templates

by Debbie Walkowski

As you begin to use the tools in Works 4.0 for Windows 95, you will create documents that you want to save and reuse—perhaps many times. There are several ways to create documents: by using a TaskWizard to build the framework of the document for you, by using a template as a model, or by building it from "scratch." Whichever method you use, you need to understand how Works handles documents and how to save, rename, copy, and recall a document whenever necessary.

In this chapter, you learn how to

- Create, save, duplicate, open, and close documents
- Use TaskWizards to accomplish specific jobs
- Create models for documents using templates

Working with Documents

A document is a collection of information that is stored on your computer's hard disk or a floppy disk. As you use Works—regardless of the application you use—you create, name, save, and copy documents as well as open existing documents.

Creating New Documents

In Chapter 2, "Getting Started with Works for Windows," you are introduced to the Works Task Launcher dialog box, which appears when you start the Works program. At this point, you know that you can create a new Works document by clicking an application button (see fig. 3.1). If you are already working on a document and want to create a new one, you access the Works Task Launcher dialog box by choosing File, New or by clicking the Task Launcher button on the toolbar, which instantly displays the Works Task Launcher dialog box.

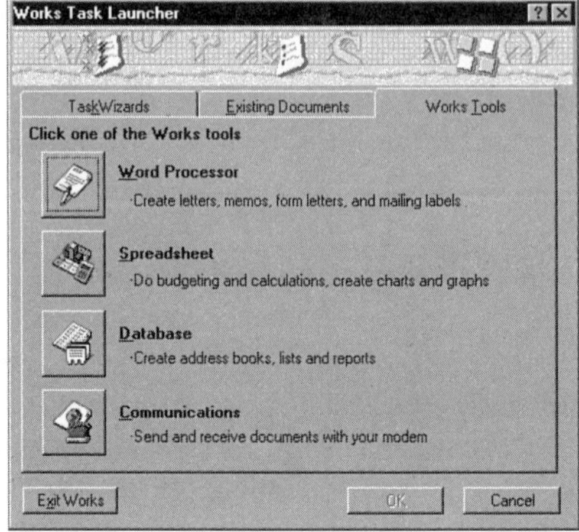

Fig. 3.1
Click the Existing Documents tab to open a saved document. Click the TaskWizard tab to use a TaskWizard for a specific task.

When you create a new document, the title bar contains a temporary document name that reflects the application you are using. For instance, when you create a new word processor document, it is called Unsaved Document 1 until you name and save the document. Subsequent new word processor documents that you create are called Unsaved Document 2, Unsaved Document 3, and so on. Spreadsheet documents are called Unsaved Spreadsheet 1, Unsaved Spreadsheet 2, Unsaved Spreadsheet 3, and so on. New database and communications documents are called Unsaved Database 1 and Unsaved Communications 1, respectively, where the number is incremented with each subsequent document you create. You give the document a permanent name when you save it, as described in the next section.

Naming and Saving Documents

As you begin using the applications in Works, you will want to save the information you create. Until you save a document, it is stored only in your computer's memory. An interruption in power or a problem with your computer might cause you to lose your work before you have saved it, so you should get in the habit of saving documents often. When you save a document, you assign it a permanent document name.

If you've used earlier versions of Works, you know that you previously saved documents with a file type (extension)—that is, WPS for word processor documents, WKS for spreadsheet documents, WDB for database documents, and WCM for communications documents. With Windows 95, you no longer have to specify a file type when you save a document. Works still uses these file types, but they are not displayed with the file name and don't need to be specified when you open a saved document.

In all of the Works applications, there are two commands on the File menu for saving documents: Save and Save As. Typically, choose File, Save to save a new document and choose File, Save As only when you want to change how or where the document is saved. Choosing File, Save As displays the Save As dialog box shown in figure 3.2. The first time you save a document, you can choose either File, Save or File, Save As. In either case, the Save As dialog box is always displayed so you can give the document a permanent name.

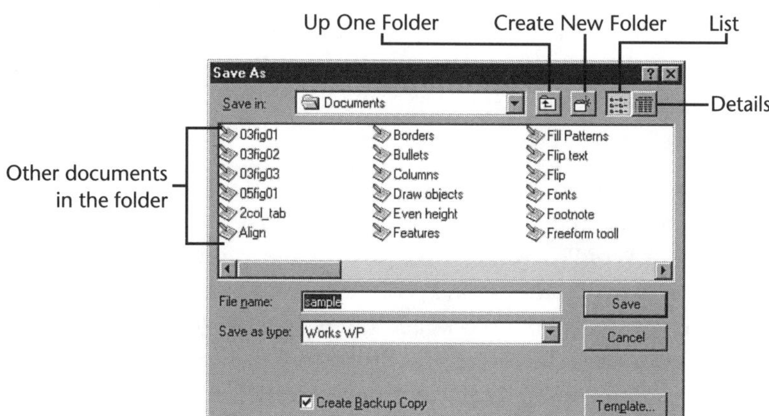

Fig. 3.2
Name your document in the File Name text box.

In the Save In box, notice that an open document folder icon appears to the left of the Documents folder name. The Documents folder is inside of the Msworks folder. Unless you choose a different folder, this is where your Works documents will be saved. (The list box displays other documents already saved in the Documents folder.) In general, you should always save your work in Documents unless you create other folders inside the Msworks folder. For example, if you primarily create letters and invoices and want to file them separately, you might create folders called Letters and Invoices.

To choose a different existing folder, open the Save In box by clicking the down arrow. Works displays a "map" of all the disks on your computer and the Msworks folders (see fig. 3.3). If you prefer to create a new folder, point to the folder in which you want to place the new folder, then click the Create New Folder button. Type a name for the new folder and press Enter. Then you can save the current document in the new folder.

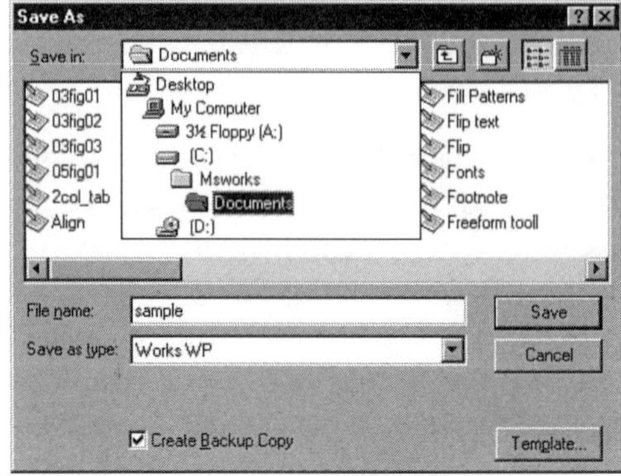

Fig. 3.3
The Save In drop-down list displays the disks and folders on your computer.

Tip
Click the Up One Level button when you want to view the contents of the folder at the previous level.

The File Name box is where you enter a name for your document. You can enter as many characters as you like to name the file but don't use the / , \ . < > characters.

If you anticipate using your document with another word processing program, such as a previous version of Works (for Windows or DOS), Word (for Windows or DOS), or WordPerfect, you can save the file in the appropriate file type. (The choices shown in the Save As Type box vary depending on the Works application you are using.) Works also offers Text and Text (DOS) types that allow you to save the text along with spaces, paragraph markers, punctuation, and sometimes tab settings. However, enhancements such as bold, underline, italics, subscript, superscript, and special fonts are not saved.

By checking the Create Backup Copy check box, you tell Works to save a backup copy of your document. A backup copy is an exact copy of a document as you saved it. It is stored in the same folder where you save your document. It's useful to make backup copies when you want to change a document but keep a copy of the previous version.

The final option in the Save As dialog box is the Template button. Templates are discussed in more detail later in this chapter in the section "Using Templates."

To save a Works document for the first time, follow these steps:

1. Choose File, Save or File, Save As, or click the Save button on the toolbar. The Save As dialog box shown in figure 3.2 is displayed.
2. To save the document in a folder other than Documents or on a different disk, choose a different folder or drive from the Save In drop-down list.
3. To choose a different document type, select a type from the Save As Type drop-down list.
4. In the File Name text box, type a name for the document.
5. If you want to save a backup copy of the document, check the Create Backup Copy check box.
6. If you want to save a document as a template, click the Template button, then type a name in the Save As Template dialog box that appears. Click OK.
7. Choose Save.

To save a document that has already been saved, choose File, Save or click the Save button on the toolbar. Because you have already named the document, the document is automatically saved using its current name and location, so the Save As dialog box does not appear. If you want to save the document under a different name, document type, on a different drive, or in a different folder, choose File, Save As to display the Save As dialog box again.

Note

When you save an already-saved document to a different drive or folder, or with a new document type or name, the previous document remains saved and unchanged in its original location.

The List and Detail buttons in the Save As dialog box let you view the contents of a folder in different ways. In figure 3.2, the List option is chosen, displaying a list of document names with an icon to the left of each name. The icons in figure 3.2 represent word processor documents; when you save a spreadsheet, database, or communications document, the icons are different. If you want to see the details of each document (name, size, type, and date last modified), click the Detail button. An example is shown in figure 3.4.

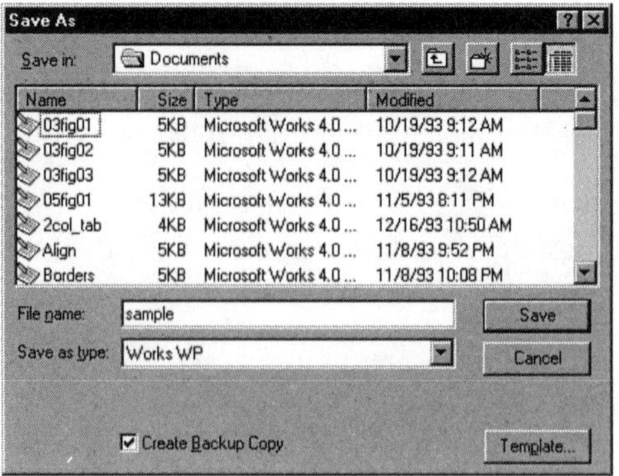

Fig. 3.4
You can see more information about each document when you choose the Detail button.

Closing Documents

After you save a document for the first time, the document continues to be displayed on-screen so you can continue working on it. The title bar now reflects the document name you specified when you saved the document. When you are finished working with a document and have saved the most recent changes, you can remove the document from the window by clicking the document window's Close button, or by choosing File, Close. When you close a document, other open documents (if any) are still visible on-screen. When you close the last open document, you see a blank Works window.

If you forget to save a document before closing it, don't worry about losing your work. Works displays a dialog box asking if you want to save the document. Choose Yes to save the most recent changes, choose No to abandon the changes, or choose Cancel to return to the document window without saving the document.

Opening Documents

Works provides several ways for you to open a saved document. Choose File, Open, or press Ctrl+O. Works displays the Open dialog box shown in figure 3.5. If other documents are already open, the next document you open becomes the active document, indicated by the highlighted title bar.

The Open dialog box is very similar to the Save As dialog box. The current folder is shown in the Look In box, and documents in that folder are listed below. (An icon representing the type of file appears to the left of each document name.) Notice that the Up One Level, Create New Folder, List, and Details buttons in the Open dialog box are identical to those in the Save As dialog box and operate in the same way.

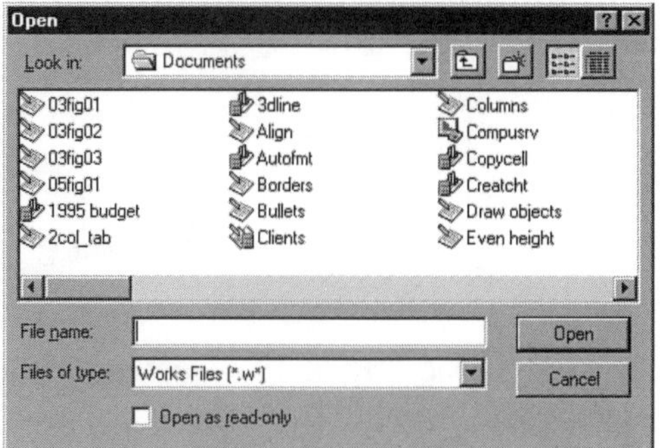

Fig. 3.5
The Open dialog box displays a list of all types of saved Works files.

The entry `Works Files (*.w*)` appears in the Files of Type box. This entry determines which documents are shown in the document list box. The asterisks are *wild cards*, or place holders, that represent any number of characters in a document name. Because all Works file types begin with w and end in two different letters, the entry `*.w*` allows for every type of Works document to be shown in the documents list. If you only want to list database documents, for example, choose Works DB (*.WDB) from the drop-down list.

To open a file, double-click the name shown in the list, or type the name in the File Name box and press Enter. To open the file only for viewing, select the Open As Read-Only option. If you try to make changes to a read-only file, an error message appears when you try to close the document. The read-only option is useful when you want to view a file but protect the information from accidental changes.

To open a saved Works document using the Open dialog box, follow these steps:

1. Choose File, Open or press Ctrl+O. The Open dialog box appears (refer to fig. 3.5).

2. To change the list of files, click the Files of Type drop-down box and choose a file type. The list of documents is updated to reflect the file type you choose.

3. If the document you want to open is stored in a different folder or drive, click the Look In drop-down box, then click the correct drive or folder.

4. In the document list box, click the name of the document you want to open and press Enter, or double-click the document name. The document opens in the appropriate document window.

Tip
It doesn't matter which application you're using when you display the Open dialog box; you can open any type of document from the Open dialog box.

Note

To prevent you from changing two separate versions of the same document at once, Works will not allow you to open more than one copy of a document at once. If you try to open an additional copy of a document that is already open, Works displays an error message.

Tip

You can open documents from Works 4.0, from a previous version of Works, or from another application that's compatible with Works (such as a text file created with a different word processor).

Another way you can open a recently-saved document is to choose the File menu and double-click the document in the list that appears at the bottom of the menu. Works lists the four most recently opened files on the File menu.

There is yet another way you can open a saved Works document. Click the Task Launcher button on the toolbar, then click the Existing Documents tab. The eight documents you have used most recently are listed. If the document you want to open appears on the list, double-click to open it. If not, click the Open a Document Not Listed Here button to display the Open dialog box and continue from there.

Finding a Lost File

If the file you want isn't listed and you can't find it in the Open dialog box, click the Task Launcher toolbar button, then the Existing Documents tab. Now click the Help Me Find a Document button. Works displays the Find Files dialog box with three tabs: Name & Location, Date Modified, and Advanced (see fig. 3.6).

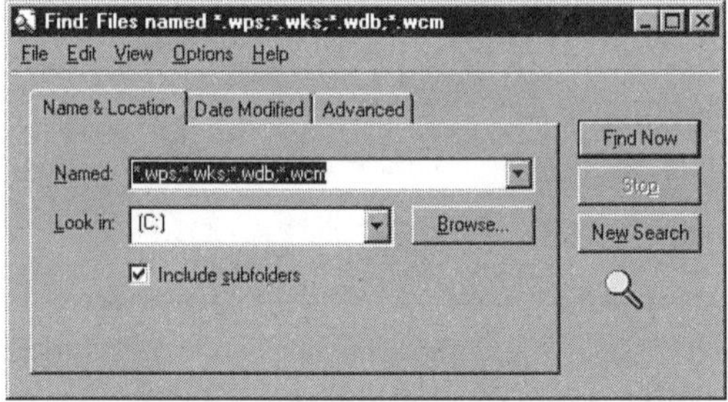

Fig. 3.6
The Find Files dialog box helps you find a "lost" document. Click a tab for the type of search you want to use.

To find the file by its name, use the Name and Location tab and enter the file name in the Named box. Use the Look In box to specify the directories or drive you want to search, for example, in C:\ or a subdirectory, or on a different drive. Use the Date Modified tab to search for a file based on the date you last worked with it. You can specify an exact date or specify within a certain number of months or days. Use the Advanced tab to find a file based on exact text contained in the document.

Duplicating Documents

When you duplicate a document, you make an exact copy of it, saving it under a different name. After it's duplicated, the two documents are entirely separate; if you make changes in one document, the other document is not affected. Duplicating can be especially helpful when you need to create two or more similar—but not exactly the same—copies of a document.

For example, suppose you're sending a similar letter to two clients. You can save yourself the time of typing two separate letters by creating one, duplicating it, then making the appropriate changes to the second letter. Or, suppose you prepare a monthly sales spreadsheet that is identical in structure and format each month; only the numbers change from month to month. You can prepare the spreadsheet the first month, then duplicate it each following month and change only the numbers.

Works does not have a special command for duplicating a document. In fact, you already know how to duplicate a document: by using the File, Save As command you learned about earlier. To duplicate a document, follow these steps:

1. Open the document you want to duplicate.
2. Choose File, Save As. The Save As dialog box appears (refer to fig. 3.2).
3. In the Save In box, choose the appropriate folder and drive where you want to store the duplicate document.
4. In the File Name box, type a unique name for the document.
5. Choose Save. Works closes the original document and leaves the new document open on-screen.

Opening Documents Automatically When You Start Works

If you frequently work with the same documents each time you use Works, you'll find the Save Workspace option a handy feature. Using this feature, Works automatically saves as a group the documents you specify, and reopens them each time you start the program. The document windows appear on-screen in the same size and arrangement in which you saved them. You can save up to eight open documents of any type (word processor, spreadsheet, database, or communications) as a workspace.

Tip
This feature saves you time and energy—you don't have to reopen and arrange each document.

To save a workspace, follow these steps:

1. Open all the documents you want to save.
2. Arrange the document windows on-screen just as you want them.
3. Choose Tools, Options. The Options dialog box appears.
4. Click the View tab.
5. Select the Use Saved Workspace at Startup check box, then click the Save Workspace button.
6. Click OK.

The next time you start Works, the documents you saved as a workspace are automatically reopened.

You can save a new workspace at any time by following the previous steps with a new set of documents on-screen. If at some point you choose not to use the saved workspace, follow the same steps—but deselect the Use Saved Workspace at Startup check box.

Troubleshooting

I named my database document CLIENTS.WDB but I can't find it in the Documents folder.

You might have inadvertently selected a different folder or drive, or typed the document name incorrectly when you saved the document. To find the document, click the Task Launcher button, choose the Existing Documents tab, then choose the Help Me Find a Document button.

I made some changes to an existing document, then duplicated the document by saving it under a different name, but the changes I made weren't saved in the original document.

You didn't save the changes you made to the original document before you duplicated it. Before you duplicate a document, *always* save the changes you make if you want them saved in both documents.

Using TaskWizards

Before you've had time to master the tools in Works, you might find yourself up against a deadline to complete an important job. Sometimes the effort involved in setting up the layout of such documents can be more time-consuming than supplying the data or information itself. A *TaskWizard* is a tool in Works that helps you create these and other challenging types of documents.

TaskWizards are a wonderful invention for users who are new to Works, who don't have a lot of time to create a complex document, or who don't feel confident in their ability to create a stylish, professional-looking document. For these users, TaskWizards are life savers. They do all the thinking, planning, designing, and layout of a document for you. All you do is choose from suggested styles and fill in the document's unique information.

When you use a TaskWizard, an on-screen "script" asks questions that you respond to interactively. Using the information you supply, the TaskWizard either completes a task or creates the framework of a document for you.

Works includes a wide variety of TaskWizards. It is well worth your time to review the entire list of TaskWizards thoroughly. You'll get great ideas for documents you never thought of creating. In the Works Task Launcher dialog box, you'll find TaskWizards listed under each of the following categories:

Common Tasks
Correspondence
Envelopes and Labels
Business Management
Names and Addresses
Household Management
Students and Teachers
Billing
Employment
Volunteer/Civic Activities

You can create the following types of documents using TaskWizards:

(Word Processor)

Bibliography
Brochure
Certificate
Envelopes
Flyer
Form Letter
Labels
Letterhead
Memo

Newsletter
Proposal Forms
Proposal Letter
Resume
Return Address Labels
School Reports/Thesis
Start from Scratch
Statements
Tests

(Spreadsheet)

Bids
Employee Time Sheet
FAX Cover Sheet
Grade Book
Invoice
Mortgage/Loan Analysis
Order Form
Price List
Quotations
Schedule
Start from Scratch

(Database)

Accounts
Address Book
Business Inventory
Customers or Clients
Employee Profile
Home Inventory
Phone List
Sales Contacts
Start from Scratch
Student & Membership Information
Suppliers & Vendors

Tip
The TaskWizards tab automatically appears whenever you start Works.

To use a TaskWizard, click the Task Launcher toolbar button. The TaskWizards tab is automatically selected. Click a category to display a list of TaskWizards. To see a description of the type of document the Wizard creates, highlight the name. The description appears on the right side of the dialog box. To start a TaskWizard, double-click a document name in the list.

Although all TaskWizards operate virtually the same way, by presenting a series of questions and choices, each TaskWizard asks different questions based on the type of document you are creating. The next three figures give you an idea of how the Resume TaskWizard works.

Tip
TaskWizards are an important feature to remember when you're in a crunch for time. You can create your document in a fraction of the time it might take to create it from scratch.

The first screen of the Resume TaskWizard lets you choose one of three resume styles: chronological, qualifications, or curriculum vitae (which is Latin for "course of one's life"). When you click on a style, a sample of that style is displayed on the right side of the screen (see fig. 3.7). Beneath the sample is a short description of the style that points out its benefits and emphasis. Choose a style and then click Next.

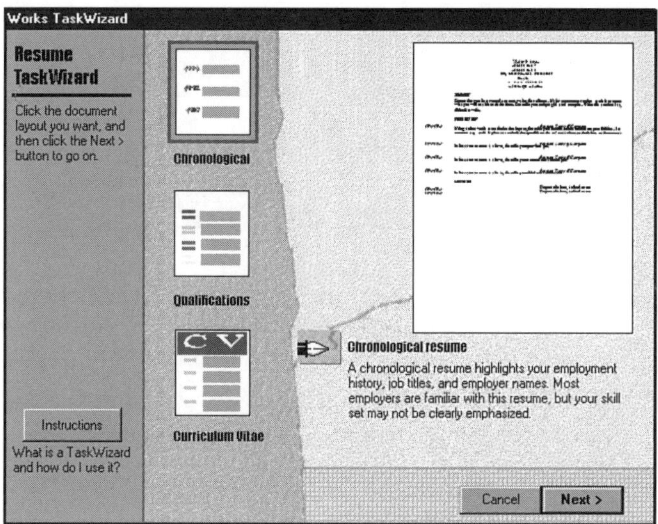

Fig. 3.7
If you need help, choose the Instructions button to receive on-screen help.

Figure 3.8 shows the next screen—the heart of the resume. Here you choose a letterhead style, or use your own personal letterhead. You determine the layout of the resume, the style of the headings, and the content of the resume (for example, the number of jobs and schools to include on the resume).

So you don't forget to complete any elements of the resume, it's best to work your way through the Letterhead, Layout, Headings, and Entries options in that order. Click on one of these options, then click the Create It! button. This takes you to a detailed screen where you can choose specific settings. When you are finished, click OK. You return to the screen shown in figure 3.8. Continue progressing through the screens by responding to the questions and clicking the appropriate buttons in the lower-right corner of the screens. When you finish, the TaskWizard creates the document for you and displays it as the active document on your screen.

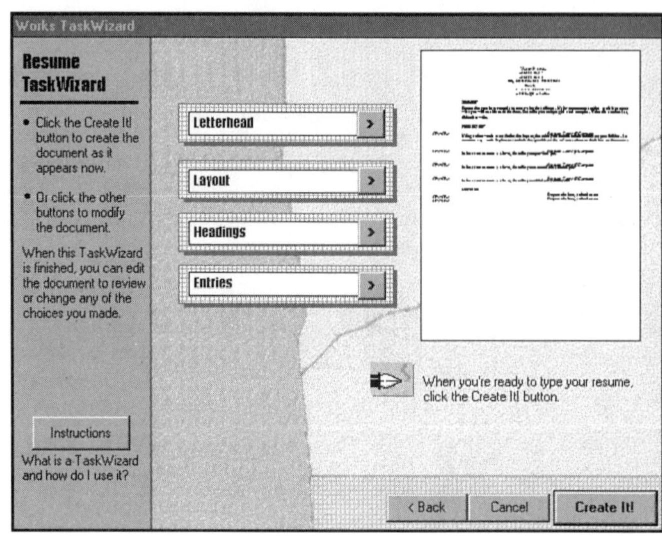

Fig. 3.8
The second Resume TaskWizard screen lets you specify a style for the letterhead, layout, headings, and entries.

Tip
The Resume TaskWizard can produce many resumes that look different. The look you get depends entirely on the choices you make throughout the TaskWizard.

The "finished" resume is shown in figure 3.9. The TaskWizard builds the structure and some of the elements of the document (such as the name/address block and the headings). In the place of job descriptions, company names, schools, dates, and so on, the TaskWizard inserts sample text as a placeholder. Replace the sample text with your own unique information and you have a finished, professional-looking resume.

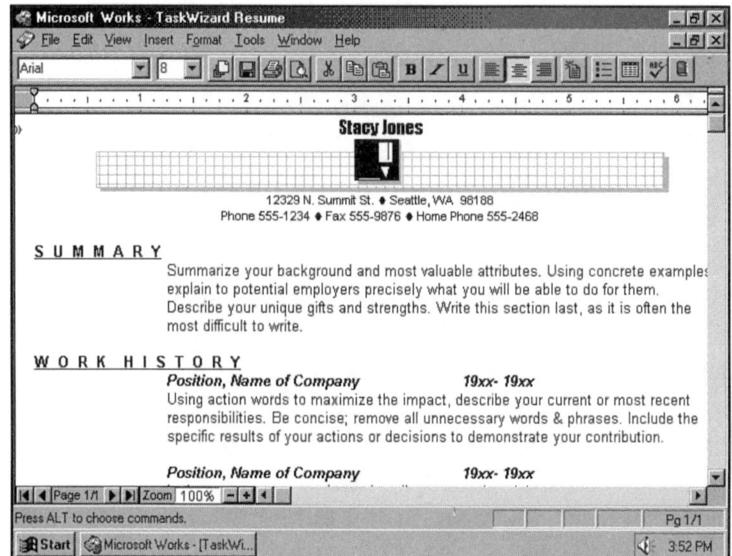

Fig. 3.9
A resume generated by the Resume TaskWizard conveys your personal style based on your responses to the TaskWizard's questions.

Using Templates

A *template* is a model, pattern, or guide. In the context of Works, you use a template to create a Works document much the same way a tailor might use a pattern to make a suit or a woodworker might use a template to create four matching table legs. A template is any type of model that can be used over and over again for different projects. A template has two purposes: to provide consistent results each time you use it, and to save you the trouble of "reinventing the wheel" for each new project.

A fax cover sheet and a purchase order form are good examples of business documents that can be created from templates. They both require the same information each time you use them, and preferably, the format of both documents should be consistent each time you create a new one.

To make a template, you create the *framework* of the document, including all repetitive text and formatting. (Essentially, you create a form.) You can create the document "from scratch" or use a TaskWizard to help you build the document. When you complete the document, you save the document as a template. (Works recommends you store all templates in the Template folder under Msworks.) When you want to use the template to create a working document, Works opens a copy of the template as a new document. You fill in the document with unique information; the original template remains unchanged.

To create a template, follow these steps:

1. Open the word processor, spreadsheet, or database and create the repetitive parts of the document exactly as you want the template to appear.
2. Choose File, Save As. The Save As dialog box appears.
3. In the Save In box, choose the Template folder.
4. Choose the Template button. The Save As Template dialog box appears.
5. In the Template Name box, enter a name for the template document.
6. If you want the template to be the default document when you open the Works word processor, spreadsheet, or database, click the Use This Template for New Word Processor Documents check box.
7. Choose OK.

To use the template, click the Task Launcher toolbar button. Scroll to the bottom of the TaskWizards list and double-click User Defined Templates, then double-click the template name. Works creates a new "blank" document using the template.

Note

If you previously used Works 3.0 and have upgraded to Works 4.0, you might have already created many useful templates. You can open and use these templates in Works 4.0. To make the templates easily accessible, copy or move them from their previous directory to the Templates folder under MSWorks.

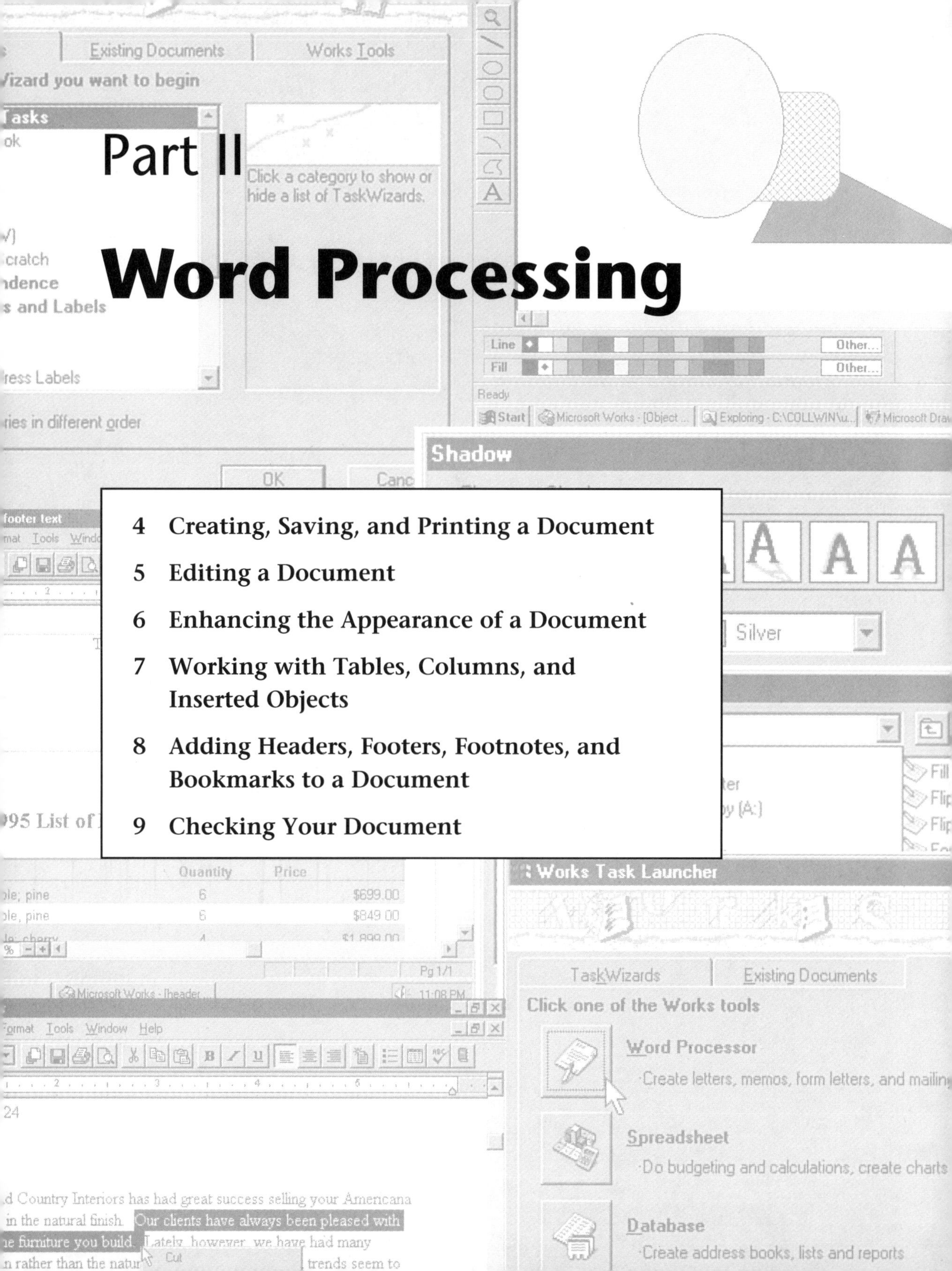

Part II

Word Processing

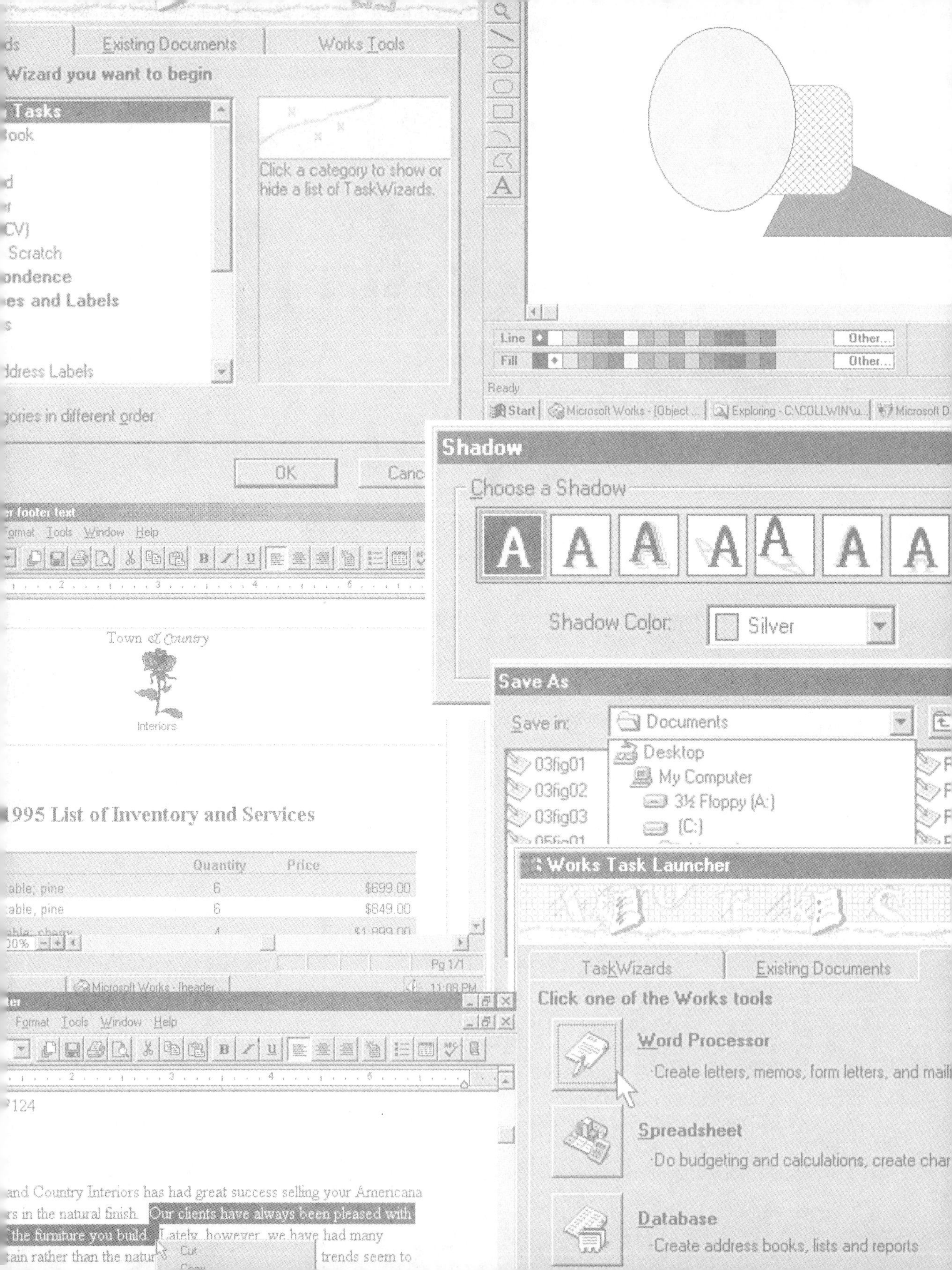
Existing Documents
Works Tools
Wizard you want to begin
Tasks
Click a category to show or hide a list of TaskWizards.
Scratch
ondence
es and Labels
ldress Labels
jories in different order
OK
Canc
Line
Fill
Other...
Other...
Ready
Start
Microsoft Works - [Object ...
Exploring - C:\COLLWIN\u...
Microsoft D
Shadow
Choose a Shadow
Shadow Color:
Silver
Save As
Save in:
Documents
Desktop
My Computer
3½ Floppy (A:)
(C:)
03fig01
03fig02
03fig03
r footer text
Format Tools Window Help
Town & Country
Interiors
1995 List of Inventory and Services
Quantity
Price
able, pine
6
$699.00
able, pine
6
$849.00
Pg 1/1
Microsoft Works - [header...
11:08 PM
Works Task Launcher
TaskWizards
Existing Documents
Click one of the Works tools
Word Processor
Create letters, memos, form letters, and mail
Spreadsheet
Do budgeting and calculations, create char
Database
Create address books, lists and reports
Format Tools Window Help
124
and Country Interiors has had great success selling your Americana
rs in the natural finish. Our clients have always been pleased with
the furniture you build. Lately, however, we have had many
tain rather than the natur
trends seem to

Chapter 4

Creating, Saving, and Printing a Document

by Debbie Walkowski

In Chapters 1, 2, and 3, you learn about the components of Works, how to get around in the program, how to work with menus, toolbars, and windows, and how to get help when you need it. You also learn how to create, name, save, duplicate, open, and close documents. Now you're ready to actually start creating files using the word processor.

In this chapter, you learn about the following:

- Using the word processing window
- Entering text
- Moving around in a document
- Correcting minor errors
- Printing a document

The Word Processor Window

As you learn in Chapter 2, "Getting Started with Works for Windows," each of the applications in Works displays a unique document window inside the Works window. Figure 4.1 shows the basic word processing window that opens when you choose the Word Processor button from the Works Tools tab in the Works Task Launcher dialog box. The document window defaults to Page Layout view. The white area of the screen represents the page; the faint dotted lines outline the text area on the page and the header area. In the figure, the window is maximized so that the Works window and the word processing window blend together to become one. The title bar, (shared by both windows) indicates the temporary file name, `Unsaved Document 1`.

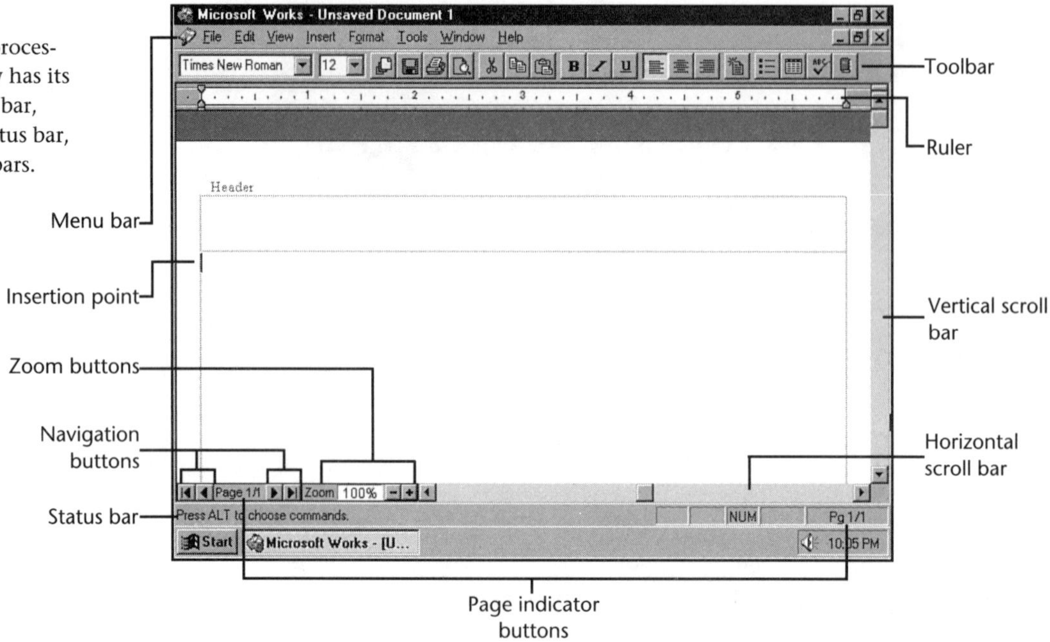

Fig. 4.1
The word processor window has its own menu bar, toolbar, status bar, and scroll bars.

The large rectangular area is the text area where you enter the content of a document. The blinking vertical bar is the *insertion point*, the point at which characters are inserted when you type.

The ruler illustrates the width of a document and indicates where right and left margins, indents, and tabs are located. If you do not see the ruler on your screen, the ruler option is probably turned off. To display the ruler, choose View, Ruler. When a check mark appears next to the Ruler command, the ruler displays on your screen.

▶ See "Examining the Ruler in the Document Window," p. 106

Like all other document windows, the word processor window has both a vertical and a horizontal scroll bar so you can scroll a long document up and down or a wide document left and right. Click the scroll arrows at either end of the scroll bar to shift your view of the document in the direction of the arrow. The page indicator buttons tell you the current page where the insertion point is located and the total number of pages (such as page 5 of 10, noted as 5/10). The navigation buttons move in certain increments. Just to the left of the page indicator are the Beginning of Document and Previous

Page buttons. To the right of the page indicator are the Next Page and End of Document buttons. Click these buttons to help you navigate the document quickly.

Also next to the horizontal scroll bar is a Zoom indicator, a Zoom button, and + and – buttons. The Zoom indicator shows the current zoom percentage (100%). When the zoom percentage is 100%, you are seeing the document at actual size. If the document is displayed at 70%, you are seeing it at 70% of its actual size. To zoom in closer on a document, click the + button; to zoom out, click the - button. Or, click the Zoom indicator and a pop-up menu appears from which you can choose a zoom percentage or enter a custom setting.

The status bar includes a page indicator just like the one in the horizontal scroll bar. The left end of the status bar provides brief instructions (such as `Press ALT to choose commands.`), or describes the current highlighted menu command. For instance, if you choose File, Print, the status bar reads `Prints the Current Document`. When you first learn to use Works, the messages in the status bar can be a handy feature to help you remember command functions. When you press the Num Lock and Caps Lock keys, indicators also appear on the status bar (to the left of the page indicator).

The Word Processor Menus

As you learn in Chapter 2, every Works application has a set of menus: File, Edit, View, Insert, Format, Tools, Window, and Help. Although the menu names are the same from application to application, the actual commands on the menus vary slightly. Table 4.1 describes the types of commands you find on the word processor menus.

Table 4.1 The Word Processor Menus

Menu Name	Command Functions
File	On this menu, you find all the commands necessary for creating, opening, saving, and printing files. Recall from Chapter 3, that the four most recently opened files are always listed at the bottom of the File menu, providing a quick way to open a file. You also use this menu to exit Works and send documents by electronic mail.
Edit	This menu contains commands for cutting, copying, and pasting text, and for undoing the most recent change to a document.

(continues)

Table 4.1 Continued

Menu Name	Command Functions
View	These commands determine how a document is displayed, for instance, in Normal View or Page Layout view. Use this menu to display or turn off the ruler, the toolbar, hidden characters, and so on. Commands for displaying footnotes, headers, and footers also appear on this menu.
Insert	Use this menu to insert any type of graphics object (such as a drawing, clip art, word art, chart, or spreadsheet) in a document. This menu also contains commands for inserting page breaks, special characters, footnotes, EasyText, and so on.
Format	These commands allow you to choose a font and text style, specify a paragraph's format, set tabs, add a border to selected text, create columns of text, create bullets, and format a picture. Easy Formats are also available from this menu.
Tools	This menu contains special tools for working with a word processor document. Here you have access to your address book, the spell checker, thesaurus, hyphenation, and word count features in Works. You also use this menu to create envelopes or labels, repaginate, dial a phone number, customize the toolbar, and other Works options.
Window	Use these commands to help you arrange all open documents on your screen and to select the active window.
Help	The Help menu offers an Index, Contents, Introduction to Works, and How to Use Help. You also use this menu to hide help.

The Word Processor Toolbar

As with menus, each Works application has a unique toolbar as well. Each button on the toolbar represents a particular command. Just click the button to activate the command. Table 4.2 describes the function of each of the word processor buttons.

Tip

Recall from Chapter 2 that you can display the name of a button by pointing to (not clicking) the button on the toolbar. A brief description also appears in the status bar.

Table 4.2 The Buttons on the Word Processor Toolbar

Button	Function
Times New Roman	Displays a drop-down list of all available fonts.

Button	Function
12	Displays a drop-down list of all available point sizes for the current font.
	Displays the Works Task Launcher dialog box.
	Saves the file using the current file name and settings. If the document has not yet been saved, the Save As dialog box appears.
	Prints the active document using the current print settings.
	Click this button to preview your document before printing.
	Cuts the selected text and places it on the Clipboard.
	Copies the selected text to the Clipboard.
	Inserts (pastes) the contents of the Clipboard in a document at the location of the insertion point.
B	Applies bold to selected text.
I	Applies italics to selected text.
U	Applies underline to selected text.
	Left-aligns selected text.
	Centers the selected text between the left and right margins.
	Right-aligns selected text.

(continues)

Table 4.2 Continued

Button	Function
	Applies an EasyFormat to the selected text.
	Places a bullet to the left of the selected paragraph.
	Displays a dialog box in which you specify a spreadsheet or table to insert in your document.
	Begins spell checking the current document.
	Runs the Address Book TaskWizard.

Troubleshooting

I don't see a toolbar in my word processor window.

In Works, you can choose to display the toolbar or turn it off. If the toolbar isn't visible in the word processor window, choose View, Toolbar. (The toolbar is visible in the window when a check mark appears to the left of the Toolbar option.)

On my toolbar, I can't find all of the buttons listed in Table 4.2.

The buttons listed in Table 4.2 appear on the standard toolbar. If the toolbar has been customized, some of the standard buttons might not be shown. To reset the toolbar to the standard buttons, choose Tools, Customize Toolbar. When the Customize Works Toolbar dialog box appears, choose the Reset button, and then choose OK. Works resets the toolbar to its standard buttons.

Entering Text

Entering text in a word processing document is one of the simplest things you can do; you just start typing. Characters appear on the screen to the left of the insertion point, and the insertion point moves to the right as you type. When you reach the end of the first line, continue typing. Works automatically *wraps* text to the next line—you don't have to press Enter at the end of each line. The only time you need to press Enter is when you want to return the insertion point to the left margin to begin a new line or paragraph.

As you type a document on a word processor, the characters you type appear on the lines that are visible in the text area of the window. When you fill those lines, the document scrolls upward to reveal a larger blank working area. For example, if you typed three pages of text without stopping, the window would display the third page and the insertion point would be located to the right of the last character you typed. Before you can make changes in a document, you must know how to move the insertion point to any location, as you learn in the next section.

Moving Around in a Document

If you type a letter on a typewriter and realize you made an error on the first line, you roll the platen backward to the first line to correct the error. In a sense, you do the same thing on a word processor, except that you move the insertion point. After you move the insertion point, you can insert new text, erase existing text, or select text that you want to move or copy.

Using the Keyboard, Mouse, and Scroll Bars

The easiest way to move the insertion point is with the arrow keys. The up- and down-arrow keys move the insertion point up or down one line at a time. The left- and right-arrow keys move the insertion point left or right one character at a time. You can press and hold any of these keys to repeat the action. But the arrow keys do not always provide the most efficient way to move through a document. For instance, what if you want to move the insertion point five pages back? It could take a long time using just the up-arrow key. You can take larger jumps using the Page Up and Page Down keys, which move the insertion point one window backward and one window forward, respectively. These keys also repeat when you hold them down. Another way to move the insertion point is to use the navigation buttons on the horizontal scroll bar (refer to fig. 4.1). These are the Beginning of Document, Previous Page, Next Page, and End of Document buttons. Click any of these buttons to move quickly through a document.

The scroll box inside the vertical scroll bar indicates your approximate position in a document. For example, if a document is 10 pages long and the scroll box is located half way down the vertical scroll bar, you are probably viewing page 5. Using the mouse, drag the scroll box to the approximate location in the document you want to view, then click anywhere within the working area to move the insertion point. You can also move the document up or down one line at a time by clicking the arrows at either end of the vertical scroll bar.

Note

Scrolling alone does not move the insertion point, it only shifts your view of the document. To move the insertion point, you must click inside the window.

Before most computer programs supported a mouse, you used the keyboard to navigate a document. These keyboard shortcuts, listed in Table 4.3, still work for those who prefer the keyboard to the mouse.

Table 4.3 Keys for Moving the Insertion Point

Keys	Moves Insertion Point
Home	To the beginning of the current line
End	To the end of the current line
Ctrl+Home	To the beginning of the document
Ctrl+End	To the end of the document
Ctrl+right arrow	To the beginning of the next word
Ctrl+left arrow	To the beginning of the previous word
Ctrl+up arrow	To the beginning of the previous paragraph
Ctrl+down arrow	To the beginning of the next paragraph
Right arrow	One character to the right
Left arrow	One character to the left
Up arrow	One line up
Down arrow	One line down
PgUp	Up one window
PgDn	Down one window

Using the Go To Command

When you want to move to a specific page in a document, choose Edit, Go To. When you choose this handy feature, the Go To dialog box appears (see fig. 4.2). Type the page number you want in the Go To box and click OK. Works moves the insertion point to the beginning of the page you specify.

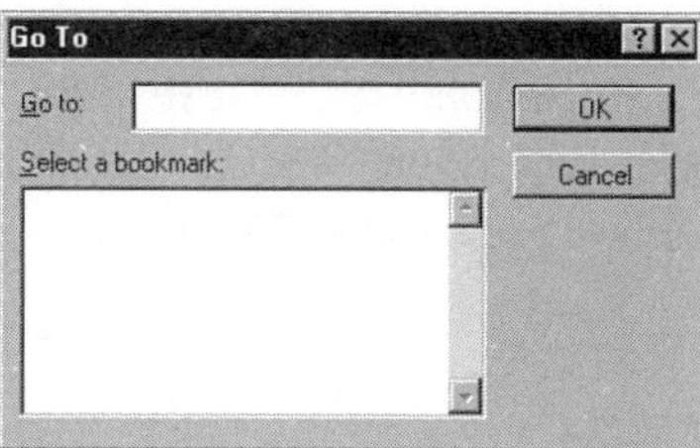

Fig. 4.2
The Go To dialog box lets you move directly to a specific page in a document.

Note

If your document contains bookmarks, you can use the Go To dialog box to move directly to the bookmark you specify rather than to a page. Chapter 8, "Adding Headers, Footers, Footnotes, and Bookmarks to a Document," discusses how to insert bookmarks in a document.

Tip
To display the Go To dialog box quickly, press F5 or Ctrl+G.

Correcting Minor Errors

When you're entering new text, it's easiest to correct minor errors as you type. Minor errors are those that you become aware of quickly and therefore can change quickly and easily without moving around in the document too much. These include typing mistakes, punctuation errors, or a minor change to a word or phrase. (To make major changes, such as extensive editing of a document, refer to Chapter 5, "Editing a Document," for more efficient methods of changing existing text.) To correct minor errors, use the Backspace or Delete key.

To delete the character to the left of the insertion point, press the Backspace key. Like the arrow keys, the Backspace key repeats when held down, so you can delete a sequence of characters quickly. If you prefer, you can use the Delete key to delete the character to the right of the insertion point. Use the arrow keys to position the insertion point, then press Delete. The Delete key also repeats when held down.

Caution

Be careful when holding down either the Backspace or Delete key! On a fast computer, these keys can delete very quickly and, in a matter of seconds, remove more characters than you intend.

Printing a Document

No matter what kind of document you create using the word processor, printing is something you do quite often. You might print short and simple documents only once. Longer and complex documents that must be reviewed in draft stages, you might print several times before the final product is produced. In any case, you should review the document's page and print settings before printing.

Choose File, Page Setup to display the Page Setup dialog box. In this dialog box you specify the page, header, and footer margins; the source, size, and orientation for the paper you are printing on; the page numbering and footnote options, and other standard settings for your particular printer. (You learn how to create headers, footers, and footnotes in Chapter 8.) When all page settings are correct, preview the document to make a final check before printing. In the following section you learn how to specify page settings.

Note

The settings you choose in the Page Setup dialog box affect only the current document.

Setting Margins

Page margins are the white spaces that surround the text on the printed page. To set page margins for the document you are printing, use the Page Setup dialog box shown in figure 4.3. The upper half of the dialog box (labeled Sample) shows a page sample that contains dummy text. As you choose different dialog box settings, the dummy text changes to reflect those choices. The lower half of the dialog box has three tabs: Margins; Source, Size & Orientation; and Other Options. In the figure, the Margins tab is selected and the default margin settings are displayed: one inch for top and bottom margins, and 1.25 inches for left and right margins. The default margin settings are typical for most types of documents—from letters and memos to reports and resumes. You seldom need to change these settings.

For some documents, however, you will change the default margin settings. For example, suppose you want all documents that you print on your company letterhead to align with the logo, name, address, and other graphic elements on your letterhead. After some careful measuring, you might find that the left and right margins need to be 1 inch, the top margin 1.25 inches, and the bottom margin .75 inch. Or, suppose that when you print your resume using default margin settings, the last two lines get bumped to a second page. If you want your resume to be a single page, you can probably get all of the text on one page by slightly altering the page margins.

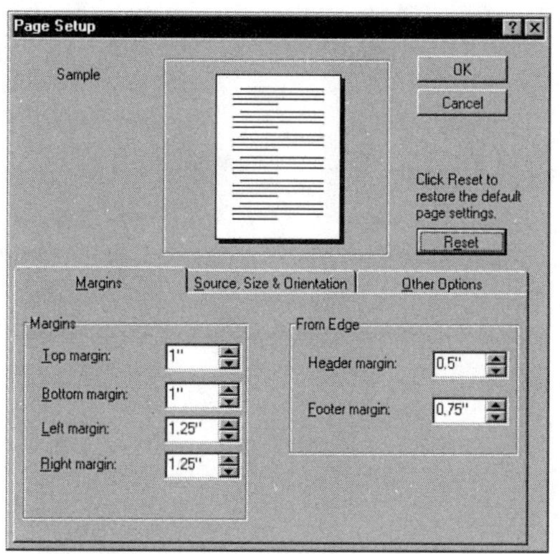

Fig. 4.3
You can change the margin width in the Page Setup dialog box.

To change margin settings for the current document, follow these steps:

1. Choose File, Page Setup. The Page Setup dialog box shown in figure 4.3 appears.
2. Choose the Margins tab.
3. In the appropriate margin boxes, type the setting you want to use in inches (or click the up/down arrow in the box). Type a decimal for fractions of an inch (such as 1.25 for 1-1/4 inches). The Sample area of the dialog box changes to reflect the settings you choose.
4. When all margin settings are correct, choose OK. Works automatically reformats your document using the new margin settings.

Tip
In the Page Setup dialog box, choose Reset to restore the default page settings.

If you decide to include a header or footer in your document, change the header and footer margins the same way you change any other margin. Determining whether you need to alter header and footer margins is discussed in Chapter 8.

Note

If you commonly work with centimeters or other units of measurement rather than inches, you can change the Works default units setting. Choose Tools, Options to display the Options dialog box. Click the General tab. In the Units box, choose a unit of measurement, then choose OK. Note that the unit of measurement you choose applies to *all* applications in Works, not just the one you're currently working in.

Setting Paper Source, Size, and Orientation

Before printing a document, you must specify in Works which paper source to use, the size of the paper you're printing on, and the direction you want the print to appear on the page. To change the paper source, paper size, and print orientation, use the Page Setup dialog box (see fig. 4.4). In the figure, the Source, Size & Orientation tab is selected and the default settings are displayed.

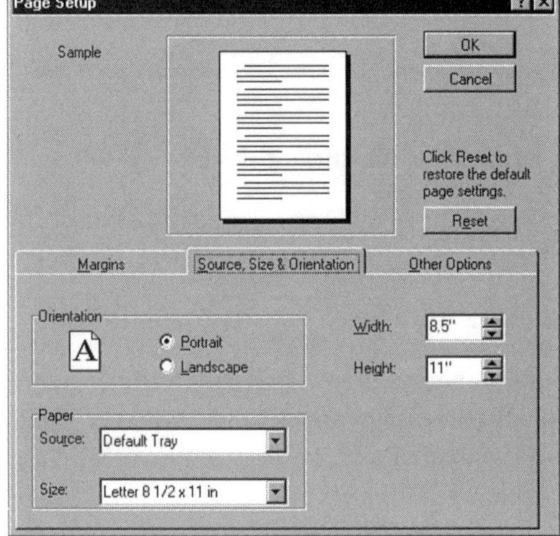

Fig. 4.4
The page in the Sample area reflects the settings you choose.

Depending on the type of printer you are using, choose the correct paper source (such as the default tray, auto sheet feeder, manual feed) from the Paper Source drop-down list. The Paper Size list offers a variety of standard paper and envelope sizes. Choose a size from the list.

Paper orientation refers to the direction the document is printed on the paper. Most documents printed on standard 8-1/2 × 11 inch paper are printed in *portrait* orientation (using the 11-inch dimension as the height of the paper). For documents that are printed in *landscape* orientation, the paper is rotated 90 degrees so that the 8-1/2 dimension is used as the height of the paper. (Of course, the paper is not actually rotated in your printer, your printer simply prints the image "sideways.") The default orientation is Portrait; to print in landscape mode, choose the Landscape button. The paper in the Sample area of the dialog box rotates. Notice, also, that for the paper size you specified, the settings in the Width and Height boxes automatically reverse.

To change source, size, and orientation settings, follow these steps:

1. Choose File, Page Setup. The Page Setup dialog box appears.
2. Choose the Source, Size & Orientation tab. The dialog box shown in figure 4.4 appears.
3. Choose a paper source from the Paper Source drop-down list.
4. Choose a paper size from the Paper Size drop-down list.
5. Choose a paper orientation by clicking either the Portrait or Landscape option button.
6. When all settings are correct, choose OK.

Setting Other Page Options

The third tab in the Page Setup dialog box is Other Options (see fig. 4.5). Use the settings on this tab to specify the page number on the first page of the document, whether you want headers or footers to print on the first page, and where you want footnotes to be printed.

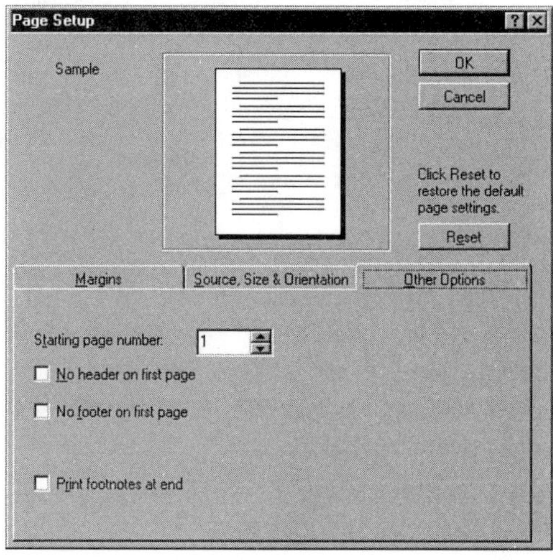

Fig. 4.5
The Other Options tab displays miscellaneous page settings.

Tip
You learn more about using page numbers and footnotes in Chapter 8, "Adding Headers, Footers, Footnotes, and Bookmarks to a Document."

The page number on the first printed page of your document can be a number other than 1. To start page numbering with the number 5, for instance, enter **5** in the Starting Page Number box. If you don't want the header or footer to be printed on the first page of your document, select the appropriate box. When you include footnotes in your document, they generally appear at the bottom of each page where they are inserted. If you prefer, you can print all footnotes at the end of a document by selecting the Print Footnotes at End check box. After choosing page number and footnote settings, choose OK.

Previewing a Document

One of the most important steps you can take before printing a document is to *preview* it. Previewing allows you to see on-screen how your document will look on the printed page. When you preview a document, Works displays a full-page view, one page at a time, of the document. This is your chance to see that margins are the appropriate size, line spacing is good, page separations are correct, header and footer text is positioned appropriately, inserted objects appear in the proper locations, and so on. When included in a document, all of these elements appear on the preview screen.

To preview a document, choose File, Print Preview or click the Print Preview toolbar button. The current document appears in a preview screen like the one shown in figure 4.6.

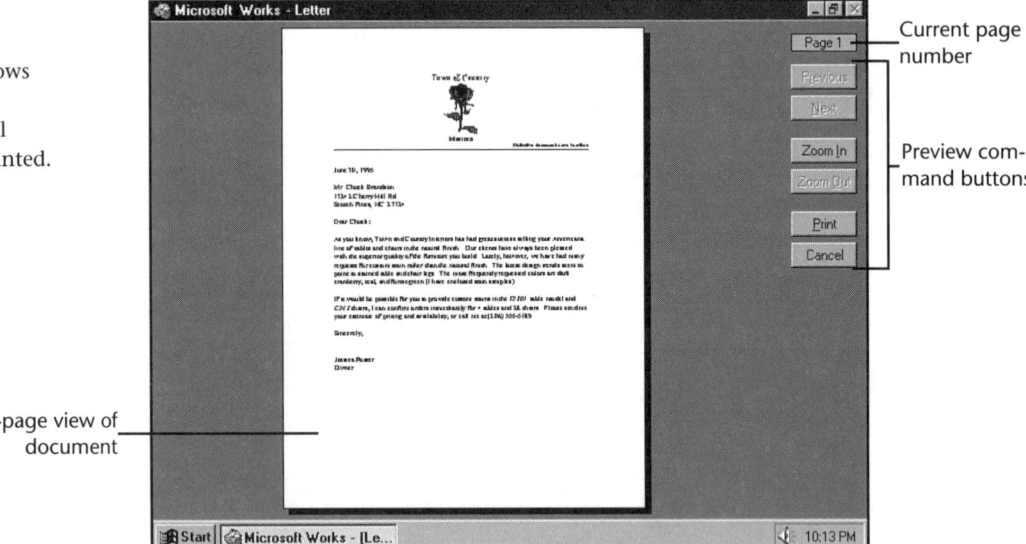

Fig. 4.6
Previewing a document shows you how the document will look when printed.

The actual text displayed in the preview screen can be difficult to read because it is reduced, but reading the text isn't the important consideration here; checking the document's layout is. If you think you spot a problem, however, you can zoom in on the document. Move your mouse around onscreen—notice that the mouse pointer changes to a magnifying glass when it is pointing anywhere on the page. Click the left mouse button once anywhere on the page to zoom in on the document, or click the Zoom In button. If you need to magnify the document further, click the left mouse button once more anywhere on the page, or click the Zoom In button again. To zoom back out, click the mouse button a third time, or click the Zoom Out button.

Tip
The Zoom Out button is only available after you have zoomed in on a document.

If your document is longer than one page, display the page you want to preview by clicking the Previous or Next button, or use the Page Up and Page Down keys on the keyboard. When you're ready to print the document, you can print directly from the preview screen by choosing the Print button. This button displays the Print dialog box. You learn how to use the Print dialog box in the next section. To close the preview screen, click the Cancel button.

Printing

When you're ready to print a document, choose File, Print, which displays the Print dialog box shown in figure 4.7. Use the Print dialog box to specify the printer you're using, the particular pages you want to print, the number of copies you want to print, the quality of printing you want to use, and whether you want to print the document itself or an envelope. The printer that is currently selected is shown at the top of the dialog box. If the printer shown is not correct, select the correct printer from the Name drop-down list.

Tip
The printer must be powered and online before you print. If not, a printer error message appears.

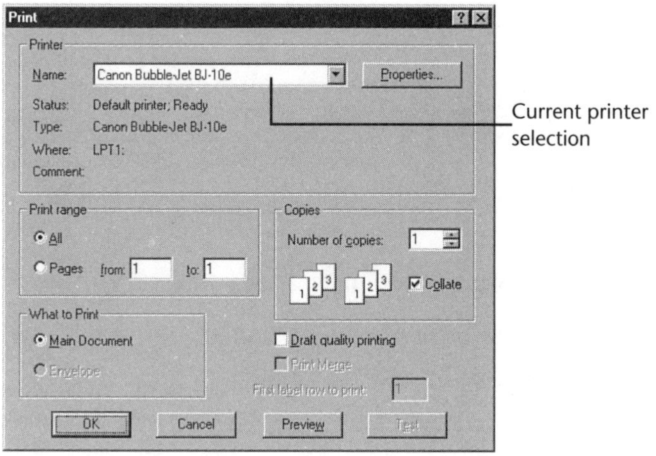

Current printer selection

Fig. 4.7
If you have access to multiple printers, be sure to check the printer name in the Print dialog box before printing.

Note

If you have access to more than one printer on your computer and switch printers often, it's a good idea to click the Properties button in the Printer Setup dialog box. This is where you specify the paper size, orientation, and settings for printing graphics for the current printer.

Notice that a Preview command button is available in the Print dialog box. If you forget to preview a document before choosing File, Print, you can choose the Preview button. Use the Test button when you merge documents. Table 4.4 describes the options in the Print dialog box. Refer to Chapter 28, "Creating Form Letters and Mailing Labels," for information on merging documents.

Table 4.4 Print Dialog Box Options

Option	Description
Number of Copies	The default setting is 1; to print more than one copy of the current document, enter a number.
Print Range: All	The default setting is to print all pages of the current document.
Print Range: Pages	To print selected pages, choose the Pages option button, then enter the first page to print in the From box and the last page to print in the To box.
Main Document	Prints the document itself rather than an envelope. This is the default setting.
Envelope	Choose this option to print envelopes.
Print merge	Allows you to merge a word processor document with a database document.
Draft quality printing	If your printer is capable of printing draft quality, choose this setting to print more quickly but at a lower print quality.

To print a document, follow these steps:

1. Open the document you want to print.
2. Choose File, Page Setup to specify print margins, paper source, size, orientation, and other print settings (as described earlier).

3. (Optional) Click the Preview toolbar button to view the document before printing.
4. Choose File, Print. The Print dialog box appears (refer to fig. 4.7).
5. Choose the appropriate print settings, then choose OK.

Tip
You can also print directly from the Preview screen by clicking the Print button.

Closing a Document

When you're finished working with a document, you can close it by choosing File, Close or double-click the document window's icon. Closing a file closes only the current document window—you can continue using Works. If you prefer to exit Works altogether, choose File, Exit Works. Refer to Chapter 3, "Working with Documents, TaskWizards, and Templates," for a discussion of closing and opening files. ❖

Chapter 5

Editing a Document

by Debbie Walkowski

The beauty of using a word processor to create text documents is that you can change a document as often as you change your mind. You can insert new text, delete existing text, rearrange sentences or paragraphs, and copy portions of text anywhere within a document.

In this chapter, you learn how to:

- Open an existing document
- Select text to delete, move, or copy
- Delete, insert, and type over existing text
- Automatically replace selected text
- Move and copy text
- Undo changes

Opening an Existing Document

When you use a word processor to type letters, memos, reports, and other text documents, you don't have to finish the document all at one time. You can enter as much text as you like (including mistakes), save the document and close it, then come back to it again later. You might reopen a document a dozen or more times before it's finally complete.

◀ See "Opening Documents," p. 52

◀ See "Opening Documents Automatically When You Start Works," p. 55

As you learn in Chapter 3, "Working with Documents, TaskWizards, and Templates," there are several ways you can open an existing document. You can select the document from the list that appears in the Works Task Launcher dialog box (under Existing Documents up to eight of the most recently used files are displayed) or by clicking the Open a Document Not Listed Here button in the Works Task Launcher dialog box. In the Word Processor window, you can choose File, Open, or click one of the four document names that appears at the bottom of the File menu.

Selecting Text

Whenever you want to make changes to text—whether you're deleting, moving, or copying—you must select it first so that Works knows what portion of text you want to change. When you select—or *highlight*—text, the background color behind the text changes (usually to black) so that the text appears highlighted (in white). Figure 5.1 shows an example of highlighted text. There are a variety of methods for selecting text using the mouse, the keyboard, or both. The method you choose depends on your own personal preference and the amount of text you are selecting.

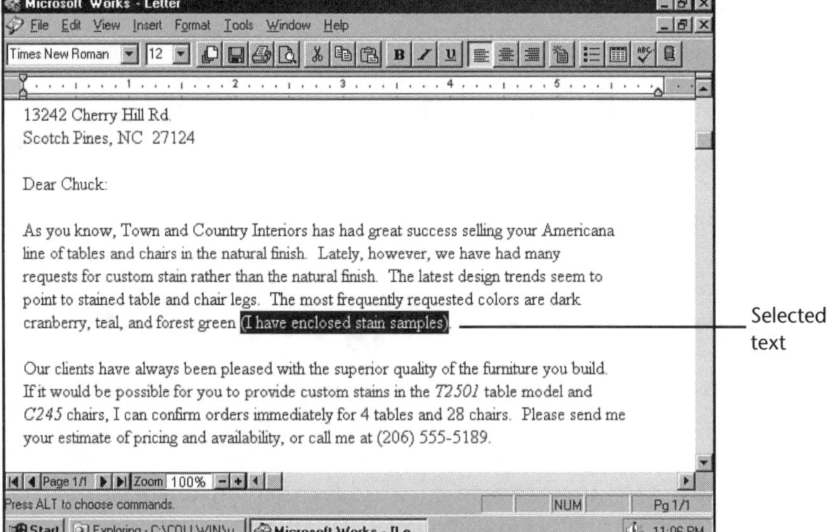

Fig. 5.1
The selected text is highlighted.

Using the Mouse

One method of selecting text is to click and drag the mouse pointer over the portion of text you want to select. This is the best method to use when you are selecting irregular areas of text. As you move the mouse, the text that you drag the pointer across is automatically highlighted. If you move the mouse vertically through lines of text, one line at a time is added to the selection. If you move the mouse horizontally across words on the same line, one word at a time is added to the selection. When the portion of text you want to select is highlighted, release the mouse button.

Tip
Recall from Chapter 1, "Introducing Works for Windows," that "click and drag" means to click the left mouse button and hold it down as you move the mouse pointer.

Note

Works selects entire words at a time because the Automatic Word Selection option is selected by default. (This setting appears on the Editing tab when you choose Tools, Options.) If you prefer to have Works select a character at a time rather than an entire word, deselect the Automatic Word Selection option.

Another way to select text is with a single click or a double-click in the correct location. To select a single line of text, click in the left margin next to the line; to select an entire paragraph, double-click in the left margin next to the paragraph. Be sure to release the mouse button to avoid selecting unwanted text. To select an entire word, double-click anywhere on the word. To select a complete sentence, press and hold the Ctrl key and click anywhere in the sentence. To select an entire document, press and hold the Ctrl key, then click anywhere in the left margin. By pressing and holding the Shift key, you can also select text from the location of the insertion point to the location where you click. These methods are summarized in Table 5.1.

Table 5.1 Selecting Text by Clicking the Mouse

To Select	Do This
One word	Double-click anywhere on the word
One line	Click in the left margin next to the line
One paragraph	Double-click in the left margin next to the paragraph
One sentence	Press and hold the Ctrl key, then click anywhere in the sentence
Entire document	Press and hold the Ctrl key, then click anywhere in the left margin
From insertion point	Press and hold the Shift key, then click where you want the selection to end

Using the Shift Key

If you prefer not to select text using the mouse, you can select text using a combination of the Shift key and the Page Up, Page Down, Home, End, and arrow keys. When the text is highlighted, release all keys on the keyboard. Using the "Shift" method to select text is sometimes easier than using the mouse because you don't need to reach for the mouse and take your hands away from the keyboard. Again, the method you use often comes down to personal preference. The Shift key methods of selecting text are summarized in Table 5.2.

Table 5.2 Using the Shift Key To Select Text

To Select	Press and hold the Shift key, then...
One character at a time	Press the right- or left-arrow key
One line	Press the up- or down-arrow key
To the beginning of the current line	Press Home
To the end of the current line	Press End
To the previous paragraph	Press Ctrl+up arrow
To the next paragraph	Press Ctrl+down arrow
To the beginning of the document	Press Ctrl+Home key
To the end of the document	Press Ctrl+End key

If you select the wrong text, or decide you don't need to select text, you can cancel a selection by pressing any of the arrow keys or clicking anywhere in the document. Before canceling a selection, however, be sure to release the mouse button and any keyboard keys that you pressed while making the selection, otherwise you might inadvertently extend the selection.

Deleting and Inserting Text

In Chapter 4, "Creating, Saving, and Printing a Document," you learn about two simple keys that help you change text: Backspace and Delete. These keys are useful for making minor changes in a document such as correcting a word or phrase. But sometimes you need to make major changes—like deleting several paragraphs, or rewording several sentences. These types of changes call for more efficient methods of revising text.

Deleting Large Areas of Text

If the Backspace and Delete keys were the only keys you could use to delete large areas of text, you could spend a great deal of time deleting! Fortunately, selecting text makes it easy to delete large amounts of text; you select the text first, then delete it using Edit, Cut.

Using the Cut command removes the selected text from the document—much the same way you might remove a section of text using scissors. If the text you remove is in the middle of a paragraph, the text that follows the selection is automatically realigned with the surrounding text. Although the text that you cut is removed from the document, it isn't permanently lost. It is stored on the Clipboard, a temporary storage area for text that you cut or copy. The Clipboard is a convenient "safety net"; there might be times when you delete the wrong text by mistake. When this happens, you can bring the text back, as you'll learn later in this chapter in "Undoing Changes."

To select the text to cut, use any of the selection methods you just learned. Be sure to select the appropriate lines and spaces surrounding the text that you want to cut. For example, if you are cutting a paragraph, you need to select the blank line that precedes or follows the paragraph, otherwise you'll be left with two blank lines between the two remaining paragraphs. If you are selecting several sentences, be sure to select the space or spaces that follow the last sentence (see fig. 5.2).

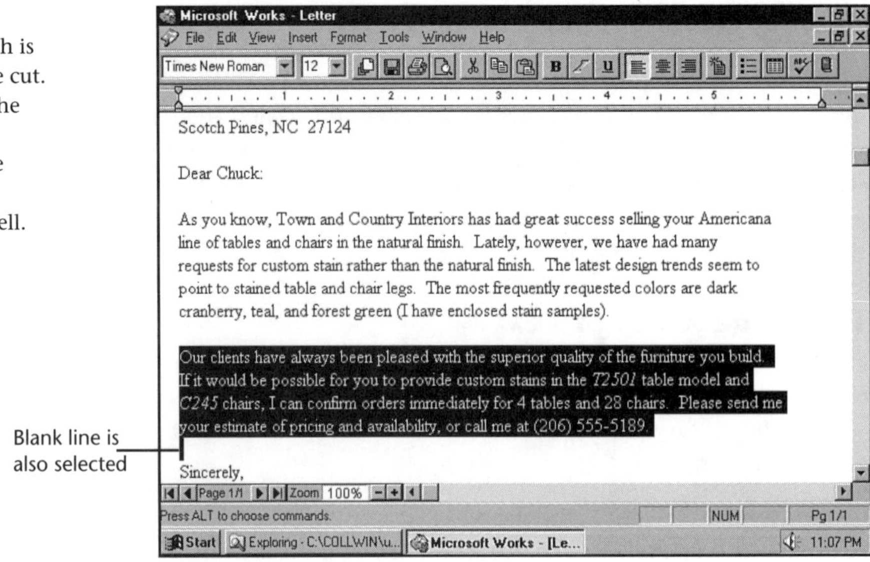

Fig. 5.2
The paragraph is selected to be cut. Notice that the blank line following the paragraph is selected as well.

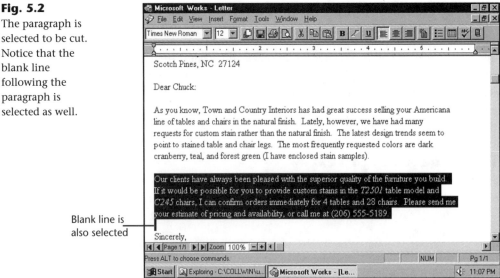

To delete text from a document, follow these brief steps:

1. Select the text you want to delete, including the appropriate blank lines and spaces.

2. Choose Edit, Cut, or click the Cut toolbar button.

> **Caution**
>
> Don't use the Delete key on the keyboard in place of the Cut command. The Delete key deletes selected text from your document, but does *not* place it on the Clipboard. Using the Delete key permanently removes the selected text from the document and you cannot retrieve it.

Inserting Text and Typing Over Text

The Works word processor operates in *insert mode* by default. In this mode, any new text you type in a document is automatically inserted beginning at the insertion point. For example, if the insertion point is located in the middle of a paragraph when you begin typing, existing text is shifted to the right to make room for the new text you type. Insert mode is the "safest" mode in which to work because you don't risk changing or losing any existing text. You don't have to set the word processor to operate in insert mode; it operates automatically in insert mode.

The alternative to insert mode is *overtype* mode. In this mode, any text to the right of the insertion point is automatically replaced by new text that you type. Overtyping is a method you might choose when you know you want to replace an existing phrase, sentence, or paragraph with new text. Overtyping saves you the trouble of selecting and deleting existing text, then inserting new text.

In contrast to insert mode, overtype mode is riskier to use because it automatically replaces existing text. If you forget that you are using overtype mode and begin typing in the middle of a sentence or paragraph, you can't retrieve the original text; it is permanently replaced by the new text you type.

Tip
If you just want to delete text without replacing it, using the Cut command is the best option.

To use overtype mode, choose Tools, Options. In the Options dialog box, choose the Editing tab, then select the Overtype check box and click OK. The OVR indicator appears near the right end of the status bar. To switch back to insert mode, deselect the Overtype option.

Note

You can quickly turn overtype mode on by pressing the Insert key on your keyboard or the Zero key (0) on the auxiliary key pad. Again, the OVR indicator appears on the status bar. The Insert and Zero (0) keys toggle on and off, so press it again to turn overtype mode off.

Automatically Replacing Selected Text

Another check box you can select in the Editing tab of the Options dialog is Typing Replaces Selection. Using this option, all text that you select is automatically replaced by new text that you type. For instance, if you select a sentence, then begin typing, the sentence is automatically removed from the document and replaced by the new text that you type. This feature saves you the trouble of deleting selected text before you type new text. However, if you are new to word processing or if other word processors you've used did not operate this way, you might want to get comfortable with Works before using this feature. Although it is a time-saver, it is somewhat risky to use because it automatically deletes selected text.

Moving and Copying Text

When you use a word processor to create and revise documents, moving and copying are editing changes you make frequently. With a few simple keystrokes, you can move or copy any selection of text, anywhere in a document. These features make it easy for you to completely rearrange a document without losing any of its original text.

You can move and copy text using menu commands or using a special mouse technique called drag-and-drop. You learn both methods in the following sections.

When you move text in a document, you must select it first, then choose a new location for it. The selected text is *inserted* at the location you choose, and the existing text is shifted to make room for the new text. The text surrounding the area from which you removed the text is automatically re-aligned as if the text you removed never existed.

When you copy text, you must select it first, then choose the location where you want the text to be duplicated. The original text that you select remains intact in its original location in the document. The new text that you copy is inserted at the location you choose.

Whether you're moving or copying text, it's important to remember to select the proper spacing along with the text you select. For example, when you want to move or copy an entire paragraph, select the blank line that precedes or follows the paragraph when you make your selection. Otherwise, the spacing will be incorrect when you insert the text in its new location. The same is true when you are moving or copying a word, phrase, or sentence. Select the space before or after the word, phrase, or sentence along with the text itself.

Moving and Copying Using Menu Commands

When you move text, choose Edit, Cut to remove the text from its original location, then choose Edit, Paste to insert the text in its new location (see fig. 5.3 and fig. 5.4). While you're in the process of moving text, Works uses the Clipboard as a temporary storage area for the selected text.

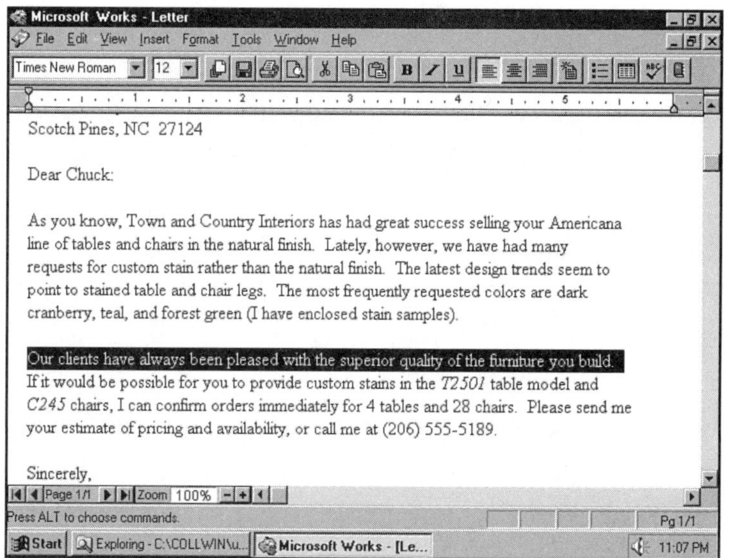

Fig. 5.3
A sentence is highlighted for moving.

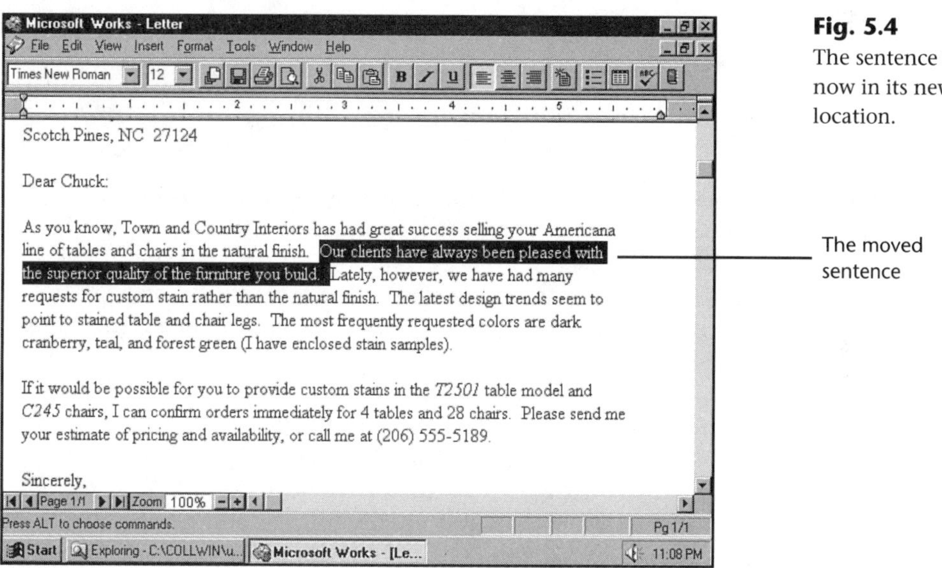

Fig. 5.4
The sentence is now in its new location.

Follow these steps to move text:

1. Select the text you want to move, including the appropriate spaces and blank lines surrounding the text.

2. Choose Edit, Cut; or click the Cut button on the toolbar. The selected text is removed from the document and placed on the Clipboard.

3. Move the insertion point to the location where you want to move the text.

4. Choose Edit, Paste; or click the Paste button on the toolbar. Works inserts the selected text where the insertion point is located.

Tip
The keyboard shortcut for Edit, Cut is Ctrl+X; for Edit, Paste, Ctrl+V; and for Edit, Copy, Ctrl+C.

When you copy text, you use the Copy and Paste commands on the Edit menu. Again, Works uses the Clipboard to store a copy of the selected text until you choose a location to paste it. Here's how to copy a selection:

1. Select the text you want to copy, including the appropriate spaces and blank lines surrounding the text.

2. Choose Edit, Copy; or click the Copy button on the toolbar. The selected text is copied to the Clipboard.

3. Move the insertion point to the location where you want to copy the text.

4. Choose Edit, Paste; or click the Paste toolbar button. Works inserts the selected text where the insertion point is located. The original text you selected remains intact in its previous location.

Caution

When you move or copy text in a document, be sure to complete the operation before doing any other editing. That is, paste the selection somewhere in the document immediately after you cut or copy it, otherwise you might lose it. The Clipboard can hold only one selection of text at a time. If you cut a paragraph, then cut a sentence without first pasting the paragraph, the sentence replaces the paragraph on the Clipboard.

One of the new features in Works 4.0 is support for the right mouse button. When you click the right mouse button in the middle of a document, Works pops up a shortcut menu that lists many editing commands, including Cut, Copy, and Paste commands (see fig. 5.5). You use shortcut menus the same way as regular menus; they are just quicker to use because they pop up right where you click on the screen. So, for example, to move a paragraph, you select the paragraph, click the right mouse button, and choose Cut. Reposition the insertion point in the document, then click the right mouse button again and choose Paste. Try it and see how much faster it is than selecting commands from the Edit menu.

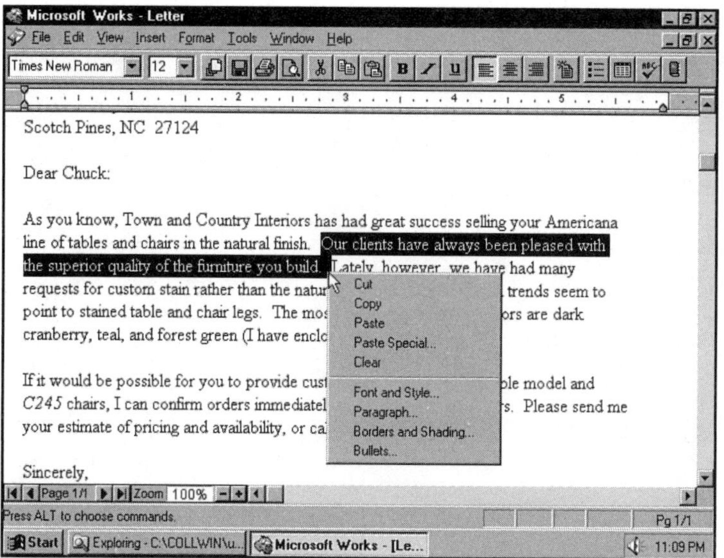

Fig. 5.5
Display this shortcut menu by right-clicking in the document.

Moving and Copying Using Drag-and-Drop

If you prefer to use the mouse rather than menu commands to move and copy text, you can use the drag-and-drop method. Using this technique, you select the text to move or copy, then drag it to its new location. This feature is turned on by default when you start Works.

To use drag-and-drop, you must first select the text you want to move or copy. When you point to the highlighted text, notice that the standard arrow mouse pointer changes to an arrow labeled DRAG (see fig. 5.6). This lets you know that Works is ready for you to drag the selection to a new location.

To move text, you simply click anywhere on the selection (remember to hold down the mouse button). When you click on the selection, the mouse pointer label changes to MOVE. Now drag the mouse to the location where you want the text to begin. (If you watch the screen closely, you see that you are actually dragging the insertion point.) After the insertion point is pointing where you want to insert the text, release the mouse button. The selected text moves automatically.

To copy text, use the same procedure but press and hold the Ctrl key as you drag the selection. When you click in the selection with the Ctrl key pressed, the mouse pointer label says COPY rather than MOVE.

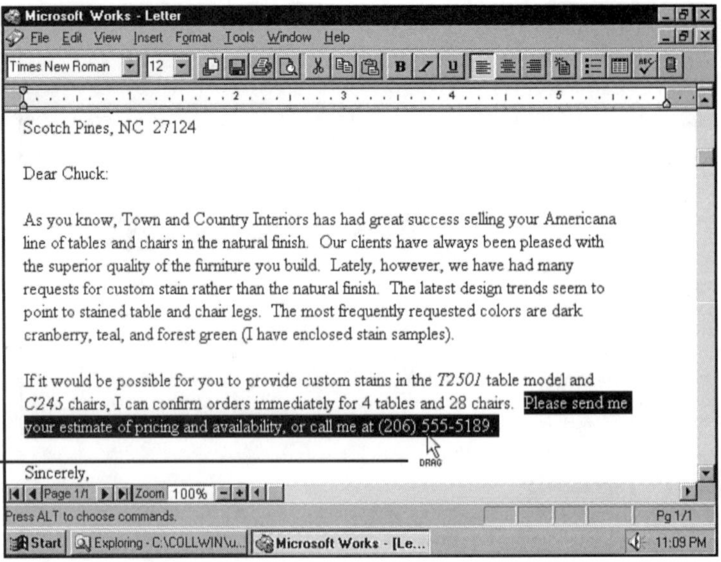

Fig. 5.6
The DRAG label indicates that Works is ready for you to move or copy the selection.

DRAG label

To use drag-and-drop to move or copy text, follow these steps:

1. Select the text you want to move or copy.
2. To move text, click anywhere on the selected text until you see the MOVE label.

   To copy text, press and hold the Ctrl key, then click anywhere on the selected text until you see the COPY label.
3. Drag the selection to its new location, then release the mouse button (and the Ctrl key, if you are copying). Works moves or copies the text to its new location.

Troubleshooting

I tried to move a paragraph to another page in my document, but when I chose the Paste command, Works pasted a word. What happened?

You cut your paragraph from the document, then cut a word before you pasted your paragraph in the new location. When moving text, you must complete the move before you cut additional text, because the Clipboard holds only one selection at a time.

Undoing Changes

Fortunately, Works provides a way for you to undo changes that you make by using the Undo command on the Edit menu. This command reverses the most recent editing changes you make in a document. Editing changes include typing, replacing text, deleting, moving, and copying. (Note that you *cannot* undo overtyping.) Although Undo is useful in all these cases, you will probably most appreciate Undo when you delete text by mistake. For example, if you select and delete several paragraphs by mistake, you can bring them back by using the Undo command.

The most important thing to remember about Undo is that you must use it *immediately* after the editing change you make. If you delete several paragraphs and then type a new word, using Undo will remove the new word you typed; it will not bring back your paragraphs. You must select Undo immediately after deleting the paragraphs in order to bring them back.

Suppose you delete a paragraph by mistake, retrieve it using Undo, then decide you really do want to delete the paragraph. You could select and delete the paragraph again, or you could just choose Undo again. The Undo command toggles between Undo and Redo for cases when you undo a change by mistake. You can change your mind back and forth as many times as you like using Undo and Redo (for instance, deleting and retrieving a paragraph), but after you make a *new* editing change, the previous change becomes part of the document.

Note

In the word processor, the Undo command also works to reverse formatting changes, including changes to the font, size, style (such as bold, underline, and italics), color, alignment, and so on. You learn more about using these features in Chapter 6, "Enhancing the Appearance of a Document."

Chapter 6

Enhancing the Appearance of a Document

by Debbie Walkowski

Have you ever noticed how difficult it is to read a document that has characters of the same width, that makes no size or style distinction between body text and headings, and uses no enhancements such as borders, shading, bold, italic, or underlining? Not only is it difficult to stay awake while reading such a document, you often have trouble grasping what you're reading. You might find yourself reading sentences over and over again. Adding these elements to a document is not just for the sake of appearance; it also makes the document more readable and easier to comprehend.

This chapter explores the many ways you can enhance a document by altering text attributes such as the font, size, color, style, or position. You can enhance paragraphs by choosing indent settings, alignment styles, and line spacing, or adding borders and shading.

This chapter discusses the following topics:

- Adding and removing character styles
- Copying a character style
- Choosing preset and custom paragraph styles
- Bordering paragraphs
- Setting paragraph breaks and line spacing
- Copying a paragraph style
- Inserting page breaks

Working with Text

The changes you make to enhance the appearance of a document are known as *format* changes. The word processor in Works includes a Format menu that contains a variety of format commands (see fig. 6.1). Using these commands, you can change the *character style* of selected text (the style for individual characters, words, or a specific selection of text), or you can change the format of entire paragraphs. In this section, you learn how to change the character style of selected text.

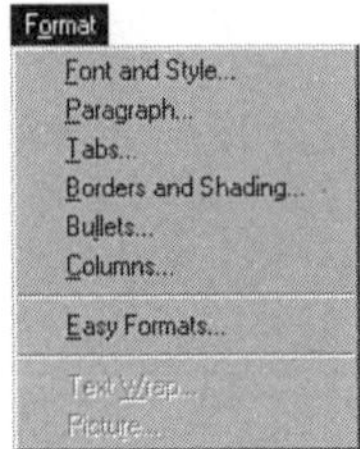

Fig. 6.1
The Format menu in the Works word processor.

You can also access some formatting commands from the shortcut menu, which you display by right-clicking in the document window. The shortcut menu is shown in figure 6.2.

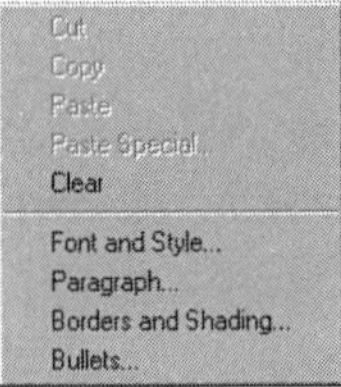

Fig. 6.2
The shortcut menu contains some formatting commands.

You can use several methods to change the character style of selected text: menu commands, toolbar buttons, or keyboard shortcuts. This section discusses menu commands first. Figure 6.3 shows the Format Font and Style dialog box, which appears when you choose Format, Font and Style. You can also display this dialog box by right-clicking in the document to display the shortcut menu, then choosing the Font and Style option.

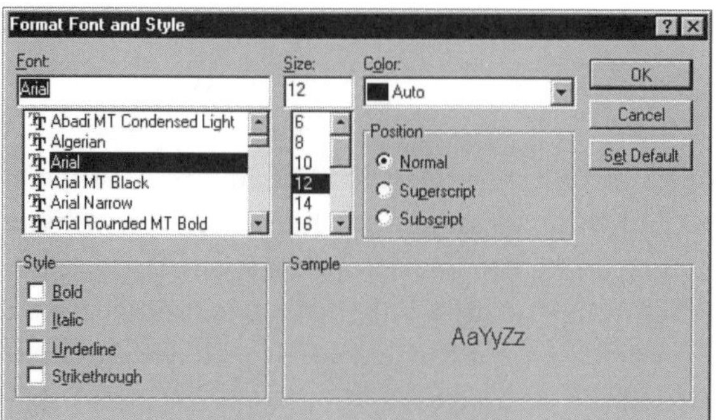

Fig. 6.3
The Format Font and Style dialog box lets you change the font, size, color, and style of text. The Sample area displays the choices you make.

Note

If you installed all available fonts when you installed Works, the complete list appears in the Font Selection box. If you installed selected fonts, only those that you installed appear in the list. You can install additional fonts by choosing Start, Programs, Microsoft Works 4.0, Microsoft Works 4.0 Setup.

Choosing a Character Style

In the Format Font and Style dialog box, you see settings for the font, size, color, style, and position of text. The following list describes these attributes:

- *Font.* In Works, a font refers to a specific style or design for a set of characters that Works displays on-screen and prints on paper. Each font has a particular shape or other characteristics that distinguish the font from other fonts.

  Note

  In addition to the fonts Works provides, you can add fonts through Windows or other programs. When you add other fonts, they are included in the Font list in the dialog box. Some printers can print only a limited number of fonts. Whether you can print all of the screen fonts available through Works depends entirely on the capabilities of your printer.

- *Size.* Most fonts are available in different sizes and are measured in points. (A point is equal to 1/72 of an inch.) The most common point sizes for body text in a typical document (such as a letter or report) are 10 or 12. Other elements in a document, such as titles or headings, often appear in larger sizes, such as 14, 16, 18, or 24 points.

- *Color.* If you have a color monitor, you can display selected text in a variety of colors. If you have a color printer, you also can print the colors that you display in your document.
- *Style.* In Works, a text style refers to bold, italic, underline, or strikethrough. Bold, italic, and underline are common styles used to emphasize text. Strikethrough is a special style often used in legal documents. Strikethrough prints a line through text, indicating that the text is marked for deletion, but the text still is readable. ~~Strikethrough has been applied to this sentence~~.
- *Position.* The position of text refers to its placement on the line. The superscript option raises a selected character slightly above the normal line level. Superscript often is used in documents that contain scientific notations such as 3×10^{23}. In contrast, the subscript option drops a selected character slightly below the normal line level, as in H_20, the symbol for water.

In the Format Font and Style dialog box, font, size, and color choices are available from list boxes. Option buttons represent positions because you can select only one position at a time. However, check boxes represent text styles (bold, italic, underline, and strikethrough) because you can select more than one style simultaneously. As you make font, size, color, style, and position choices, the Sample area of the dialog box displays the choices you make. This area is especially helpful for viewing the unique design of a particular font and the relative size of characters.

If you use a particular font, size, color, or style for standard text in most of the documents you create, the Set Default button will be particularly helpful to you. When you click this button, Works uses the current settings in the Format Font and Style dialog box as the default settings for all new documents you create. This saves you the time and trouble of changing format settings each time you create a new document.

Changing the Character Style of Existing Text

You might type all the text of a document before you apply any character styles, especially if the document goes through several draft phases before final printing. (You don't want to spend time formatting a document only to change or cut portions.)

To apply a character style to existing text using menu commands, follow these steps:

1. Select the text you want to format.
2. Choose Format, Font and Style, or choose the Font and Style command from the shortcut menu.
3. From the Font, Size, and Color lists, select one option each.
4. Choose one Position option (Normal, Superscript, or Subscript).
5. From the Style area, select any styles you want to apply to the selected text.
6. When the Sample area reflects the text as you want, choose OK. Works automatically reformats the selected text.

The toolbar helps you execute commands quickly and avoid using dialog boxes. When choosing a character style for text, use the toolbar buttons to speed up your work. The word processor toolbar has buttons for font name and size, as well as bold, italic, and underline (see fig. 6.4).

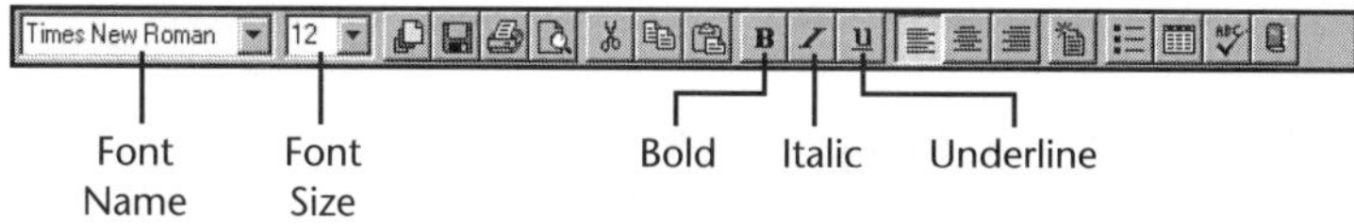

Fig. 6.4
You can choose a character style from the word processor toolbar.

The Font Name and Font Size buttons contain drop-down lists from which you select a font and point size, respectively. To change a font or size, select the text you want to change, and then select an item from each drop-down list. To add bold, italic, or underline to text in a document, select the text first, then click the appropriate button. Note that the bold, italic, and underline buttons toggle on and off, so if you want to remove an attribute, select the affected text, then just click the appropriate button again.

Tip
When text contains several attributes, you can remove all attributes quickly by selecting the text and then pressing Ctrl+space bar. This changes selected text back to plain text and saves you the trouble of removing each attribute individually. It will not, however, change the font or font size.

Note

The disadvantage of using the toolbar rather than the menu command is that you cannot preview the font and size like you can in the Sample area of the Format Font and Style dialog box.

If you customize your word processor toolbar, you can add buttons for strikethrough, subscript, and superscript. To customize your toolbar, refer to Chapter 2, "Getting Started with Works for Windows."

◄ See "Customizing the Toolbars," p. 33

If you use your keyboard more than your mouse, you can apply some character styles using the keyboard shortcuts listed in table 6.1. To use a keyboard shortcut, select the text you want to format, then press the key sequence shown in table 6.1. Note that all the shortcuts listed except Ctrl+space bar (for plain text) toggle on and off.

Table 6.1 Keyboard Shortcuts for Character Styles

Key Combinations	Character Style
Ctrl+B	Bold
Ctrl+U	Underline
Ctrl+I	Italic
Ctrl+Plus Sign (+)	Superscript
Ctrl+Equal Sign (=)	Subscript
Ctrl+space bar	Plain text (removes all character styles)

Note

Although the toolbar and keyboard shortcuts for character styles are helpful, they do not replace all menu commands for text character styles. For instance, if you want to change the color of text, you still must use the Format Font and Style dialog box because color has no toolbar button or keyboard shortcut.

Choosing a Character Style for New Text

Because character styles are attributes you can apply and remove from text, you can select styles before you enter new text just as easily as you can add styles to existing text. The time at which you choose to apply character styles is purely a matter of personal preference. Sometimes when you create a new document, you don't know the character style you want to use, so you apply the character style later. If you already know the character style you want to use, you might want to apply the character style as you type.

Except for selecting the text first, you apply a character style to new text the same way you apply a character style to existing text. Place the insertion point where you want the new character style to begin, select the character style options you want to use, then begin typing. All new text you type conforms to the character style you specify until you perform one of the following actions:

- Change the character style
- Move the insertion point to an area of the document that uses a different character style

Suppose that your document contains one paragraph typed in Arial 14-point bold, then you select Courier 12 point for new text. Courier 12 point remains in effect for all new text until you change the character style again or move the insertion point back into the paragraph typed in Arial.

Removing Character Styles from Existing Text

As you begin experimenting with character styles, you might change your mind many times. You might decide to change character styles you applied, or you might decide to remove character styles altogether. Attributes you add to text (such as bold, italic, underline, strikethrough, subscript, and superscript) toggle on and off, whether you select the setting using the Format Font and Style dialog box, toolbar, or a keyboard shortcut. To remove any of these character styles, select the affected text. Then select the dialog box option, the toolbar button, or the keyboard shortcut to remove the attribute.

Unlike attributes that are added to text, attributes such as font, size, and color change the characteristics of text. Technically, you cannot remove these attributes from text, but you can change them. Select the affected text, then choose Format, Font and Style, or the Font and Style command from the shortcut menu to change any or all of these attributes.

Copying a Character Style

In Chapter 5, "Editing a Document," you learn how to copy a selection of text from one location in a document to another. Instead of copying text, however, you might want to copy a character style from one selection to another. For example, suppose you're creating a report that contains special cautions and notes. You want to identify each caution and note paragraph easily in the text, so you use a special font, size, color, and style to distinguish cautions and notes from the body text. Without the capability to copy a character style, you would need to select and apply the font, size, color, and style each time you typed a new caution or note paragraph.

The fact that you can copy character styles and text attributes gives you several advantages. First, copying saves you the trouble of remembering (or checking each time) the attributes you assigned to text. Second, this method is fast—it copies all attributes at one time. And third, copying eliminates the likelihood of errors; you cannot possibly get the character style wrong when you copy it.

To copy a character style, follow these steps:

1. Select the text that uses the character style you want to copy. (You don't need to select all the text, such as an entire paragraph. Just select any portion that uses all the attributes you want to copy.)

2. Choose Edit, Copy, or choose the Copy command from the shortcut menu.

3. Select *all* the text to which you want to copy the character style.

4. Choose Edit, Paste Special or choose the Paste Special command from the shortcut menu. Works displays the Paste Special dialog box shown in figure 6.5.

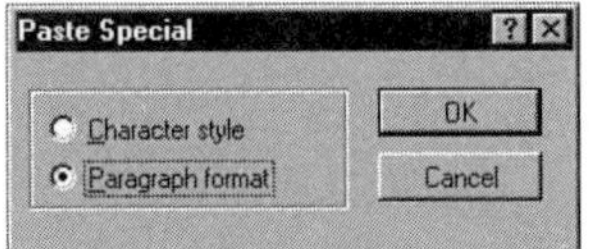

Fig. 6.5
Using the Paste Special dialog box, you can copy either a character style or a paragraph format to selected text.

5. Choose the Character Style button, then click OK. Works automatically applies the character style to the selected text.

You also can copy a character style to a blank line where you intend to enter new text. Follow the previous steps, but instead of selecting text in step 3, move the insertion point to where you want the copied character style to take effect. Complete steps 4 and 5, and then begin typing. All new text you type conforms to the copied character style until you change the character style or move the insertion point to text that uses a different style.

Troubleshooting

I set a specific character style for a new paragraph I typed, but now I don't know how to turn it off.

When you set a character style for new text, the style remains in effect until you change it. You don't "turn off" a character style—you define a new one. If you want to switch to a style you used previously in the document, copy the character style to the location where you want the style to begin.

I selected some text and then pressed Ctrl+space bar to remove all style characteristics. Works removed the bold, underline, and color, but not the special font I used.

Bold, underline, italic, subscript, superscript, and color are attributes you can add to text; therefore, you can remove them from text. Technically, you cannot remove a font from text, but you can change the font. Select the text, then choose a new font from the Format Font and Style dialog box or from the Font Name toolbar button.

I changed some text from Times New Roman 12 to Arial 12, but now the text is much smaller than it was before. Why?

Even though you chose 12 point for both fonts, they don't necessarily appear the same size. Because fonts have unique designs with unique style characteristics, they often vary greatly in size from font to font. Use whatever point size seems appropriate for the particular document and font.

Working with Paragraphs

In the first half of this chapter, you learned how to change the format or character style of text. You select the text, then apply certain attributes to enhance the text's appearance or convey a specific meaning (as with subscript and superscript). In the next half of this chapter, you learn about certain attributes you can apply to paragraphs rather than to selected text. These attributes, such as indentation, bullets, alignment, line spacing, borders, and so on, are known as the *paragraph format*.

Paragraph formats not only improve the appearance of your document, they make the information more accessible by defining a *structure* within the text and distinguishing particular types of text. You can apply a variety of formats to paragraphs, and you can copy paragraph formats just like you can copy character styles.

Before you begin applying formats to text in a document, you need to understand how the *ruler* in the word processor window works.

Examining the Ruler in the Document Window

◀ See "Printing a Document," p. 74

Tip

If the ruler is not displayed on your screen, choose View, Ruler to display it.

The ruler in the word processor window serves several purposes. First, it acts as a guide to the width of a document, indicating in inches the size of margins and the text area. Second, it indicates the right and left indentation of paragraphs throughout a document. Third, it indicates where tabs are set.

Unless you change a document's Page Setup, which determines margin settings, Works uses left and right margins of 1.25 inches each. On standard 8 1/2 × 11-inch paper, six inches remain across the paper for text. The highlighted, or white, part of the ruler runs from the 0 marker to the 6-inch marker on the ruler, indicating your working, text area in the document (see fig. 6.6). The gray parts of the ruler measure the edges of the paper beyond the text area; in other words, the margins.

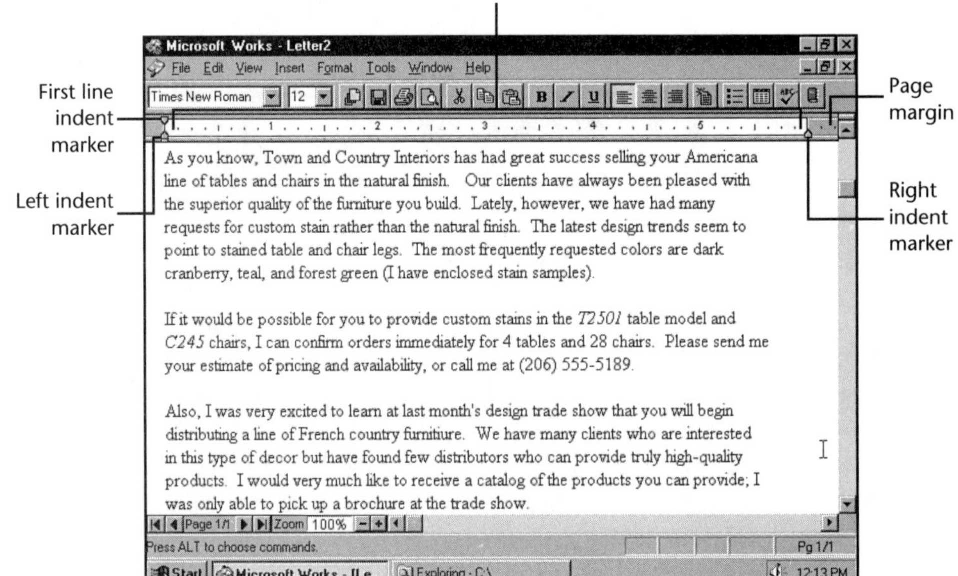

Fig. 6.6 Ruler markers indicate the format of a paragraph.

The markers at the zero point and the 6-inch point are called *indent markers*. Indent markers indicate the points at which text indents from the left and right margins. Two indent markers appear at the zero point; the bottom one, the left indent marker, marks the indentation of the current paragraph. The top marker, the first line indent marker, marks the indentation of only the first line of the current paragraph (refer to fig. 6.6). Only one marker appears at the 6-inch point, the right indent marker, which indicates the point at which text indents from the right margin. Figure 6.6 illustrates the default settings: left indent at 0, first line indent at 0, and right indent at 6. Later in this chapter, you learn how to set the indentation of paragraphs by moving these markers on the ruler (see "Indenting Paragraphs").

Note

At any given time, the settings shown on the ruler reflect the paragraph where the insertion point is currently located. As you move the insertion point through the paragraphs of a document, the indent markers on the ruler change for paragraphs that indent differently.

Choosing Paragraphs To Format

Before you can apply a format to a paragraph, you first must let Works know which paragraph you want to format. To do this, just place the insertion point anywhere in the paragraph. Or you can select any amount of text in the paragraph; selecting the entire paragraph isn't necessary.

You might want to apply the same format to several paragraphs in a document. When the paragraphs are contiguous, you can apply a format to all paragraphs at one time by selecting at least a portion of text in all paragraphs. For example, if you want to format three consecutive paragraphs, you can select the last line in the first paragraph, all of the second paragraph, and the first line of the third paragraph (see fig. 6.7). You can select all text in all three paragraphs if you like, but it isn't necessary to do so. When paragraphs are not contiguous, you must apply the format to each paragraph individually or copy the format from one paragraph to another. Copying the attributes of a paragraph is discussed in "Copying a Paragraph Style," later in this chapter.

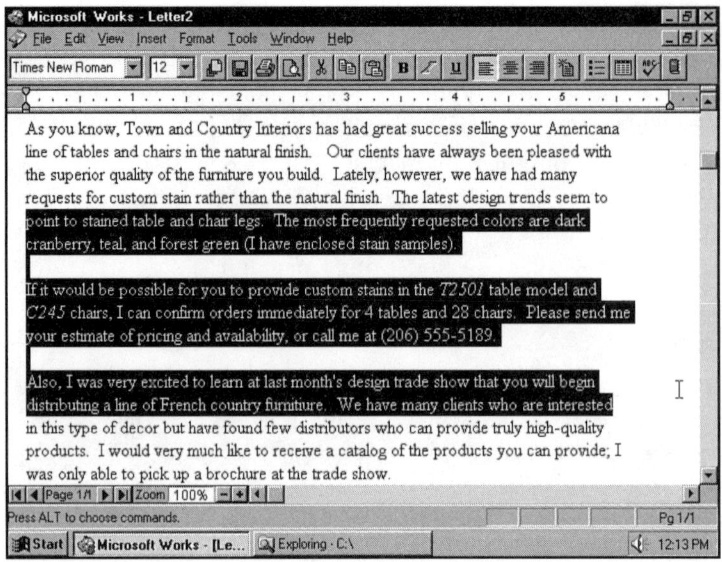

Fig. 6.7 Select a portion of text in the paragraphs you want to format—all three paragraphs will be formatted.

Setting Paragraph Alignment

Alignment refers to the way the left and right edges of a paragraph line up. For instance, the paragraph you are reading is left-aligned; the characters at the left margin align vertically and the characters at the right margin are ragged. Left-aligned text is most commonly used in business documents because it is considered easy to read and not too stiff or formal.

In Works, you can left-align, right-align, center, or justify paragraphs. A right-aligned paragraph is just the opposite of a left-aligned paragraph—characters at the right margin align vertically and characters at the left margin are ragged. Right alignment sometimes is used in brochures, flyers, or other advertising literature for its stylistic effect. A centered paragraph positions each line at the midpoint between margins, leaving ragged left and right edges. In a justified paragraph, characters at both the right and left margins align vertically by adjusting the space between letters on each line. Justified text conveys a more formal appearance than left-aligned text. Figure 6.8 shows an example of each of these alignment styles.

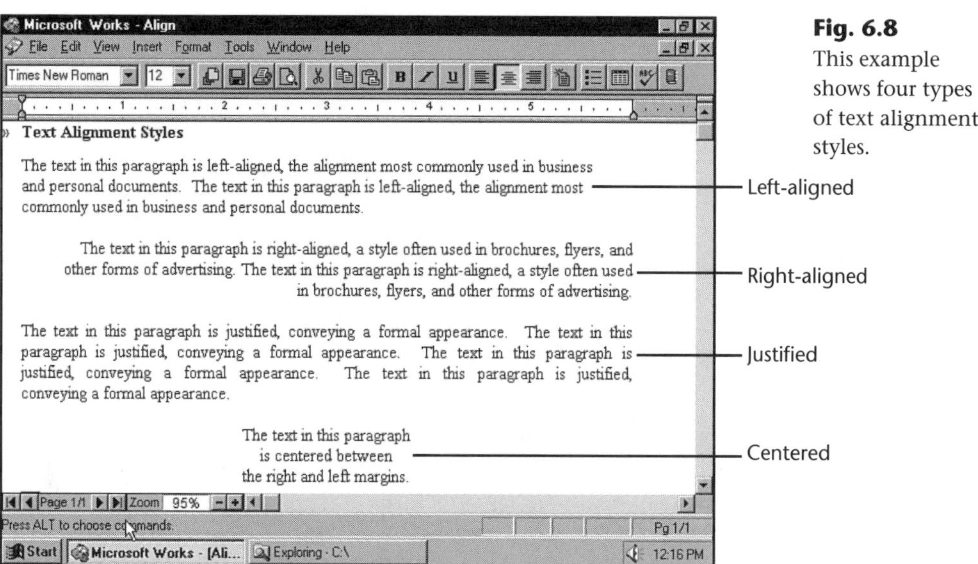

Fig. 6.8
This example shows four types of text alignment styles.

You can use menu commands, toolbar buttons, or keyboard shortcuts to align paragraphs. To set alignment of a paragraph using menu commands, follow these steps:

1. Place the insertion point anywhere in the paragraph you want to align. To align two or more contiguous paragraphs at a time, select at least a portion of text in each paragraph.

2. Choose Format, Paragraph, or choose the Paragraph command from the shortcut menu. The Format Paragraph dialog box appears (see fig. 6.9). (If the Indents and Alignment tab is not showing, choose it now.)

3. From the Alignment area, select Left, Center, Right, or Justified.

4. Choose OK. Works realigns the current paragraph.

Because the alignment feature is frequently used in documents, the word processor toolbar contains the left-align, center, and right-align buttons.

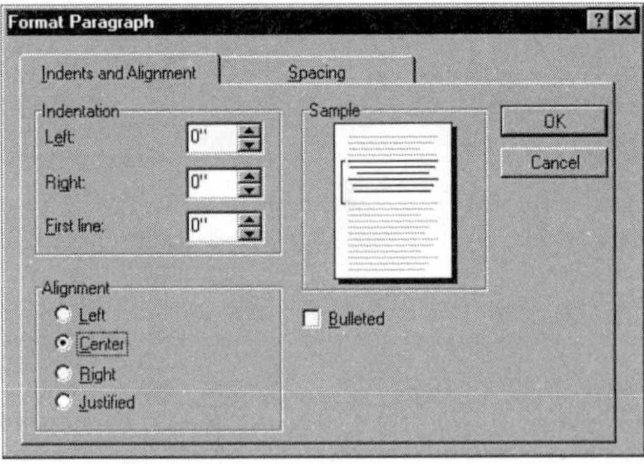

Fig. 6.9
Use the Indents and Alignment tab to set text alignment.

Aligning a paragraph using a toolbar button is easy. Place the insertion point anywhere in the paragraph, and then click an alignment button. Works immediately realigns the paragraph without displaying any dialog boxes. Also, remember that you can customize the toolbar by choosing Tools, Customize Toolbar. When you choose the Format category in the Customize Works Toolbar dialog box, one of the buttons you can add to the toolbar is for justified text.

◀ See "Customizing the Toolbars," p. 33

If you prefer to use the keyboard, you can set paragraph alignment using a keyboard shortcut. Move the insertion point anywhere in the paragraph you want to align, then press one of the following key sequences:

Key Sequence	Function
Ctrl+L	Left-aligns the current paragraph
Ctrl+E	Centers the current paragraph
Ctrl+Shift+R	Right-aligns the current paragraph
Ctrl+J	Justifies the current paragraph

Indenting Paragraphs

Another way to add structure to a document is by changing the indentation of paragraphs. As you learned earlier in this chapter, the ruler in the word processor window contains right indent, left indent, and first line indent markers. These markers indicate the indentation of the paragraph where the cursor is currently located. For example, figure 6.10 shows the selected paragraph is left-indented 1/2 inch and right-indented 1 inch. The first line of the paragraph is indented 1 inch.

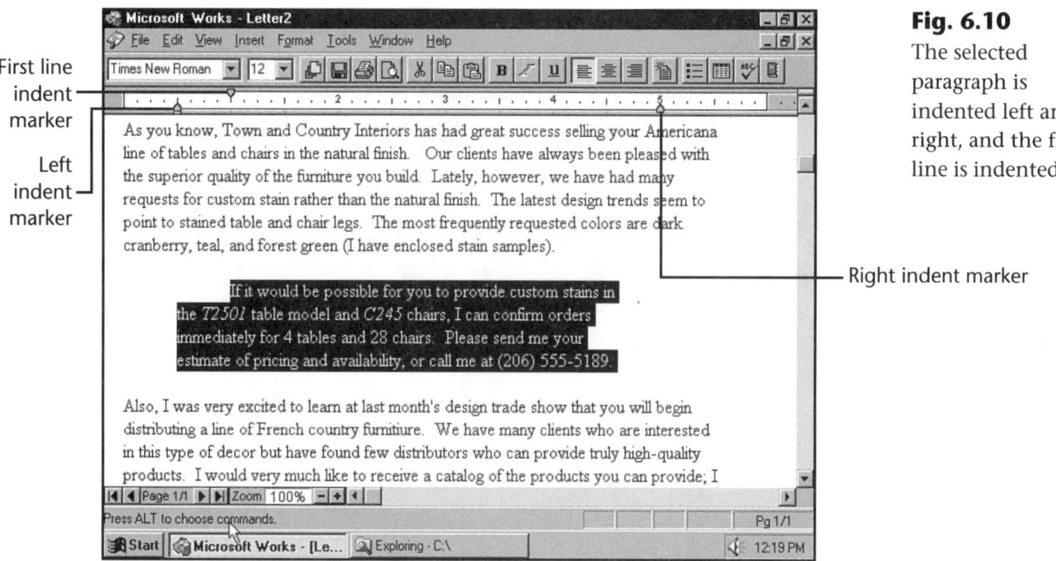

Fig. 6.10
The selected paragraph is indented left and right, and the first line is indented.

A quicker and easier way to change a paragraph's indentation is to drag the indent markers along the ruler. Suppose you wanted to change the selected paragraph in figure 6.10 back to a "standard" format; that is, no first line, right, or left indentation. Use these steps:

1. Place the insertion point anywhere in the paragraph.
2. Hold the Shift key down, then click the left indent marker and drag it back to 0. Release the Shift key.
3. Drag the first line indent marker back to 0.
4. Drag the right indent marker back to 6.

It's as simple as that; the paragraph reformats right before your eyes. But why do you have to hold the Shift key down to move the left indent marker? If you don't, the first line indent marker moves with the left indent marker—maintaining its relative position. This is because Works always measures the first line indent relative to the left indent. So, for example, if you want to always maintain the 1/2 inch indentation on the first line of the paragraph, drag the left indent marker *without* holding the Shift key down; the first line indent marker will move right along with it.

If you prefer to set paragraph indentation using a more precise method, you can choose Format, Paragraph, Indents and Alignment, and then set indentation using the dialog box (see fig. 6.11). Using the up and down arrows in the

Left, Right, and First Line boxes, you can specify indentation to 1/10th of an inch. If you want to use even smaller increments, you can type a number (such as 1.325) in the boxes. As you change the settings in these boxes, the Sample area changes to reflect the new settings. When the settings are correct, click OK.

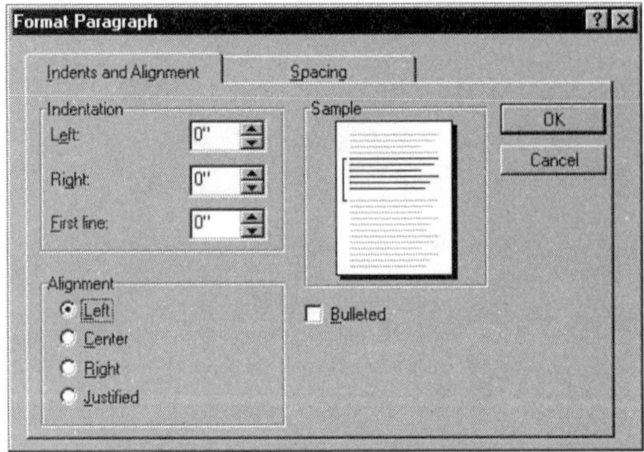

Fig. 6.11 Use the Indents and Alignment tab in the Format Paragraph dialog box to change a paragraph's indentation.

Perhaps the quickest way to indent a paragraph is to use the keyboard shortcuts listed in table 6.2. Use these shortcuts when you only want to indent the paragraph from the left margin without changing the first line indent or right indent.

Table 6.2 Keyboard Shortcuts for Indentation

Press	To
Ctrl+M	Move the indentation of the current paragraph to the right in 1/2-inch increments.
Ctrl+Shift+M	Move the indentation of the current paragraph back to the left in 1/2-inch increments.

Setting Line Spacing and Paragraph Breaks

Two additional factors that affect the appearance of a document are line spacing and paragraph breaks. *Line spacing* refers to the amount of space between lines. A *paragraph break* is the point where a paragraph divides when it falls near the bottom of a page. In this section, you learn how to adjust both of these settings using the Spacing tab in the Format Paragraph dialog box, shown in figure 6.12. To display this dialog box, choose Format, Paragraph, Spacing.

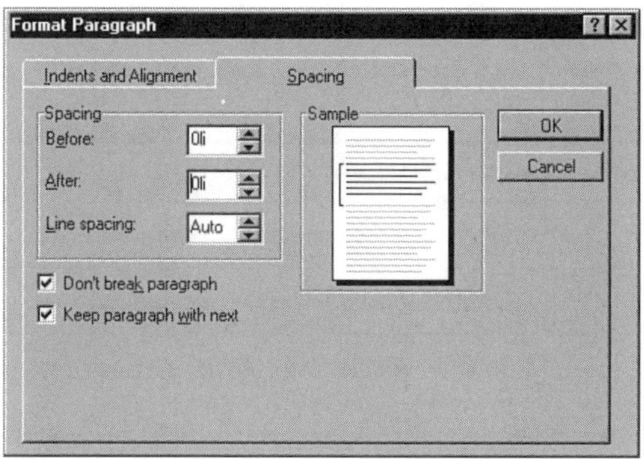

Fig. 6.12
Use the Spacing tab in the Format Paragraph dialog box to control spacing of lines, spacing before and after paragraphs, and the location of paragraph breaks.

Most common business documents, such as letters and memos, are single-spaced documents; the amount of space between lines is just enough to make the document readable. Single-spaced documents, however, do not allow much room for writing between the lines, which is why most draft documents are double-spaced. For example, reports and proposals often are double-spaced—at least in the beginning stages—because many people might review the document. In addition to being easier to read, a double-spaced document is much easier to review, edit, and add comments to than a single-spaced document.

In Works, you have complete control over the line spacing used in your documents; you aren't limited to single or double spacing. On the Spacing tab in the Format Paragraph dialog box, the Line Spacing option is represented in number of lines. The default setting is *Auto*, which means the line space is equal to the height of the largest character in the current font and size. (If you change the font and size of the current text, Works automatically adjusts the line spacing.) You can enter any whole positive number for Line Spacing (2, 5, 10, and so on) or any number fraction (1.3, 3.2, 5.8, and so on). To return to the default setting, choose Auto.

Note

If you prefer to set line spacing using a different unit of measurement, you can type a designator following the number you enter, such as 3 cm for 3 centimeters. You can enter *in* or " for inches, *cm* for centimeters, *mm* for millimeters, *pi* for picas, or *pt* for points.

Besides using the Format Paragraph dialog box, you can set a paragraph to single, double, or one-and-one-half spaced lines quickly by using the following key sequences. Just place the insertion point anywhere in the paragraph, and then press one of the following key sequences:

Key Sequence	Function
Ctrl+1	Single spaces the current paragraph
Ctrl+2	Double spaces the current paragraph
Ctrl+5	Sets the spacing of the current paragraph to one-and-one-half

In addition to line spacing, you can specify the number of lines that precede and follow a paragraph. This setting is especially helpful for chapter names, titles, headings, opening paragraphs, and so on. You might want these document elements set off with extra space, and the Before and After settings enable you to define this space. Like the Line Spacing setting, the Before and After settings are measured in number of lines. For example, if you want one blank line to precede a document heading and two blank lines to follow the heading, enter 1 and 2 respectively in these boxes.

The two check boxes below the Spacing area determine how paragraphs break in a document. You can choose not to break a particular paragraph (Don't Break Paragraph), and you can choose to keep a paragraph together with the paragraph that follows it (Keep Paragraph With Next). For example, suppose you write a letter that includes an address near the bottom of the page where the reader can write for more information. If a page break causes the first line of the address to appear at the bottom of the page and the rest of the address appears at the top of the next page, choose the Don't Break Paragraph option to keep the address lines together. Or suppose that the last paragraph on a page in your document ends in a colon and has a bulleted list of items following. You don't want a page break to occur between these two paragraphs, so you select the first paragraph, and then select the Keep Paragraph With Next option.

Keep your eye on the Sample area as you select your settings—the settings you choose are reflected here. For example, if you set line spacing to 2, the sample paragraph switches to double-spaced text. When you select the Don't Break Paragraph option, a bracket appears to the left of the sample paragraph in the Sample area indicating the paragraph should not be broken.

Use the following steps to set line spacing and paragraph breaks:

1. Place the insertion point in the paragraph you want to format. To format contiguous paragraphs, select at least a portion of text in each paragraph.
2. Choose Format, Paragraph. The Format Paragraph dialog box appears. (If the Spacing tab is not selected, choose it now.)
3. In the Spacing area, set the amount of space in the Line Spacing, Before, and After boxes.
4. If you want to prevent the current paragraph from splitting in a page break, select the Don't Break Paragraph check box.
5. If you want to keep the current paragraph together with the paragraph that follows, select the Keep Paragraph With Next check box.
6. Choose OK. Works adjusts line spacing and page breaks according to the choices you make.

Bordering a Paragraph

Documents often contain special types of text that need to be very visible and accessible. One way to make a paragraph stand out is to place a border around it. For example, the troubleshooting and cautions in this book contain important information you don't want to overlook. To make sure you don't miss them, each troubleshooting and caution has a border. Using Works, you can create a border using a single line, double line, bold line, or a color.

The term *border* is somewhat misleading; it implies that a line completely surrounds a paragraph. This type of border is called an *outline* border. But in Works, you also can create *partial* borders that fall on the top, bottom, left, or right sides of a paragraph. Or you can use any combination of the four partial borders. For example, you might want to use a bottom border to set off chapter names in a multi-chapter document, or you might want to use right and left borders to set off notes and cautions. A creative way to use a left or right border in a draft document is to mark all paragraphs in which a change has occurred. This type of border commonly is called a *change bar* or *revision mark*. Figure 6.13 illustrates some sample border styles.

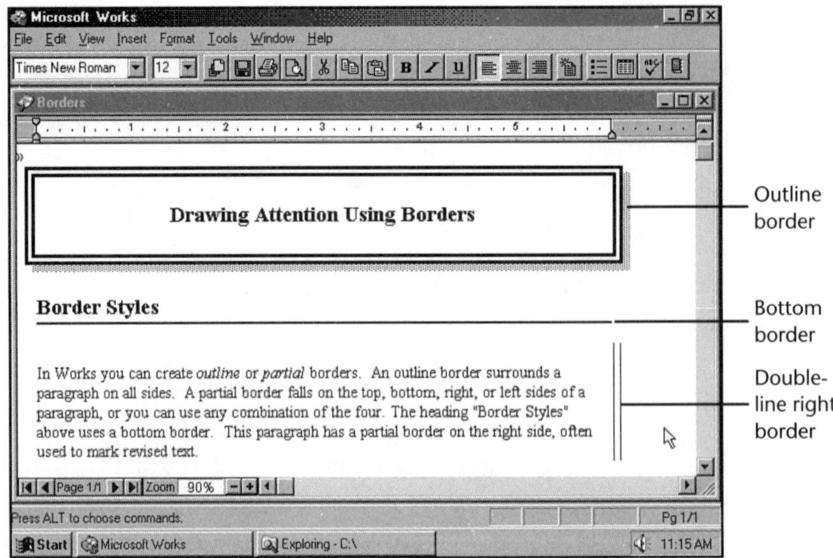

Fig. 6.13
Use borders creatively to add style, draw attention, or mark revised text.

Note

You can add a border to a single-line paragraph, a multiple-line paragraph, several contiguous paragraphs, or an entire page, but you cannot border individual words in a line of text.

To define a line style, color, and border, choose Format, Borders and Shading. The Borders and Shading dialog box appears (see fig. 6.14). To create an outline border, select the Outline or Outline With Shadow check box. To create a partial border, select any combination of the Top, Bottom, Left, and Right check boxes. In the Line Style box, click on one of the styles shown. To change the color of the border, select a color from the Color list. Note that unless you have a color printer, the color is visible only on-screen.

Use the following steps to add a border to text:

1. Place the insertion point anywhere in the paragraph you want to border. To border contiguous paragraphs, select a portion of text in each paragraph.

2. Choose Format, Borders and Shading, or choose Borders and Shading from the shortcut menu. The Borders and Shading dialog box is displayed. (If the Borders tab is not selected, click it now.)

3. Select a border style form the Border area.
4. Select a style from the Line Style area.
5. Select a color from the Color list.
6. Choose OK. Works adds the specified border to the current paragraph.

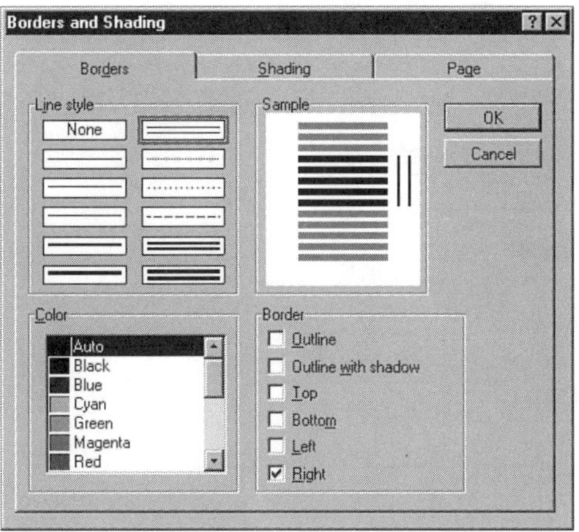

Fig. 6.14
Use the Borders tab in the Borders and Shading dialog box to select a border, line style, and color.

Note

To remove a border, choose None in the Line Style area.

Troubleshooting

I used an outline border on a paragraph that split between two pages. Now half the border appears at the bottom of the first page and the other half appears at the top of the next page. Why did this happen?

A border around a paragraph doesn't prevent the paragraph from splitting if it falls near a page break. To avoid this situation, select the bordered paragraph, then choose Format, Paragraph, Spacing. In the dialog box, select the Don't Break Paragraph option.

Bordering a Page

A new feature in Works 4.0 allows you to quickly add a border to an entire page. To use this option, you use the Borders and Shading dialog box again, this time choosing the Page tab (see fig. 6.15).

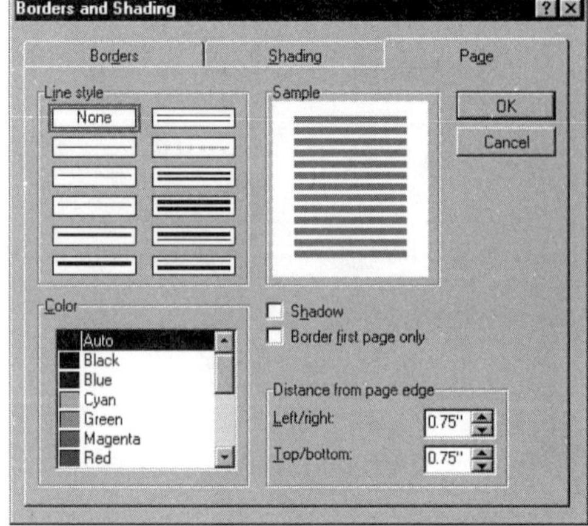

Fig. 6.15
In the Borders and Shading dialog box you can choose a page border, line style, and color for an entire page.

The Page tab is very similar to the Borders tab shown in figure 6.14; you choose a line style and color for the border. You also can choose to add a shadow to the border, or border only the first page. In the Distance From Page Edge box, you can specify exactly where you want the border to fall on the page. (If you don't alter the settings in this box, Works automatically adds a page border at the page margins.)

To create a page border, follow these steps:

1. Place the insertion point anywhere on the page you want to border.
2. Choose Format, Borders and Shading, or choose Borders and Shading from the shortcut menu. The Borders and Shading dialog box appears. (If the Page tab is not selected, click it now.)
3. Select a style from the Line Style box.
4. Select a color from the Color list.
5. Choose Shadow or Border First Page Only if you want either of these options.
6. To change the position and size of the border, enter the appropriate settings in the Left/Right and Top/Bottom boxes.
7. Choose OK. Works adds a border to the current page.

Tip
To quickly check whether your border is correct, click the Preview toolbar button, then click Close to return to your previous view.

Copying a Paragraph Style

Just as copying a character style can save you time and ensure consistency, copying a paragraph style can do the same. When you spend time setting up indent markers, choosing paragraph alignment, defining line spacing, and specifying paragraph breaks for a single paragraph, you can copy the style to another paragraph faster than redefining it. When you copy a paragraph style, the paragraph to which you copy takes on all the indents, alignment, spacing, and paragraph breaks of the paragraph from which you copy.

You copy a paragraph style in much the same way you copy a character style. Follow these steps:

1. Select the *entire* paragraph from which you want to copy the paragraph style.
2. Choose Edit, Copy, or choose the Copy command from the shortcut menu.
3. Place the insertion point anywhere within the paragraph to which you want to copy the paragraph style.
4. Choose Edit, Paste Special, or choose Paste Special from the shortcut menu. The Paste Special dialog box opens.
5. Select the Paragraph Format option, then choose OK. Works applies the copied paragraph style to the selected text.

Tip
If Works displays an error message saying you must copy an entire paragraph, you didn't select the entire paragraph in step 1. Select the entire paragraph, then repeat steps 2-5.

Working with EasyFormats

To save you the trouble of setting up some commonly used formats, Works includes 24 predefined formats called *EasyFormats*. These easy-to-use formats take the guesswork out of creating formats from scratch. EasyFormats are especially helpful to beginning users who don't feel comfortable experimenting with formatting, and for users who are in a hurry and need to get a polished document done quickly.

Perhaps the most common paragraph format is the simple indented paragraph in which the first line is indented 1/2 inch and the remaining lines are left-aligned. Another format used frequently is called a *hanging indent*, in which the first line of a paragraph is left-aligned and the remaining lines are indented 1/2 inch. Hanging indents are often used to format numbered or bulleted lists. A third type of commonly used format is one that indents a paragraph 1/2 inch on both the right and left sides. This type of format is often used for quotations to distinguish them from body text in a document.

In addition to these three formats, Works includes nearly two dozen other EasyFormats that you might not use frequently but you will appreciate nevertheless. Some are more complex to set up than the more commonly used formats and therefore can save you valuable time.

Choosing an EasyFormat

To use an EasyFormat, you simply select the text you want to format, then choose an EasyFormat from the Easy Formats dialog box (see fig. 6.16). In the dialog box, the list on the left includes all 24 EasyFormats. The Sample area on the right shows a sample page with dummy text that adjusts to the format you choose. The font and style used by the format are displayed just below the sample page. The Description area gives a detailed list of the actual format characteristics; the font name and size, color, alignment, indentation, line spacing, bordering, and so on.

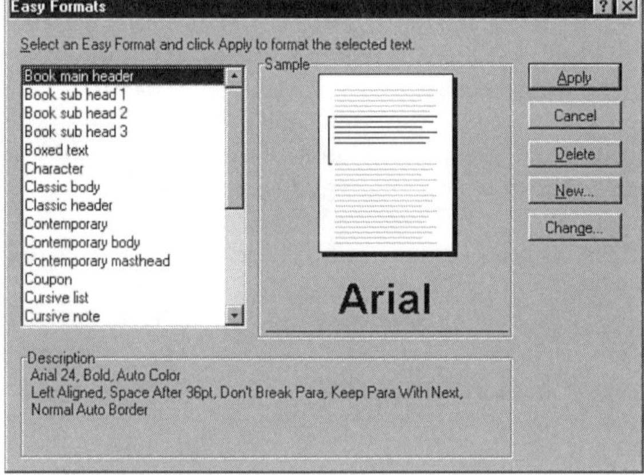

Fig. 6.16
The Arial font was used in this example, which you can see in the Sample area.

To use an EasyFormat, follow these steps:

1. Place the insertion point anywhere in the paragraph you want to format.

2. Choose Format, EasyFormats. The EasyFormats dialog box appears.

3. Click an EasyFormat. The sample area displays how the format will look.

4. Click Apply.

The paragraph you selected automatically reformats using the EasyFormat characteristics. If you want to change any of the characteristics, use the steps you learned earlier in this chapter for changing text attributes (such as font, size, color) or paragraph attributes (such as alignment, line spacing, border, shading).

Troubleshooting

Can I quickly set up the paragraph formats required to type a typical three- or four-level outline (I, II, III, A, B, C, 1, 2, 3, a, b, c, and so on)?

Yes. Just follow these steps:

1. For the I section of your outline, select the Hanging Indent EasyFormat from the EasyFormats dialog box, which creates a 1/2-inch hanging indent. Type **I.** and press tab. Then type your outline text.
2. When you're ready to type section A at the next outline level, press Ctrl+M to move the hanging indent 1/2 inch to the right. (Ctrl+M is a keyboard shortcut for what Works calls a *nested* indent, an indent identical to the preceding indent except bumped 1/2 inch to the right.)
3. When you're ready to type point 1 under section A, press Ctrl+M again. Works moves the hanging indent to the right 1/2 inch.
4. To move back to the preceding outline level, press Ctrl+Shift+M, which moves the hanging indent back to the left 1/2 inch.
5. Press Ctrl+Shift+M again to move the hanging indent back another 1/2 inch.

Creating Custom EasyFormats

EasyFormats are excellent time-savers when they meet your needs but, in some cases, you might need to create a custom format. For instance, suppose you regularly type detailed instructions for lab technicians and the instructions include many cautionary notes. You want to be sure the reader notices these cautions, so you design a custom format that uses a shaded box with a double-line red border. Because you want to use the format over and over again, you name it Caution and add it to the existing list of EasyFormats.

The easiest way to create a new EasyFormat is to use an existing one as a starting point. For example, if the Boxed Text EasyFormats is similar to the one you want to create for your Caution notes, you can start with the settings for Boxed Text and modify them where necessary.

To create a new EasyFormat, use these steps.

1. Select the paragraph you want to format, then apply the EasyFormat that most closely resembles the format you want to create.
2. Choose Format, EasyFormats.
3. Click New. Works displays the New Easy Format dialog box shown in figure 6.17. The current EasyFormat appears in the Sample area. A description of the format appears in the Format Settings box.
4. Type a name for the new EasyFormat.
5. Choose the Font, Borders, Shading, Paragraph, Bullets, or Tabs buttons to modify the format settings.
6. When all settings are correct, click Done. The EasyFormats dialog box appears.
7. Scroll through the list to find the new EasyFormat you just created.
8. Click Apply.

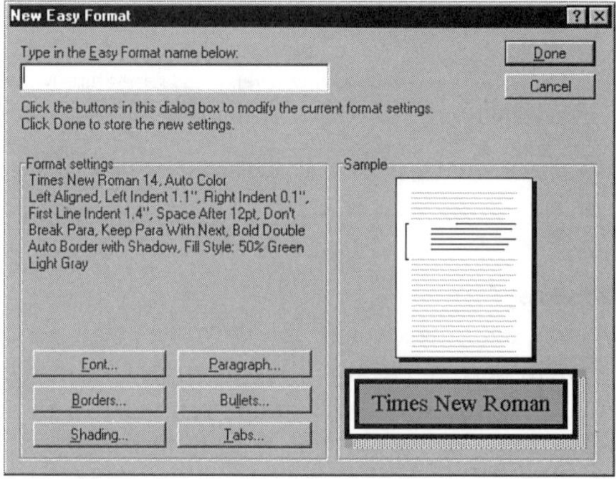

Fig. 6.17
Use the New Easy Format dialog box to add a new format to the existing list.

If you create a new EasyFormat and later decide you want to delete it, just highlight it on the list and click the Delete button.

Changing an EasyFormat

In addition to creating new EasyFormats, you can change any attribute of an existing EasyFormat. The process for changing an EasyFormat is quite similar to that of creating one. Just choose Format, EasyFormats, highlight the format you want to change, and click the Change button. Works displays the Change Easy Format dialog box, which looks identical to the New Easy Format dialog box except for the title. Use the same steps to change the format, then click Done when all settings are correct.

Creating Lists

Documents often contain lists—lists of items, lists of numbers, lists of names. Lists are usually single-column; however, sometimes they include more than one column.

Creating a Bulleted List

The documents you type often include a list of items preceded by bullets. This format is so common that Works provides a Bullets button on the toolbar.

There are two ways to create a bulleted list. One way is to type the list items first (pressing Enter after each item), select all items, then click the Bullets button. If you decide later to remove the bullets, select all the items in the list, then click the Bullets button again.

The second way to create a bulleted list is to click the Bullets button first, then begin typing items. Press Enter after each item and Works automatically inserts the bullet at the beginning of the line. After you type the last item, press Enter again. When the bullet appears at the left margin, click the Bullets button to turn off the Bullets format.

After typing a bulleted list, notice the indent markers on the ruler (see fig. 6.18). The left indent marker is positioned at 1/2 inch; the first line indent marker is positioned at zero. This is known as a *hanging* indent because the first line *hangs* to the left of the rest of the paragraph. The position of the left indent marker is what causes long (multiple line) entries to wrap at the 1/2-inch point instead of wrapping at the left margin (zero).

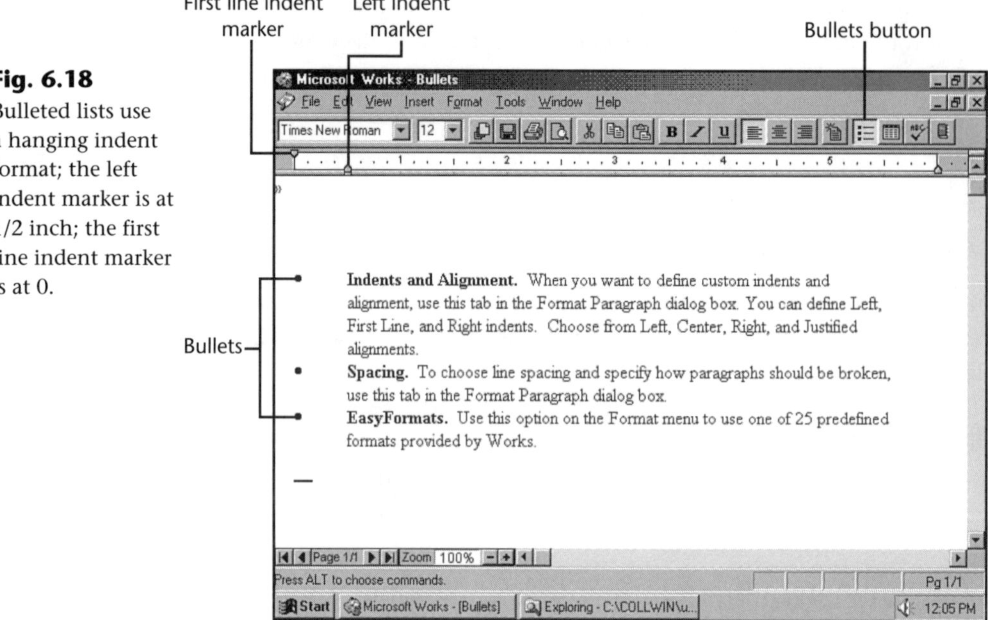

Fig. 6.18
Bulleted lists use a hanging indent format; the left indent marker is at 1/2 inch; the first line indent marker is at 0.

Choosing a Bullet Style

Although the bullet style shown in figure 6.18 is probably the most commonly used style, it is not the only style available in Works. You can choose from a variety of bullet styles by using the dialog box shown in figure 6.19.

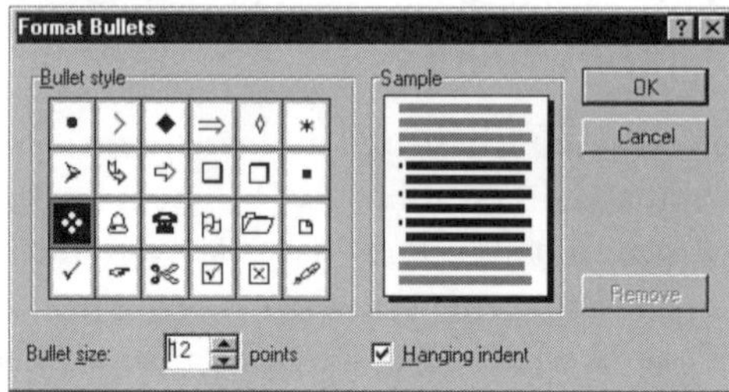

Fig. 6.19
The Format Bullets dialog box offers a variety of bullet styles and sizes.

To change a bullet style, use these steps:

1. Choose Format, Bullets to display the Format Bullets dialog box shown in figure 6.19.

2. Click a bullet style.

3. (Optional) In the Bullet Size box, click the up- or down-arrow key, or type a new size.

4. To turn off the hanging indent option, deselect the Hanging Indent check box.

5. Click OK.

Creating a Numbered List

A numbered list is similar to a bulleted list in that it uses a hanging indent format (see fig. 6.20). The Works toolbar, however, does not include a Numbers button, so you must type the numbers yourself after you set up the hanging indent format.

Use these steps to create a numbered list.

1. Type the items you want in the list, pressing Enter after each entry.

2. Select all items in the list.

3. Press and hold the Shift key, then drag the left indent marker on the ruler to the 1/2 inch point.

4. Move the insertion point back to the first item in the list.

5. Type **1.** and press Tab.

6. Move the insertion point to the next item in the list.

7. Type **2.** and press Tab.

8. Repeat this process for all items in the list.

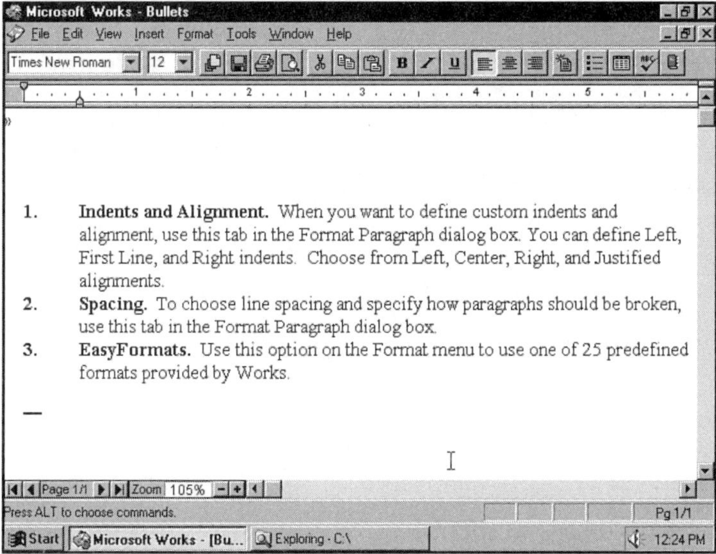

Fig. 6.20
A numbered list uses a hanging indent format.

Creating Lists Using Tabs

In addition to using indent markers, you can create simple one- or multi-column lists in Works using *tabs*. A tab marks a location on a line in a document. When you press the Tab key, the insertion point moves immediately to that location. Tabs let you align data or text in columns.

If you can create lists by changing the left indent marker or by setting tabs, what's the difference between the two and what's the preferred method? The difference is that a left indent marker marks the point at which *all* lines in a paragraph will be wrapped; a tab does not. If you place the left indent marker at 1/2 an inch, all lines of the paragraph will wrap at 1/2 inch. In contrast, if you press Tab to indent text at 1/2 inch and keep typing past the end of the line, the following lines wrap back at the left margin, not at the 1/2 inch tab.

The ruler in Works includes default tab settings, or you can set custom tabs. Although the ruler doesn't display them, default tabs occur at half-inch intervals on the ruler. (Later, you learn how to change this interval.) Custom tabs always appear on the ruler, and you can set a custom tab at any ruler location.

Works offers four types of custom tabs: left, center, right, and decimal. The names refer to the alignment of text or data in a column. For example, when you type data at a left tab, all data in the column is left-aligned at the tab location; when you type decimal numbers at a decimal tab, the decimal points in the column are aligned. Notice that both columns of data in the list shown in figure 6.21 are left-aligned.

Left-alignment works well for the first column of text. However, it does not work well for the second column, which includes numbers. Numbers are not generally left-aligned. In figure 6.22, the list is redone using a decimal tab for the Sales figures.

Notice in figures 6.21 and 6.22 that the tab marks for each type of tab (left and decimal) appear on the ruler. In these figures, you see an L-shaped marker, used for a left tab, and the upside down T shape with a decimal point next to it for a decimal tab. The two types of tabs not shown in these figures include a right tab, which is the mirror-image of the L-shaped tab, and the center tab, represented by an upside-down T shape (without the decimal point).

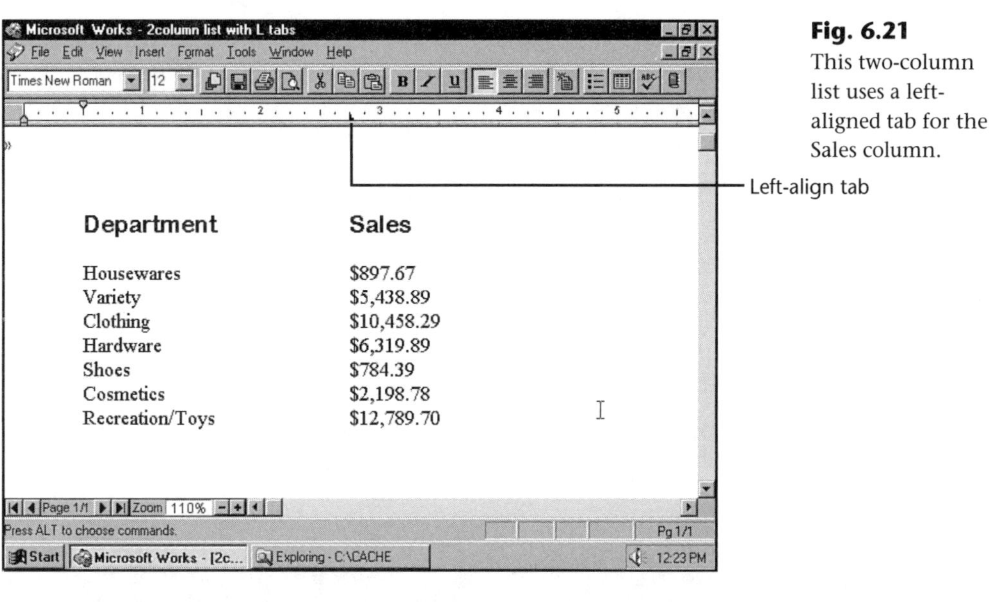

Fig. 6.21
This two-column list uses a left-aligned tab for the Sales column.

II

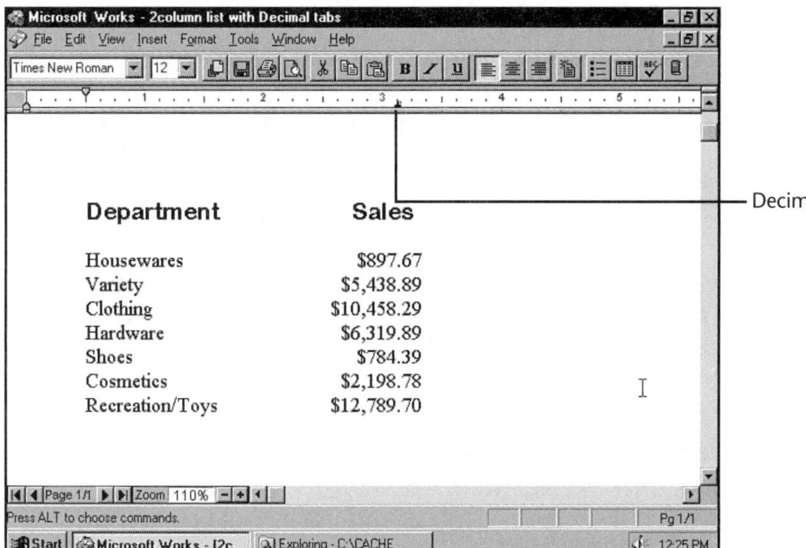

Decimal tab

Fig. 6.22
The decimal tab changes the alignment of numbers (compare to figure 6.21).

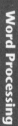

To set tabs for multiple columns in a list, follow these steps:

1. Move the insertion point to the line where you want your table to begin.

2. To set left tabs, click the proper location on the ruler. Works inserts a left tab marker on the ruler.
3. Choose Format, Tabs to open the Tabs dialog box.
4. In the Position box, enter a number in inches indicating the location of the tab on the ruler.
5. In the Alignment box, select Left, Center, Right, or Decimal.
6. Choose the Set button. If you make a mistake, choose Clear or Clear All.
7. To set an additional tab or tabs, repeat steps 4 through 6.
8. To change the default tab interval, enter a setting in the Default Tab Stops box.
9. When all tabs are set, correctly, choose the Close button.

Note

Because inches often convert to unfamiliar decimal numbers (such as 1.62 for 1 5/8 inches), you might have difficulty positioning a tab correctly when you type a setting in the Position box. You might make several guesses before getting the tab in exactly the position you want. To save time and avoid experimenting with different settings, double-click the ruler where you want to set the tab. The Tabs dialog box opens and the tab you set is highlighted so that you can change its alignment, if necessary.

The tabs you set apply on the line where the insertion point is located. Begin typing the data for your list, pressing Enter to add a new line. Like character style and paragraph formats, tabs remain in effect until you change or remove them.

Moving and Deleting Tabs

Sometimes after you enter all the data for a list, you might want to move tabs that are not positioned correctly. Or you might decide to add or delete a column of data, requiring that you add or delete a tab. Works makes moving and deleting tabs easy because you can drag the tab mark right on the ruler.

Before you move or delete a tab, you must select the lines that the ruler tabs affect. For example, if your list contains one line of column headings, one blank line, and eight lines of data, select all 10 lines before changing tab settings. If you forget to select a line, your tab changes affect only the line containing the insertion point; the remainder of the list continues to use the original tab settings. If you select only a portion of the list, the changes you make apply only to the text you select.

After selecting text, you move a tab by dragging it to a new location on the ruler. The tab automatically assumes its new position on the ruler. To delete a tab, drag the tab off the ruler (up or down). Works automatically realigns the data in the list based on the new tab settings. If you move or delete a tab by mistake, you can restore it by choosing Edit, Undo or by pressing Ctrl+Z.

Note

Before deleting a tab, you might want to delete the data in the column first. If you delete the tab first, the list reformats using one less tab, and the alignment of columns is thrown off. Finding the correct data to delete then becomes difficult. You can avoid this problem by deleting the data first—then deleting the tab.

You also can use the Format Tabs dialog box to move or delete tabs. To move a tab, highlight the tab in the Tab Stop Position list. Move the insertion point into the Tab Stop Position box and type a new setting for the tab. For example, to move a tab from 3" to 3.5", highlight the 3" tab in the Position list, and then change the 3" entry to 3.5". Choose the Set button to save the new setting, and then choose Close.

To delete a tab, highlight the tab in the Position list, and then choose the Clear button. Works removes the tab from the Position list. Repeat these steps to delete additional tabs and then choose Close to return to your document.

Using Tab Leaders

Sometimes using a leader can make the data in a list easier to read and follow. A leader is a dotted line (or other character) that fills the space between columns in a list. Leaders help your eye track a row of data from one column to another. In figure 6.23, you see the same department sales figures shown in figures 6.21 and 6.22, but the columns are farther apart. Without the dot leader, it would be more difficult for your eye to follow the row across to find the correct dollar figure in the second column. The dot leader makes it easy to see which dollar figures go with each department.

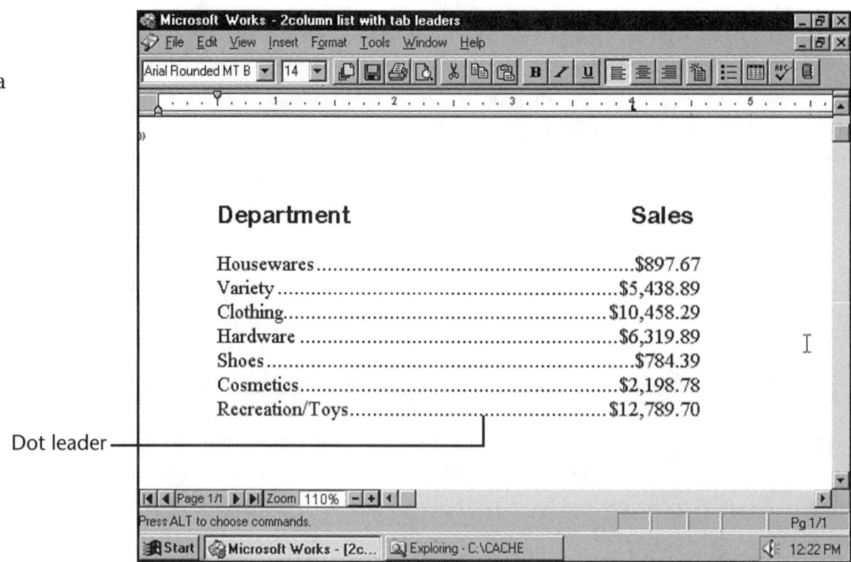

Fig. 6.23
A leader helps your eye track a row in a list.

To add a leader to a tab, select a style from the Leader box after you set the tab. Works automatically fills the space preceding the tab with the leader character you select.

Troubleshooting

I changed the tab position of several tabs in my list, but only part of my list reformatted. What happened?

You didn't select the entire list before you moved the tabs. If you haven't made any other changes to the document, choose Edit, Undo to restore the original settings. If you aren't able to use Undo, select the entire list and then reset all tabs to the new positions you want to use.

How can I center my column headings above the lists in my columns?

Works doesn't have a feature that automatically centers headings above columns. To make the headings appear centered over the columns, type the list first, and then type the headings using different tab settings than the list. You might need to experiment a little to find the correct position. Be sure to set the font and size you want to use before setting the tabs, and then preview the document before printing.

Inserting Page Breaks in a Document

As you create a document, Works keeps track of the number of lines you type relative to the page size and margin settings you are using. The program calculates where page breaks should occur and inserts a page break marker, a chevron character at the proper location in the left margin (see fig. 6.24). The page breaks that Works inserts are called *automatic* page breaks.

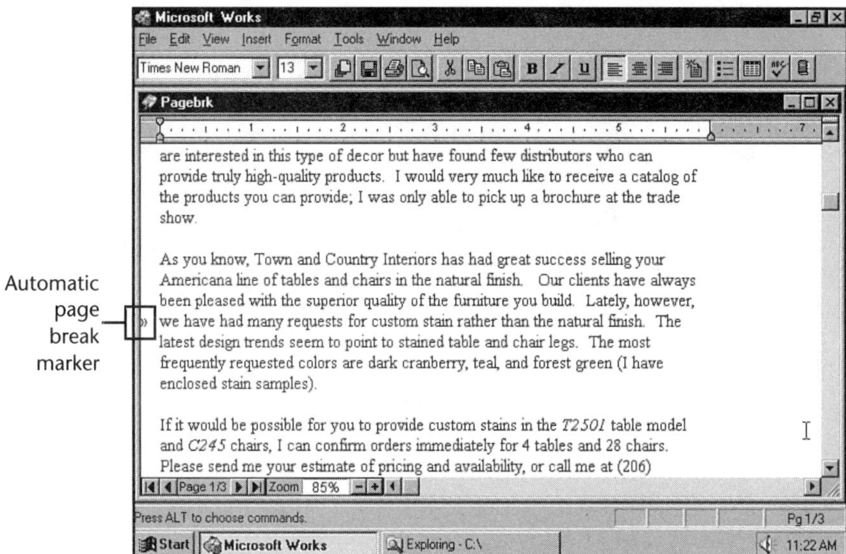

Fig. 6.24
A chevron character marks automatic page breaks in the left margin.

Because Works does not always break a page where you want, you can insert page breaks anywhere in a document. For example, suppose that Works inserts a page break following a section heading and the first paragraph in the section bumps to the next page. You probably want to insert a page break just before the section heading so that the heading and the first paragraph appear on the same page.

Page breaks that you insert are called *manual* page breaks and are indicated on-screen by a dashed line that runs horizontally across the document (see fig. 6.25). Manual page breaks are sometimes called *hard* page breaks. Works cannot adjust hard breaks; only you can move or delete them. When you insert a manual page break, Works automatically adjusts automatic page breaks throughout the document.

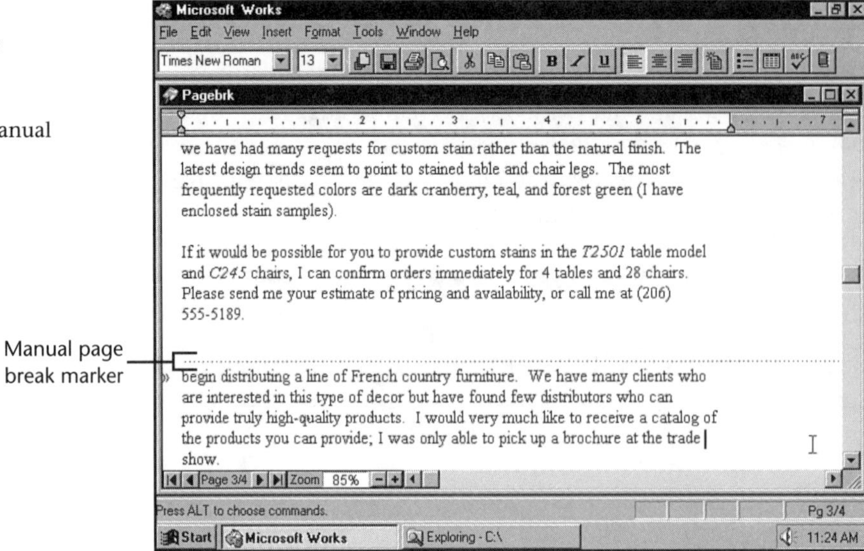

Fig. 6.25
A dashed line across the document indicates a manual page break.

Follow these steps to insert a manual page break:

1. Place the insertion point at the left-most character on the line that you want to appear on the new page.

2. Choose Insert, Page Break; or press Ctrl+Enter. Works inserts a manual page break marker (a dashed line) in the document above the line with the insertion point.

To remove a manual page break, move the insertion point to the beginning of the dashed line, then press the Delete key. When you delete a manual page break, Works automatically adjusts all automatic page breaks.

Troubleshooting

How can I delete an automatic page break that Works inserts in my document?

You cannot delete an automatic page break, but you can insert a manual break, which causes the automatic page break to readjust.

Why does the document I just printed contain many misplaced page breaks?

The document might contain manual page breaks you inserted before you revised the document. When a document undergoes extensive revision—adding and deleting large amounts of text—Works automatically adjusts the automatic page breaks but not the manual page breaks. Only you can move or delete manual breaks. When you know a document will undergo extensive revisions, don't insert manual page breaks until the content and structure of the document are stable. Also, don't forget to preview your document before printing so you can see where page breaks occur.

Chapter 7

Working with Tables, Columns, and Inserted Objects

by Debbie Walkowski

In Chapter 6, you learned many different techniques for improving the appearance and readability of a document. In this chapter, you learn additional techniques that enhance a document's appearance, but these techniques deal more specifically with the *layout* of a document. For example, some types of documents lend themselves well to multi-column text rather than full-page text. Newsletters are a good example of multi-column text. In other documents such as reports, manuals, or proposals, multi-column tables provide an appropriate way to convey information. In either case, pictures can add a great deal to a document, conveying in an instant information that is not readily accessible in words. In this chapter, you learn the techniques for creating tables, multi-column text, and incorporating pictures and other objects into a document.

This chapter discusses the following topics:

- Creating multi-column tables
- Formatting a document in multiple columns
- Inserting objects in a document
- Wrapping text around objects

Working with Tables

What is a table? In simplest terms, a table is nothing more than rows and columns of text or data. Ideally, a tabular arrangement makes information easier to understand than if it were presented as text. Tables are designed to convey concise bits of information—and their relationship to one another—at a glance.

Inserting a Table

In previous versions of Works, you created tables using tabs. Works 4.0 has a new built-in table generator that lets you create multi-column tables effortlessly. You just use the Insert Table dialog box shown in figure 7.1 to choose a table format, then specify the number of rows and columns. Works inserts the framework for the table into your word processor document. You fill in the rows and columns with your data.

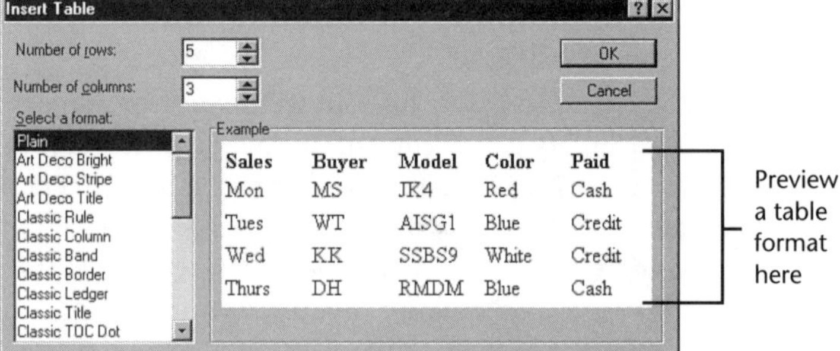

Fig. 7.1
The Insert Table dialog box lists a variety of formatting styles.

To insert a table in a document, use these steps:

1. Move the insertion point to the location where you want the table in your document.
2. Click the Insert Table toolbar button, or choose Insert, Table. The Insert Table dialog box shown in figure 7.1 appears.
3. Enter the number of rows to include in the table.
4. Enter the number of columns to include in the table.
5. From the Select a Format list, choose a table format.
6. Click OK.

The predesigned table formats in Works are wonderful. They save you the trouble of choosing colors, styles, fonts, and so on, to format a table. The wide variety of formats lets you choose the one that is most appropriate for the data in your table. For instance, some table formats emphasize rows of data while others emphasize columns. Highlight a format name to see an illustration in the Example area of the dialog box.

Figure 7.2 shows a five-column table created using the Insert Table command. The table format shown in figure 7.2 is Plain; the font is Times New Roman 12, column headings are set in bold, and rows and columns are not bordered or lined. This is the simplest format Works provides for tables.

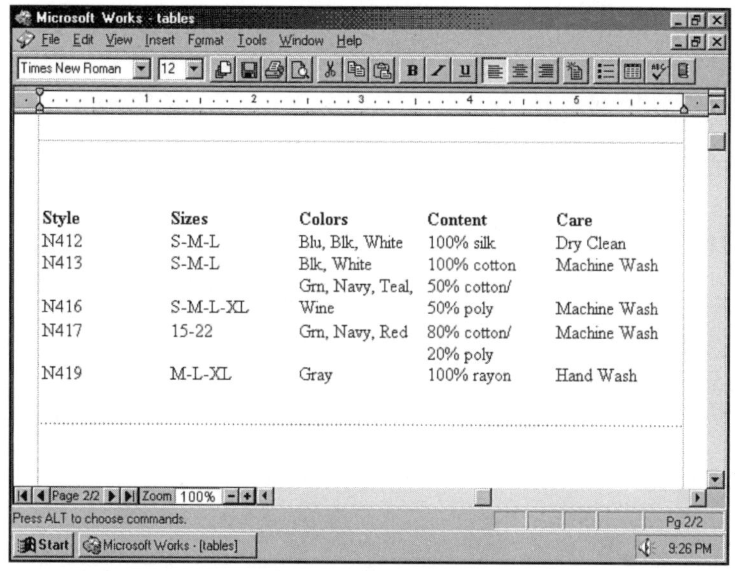

Style	**Sizes**	**Colors**	**Content**	**Care**
N412	S-M-L	Blu, Blk, White	100% silk	Dry Clean
N413	S-M-L	Blk, White	100% cotton	Machine Wash
N416	S-M-L-XL	Grn, Navy, Teal, Wine	50% cotton/ 50% poly	Machine Wash
N417	15-22	Grn, Navy, Red	80% cotton/ 20% poly	Machine Wash
N419	M-L-XL	Gray	100% rayon	Hand Wash

Fig. 7.2
This format is appropriate when you want a very uncomplicated, unadorned table.

In figure 7.3, you see the same table presented in the Classic Band format. This is a good example of a format that emphasizes rows rather than columns of data. It presents the column headings on a blue background, and the rows of data on alternating white and gray backgrounds. This color format makes it easy for your eye to follow each item across the table.

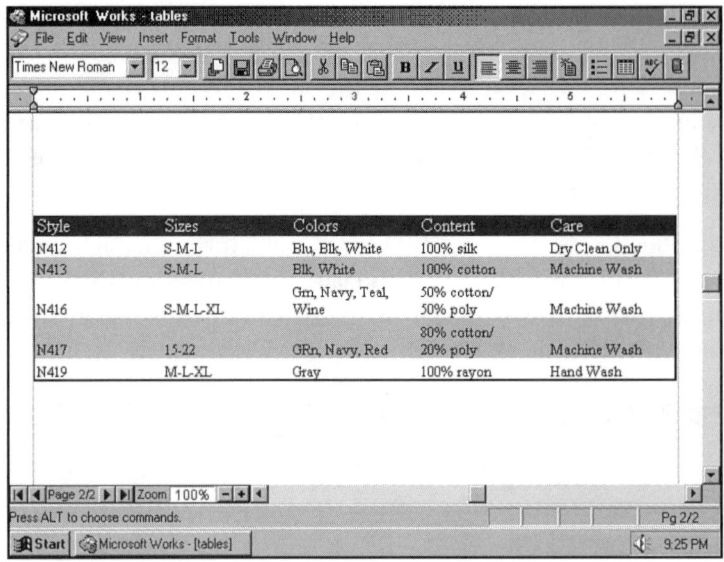

Style	Sizes	Colors	Content	Care
N412	S-M-L	Blu, Blk, White	100% silk	Dry Clean Only
N413	S-M-L	Blk, White	100% cotton	Machine Wash
N416	S-M-L-XL	Grn, Navy, Teal, Wine	50% cotton/ 50% poly	Machine Wash
N417	15-22	GRn, Navy, Red	80% cotton/ 20% poly	Machine Wash
N419	M-L-XL	Gray	100% rayon	Hand Wash

Fig. 7.3
This is the same table, displayed in the Classic Band format.

Entering and Editing Data

With the table inserted in your document, you're ready to begin entering your data. When you select the table, you can see the row and column dividers (see fig. 7.4). The standard word processor replaces the spreadsheet toolbar. This is because the table feature in the word processor actually places a spreadsheet in your document. Thus, you operate in the table the same way you do in a spreadsheet document. That is, you type text or numbers in each *cell* (the intersection of a row and column). To edit the table, click anywhere inside it. A selection box appears around the current cell.

Table 7.1 summarizes some of the most common text entry and editing techniques for spreadsheets. For complete instructions about entering and editing data in a spreadsheet, refer to Chapter 10, "Creating, Saving, and Printing a Spreadsheet."

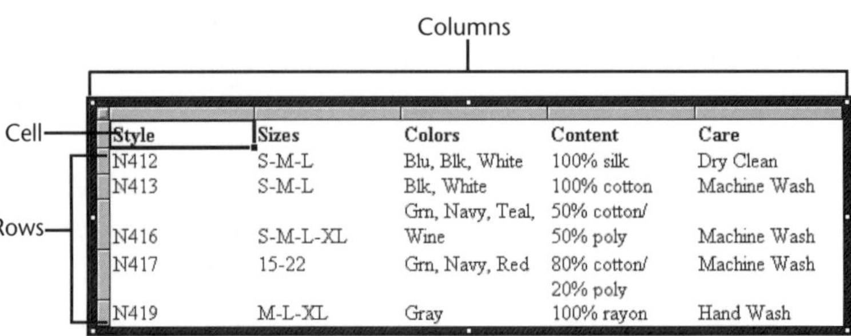

Style	Sizes	Colors	Content	Care
N412	S-M-L	Blu, Blk, White	100% silk	Dry Clean
N413	S-M-L	Blk, White	100% cotton	Machine Wash
N416	S-M-L-XL	Grn, Navy, Teal, Wine	50% cotton/ 50% poly	Machine Wash
N417	15-22	Grn, Navy, Red	80% cotton/ 20% poly	Machine Wash
N419	M-L-XL	Gray	100% rayon	Hand Wash

Fig. 7.4
A table, when selected, is actually a spreadsheet within a word processor document.

Table 7.1 Text Entry and Editing Techniques for Spreadsheets

To:	Do This:
Move to the next cell	Press Tab in the current row
Select a cell	Click it
Select a row	Click the row marker at the far left of the row
Select a column	Click the column marker at the top of the column
Select the entire table	Click the square in the upper-left corner of the table
Edit an entry	Highlight the cell; use the Backspace key to delete characters; type new characters
Change the font, alignment, number format, border, or shading	Highlight the cells you want to change, then choose Format from the shortcut menu. In the Format dialog box, click the tab for the change you want to make
Adjust column width	Point to the column divider until the Adjust pointer appears, then click and drag the column divider
Adjust cell width	Point to the row divider until the Adjust pointer appears, then click and drag the row divider

When you are finished entering data and editing data in a table, click anywhere in the document to move outside of the table. When you do, the word processor toolbar returns to the screen.

Using an Existing Spreadsheet for a Table

Another way to include a table in a document is by using an existing spreadsheet, created using the spreadsheet application in Works. Works lets you incorporate spreadsheets using one of two methods. You can *embed* a spreadsheet, which gives you full access to the Works spreadsheet functions from inside the word processor window. Or you can *link* an existing spreadsheet, which ensures that the spreadsheet in your word processor document updates automatically when you change the spreadsheet in the window. To learn how to use linking or embedding, refer to Chapter 26, "Using the Works Tools Together."

Tip

You can resize a table by dragging one of its frame *handles*. For specific instructions about sizing a table or other type of object, see the section "Selecting, Sizing, and Moving Objects," later in this chapter.

Creating Columns of Text

Certain types of documents lend themselves well to multiple columns of text; newspapers and magazines use this style almost exclusively. You can use the same style to create newsletters, articles, brochures, or other types of documents.

When you format a document for multiple columns, you determine the number of columns and the amount of space between columns. The columns apply to the entire document except headers and footers. (You cannot use multiple columns on selected pages of a document.) Based on the number of columns you specify, the page size, and the margin settings, Works automatically calculates the width of the columns. You also can add a vertical line between columns. An example of a multi-column document is shown in the Preview screen in figure 7.5.

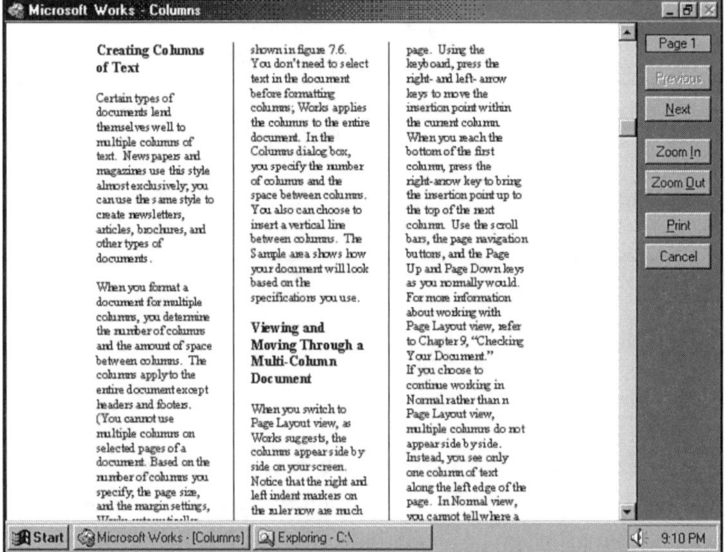

Fig. 7.5
Print Preview shows how a three-column document looks.

Choosing Column Specifications

To create a multi-column document, choose Format, Columns. The Format Columns dialog box appears (see fig. 7.6). You don't need to select text in the document before formatting columns; Works applies the columns to the entire document. In the Format Columns dialog box, you specify the number of columns and the space between columns. You also can choose to insert a vertical line between columns. The Sample area shows how your document will look based on the specifications you use.

To specify columns in a document, follow these steps:

1. Choose Format, Columns to display the Format Columns dialog box shown in figure 7.6.

2. In the Number of Columns text box, enter the number of columns to use.

3. In the Space Between text box, enter a measurement in inches.

4. To print a vertical line between columns, select the Line Between Columns check box.

5. Click OK. Works displays a message suggesting that you switch to Page Layout view to view the document.

6. Choose Yes. Works displays the columns on your screen. If you choose No, the columns are not displayed on the screen. Switch to Page Layout view or Print Preview to view them.

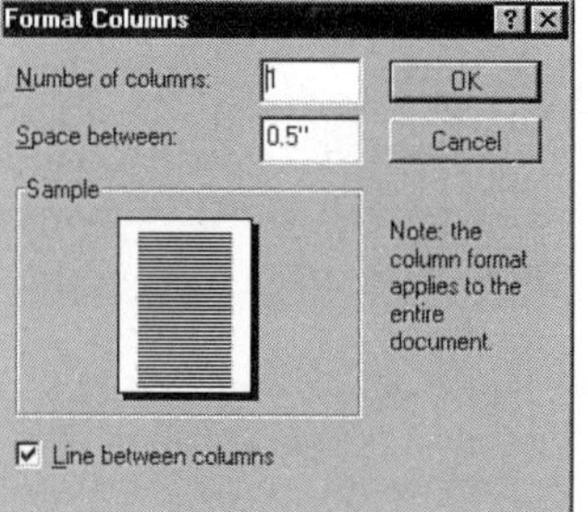

Fig. 7.6
Use the Format Columns dialog box to set the number of columns, the space between columns, and whether you want a vertical line between columns.

Viewing and Moving through a Multi-Column Document

When you switch to Page Layout view, as Works suggests, the columns appear side by side on your screen. Notice that the right and left indent markers on the ruler now are much closer together than normal—the markers define the width of a single column (see fig. 7.7). If you specify a vertical line between columns, you don't see it in Page Layout view, but the line is visible when you preview the document.

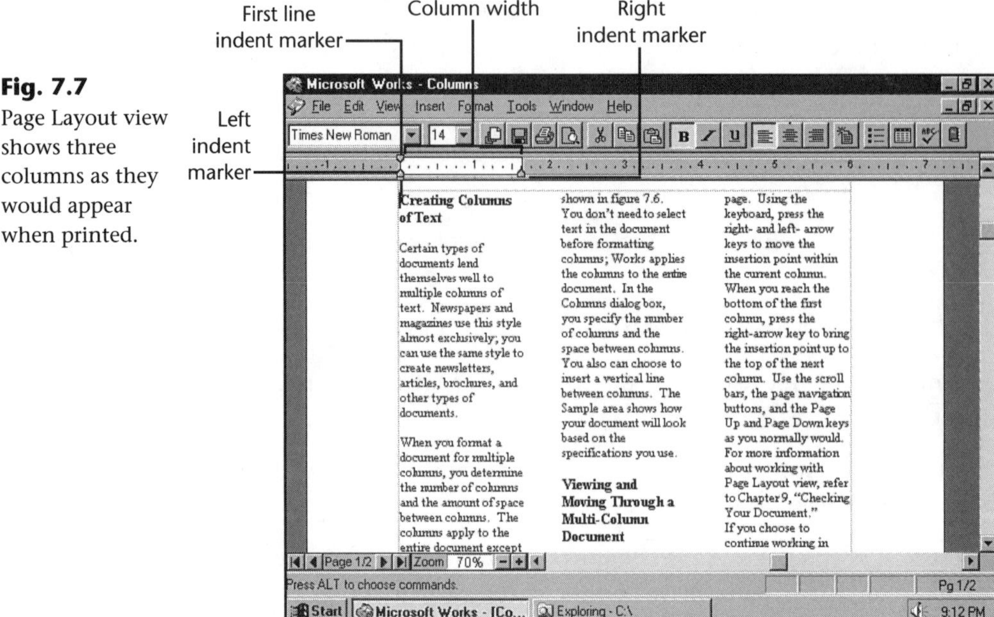

Fig. 7.7
Page Layout view shows three columns as they would appear when printed.

To move the insertion point using the mouse, click anywhere on the page. Using the keyboard, press the right- and left-arrow keys to move the insertion point in the current column. When you reach the bottom of the first column, press the right-arrow key to bring the insertion point up to the top of the next column. Use the scroll bars, the page navigation buttons, and the Page Up and Page Down keys as you normally would.

◄ See "Changing Your View of a Document," p. 39

If you choose to work in Normal rather than Page Layout view, multiple columns do not appear side by side. Instead, you see only one column of text along the left edge of the page. In Normal view, you cannot tell where a new column begins or ends.

Creating a Title Across Multiple Columns

If a multi-column format affects the entire document, how can you enter a title or a headline that runs across the top of all columns, as shown in figure 7.8? You can do it by using WordArt, a tool built into Works that lets you add creative and artistic text to documents.

This section is not intended to provide a detailed discussion of WordArt and how to position it in your document. The instructions below briefly describe how to add a WordArt title across columns like the one shown in figure 7.8. To learn the details of using WordArt, refer to Chapter 25, "Using WordArt and Note-It." To learn more about positioning objects in a document, refer to the section "Working With Inserted Objects" later in this chapter.

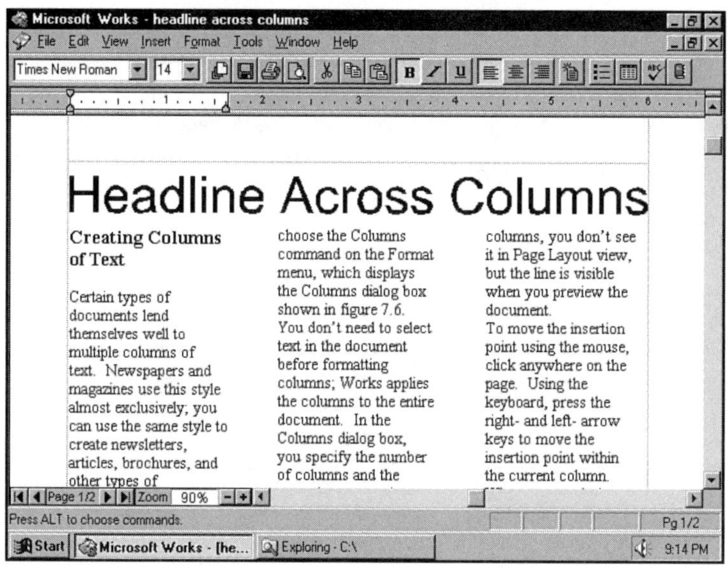

Fig. 7.8
A headline or title can span all three columns.

1. Place the insertion point at the top of the page where you want to insert a headline or title.

2. Choose Insert, WordArt.

3. In the WordArt pop-up window, type the headline or title text. Use the WordArt toolbar to change the font and size of the entry.

4. Click the Close button in the WordArt window. The WordArt object is placed in your word processor document and selected.

5. Choose Format, Text Wrap.

6. In the Text Wrap dialog box, choose Absolute, then click OK.

7. With the WordArt object still selected, click and drag the gray handle on the right side of the object to the right margin of the document. If necessary, drag the bottom gray handle to change the height of the WordArt object.

Troubleshooting

I can't figure out the maximum number of columns I can use in a document.

Works doesn't define a maximum number because the program calculates the placement of columns based on the space between columns and the margin widths. If your margins are narrow and the space between columns is minimal, obviously Works can create more columns. The maximum number depends entirely on these factors. Works displays an error message when it is unable to create the number of columns you specify.

I want to format my document with two columns, but I want the left column to be wider than the right one. How can I do this?

Although you can alter the left indent, first line indent, and right indent markers for a specific column, all columns in a word processor document are the same width; you cannot make one column wider or narrower than another.

I want to enter the same title across each page of my multi-column newsletter. How can I create this title if Works applies multiple columns to the entire document?

You can enter the title of your newsletter in a header. Multi-column formatting does not affect headers. For information about creating headers, refer to Chapter 8, "Adding Headers, Footers, Footnotes, and Bookmarks to a Document."

Changing or Removing Columns

Multiple columns are as easy to change or remove from a document as they are to define. Choose Format, Columns, then enter a number (enter 1 to take away all multiple columns) in the Number of Columns box and choose OK. Works reformats the document according to the number of columns you specify.

Working with Inserted Objects

One of the most dramatic ways to make a document more visually appealing is to include graphic elements and illustrations. As discussed in Chapter 1, Works provides a variety of ways to include such items. Using ClipArt, you can include a prepared drawing to add humor, draw attention, or illustrate a point. With Microsoft Draw, you can create your own drawings that are custom-designed to achieve the same purpose. WordArt's unique capability to bend and shape text offers a creative way to dress up and stylize titles, banners, headlines, or logos. And finally, the Note-It feature in Works enables you to insert eye-catching icons in a document that reveal a hidden note when you click the icon.

Inserting Objects in a Document

All four of the mini-applications insert objects into your document. The method for inserting an object varies from application to application. For example, when you create a drawing using Microsoft Draw, a separate drawing window appears on-screen. You use the drawing commands and tools to create your drawing, then insert the object into your document. Like Microsoft Draw, WordArt uses a separate window as well as its own menu bar and toolbar. To insert a note in a document, you use the Note-It dialog box to select a note style and enter the note text. ClipArt also uses its own dialog box from which you can preview and choose the file to insert.

Because the method for inserting objects varies from one application to another, the focus of this section is not to describe in detail how to insert objects—later chapters discuss these details. Rather, the important thing to understand is what actually happens when you insert an object. Because an object has height and width, it disrupts the surrounding text when placed at the insertion point. The insertion point might be on a blank line, at the end of a line of text, or in the middle of a paragraph. Regardless of the insertion point's position, the height of the current line increases to accommodate the height of the object. Therefore, you must determine the best size and position for the object, then specify how you want to format the surrounding text.

Refer to Chapter 24, "Using Microsoft Draw and ClipArt," for details about creating and inserting Microsoft Draw drawings and choosing ClipArt files. Refer to Chapter 25, "Using WordArt and Note-It," for information about using WordArt and Note-It.

Selecting, Sizing, and Moving Objects

After you insert an object in a document, the object occupies space in the document. Because all objects have height and width, they generally occupy more space than a single line of text. Before you can determine how to format the surrounding text, you need to know how to select, move, and resize an object, if necessary.

To select an object, click anywhere on the object. The object's *frame* (the rectangular shape that surrounds the object) becomes visible. Regardless of the size of a particular object, all objects have a rectangular shape when you select them. At the corners and midpoints around the frame are *handles*, used for resizing the object (see fig. 7.9).

Fig. 7.9
An object's frame and handles appear when you select the object.

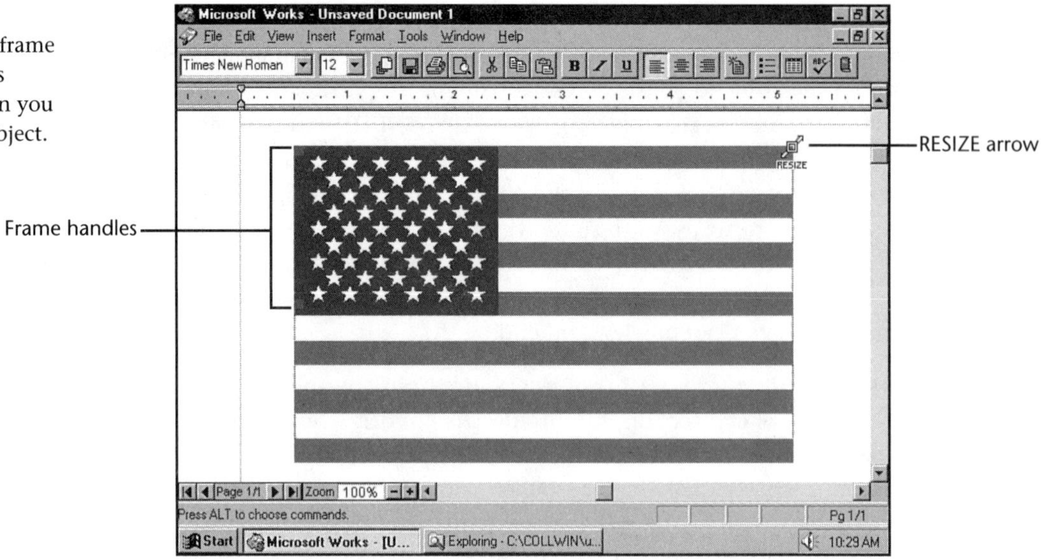

RESIZE arrow

Frame handles

You can resize an object in several ways. First, select the object so its frame and handles are visible. When you place the mouse pointer on any of the handles, the pointer changes to a RESIZE arrow (refer to fig. 7.9). Click and drag a side, top, or bottom handle to resize in one dimension only. For instance, drag the top or bottom handle to make the object longer or shorter. Release the mouse button when the object is the size you want. To resize an object while maintaining its height-to-width ratio, click and drag any of the corner handles. The object resizes in two dimensions at the same time.

Rather than sizing an object using the mouse, you can specify exact dimensions for the object. To specify dimensions or to scale an object from its original size, select the object, then choose Format, Picture, which displays the Format Picture dialog box (see fig. 7.10). If the Size tab is not selected, click it now.

Fig. 7.10
Use the Size tab to specify an object's exact dimensions and scale.

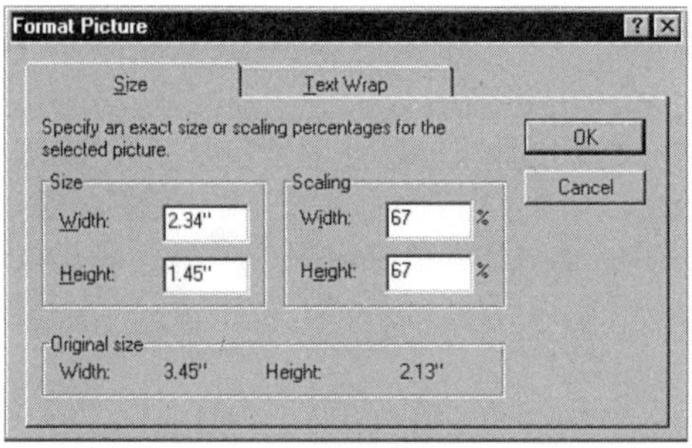

The Original Size section lists the original width and height of the object. In the Size section, you can enter numbers in the Width and Height boxes. Or, if you prefer to scale the object, enter percentages in the Width and Height boxes in the Scaling section. After you size the object correctly, choose OK to return to the document window.

To move an object, you simply drag it to the proper location. When you point anywhere on the object, the I-beam mouse pointer changes to an arrow labeled DRAG. Click the object and hold down the left mouse button; the DRAG label changes to MOVE. Drag the object in any direction until it is where you want it. Don't worry yet about the placement of the surrounding text; you'll learn how to position it next.

Wrapping Text around Inserted Objects

Because most objects occupy more space than a single line of text in a document, you must make choices about how you want to format the surrounding text. Works offers two options for formatting the text that borders an inserted object: *inline* or *absolute*. These options are illustrated in figure 7.11, where the Format Picture dialog box is shown with the Text Wrap tab selected.

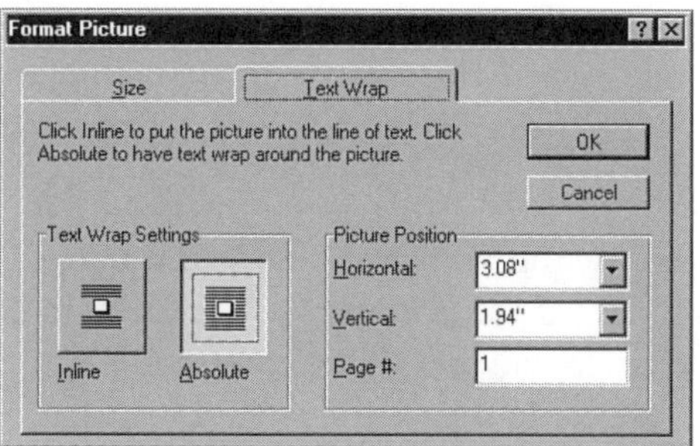

Fig. 7.11
Use the Text Wrap tab to specify how you want text formatted around a picture.

The Inline text wrapping option positions an object on the same line as the text that immediately precedes and follows the object. The height of the object determines the height of that line because Works treats the object as though it were a character on the line. The Absolute text wrapping option surrounds all sides of the object with text (see fig. 7.12).

II

Word Processing

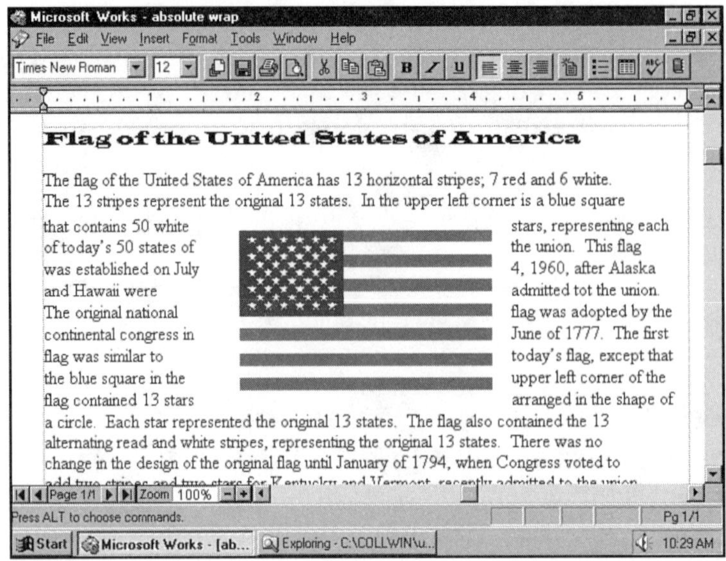

Fig. 7.12
With Absolute text wrapping selected, the text flows around the object.

The settings in the Picture Position area are available only when you select the Absolute option. Initially, the Horizontal box shows where the object is positioned relative to the left edge of the paper; the Vertical box shows where the object is positioned relative to the top edge of the paper. The Page # box shows the page number where the object is located. In figure 7.11, for example, the object is 3.08" from the left edge of the paper and 1.94" from the top of the paper.

If you prefer, you can use the Horizontal and Vertical boxes to position an object for you. The boxes are drop-down lists that contain the choices Left, Center, and Right (Horizontal) and Top, Center, and Bottom (Vertical). If you want your object to appear in the exact center of the page, for example, you can select the Center setting in both the Horizontal and Vertical boxes. If you want the object to appear in the lower-left corner of the page, select the Left setting in the Horizontal box and the Bottom setting in the Vertical box. To change the page on which the object appears, enter a new page number in the Page # box.

Troubleshooting

How can I place text only above and below my object and center the object horizontally? (I don't want any text on the line with the object.)

Works doesn't have an automatic setting for this arrangement, but you can achieve it. Place the object on a line of its own between the two lines of text that you want to border the object. Select the Inline wrap option. In the document, select the object and then select the Center alignment button on the toolbar. The object is centered and bordered on top and bottom by text.

Sometimes when I select the Absolute setting, my screen shows a large space between lines of text at the top of my object. Will this cause a problem when I print my document?

No. If you preview your document, you can see that the spacing between lines adjusts correctly.

Chapter 8

Adding Headers, Footers, Footnotes, and Bookmarks to a Document

by Debbie Walkowski

Chapters 6 and 7 discuss how to enhance documents by using various character and paragraph styles, alignment, borders, columns, tables, and inserted objects. All these features improve the appearance of a document. The features discussed in this chapter are also enhancements, but they improve the *readability* of a document.

This chapter discusses the following topics:

- Inserting headers and footers
- Adding footnotes
- Using a bookmark to mark a location in a document

Using Headers and Footers in a Document

Before you print a document, you might want to include a title, page number, date, time, or other information that prints at the top or bottom of each page. Repetitive text that appears at the top of each page is called a *header*.

Text that appears at the bottom of each page is called a *footer*. We often think of a header or footer as a page number, but headers and footers can include any kind of information you want to repeat on each page. For example, you might want to include the current date, current time, the document name, or instructions such as *Company Confidential*. You can even include objects (such as ClipArt, a drawing, or WordArt) in a header or footer, and you can apply formatting, font, style characteristics, borders, and shading, just like you do to regular text in a document.

A header or footer prints in the top or bottom page margin areas and can be a single line of text or multiple lines (up to 1/3 the page length). In some cases, such as when your document contains a title page, you might want to eliminate the header and footer from the first page of the document.

Headers and footers are visible in the document window in either Page Layout view or Normal view. The primary difference between the two views is that in Page Layout view, headers and footers appear on every page of a document. The header and footer areas are bordered on the screen by a faint dotted outline and labeled *Header* or *Footer*. An example of a header in Page Layout view is shown in figure 8.1

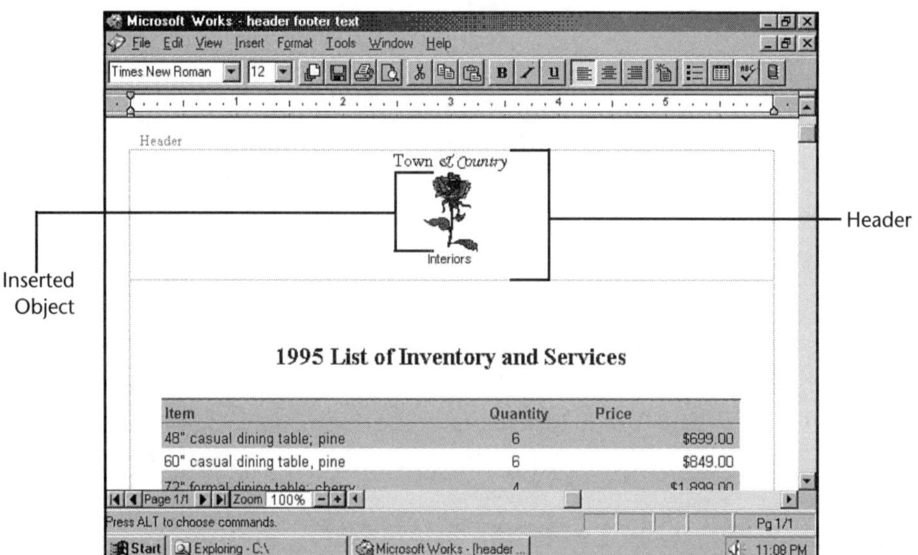

Fig. 8.1
In Page Layout view, you can see headers and footers at the top and bottom of every page in a document.

In Normal view, headers and footers appear only at the top of the first page of a document; they do not display on subsequent pages. The header text appears next to an H marker in the left page margin; the footer text appears next to an F marker. An example of header and footer text in Normal view is shown in figure 8.2. The header includes a ClipArt picture.

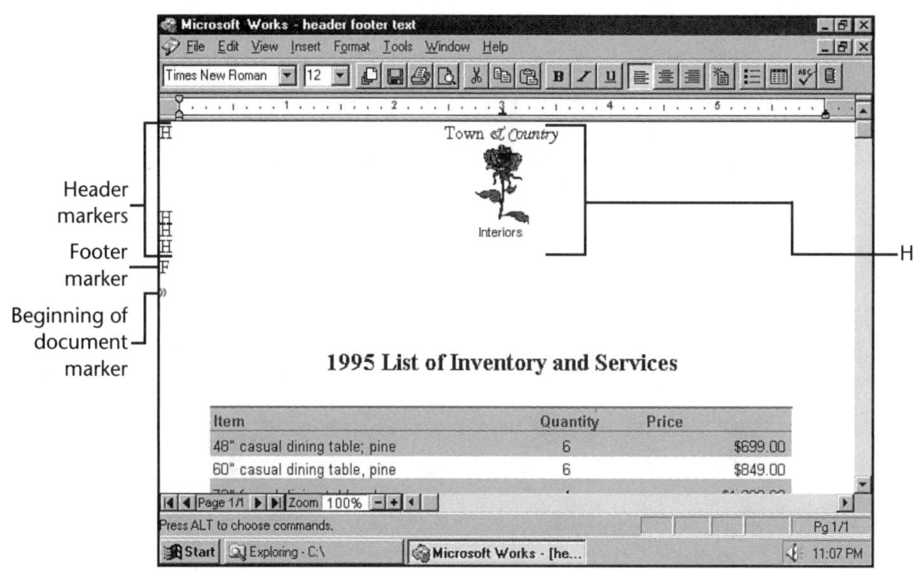

Fig. 8.2
In Normal view, header and footer text appears next to the H and F markers in the left margin.

Creating a Header or Footer

In Works, you can create a header or footer in Normal view or Page Layout view. To create a header or footer in Normal view, scroll to the top of the first page and click next to the H or the F marker in the left margin. If you want the header or footer to be several lines long, press Enter at the end of each line. When the text is typed, you can use the Format menu to change the font, size, color, alignment, and so on. All changes are visible on the screen in Normal view. When you are finished creating the header or footer, click anywhere in the document area or on the first line to the right of the Beginning of Document marker (>>) (refer to fig. 8.2).

◄ See "Changing Your View of a Document," p. 39

◄ See "Working with Inserted Objects," p. 142

► See "Using ClipArt," p. 513

To create a header or footer in Normal view, follow these steps:

1. Choose View, Normal.
2. If the H and F markers are not visible, choose View, Header or View, Footer. Works moves to the top of the document.
3. Click next to the H or F that appears in the left margin.
4. Type the text for the header or footer, and press Enter when you want to begin a new line.
5. Format the text as you want it.
6. If you choose, use the Insert menu to include ClipArt, a drawing, or WordArt in your header or footer.

Tip
You can move quickly to the top of the document by pressing Ctrl+Home.

7. When the header or footer is complete, click next to the Beginning of Document marker at the top of the first page to begin entering text, or click anywhere in the text area of the document to continue editing.

To create a header or footer in Page Layout view, use these steps:

1. Choose View, Page Layout.
2. If the header or footer is not visible, scroll to the top or bottom of any page.

> **Note**
>
> In Page Layout view, you can create or change a header or footer on *any* page, not just on the first page.

3. Click inside the Header or Footer area.
4. Type the text for the header or footer, pressing Enter when you want to begin a new line.
5. Format the text as you want it.
6. If you want, use the Insert menu to include ClipArt, a drawing, or WordArt in your header or footer.
7. When the header or footer is complete, click anywhere inside the text area of the document.

Regardless of the view you use to create a header or footer, you can edit, format, and enhance the text just like you can modify any other text in a document. You can choose a different font, point size, or text color, and you can apply bold, underline, or italic. You can even add a border or shading to a header or footer.

Inserting Special Information in Headers and Footers

Page numbers, the current date (or date of printing), the current time (or time of printing), and the document name are elements that are commonly included in headers and footers. Works can insert these elements for you automatically. To include any of these elements in a header or footer, choose the appropriate command from the Insert menu (see fig. 8.3).

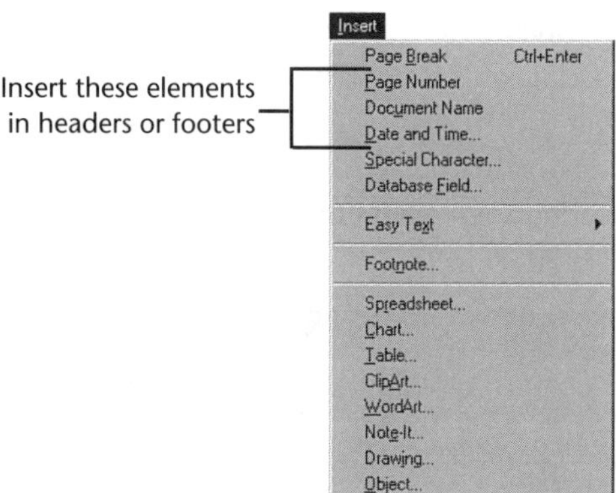

Fig. 8.3
The Insert menu contains commands for inserting the date, file name, and page numbers in a document.

When you choose Insert, Page Number or Insert, Document Name, Works automatically inserts a `*page*` or a `*filename*` placeholder wherever the insertion point is located. When you're ready to print the document, Works inserts the correct page number on every page and the document name in the location of these place holders. An example of these place holders is shown in figure 8.4.

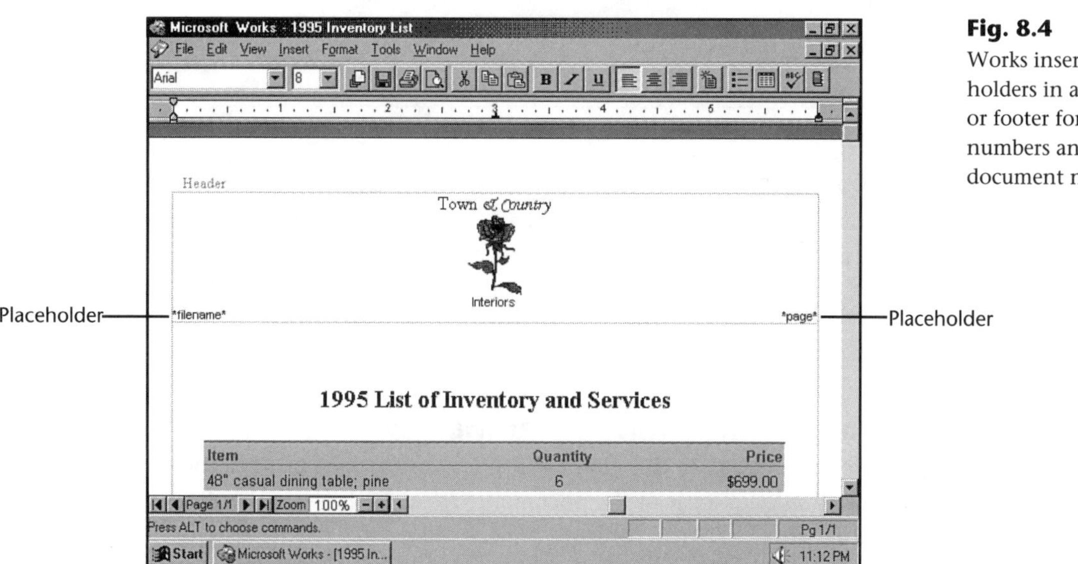

Fig. 8.4
Works inserts placeholders in a header or footer for page numbers and the document name.

When you choose Insert, Date and Time, Works displays the Insert Date and Time dialog box shown in figure 8.5. This dialog box displays a wide variety of date and time formats, including numeric or text formats, date and time separately, or date and time together. To insert a date or time, highlight a format, then click Insert. Rather than inserting a placeholder, Works inserts the actual current date or time in the header or footer.

Because you often don't print a document the same time you create it, Works lets you specify if you want the date and time to be updated when the document is printed. If you do, select the Automatically Update When Printed check box. When you leave this box blank, Works prints the date and time that was current when you inserted these elements in the document.

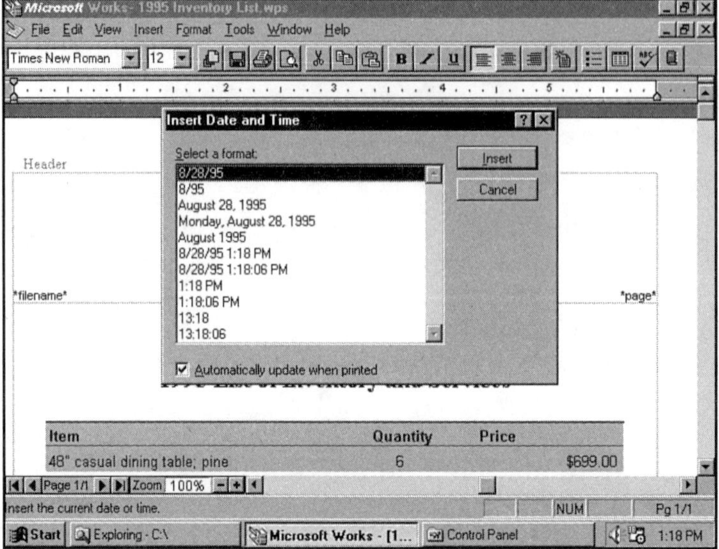

Fig. 8.5
The Insert Date and Time dialog box offers a wide variety of date and time formats.

Removing a Paragraph Header or Footer

Sometimes you decide you don't need a header or footer after you've created it. To delete a header or footer (in either Normal view or Page Layout view), select all of the text, then press Delete. In Normal view, the H and F markers remain on the screen. In Page Layout view, the Header and Footer areas remain visible on the screen but are empty.

Altering Header and Footer Margins

As you learned earlier in this chapter, headers and footers print in the top and bottom margin areas of the document. The default top and bottom margin settings are one inch. Within that space is a default header margin of .5 inch and a default footer margin of .75 inch. Therefore, a header or footer must fit within these margins in order to print correctly. Because a one-line header always fits within a .5 inch margin and a one-line footer always fits within a .75 inch margin, you never need to adjust margins for a one-line header or footer. However, headers and footers can be multiple lines and, therefore, margins might require adjustment.

Figure 8.6 illustrates how Works measures margins. The top margin is the distance from the top edge of the paper to the first line of body text in the document. The header margin is the distance from the top of the paper to the first line of text in the header. The bottom margin is the distance from the bottom of the paper to the last line of text in the body of the document. The footer margin is the distance from the bottom edge of the paper to the first line of text in the footer.

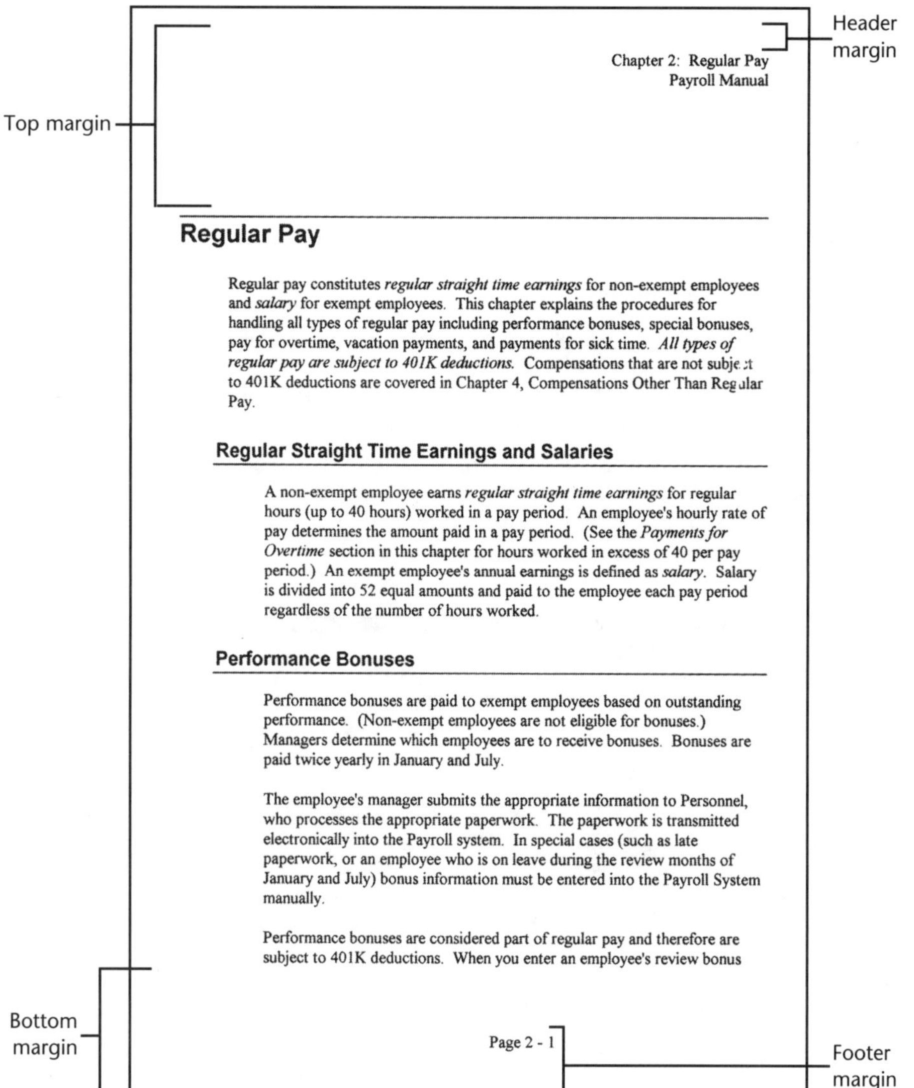

Chapter 2: Regular Pay
Payroll Manual

Regular Pay

Regular pay constitutes *regular straight time earnings* for non-exempt employees and *salary* for exempt employees. This chapter explains the procedures for handling all types of regular pay including performance bonuses, special bonuses, pay for overtime, vacation payments, and payments for sick time. *All types of regular pay are subject to 401K deductions.* Compensations that are not subject to 401K deductions are covered in Chapter 4, Compensations Other Than Regular Pay.

Regular Straight Time Earnings and Salaries

A non-exempt employee earns *regular straight time earnings* for regular hours (up to 40 hours) worked in a pay period. An employee's hourly rate of pay determines the amount paid in a pay period. (See the *Payments for Overtime* section in this chapter for hours worked in excess of 40 per pay period.) An exempt employee's annual earnings is defined as *salary*. Salary is divided into 52 equal amounts and paid to the employee each pay period regardless of the number of hours worked.

Performance Bonuses

Performance bonuses are paid to exempt employees based on outstanding performance. (Non-exempt employees are not eligible for bonuses.) Managers determine which employees are to receive bonuses. Bonuses are paid twice yearly in January and July.

The employee's manager submits the appropriate information to Personnel, who processes the appropriate paperwork. The paperwork is transmitted electronically into the Payroll system. In special cases (such as late paperwork, or an employee who is on leave during the review months of January and July) bonus information must be entered into the Payroll System manually.

Performance bonuses are considered part of regular pay and therefore are subject to 401K deductions. When you enter an employee's review bonus

Page 2 - 1

Fig. 8.6 Headers and footers must fit within top and bottom margins

Note

Header and footer margins are not the same size. A footer margin includes the footer text but a header margin does not include header text. This is an important point to remember when adjusting header and footer margins. Also, because headers and footers print within the top and bottom page margins, header and footer margin measurements must be less than or equal to top and bottom page margin measurements.

In Chapter 4, you learn how to adjust top, bottom, left, and right margins using the Page Setup dialog box (see fig. 8.7). In the same dialog box, you use the Header Margin and Footer Margin boxes to adjust header and footer settings.

To adjust top, bottom, header, and footer margins, use the following steps:

1. Choose File, Page Setup.
2. Choose the Margins tab at the bottom of the dialog box.
3. In the Top Margin, Bottom Margin, Header Margin, and Footer Margin boxes, type the setting you want to use in inches, or click the up/down arrows. Type a decimal for fractions of an inch (such as 1.25 for 1 1/4 inches).
4. After all margin settings are correct, choose OK.

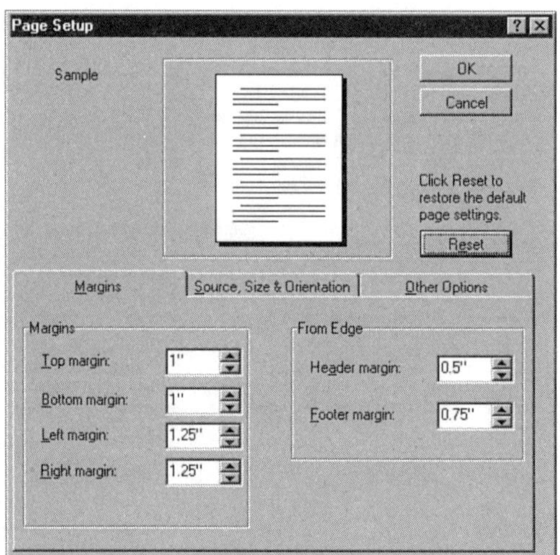

Fig. 8.7
Use the Margins tab in the Page Setup dialog box to adjust header and footer margins.

Troubleshooting

My two-line header is printing correctly, but my two-line footer is printing too close to the bottom of the page. My top and bottom margins are set at 1.25 inches, and my header and footer margins are set at .5 inch. What's wrong?

Your bottom margin setting is large enough, but remember that the footer margin is the space from the bottom of the page to the *top* of the footer—the footer margin includes the footer text, unlike the header margin. Try increasing the footer margin to .87 inch or larger.

Adding Footnotes to a Document

Footnotes are often used in reports, proposals, and other documents to cite the source of information or to provide additional information, comments, or remarks about a topic in the body. A footnote marker appears in the body of the document where you place the marker, and the actual footnote text prints at the bottom of the page or at the end of the document. You can use numbered footnote markers, or you can specify another character to mark the location of a footnote.

When you insert a footnote in Normal view, Works displays a footnote pane at the bottom of the document window (see fig. 8.8). Works inserts the matching footnote marker and places the insertion point next to the marker in the footnote pane. In the footnote pane, you can enter, edit, and format the footnote text just like any other text in the document. After you complete the footnote, move the insertion point back into the body of the document and continue working. You can close the footnote pane by choosing the Footnotes command on the View menu. This command toggles the footnote pane on and off; choose the command another time to view footnotes again.

If you are using Page Layout view when you create a footnote, Works inserts the matching footnote marker and moves the insertion point to the bottom of the page where you can enter, edit, and format the footnote text. After you complete the footnote, move the insertion point back into the body of the document to continue working (see fig. 8.9). Footnotes print in the body text area of the page, so they are not affected by top, bottom, header, or footer margins.

Fig. 8.8
In Normal view, you can enter, edit, and format footnote text in the footnote pane.

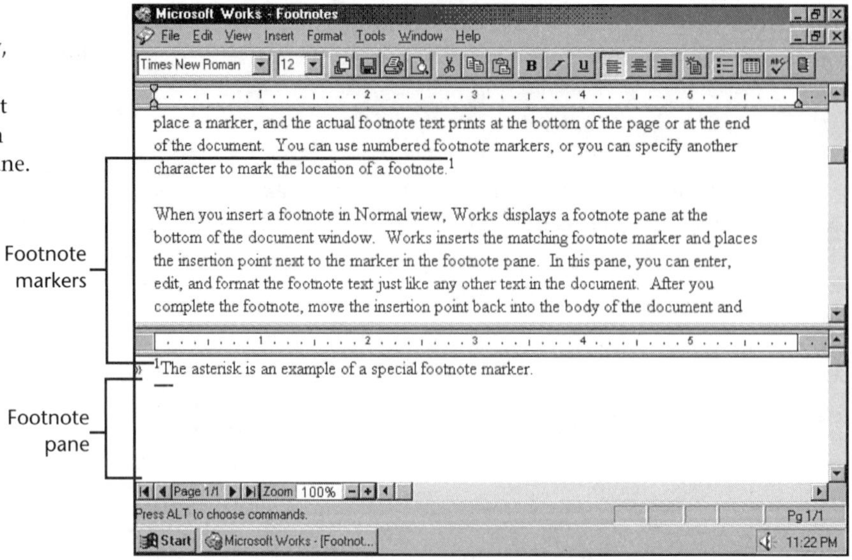

Footnote markers

Footnote pane

Creating a Footnote

To insert a footnote in a document, you use the Insert Footnote dialog box shown in figure 8.10. In this dialog box, you select Numbered or Special Mark for the footnote marker. A special mark is a character other than a number, such as an asterisk.

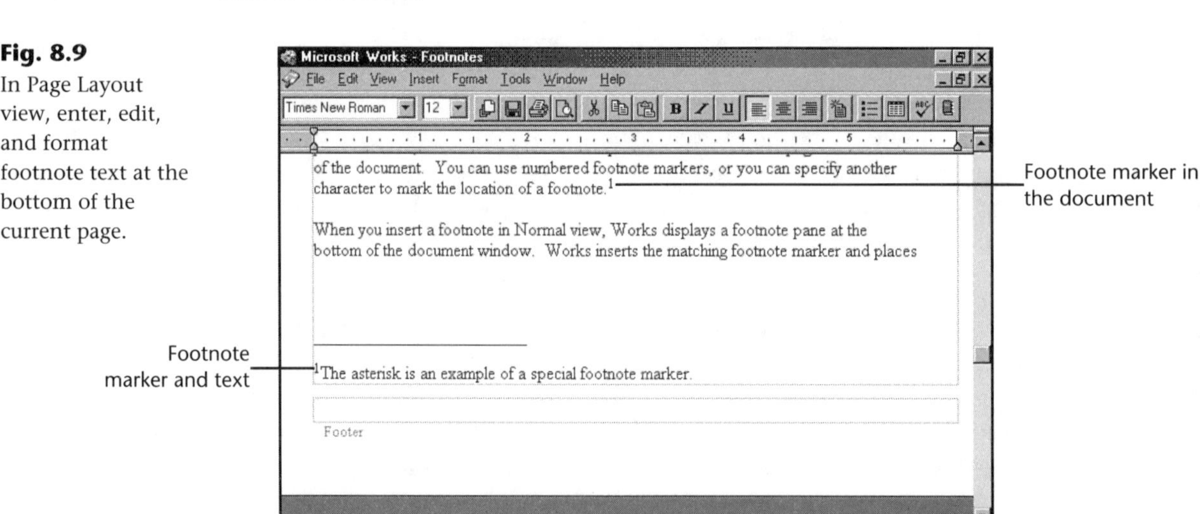

Fig. 8.9
In Page Layout view, enter, edit, and format footnote text at the bottom of the current page.

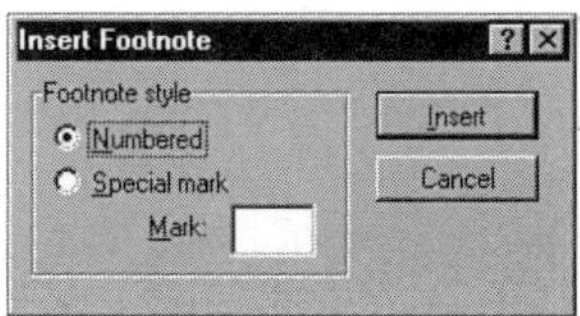

Fig. 8.10
Choose the type of footnote marker that works best with your document.

Follow these steps to create a footnote:

1. Move the insertion point to the location in the document where you want to insert the footnote marker.
2. Choose Insert, Footnote. The Footnote dialog box shown in figure 8.10 opens.
3. Select Numbered or Special Mark. If you select Special Mark, type the character in the Mark box.
4. Choose OK.

Works returns to your document. In Page Layout view, the insertion point moves to the bottom of the page. In Normal view, the insertion point moves into a footnote pane at the bottom of the document window. You now can enter, edit, and format the footnote text.

After you complete the footnote, you must move the insertion point back into the body of the document to continue working. In Page Layout view, just click in the document text area of the screen. In Normal view, choose View, Footnotes to return to the document text area.

Moving or Copying a Footnote

Sometimes you might want to move a footnote in a document from one location to another, or you might want to copy a footnote to another page. You can move and copy footnotes in Works just like you move or copy any other text in a document. The important thing to remember is to select and move or copy the footnote marker in the body of the text rather than the footnote text itself. After you select the marker and move or copy it, Works removes the footnote marker and footnote text from the original location. In the case of a move, Works places the footnote marker and the footnote text in the location where you paste it. If the order of footnotes changes, Works automatically renumbers footnotes appropriately.

Deleting a Footnote

You cannot delete a footnote by selecting and cutting the footnote text from the bottom of the page or the footnote pane. If you try to delete the footnote, Works beeps and won't let you delete the text. You must delete a footnote by selecting the footnote marker in the body of the document then deleting the marker. (Choose Edit, Cut; click the Cut toolbar button; or press Delete.) Works removes the text and marker from the list of footnotes and, in the case of numbered footnotes, automatically renumbers all remaining footnotes.

Printing Footnotes at the End of a Document

By default, Works assumes you want to print footnotes at the bottom of the appropriate page in a document. For some documents, however, you might decide to print all footnotes at the end of a document. To choose this option, choose File, Page Setup to display the Page Setup dialog box shown in figure 8.11. If the Other Options tab is not selected, click it now.

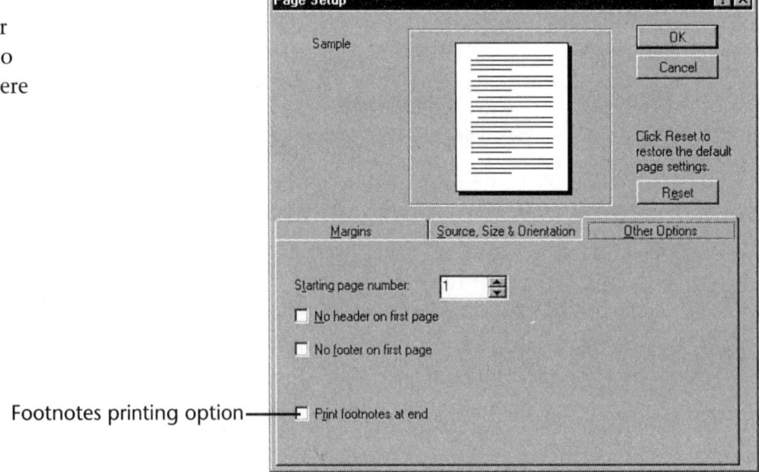

Fig. 8.11 Use the Other Options tab to designate where you want footnotes to print.

Follow these steps to print footnotes at the end of a document:

1. Before printing your document, choose File, Page Setup. Works displays the Page Setup dialog box.
2. Choose the Other Options tab to open the dialog box shown earlier in figure 8.10.
3. Select the Print Footnotes at End check box.

4. Choose OK.
5. Print your document as you usually do.

To restore footnotes to their respective pages, deselect the Print Footnotes at End check box before printing again.

Troubleshooting

How many footnotes can I print on one page?

Because footnotes print in the body text area of a document, Works doesn't have a maximum number of footnotes. However, to maintain some balance on a page, you probably don't want footnotes to occupy more than half the page.

I created numbered footnotes in my document. Can I change them to character footnotes?

Yes. Select the footnote marker in the body of the document and choose Insert, Footnote to insert a new footnote, changing the marker to a character. If you switch to character footnote markers, however, you should change all footnote markers throughout the document. If you mix numbered and character footnotes in a document, Works counts the character footnotes in sequence with the numbered ones.

Using Bookmarks

Just as you can place a paper bookmark in a book to mark the last page you read, you can insert an electronic *bookmark* in a document to mark a location where you want to return later. Using a bookmark lets you return instantly to the location you mark. Without using a bookmark, you can search for a location, but if you don't remember a particular word or phrase to search for, you might spend a long time looking for your place.

In Works, you assign a name to a bookmark using the Bookmark Name dialog box shown in figure 8.12. To find the bookmark in the document, you use the Go To dialog box, which lists the names of all bookmarks.

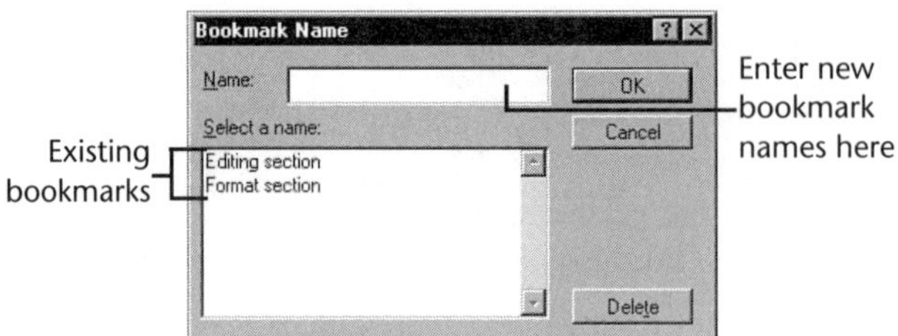

Fig. 8.12 Define bookmark names in the Bookmark Name dialog box.

Creating and Returning to a Bookmark

To create a bookmark, follow these steps:

1. Move the insertion point to the location in the document where you want to place a bookmark.
2. Choose Edit, Bookmark. Works displays the Bookmark Name dialog box.
3. In the Name text box, enter the name for the bookmark. Existing bookmarks are listed in the Select a Name box.
4. Choose OK.

Works invisibly marks the location in the document; you don't see bookmarks on the screen. To return to a bookmark, choose Edit, Go To or press F5. In the Go To dialog box that appears, double-click the bookmark name in the Select a Bookmark list, or highlight the bookmark name and choose OK. Works immediately moves the insertion point in the document to the location of the bookmark.

Removing a Bookmark

When you no longer want to use an existing bookmark, you can delete it by following these steps:

1. Choose Edit, Bookmark. The Bookmark Name dialog box opens.
2. In the Select a Name list, highlight the bookmark you want to delete.
3. Click the Delete button. Works deletes the bookmark.
4. Repeat steps 2 and 3 to delete additional bookmarks.
5. After you finish deleting bookmarks, choose OK. ❖

Chapter 9

Checking Your Document

by Debbie Walkowski

Nothing is worse than reading a printed document that contains spelling and typing mistakes, formatting errors, and words or phrases that are used over and over again. Works contains several tools to assist you in producing clean, error-free documents. The two most commonly used tools are the spelling checker and the thesaurus. Works also has tools that help you find and replace text in a document and count the number of words in a document. To help you spot formatting problems, Works lets you display the hidden characters it inserts in a document.

The best time to perform many of these checking tasks is after the content of the document is stable and before you print it; however, you can perform these tasks any time.

In this chapter, you learn how to do the following:

- View hidden characters
- Search for and replace characters, words, or phrases
- Check spelling and word usage
- Count words

Viewing Hidden Characters

As you create a document, Works inserts *invisible* characters whenever you press the Tab key, the Enter key, or when you insert other special characters (such as non-breaking hyphens and spaces, and end of line markers) that are not visible on-screen. For example, you learned in Chapter 6 that pressing the Tab key moves the insertion point in your document to the location of the tab. The area between the tab and the original location of the insertion point does not contain spaces; the entire area is a special character that Works records in your document as a Tab. Works inserts another invisible character, the paragraph marker, when you press Enter. When you press Shift+Enter, Works inserts an end-of-line marker in your document.

As you check the format and spacing of a document, you might find it useful to see these invisible characters. For example, suppose you created a multi-column list using tabs, and the data in the table is not lining up correctly. Viewing the hidden tabs can help you correct the alignment problem; you might have a tab or space in the wrong location. Or suppose you notice a short line in the middle of a paragraph. The line might contain an end-of-line marker rather than a space. Examples of these errors and other invisible characters are shown in figure 9.1.

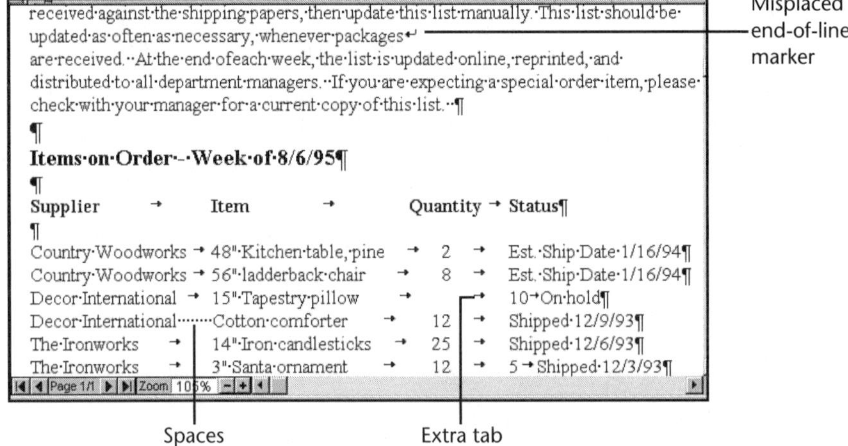

Fig. 9.1
Displaying hidden characters can help you correct errors in a document.

To display hidden characters in a document, choose View, All Characters. This command affects all open documents and any documents that you open or create after choosing the command. This command remains in effect until you change it. A check mark appears next to the All Characters command on the View menu when the option is selected. To remove hidden characters from the screen, choose View, All Characters again.

Another useful feature of a word processor is its capability to search for and replace characters in a document. Imagine typing a 50-page sales proposal on a typewriter—then discovering that you misspelled the client's company name throughout the document. Correcting every occurrence of the company name would be trouble enough, but *finding* every occurrence of the company name would take a great deal of time as well. With Works, you can find every occurrence easily, replace all occurrences, or replace only selected occurrences.

Tip
If you frequently need to display hidden characters in a document, you can add the Show All button to your toolbar. Refer to Chapter 2 for instructions on customizing the toolbar. The Show All tool is located under the View category in the Customize Works Toolbar dialog box.

The two commands that enable you to search for and replace text in a document are Edit, Find and Edit, Replace. Choosing Edit, Find lets you search for text without replacing it. Choosing Edit, Replace finds the text you specify and enables you to replace all occurrences or selected occurrences. Whether you are finding or replacing, you can specify a single character, word, phrase, or any string of characters, such as a part number like 120-NB98.

Both the Edit, Find and Edit, Replace commands enable you to specify whether you want Works to search for the whole word only or match the case (uppercase or lowercase characters) of the word. Depending on the text you are searching for, these options can help you zero in on your search text more quickly. For example, if you want to replace the word "in" with the word "on" throughout a document, Works finds every occurrence of the characters "in," even if they are contained within a word. So if your document contains the words "within," "searching," "again," and "instance," Works finds all these words. However, when you check the Find Whole Words Only box, Works finds only occurrences of the word "in." Use this option when the characters you are searching for are also contained within other words. If you are searching for a word like "tomorrow," you won't find this sequence of characters contained in another word, so you don't need to use the Find Whole Words Only option.

In some situations, you might want to specify that Works match the case of a word you're searching for. For example, if you are searching for the name "Young" in a document, you might want to check the Match Case box if the document is about children and also contains occurrences of the word "young." By checking the Match Case box, Works finds only the occurrences of the name "Young" because it is capitalized.

Finding Text

The Edit, Find command displays the Find dialog box shown in figure 9.2. Use Edit, Find to find any type of text in a document. For instance, suppose that in the sales proposal you are creating, you know you mentioned training costs, but you cannot find it anywhere in the text. Using Edit, Find, you can search for the word "training" and find the page that discusses this topic. You don't want to replace text; you simply want to find a specific topic in a document.

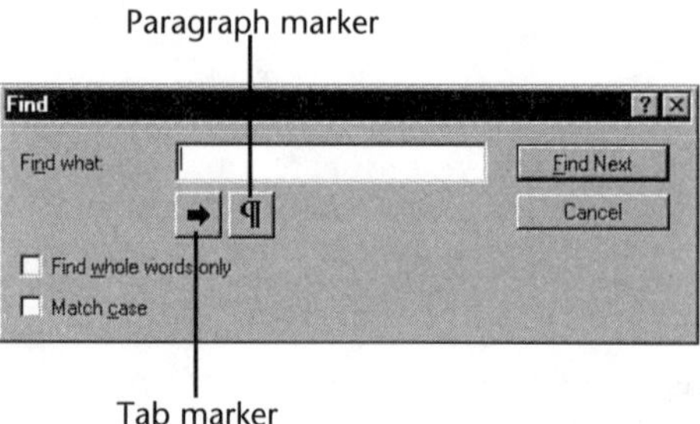

Fig. 9.2
Find any word, phrase, or character string using the Find dialog box.

Note

For information about the Tab and Paragraph Marker buttons in the Find dialog box, refer to the section "Using Wild Cards and Special Characters in a Search," later in this chapter.

When you find text in a document, Works locates the first occurrence of the text and highlights it, leaving the Find dialog box on the screen. To find additional occurrences, choose the Find Next button. When you find the last occurrence, Works displays a message saying it reached the end of the document.

Note

If you begin searching in mid-document, Works offers to continue searching from the beginning of the document when you reach the end.

To find text in a document, follow these steps:

1. Move the insertion point to the beginning of the document.
2. Choose Edit, Find. The Find dialog box shown in figure 9.2 opens.
3. In the Find What text box, enter the word, phrase, or character string to find.

4. To match the whole word or the case of the text, check the Find Whole Words Only check box or the Match Case check box.

5. Choose the Find Next button. Works finds the first occurrence of the text.

6. Repeat step 5 to find additional occurrences.

7. After you finish searching, close the Find dialog box by choosing the Cancel button.

Tip
Press Shift+F4 to search for the last text you entered in the Find dialog box. This keyboard shortcut is useful when you finish a search, close the Find dialog box, and then realize you want to continue searching.

You can add a Find button to your toolbar by customizing the toolbar. Refer to Chapter 2, "Getting Started with Works for Windows," for instructions on customizing the toolbar. The Find button is located in the Edit category of the Customize Works Toolbar dialog box.

Replacing Text

Choosing the Edit, Replace command displays the Replace dialog box shown in figure 9.3. In the dialog box, you specify the word or phrase you're looking for as well as the replacement text. You can choose to replace all occurrences of the text you're looking for (using the Replace All button), you can replace occurrences selectively, or you can skip one occurrence and go on to the next.

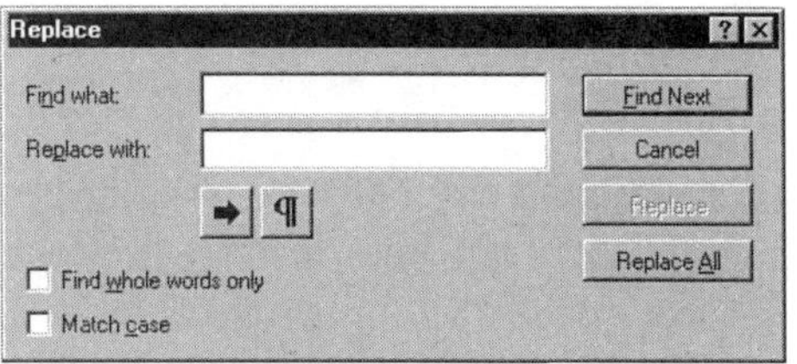

Fig. 9.3
Use the Replace dialog box to specify the text to find as well as the replacement text.

> **Note**
>
> For information about the Tab and Paragraph Marker buttons in the Replace dialog box, refer to the section "Using Wild Cards and Special Characters in a Search," later in this chapter.

To replace text in a document, follow these steps:

1. Move the insertion point to the beginning of the document.

2. Choose Edit, Replace. The Replace dialog box shown in figure 9.3 opens.

3. In the Find What text box, enter the word, phrase, or character string to find.

4. In the Replace With text box, enter the replacement text.

5. To match the whole word or case of the text Works searches for, check the appropriate check box.

6. Choose the Find Next button. Works finds the first occurrence of the text.

7. If you want to replace all occurrences of the text, choose the Replace All button. If you want to replace only the current occurrence, choose the Replace button. If you want to find the next occurrence without replacing the current one, choose the Find Next button.

8. Repeat step 7 until you finish searching for and replacing text. A message appears after Works has searched the entire document.

9. Close the Replace dialog box by choosing the Cancel/Close button.

Note

Unlike the Find command, the Replace command does not go back to the start of the document if you start Replace in mid-document. Also, the text that was last entered in the Find What box (whether in the Find or Replace dialog box) remains in the Find What box whenever you use the Find or Replace command again.

You can add a Replace button to your toolbar by customizing the toolbar. Refer to Chapter 2, "Getting Started with Works for Windows," for instructions on customizing the toolbar. The Find button is located in the Edit category of the Customize Works Toolbar dialog box.

Using Wild Cards and Special Characters in a Search

When you're uncertain about the spelling of a word you're searching for, you can use a wild card to represent any single character. For instance, if you enter **t?p**, Works finds *tap*, *tip*, and *top*. If you enter **t???p**, Works finds all five-letter words that begin with *t* and end with *p*. Wild cards can be very useful for finding names like Anders*o*n or Anders*e*n when you're not sure of the spelling.

In addition to searching for unknown characters with wild cards, searching for special and hidden characters in a document can be extremely useful. For instance, earlier in this chapter you learned how a misplaced tab or paragraph marker can throw off the alignment of a table or paragraph. If a document contains many of these errors, searching for these characters can save you a great deal of clean-up time.

The Find and Replace dialog boxes both contain Tab and Paragraph Marker buttons. These buttons allow you to search for these two hidden characters. When you click the Tab button, Works inserts ^T in the Find What box. Likewise, when you click the Paragraph Marker button, Works inserts ^P in the Find What box. These are codes that enable Works to search for these hidden characters. Because searching for these two characters is so common, Works provides buttons in the Find and Replace dialog boxes for both of these hidden characters.

In addition to tabs and paragraph markers, there are other special or hidden characters you might want to search for. These are listed in table 9.1, along with wild-card characters you can use to represent other characters. To search for one of these characters, type the code in the Find What box of the Find or Replace dialog boxes.

Table 9.1 Wild Cards and Special Character Codes

To find this character...	Type this code...
Any single character	?
Question mark	^?
End-of-line marker	^n
Page break	^d
White space (space between words)	^w
Optional hyphen	^-
Nonbreaking space	^s
Caret (^)	^^

Note

A non-breaking space is one that does not break if it occurs at the end of a line. For example, in the street address *2546 196th Avenue*, you might prefer to insert non-breaking spaces between the house and street numbers so the address is not split between two lines.

Troubleshooting

I know I typed the word ***reflection*** *in my document, but when I used the Find command to search for it, Works found nothing. Why?*

Works can miss a word for several reasons. If you select text before you choose the Find command, Works searches only the selection. Or you might have misspelled the word, in which case Works would not find it. You might want to search for only a portion of the word such as *reflec*, or use wild cards to search for the word.

Checking Your Spelling

The spell checker in Works checks all the words in your document against a dictionary file that contains hundreds of thousands of words. When the spell checker finds a word not in the dictionary file, Works highlights the word in your document and displays the Spelling dialog box shown in figure 9.4.

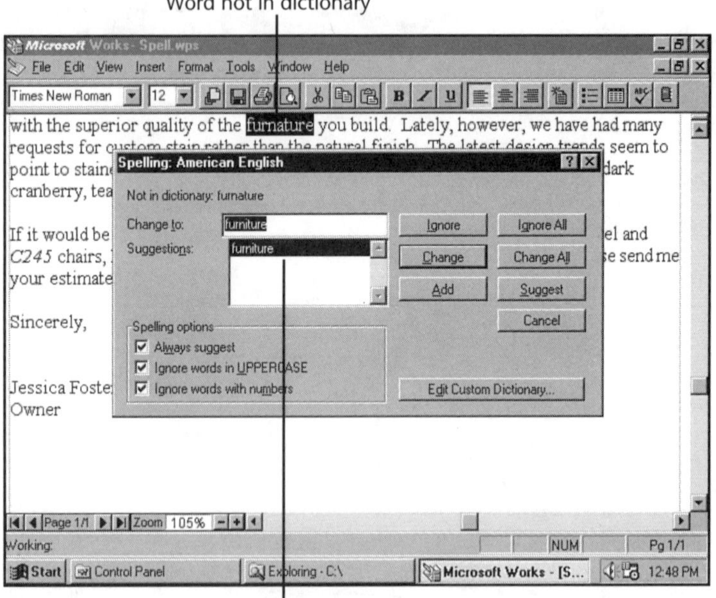

Fig. 9.4
The Spelling dialog box displays the unrecognized word and suggested replacement words.

When Works finds an unrecognized word, the word might have one of the following problems:

- Misspelling
- An unknown word (not in the dictionary)
- Incorrect hyphenation
- Irregular capitalization (such as wOrks)
- A repeated word

The word in question is highlighted in the document, and the word also appears at the top of the Spelling dialog box next to Not in Dictionary. If the Always Suggest check box is marked, the Suggestions list shows words you might use as replacement words. Of these words, the spell checker picks the most likely replacement word and places it in the Change To text box. You can choose a different word if you like. If a word is completely unrecognized, the Suggestions and Change To areas remain blank. The command buttons on the right side of the dialog box offer eight options to correct the error found in the document (see table 9.2 for descriptions of these buttons).

Other check boxes in the Spelling dialog box include Ignore Words in UPPERCASE and Ignore Words with Numbers. Both of these options come in handy when a document contains part or model numbers, addresses, or telephone numbers.

Table 9.2 Spell Checker Command Buttons

Button	Description
Ignore	If the highlighted word is spelled correctly, use this button to leave the word unchanged and continue checking the document.
Ignore All	If the highlighted word is spelled correctly and it occurs frequently in the document, use this button to leave the highlighted word and all subsequent occurrences of the word unchanged.
Change	Choose this button if you want to replace the highlighted word with the word shown in the Change To box.
Change All	Choose this button if you want to replace the highlighted word and all other occurrences of the same word throughout the document with the word shown in the Change To box.

(continues)

Table 9.2 Continued

Button	Description
Add	If you want to add a word to the dictionary, choose this button. For instance, if the name of your company is Smithson Tool Works, the dictionary will always question "Smithson" as a misspelled word unless you add it to the dictionary file.
Suggest	If the Always Suggest check box is not selected, choose this button to see a list of suggested replacement words.
Cancel	Close the spell checker without checking the remainder of the document.
Help	Display the help topic that describes the spell checker dialog box.

To use the spell checker, follow these steps:

1. Move the insertion point to the beginning of the document.

2. Choose Tools, Spelling; press F7; or click the Spelling Checker button on the toolbar. The Spelling dialog box shown in figure 9.4 opens. The first unrecognized word is highlighted in the document and shown at the top of the dialog box.

3. If the word is spelled correctly, choose the Ignore, Ignore All, or Add button.

   If the word is spelled incorrectly, select a replacement word from the Suggestions list or use the word shown in the Change To box. (If the Always Suggest check box is not checked, you can display a list of suggested words by choosing the Suggest button.) If no words are suggested, type the correct spelling in the Change To box, then choose the Change or Change All button.

4. After you choose a command button, Works highlights the next unrecognized word in the document. Repeat step 3 until Works displays a message saying it has reached the end of the document.

5. Choose OK to dismiss the message and return to your document.

If you start the spell checker anywhere other than at the beginning of a document, Works checks spelling from the location of the insertion point to the end of the document. Works then displays a message signaling the end of the document and asks if you want to continue checking from the beginning of the document. Choose OK to continue or Cancel to close the spell checker.

You also can use the spell checker to check only a selection of text in a document. even just a single word. Select the text you want to check, then choose Tools, Spelling, or click the Spelling Checker toolbar button.

Finding the Right Word with the Thesaurus

A *thesaurus* is a list of words with their synonyms and other related words. A thesaurus helps you find just the right word to use in a particular context; it also helps you improve the style and readability of a document by eliminating overuse of the same word. To use the thesaurus, place the insertion point in or next to a word in a document for which you want to find a synonym, then choose Tools, Thesaurus. Works displays the Thesaurus dialog box shown in figure 9.5.

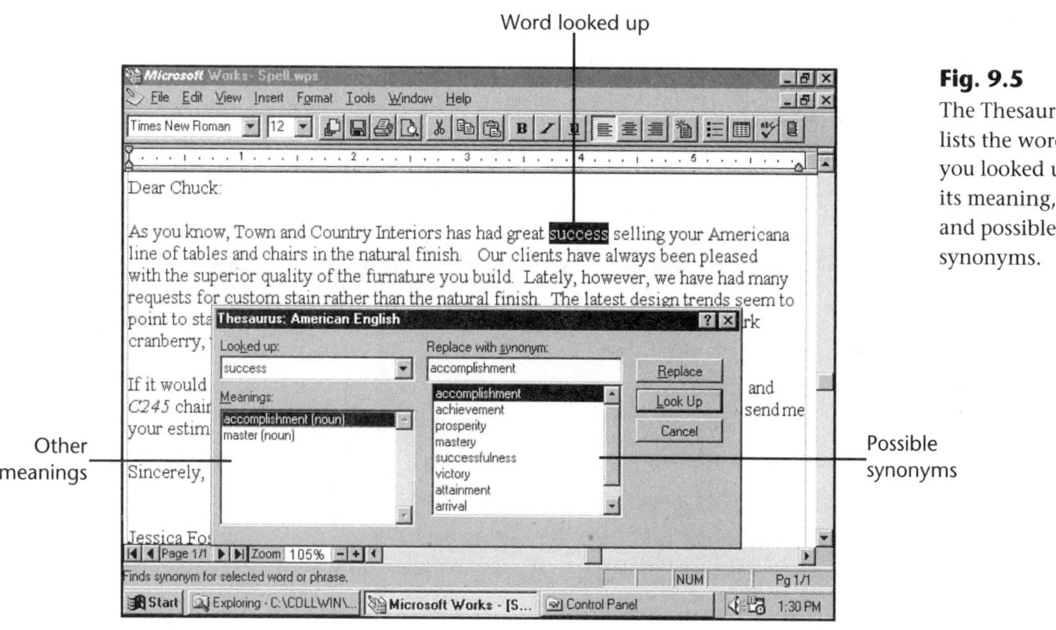

Fig. 9.5
The Thesaurus lists the word you looked up, its meaning, and possible synonyms.

The Meanings list box shows possible meanings for the selected word. Because some words often have several meanings, you begin by selecting the appropriate meaning then selecting a synonym from the Replace With Synonym box. The list of synonyms changes depending on the meaning you choose. If you want to change the word you're looking up, highlight a word in either list (meaning, or synonyms) and click Look Up. Works generates a new list of meanings and synonyms.

Tip
If you use the Thesaurus frequently, consider adding the Thesaurus button to your toolbar (see Chapter 2 for instructions on adding buttons to the toolbar). The Thesaurus button is in the Tools category of the Customize Works Toolbar dialog box.

To use the thesaurus, follow these steps:

1. In the document, move the insertion point in or near the word you want to look up.

2. Choose Tools, Thesaurus or press Shift+F7. The Thesaurus dialog box opens (refer to fig. 9.5).

3. In the Meanings box, highlight the word that most closely resembles the meaning of the selected word in its context.

4. In the Replace with Synonym list, highlight the word you want to use as the replacement.

5. If none are appropriate, you can type a word that you choose in the Replace with Synonym box.

   If you want to look up a different word, highlight the word, click the Look Up button, and repeat Step 4.

6. Choose the Replace button to change the selected word in the document to the highlighted synonym. Works returns to your document and changes the highlighted word.

Tip
If you count words frequently in a document, consider adding the Word Count button to your toolbar (see Chapter 2). The Word Count button is in the Tools category of the Customize Works Toolbar dialog box.

Counting Words in a Document

In some situations, you might want to count the number of words in a document. For instance, if you are writing a 500-word essay or submitting a 1,000-word article for publication, Works can tell you how close you are to your limit. To count the number of words in an entire document, choose Tools, Word Count. Works displays a message indicating the total number of words in the document. The number includes footnotes, header text, and footer text. You can also count the number of words in a selection of text by first selecting the text before you choose the Word Count command. Note that Works counts the exact number of words and does not estimate word length.❖

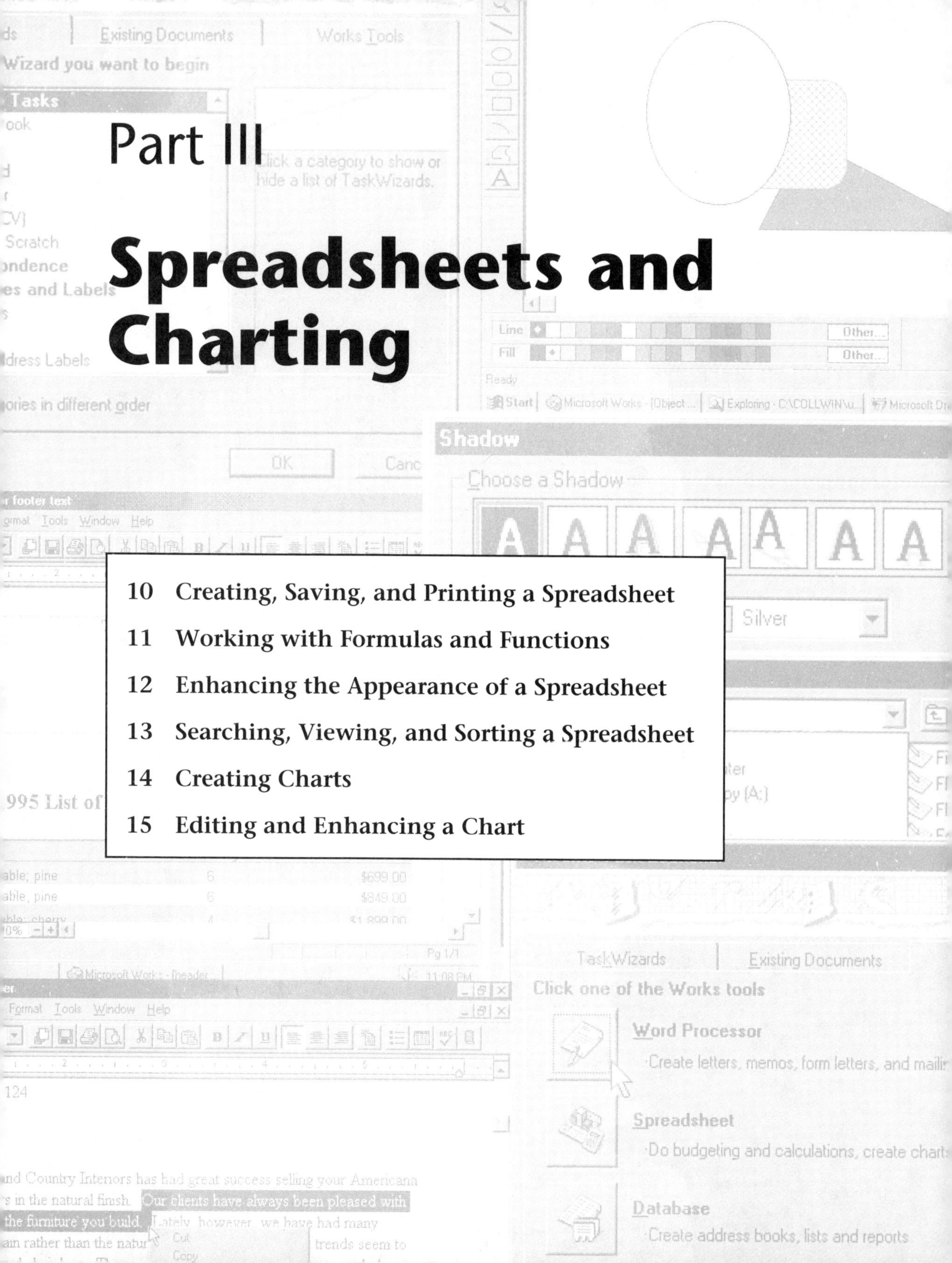

Part III

Spreadsheets and Charting

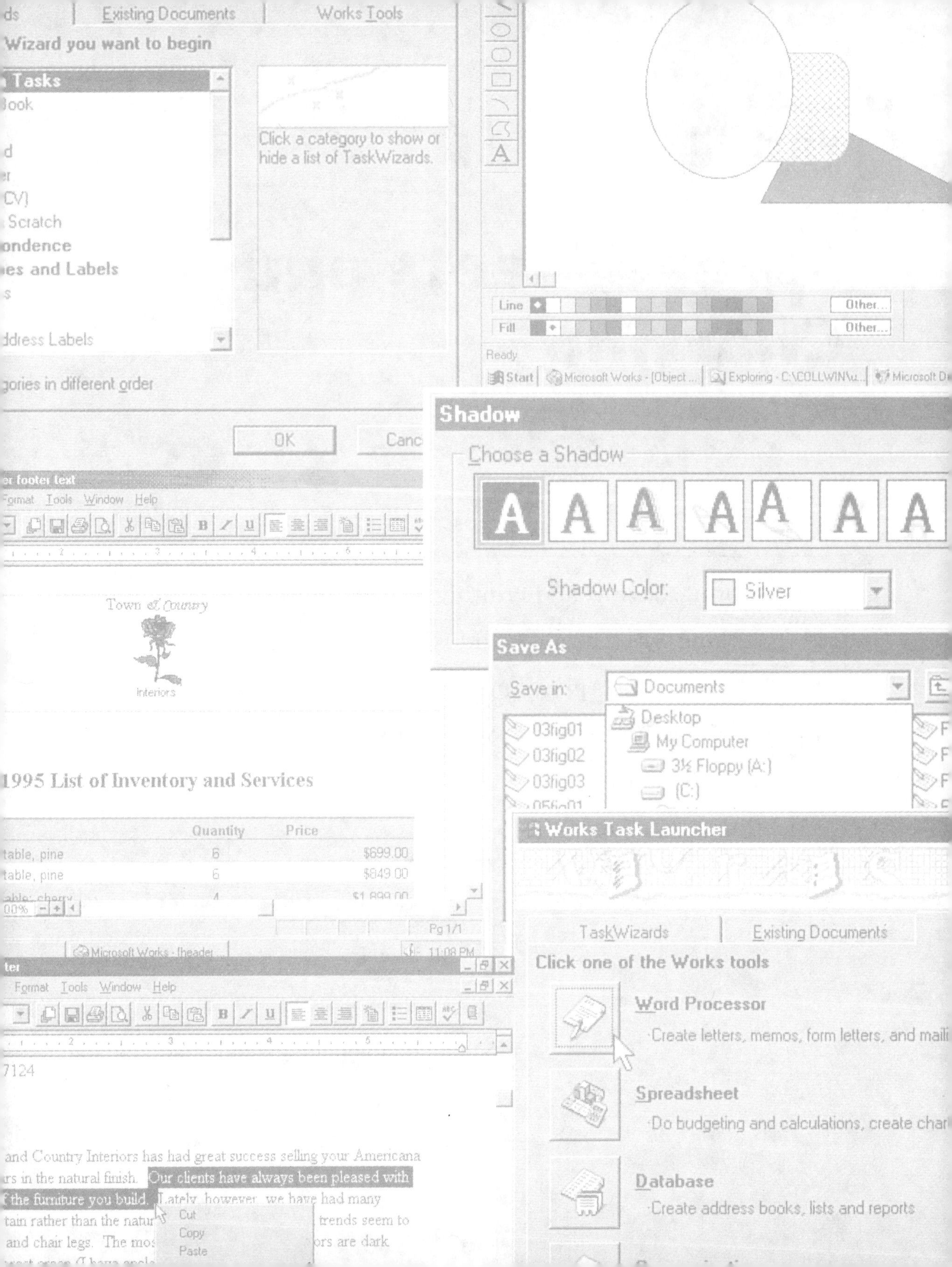

Existing Documents
Works Tools
Wizard you want to begin
Tasks
Click a category to show or hide a list of TaskWizards.
Scratch
ondence
es and Labels
ddress Labels
gories in different order
OK
Canc
Line
Other...
Fill
Other...
Ready
Start
Microsoft Works - [Object ...
Exploring - C:\COLLWIN\u...
Shadow
Choose a Shadow
Shadow Color:
Silver
er footer text
Format Tools Window Help
Town & Country
Interiors
Save As
Save in:
Documents
Desktop
My Computer
3½ Floppy (A:)
(C:)
03fig01
03fig02
03fig03
1995 List of Inventory and Services
Quantity
Price
table, pine
6
$699.00
table, pine
6
$849.00
Works Task Launcher
Pg 1/1
11:08 PM
Microsoft Works - [header
TaskWizards
Existing Documents
Click one of the Works tools
Word Processor
Create letters, memos, form letters, and maili
Spreadsheet
Do budgeting and calculations, create char
Database
Create address books, lists and reports
ter
Format Tools Window Help
7124
and Country Interiors has had great success selling your Americana
rs in the natural finish. Our clients have always been pleased with
the furniture you build. Lately, however, we have had many
tain rather than the natur
trends seem to
and chair legs. The mos
ors are dark
Cut
Copy
Paste

Chapter 10

Creating, Saving, and Printing a Spreadsheet

by Judy Petersen

A spreadsheet is an electronic version of an account worksheet that performs numeric calculations automatically. You can use a spreadsheet to create standard financial reports such as income statements, balance sheets, and cash flow statements, or to perform scientific and statistical calculations. If you want a refresher on the basic capabilities of the spreadsheet, refer to Chapter 1, "Introducing Works for Windows." The topics covered in this chapter help you create, save, and print spreadsheets.

In this chapter, you learn about the following:

- What's behind spreadsheet menus and the toolbar
- How to move around in a spreadsheet
- How to enter and edit text and numbers in spreadsheet cells
- How to create simple formulas
- Creating a spreadsheet template
- Customizing spreadsheets
- How to save and print a spreadsheet

Examining the Spreadsheet Window

As discussed in Chapter 2, "Getting Started with Works for Windows," each of the tools in Works displays a unique document window inside the Works application window. When you maximize the document window, the two windows blend together and share the title bar. The buttons at either end of the title bar in the document window are relocated to either end of the menu bar. A sample spreadsheet is shown in figure 10.1. You can open a new spreadsheet window by choosing the Spreadsheet icon from the Works Tools page box in the Works Task Launcher dialog box.

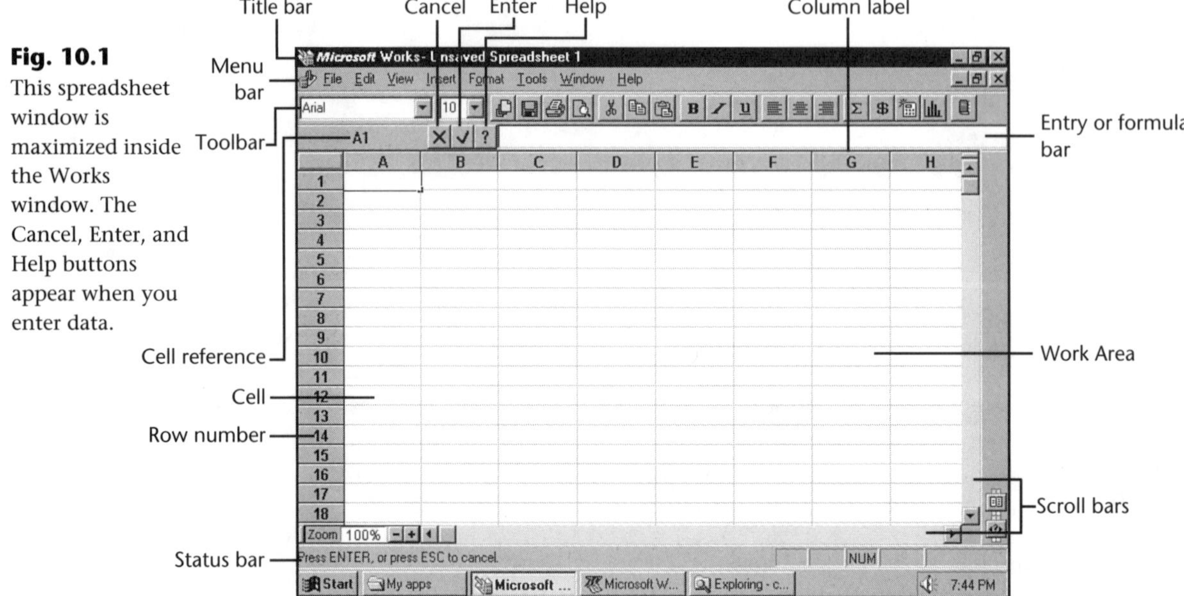

Fig. 10.1
This spreadsheet window is maximized inside the Works window. The Cancel, Enter, and Help buttons appear when you enter data.

The working area of the spreadsheet window is divided into rows and columns. The spreadsheet is bordered on the bottom with a horizontal scroll bar and right with a vertical scroll bar, on the left with row numbers, and on the top with column labels. Above the working area are, in order, the title bar, menu bar, and toolbar. The following are the various elements of the spreadsheet window:

- *Work area, row numbers, and column labels.* The work area in a spreadsheet file is a grid of rows and columns. On average, the spreadsheet window displays seven or eight columns and up to 20 rows at a time. (The exact number depends on your monitor and the resolution you are using, the width of columns, the height of rows, and the current Zoom setting.) Although the portion of the spreadsheet that you see might seem rather small, the entire spreadsheet is actually quite large: 256 columns by 16,384 rows. The columns are labeled A through Z, then are labeled AA, AB, AC...AZ; BA, BB, BC...BZ; CA, CB, CC...CZ; and so on until the last column, IV. Row numbers run consecutively from 1 to 16,384.

- *Cell.* A cell is the point at which columns and rows intersect; it is the "box" into which you enter data. A cell reference is its *address*, the column letter and row name. For example, C19 is the address for the cell at the intersection of column C and row 19. The cell you are currently using is called the *active* cell and is easily identified by its bold border. When you select a *cell range*—two or more cells—Works highlights the range.

- *Mouse pointer.* When pointing anywhere in the work area, the mouse pointer in the spreadsheet tool is a large, bold cross that's easy to find anywhere on-screen. When you point to a menu command or a tool on the toolbar, the mouse pointer changes to an arrow. When you point to the formula bar (described later in this list), the mouse pointer changes to an I-beam so you can enter text or numbers.

- *Title bar.* The title bar in the spreadsheet displays the name `Microsoft Works` followed by the name of the current file. In figure 10.1, the file name is `Unsaved Spreadsheet 1`. New spreadsheet files are named `Unsaved Spreadsheet 1`, `Unsaved Spreadsheet 2`, and so on, until you rename and save the files. The file extension Works adds to spreadsheet files is WKS.

- *Menu bar.* The menu bar displays the names of the drop-down menus that hold spreadsheet commands. For instance, the File menu contains commands for working with files, like Print and Save. Menus are described in more detail in the section "Looking at the Spreadsheet Menus."

- *Toolbar.* The buttons on the toolbar represent spreadsheet commands that are used frequently. Using a mouse, you can click on a toolbar button rather than selecting a command from a menu. The toolbar buttons are described in detail in the section "Looking at the Spreadsheet Toolbar."

- *Scroll bars.* Use the horizontal and vertical scroll bars to display different parts of the worksheet. Click the arrows on the vertical scroll bar to display one more row at a time; click the arrows on the horizontal scroll bar to display one more column at a time. Click the background of a scroll bar to scroll the display one screen at a time. Drag the scroll button to scroll more than a single screen.

Tip
To cancel an entry, you can also press the Esc key; to accept the entry so that it is entered in a cell, press the Enter key.

- *Cell reference, Cancel button, Enter button, Help button, and Formula bar.* In the cell reference area, Works displays the address of the active cell or cell range. In the formula bar, Works displays the entry in the active cell. If the cell contains a formula, the result of the formula is shown in the cell itself, and the formula is shown in the formula bar. You use the formula bar to enter and edit information in cells. When entering or editing data in a cell, Cancel and Enter buttons appear between the cell reference area and formula bar. Use the Cancel button to cancel the entry shown in the formula bar; use the Enter button to accept the entry.

- *Status bar.* The status bar provides brief instructions (such as `Press ALT to choose commands, or F2 to edit.`) or describes the current menu command that is highlighted. The boxes at the right end of the status bar are indicators that display when Num Lock is toggled on, and when Extend Selection, Edit, or Point modes are active.

Looking at the Spreadsheet Menus

The menus in the spreadsheet are identical to many of those used in other Works tools. The commands on each menu, however, perform unique functions in the spreadsheet program. Table 10.1 describes the spreadsheet menus.

Table 10.1 The Spreadsheet Menus

Menu Name	Command Functions
File	Here are all the commands necessary for creating, opening, saving, printing, or sending files. The four most recently opened files are always listed at the bottom, providing a quick way to open the files you are currently using. (Refer to Chapter 3, "Working with Documents, TaskWizards, and Templates," for information on working with files.)
Edit	This menu contains commands for cutting, copying, and pasting data and for undoing the most recent change to a spreadsheet. You also use this menu to select rows and columns, to find and replace data in a spreadsheet, and to fill a range of cells with data.
View	These commands change how a spreadsheet displays; for example, with gridlines or showing formulas in place of data, with or without the toolbar, ruler, or other screen features. Use this menu to create headers and footers for a spreadsheet, and to switch between Chart and Spreadsheet views. Use Zoom to reduce or enlarge the amount of spreadsheet that is displayed.

Table 10.1 The Spreadsheet Menus

Menu Name	Command Functions
Insert	Use this menu to insert page breaks, rows and columns, functions, and range names into a spreadsheet.
Format	On the Format menu, you find commands for font and style, number formats, borders, alignment, patterns, row height, and column width. From the Format menu, the AutoFormat command lets you apply specially designed formats to spreadsheets. Use the Format menu as well to set the print area so you can print only a selected portion of a larger spreadsheet.
Tools	This menu contains special tools for working with a spreadsheet. Use these commands to check the spelling in a spreadsheet, sort a spreadsheet, recalculate a spreadsheet, and work with charts. You also use this menu to customize the toolbar and other Works options and use the Address Book. A special command on this menu, Dial This Number, automatically dials a phone number for you if the number is in a cell of the spreadsheet.
Window	Use these commands to arrange all open documents on-screen and to make another open document window active.
Help	The Help menu lists a variety of help topics, including an overview of the spreadsheet tool.

Looking at the Spreadsheet Toolbar

Just as each Works tool has unique menus, each has unique buttons on its toolbar. Each button on the toolbar represents a particular command. Just click the button to activate the command. Table 10.2 describes the function of each of the default spreadsheet tools.

Table 10.2 The Buttons on the Spreadsheet Toolbar

Button	Function
Times New Roman	Displays a drop-down list of all available fonts.
12	Displays a drop-down list of all available point sizes for the current font.
	Displays the Works Task Launcher dialog box.

(continues)

Table 10.2 Continued

Button	Function
	Saves the file using the current file name and settings. If a spreadsheet has not yet been saved, the Save As dialog box appears.
	Prints the current spreadsheet using the current print settings.
	Previews your spreadsheet before printing.
	Removes (cuts) the selected text to the Clipboard.
	Copies the selected text to the Clipboard.
	Inserts (pastes) the contents of the Clipboard into the spreadsheet at the location of the insertion point.
B	Applies bold to the contents of the selected cell.
I	Applies italics to the contents of the selected cell.
U	Applies underline to the contents of the selected cell.
	Left-aligns selected cell entry.
	Centers selected cell entry.
	Right-aligns selected cell entry.
Σ	Automatically sums the nearest row of numbers or column of numbers.
$	Automatically formats the data in selected cells using the dollar symbol ($) and two decimal places.
	Displays the Easy Calc Wizard in which you create a formula.
	Click this button to create a new chart using selected data in the current spreadsheet.
	Displays the Address Book TaskWizard.

Troubleshooting

I don't see a toolbar in my spreadsheet window.

In Works, you can choose to display the toolbar or turn it off. If the toolbar isn't visible in the spreadsheet window, choose View, Toolbar.

The buttons listed in table 10.2 appear on the standard toolbar. If the toolbar has been customized, some of the standard buttons might not appear. To reset the toolbar to the standard tools, choose Tools, Customize Toolbar. When the Customize Works Toolbar dialog box appears, choose Reset and then choose OK. Works resets the toolbar to its standard tools.

Moving Around the Spreadsheet

To move around in the spreadsheet work area, you can use the mouse, the arrow keys, the scroll bars, or the keyboard shortcuts listed in table 10.3. In the spreadsheet, you don't move an insertion point, you move the *highlight*, the bold border that outlines a single cell.

To use the mouse to select a cell, simply click the cell to activate it. If the cell you want isn't visible on-screen, use the scroll bars or another method to display the cell, and then click the cell.

Table 10.3 Keyboard Shortcuts for Moving Around in a Spreadsheet

Press...	To move...
Arrow keys	Up, down, right, or left one cell at a time
Tab	One cell to the right
Shift+Tab	One cell to the left
Home	To column A in the current row
Ctrl+Home	To cell A1
End	To column IV in the current row
Ctrl+End	To column IV in the last row in the spreadsheet that contains data
Page Up	Up one window

(continues)

Table 10.3 Continued

Press...	To move...
Ctrl+Page Up	Left one window
Page Down	Down one window
Ctrl+Page Down	Right one window

Selecting Cells

Before you can enter or edit data in a worksheet, you must select a cell or cell range. To select a single cell, you simply move the highlight to the cell or click it with the mouse.

A range of cells, or *cell range*, is any rectangular area of cells. It could be three columns by five rows, or 350 columns by 1,000 rows. A cell range also can be an entire column or an entire row. You select a range of cells when you want to take an action that will affect all cells in the range. For example, you might want all cells in a range to display dollar signs, or you might want to move the contents of a range of cells to a new location in the spreadsheet.

The address for a cell range is the address of the cells in opposite corners of the rectangular area, separated by a colon. The cell range A1:C3 means "cells A1 through C3" and includes cells A1, A2, A3, B1, B2, B3, C1, C2, and C3. If you begin selecting the range at cell A1, it remains outlined while the other cells in the range become highlighted. An example of a cell range is shown in figure 10.2.

There are several ways to select a cell range, as follows:

- *Drag the mouse over a range of cells.* To select a cell range with the mouse, point to the first cell in the range, press and hold the left mouse button, and drag the mouse pointer to the cell in the opposite corner of the rectangle—the last cell you want to include in the range. When you release the mouse button, the entire range is highlighted and the first cell you selected in the range is outlined.

- *Click a column label or row number.* You can easily select an entire column or row by clicking the column label at the top of the column or row number at the left end of the row. To select multiple, consecutive columns or rows, drag the mouse pointer across all column labels or row numbers you want to include in the selection. Release the mouse button when the selection is complete.

- *Use menu commands to select a row, column, or all cells in the spreadsheet.* If you prefer to use menu commands, you can select a single row, single column, or all cells in the spreadsheet by choosing Edit, Select Row, Select Column, or Select All. Works selects the row or column in which the highlight is located when you choose a command. If the highlight is in cell C13 when you choose Select Row, Works selects row 13; if you choose Select Column, Works selects column C. When you choose Select All, Works selects every cell in the spreadsheet. Note that cell C13 displays in a contrasting color to indicate the highlight location.

- *Use the shift key and an arrow key or other shortcut keys.* When you press and hold the Shift key, then move the highlight to a new cell using the keyboard or mouse, Works highlights all cells in the range from the point of the original active cell to the final cell you select. Release the Shift key when the selection is complete.

Tip
Using the Shift key and the mouse together makes it easy to select ranges. Click a cell in one corner of the desired range, then Shift+Click in the cell in the opposite corner.

- *Use the F8 key to extend a selection.* Press Ctrl+F8 to select the entire row where the highlight is located. Press Shift+F8 to select the entire column where the highlight is located. When you press Ctrl+Shift+F8, Works highlights the entire spreadsheet. You can also use F8 in combination with any of the arrow keys to extend the selection from the point of the original active cell to the final cell you select.

Microsoft Works - 1995 Net Income Statement.wks

A6:D8 "Retail Store

	A	B	C	D	E	F
1	Town and Country Interiors					
2	1995 Income Statement					
3						
4		Quarter 1	Quarter 2	Quarter 3	Quarter 4	Total
5	INCOME					
6	Retail Store	$13,987	$15,090	$19,567		$48,644
7	Prevate Clients	$33,546	$32,198	$27,908		$93,652
8	Mail Order	$5,432	$5,112	$6,298		$16,842
9	Total Income	$52,965	$52,400	$53,773	$0	$159,138
10						
11	EXPENSES					
12	Rent	$5,000	$5,000	$5,000		$15,000
13	Labor	$7,310	$6,220	$7,900		$21,430
14	Insurance	$1,500	$1,500	$1,500		$4,500
15	Cost of Goods	$21,186	$20,960	$21,509		$63,655
16	Total Expenses	$34,996	$33,680	$35,909	$0	$104,585
17						
18					NET INCOME	$54,553

Press ALT to choose commands, or F2 to edit.

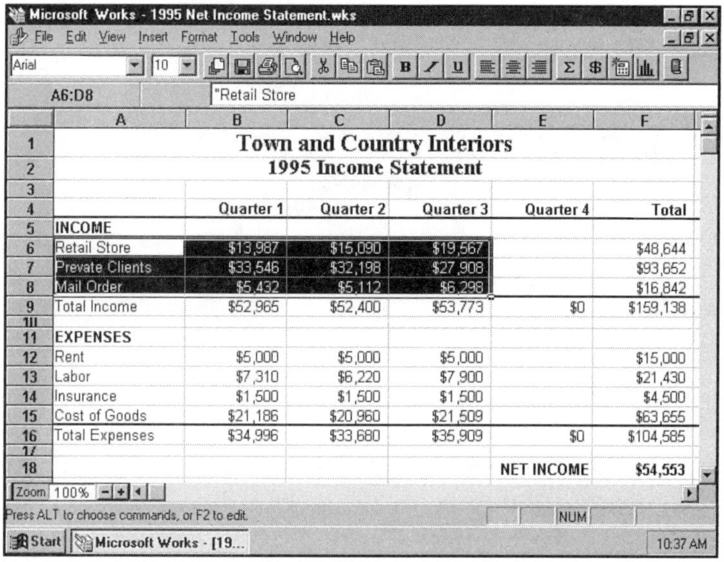

Fig. 10.2
The cell range in this figure is A6:D8—the highlighted cells.

Using Go To

When you want to move to a specific cell in a spreadsheet, often the fastest way to do so is by choosing Edit, Go To. The Go To dialog box appears as shown in figure 10.3. The keyboard shortcut for the Go To command is Ctrl+G and the function key command is F5, either of which also displays the Go To dialog box.

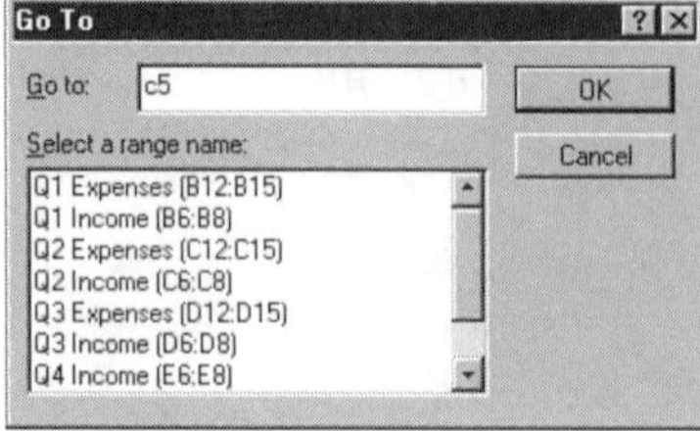

Fig. 10.3
Use the Go To dialog box to quickly move to a specific location in a spreadsheet.

In the Go To text box, type the address of the cell you want to highlight, then choose OK. You can type the address of a single cell or a cell range. Works closes the Go To dialog box and immediately highlights the cell or range you specify.

Notice that the Go To dialog box also contains a Select a Range Name list box. In Chapter 12, "Enhancing the Appearance of a Spreadsheet," you learn how to name a range of cells so you can quickly select a named cell range using the Go To command.

Entering Information in Cells

In the cells of a spreadsheet, you can enter three types of data: text, numbers, and formulas. The raw data of a spreadsheet is made up of numbers; you use text to label, explain, and describe the numbers. Formulas perform calculations and display the results.

To enter any type of data in a cell, select the cell and then type the entry. As you begin typing, an insertion point appears in the formula bar. The characters you type appear in the formula bar as well as in the cell itself. To confirm the entry, press Enter or click the Enter button on the reference bar. You can also confirm an entry and move to another cell in a single step by pressing an arrow key, the Tab key, or by clicking in a new cell, instead of pressing Enter.

You also can make entries in cells by *filling* a range of cells, or *copying* information from one cell to a range of cells. In the following sections, you learn how to enter text and numbers, how to fill a cell range, and how to copy into a range of cells. Formulas are described later in this chapter.

Entering Text

Any entry that begins with or includes a letter of the alphabet is considered a text entry. You use text in a spreadsheet to label data, add titles to a spreadsheet, and to provide instructions or explanations. *Text* entries are automatically left-aligned in cells using the *general* alignment format. If the text you type is too long to fit in a cell, it is displayed over the cell to the right if that cell is empty. If that cell contains data, the cell that contains text displays only the amount of text that fits in the cell. You can still see the complete text entry in the formula bar when the cell is highlighted. To display the entire text entry in the cell, however, you must increase the column width. See the section "Adjusting Column Width" later in this chapter.

Because you might want some numeric entries (such as phone numbers and street addresses) to be interpreted as text, you precede these entries with a quotation mark ("). Without this symbol, Works interprets the entry as a number. For example, you might want to precede a zip code with a quotation mark so that Works interprets it as text. When an entry contains both alphabetic characters and numbers (such as a part number like 12-BNC-32), Works interprets it as text. When an entry includes punctuation marks (, . : ; !) or other keyboard symbols (~ ` # $ % ^ & * ( ) _ [ ] { }) along with alphabetic characters, they also are interpreted as text.

Exceptions to these are entries that begin with the following symbols and are followed by text: the addition symbol (+), the subtraction symbol (–), the equal symbol (=), and the @ symbol. These symbols are used in formulas and functions and are therefore not valid characters to use when followed by text that is not recognized by Works as a cell address or function name. (Works displays a formula error message if you type + – = or @ followed by text.) To type a text entry such as **@ .49/each**, precede the entry with a quotation mark so that Works interprets the entry as text. Figure 10.4 illustrates valid text entries in a spreadsheet.

The only other exception is the way Works treats month names. When you enter the name of a month into a cell, it is interpreted as a number. Even the three-letter abbreviation for a month name, entered in all lowercase characters, is interpreted as a number. Works converts what you type and enters the full name for the month, with the first letter in uppercase, and right-aligns the entry.

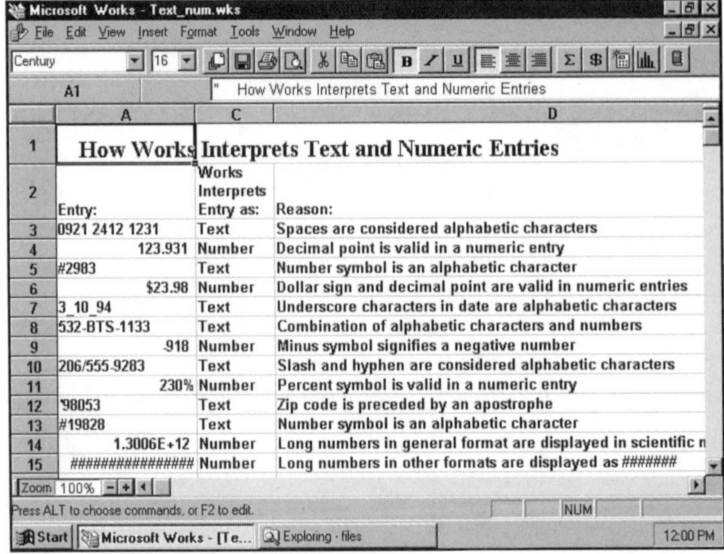

	A	C	D
1	How Works Interprets Text and Numeric Entries		
2	Entry:	Works Interprets Entry as:	Reason:
3	0921 2412 1231	Text	Spaces are considered alphabetic characters
4	123.931	Number	Decimal point is valid in a numeric entry
5	#2983	Text	Number symbol is an alphabetic character
6	$23.98	Number	Dollar sign and decimal point are valid in numeric entries
7	3_10_94	Text	Underscore characters in date are alphabetic characters
8	532-BTS-1133	Text	Combination of alphabetic characters and numbers
9	-918	Number	Minus symbol signifies a negative number
10	206/555-9283	Text	Slash and hyphen are considered alphabetic characters
11	230%	Number	Percent symbol is valid in a numeric entry
12	'98053	Text	Zip code is preceded by an apostrophe
13	#19828	Text	Number symbol is an alphabetic character
14	1.3006E+12	Number	Long numbers in general format are displayed in scientific n
15	################	Number	Long numbers in other formats are displayed as #######

Fig. 10.4
These are examples of how Works formats text and numeric entries.

Entering Numbers

> **Tip**
> To quickly insert the current date in m/d/yy format, press Ctrl+;. To insert the time in h:mm AM/PM format, press Ctrl+:.

In Works, a *number* is defined as an entry where Works can perform calculations. These include numbers, dates, and times. Works automatically right-aligns numbers in a cell using the *general* alignment format. If the entry you type is too long to fit in a cell, Works either displays ##### in the cell or displays the number using scientific notation (refer to fig. 10.4).

Any entry that contains numbers and no alphabetic characters is interpreted as a number. When a number includes commas used as thousands separators (1,320), a percent sign (6.25%), a period used as a decimal point (20.50), or a dollar symbol to signify currency ($2.00), it is also automatically interpreted as a number. Works only enters the number, including the decimal point, in the cell. Dollar signs and commas are dropped. When a number ends with a percent sign, Works converts the entry to its decimal equivalent and enters the result in the cell. To enter a negative number in a cell, precede the number with a minus sign. To type a positive number, just type the number. If you type a plus (+) sign before the number, Works assumes you want a positive number and drops the + from the entry. If you precede a number with an equal symbol (=) or an @ symbol, Works also drops the symbol and enters a positive number. Refer to figure 10.4 for examples of valid numeric entries.

Filling Cells

Because numbers are sometimes repeated or occur in a series in spreadsheets, Works offers a way for you to quickly fill cells. Filling cells speeds up your work by eliminating the need to make separate entries in individual cells. You can fill cells with identical entries to the right of the current cell or below the current cell. If your income statement spreadsheet shows the same amount each month in the rent category, for example, you can enter the amount for the first month, and then fill the cells for the remaining months with the same dollar amount.

You choose the Fill Right and Fill Down commands from the Edit menu. Both commands are very easy to use and do not display a dialog box. Figure 10.5 shows an example of cells that are filled to the right.

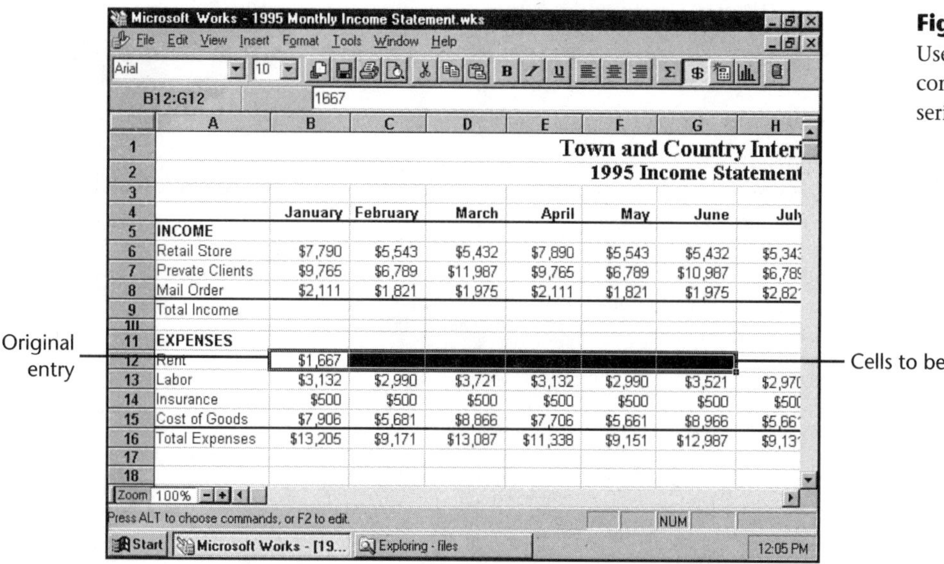

Fig. 10.5
Use the Fill Right command to fill a series of cells.

To fill a range of cells to the right of the current cell or below the current cell, follow these steps:

1. In the first cell in the range you want to fill, type the entry you want to use to fill the other cells.

2. Highlight the original cell and all cells to the right or below it that you want to fill (refer to fig. 10.5).

3. Choose Edit, Fill Right or Edit, Fill Down. Works fills the range of cells you select with the entry in the first cell.

Tip
To quickly fill a range of cells that spans multiple columns or rows, select the range of cells, type the entry, and press Ctrl+Enter.

You also can fill cells with a *series* of data. A series is a set of numbers or dates that is automatically increased or decreased by a specific amount.

Tip

To enter a series of dates, you must enter the first date in one of the following formats: 11/22/94; 11/22; 11/94; 22 November, 94; November, 1994; 22 November; November; or 1994.

For example, if your spreadsheet includes item numbers in column B that start at 1 and go through 50, you can fill in the numbers in column B by choosing Edit, Fill Series, which displays the Fill Series dialog box (see fig. 10.6). In this example, numbers are incremented by 1. (If you wanted to start with item 50 and count down to item 1, you would increment the numbers by –1.) But, suppose your spreadsheet requires column headings that show the date for every Monday over a 3-month period. Rather than checking a calendar and typing each date individually, you can type the first date in the first column, then fill the remaining columns with a series that is incremented by 7—Works automatically increments each date by seven days. For office use, you can create series that increment by workdays.

Note

If you fill cells frequently, consider adding the Fill Right, Fill Down, and Fill Series buttons to your spreadsheet toolbar. When you click the Fill Right and Fill Down buttons, Works automatically fills the selected range of cells. When you click the Fill Series button, Works displays the Fill Series dialog box.

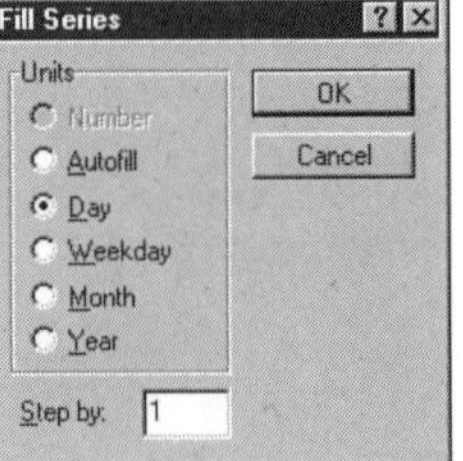

Fig. 10.6
Enter a negative number in the Step By box to specify a decreasing series.

► See "Applying a Number Format to Selected Cells," p. 240

In the Fill Series dialog box, you choose the units (Number, Day, Weekday, Month, or Year) you want to increment, and the step by which you want to increment. In the first cell of the series, you can enter any number or date in a valid date format (see Chapter 12, "Enhancing the Appearance of a Spreadsheet," for information about date formats). If you enter **7/26/95** in the first cell, select Weekday and increment by 1, for example. Works fills the cell range you select with `7/27/95`, `7/28/95`, `7/31/95`, `8/1/95`, and so on.

To fill a range of cells with a series, follow these steps:

1. In the first cell in the range you want to fill with a series, type the first date, day, or number in the series.

2. Select the first cell and all cells to the right or below the first cell that you want to fill with a series.
3. Choose Edit, Fill Series. The Fill Series dialog box shown in figure 10.6 appears.
4. In the Units area, choose an option.
5. In the Step By box, enter a positive number to increase the series or a negative number to decrease the series.
6. Choose OK. Works fills the selected range of cells with the series you specify.

Using the Autofill Feature

Autofill is available in Works for Windows 4.0 to fill cells with a series of numbers without the bother of providing information in a dialog box. Autofill works by dragging the first or first two entries using the small box in the lower-right corner of the selected cell or cells. When you move the mouse pointer over the box in the lower-right corner of the selected cell, the pointer changes to crosshairs and the word FILL appears (see fig. 10.7). Now drag the corner until the light gray outline includes all the cells in the column or the row you want to include. Release the mouse button and the outlined cells fill with data.

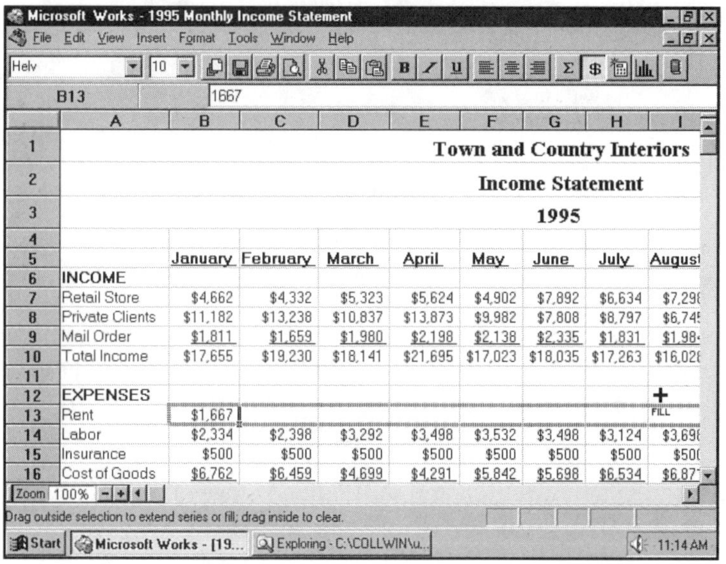

Fig. 10.7 Drag using the FILL handle to copy an entry or fill with a series of numbers.

When the selected cell contains the name of a month, a day, a date, or a quarter number in the format Q*n*, Autofill automatically increments the value as it fills the number of cells you indicate. Also, when text is followed by a number, Autofill repeats the text and the number is incremented. This creates an interesting result with quarterly numbering. Using Q immediately followed by a number causes the number to increase to 4, then start numbering again at 1, while the text "Quarter" is not recognized by Autofill the same way.

Filling with Autofill causes the format of the text, such as italics, uppercase, or currency, to be copied. Using Autofill, you can enter the first value shown in these examples to fill with the information that follows.

November	MONDAY	Q1	10/4/95	*Text* 1	*Text* 1.1
December	TUESDAY	Q2	10/5/95	*Text* 2	*Text* 1.2
January	WEDNESDAY	Q3	10/6/95	*Text* 3	*Text* 1.3
February	THURSDAY	Q4	10/7/95	*Text* 4	*Text* 1.4
March	FRIDAY	Q1	10/8/95	*Text* 5	*Text* 1.5

Note

It's possible to Autofill several rows or several columns at the same time. You can, for example, enter the first value in each of the above columns in adjacent cells, select the six cells and the cells you want to fill, then follow the steps for using the Autofill feature beginning with step 2.

To fill a range of cells using the Autofill feature, follow these steps:

1. In the first cell of the range you want to fill, type the entry that you want to use to fill the other cells.

2. Move the pointer over the small box in the lower-right corner of the first cell until the pointer changes to crosshairs and the word `FILL` appears. Drag the Autofill outline to enclose all the cells to the right or below the first cell that you want to fill.

3. Release the mouse button and the outlined range of cells fills with values.

Note

Autofill can be used as a quick substitute for Fill Down and Fill Left. If the information in the first cell is not recognized by Autofill as a value that can increment, all the cells in the range are filled with the same entry.

Autofill can also be used to fill with information that increments at an interval greater than one unit, just as with the Fill Series command. You provide the amount to increase or decrease the series of values by entering the first value in the first cell, and in the next cell enter a value that differs from the first below or to the right.

To fill a range of cells with a series of values, follow these steps:

1. In the first cell in the range you want to fill, enter the value to begin the series.
2. In the cell below or to the right of the first cell, enter the next value in the series.
3. Select both cells. Use the box in the lower-right corner of the highlight to drag the Autofill outline to enclose all cells you want to fill.
4. Release the mouse button to fill the range with values.

You can use Autofill to fill up and to the right. The result, however, is that the values decrease instead of increase so that the smaller value is at the top or left cell of the range. To fill with values that decrease, provide a start value and then in the next cell enter a smaller value, then use the Autofill feature.

Moving and Copying Cell Entries

While the Fill Down and Fill Right commands allow you to fill an adjacent range of cells with identical data, the Copy command lets you copy identical data to a separate range of cells. Copying saves you the trouble of retyping identical entries in a spreadsheet and eliminates the possibility of errors while retyping. You can copy data from one or several cells in the *source* range to a *destination* range. Remember that when you copy data, the data remains unchanged in its source range and is duplicated in the destination range.

In Works, you can copy cell entries using menu commands (Copy and Paste on the Edit menu), the Copy and Paste toolbar buttons, or you can use the drag-and-drop method with the mouse. In either case, you select the source and destination ranges displayed in figure 10.8.

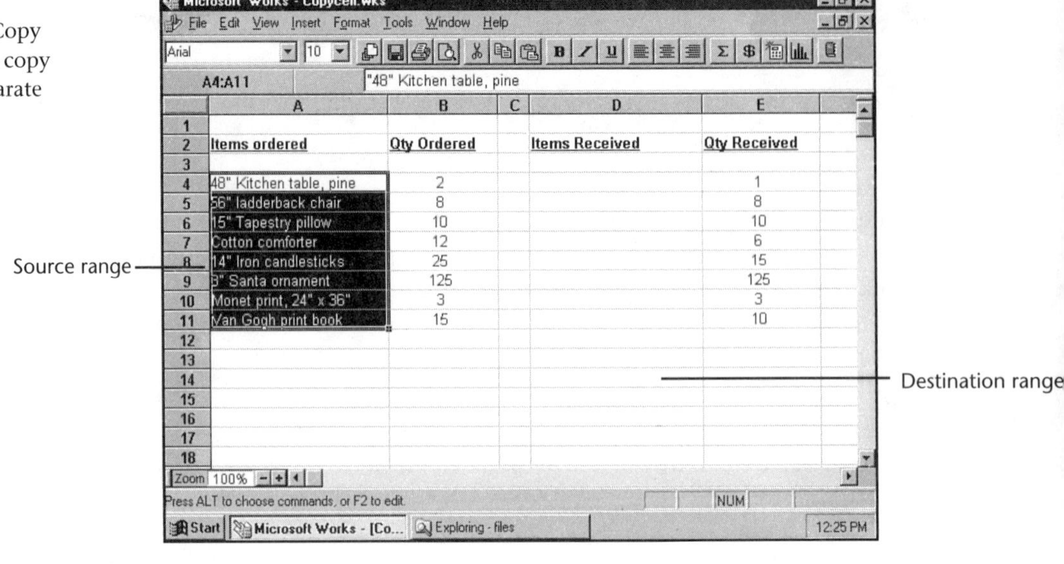

Fig. 10.8
Choose the Copy command to copy data to a separate range.

To use menu commands to copy cell data, follow these steps:

1. Select the range of cells you want to copy. Works highlights the selection.

2. Choose Edit, Copy, or click the Copy button on the toolbar.

3. Move the highlight to the first cell in the destination range.

4. Choose Edit, Paste, or click the Paste button on the toolbar. The selection is copied to the destination range of cells.

After you enter all the information in a spreadsheet, a better way to arrange the data is sometimes more obvious. The Cut command lets you remove data so it can be relocated to a separate range of cells, saving you the trouble of clearing data from one area and retyping the same information in another area. Just as when you copy data, you can move data from one or several cells in the source range to a destination range. You can move cell entries using menu commands (Cut and Paste on the Edit menu), the Cut and Paste toolbar buttons, or you can use the drag-and-drop method with the mouse.

Table 10.4 shows the keyboard shortcuts for the Cut, Copy, and Paste commands. To use a keyboard shortcut, select the cell or range of cells you want to move or copy and then press the appropriate key sequence. Place the highlight at the destination location and press the Paste key sequence.

Table 10.4 Keyboard Shortcuts for Moving and Copying Entries

Key Sequence	Character Style
Ctrl+X	Cut
Ctrl+C	Copy
Ctrl+V	Paste

To use menu commands to move cell data, follow these steps:

1. Select the cell or range of cells containing data you want to move.
2. Choose Edit, Cut, or click the Cut button on the toolbar.

3. Move the highlight to the first cell in the destination range.
4. Choose Edit, Paste, or click the Paste button on the toolbar. The selection is moved to the destination range of cells.

To use drag-and-drop to move data, first select the cells containing the source data, then point to the border surrounding the cells until the mouse pointer changes to an arrow labeled `DRAG`. Press and hold the left mouse button on the border of the selected cells and the pointer is now labeled `MOVE`. Drag the selection to its new location. As you drag, the data in the cells isn't shown, only a border outlining the shape of the selected range (see fig. 10.9). Position the selection in the correct destination range, then release the mouse button. The selection is moved to the destination range. To copy the contents of the selection, follow the same procedure except when `DRAG` appears, press and hold the Ctrl key when you click the border of the selected cells so the mouse pointer is labeled `COPY`. Drag the selection to the location where you want the data copied.

Caution

Any data that exists in the destination range is overwritten by the data you copy. This is true whether you use the Copy and Paste menu commands or the drag-and-drop method.

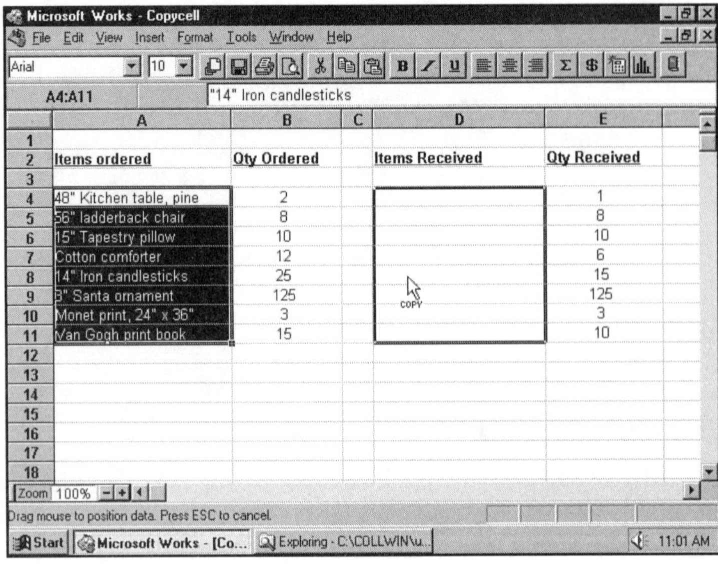

Fig. 10.9 The selected cells are being dragged to the destination range to be copied.

◄ See "Undoing Changes," p. 95

Pasting data in a new location can bring unexpected results. You might choose the wrong cell and overwrite something important. Moving data can cause calculations to produce inaccurate results. Check your spreadsheet carefully for errors immediately after you use the Paste command. If you find a problem, simply choose Edit, Undo Paste or press Ctrl+Z to undo the paste operation and try again.

Troubleshooting

How can I get Works to treat my account number 9843 3498 0021 as a number rather than as text?

The spaces cause Works to interpret the entry as text. The only way to get Works to format this entry as a number is by removing the spaces.

When I choose the Fill Right command (or Fill Down), nothing happens in my spreadsheet. What's wrong?

► See "Applying a Number Format to Selected Cells," p. 240

You might have forgotten to select cells, or you might have selected the wrong cells. Before choosing the Fill Right or Fill Down commands, you must select the cells you want to fill, including the cell that contains the data you want to use.

I entered 10-93 as the date in a cell. When I fill adjacent cells using Autofill or the Fill Series command, the series is not correct for the date I entered. What's wrong?

To fill a series of cells with a date, the date you enter in the first cell must be typed in a valid date format. 10-93 is not a valid date format, but 10/93 is. See Chapter 12, "Enhancing the Appearance of a Spreadsheet," for more information about formatting dates.

Adjusting Column Width

By default, Works sets the width of all columns in a new spreadsheet to 10. Depending on the font and point size you use, and the data you enter in your spreadsheet, 10 spaces might not be an appropriate width, and a cell might not actually display 10 characters because most fonts are proportionally spaced. When the contents of cells do not display completely in the column, you can increase or decrease the width of all columns in a spreadsheet, or you might want to vary the width of columns on an individual basis.

Tip
To quickly adjust the column width for the widest entry in the entire column, double-click the column label.

Note

You learned earlier in this chapter that Works displays ###### or scientific notation when a number is too wide to fit in a cell. And you learned that long text entries are not displayed entirely if there is data in the cell immediately to the right.

Works provides several methods for adjusting the width of spreadsheet columns. You can adjust the width of a column by dragging the column label border, or you can choose Format, Column Width, which displays the Column Width dialog box shown in figure 10.10.

Fig 10.10
The Column Width dialog box offers the default width of 10 and buttons to restore the standard width or let Works find the best fit.

In the dialog box, you can specify an exact column width or you can have Works determine the best width by choosing the Best Fit option. If you select a single cell in the column, the Best Fit option sizes the column to fit the entry in the selected cell. If you select the entire column, the Best Fit option sets the column width to accommodate the widest entry in the column.

To adjust column width using the Column Width dialog box, follow these steps:

1. In the spreadsheet, select any cell in the column you want to adjust. To adjust a column to the widest entry in the column, select the entire column. To adjust multiple columns at once, select multiple columns.

2. Choose Format, Column Width command. The Column Width dialog box shown in figure 10.10 appears.

3. In the Column Width text box, enter a number.

   Or

   Select the Best Fit check box to have Works determine an accurate column width.

4. Choose OK. Works automatically adjusts the column width.

Note

When you change column widths with the mouse, you cannot achieve the same uniformity or precision that is available by specifying an exact point size. The eye of the average viewer will notice irregular column widths. Try setting all columns to a uniform width first. Then use the mouse to change the one or two columns that are significantly different.

When you want to adjust the width of a single column, or several columns individually, using the mouse to drag the column label border is the easiest method. Use the mouse pointer to point to the border to the right of the column letter. If you want to adjust column B, for example, point to the border between the labels for columns B and C. The mouse pointer changes to a left/right arrow labeled ADJUST (see fig. 10.11). When you see this new pointer, click and drag the column border right or left to adjust the column width. Release the mouse button when the column is the size you want.

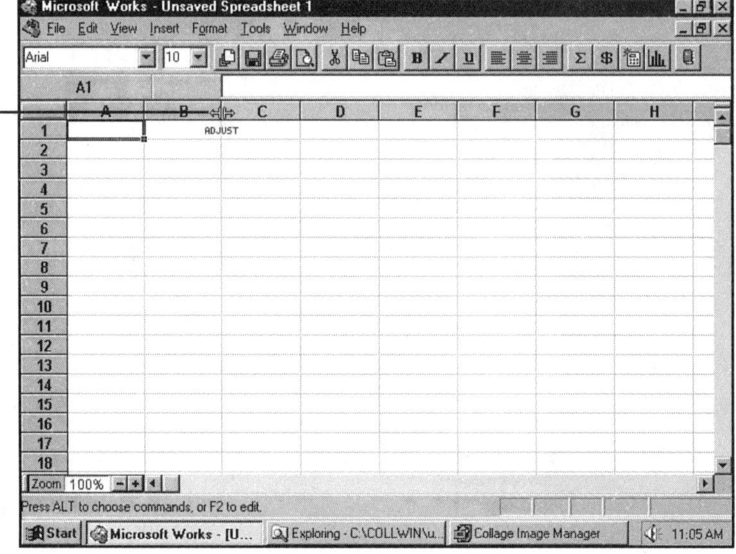

Fig. 10.11 It's easy to adjust column width by dragging the column border.

Troubleshooting

I used the Best Fit option to size my column, then typed a longer entry in a cell in the same column. Why didn't Works automatically readjust the column width since I chose the Best Fit option?

Works does not automatically readjust the column width if you change data in a column after sizing the column. To adjust the column for the new entry you type, you must select the Best Fit option again in the Column Width dialog box, or double-click the column label.

Because my column wasn't wide enough to display a large number, Works displayed the number exponentially. I widened the column so Works could display the actual number, but it still displays the exponential number. How can I change this?

If the number contains 11 digits or less, Works displays the actual number if the column is wide enough. If the number contains 12 digits or more, it is always displayed exponentially, unless you apply the Fixed format to the cell using Format, Number.

► See "Applying a Number Format to Selected Cells," p. 240

Editing Cell Entries

As in any file you create—whether it's a word processor document or a database file—you will inevitably want to change, or edit, data in a spreadsheet. Editing includes changing, moving, and deleting entries in cells, and inserting, moving, and deleting rows and columns. The following sections discuss each of these topics.

Changing Cell Entries

You can change an entry in a cell as easily as you entered it by simply selecting the cell, and then entering new data. The new entry you type automatically overwrites the original entry. This is the quickest method to use when you want to change an entire entry. But sometimes, particularly when a cell contains a long entry, you might want to make a simple change within an entry itself. For example, if the title of your spreadsheet is "1994 Income Statement for Town and Country Interiors" and you want to change the date to 1995, there is no reason to retype the entire entry, just change 1994 to 1995.

Tip
When you delete or clear the contents of a cell, any formatting you have already applied, such as the font, number format, and alignment, is unaffected.

To edit an entry in a cell, select the cell, then press F2 or double-click in the cell. The insertion point is visible at the right end of the entry in the cell. You can also click in the formula bar rather than pressing F2 and the insertion point appears wherever you click. Use the right and left arrow keys to position the insertion point, then delete and retype the characters you want to change. If you want to delete a block of text in an entry, select the characters to delete in the formula bar and then press Delete. To confirm the change, press Enter or click the Enter button on the reference bar. (You can also click anywhere in the formula bar where the cell contents are displayed.)

Clearing Cells

An alternative to editing or retyping an entry in a cell is to delete or *clear* the cell contents. Clearing the cell deletes the data in the cell but retains the cell in the spreadsheet. (You can't delete the cell itself from a spreadsheet.) You can clear a single cell at a time or a selected range of cells at once. To quickly clear a cell or cell range, select the cells and press Delete on the keyboard, or click the Cut button on the toolbar. To clear a single cell or a range of cells using menu commands, use the following steps:

1. Select the cell or cell range you want to clear.
2. Choose Edit, Clear. The data in the selected cells is removed.

Inserting Columns and Rows

Another common change you make in a spreadsheet is to insert columns or rows. You might decide to add data to the original spreadsheet, or perhaps you forgot to include some important data when you created the spreadsheet. You also can insert blank columns and rows to improve the appearance and layout of a spreadsheet. When you insert a column, the existing columns are moved to the right; when you insert a row, Works moves the existing rows of data down. Works automatically adjusts any formulas in the moved columns and rows.

Figure 10.12 shows a spreadsheet that includes four rows of expenses. Suppose you want to add a row between the Labor and Insurance rows. Works inserts a row *above* the current row, so you would select the Insurance row, and then insert a new row. Or, suppose you want to insert a column between columns A and B. Works inserts a column *before* the current column, so you would select column B, and insert a column.

To insert a row in a worksheet, follow these steps.

1. Select the entire row where you want to insert a new row.

2. Choose Insert, Insert Row. Works inserts a new row immediately above the row you selected in step 1.

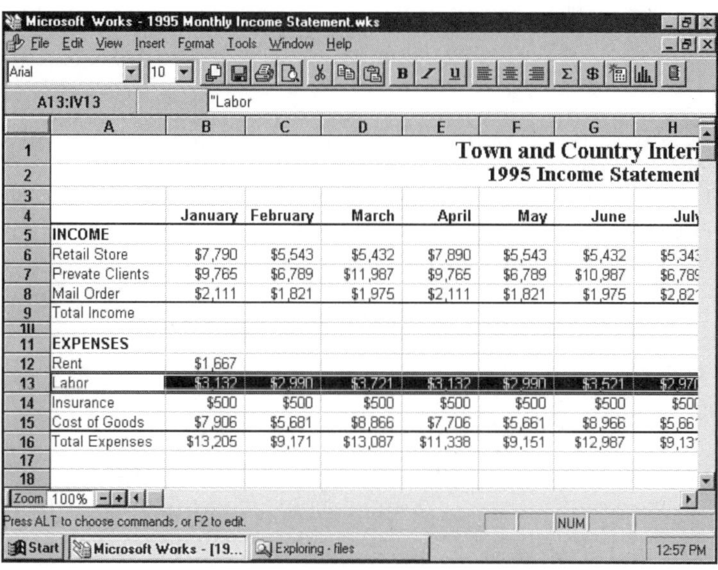

Fig. 10.12
Select any cell in the highlighted row to insert a row above it.

To insert a new column in a worksheet, follow these steps:

1. Select the entire column where you want to insert a new column.

2. Choose Insert, Insert Column. Works inserts a new column immediately before the column you selected in step 1.

Note

If you insert rows and columns frequently in a spreadsheet, you can add buttons to your toolbar for inserting and deleting rows and columns. These buttons appear in the Insert category of the Customize Works Toolbar dialog box.

◀ See "Customizing the Toolbars," p. 33

If you select a single cell rather than an entire row or column in the above steps, Works doesn't know what you want to insert and enables both Row and Column commands on the Insert menu.

Deleting Columns and Rows

Deleting columns and rows in a spreadsheet is just as common a task as inserting them. The principle for deleting columns or rows is similar to inserting. If you select an entire row first, Works assumes you want to insert or delete the entire row. But if you select only a single cell, Works enables both the Row or Column commands. When you delete a row or column, existing rows are moved up and existing columns are moved to the left to fill the void.

To delete a single row or multiple rows, follow these steps:

1. In the spreadsheet, click the number of the row to delete. To select more than one row, click and drag the mouse pointer across all row numbers you want to include in the selection.

2. Choose Insert, Delete Row. Works automatically deletes all selected rows.

To delete a single column or multiple columns, follow these steps:

1. In the spreadsheet, click the label of the column to delete. To select more than one column, click and drag the mouse pointer across all column labels you want to include in the selection.

2. Choose Insert, Delete Column. Works automatically deletes all selected columns.

Moving Columns and Rows

In addition to inserting and deleting, you will find that moving columns and rows is a common editing task. Moving is simply rearranging to make a worksheet more readable or perhaps to place items in a logical order. You can move a single column or row, and you can move several at once.

When you move columns or rows in a spreadsheet, Works makes room for the moved data by *inserting* it. If you select column A to move it to column D, for example, Works doesn't overwrite column D, it inserts a new column before column D and places the data from column A in the new column. Therefore, the original column A becomes column C. The original columns B and C are shifted to the left to fill in the void left by column A. Column B becomes column A, and column C becomes column B. This process is illustrated in figures 10.13 and 10.14.

Works operates the same way when moving rows: the row you move is inserted above the row you select, and the remaining rows are shifted to fill in the void. While it might seem confusing that Works actually inserts columns or rows that you move, inserting is much safer than overwriting data in the new location, which might cause you to lose data.

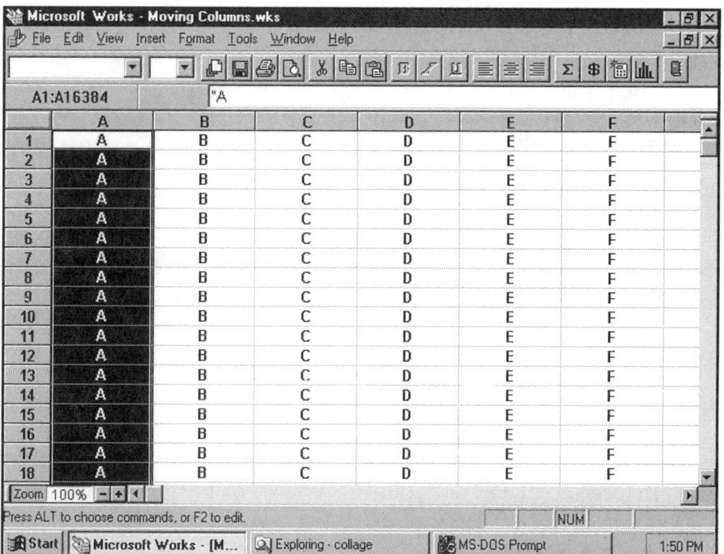

Fig. 10.13
Column A is selected to be moved to before column D.

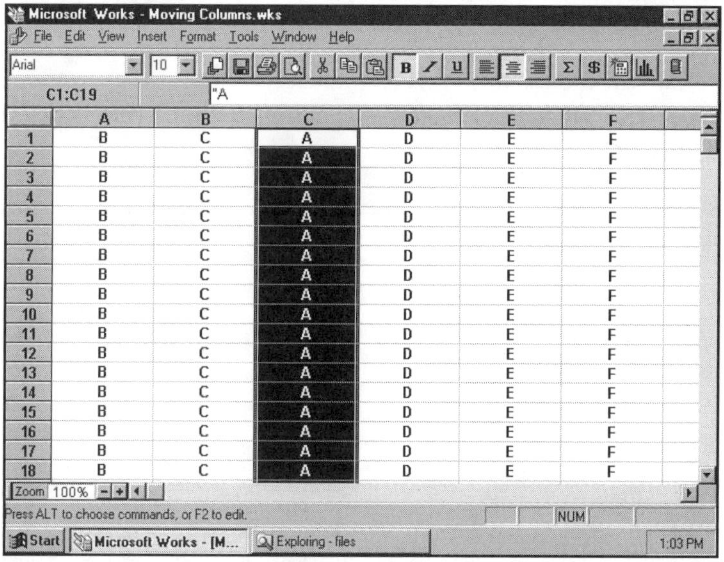

Fig. 10.14
Columns B and C shifted to the left after column A was moved.

In Works, you can move a row or column using the Edit, Cut and Edit, Paste commands or using the drag-and-drop method. To move a row or column using menu commands, follow these steps:

1. In the spreadsheet, select the row or column you want to move. To move multiple rows or columns at once, select all rows or columns you want to move. Works highlights the cells.

2. Choose Edit, Cut; click the Cut button on the toolbar; or press Ctrl+X. Works removes the selected row or column from the spreadsheet and shifts the remaining rows or columns to fill the void.

3. Select the cell at the beginning of the row or column where you want to move the data.

4. Choose Edit, Paste; click the Paste button on the toolbar; or press Ctrl+V. Works inserts the moved row above the row you select; Works inserts a moved column before the column you select.

Using the drag-and-drop method is a quicker, more visual method of moving rows or columns. Follow these steps:

1. Select the row or column you want to move. To move multiple rows or columns, select all rows or columns you want to move at once. Works highlights the cells.

2. Point to the selection border until the mouse pointer changes to an arrow labeled DRAG. Click and drag the selection to its new location. The mouse pointer is now labeled MOVE.

3. Release the mouse button when the selection is properly positioned. Works shifts remaining rows and columns to fill the void left by the moved cells.

Troubleshooting

How can I delete a single cell from a spreadsheet?

Because a cell occurs at the intersection of a row and column, you can't delete a single cell from a spreadsheet, you can only delete an entire row or column. You can clear a cell's contents by choosing Edit, Clear; by clicking the Cut key on the toolbar; or by pressing Delete.

How can I insert multiple rows or columns in a spreadsheet at once?

To insert more than one row or column at a time, highlight the number of rows or columns you want to insert, then choose Insert, Insert Row or Insert, Insert Column. Works automatically inserts the number of rows or columns you highlight. For example, to insert three rows at row 17, highlight rows 17, 18, and 19, then select Insert, Row.

Entering Simple Formulas

Spreadsheets are of little value without their capability to perform mathematical calculations through the use of *formulas*. A formula is an equation that performs a calculation on one or more values and returns a result. In Works, you can use formulas to perform basic arithmetic calculations such as addition, subtraction, multiplication, and division. Or you can perform more complex calculations through the use of *functions*, which are prepared equations designed to perform a specific task. For example, rather than trying to create a formula yourself, you would use the PMT function to calculate the periodic payment for a loan or an investment. You learn more about functions in Chapter 11, "Working with Formulas and Functions."

Figure 10.15 shows an example of a simple spreadsheet that doesn't include any formulas. Income and Expenses in columns B, C, and D need to be totaled.

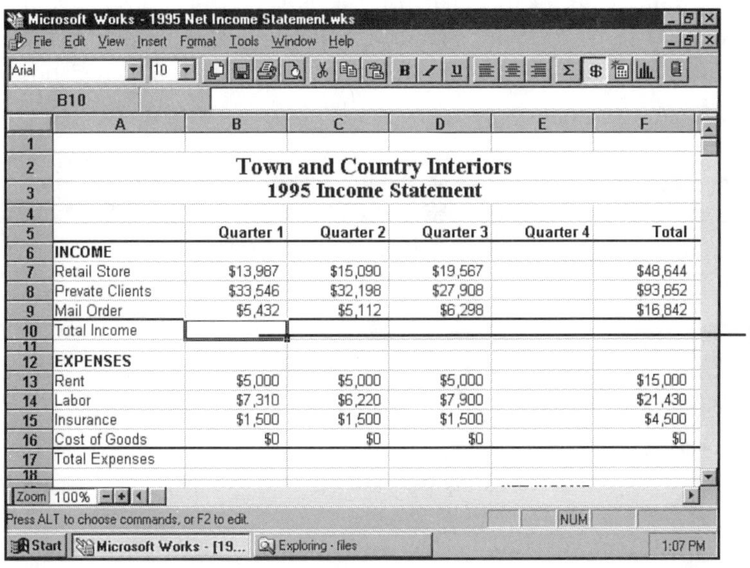

	A	B	C	D	E	F
1						
2	Town and Country Interiors					
3	1995 Income Statement					
4						
5		Quarter 1	Quarter 2	Quarter 3	Quarter 4	Total
6	INCOME					
7	Retail Store	$13,987	$15,090	$19,567		$48,644
8	Prevate Clients	$33,546	$32,198	$27,908		$93,652
9	Mail Order	$5,432	$5,112	$6,298		$16,842
10	Total Income					
11						
12	EXPENSES					
13	Rent	$5,000	$5,000	$5,000		$15,000
14	Labor	$7,310	$6,220	$7,900		$21,430
15	Insurance	$1,500	$1,500	$1,500		$4,500
16	Cost of Goods	$0	$0	$0		$0
17	Total Expenses					

Fig. 10.15
Enter formulas in cells B10:D10 and cells B17:D17 to sum the columns.

All formulas must begin with an equal symbol. This symbol is followed by a combination of cell references or specific values, and arithmetic operators such as + for addition, – for subtraction, / for division, and * for multiplication. For example, the formula `=B8*12` multiplies the value in cell B8 by 12 and displays the result in the cell where the formula is located. In figure 10.15, cells B10 through D10 need summation formulas to total the income figures for Quarter 1, Quarter 2, and Quarter 3, so the formula in cell B10 should read =B7+B8+B9.

The real power of a spreadsheet program is the capability to use cell references in a formula. A formula that contains a cell reference is not restricted to using a specific number but uses whatever value is found in the cell. The cell that is referenced in a formula might contain, for example, the current interest rate (a value that can fluctuate frequently). When the bank notifies you of the new interest rate, you just enter the new rate in its cell and the formula containing a reference to this cell immediately displays a new result. Or you might create a spreadsheet to analyze the financial status of your business each month based on the total sales for the month. Each month you can enter that month's sales in the total sales cell and all the formulas that reference that cell recalculate to display up-to-date results.

When a formula contains more than one operator, Works uses standard algebra rules to evaluate the formula, including evaluating values in parentheses first. For example, in the formula =(C13+5)*35/E4, C13+5 is evaluated before the rest of the formula. When parentheses are nested, the innermost set of parentheses is evaluated first. Operators are evaluated in the order shown in Table 10.4.

Table 10.4 Operators and Their Order of Evaluation

Operator	Order of Evaluation
– (negative) and + (positive)	First
^ (exponent)	Second
* (multiplication) and / (division)	Third
+ (addition) and – (subtraction)	Fourth
=, <>, <, >, <=, >=	Fifth
#NOT#	Sixth
#OR#, #AND#	Seventh

There are a number of ways to create even the simplest formula that sums a column of numbers. You can type the cell references and operators—in this example, type **=B7+B8+B9** in cell B10. However, typing cell references can lead to errors. A faster and more accurate way to create the formula is to "point" to the cells using the arrow keys. Place the highlight in cell B10 and press = (don't press Enter yet). Using the up-arrow key, highlight cell B7, then type the plus symbol. The highlight jumps back to cell B10 and the formula now reads =B7+. Use the up-arrow key to highlight cell B8, then press the plus symbol. Again, the highlight jumps back to cell B10 and the formula now reads =B7+B8. Repeat this process, highlighting cell B9, then press Enter. When you press Enter, the formula is complete and the result of the formula appears in cell B10. The formula itself rather than the calculated result displays in the formula bar. If you prefer, you can use the mouse rather than the up-arrow to point to the cells you want to include in the formula.

After you enter a formula in the spreadsheet, the formula is recalculated every time you make an entry or edit data in the spreadsheet. If you change values used in the formula, the formula immediately displays the new result.

Using the Autosum Button

Because summation is such a common formula in spreadsheets, Works includes a handy toolbar button called Autosum. It uses the SUM function, which automatically sums the values in the specified range of cells. The Autosum button is intelligent; it "reads" the context of the spreadsheet and guesses which cell values you want to sum. An Autosum function looks like this:

Σ

=SUM(B7:B9)

The equal symbol designates the entry as a formula, the SUM part of the formula is the name of the function being used, and the cells referenced in parentheses are the range of cells whose values will be totaled.

To use the Autosum button, select the cell where you want the formula result to appear. Click the Autosum button on the toolbar, or press Ctrl+M (the keyboard shortcut for the Autosum button). Works highlights the range of cells it thinks you want to total and places a formula like the one previously shown in the current cell. The cells referenced in the parentheses are the cells Works highlights (see fig. 10.16). If the cell range is correct, press Enter or click the Autosum button again to complete the formula. Works displays the result in the active cell and the formula appears in the formula bar.

The Autosum function first looks above the current cell to find an appropriate range to sum and then looks to the left. The Autosum feature works even if there are one or more blank cells between the highlighted cell and the range of values. If a range is not found, =SUM() appears in the cell and the formula bar. Enter the correct cell range in the parentheses to complete the formula.

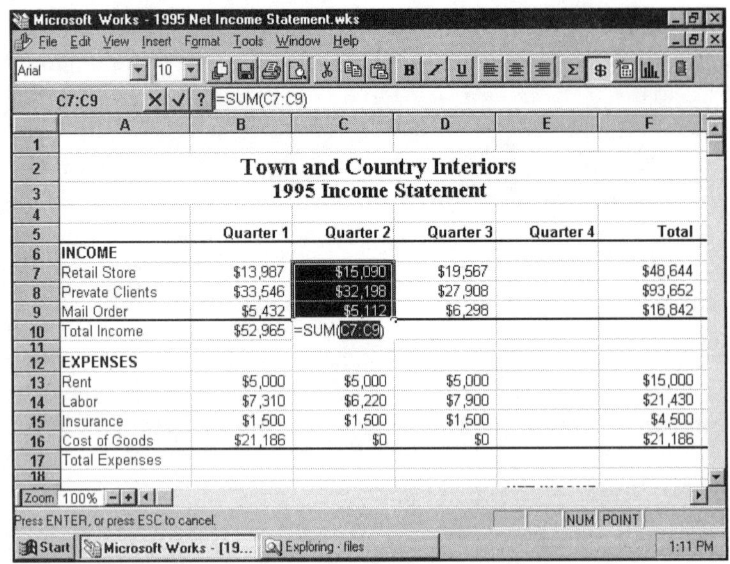

Fig. 10.16 AutoSum highlights cells to sum and displays the formula in the current cell.

Troubleshooting

The cell range that Autosum suggests isn't the range I want to sum.

Sometimes, because of the way the data in your spreadsheet is arranged, Works is not able to accurately guess the range of cells to sum. When this happens, you must type or highlight the correct range to complete the formula.

Works keeps displaying the message `Missing Operand`. *What's wrong with my formula?*

The formula ends with an operator (such as +, –, *, /) instead of an *operand.* An operand is a number or a cell reference. Remove the final operator from the formula, or add an operand following the operator.

Saving a Spreadsheet

After you begin creating real spreadsheets, you will want to save your work. You learned in Chapter 3, "Working with Documents, TaskWizards, and Templates," that you choose a permanent name for a file, a location to store it, and a file type the first time you save a file. Until you save a spreadsheet, any data that you enter is vulnerable. An interruption of power or an equipment failure could cause an unsaved file to be lost, so it's important to remember to save a file frequently and to save the first time as soon as you begin entering information.

Note

Now is the time to take advantage of the capability of Windows 95 to save files using long file names. As you study the various figures throughout this book, check the Works title bar for examples of effective long names.

If you think you might use your spreadsheet file with another spreadsheet program, you can save the file in the appropriate file format. Works allows you to save a spreadsheet in any of the formats in the following list. The Text & Commas, Text & Tabs, and Text & Tabs (DOS) options are used primarily when you want to transfer spreadsheet data to a database file.

The following formats are available for saving spreadsheet files:

Works SS (Works spreadsheet)

Works for Windows 3.0 SS

Works for Windows 2.0/Works for DOS SS

Text & Commas

Text & Tabs

Text & Tabs (DOS)

Excel 4.0/5.0 SS

Lotus 1-2-3

Works 3.0 for Macintosh SS (*.ss)

Works 4.0 for Macintosh SS (*.ss)

Printing a Spreadsheet

► See "Adding Headers and Footers to a Spreadsheet," p. 254

You can print a portion of a spreadsheet or an entire spreadsheet at any time—while you're in the process of creating it or after it's finished. In any case, you should always review page and print settings before printing. Choose File, Page Setup to display the Page Setup dialog box. In this dialog box, you specify the page, header, and footer margins; the source, size, and orientation for the paper you are printing on; page numbering and footnote options; and other standard settings for your particular printer. When all page settings are correct, it's a good idea to preview your spreadsheet as a final check before printing. You learn how to specify page settings in the following sections.

Note

The settings you choose in the Page Setup dialog box affect only the current spreadsheet file.

Setting a Print Area

Often, you don't need to print an entire spreadsheet—only a portion of it. Printing a selected portion of a spreadsheet is a very useful feature, especially when a spreadsheet becomes rather large.

► See "Using Range Names," p. 233

The portion of a spreadsheet that you print is called the *print area*. Normally, the print area includes all cells in the spreadsheet. When you want to print only a portion of a spreadsheet, however, you specify a different print area. To set the print area, use these steps:

Tip
If you frequently print portions of a spreadsheet rather than an entire spreadsheet, you can add the Set Print Area button to your toolbar.

1. Select the cells you want to include in the print area.
2. Choose Format, Set Print Area. Works displays a dialog box asking you to confirm the current selection as the print area.
3. Choose OK.

When you define a print area, Works assigns the range name `Print Area` to the cells you select. (To learn more about naming a range of cells, refer to Chapter 11, "Working with Formulas and Functions.") When you're ready to print the file, Works prints only those cells in the designated print area.

To change the print area back to the entire spreadsheet, use the following steps:

1. Choose Insert, Range Name. Works displays the Range Name dialog box.
2. In the Select a Name list, select Print Area and then choose the Delete button. Works removes Print Area from the list of range names.
3. Choose the Close command to close the Range Name dialog box.

Setting Margins

◄ See "Customizing the Toolbars," p. 33

Page margins are the white space that surrounds the text on the printed page. To set page margins for your spreadsheet, you use the Page Setup dialog box shown in figure 10.17. Unless you change margin settings, the Page Setup dialog box shows the default margins that Works uses: 1 inch for top and bottom margins, and 1.25 inches for left and right margins. The Sample area of the dialog box displays a graphics representation of these settings.

For some spreadsheets, however, you might want to change the default margin settings in order to fit more data on a page. Also, when you print a range of cells that is smaller than a single page, change the margins to center the material on the page for a more pleasing appearance.

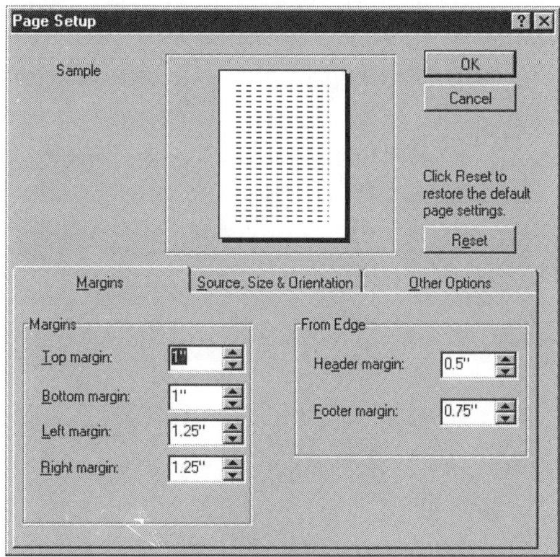

Fig. 10.17
The Page Setup dialog box displays margin settings for the current spreadsheet.

To change margin settings, follow these steps:

1. Choose File, Page Setup. The Page Setup dialog box appears.
2. In the dialog box, choose the Margins tab (the options shown in figure 10.17 appear).
3. In the appropriate margin boxes, type the setting you want to use in inches. Type a decimal fraction for fractions of an inch (such as 1.25 for 1-1/4 inches) or click the arrow buttons to increase or decrease the current setting 0.1 inch per click. The Sample area of the dialog box reflects the settings you choose.
4. When all margin settings are correct, choose OK. Works automatically reformats your spreadsheet using the new margin settings.

Note

If you commonly work with centimeters or another unit of measure rather than inches, you can change the Works default units setting. Choose Tools, Options to display the Options dialog box. Choose the General tab. In the Units box, choose a unit of measure, and then choose OK. Notice that the unit of measure you choose applies to *all* tools in Works.

Setting Paper Source, Size, and Orientation

Before printing a spreadsheet, you must specify in Works which paper source to use, the size of the paper you're printing on, and the direction you want the print to appear on the page. To change the paper source, paper size, and print orientation, you use the Page Setup dialog box shown in figure 10.18. In the figure, the Source, Size, and Orientation tab is selected and you can see the default settings. The page in the Sample area reflects the current paper size and orientation settings.

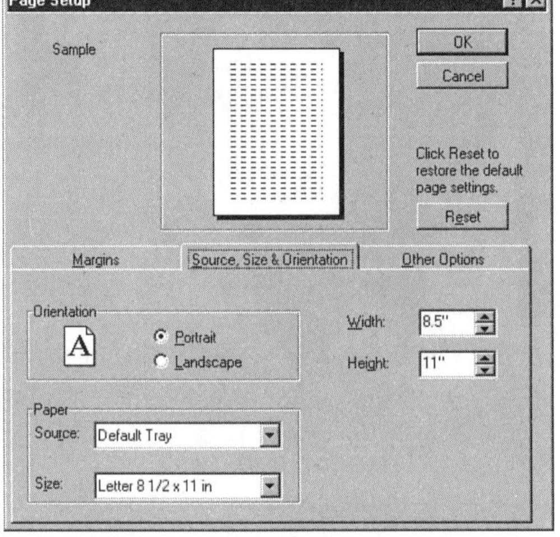

Fig. 10.18 Here you can change the paper source, size, and orientation settings for the current spreadsheet.

Depending on the type of printer you are using, you can choose the correct paper source (such as the default paper tray, second paper tray, and envelope feeder) from the Paper Source drop-down list. The Paper Size list offers a variety of standard paper and envelope sizes that the current printer can use. Choose a size from the list or enter the correct size in the Width and Height boxes.

Paper orientation refers to the direction the print will appear on the paper. Most documents printed on standard 8-1/2 × 11 inch paper are printed in *portrait* orientation, or using the 11-inch dimension as the *height* of the paper. Spreadsheets, however, often have more columns of data than rows, and therefore look better when printed in landscape orientation. For documents that are printed in landscape orientation, the paper is rotated 90 degrees so that the 8-1/2 dimension is used as the height of the paper. (The paper is not actually rotated in your printer, your printer simply prints the image "sideways.") The default orientation is Portrait; to print in landscape mode, choose the Landscape option. The paper in the Sample area of the dialog box rotates. Notice, also, that for the paper size you specified, the settings in the Width and Height boxes automatically reverse.

To change source, size, and orientation settings, follow these steps:

1. Choose File, Page Setup. The Page Setup dialog box appears.
2. In the dialog box, choose the Source, Size, and Orientation tab. The dialog box shown in figure 10.18 appears.
3. Choose a paper source from the Paper Source drop-down list. Choose a paper size from the Paper Size drop-down list, or specify a custom size in the Width and Height boxes. Choose a paper orientation by clicking either the Portrait or Landscape option. The Sample area of the dialog box reflects the settings you choose.
4. When all settings are correct, choose OK.

Setting Other Page Options

The third tab in the Page Setup dialog box is Other Options (see fig. 10.19). Use the settings on this tab to print gridlines or to print row and column headers (row numbers and column labels) and to set the beginning page number.

By default, Works does not print the gridlines that appear on the screen when you print a spreadsheet. However, printing gridlines can sometimes make a spreadsheet easier to read. To print gridlines, select the Print Gridlines check box and then choose OK.

Printing row and column headers containing the row numbers and column letters can also make a spreadsheet easier to read. This option is helpful when you are still making changes to a spreadsheet and printing draft copies as you work. The row and column headers can help you find the right cell when you go back to the screen to make corrections. To use this option, select the Print Row and Column Headers check box, then choose OK.

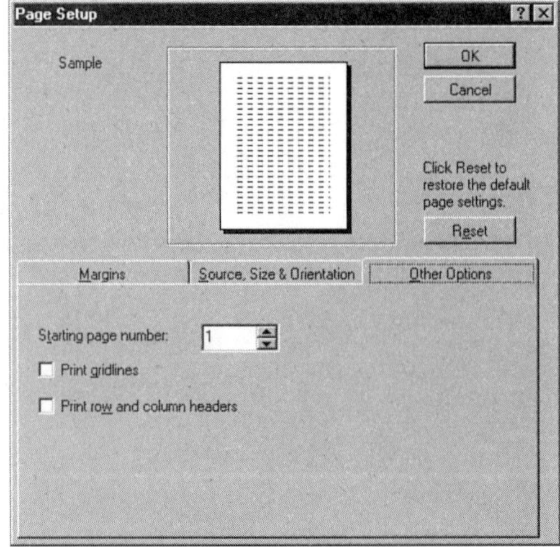

Fig. 10.19 The Other Options tab displays miscellaneous page settings.

Previewing a Document

One of the most important steps you can take before printing a spreadsheet is to *preview* it. Previewing allows you to see on the screen how your spreadsheet will look on the printed page. When you use the preview screen, Works displays a full-page view—one page at a time—of the spreadsheet. This is your chance to see that margins are the appropriate size, row heights and column widths are acceptable, page separations are correct, header and footer text is positioned correctly, and so on. All of these elements appear on the preview screen.

To preview your spreadsheet, choose File, Print Preview or click the Print Preview button. The current document appears in a preview screen like the one shown in figure 10.20.

The actual text and numbers displayed in the preview screen can be difficult to read because they are so small, but reading the text isn't the important consideration here—checking the layout is. If you think you spot a problem, however, you can zero in on a particular location. Notice in figure 10.20 that the mouse pointer changes to a magnifying glass when it is pointing anywhere on the page. Click the left mouse button anywhere on the page to zoom in on that location in the spreadsheet, or choose the Zoom In button. If you need to magnify the spreadsheet further, click the left mouse button once more anywhere on the page, or click the Zoom In button again. Use the scroll bars, if necessary, to view a part of the spreadsheet that isn't visible. To zoom back out, click the mouse button a third time anywhere on the page, or click the Zoom Out button.

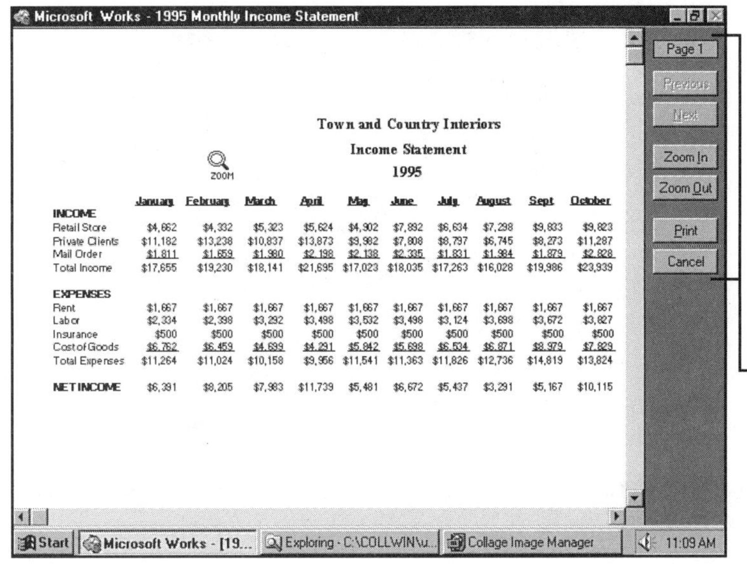

Town and Country Interiors
Income Statement
1995

	January	February	March	April	May	June	July	August	Sept	October
INCOME										
Retail Store	$4,662	$4,332	$5,323	$5,624	$4,902	$7,892	$6,634	$7,298	$9,833	$9,823
Private Clients	$11,182	$13,238	$10,837	$13,873	$9,982	$7,808	$8,797	$6,745	$8,273	$11,287
Mail Order	$1,811	$1,659	$1,980	$2,198	$2,138	$2,335	$1,831	$1,984	$1,879	$2,828
Total Income	$17,655	$19,230	$18,141	$21,695	$17,023	$18,035	$17,263	$16,028	$19,986	$23,939
EXPENSES										
Rent	$1,667	$1,667	$1,667	$1,667	$1,667	$1,667	$1,667	$1,667	$1,667	$1,667
Labor	$2,334	$2,398	$3,292	$3,498	$3,532	$3,498	$3,124	$3,698	$3,672	$3,827
Insurance	$500	$500	$500	$500	$500	$500	$500	$500	$500	$500
Cost of Goods	$6,762	$6,459	$4,699	$4,291	$5,842	$5,698	$6,534	$6,871	$8,979	$7,829
Total Expenses	$11,264	$11,024	$10,158	$9,956	$11,541	$11,363	$11,826	$12,736	$14,819	$13,824
NET INCOME	$6,391	$8,205	$7,983	$11,739	$5,481	$6,672	$5,437	$3,291	$5,167	$10,115

Preview command buttons

Fig. 10.20 Previewing a document shows you how the document will appear when you print it. This spreadsheet is in landscape page orientation.

If your spreadsheet is longer than one page, display the page you want to preview by clicking the Previous or Next button, or use the Page Up and Page Down keys on the keyboard. When you're ready to print the spreadsheet, you can print directly from the preview screen by clicking the Print button. This button displays the Print dialog box.

Printing

When you're ready to print your spreadsheet, choose File, Print, which displays the Print dialog box shown in figure 10.21. You use the Print dialog box to specify the number of copies you want to print, the particular pages you want to print, and the quality of printing you want to use. The printer that is currently selected is shown at the top of the dialog box.

To print a spreadsheet, follow these steps:

1. Open the spreadsheet file you want to print.
2. (Optional) Choose File, Page Setup to specify print margins, paper source, paper size, paper orientation, and other print settings.
3. (Optional) Choose File, Print Preview to preview the spreadsheet.

4. Choose File, Print (or choose the Print button from the Print Preview dialog box). The Print dialog box shown in figure 10.21 appears.

5. Select the appropriate print settings and choose OK.

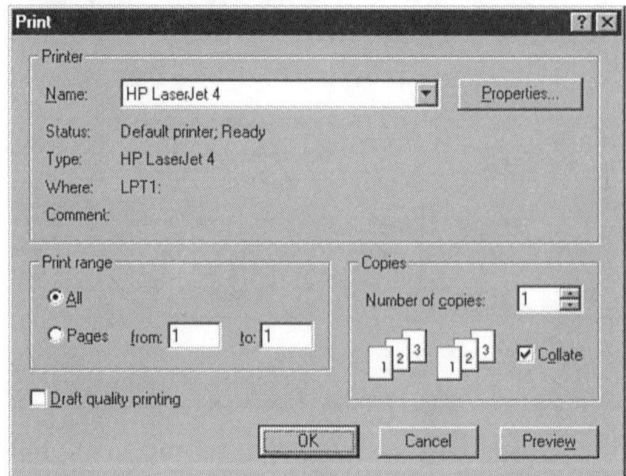

Fig. 10.21
If the printer shown is wrong, select the correct printer from the Name drop-down list.

Creating a Default Spreadsheet Template

Many users find that after working with a program for a while, they create the same or similar spreadsheets over and over. Time records, pay sheets, and monthly or weekly reports of various types are examples of this repetitive work. After you have created the same spreadsheet enough times to have worked out the kinks and devised the formulas that generate the information your business needs, you might consider saving the spreadsheet as a form—with all the labels, titles, and formulas but without the data. Later, you retrieve the form spreadsheet, enter the current data, and the formulas stored in the form automatically display the results. However, you might forget the spreadsheet is a form and accidentally overwrite the original file when you save the completed spreadsheet.

When you have created a form spreadsheet, Works makes it possible for you to save the spreadsheet as a template. Thereafter, the template is included in the User Defined Templates category in the list of TaskWizards (available in the Works Task Launcher dialog box). When you need to create the next month's report, you can choose your form by name in the Works Task Launcher dialog box. Selecting a template opens a *copy* of the form document. The data you add does not change the template. When you save the completed spreadsheet the template is not overwritten; it remains available for you to use again and again.

After you save the spreadsheet as a template, you can configure Works to use it as the *default* template. Also called an AutoStart template, Works opens the default template every time you start Works. Works completely bypasses the Works Task Launcher dialog box. Perhaps you have designed a logo or title area that you use at the top of most of your work. An excellent choice for a default template might be a spreadsheet with this logo or title and the specific header and footer you prefer already set up.

To save a spreadsheet as a template and specify it as the default template, follow these steps:

1. After you have created the spreadsheet as you want the template to appear, choose File, Save As to display the Save As dialog box.
2. If you have not previously saved the spreadsheet or need to change its current name, enter a name for the spreadsheet file in the File Name text box.
3. Select the Template button to display the Save As Template dialog box.
4. Enter a name for the template file in the Type a Name for the New Template Below text box.
5. To designate the template as the default template, choose the check box labeled Use This Template for New Spreadsheet Documents.
6. Choose OK to close the Save As dialog box.

Your new template now appears at the end of the TaskWizards list in the Works Task Launcher dialog box under the User Defined Templates category. If you indicated you want it used as the default template, the template appears every time you open a new spreadsheet window.

Tip
As helpful as the default template feature is, be sure you want to use this form to create a new spreadsheet most of the time. Otherwise, you will create more rather than less work for yourself by making that report the default template.

Customizing the Spreadsheet Display

There are almost as many ways to work in a spreadsheet as there are users. For example, you might not want zeros to display in your forms when formulas result in zero. You can choose to edit entries only in the cell if you want the entry bar removed from the screen. You can turn off drag-and-drop editing, and you can control the number of decimal places proposed when you choose a number format.

To configure Works so your spreadsheet preferences are in effect, choose Tools, Options. If a spreadsheet is active, the Data Entry tab is selected (see fig. 10.22).

In the Cell Data Entry Modes section of the dialog box you can choose the following options:

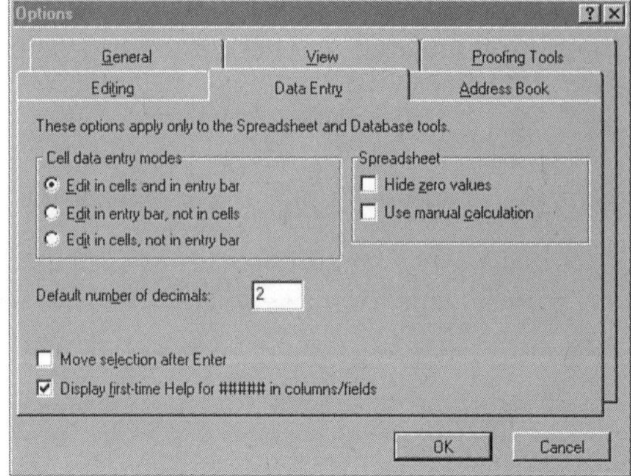

Fig 10.22
You can control the behavior of many spreadsheet features in the Data Entry tab of the Options dialog box.

- *Edit in Cells and in Entry Bar.* To edit the contents of a cell, double-click a cell or click the I-beam cursor in the cell contents in the entry bar.
- *Edit in Entry Bar and Not in Cells.* You can only edit the contents of a cell in the entry bar.
- *Edit in Cells and Not in Entry Bar.* Double-click a cell to edit its contents. The entry bar is no longer displayed after you choose this option.

In the Spreadsheet section, you can choose these options:

- *Hide Zero Values.* Depending on the formula, when cells that are referenced in a formula are empty, the formula displays a zero. Choose this option to have these cells display as empty as long as the results are zero.
- *Use Manual Calculation.* In very large spreadsheets, operations such as pasting a column of formulas can be very slow. Use manual calculation to perform the desired operation and then calculate the spreadsheet later. To calculate, press F9 or toggle this selection off and enter a value in a cell.

The following options are also available in the Data Entry tab of the Options dialog box:

- *Default Number of Decimals.* Some users rarely display numbers to two decimal places. Enter the number of decimal places you most frequently use in the text box. This option controls the number of decimal places offered when you choose the number format for the contents of a cell.
- *Move Selection After Enter.* Choose this option to cause the highlight to move down one cell when you enter a value in a cell. Even when selected, you can press the left, up, or right arrow keys to enter a value in a cell and move the highlight left, up, or right.
- *Display First-Time Help for ##### in Columns/Fields.* This option assures that the first time a numeric entry displays as ##### because it is too long to display in the cell, a First-Time Help dialog box appears. It has a button you click to see a step-by-step demo that shows you how to change the column width to fix the display.

A final option that controls several useful features is on the General tab. The Enable Drag-And-Drop Editing option, turned on by default, enables you to cut, copy, and paste by dragging the selection to a new location. Before you decide to turn this off, realize that it also enables the new Autofill feature where you drag using the selection's fill handle. ❖

Chapter 11

Working with Formulas and Functions

by Judy Petersen

Using Works, you can create more complex formulas than the simple formulas described in Chapter 10, "Creating, Saving, and Printing a Spreadsheet." Even greater calculating power can be achieved by using functions in your formulas. You also can name cell ranges and use the range name in your formulas. Using functions and range names simplifies the task of creating formulas in a spreadsheet.

In this chapter, you learn how to

- Understand how formulas work
- Understand relative and absolute cell addressing
- Move, copy, and delete formulas and data
- Use functions in formulas
- Name a range of cells

Understanding How Formulas Work

In Chapter 10, "Creating, Saving, and Printing a Spreadsheet," you learn some basic steps for creating a simple formula. You learn that a formula begins with an equal symbol and is followed by a combination of values, cell references, and operators. You also learn that the contents of parentheses are evaluated first in a formula and that operators are evaluated in a specific order. Chapter 10 also describes how to create a simple formula by typing or pointing to cell references and entering operators, or by using the Autosum button on the spreadsheet toolbar.

The formulas shown in Chapter 10 are simple summation formulas—but spreadsheet formulas are often more complex than that. Formulas can reference many cells and ranges in the spreadsheet, constant values, operators, and parentheses, such as in a formula like =(3*4^3)-(3*(D18*A4)+(3*E7))+25. You can create complex formulas by pointing to cells when you want to use a cell reference, and typing operators, constants, and parentheses where appropriate—but they require extra care when creating them. Another factor that makes formulas more complex is a concept called relative and absolute cell addressing. In the following section, you see how relative and absolute cell addressing affect a formula.

Note

As you create more complex formulas, it becomes increasingly important to use parentheses freely—not only to ensure that the calculation is performed in the proper order, but also because the formula will be easier for you and others to read and understand.

Relative and Absolute Cell Addressing

Let's say the cell D17 contains the formula `=D14-D15`, where the value in D15 is subtracted from the value in D14, and the result is displayed in D17. The cell references in this formula are called *relative* references because Works doesn't interpret them literally. To Works, the formula in D17 means "find the value in the cell 2 rows up and subtract it from the value in the cell 3 rows up, then display the result here."

Rather than operating on specific values, a formula that uses relative addresses "follows directions" to find the values on which to calculate a result. If you copy the formula `=D14-D15` to cell F5, for example, Works automatically changes the formula to `=F2-F3` to set up the same directions to follow and calculates a result based on the values found in those cells.

When it's important for a formula to calculate using specific values in specific cells, you create a formula with *absolute* references. Figure 11.1 illustrates why you need to use absolute cell references in some formulas. In the figure, the worksheet lists a markup percentage (200%) in cell B4. Column B shows wholesale prices for the items listed in column A, and column C is where the retail price is calculated by multiplying the retail price by a markup percentage. In cell C9, the formula reads `=B9*B4`, which translates to $350×200%. This formula calculates the correct retail price in cell C9. For this cell, the formula really says "find the value in the cell one column to the left ($350) and multiply it by the value in the cell one column to the left and five rows up (200%)." Given the location of the formula and the position of the values in the spreadsheet, this formula calculates correctly.

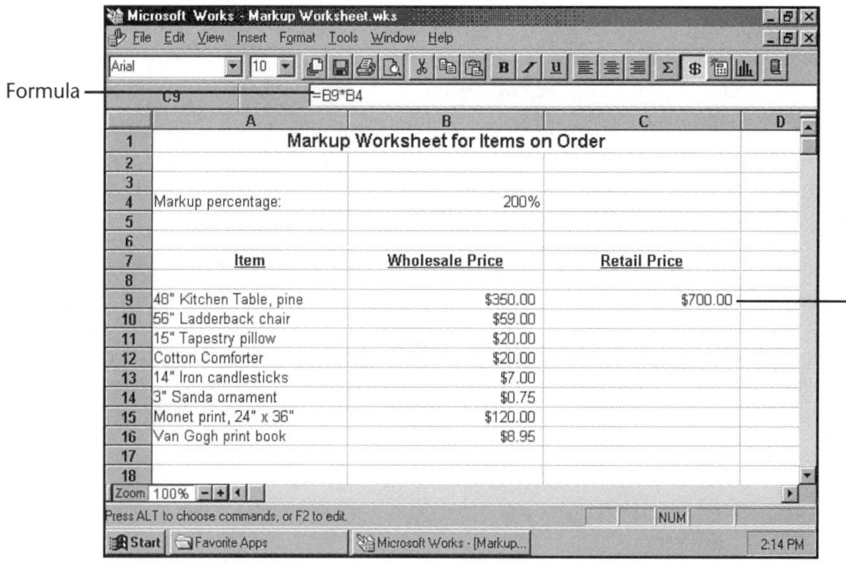

Fig. 11.1
The formula in cell C9 calculates the correct result for the price of the merchandise.

But suppose you copy the formula in C9 to C10, thinking it will multiply $59 (in B10) by 200% (in B4). The formula no longer calculates correctly (see fig. 11.2). Because the original formula in C9 contains relative cell addresses, the formula copied to cell C10 reads `=B10*B5`, which is incorrect. Because there is no value in cell B5, the formula evaluates to zero.

If you copy the formula from C9 all the way through cell C16, you find that the formula starts multiplying retail prices by retail prices rather than by the markup percentage—all because of the location of the cells. Formula errors like these can lead to significant errors in results in a spreadsheet. The way to fix this problem is to use an absolute cell reference. That is, you want to multiply *all* of the retail prices in Column B by the markup percentage shown in cell B4, so the cell reference to cell B4 in all formulas should be an absolute reference.

Creating Formulas with Relative and Absolute Addresses

Formulas with relative cell references look like all the formulas you have seen up to this point—they don't contain any special characters, just simple cell references. When you create a formula by pointing to cell references with the mouse or arrow keys, Works automatically inserts relative cell references in the formula. To create a formula with absolute cell references, you insert dollar signs preceding the column and row references. To make the formula =B9*B4 *always* reference cell B4, for example, you write the formula as =B9*B4. The dollar sign preceding the B "locks" the cell reference to column B; the dollar sign preceding the 4 locks the reference to row 4. A "locked" cell reference is what Works refers to as an *absolute* reference. This means that if you copy the formula from cell C9 to cell C10, it now reads =B10*B4, which is exactly how you want it to read. If you copy the formula to C11, it reads =B11*B4. You can now copy this formula to all cells from C10 through C16, and the retail prices will be calculated correctly. Figure 11.3 shows the results.

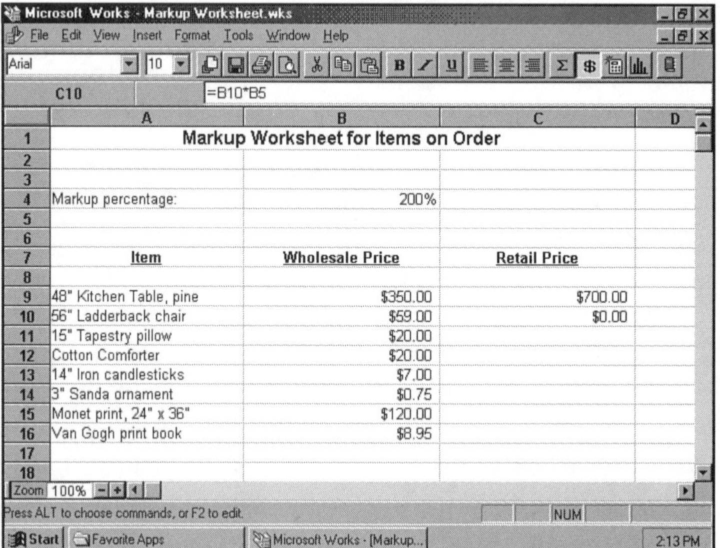

Fig. 11.2
When copied to C10, the formula from C9 is incorrect and evaluates to zero.

To create a formula with absolute cell references, you either type the correct cell reference, including dollar signs, or you create the formula using relative references, and then add the dollar signs by editing the formula. To ensure the accuracy of the cell references, it's often best to create a formula with relative references by pointing to the correct cells, and then add the dollar signs when you edit the formula.

In Works, you also can create a *mixed* cell reference, such as $B4 or B$4. In a mixed cell reference, only one reference—either the row or the column—is absolute; the other is not. In the reference $B4, the reference to column B is absolute but the row reference is not. The reference B$4 is just the opposite—the reference to row 4 is absolute but the column reference is not. To copy the formula in figure 11.3 correctly, for example, only the row number needs to be absolute.

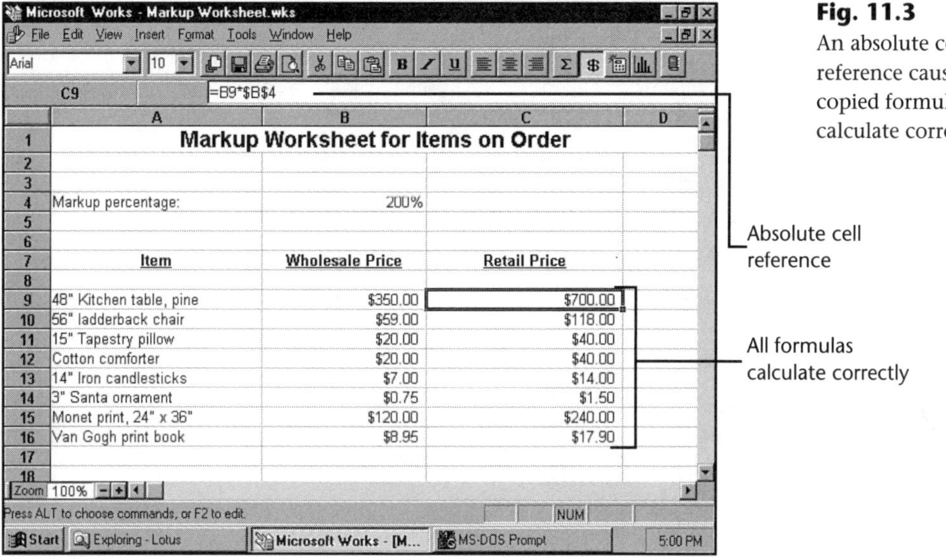

Fig. 11.3
An absolute cell reference causes all copied formulas to calculate correctly.

You can also quickly insert the dollar signs for absolute references by pressing the F4 key as you create a formula. When you point to a cell, such as C3, the cell reference is highlighted in the formula bar. Press F4 once to make the cell reference absolute. If you press F4 repeatedly, Works cycles through the following list of absolute, mixed, and relative references, creating them automatically for you:

Press F4 once	C3
Press F4 twice	C$3
Press F4 three times	$C3
Press F4 four times	C3

Using F4 works only when entering the formula in the entry bar or when using Easy Calc, which is described later in this chapter. You cannot use F4 when editing a formula to change or add another cell reference.

To complete the formula, insert operators and parentheses as you normally would.

Troubleshooting

The current Social Security rate is stored in a cell I named SS. When I multiply the first employee's gross pay by SS and copy this formula to the rows for the additional employees, the result for all but the first employee is $0. Why doesn't this work?

If you copy a formula containing a named range, Works adjusts the range reference in the copy. Because the range now referenced is empty, the calculated result is 0. You can also make range names absolute. Simply start the range name with a $ sign. Now when you copy the formula, all copies refer to the cell named SS.

Moving Formulas and Cells Referenced by Formulas

When you move a formula in a spreadsheet, Works does not change any of the cell references in the formula. If, for example, you move the formula =B10*B4 from cell C10 to cell K32, the formula still reads =B10*B4. In most cases, you still want the formula to calculate a result on the same values, it's only the *location of the answer* that you are changing. Based on the principle that you still want to perform the same calculations regardless of the location of the formula, Works does not change the cell references in a moved formula.

On the other hand, when you change the location of *data* in a spreadsheet, Works may or may not change any formula cell references. If the cell reference of the data you move is part of the formula, Works assumes that you still want to perform the same calculation, but the data is now located in a different cell, so the cell reference in the formula must be changed. For example, if you move the value of 200% in cell B4 to cell B3, Works changes the reference in the formula =B10*B4 to =B10*B3. This change ensures that the same calculation is performed now that the data (200%) is located in a different cell.

However, if you move data located inside a range of cells, no change is made in the formula. If, for example, the cell C11 contains the summation formula =sum(C3:C10) and you move the contents of cell C7 to another location, Works does not change the formula. In this example, where a range reference is used in the formula, Works changes the formula only if the cell C3 or C10 is moved. Check the original formula carefully to make sure any changes in the formula give correct results.

> **Caution**
>
> Moving the contents of cells that define a range, such as the cells C3 or C10 in the previous example, can change the entire concept of your formula. Here, moving C3 to D3 causes Works to change the formula to =sum(D3:C10), *doubling* the number of cells that are included in the formula. When you move data, be sure to proofread the results carefully before relying on the calculations in the spreadsheet.

Copying Formulas and Cells Referenced by Formulas

When you copy a formula in a spreadsheet, you usually want the formula to perform the same type of calculation but use different data. In figure 11.4, for example, you might copy the formula in cell B10, `=SUM(B7:B9)`, to cells C10 through M10 to sum total income for the months of February through December. When you copy the formula, you expect it to accurately total the figures in columns C through M, not use the data from column B. To accomplish this, Works must adjust all relative cell references in a formula. So, if you copy `=SUM(B7:B9)` from B10 to C10, the formula reads `=SUM(C7:C9)`; copied to D10, the formula reads `=SUM(D7:D9)`, and so on.

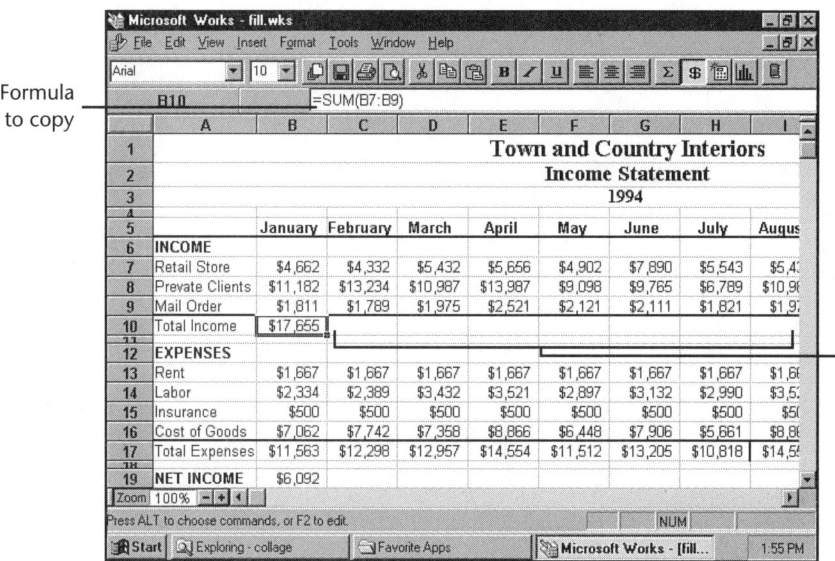

	A	B	C	D	E	F	G	H	I
5		January	February	March	April	May	June	July	Augus
6	INCOME								
7	Retail Store	$4,662	$4,332	$5,432	$5,656	$4,902	$7,890	$5,543	$5,4
8	Prevate Clients	$11,182	$13,234	$10,987	$13,987	$9,098	$9,765	$6,789	$10,9
9	Mail Order	$1,811	$1,789	$1,975	$2,521	$2,121	$2,111	$1,821	$1,9
10	Total Income	$17,655							
12	EXPENSES								
13	Rent	$1,667	$1,667	$1,667	$1,667	$1,667	$1,667	$1,667	$1,6
14	Labor	$2,334	$2,389	$3,432	$3,521	$2,897	$3,132	$2,990	$3,5
15	Insurance	$500	$500	$500	$500	$500	$500	$500	$5
16	Cost of Goods	$7,062	$7,742	$7,358	$8,866	$6,448	$7,906	$5,661	$8,8
17	Total Expenses	$11,563	$12,298	$12,957	$14,554	$11,512	$13,205	$10,818	$14,5
19	NET INCOME	$6,092							

Fig. 11.4
When copied to C10 through M10, the formula in B10 calculates accurately.

Range to which formula will be copied

Note

When you copy a formula that contains absolute cell references, such as C9*B4, the relative part of the formula (C9) is automatically adjusted, but the absolute portion of the formula (B4) remains unchanged.

Clearing and Deleting Cells Referenced in a Formula

If you delete the contents of a cell that is referenced by a formula, the value of that cell becomes zero, but the cell references in the formula remain unchanged. This is true whether you choose Edit, Clear or just press the Delete key to remove the data. Suppose the formula cell C14 contains the formula =C10*C11 and you clear the value in C10. The formula now operates on a zero value in C10, but the cell references in the formula are still C10 and C11. This change is no different than if you change the value in C10 to 2 or 1,345,872.93. Zero is a value like any other value, and the formula remains unchanged.

If you delete a row or column that contains a cell referenced by a formula, the formula displays ERR in the cell where the formula is located. When you delete a row or column, the referenced cell no longer exists. Because the formula doesn't know where to find the cell, it can't calculate correctly, so Works must display the ERR value. This is your cue to adjust the cell reference in the formula so it can calculate correctly.

Note

When a formula displays ERR, the cell references in the formula have changed to ERR. Inserting or adding new data will not cause the formula to work again. You must edit or replace the formula to replace ERR with a cell reference.

If, on the other hand, you delete a row or column that contains a cell included in a formula but not specifically referenced, the result recalculates to reflect the now absent data, but the formula itself does not change.

Troubleshooting

I deleted a column and now several cells contain ERR. *Is there any way to restore my data?*

Yes, if you notice the change immediately. Choose Edit, Undo (or press Ctrl+Z) to restore the deleted column. Now check the formulas in the cells that displayed ERR and edit the formulas so they no longer include references to cells in the column you want to delete.

Using Easy Calc

Entering formulas to perform simple tasks, such as adding two numbers, is simple as long as you remember to start with an equal sign. Creating more complex formulas takes practice and, when an occasional formula doesn't work, some troubleshooting may be in order. Usually the problem is a misplaced parenthesis or an incorrect operator. Until you become comfortable writing formulas, the Easy Calc Wizard shown in figure 11.5 is available to handle the structural details for you.

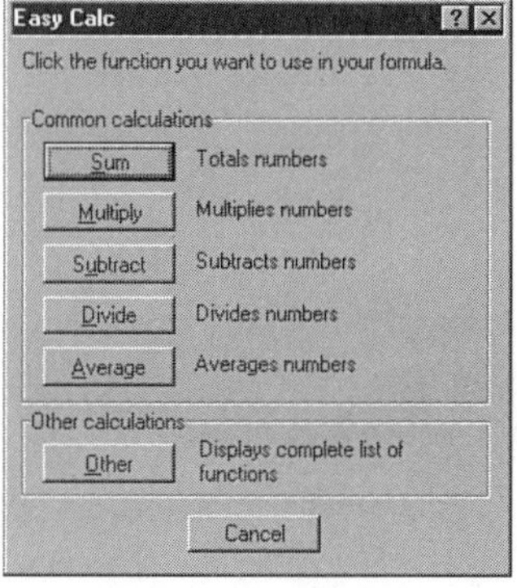

Fig. 11.5
In Easy Calc, you only have to choose the type of formula to create and provide the values.

Start Easy Calc by choosing Tools, Easy Calc or by clicking the Easy Calc button on the toolbar. The Easy Calc dialog box provides buttons to Sum, Multiply, Subtract, Divide, or Average the values you want to use. For more complex calculations, you can choose Other to open the Insert Function dialog box. Select what operator you want Works to use and in the next Easy Calc screen, click the cells containing the values you want to include in the formula. As you select each cell in order, Easy Calc adds the cell reference in the List of Values text box. Between each cell reference, Easy Calc inserts the operator you selected initially. Choose Next. In the Result In text box, enter the address of the cell where you want the formula written. If you select the cell to hold the formula before you choose Easy Calc, the address is already filled in for you.

To use Easy Calc to insert a formula in a spreadsheet, follow these steps:

1. Select the cell where you want the result to display.
2. Choose Tools, Easy Calc or click the Easy Calc button on the toolbar. The Easy Calc dialog box in figure 11.5 appears.
3. From the Common Calculations list, choose Sum, Multiply, Subtract, Divide, or Average. The Easy Calc dialog box changes to a display similar to the one for Subtract shown in figure 11.6.

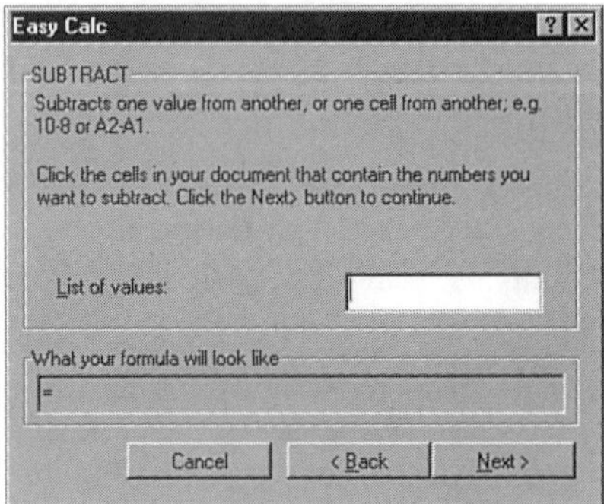

Fig. 11.6
As you click each cell containing a value, the cell reference is added to the List of Values text box. The actual formula appears in the What Your Formula Will Look Like box.

4. Click each cell containing a value you want included in the formula. If the formula subtracts or divides, click each cell in the correct order. If the formula allows you to enter a range, you can drag the mouse to select the range. Choose the Next button.

> **Note**
>
> If the Easy Calc dialog box hides your view of the data you want to calculate, move the dialog box out of the way by dragging the title bar of the dialog box.

5. In the next Easy Calc screen, check the Result In box to verify the cell reference matches where you want the result to display. Enter the correct cell reference, if necessary.
6. Choose the Finish button. Works displays the function result in the current cell.

The final option available in Easy Calc is the Other button. Use Other to move directly to the Functions dialog box, which is the subject of the next section.

Using Functions in Formulas

As you learned in Chapter 10, functions are prepared equations designed to simplify the task of creating formulas in a spreadsheet. Functions perform such common tasks as finding the sum of a range of numbers (SUM); and can be as complex as finding the net present value of an investment based on constant future cash flows (NPV). Rather than trying to create a complex formula yourself, insert a function into a spreadsheet to perform a specific type of calculation. Works contains 76 built-in functions that you select from the Function dialog box (see fig. 11.7), which displays when you choose Insert, Function. The functions cover a broad range of categories, including financial, logical, statistical, and math and trigonometry. For a complete summary of all 76 functions included in Works, refer to the Appendix, "Works for Windows Functions."

Σ

Functions consist of a function name, which is usually followed by one or more *arguments* that represent the values upon which the function operates. An argument can be a constant value, a reference to a cell that contains a value, a reference to a cell that generates a value, a range of cells, or a named range. When you insert a function in a spreadsheet, it begins with an equal sign, followed by the function name, followed by the arguments enclosed in parentheses. Within the parentheses, arguments are separated by commas and no spaces. For example, the present value function, before you enter cell references or values, looks like this:

PV(payment,rate,term)

When you use the PV function and substitute the arguments with values or cell references, the formula might look like this:

=PV(25000,7.75%,4)

Or this:

=PV(C2,C6,C3)

A handful of functions, such as PI and NOW, do not accept arguments; however, the open and close parentheses must still follow the name of the function. When you enter one of these functions, do not type anything—even a space—between the open and close parentheses.

The easy way to insert a function in a spreadsheet is to use the Insert Function dialog box shown in figure 11.7. In the dialog box, functions can be listed by category. The Choose a Function list box lists function names and their arguments. The Description box briefly describes the purpose of the function that's currently selected.

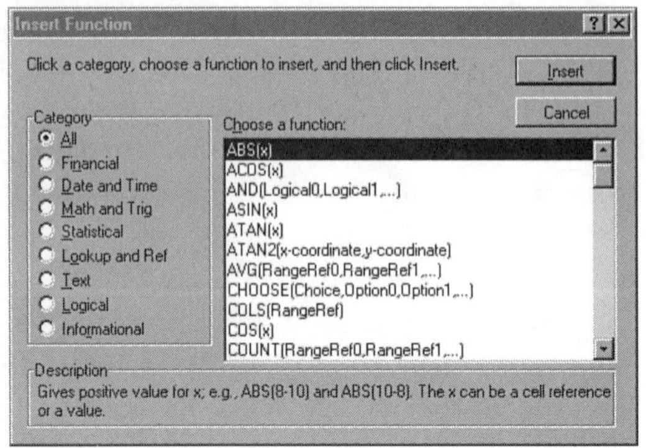

Fig. 11.7
The Choose a Function list box shows an alphabetized list of functions for the selected Category.

To insert a function in a spreadsheet, follow these steps:

1. Move the cell selector to the cell where you want the result to be displayed.

2. Choose Insert, Function. Alternatively, click the Easy Calc button then choose Other. The Function dialog box in figure 11.7 appears.

3. From the Category list, choose a category.

4. From the Choose a Function list box, highlight the function you want to use. Look at the Description box for an explanation of the function to be sure you selected the right one.

5. When you find the right function, choose Insert. Works inserts the function, including all of its arguments, in the current cell. The equal symbol is inserted before the function name to make the entry a formula. In the cell, the first argument is highlighted.

6. In the cell, replace each argument with the correct value or cell reference, then press Enter or click the Enter button. Works displays the function result in the current cell.

Tip
If you use functions frequently, consider adding the Function button to the toolbar, which displays the Function dialog box when you click it (see Chapter 2).

If you make an error as you enter a function, Works displays a dialog box alerting you to the error. When you click OK or press Enter, Works highlights the error in the formula bar so you can correct it.

Note

The characters in a cell are so small and thin that some users find it difficult to highlight each formula argument with the mouse before typing a replacement value. When you use the Insert Function dialog box to create a function, the first argument name is highlighted. Enter the value for the first argument, then try pressing Enter twice. The first Enter causes the error message to appear, the second Enter selects the OK button, returning you to the function with the next argument name already selected and ready for you to type a value for the argument. Repeat this process for each argument name until all argument names are replaced with a value.

Using Range Names

A handy feature of Works allows you to assign a *range name* to a cell or range of cells. Using a range name, you can identify cells by a name you recognize rather than a cell reference like C14:F18 or K37. Suppose you enter raw data similar to the spreadsheet shown in figure 11.8. You might consider naming cells B7:B9 "Q1 Income" and cells B13:B16 "Q1 Expenses." Or you might name cells B10:E10 "Total Income" and cells B17:E17 "Total Expenses."

There are a number of advantages to naming ranges instead of using cell references.

- A typographical error in a cell address will cause the formula result to be incorrect. If you make a mistake when typing a range name, an error message is displayed.
- A formula that subtracts "expenses" from "income" is easier to read and understand than =D7-D25. It also clarifies to others who might use the spreadsheet exactly what the formula does.
- When you insert or delete rows and columns, Works adjusts range name addresses to reflect the new location. You can continue to enter the range names without having to check where the data is now located.
- After you name a range of cells, you can quickly find and highlight a named range using the Go To (F5) command.

Fig. 11.8
A number of ranges in this example can be named to simplify creating formulas.

	A	B	C	D	E	F
1	Town and Country Interiors					
2	1995 Income Statement					
3						
4		Quarter 1	Quarter 2	Quarter 3	Quarter 4	Total
5	INCOME					
6	Retail Store	$13,987	$15,090	$19,567		$48,644
7	Prevate Clients	$33,546	$32,198	$27,908		$93,652
8	Mail Order	$5,432	$5,112	$6,298		$16,842
9	Total Income	$52,965	$52,400	$53,773	$0	$159,138
10						
11	EXPENSES					
12	Rent	$5,000	$5,000	$5,000		$15,000
13	Labor	$7,310	$6,220	$7,900		$21,430
14	Insurance	$1,500	$1,500	$1,500		$4,500
15	Cost of Goods	$21,186	$20,960	$21,509		$63,655
16	Total Expenses	$34,996	$33,680	$35,909	$0	$104,585
17						
18					NET INCOME	$54,553

Q1 income — Total income — Total expenses — Q1 expenses

Creating, Editing, and Deleting Range Names

You can assign a name to a single cell or any range of cells in a worksheet. Range names can be up to 15 characters and can include any combination of letters, numbers, spaces, and other symbols like *, #, and +. You can use any combination of upper- and lowercase letters.

> **Caution**
>
> Plan carefully before using symbols in range names. If you use arithmetic operators like +, -, *, and / in a range name. For example, say you name a range *Income-Expenses*, and also have ranges named *Income* and *Expenses* in the same spreadsheet. In this case, entering the formula =Income-Expenses causes the contents of the range named *Income-Expenses* to be displayed rather than the results of the subtraction operation (subtracting the cell contents of the *Expenses* range from the cell contents of the *Income* range) as you may have intended.

To assign a range name to a cell or range of cells, choose Insert, Range Name to display the Range Name dialog box (see fig. 11.9). In the dialog box, all existing range names are shown in the Select a Name list box along with their respective cell ranges.

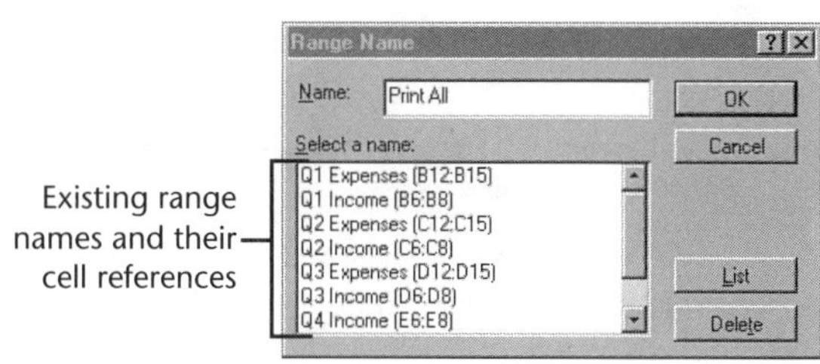

Fig. 11.9
Use the Range Name dialog box to list all existing names and create new ones.

To name a cell range, follow these steps:

1. Select the cell or cell range you want to name.
2. Choose Insert, Range Name. The Range Name dialog box in figure 11.9 appears.
3. In the Name box, enter a name for the selected cell or range.
4. Choose OK. Works adds the new name to the Select a Name list and closes the dialog box.

   When you change a spreadsheet by inserting or deleting rows and columns, Works automatically adjusts range name cell references. In these cases, you don't need to adjust the cell references in a named range. But suppose you selected the wrong cells when you created the range, or suppose you decide to add more cells to an existing range. You can change the cell reference for a named range by following these steps:

Tip
Be careful deleting a range name because you can't use Edit, Undo to restore a deleted name.

When you change a spreadsheet by inserting or deleting rows or columns or moving a named range, Works adjusts range name cell references for you. But suppose you selected the wrong cells when you created the range or you decide to add more cells to an existing range. You can change the cell reference for a named range by following these steps:

1. Select the new cell or cell range you want to use for an existing named range. Or, to edit a range name, select the cell or cell range for the existing named range.
2. Choose Insert, Range Name. The Range Name dialog box in figure 11.9 appears.
3. In the Select a Name list box, highlight the named range for which you want to change the cell reference or range name.
4. To change the range name, edit the name, and choose OK. Works creates a named range with the cell reference or name you specified.

Tip
If you use range names frequently, you can customize your toolbar by adding the Range Name button, which displays the Range Name dialog box when you click it (see Chapter 2).

When you change a range name, the original named range remains in effect. If you make extensive changes in a spreadsheet, you might find that you no longer need some of the named ranges you created. Working with range names will be easier if you delete names from the Range Name dialog box you no longer need. You can delete a range name at any time by opening the Range Name dialog box, highlighting the range to delete in the Select a name list, and choosing the Delete button.

Listing Range Names

After you recognize the value of range names, you will find yourself creating a large number of them in some spreadsheets. When a spreadsheet contains many range names, often it's helpful to include them as a list somewhere in a blank area of your spreadsheet. Use the list to help you avoid creating duplicate range names and to remember what cells are already named. Later, you can print that area of the spreadsheet and have a permanent record of the range names and their respective cell references.

To create a list of range names, first choose a blank area of the spreadsheet where the list will fit without overwriting other data in the spreadsheet. (If the area you choose contains data, Works *will* overwrite it, although a warning that this will happen always displays.) Place the cell selector in the cell where you want the list to begin, then display the Range Name dialog box. In the dialog box, click the List button. Works inserts a two-column list like the one in figure 11.10.

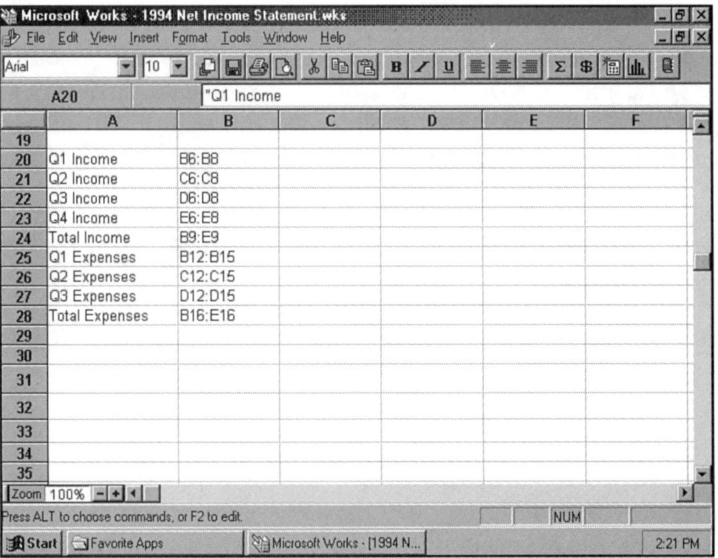

Fig. 11.10
Use the List button in the Range Name dialog box to paste a list of range names into your spreadsheet.

Using Range Names in Formulas

Using range names in a formula can make the formula easier to create as well as interpret. The formula =SUM(Q1 Expenses) is much more descriptive than the formula =SUM(B7:B9). You use range names in a formula just like you use a constant value or a cell reference. In other words, you can combine range names in a formula with other range names, cell references, operators, and constants. Figure 11.11 illustrates the formulas that were used to complete the totals in the income statement spreadsheet. In cell B17, the formula is =SUM(Q1 Expenses). Net income figures in cells B19:D19 were calculated using the formula =Total Income-Total Expenses.

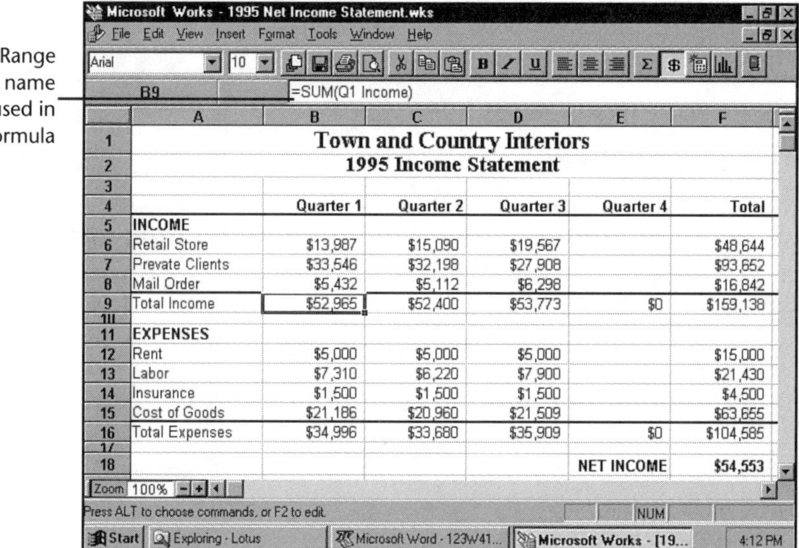

	A	B	C	D	E	F
1	Town and Country Interiors					
2	1995 Income Statement					
3						
4		Quarter 1	Quarter 2	Quarter 3	Quarter 4	Total
5	INCOME					
6	Retail Store	$13,987	$15,090	$19,567		$48,644
7	Prevate Clients	$33,546	$32,198	$27,908		$93,652
8	Mail Order	$5,432	$5,112	$6,298		$16,842
9	Total Income	$52,965	$52,400	$53,773	$0	$159,138
10						
11	EXPENSES					
12	Rent	$5,000	$5,000	$5,000		$15,000
13	Labor	$7,310	$6,220	$7,900		$21,430
14	Insurance	$1,500	$1,500	$1,500		$4,500
15	Cost of Goods	$21,186	$20,960	$21,509		$63,655
16	Total Expenses	$34,996	$33,680	$35,909	$0	$104,585
17						
18					NET INCOME	$54,553

Fig. 11.11
Formulas that use range names are easier to interpret.

Using Range Names with the Go To Command

In Chapter 10, you learn to use the Edit, Go To (F5) command to move the cell selector to a cell or cell range. You also can use the Go To command to highlight a named range in a spreadsheet. When you create range names, the names appear in the Go To dialog box as well as the Range Name dialog box. To highlight a named range, choose Edit, Go To or press F5, and then highlight the range name you want to go to and click OK. Works selects the named range you select.

Tip
If you need to print several separate areas of a worksheet, consider naming each one. You need only use Go To to highlight the range you want to print, then select Set Print Area. After printing that data, repeat beginning with Go To for the next area you want to print.

Note

One powerful use for range names is to name a cell that contains a constant, such as the current social security rate or the interest your bank charges on your line of credit. When you use these range names in a formula and then want to copy the formula, be sure you make the range name absolute by typing a dollar sign in front of the range name.

Troubleshooting

What happens to a formula that uses a range name if I delete the name?

The formula still calculates correctly. Works replaces the range name in the formula with the actual cell reference that was used by the name.

I accidentally overwrote some data in my spreadsheet when I created a list of range names. Is there any way to restore my data?

The Undo command isn't available after you insert a list of range names in a spreadsheet. If you overwrote data with the range name list, the only way to restore the data is to close the file without saving changes, but you lose all changes that were made since you last saved the file.

Chapter 12

Enhancing the Appearance of a Spreadsheet

by Judy Petersen

In Chapter 6, "Enhancing the Appearance of a Document," you learn that enhancing a document makes it more visually appealing and easier to read and comprehend. The same is true of spreadsheets. In fact, a spreadsheet that is not enhanced can easily look like an incomprehensible sea of numbers. Using different fonts, sizes, borders, patterns, and colors to format and define a spreadsheet makes the sea much easier to navigate. This chapter discusses the variety of ways you can make a spreadsheet more attractive and readable.

In this chapter, you learn how to

- Apply a number format to numeric entries
- Align cell entries
- Choose a font, size, color, and style
- Adjust row heights
- Enhance cells with borders and patterns
- Use headers and footers in a spreadsheet
- Use AutoFormat to format spreadsheets

Applying a Number Format to Selected Cells

When you enter a number in a spreadsheet, Works automatically right-aligns the number in the cell. Works makes no assumptions about what the number represents, and therefore applies no other notations, such as dollar signs, commas, percent symbols, and so on. When you choose to apply a particular combination of these and other notations to a cell entry, or use the default way Works displays numbers, that combination is called a *number format*. For example, if you choose the Currency format for a cell, Works adds a dollar sign, thousands separator, and the number of decimal places you specify to the cell's contents. Works applies the default General format when you haven't specified another format for a cell. The General format right-aligns numbers and left-aligns text but applies no notations.

You apply a format to a cell or cell range by choosing the Number command on the Format menu, which displays the Number tab of the Format Cells dialog box (see fig. 12.1). Available formats are displayed in the Format list box. Most number formats offer display options, such as the number of decimal places to display, or a style, such as the way the day, month, and year appear in a date format. Formats and options are described in table 12.1.

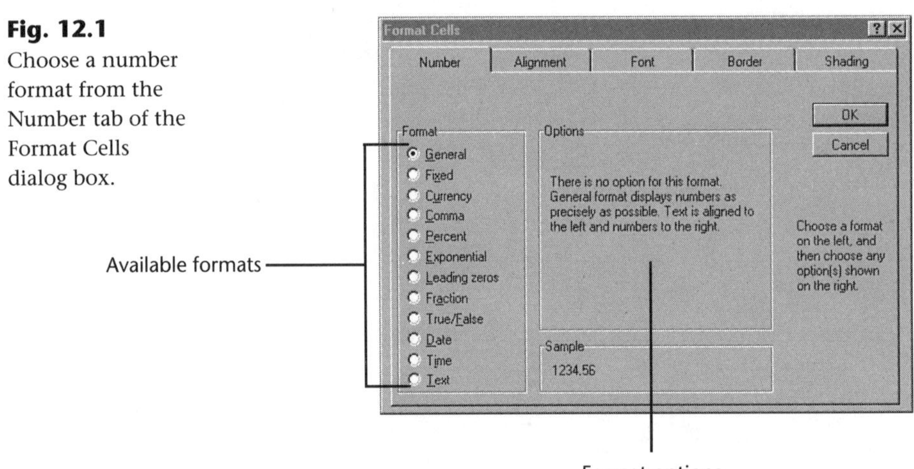

Fig. 12.1
Choose a number format from the Number tab of the Format Cells dialog box.

Table 12.1 Number Formats

Format	Effect
General	Text is left-aligned and numbers are right-aligned. Uses scientific notation when a number is too long to be displayed in a cell. General is the Works default format. Fixed rounds the display of numbers to the number of decimal places you specify. If you specify two places, for example, 34.2391 is displayed as 34.24. Negative numbers are preceded by a minus (–) symbol.
Currency	Numbers are preceded by a dollar symbol ($); large numbers use commas as thousands separators. Use this setting to choose the number of decimal places and to display negative numbers in red.
Comma	Inserts commas as thousands separators. Negative numbers appear in parentheses rather than with a minus (–) symbol. As an option, use this setting to display negative numbers in red.
Percent	Follows a number with a percent symbol (%). Automatically moves decimal points two places to the right. If you enter .081, Works displays 8.1%. You specify the number of decimal places to use.
Exponential	Displays numbers using scientific notation. If you enter 7898.23, Works displays 7.90E+03. You specify the number of decimal places to use.
Leading zeros	Displays the number you enter with leading zeros, for example, 03/04/95 rather than 3/5/95. You specify the number of digits (up to 8) to display. Use this format when you want to display leading zeros of zip codes, invoice numbers, part numbers, and so on.
Fraction	Displays numbers as fractions, rounded to the fraction you specify (1/2, 1/3, 1/8, 1/10, 1/16, 1/32, 1/100), or you can choose to display all fractions. If you enter 2.781 and choose the 1/4 setting, works displays 2 3/4.
True/False	Displays numbers as logical values, either TRUE or FALSE. All zeros that appear are displayed as FALSE. All non-zero numbers are displayed as TRUE.
Date	Displays entries in the date format you specify. Choose from three numeric formats, such as 3/20/95, or four text formats, such as March 20, 1995.

(continues)

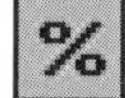

Tip

Another way to access the Format Cells dialog box is to right-click a cell (or selected cells) and choose Format from the shortcut menu that appears.

Tip
If you work with number formats frequently, you can add Percent and Comma buttons to the toolbar to format numbers quickly. To customize the toolbar, refer to Chapter 2, "Getting Started with Works for Windows."

Table 12.1 Continued

Format	Effect
Time	Displays entries in the time format you specify. Choose between 12- and 24-hour formats and whether to include seconds in the display.
Text	Formats the entry as text rather than as a number. This format is useful when you want to sort entries such as phone numbers and postal codes.

When you specify a number of decimal places for the display of a number, only the display is affected. Works stores any additional numbers you enter to the right of the decimal or that result from a calculation. The actual cell contents, rather than digits displayed, are used for further calculations. To display a result with more precision, increase the number of decimal places in the numeric format.

You can apply a number format to cells that already contain data, or to cells before you enter data. Select the range of cells to format, then choose Format, Number. Choose a format from the Format box, then specify options for the format, if applicable. When all settings are correct, choose OK.

A Currency button is included on the standard toolbar. When you click this button, Works formats the selected cells with dollar signs, commas (if applicable), and two decimal places. If you don't want two decimal places, use the Number tab in the Format Cells dialog box to specify the number of decimal places for the Currency option.

Aligning Entries within Cells

As you learned earlier in this chapter, Works automatically applies the General format to all entries you make in a spreadsheet. The General format causes text to be left-aligned and numbers to be right-aligned in a cell. Often, you may want to change the alignment of entries to improve the overall appearance of a spreadsheet or make data easier to read. For example, spreadsheet titles look best when centered across the columns containing data, and column labels are usually centered or right-aligned above columns of data.

In a spreadsheet, you can change the horizontal and vertical alignment of cell entries. If text does not fit in a cell, you can choose to wrap it. When you choose to wrap text, Works adds enough additional lines to the cell to move the extra text to the extra lines.

Setting Horizontal Alignment of Entries

To align entries horizontally, you can left-align, right-align, or center an entry in a cell; fill a cell; or center an entry across a selection of columns. These options are available in the Alignment tab of the Format Cells dialog box and appear when you choose Format, Alignment (see fig. 12.2).

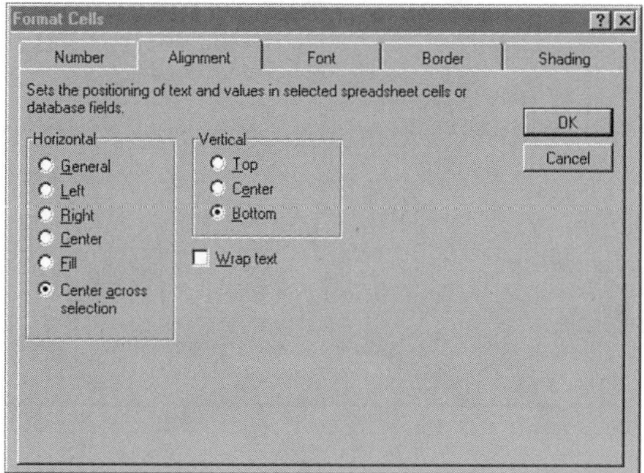

Fig. 12.2
Choose an alignment style from the Format Cells dialog box.

When you choose the Left option, both text and numeric entries are left-aligned. When you choose Right, text and numbers are right-aligned. The Center option centers an entry within the width of a cell. If the entry is too long to display within the borders of the cell, a text entry "spills over" into the cells immediately to the left and right of the current cell, provided those cells are empty. If the cells to the left and right contain data, the centered entry appears cut off on both the right and left edges of the cell. You can view the entire entry by selecting the cell and then checking the formula bar.

The Fill option duplicates the cell entry as many times as possible until the cell is filled. For instance, if you type **#** in a cell and use the Fill option, Works fills the cell with # characters. If you type **ABC** in a cell formatted with the Fill option, Works displays ABCABC in the cell until the cell is filled.

When you choose the Center Across Selection option, illustrated in figure 12.3, Works centers an entry across the range of cells you select. Use this option to center a spreadsheet title across the columns contained in a spreadsheet. If cell A2 contains the title "1996 Sales Forecast" and you select cells A2:G2, Works centers the title between the left boundary of cell A2 and the right boundary of cell G2.

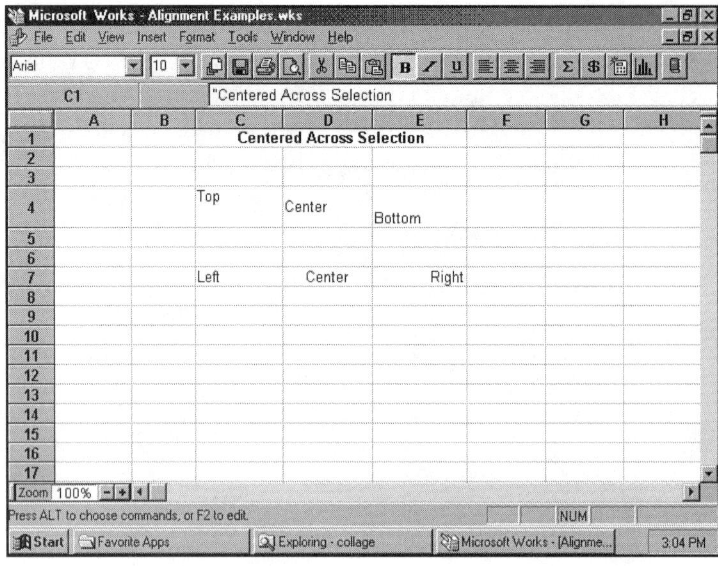

Fig. 12.3 Examples of horizontal and vertical alignment within a cell. Above the examples is a title that is centered across the three columns of data.

To change the horizontal alignment of entries in a cell or cell range, follow these steps:

1. Select the cell or cell range for which you want to align entries.
2. Choose Format, Alignment. The Alignment tab of the Format Cells dialog box shown in figure 12.2 appears.
3. In the Horizontal box, choose an alignment style.
4. Choose OK.

Left, center, and right alignment buttons are available on the spreadsheet toolbar. To use these buttons rather than the Format Cells dialog box, select the cell or cells for which you want to change the alignment, and then click the appropriate toolbar button. If you choose to customize the toolbar, you can add the Center Across Selection button to the toolbar. (Refer to Chapter 2, "Getting Started with Works for Windows," for information on customizing the toolbar.)

Setting Vertical Alignment of Entries

All spreadsheet cells have height as well as width. When you enter data into cells, Works automatically aligns entries along the bottom edge of a cell. This is generally where you want an entry to be aligned because the default row height is appropriate for the height of the current font. However, in some cases, particularly when you are using a large row height or a special font, you may want an entry to be vertically aligned along the top of a cell or through the horizontal center of a cell. Examples of each style are shown in figure 12.3. To change the vertical alignment of an entry, choose Format, Alignment, and then choose the Top, Center, or Bottom option in the Vertical section of the Alignment tab of the Format Cells dialog box.

Wrapping Text within a Cell

When a cell contains a text entry that's too long to display completely, you can increase the column width to display the entire entry. Often, however, increasing column width isn't a practical solution because the spreadsheet becomes too wide. A more practical solution is to wrap text within the cell, which increases the row height but allows you to maintain a cell's column width. Wrapping text within a cell is commonly used for column headings (see fig. 12.4).

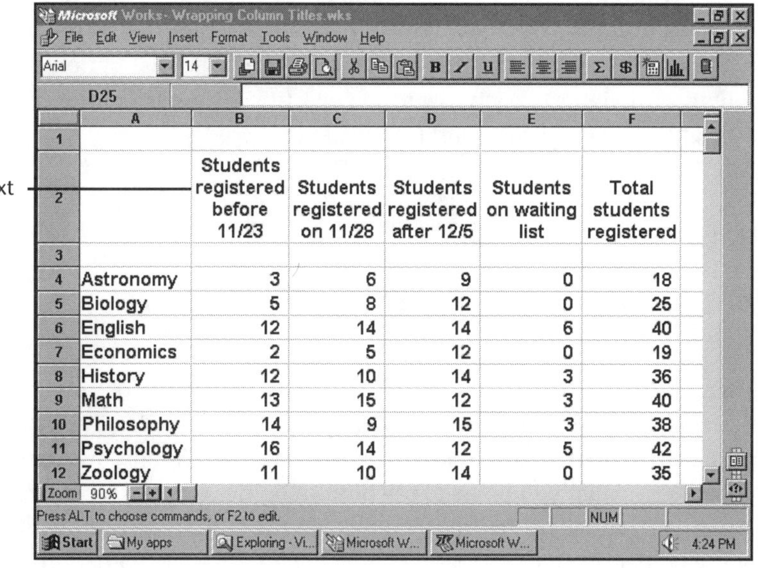

	A	B	C	D	E	F
1						
2		Students registered before 11/23	Students registered on 11/28	Students registered after 12/5	Students on waiting list	Total students registered
3						
4	Astronomy	3	6	9	0	18
5	Biology	5	8	12	0	25
6	English	12	14	14	6	40
7	Economics	2	5	12	0	19
8	History	12	10	14	3	36
9	Math	13	15	12	3	40
10	Philosophy	14	9	15	3	38
11	Psychology	16	14	12	5	42
12	Zoology	11	10	14	0	35

Fig. 12.4
Wrapped column headings allow reasonable column widths in a spreadsheet.

To wrap text within a cell or cell range, select the cells and then choose Format, Alignment. In the Alignment tab, choose the Wrap Text check box and then click OK. Works automatically wraps existing text within the cell and adjusts row height as appropriate.

Adjusting Row Height

When you open a new spreadsheet file, Works uses the standard row height, which adjusts the height of each row automatically to accommodate the font and point size you choose. The row height throughout a spreadsheet is initially set at 12 points. Because the default font and size for spreadsheets is Arial 10, a row height of 12 adequately accommodates all new entries you type. If you change the font or point size, Works automatically adjusts the row height for the font and size you choose. For example, if you change the font throughout your spreadsheet to Times New Roman 12, Works automatically sets the row height throughout the sheet to 15. (The three extra points allow for spacing.) If you enter a title on row 1 in Arial 16, Works adjusts the row height of row 1 to 20 points.

You can specify an exact row height by selecting the row or rows you want to adjust and then choosing the Row Height command from the Format menu. The Format Row Height dialog box in figure 12.5 appears. In the Row Height text box, type a number in points. If you choose the Best Fit button, Works automatically adjusts the row height for the largest font used in the row. If you select multiple rows that use different fonts, the Best Fit option assigns different row heights to each row in the selection. To return to the default row height, choose the Standard button.

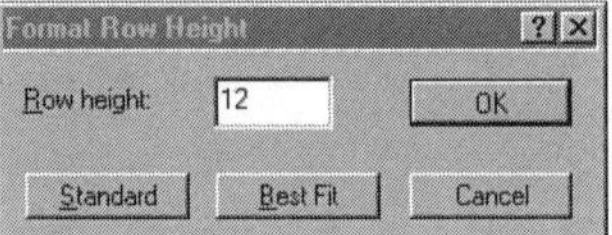

Fig. 12.5
Use the Format Row Height dialog box to specify an exact row height or best fit.

In Chapter 10, "Creating, Saving, and Printing a Spreadsheet," you learn that you can adjust column width by dragging the column border. The same is true for rows. The standard mouse pointer changes to an up/down arrow labeled ADJUST when you point to the bottom border of a row label (see fig. 12.6). When you see this pointer, hold down the left mouse button and then drag the border down to increase the row height; drag the border up to decrease row height. Release the mouse button when the row is the height you want.

◀ See "Adjusting Column Width," p. 197

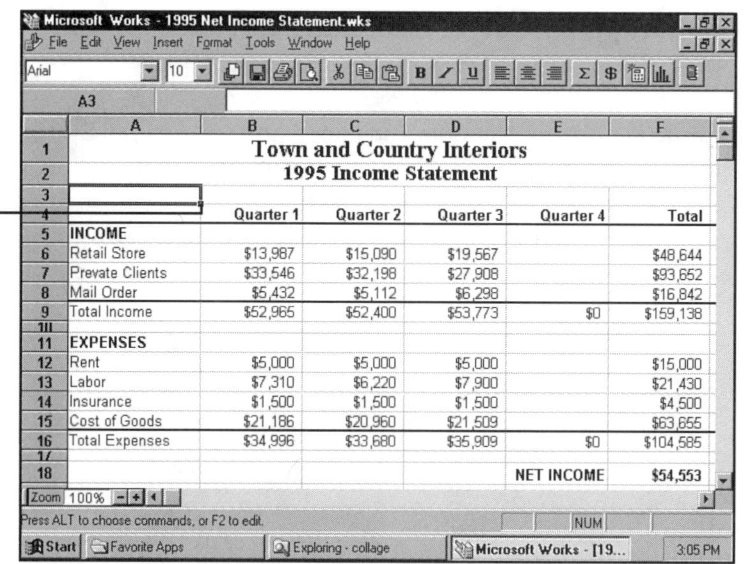

Fig. 12.6
Drag the bottom border of a row to adjust row height.

Troubleshooting

I typed my spreadsheet title in cell C3, then centered it across columns A through G, but the title isn't centered. What's wrong?

To accurately center an entry across a selection of cells, you must type the entry in the first cell in the range across which you want to center the entry. In this example, if you want to center the title across columns A through G, type your title in cell A3, not C3. When the title appears in cell C3, Works ignores columns A and B when centering because your entry doesn't appear there.

I typed a spreadsheet title in cell A3 and centered it across columns A through F, but the title is still not centered correctly. What's wrong?

Check to see that the title doesn't include any unnecessary spaces before or after the text. Adding spaces to an entry will throw off center alignment across selected cells.

When I wrap text within a cell, Works breaks text in the middle of a word. How do I avoid this error?

Whenever you use the Wrap Text option, you still need to adjust column width to format the text correctly. To prevent Works from breaking text in the middle of a word, make the column as wide as the longest word in the cell. Notice in figure 12.4, the width of columns B through F was adjusted to fit the longest word, *registered*, in each entry.

Choosing a Character Font, Size, Color, and Style

To emphasize data, draw attention, and make a spreadsheet more visually appealing, you can choose a font, size, color, and style for selected cells or all cells. To apply these characteristics, you can use any of three methods: menu commands, buttons on the toolbar, or keyboard shortcuts. When using menu commands, choose Format, Font and Style. Use the Font tab of the Format Cells dialog box, shown in figure 12.7.

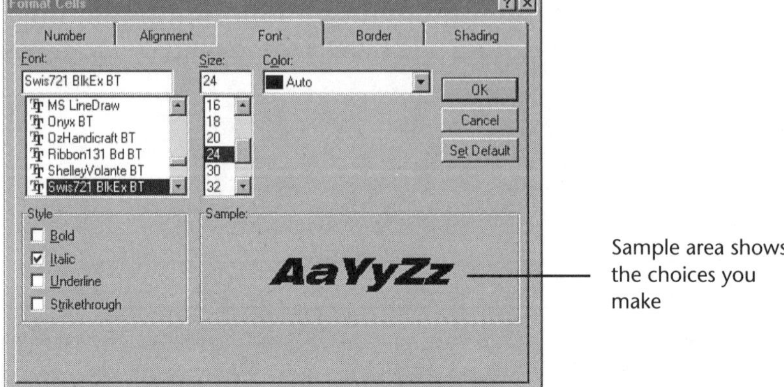

Fig. 12.7
In the font tab of the Format Cells dialog box, you can choose a different font, change the size, choose a style, and even select other colors.

In the dialog box shown in figure 12.7, you see settings for the font, size, color, and style. These attributes are described in this list:

- *Font*. A font refers to a specific typeface or design for a set of characters that Works displays on-screen and prints on paper. Each font has a particular thickness, ornamentation, or other characteristics that distinguish it from other fonts. **For example, this sentence appears in the Impact font.**
- *Size*. Most fonts are available in different sizes and are generally measured in *points*. (A point is equal to 1/72 of an inch.) The most common point sizes for use in the body of a spreadsheet are 10 or 12. Other elements in a spreadsheet, such as titles or row and column labels, often appear in larger sizes, such as 14, 16, 18, or 24 points.
- *Color*. If you have a color monitor, you can display selected cells in a variety of colors. If you have a color printer, you also can print the colors that you display in your spreadsheet.

- *Style*. In Works, a text style refers to bold, italic, underline, or strikethrough. Bold, Italic, and Underline are the most common styles used to emphasize entries. Strikethrough prints a line through an entry, indicating that the entry is proposed for deletion, but the entry itself is still readable.

In the Font tab of the Format Cells dialog box, font, size, and color choices are available from list boxes. Text styles (bold, italic, underline, and strikethrough) are represented by check boxes because you can choose more than one style simultaneously. As you make font, size, color, and style choices, the Sample area of the dialog box displays the choices you make. The Sample area is especially helpful for viewing the unique design of a particular font and the relative size of characters.

To apply a character style to cells that contain data or to empty cells, follow these steps:

1. Select the cells to which you want to apply a character style.
2. Choose Format, Font and Style. The Font tab of the Format Cells dialog box in figure 12.7 appears.
3. Select one option from each of the Font, Size, and Color lists.
4. From the Style box, choose as many styles as you want to apply to the selected cells.
5. When the text shown in the Sample area appears as you want, choose OK. Works automatically reformats the selected cells.

Tip
Another way to display the dialog box is to right-click the selected cell (or cells) and choose Format from the shortcut menu that appears. Then, click the Font tab.

If you prefer to use the toolbar to apply a character style, buttons are available for font and size, as well as for bold, italic, and underline (see fig. 12.8).

The font and size buttons on the toolbar contain drop-down list boxes from which you select a font and point size. To change a font or size, select the cells you want to change and then select an item from each drop-down list. To add bold, italic, or underline to cell entries, select the cells first, then click the appropriate toolbar button.

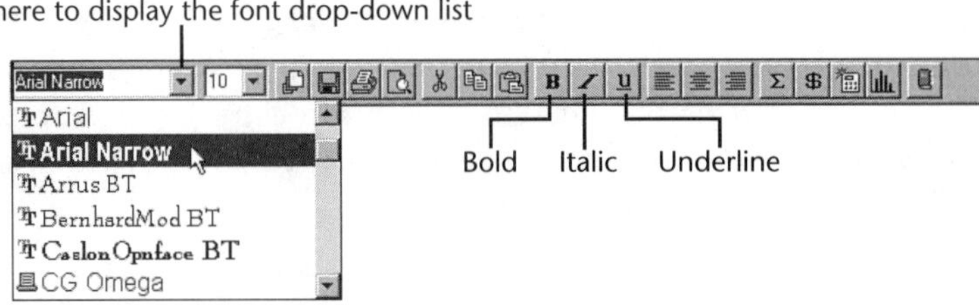

Fig. 12.8 Choose a character style from the spreadsheet toolbar.

Tip You can customize your spreadsheet toolbar to add a button for the strikethrough style. Refer to Chapter 2, "Getting Started with Works for Windows."

Works provides keyboard shortcuts for the character styles shown in table 12.2. To use a keyboard shortcut, select the cells you want to format and then press the appropriate key sequence.

Table 12.2 Keyboard Shortcuts for Character Styles

Key Sequence	Character Style
Ctrl+B	Bold
Ctrl+U	Underline
Ctrl+I	Italic
Ctrl+space bar	Plain text (remove all character styles)

Tip To quickly check the format of a cell, select the cell and then check the toolbar to see the name of the font and the point size—and whether any style or alignment buttons are selected.

Note

The toolbar and keyboard shortcuts for character styles are helpful, but if you want to change the *color* of text, you still must use the Font tab of the Format Cells dialog box shown in figure 12.7 because no toolbar buttons or keyboard shortcuts are available for color.

Attributes that you add to text (such as bold, italic, underline, and strikethrough) toggle on and off, whether you choose the setting using the Font tab in the Format Cells dialog box, the toolbar, or a keyboard shortcut. To remove any of these character styles individually, select the affected cells and then select the dialog box option, the toolbar button, or the keyboard shortcut again to remove the attribute.

When cells contain several attributes and you want to remove *all* the attributes, the quickest way is to select the text and then press Ctrl+space bar. This keyboard shortcut changes all selected cells back to plain text and saves you the trouble of removing each attribute individually. If you have changed the font used in the selected cells, Works restores the default Arial 10 font.

Adding Borders and Patterns to Cells

In a spreadsheet, you often want to draw attention to a particular cell or cells. In an income statement, for example, you might want to highlight the Net Income/Net Loss row so the reader can instantly focus on "the bottom line." One way to make a cell or cell range stand out is to place a border around it. With Works, you can border cells using a variety of line styles and add a color if you like.

Tip
Another way to display the Border tab of the Format Cells dialog box is to right-click the selected cell (or cells) and choose Format from the shortcut menu that appears. Then click the Border tab.

The term *border* is somewhat misleading because it implies that a line completely surrounds a cell. This type of border is called an *outline border*. But in Works, you also can create *partial borders* that fall on the top, bottom, left, or right sides of a cell, or you can use any combination of the four.

To add a border and define its style and color, you use the Border tab of the Format Cells dialog box, which appears when you choose Format, Border (see fig. 12.9). To create an outline border, choose Outline. To create a partial border, choose any combination of the Top, Bottom, Left, and Right options. In the Line Style box, choose a style. To add color to the style you choose, select a color from the Color list box. Note that unless you have a color printer, the color is visible only on-screen.

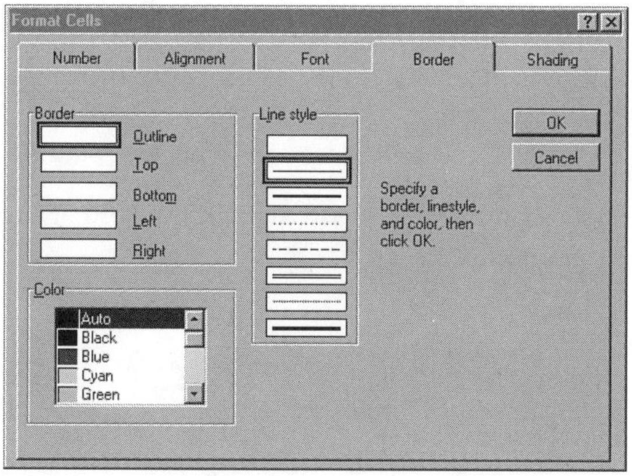

Fig. 12.9
Use the border tab of the Format Cells dialog box to choose a border, style, and color.

To add a border to spreadsheet cells, follow these steps:

1. Select the cell or cell range you want to border.
2. Choose Format, Border. The Format Cells dialog box appears with the Border tab displayed (refer to fig. 12.9).
3. Choose the Outline option to create an outline border. Or choose any of the Top, Bottom, Left, and Right options to create a partial border.

4. Select a style from the Line Style box.
5. Select a color from the Color list box.
6. Repeat steps 3 through 5 to add a border to more than one side of the cell if you want a different line style or color for other sides of the cell.

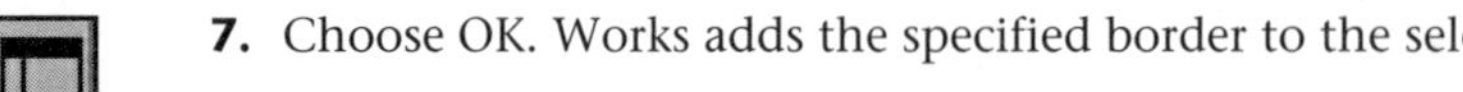

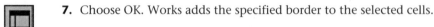

7. Choose OK. Works adds the specified border to the selected cells.

To remove a border, use the preceding steps but select the blank line style box to clear all borders from the Outline, Top, Bottom, Left, and Right options.

Tip
If you work with borders frequently, you can customize your toolbar by adding the Border button, which displays the Border tab of the Format Cells dialog box when you click it. For instructions on customizing the toolbar, refer to Chapter 2, "Getting Started with Works for Windows."

Another way to make cells stand out is to add a pattern. A *pattern* shades the background of a cell, leaving the entry in the cell readable. You can add a pattern to individual cells or to a range of cells by choosing a pattern style, a foreground color, and a background color from the Shading tab of the Format Cells dialog box (see fig. 12.10). Open this box by choosing Format, Shading. If you choose a solid pattern, the selected cells display only the foreground color. You can choose a foreground color and a background for both shading and patterns. If you choose a shading, you can create interesting color blends. The Sample area shows an example of the pattern and colors you choose.

Use the following steps to add a pattern to a cell or cell range. As you make choices in the dialog box, be sure to check the Sample area, which illustrates the choices you make:

1. Select the cell or cells to which you want to apply a pattern.
2. Choose Format, Shading. The Shading tab of the Format Cells dialog box appears (refer to fig. 12.10).

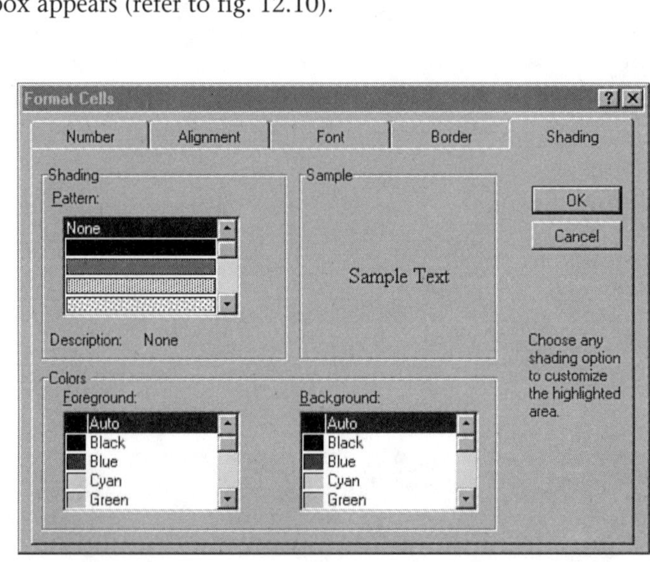

Fig. 12.10
Choose cell pattern and colors in the Shading tab of the Format Cells dialog box.

3. In the Pattern list box, select a pattern style.

4. In the Foreground list box, select a color for the pattern foreground.

5. In the Background list box, select a color for the pattern background.

6. When you create a pattern you like, choose OK.

Note

Remember that you can only print the colors you apply if you have a color printer. However, many printers effectively print shades of gray. Experiment with color selections and your printer to find printed output that works with your data.

Consider changing the color of the font to create an effective contrast with the shading or pattern you choose. The report shown in figure 12.11 illustrates an interesting combination of shading, border, and font color choices. The double-line outline border is applied to the cell range where the titles are displayed, the range is shaded solid black, and the font color is white.

To switch a pattern back to the colors used in your current color scheme, select the affected cells and then choose Format, Shading. In the Foreground and Background list boxes, choose the Auto option. To remove a pattern entirely, select the cell or cell range from which you want to remove a pattern, then display the Shading tab of the Format Cells dialog box and choose None as the option in the Pattern list box. Works removes the pattern from the selected cells.

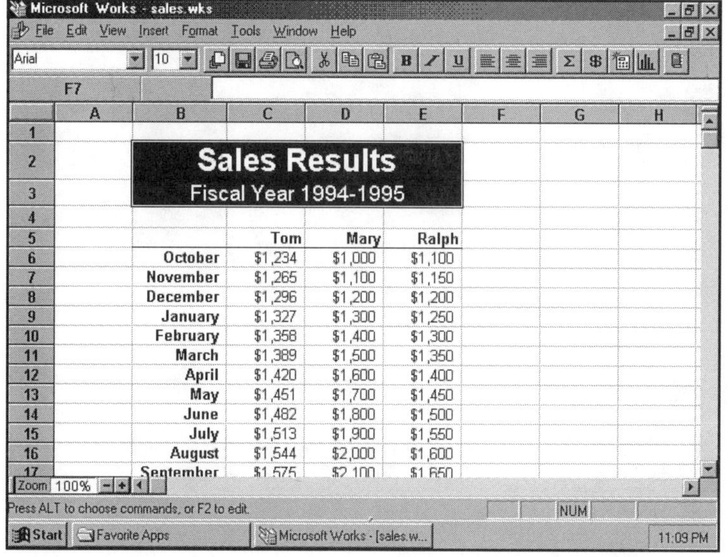

Fig. 12.11
The title of this report uses a solid background with white font and a double-line outline to soften the edges of the background.

Adding Headers and Footers to a Spreadsheet

Before you print a spreadsheet, you may want to add a title, page number, date, or other information at the top or bottom of each page. Repetitive text that appears at the top of each page is called a *header*. Text appearing at the bottom of the page is called a *footer*. You can add a header, footer, or both to any spreadsheet. (You may want to include a reminder such as "Do Not Copy.")

Headers and footers print within the top and bottom margin areas of your spreadsheet. If your spreadsheet is longer than one page and you don't want a header or footer on the first page, you can eliminate them from the first page.

In a spreadsheet, a header or footer cannot be longer than one line of text. You can insert special codes that automatically print the current date, current time, page numbers, file name, and so on, but you cannot change the font or add effects such as bold, underline, or italics.

You enter the text for a header or footer in the Headers and Footers dialog box, displayed when you choose View, Headers and Footers. When you close the dialog box, the header or footer is visible only on the Print Preview screen (see fig. 12.12).

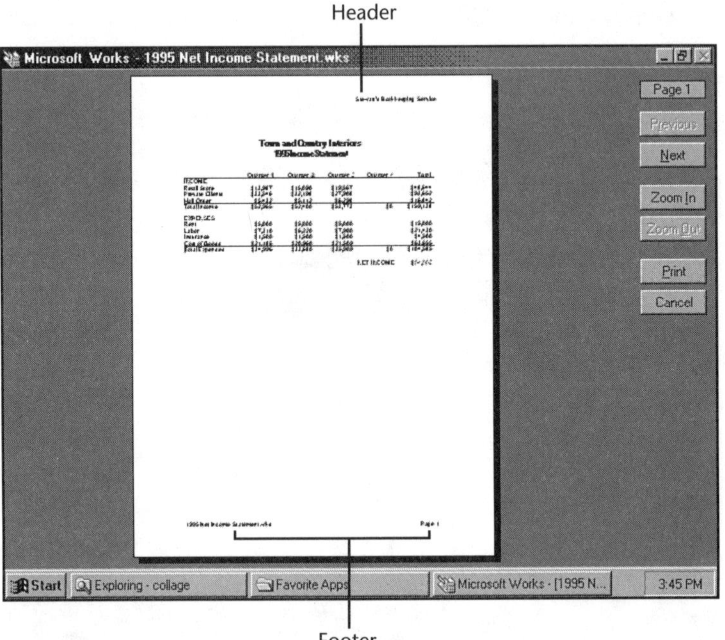

Fig. 12.12 Spreadsheet headers and footers are visible only on the Print Preview screen.

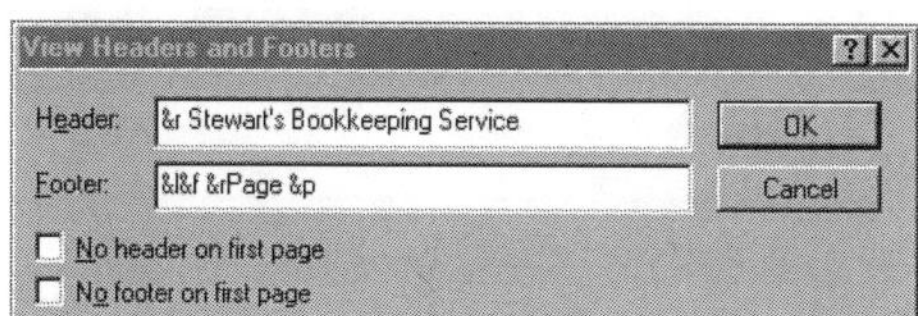

Fig. 12.13
Type the text for a header, footer, or both in the View Headers and Footers dialog box.

To create a header, footer, or both, follow these steps:

1. Choose View, Headers and Footers. The View Headers and Footers dialog box in figure 12.13 appears.
2. In the Header box, type the text you want to use for the header.
3. In the Footer box, type the text you want to use for the footer.
4. To eliminate a header or footer on the first page of your document, choose the No Header on First Page or No Footer on First Page check boxes.
5. Choose OK.

Adding Special Text and Formatting Headers and Footers

Works automatically centers all header and footer text in a spreadsheet. To align the text differently, you insert special codes, as shown in table 12.3, into your entries in the View Headers and Footers dialog box. Some codes align text and other codes insert special text such as a page number, file name, or current date. For codes that align text, you enter the code immediately preceding the text. For example, you can specify that Works right-align your text by entering **&r** immediately preceding the text that you want right-aligned. For codes that insert text, you simply type the code, such as **&f**, which prints the file name in the header or footer. You also can combine codes, where appropriate. If you want Works to insert the file name of the current document and right-align it, type **&r&f**. To make the codes easier to read, you can separate two codes with a space if you like (as in **&r &f**). The codes can be typed with either upper- or lowercase letters.

◄ See "Using Headers and Footers in a Document," p. 149

Table 12.3 Format and Alignment Codes

Code	Function
&l	Left-aligns the text that follows the code
&r	Right-aligns the text that follows the code
&c	Centers the text that follows the code
&f	Prints the file name
&p	Prints page numbers
&t	Inserts the time at the time of printing
&d	Inserts the date at the time of printing (such as 3/2/95)
&n	Inserts the long form date at the time of printing (such as 2 March 95)
&&	Prints an ampersand (&)

Changing and Deleting a Header or Footer

You can change the content of a spreadsheet header or footer, as well as the alignment or any special text you included. To change a header or footer, simply recall the View Headers and Footers dialog box and then make the appropriate changes in the Header and Footer text boxes.

Troubleshooting

*In my header, I entered the codes **&r &f** to right-align the document's file name, but when I printed the document, the header read* `& f` *at the right margin. What happened?*

You typed the *&r* code correctly, but you typed a space between the & and the *f*, so Works interpreted the two characters literally. When inserting codes, you can put a space between separate codes to make them easier to read, but be careful not to put a space within a code itself.

Using AutoFormat

If you're not inclined to bother with formatting a spreadsheet yourself, you can have Works do it for you. Works includes 14 predefined format styles that are available in the AutoFormat dialog box, displayed when you choose

Format, AutoFormat (see fig. 12.14). The Example area shows how the selected style looks. Each format applies a special font, size, and style to text and numbers and adds borders and patterns to make the spreadsheet more attractive. Subtotal and total rows are sometimes formatted in distinctive ways to make these particular numbers stand out.

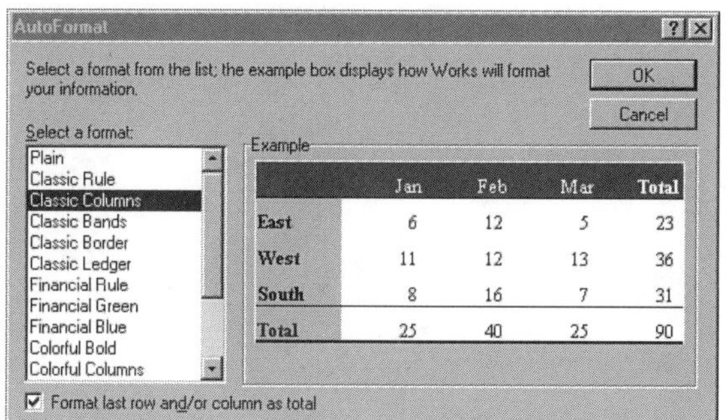

Fig. 12.14
You can choose a spreadsheet format from the AutoFormat dialog box.

To apply an AutoFormat to a spreadsheet, follow these steps:

1. Select the entire range of cells you want to format.

2. Choose Format, AutoFormat. Works displays the AutoFormat dialog box in figure 12.14.

3. In the Select a Format list box, highlight a format style. The Example area illustrates the style you choose.

4. To specify that Works not show totals in the formatted table, choose the Format Last Row and/or Column as Total check box.

5. When you find a format you want to use, choose OK. Works applies the format to the selected cells in the spreadsheet.

Tip
If you use AutoFormat frequently, you can customize your toolbar to add the AutoFormat button, which displays the AutoFormat dialog box when you click it. For instructions on customizing the toolbar, refer to Chapter 2, "Getting Started with Works for Windows."

When you apply an AutoFormat, all formatting of the selected cells changes, so give consideration to the area of the spreadsheet you want to format. Notice in the Example area of the AutoFormat dialog box that all the styles available format the top row as column labels. You probably do not want to include the title of the spreadsheet in the range of cells you select to AutoFormat. Also, only the Financial Blue, Financial Green, and Financial Rule formats include Currency format for numbers. All other styles use General format. To avoid extra work, first apply the AutoFormat you want, then format numbers and add any additional formatting.❖

Chapter 13

Searching, Viewing, and Sorting a Spreadsheet

by Judy Petersen

After you enter all the numbers, text, and formulas in a spreadsheet, you can work with the data in several ways that make your job easier. For instance, when you need to find a specific entry in a spreadsheet—especially a large one—it's easier to have Works search the spreadsheet for you instead of doing it yourself. You also can make it easier to see your work by magnifying or reducing the spreadsheet. When you are ready to print, the output may be easier to understand if you remove the gridlines, or hide columns or rows that contain data you do not want as part of the current printout.

Entering data in large spreadsheets is easier if you freeze row and column headings or split the spreadsheet window. Occasionally, it's useful to see the formulas you are using rather than the calculated results. Another function that is useful in spreadsheets is to sort the information after you enter it. Finally, even though a spreadsheet is mostly numbers, you can still use the spell check feature, just to be sure.

In this chapter, you learn about the following topics:

- Finding and replacing information in a spreadsheet
- Zooming in on an area of your spreadsheet
- Hiding rows or columns in a spreadsheet
- Hiding gridlines
- Freezing row and column headings
- Displaying formulas rather than cell values
- Sorting spreadsheet data

Searching a Spreadsheet

One of the most useful features in the Works spreadsheet component is its capability to search for and replace characters. You can search a spreadsheet to find specific text or a specific value, or to find cells or cell ranges referenced in a formula. You can search for a partial entry or an entire entry. After you find the information you're looking for, you can replace it with new information if you want.

The two commands that enable you to search for and replace text or values are Find and Replace, both located on the Edit menu. The Find command enables you to search for text or a value without replacing it. The Replace command finds the text or value you specify and replaces all occurrences or selected occurrences with a new entry.

Both the Find and Replace commands enable you to specify whether you want Works to search a spreadsheet by rows or by columns. When you choose By Rows, Works searches left to right through the spreadsheet one row at a time. If you think the text or value you're looking for is located near the top of the spreadsheet, choose the By Rows option to find the information quickly. When you choose By Columns, Works searches a spreadsheet from top to bottom one column at a time. If you think the text or value you're looking for is located in the first few columns of the spreadsheet, choosing the By Columns option may help you find the information more quickly.

In both the Find and Replace dialog boxes you also specify whether you want Works to search the values of a spreadsheet or the formulas. When you choose the Values option, Works searches the cells for the text or value you specify. When you choose the Formulas option, Works searches the actual formulas rather than displayed values until it finds the information you are looking for.

Finding Text

Choosing the Find command displays the Find dialog box shown in figure 13.1. Use the Find command to locate any text or value in a spreadsheet without replacing it with new information. For instance, suppose you entered the value 10,532 somewhere in your spreadsheet and you want to find the exact location of that entry. Using the Find dialog box, you can search the values of the spreadsheet to find 10,532. If Works finds the value, it highlights the first cell where the value appears and closes the Find dialog box. If Works doesn't find the value, it displays the message `Works did not find a match`.

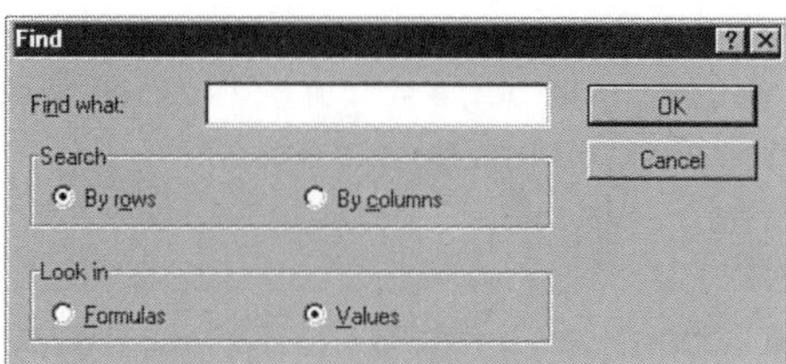

Fig. 13.1
Find any text or value in a spreadsheet's cells or formulas using the Find dialog box.

If you want to find text or a cell reference in a spreadsheet formula, choose the Formulas option in the Find dialog box. For instance, suppose you entered the formula `=Total Income-Total Expenses` somewhere in your spreadsheet and you want to change the cells referenced in that formula. You enter part or all of this formula text in the Find What text box, then choose the Formulas option and click OK. If Works finds the text, it highlights the first cell where the text appears and closes the Find dialog box.

Tip
If you use the Find feature frequently, you can add a Find button to the toolbar.

To find text, a value, or a cell or range reference in a spreadsheet without replacing it, follow these steps:

1. Select the range of cells you want to search (or select no cells to search the entire spreadsheet).
2. Choose Edit, Find. The Find dialog box shown in figure 13.1 appears.
3. In the Find What box, type the text, value, or cell reference you want to search for.
4. In the Search box, choose By Rows or By Columns.
5. In the Look In box, choose Values or Formulas.
6. Choose OK. Works finds the first occurrence in the spreadsheet.

Tip
To quickly display the Find dialog box, press Ctrl+F.

When a number format has been applied to a cell, the resulting display affects the way Find searches. For example, when you enter 12,345 into a cell, Works enters and displays `12345`. You can then format the cell with the comma or currency format to cause a comma to display. When you apply a numeric format, the displayed result is the value and what you originally entered in the cell is the formula. When you search in a spreadsheet and Works fails to find a match, run Find again but use the options in the Look In box to change where to look.

◄ See "Finding Text," p. 165

You can enter only part of the value or formula and find the entry. You can, for example, enter part of a number, a single cell reference used in a formula, or one word of a label that contains several words.

Replacing Text

Choosing the Replace command displays the Replace dialog box shown in figure 13.2. In this dialog box, you specify the text or value you're looking for as well as the replacement text. If Works finds the text or value you specify, it highlights the first occurrence and leaves the Replace dialog box on-screen. You can choose to replace all occurrences of the text you're looking for (using the Replace All button), you can replace occurrences selectively (using the Replace button), or you can skip the occurrence and go on to the next (using the Find Next button).

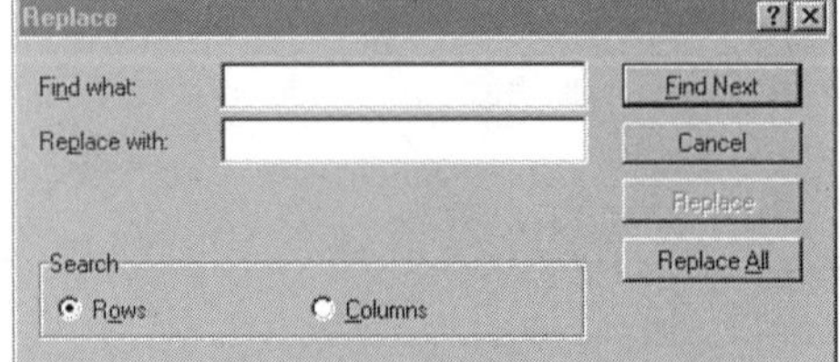

Fig. 13.2
Use the Replace dialog box to specify the text or value to find as well as the replacement text or value.

To replace text or a value in a spreadsheet, follow these steps:

1. Select the range of cells you want to search, or select none to search the entire spreadsheet.
2. Choose Edit, Replace. The Replace dialog box shown in figure 13.2 appears.
3. In the Find What box, type the text, value, or cell reference you want to search for.
4. In the Replace With box, type the replacement information.
5. In the Search box, choose Rows or Columns.
6. Choose the Find Next button. Works finds the first occurrence.

Tip
To quickly display the Replace dialog box, press Ctrl+H.

7. If you want to replace all occurrences in the spreadsheet, click the Replace All button. If you want to replace only the current occurrence, click the Replace button. If you want to find the next occurrence without replacing the current one, click the Find Next button.

8. Repeat step 7 until you are finished searching and replacing.

9. Close the Replace dialog box by choosing the Close button. (The Cancel button changes to Close when Works is finished replacing.)

Caution

The Replace command has the potential for disaster. A simple error in typing what to find or what to replace with can transform your data to gibberish. Review the results of Replace immediately and choose Undo if necessary. Unfortunately, a problem may not show up immediately. The safe way to use Replace is to *always* save the file just before beginning the Replace operation.

◄ See "Replacing Text," p. 167

Using Wild Cards in a Search

When you're uncertain of the exact text or value to search for in a spreadsheet, you can use a wild card to represent any single character. For instance, if you search for *?00*, Works finds *100*, *300*, and *500*. If you enter 1???3, Works finds all five-digit values that begin with 1 and end with 3. Wild cards can be very useful for finding text or values when you're not sure of the spelling or the exact amount of a number. To use the question mark wild card in the Find or Replace dialog box, type a question mark for each unknown character you are searching for in the Find What text box.

◄ See "Using Wild Cards and Special Characters in a Search," p. 168

The asterisk wild card is available to replace more than one character when you search in a spreadsheet. If you search for 1*6, Works finds 146, 1236, 13498756, or any other value that begins with 1 and ends with 6. Similarly, you can search for 12* and Works will find all values that begin with 12. If you enter *12, Works finds values of any length that end with 12. To use the asterisk wild card in the Find or Replace dialog box, type an asterisk for each group of unknown characters you are searching for in the Find What text box.

Troubleshooting

I know I typed the number 10,550 in my spreadsheet, but when I used the Find command to search for it, nothing was found. Why?

There could be several reasons. If you select only a portion of the spreadsheet before you choose the Find command, Works searches only the selection. If the number is located somewhere outside of the selected range of cells, Works cannot find it. Another possibility is that you entered the number incorrectly, in which case Works cannot find it. You might try using one or more wild cards to search for the value, such as 1????0 (which includes a ? for the comma).

I used the range name Total Sales in my spreadsheet, but when I searched for this text, Works didn't find it.

If Works didn't find the range name you entered, you probably specified Values rather than Formulas in the Find dialog box. Remember that range names are used in formulas only, so you must search the formulas of your spreadsheet. Be sure you check the Formulas option in the dialog box. If Works still doesn't find the range name, perhaps you misspelled it. Try finding the name using a wild card.

Viewing a Spreadsheet in Different Ways

Although the standard view of a spreadsheet on-screen is adequate for many of the editing tasks you perform, you may want to change your view of the spreadsheet for some tasks. For instance, you may want to reduce your view of a large spreadsheet so you can see more of the cells on-screen at one time. Or you may want to include sensitive information (such as employees' salaries) in the calculations in a spreadsheet but hide that information from other viewers. In the following sections, you learn these and other techniques for altering your view of a spreadsheet.

Using Zoom

One way to change your view of a spreadsheet is to magnify or reduce what is visible on-screen. This feature is called Zoom and is particularly helpful with a large spreadsheet if you want to display more cells on-screen at one time. When you choose View, Zoom, Works displays the Zoom dialog box shown in figure 13.3. The dialog box contains five preset magnification and reduction levels: 400%, 200%, 100%, 75%, and 50%. You also can use the Custom text box to specify a custom magnification level by entering any number from 25 to 1,000.

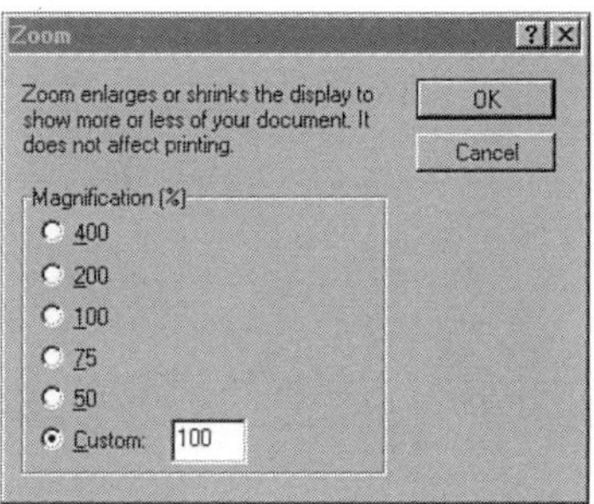

Fig. 13.3
Use the Zoom dialog box to magnify or reduce the size of your spreadsheet.

Use the following steps to use the Zoom feature on a spreadsheet:

1. Choose View, Zoom. Works displays the Zoom dialog box (refer to fig. 13.3).
2. Choose a magnification level or enter a number from 25 to 1,000 in the Custom text box.
3. Choose OK. Works displays the current spreadsheet at the magnification level you choose.

To return to normal magnification, use the preceding steps, choosing the 100% option. An example of a reduced spreadsheet is shown in figure 13.4. You can change the zoom amount by right-clicking the Zoom box in the lower-left corner of the screen. From the context menu that appears, click one of the zoom amounts. You can also use the + and – buttons to the right of the Zoom box to change the zoom amount. The Zoom split boxes are described in the next section.

◄ See "Using Zoom," p. 40

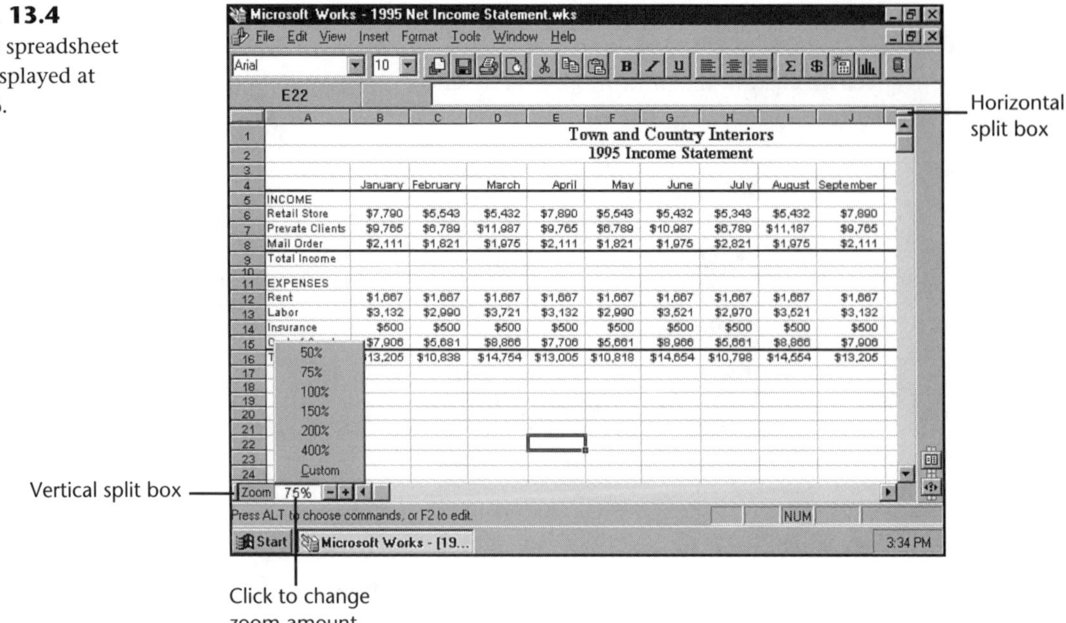

Fig. 13.4
This spreadsheet is displayed at 75%.

Splitting the Screen

As a spreadsheet grows in size when more and more information is added to it, you can split the spreadsheet window into panes to see two areas of the spreadsheet at the same time. This feature can be useful when you want to enter information in one part of the spreadsheet that is based on information in another part of the spreadsheet. Each pane includes a scroll bar so you can move to different parts of the spreadsheet in each pane.

> **Note**
>
> To make copying data from one document to another document easier, you can display both documents. For instructions on working with multiple document windows, refer to Chapter 2, "Getting Started with Works for Windows."

The horizontal split box is located immediately above the arrow button at the top of the vertical scroll bar (refer to fig. 13.4). When you point to the split button, the standard mouse pointer changes to an up/down arrow labeled ADJUST. When you see this pointer and press the left mouse button, a split bar appears. Drag the split bar down until the window is divided the way you want, then release the mouse button.

The vertical split box is located to the left of the Zoom box at the left end of the horizontal scroll bar. To split the window vertically, move the mouse pointer over the split box, press the left mouse button, and drag the vertical split bar until the window divides the amount you want.

Hiding and Redisplaying Columns and Rows

When a spreadsheet contains data that you don't want or need to display on-screen or in the printed output, you can hide entire rows or columns of data. This feature is often used in spreadsheets that contain employee information such as salaries and wages, job classifications, and other personal data that you don't want displayed on-screen. When you hide a row or column in a spreadsheet, the spreadsheet continues to calculate correctly. The row or column is not removed from the spreadsheet; it is simply hidden from view. If you print the spreadsheet, the hidden row or column is not printed.

You hide a row or column by setting the row height or column width to zero. To do so, you can use the Row Height or Column Width commands on the Format menu, or you can use the mouse to drag the row or column border to zero.

Use the following steps to hide a row or column in a spreadsheet using the menu commands:

1. Highlight a cell anywhere within the row or column you want to hide.
2. Choose Format, Row Height or Column Width. The appropriate dialog box appears.
3. In the Row Height or Column Width text box, enter the number zero, then choose OK.

You also can use the mouse to change the width of columns and the height of rows. When you point to a column or row border, the mouse pointer changes to a two-headed arrow and is labeled ADJUST. When you see this pointer, click and drag the mouse to adjust the width of a column or the height of a row. You can use this same technique to hide a column or row in a spreadsheet. Drag a column border to the left until the column disappears; drag a row border up until the row disappears.

On-screen, you can tell when a row or column is hidden because the row numbers and column labels do not appear in sequence. For instance, if you hide column E, the column labels across the top of the spreadsheet read A, B, C, D, F, G, and so on. If you hide row 4, row numbers read 1, 2, 3, 5, 6, 7, and so on. An example is shown in figure 13.5. In the figure, the column showing Quarter 4 results is still blank and so the column is hidden.

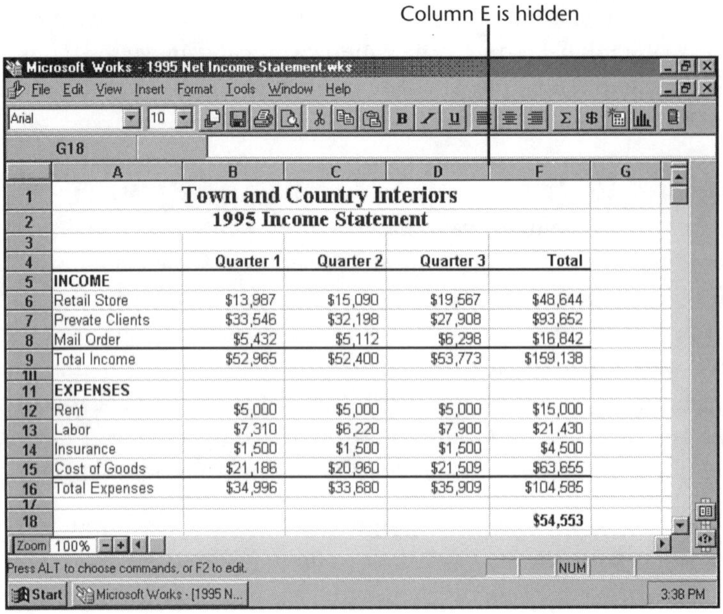

Column E is hidden

	A	B	C	D	F	G
1	Town and Country Interiors					
2	1995 Income Statement					
3						
4		Quarter 1	Quarter 2	Quarter 3	Total	
5	INCOME					
6	Retail Store	$13,987	$15,090	$19,567	$48,644	
7	Prevate Clients	$33,546	$32,198	$27,908	$93,652	
8	Mail Order	$5,432	$5,112	$6,298	$16,842	
9	Total Income	$52,965	$52,400	$53,773	$159,138	
10						
11	EXPENSES					
12	Rent	$5,000	$5,000	$5,000	$15,000	
13	Labor	$7,310	$6,220	$7,900	$21,430	
14	Insurance	$1,500	$1,500	$1,500	$4,500	
15	Cost of Goods	$21,186	$20,960	$21,509	$63,655	
16	Total Expenses	$34,996	$33,680	$35,909	$104,585	
17						
18					$54,553	

Fig. 13.5 A hidden row or column does not appear in a spreadsheet on-screen or when printed.

The only way to view the data in a hidden row or column is to restore the row height or column width to a size large enough to display the entries. You can select a hidden row or column only by using the Go To command on the Edit menu; you cannot scroll to a hidden row or column by using the arrow keys.

Tip
To quickly display the Go To dialog box, press F5 or Ctrl+G.

To restore a hidden row or column, follow these steps:

1. Choose Edit, Go To. The Go To dialog box appears.
2. In the Go To dialog box, type any cell reference in the hidden row or column. For example, to restore row 9, type any cell reference to the row such as C9. Works highlights the cell reference but doesn't display it yet.
3. Choose Format, Row Height to restore a hidden row or the Column Width command to restore a hidden column. Works displays the appropriate dialog box.
4. In the Row Height or Column Width box, type a number adequate to display the entries in the hidden row or column (you might check the height or width of other rows or columns first), or use the Best Fit option.
5. Choose OK. Works restores the hidden row or column to the spreadsheet.

Tip
If you use the Go To command frequently, you can customize your toolbar by adding a Go To button, which displays the Go To dialog box when you click it.

Hiding Gridlines

Gridlines are the vertical and horizontal lines on a spreadsheet that define the boundaries of cells. Works automatically displays gridlines whenever you create a new spreadsheet file. If you prefer not to display the gridlines in a spreadsheet, select the Gridlines command on the View menu. This command toggles the Gridlines feature on and off. To display gridlines again, choose the Gridlines command again to turn this feature back on.

Tip
If you turn gridlines on and off frequently, consider adding the Gridlines button to your toolbar. The Gridlines button is in the View category in the Customize Works Toolbar dialog box (see Chapter 2).

Freezing Row and Column Headings

When you work with average column widths, row heights, and font sizes, your screen can display approximately 6 to 10 columns and 20 to 30 rows at a time. If your spreadsheet is large (more than 10 columns or 30 rows) and requires a lot of scrolling down or to the right, you will inevitably experience the column and row headings disappearing off the screen due to scrolling. Even if you reduce the view of the spreadsheet, the screen can display only a limited number of columns and rows at one time. So if you scroll far enough down or to the right, the column or row headings eventually scroll out of your view, making it difficult to identify the data in your spreadsheet.

To avoid this problem, Works enables you to *freeze* row headings, column headings, or both by choosing Format, Freeze Titles. When you freeze row headings that appear in column A, for example, and then scroll the spreadsheet to the right, the row headings in column A remain stationary while column B and the following columns scroll to the right. Likewise, when you freeze column headings that appear in row 5, for example, and then scroll the spreadsheet down, the column headings in row 5 remain stationary while row 6 and the following rows scroll downward. Works inserts a bold line in the spreadsheet beneath the row or to the right of the column that is frozen. In figure 13.6, row and column headings are frozen.

When you choose the Freeze Titles command from the Format menu, Works freezes headings *above and to the left of* the location of the highlighted cell. For example, if you highlight cell C3, Works freezes columns A and B (above the highlighted cell) and rows 1 and 2 (to the left of the highlighted cell). If you highlight cell C1, Works freezes only columns A and B. If you highlight cell A3, Works freezes only rows 1 and 2.

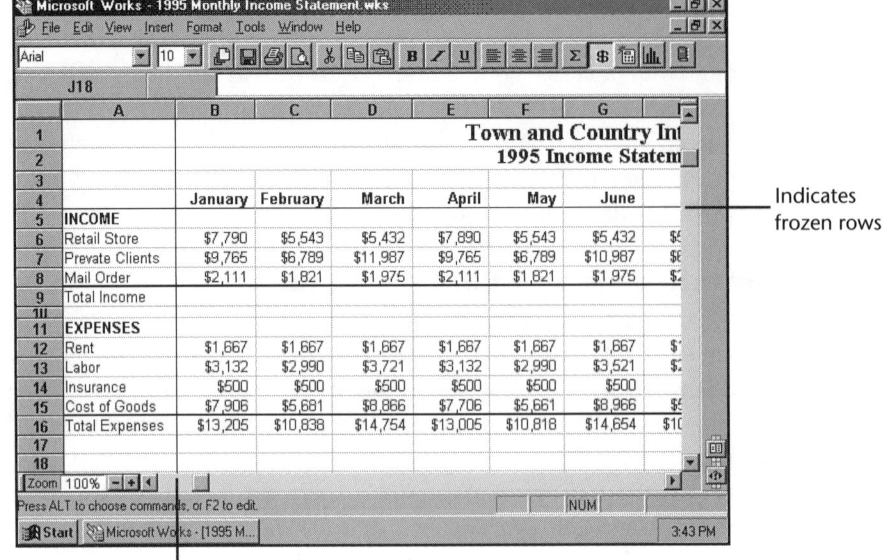

	A	B	C	D	E	F	G
1							
2							
3							
4		January	February	March	April	May	June
5	INCOME						
6	Retail Store	$7,790	$5,543	$5,432	$7,890	$5,543	$5,432
7	Prevate Clients	$9,765	$6,789	$11,987	$9,765	$6,789	$10,987
8	Mail Order	$2,111	$1,821	$1,975	$2,111	$1,821	$1,975
9	Total Income						
10							
11	EXPENSES						
12	Rent	$1,667	$1,667	$1,667	$1,667	$1,667	$1,667
13	Labor	$3,132	$2,990	$3,721	$3,132	$2,990	$3,521
14	Insurance	$500	$500	$500	$500	$500	$500
15	Cost of Goods	$7,906	$5,681	$8,866	$7,706	$5,661	$8,966
16	Total Expenses	$13,205	$10,838	$14,754	$13,005	$10,818	$14,654
17							
18							

Fig. 13.6
When row and column headings are frozen, you can identify remote rows and columns in a spreadsheet.

To freeze rows only in a spreadsheet, follow these steps:

1. Move the highlight to the leftmost column and the row *below* the last row you want to freeze. For example, to freeze rows 1 and 2, move the highlight to cell A3.

2. Choose Format, Freeze Titles. Works freezes the rows above the row you selected.

To freeze columns only in a spreadsheet, follow these steps:

1. Move the highlight to the topmost cell in the column *to the right of* the last column you want to freeze. To freeze columns A and B, for example, move the highlight to cell C1.

2. Choose Format, Freeze Titles. Works freezes the columns to the left of the column you selected.

To freeze rows *and* columns in a spreadsheet, follow these steps:

1. Move the highlight to the cell below the last row and to the right of the last column you want to freeze. For example, to freeze columns A and B and rows 1 and 2, move the highlight to cell C3.

2. Choose Format, Freeze Titles. Works freezes rows and columns above and to the left of the cell you selected.

Tip
You can add a Freeze Titles button to the toolbar if you use this feature frequently.

The Freeze Titles command on the Format menu toggles on and off. To remove frozen titles, choose the Freeze Titles command again to remove the check mark that appears next to the command on the drop-down menu. Works restores the spreadsheet to its original appearance.

Displaying Formulas

Most of the time when you work with a spreadsheet, you display actual values (formula results) in the cells. To check on the content or structure of a particular formula, you select the cell where the formula appears and then look in the formula bar for the exact formula. Sometimes, however, you may want to display *all* formulas in a spreadsheet at one time. This feature is useful when you want to check the accuracy of all formulas in a spreadsheet.

To display all formulas in a spreadsheet at one time, choose View, Formulas. Works displays formulas in all cells that contain formulas instead of displaying their calculated results. All other cells in the worksheet (cells containing text or values) display their contents but without numeric formatting such as currency or percent. An example of a spreadsheet that displays formulas is shown in figure 13.7.

If you need a record of the formulas used in a spreadsheet, you can print the spreadsheet with formulas displayed. You can also return to normal view to see values instead of formulas. To restore the spreadsheet to its normal appearance, open the View menu and again choose the Formulas command, which toggles on and off. Works restores the calculated values to the spreadsheet, and formulas appear in the formula bar when a formula cell is highlighted.

◄ See "Entering Simple Formulas," p. 205

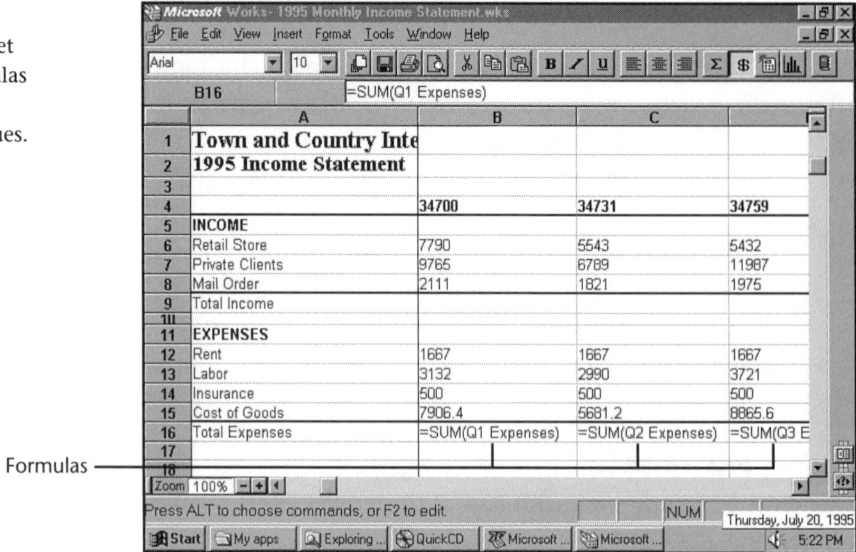

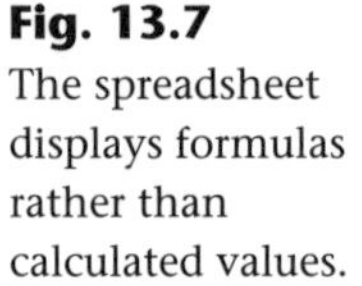
Fig. 13.7
The spreadsheet displays formulas rather than calculated values.

Sorting a Spreadsheet

When you enter new information into a spreadsheet, you often enter it in the order you receive the information. A spreadsheet can be easier to work with when you sort the information in different ways. Grouping the information differently also can make the data more useful. You may enter data from employee reports, for example, then at the end of the month sort the data by client to use for invoicing. You can rearrange entries in a spreadsheet alphabetically or numerically in ascending or descending order. Works sorts text as well as numbers, whether they are dates, times, part numbers, dollars, or other types of values. When you sort in ascending order on entries that contain both text and numbers, Works lists text entries first, then numbers. When you sort in descending order, numeric entries appear first and text entries follow.

It is not necessary to select values before sorting if you want to sort the entire spreadsheet—including report titles, column labels, and totals. To sort only a portion of the information in a spreadsheet, first select the values that you want to sort. Do not overlook data that is not currently on-screen. If you want to sort employees by their Social Security numbers, for example, and you fail to also select other information such as pay rate entered for the employee, the other information will be separated from the employee names and numbers.

After you select the values to sort, choose Tools, Sort, which displays the Sort dialog box shown in figure 13.8.

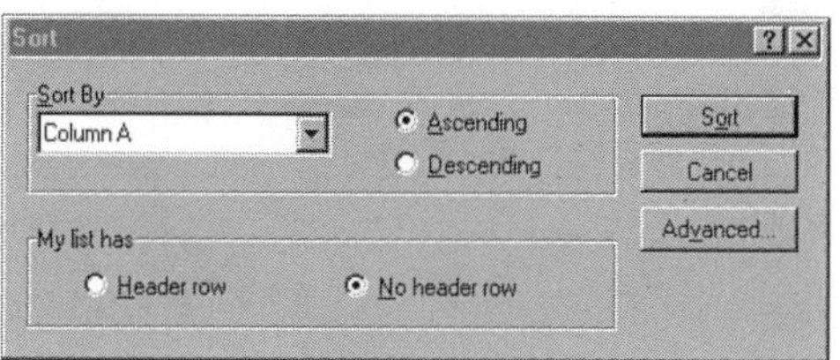

Fig. 13.8
In the Sort dialog box, indicate the column to sort.

To sort a spreadsheet, follow these steps:

1. Select the rows you want to include in the sort. For example, don't include rows that contain titles, subtitles, column totals, or blank rows.
2. Choose Tools, Sort. The Sort dialog box shown in figure 13.8 appears.
3. Choose the column (A, B, C, or other column) you want to sort from the Sort By drop-down list. Select Ascending or Descending for the sort order.
4. If you have included column labels in the selection and want them to remain at the top of the columns, choose Header Row in the My List Has area.
5. Choose OK. Works sorts the selection in the order you specify.

You can also sort a spreadsheet by columns or sort a selection that does not include entire columns or rows. When you highlight several columns or a selection of cells and then choose the Sort command, Works displays a dialog box in which you can confirm that the highlighted selection is what you want to sort. You can also choose to sort all the information in the spreadsheet. The Sort dialog box appears after you choose OK to proceed. If you fail to select any part of the spreadsheet, Works warns that you need to make a selection and offers you a demonstration on highlighting entries or sorting columns.

Choosing the Advanced button allows you to sort information by one, two, or three columns in ascending or descending order. When items in the first column you specify match, Works sorts items based on the second column. When items in the first and second column match, Works sorts items based on the third column. This concept is illustrated in figure 13.9. In the figure, a payroll spreadsheet lists employees by last name, first name, department, hourly rate, hours worked, and total.

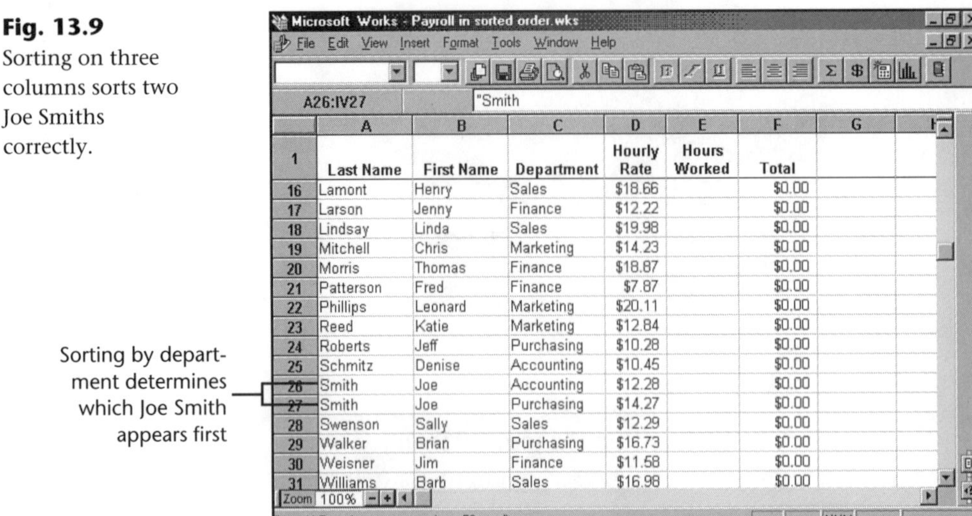

	A	B	C	D	E	F	G
1	Last Name	First Name	Department	Hourly Rate	Hours Worked	Total	
16	Lamont	Henry	Sales	$18.66		$0.00	
17	Larson	Jenny	Finance	$12.22		$0.00	
18	Lindsay	Linda	Sales	$19.98		$0.00	
19	Mitchell	Chris	Marketing	$14.23		$0.00	
20	Morris	Thomas	Finance	$18.87		$0.00	
21	Patterson	Fred	Finance	$7.87		$0.00	
22	Phillips	Leonard	Marketing	$20.11		$0.00	
23	Reed	Katie	Marketing	$12.84		$0.00	
24	Roberts	Jeff	Purchasing	$10.28		$0.00	
25	Schmitz	Denise	Accounting	$10.45		$0.00	
26	Smith	Joe	Accounting	$12.28		$0.00	
27	Smith	Joe	Purchasing	$14.27		$0.00	
28	Swenson	Sally	Sales	$12.29		$0.00	
29	Walker	Brian	Purchasing	$16.73		$0.00	
30	Weisner	Jim	Finance	$11.58		$0.00	
31	Williams	Barb	Sales	$16.98		$0.00	

Fig. 13.9 Sorting on three columns sorts two Joe Smiths correctly.

The spreadsheet is sorted by last name, first name, and department. To sort the list by last name, which appears in column A, you choose Column A from the drop-down list in the Sort By box of the Sort dialog box (see fig. 13.10). To sort the list by last name and then first name, you choose Column B from the drop-down list in the Then By box. In this example, two employees are named Joe Smith. Because their last and first names match, you must use a third column to determine the order in which these two names are sorted. To sort by department, choose Column C from the drop-down list in the second Then By box. This final sort by department ensures that Joe Smith in Accounting appears in the list before Joe Smith in Purchasing.

Sort

Sort by: Column A — Ascending / Descending

Then by: Column B — Ascending / Descending

Then by: Column C — Ascending / Descending

My list has: Header row / No header row

Sort | Cancel

Fig. 13.10 Choose the Advanced button to display this Sort dialog box to sort on one, two, or three columns.

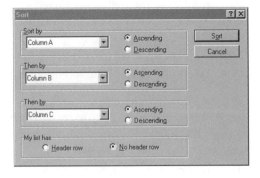

To sort a spreadsheet by more than one column, follow these steps:

1. Select the entries you want to include in the sort. For example, don't include report titles, column totals, or blank rows.
2. Choose Tools, Sort. The Sort dialog box shown in figure 13.8 appears.
3. To sort on multiple columns, choose the Advanced button to display the Sort dialog box shown in figure 13.10.
4. Choose the column (A, B, C, or other column) you want to sort from the drop-down list in the Sort By box. Select Ascending or Descending for the sort order.
5. To sort on two columns, repeat step 4 for the first Then By box.
6. To sort on three columns, repeat step 4 for the second Then By box.
7. If you included a row with column labels in the selection to sort, choose Header Row in the My List Has area.
8. Choose OK. Works sorts the spreadsheet in the order you specify.

Sometimes when you enter spreadsheet data in random order, you want to preserve that spreadsheet before you sort it. You could keep a backup copy of the spreadsheet or a duplicate copy under a different name. But another way to preserve the original random order of items in a spreadsheet is to add a column that sequentially numbers items in the spreadsheet as they were originally entered. For example, figure 13.11 illustrates the payroll spreadsheet showing data as it was originally entered (in random order). Column A was inserted to number each entry sequentially. If you sort a spreadsheet incorrectly or by mistake, this column of sequential numbers enables you to re-sort the list into its original order if necessary. Just select the rows to sort, then sort on column A in ascending order. Works re-sorts the spreadsheet in its original order.

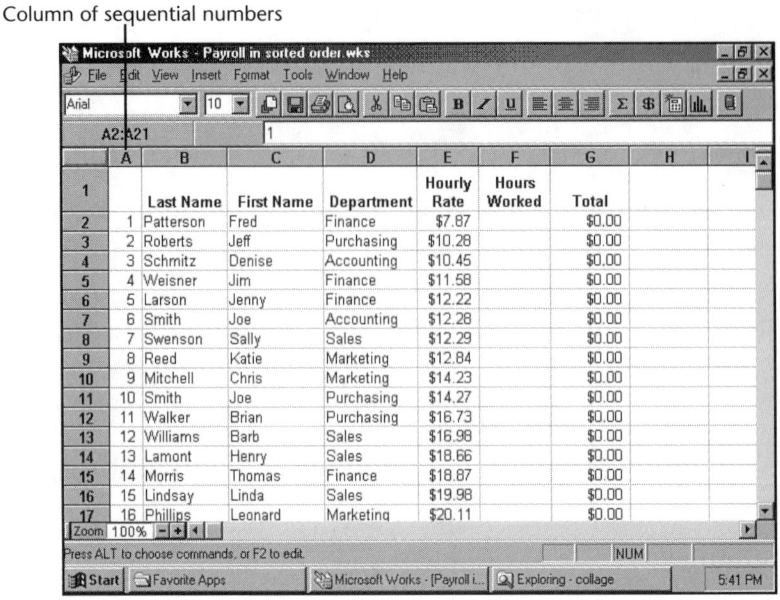

Column of sequential numbers

	A	B	C	D	E	F	G
1		Last Name	First Name	Department	Hourly Rate	Hours Worked	Total
2	1	Patterson	Fred	Finance	$7.87		$0.00
3	2	Roberts	Jeff	Purchasing	$10.28		$0.00
4	3	Schmitz	Denise	Accounting	$10.45		$0.00
5	4	Weisner	Jim	Finance	$11.58		$0.00
6	5	Larson	Jenny	Finance	$12.22		$0.00
7	6	Smith	Joe	Accounting	$12.28		$0.00
8	7	Swenson	Sally	Sales	$12.29		$0.00
9	8	Reed	Katie	Marketing	$12.84		$0.00
10	9	Mitchell	Chris	Marketing	$14.23		$0.00
11	10	Smith	Joe	Purchasing	$14.27		$0.00
12	11	Walker	Brian	Purchasing	$16.73		$0.00
13	12	Williams	Barb	Sales	$16.98		$0.00
14	13	Lamont	Henry	Sales	$18.66		$0.00
15	14	Morris	Thomas	Finance	$18.87		$0.00
16	15	Lindsay	Linda	Sales	$19.98		$0.00
17	16	Phillips	Leonard	Marketing	$20.11		$0.00

Fig. 13.11
A column that sequentially numbers entries enables you to re-sort in the original order.

To easily create a column of sequential numbers, insert a new column before column A. Type the number 1 in the cell in the first row you want to include in the sort. Then move down one cell and type the number 2 in this cell. Select these two cells and use the Autofill box in the lower-right corner of the selection to drag the selection to the last row you want to sort.

◄ See "Using the Autofill Feature," p. 191

Caution

The Sort command, like Replace, has the potential for disaster. A simple error in highlighting what to sort may result in part of the information that belongs together being unsorted and therefore separated from its companion data. Review the results of Sort immediately and choose Edit, Undo Sort if necessary. Unfortunately, problems may not be immediately obvious. The safe ways to use the Sort command are to number the rows as just described or to *always* save the file just before beginning the sort.

Checking Your Spelling

Most spreadsheets contain mainly numbers and have little information in the form of labels (text). With so little text, spelling errors are even more obvious. Fortunately, the spelling tool is available to check a spreadsheet for any typographical errors.

To use the spell check tool, choose the Spelling command from the Tools menu or click the Spell Checker button on the toolbar. If Works does not find any spelling errors, a box appears displaying the message `Spelling check finished`.

The insertion point can be anywhere in the spreadsheet when you begin spell-checking. You also may select only a portion of the spreadsheet to check. The process for checking a spreadsheet is no different than spell-checking a word processing document. For more instructions on using the Spelling command, refer to Chapter 9, "Checking Your Document." ❖

Tip
To quickly begin spell-checking your document, press F7.

Chapter 14

Creating Charts

by Judy Peterson

Spreadsheets are excellent tools for compiling, summarizing, calculating, and analyzing data. But all the data in a spreadsheet is of little value if you can't easily understand it. When data is presented in a graphical form, however, it is often much easier to interpret—even at a glance. Charts provide the means for depicting spreadsheet data in a graphical form. Charts can help you recognize trends, compare data, identify percentages of a whole, and spot relationships between two or more items.

In Works, charts are tied to data in a spreadsheet. You tell Works which data to use to create the chart, Works creates the chart for you, and then Works saves it with the spreadsheet. If you change the data in your spreadsheet, Works automatically updates the data in the chart. You can create up to eight charts for each Works spreadsheet.

In this chapter, you learn about:

- The basic chart types and their characteristics
- The elements of a typical chart
- How Works plots charts
- Creating a new chart
- Naming, deleting, and duplicating a chart
- Printing a chart

Understanding Charts

Before you begin creating charts in Works, you need a basic understanding of the chart types available in Works, the standard elements of a chart, and how Works plots data in a chart. This section includes a discussion of these topics.

Reviewing the Basic Chart Types

Works includes 12 basic chart types: area, bar, line, pie, stacked line, X-Y (scatter), radar, combination, 3D area, 3D bar, 3D line, and 3D pie charts. Each chart type has a unique purpose and characteristic. For each of the 12 chart types, you can choose from a variety of style variations. The 12 chart types are described and illustrated next. Review the figures and descriptions to choose the chart type that best illustrates your particular data.

Area charts emphasize the relative contribution of each item in a category of data. Rather than emphasizing the time period itself, an area chart emphasizes the change in data over a period of time and implies that the data is measured continuously over time. In figure 14.1, the area chart shows how each category of income contributed to total income throughout the year.

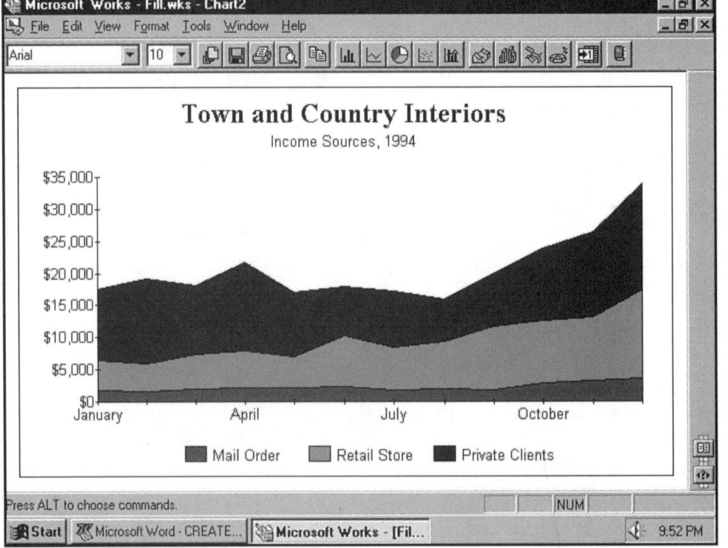

Fig. 14.1
Area charts emphasize the relative contribution of items in a category.

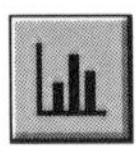

Bar charts enable you to compare distinct items or emphasize the relationship of items to one another over a period of time. Bar charts emphasize comparisons and relationships among items more than the flow of time. Unlike area charts, bar charts show clearly that the data is measured at intervals rather than continuously. Positive values appear above the horizontal axis (the x-axis); negative values appear below. Figure 14.2 illustrates 1994 expenses for Town and Country Interiors. Bar chart variations include stacked bar charts, which depict each data item as a percentage of the entire category (100%).

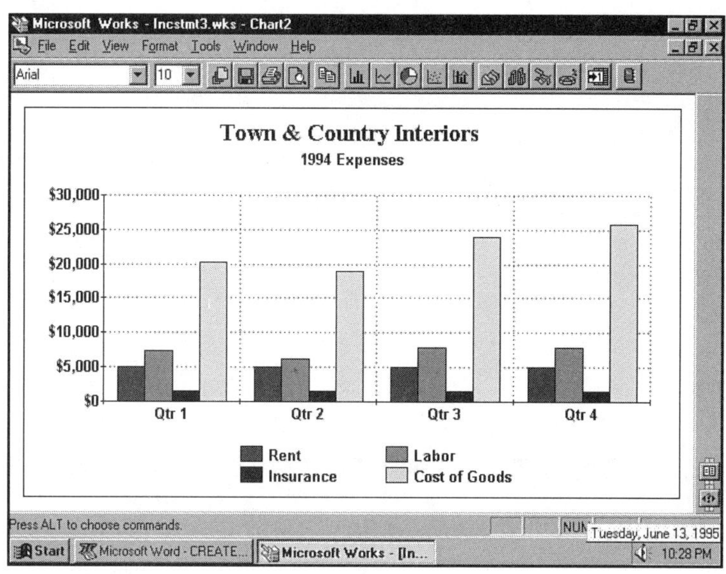

Fig. 14.2
A bar chart compares distinct items over a period of time.

Line charts are best used for illustrating trends among data items, so the x-axis usually represents time (days, months, quarters, years, and so on). Each line in the chart represents a distinct data item; markers on the line pinpoint the exact values charted. In figure 14.3, Retail Store, Private Clients, and Mail Order are the three sources of income (data items) depicted using a line chart.

Pie charts emphasize how individual parts contribute to a whole. Pie slices correspond to individual values in a spreadsheet; the entire pie corresponds to the sum of those values. Unlike area, line, and bar charts, pie charts can depict data at only one specific point in time. Pie chart variations let you explode one or all slices. Figure 14.4 depicts the total income of Town and Country Interiors for 1994 using a pie chart. The Retail Store slice is exploded.

Stacked line charts are similar to line charts except that the lines are stacked to show the total of all items shown. Works adds the values of the first line to the second line, the second line to the third line, and so on. The stacked line chart illustrates the flow of data over time unlike an area chart, which indicates the volume of data over time. Figure 14.5 shows three categories of income for the year 1994 in a stacked line chart.

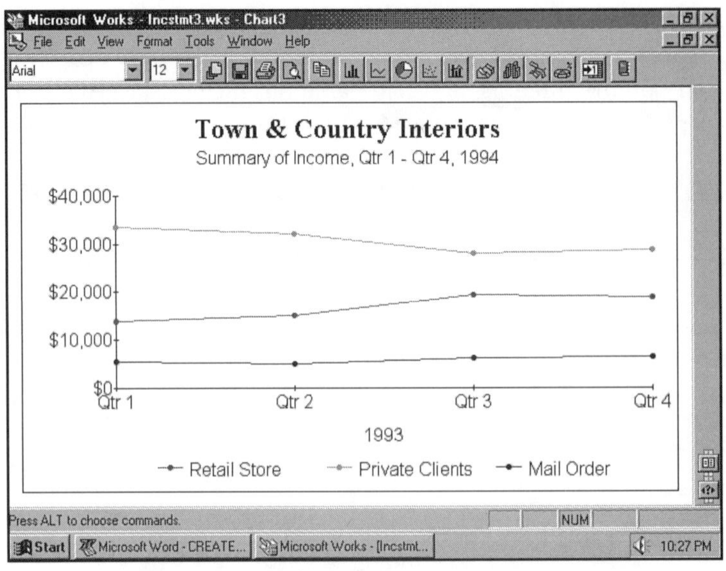

Fig. 14.3
Line charts illustrate trends among data items.

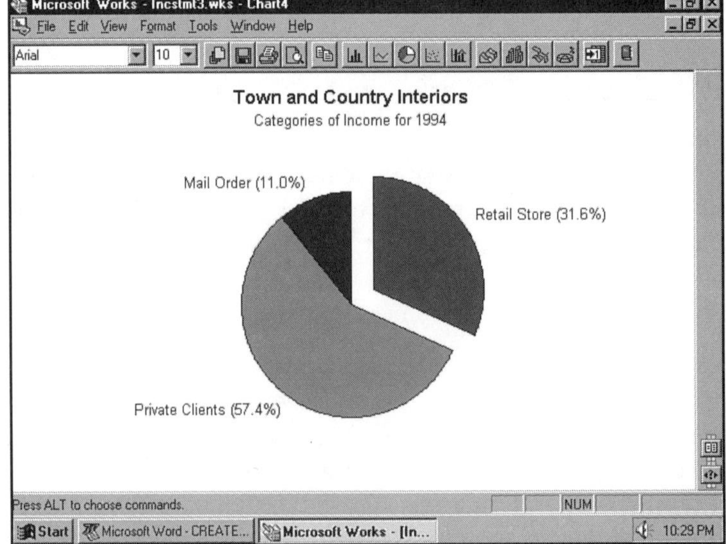

Fig. 14.4
The pie chart illustrates how parts contribute to the whole.

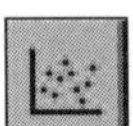

An *X-Y chart* (also called a *scatter* chart) shows the correlation between two related values (such as productivity and number of hours worked, or temperature and relative humidity). It illustrates how a change in one value affects the other. In figure 14.6, the x-y chart shows how the number of consecutive hours worked affects employees' productivity.

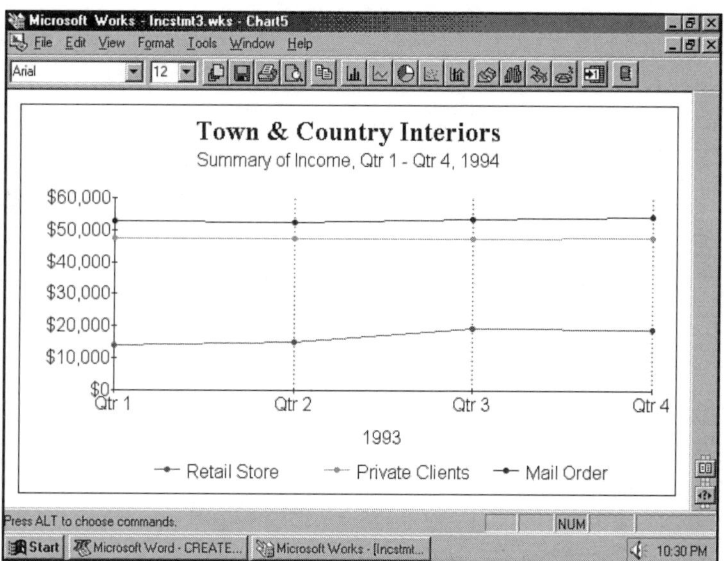

Fig. 14.5
A stacked line chart depicts the total of all items shown.

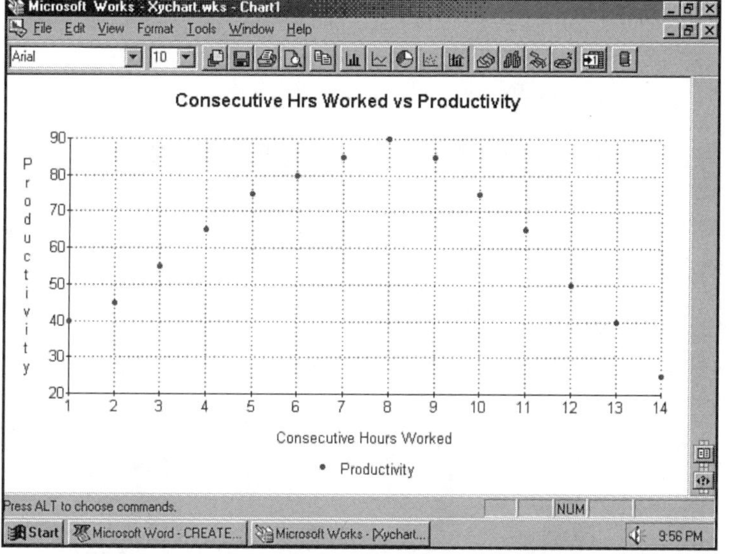

Fig. 14.6
An x-y chart shows the correlation between two related values.

Use a *radar chart* to compare two sets of data relative to a center point. For example, suppose that you want to make a purchasing decision between two cars. You rank the cars on a scale of 1 to 10 based on purchase price, options, horsepower, reliability, and cost of maintenance. The center point of the chart represents the fact that the cars are equally matched for comparison (see fig. 14.7).

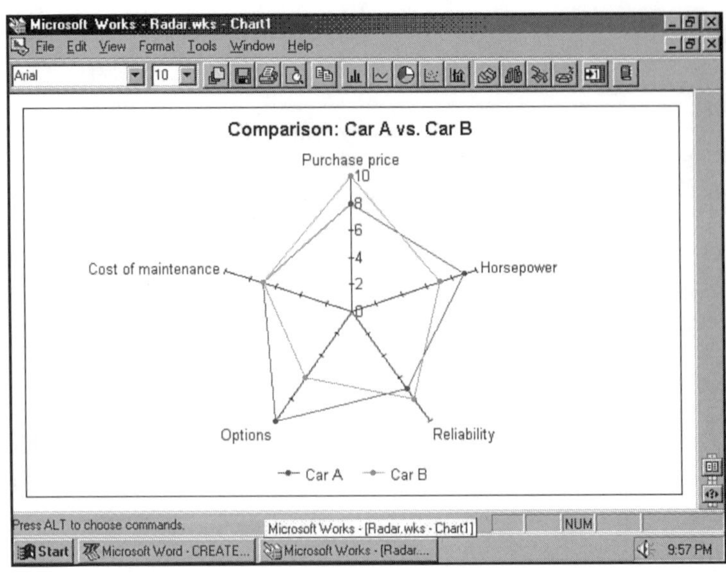

Fig. 14.7 A radar chart compares two sets of data relative to a center point.

Combination charts mix bars and lines in the same chart. They are also referred to as mixed charts. The chart in figure 14.8 displays total income as bars and total expenses as a line.

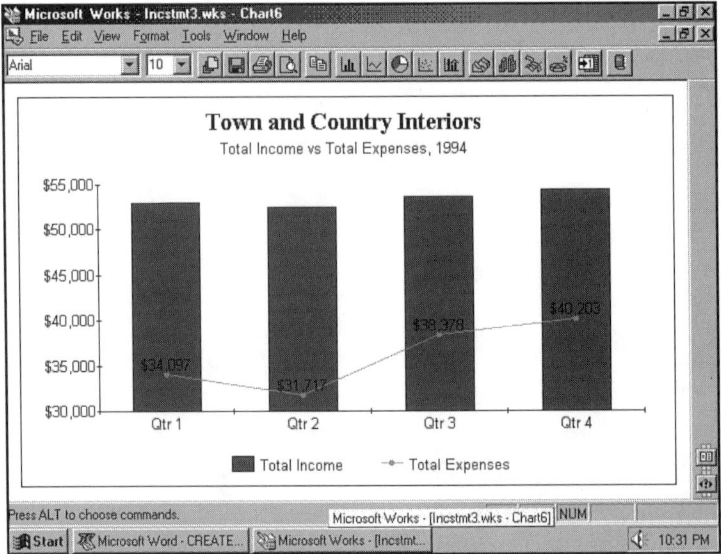

Fig. 14.8 In this combination chart, a line overlays bars.

3D area, bar, line, and pie charts are similar to their 2D counterparts (shown earlier) except that they add depth to the areas, bars, lines, and pie slices used in the charts. The 3D variation adds interest and can sometimes help emphasize data better than a 2D chart. In addition, 3D area and bar charts enable you to show each data item on its own rather than stacked. For instance, rather than stacking three types of income on top of one another, as shown in the area chart in figure 14.1, a 3D area chart enables you to depict each type of income as its own 3D area (see fig. 14.9). 3D charts should receive top consideration for use in presentations because they illustrate your data well and offer the maximum visual impact.

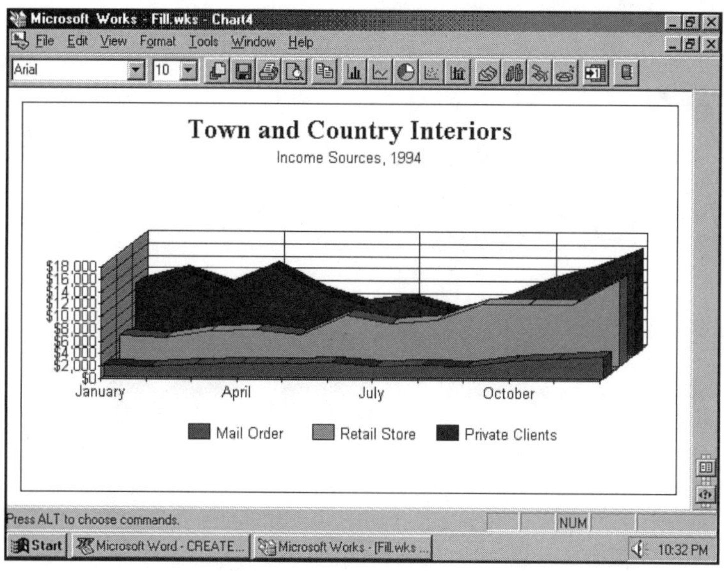

Fig. 14.9
This 3D variation shows each data item separately.

A *3D bar chart* can also depict distinct data items separately rather than side-by-side or stacked. Figure 14.10 depicts the 1994 expenses for Town and Country Interiors in a 3D bar chart. Refer to the same data charted in a 2D bar chart in figure 14.2.

3D line charts are essentially the same as 2D line charts except that they represent lines of data as ribbons. This style is especially effective for displaying lines of data that cross one another. Figure 14.11 illustrates the test scores of two different students across a nine-week period.

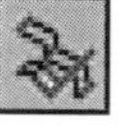

3D pie charts are essentially the same as 2D pie charts. Figure 14.12 shows the same data from figure 14.4 charted as a 3D pie with slices exploded.

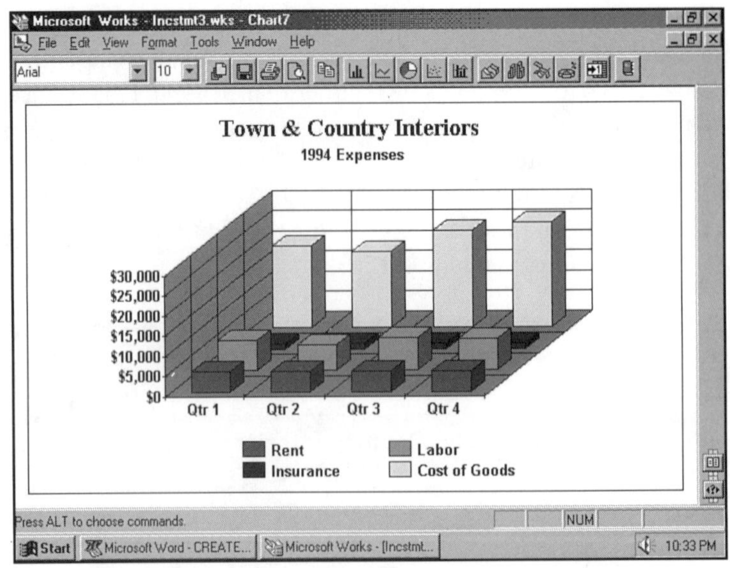

Fig. 14.10
A 3D bar chart depicts distinct data items separately.

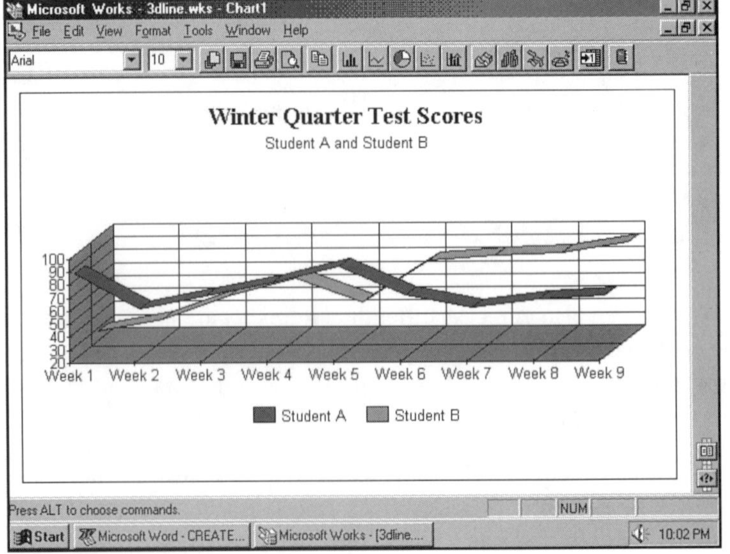

Fig. 14.11
In a 3D line chart, individual data items are represented by ribbons.

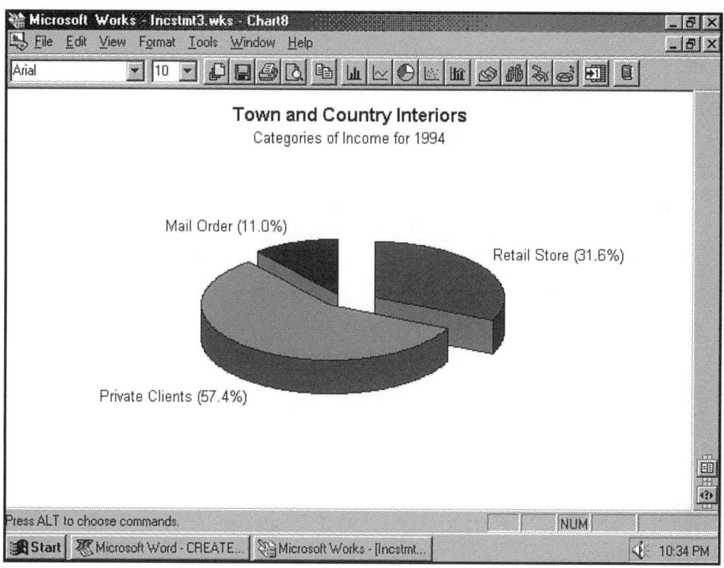

Fig. 14.12
A 3D pie chart illustrates how parts contribute to a whole.

Learning the Elements of a Chart

Before you begin creating charts, it's important to know and recognize the elements that make up a chart. Figure 14.13 shows a bar chart that includes many of the common chart elements. Most of the chart elements are optional features you can add or remove to suit your particular needs. The charts you create can contain any or all of the elements described in the following list:

- *Axes.* Except for pie charts, all charts have two axes. The horizontal axis, or *x-axis,* often represents dates. The vertical axis, or *y-axis,* often represents percentages or a quantity such as dollars. *Tick marks* mark the intervals along an axis. With some chart types, you can choose a style variation that adds a right y-axis. A right y-axis makes it easier to interpret bars or lines located on the far right side of a chart.

- *Scale.* A scale depicts units of measurement (such as dollars) along an axis. Based on the data you select to chart, Works automatically determines the maximum number, the minimum number, and the interval used in the scale.

- *Chart Titles.* The chart title identifies the content of a chart. You can enter a title by itself or include a subtitle. You can format a chart title individually using any font or point size. When you choose a font or size for a chart subtitle, the font and size are applied to all other text in a chart. In addition to chart titles, you can add titles to the horizontal and vertical axes of a chart.

- *Legend.* A legend appears at the bottom of a chart and identifies the bars, lines, pie slices, or other markers that represent data.
- *Gridlines.* Gridlines can make a chart easier to read, especially when data points are close in value. Horizontal gridlines mark the intervals along the x-axis; vertical gridlines mark the intervals along the y-axis.
- *Category labels.* Category labels identify the specific categories of data represented in a graph. For example, in figure 14.13, the categories are quarters; the bars in each category are individual data items.
- *Data labels.* Data labels mark the exact value or percentage represented by a data point. When a chart contains a lot of data, data labels can make the chart look very cluttered, so use them with care. (Data labels identify exact percentages of the pie slices shown in figure 14.12.)
- *Border.* To give a chart a more finished appearance, add a border, which surrounds the chart data, title, and legend.

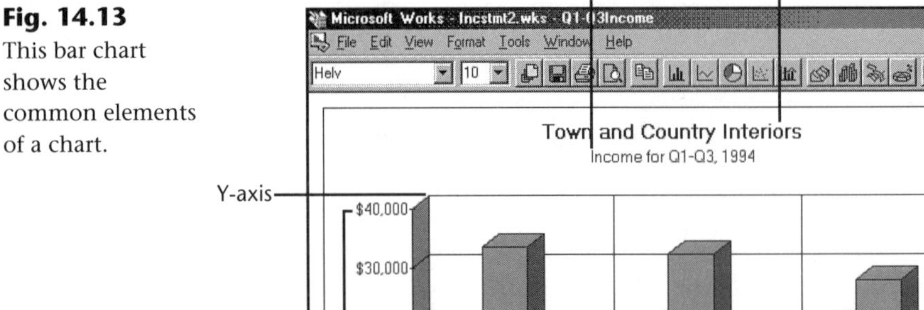

Fig. 14.13
This bar chart shows the common elements of a chart.

Knowing How Charts Are Plotted

Creating a chart in Works is a relatively straightforward task that involves selecting the range of cells to be charted. Because Works creates a bar chart automatically from the cell range you select, it is helpful to understand how Works interprets the content of the selected cell range. The example shown in figure 14.14 helps to illustrate the process.

Works determines how to create a chart based on the shape of the cell range you select and the data contained in the range (see fig. 14.14). When your selection contains more columns than rows—which is often the case—Works translates the columns into categories and places them along the x-axis. The data from the selected columns is the x series. In figure 14.14, the entire cell range selected is A2 through E5. The x-series categories are Qtr 1, Qtr 2, Qtr 3, and Qtr 4, taken from cells B2 through E2.

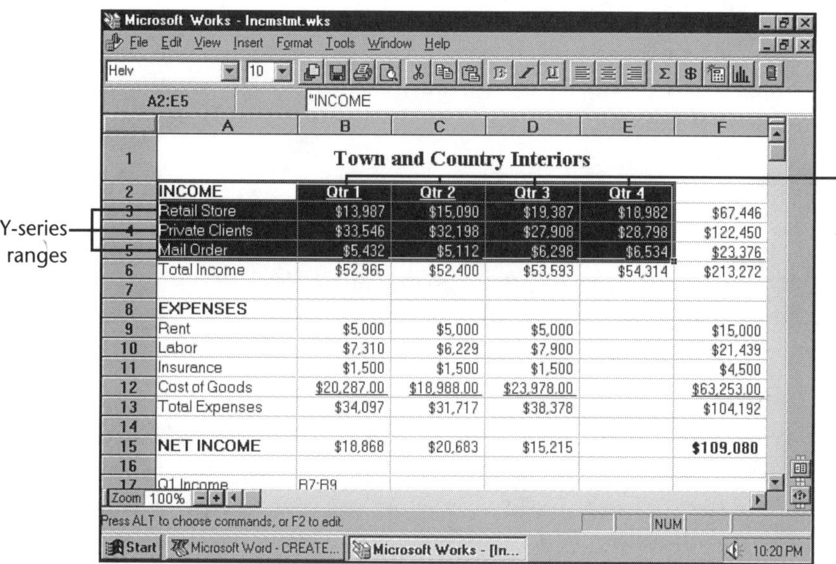

	A	B	C	D	E	F
1	Town and Country Interiors					
2	INCOME	Qtr 1	Qtr 2	Qtr 3	Qtr 4	
3	Retail Store	$13,987	$15,090	$19,387	$18,982	$67,446
4	Private Clients	$33,546	$32,198	$27,908	$28,798	$122,450
5	Mail Order	$5,432	$5,112	$6,298	$6,534	$23,376
6	Total Income	$52,965	$52,400	$53,593	$54,314	$213,272
7						
8	EXPENSES					
9	Rent	$5,000	$5,000	$5,000		$15,000
10	Labor	$7,310	$6,229	$7,900		$21,439
11	Insurance	$1,500	$1,500	$1,500		$4,500
12	Cost of Goods	$20,287.00	$18,988.00	$23,978.00		$63,253.00
13	Total Expenses	$34,097	$31,717	$38,378		$104,192
14						
15	NET INCOME	$18,868	$20,683	$15,215		$109,080
16						
17	Q1 Income	B7:B9				

Fig. 14.14 Works will translate a selection of cells into a chart.

The individual rows of data you select represent distinct *data items* (such as Retail Store, Mail Order, and Private Clients). Works plots the *data points*, or values, for each data item along the y axis. A row of cells that represents a data item is referred to as a *y series*. You can include up to six y-series data ranges in a chart. The chart produced from the spreadsheet in figure 14.14 includes three y-series ranges: Retail Store, Private Clients, and Mail Order taken from rows 3, 4, and 5.

If you include both row and column headings in your cell selection, Works translates them into the chart *legend* and x-axis *category labels*. In figure 14.14, the row headings in cells A3:A5 make up the chart legend. The category labels, as described earlier, are taken from cells B2:E2. (The Income label in cell A2 is ignored.)

Selecting Spreadsheet Data To Chart

As illustrated in figure 14.14, when the cell range you select for your chart contains more columns than rows, Works translates columns into categories along the x-axis and translates the values in each row into data points on the y-axis (represented by bars). If the range you select contains more rows than columns, Works interprets and transfers the data to the chart in exactly the opposite order: row headings transfer to the x-axis as categories, and values in columns are used to plot data points on the y-axis as bars. Regardless of the shape of the range, when the selection contains row and column headings, Works automatically creates a chart legend and adds category labels to the chart.

Recall that pie charts can only show one data item at a time, so be sure to select the correct y-series cell range if you are creating a pie chart. For instance, to use the data shown in figure 14.14 to create a pie chart, you must choose only one of the three income sources (B3:E3, B4:E4, or B5:E5), or choose the total income (B5:E6) as the y-series range. If you select more than one y-series range, Works charts the first range and ignores the remaining ranges.

Because Works interprets data automatically based on the shape of the cell range you select, it is important to remove any unnecessary blank rows or columns from the body of a spreadsheet before you create a chart. Notice in figure 14.14 that the selection does not include any blank rows or columns. Blank rows and columns in the spreadsheet cause blank categories and bars in a chart. For the same reason, do not select entire rows or entire columns when you select a cell range to be charted—they invariably contain blank cells.

Note

If it isn't possible to remove blank rows or columns from a spreadsheet, you can still plot a chart. Refer to the section "Changing X- and Y-Series Cell Ranges" in Chapter 15, "Editing and Enhancing a Chart."

Creating and Viewing a Chart

When you create a chart, it appears in a separate window but is actually part of the active spreadsheet. You can create up to eight charts in a spreadsheet. Each chart you create is given an individual name and is printed from the chart window. If you create a chart after saving its spreadsheet, you must save the file again in order to save the chart.

To create a new chart, first select the range of cells to be charted, and then choose Tools, Create New Chart or click the New Chart button on the toolbar. The New Chart dialog box appears with the Basic Options tab selected (see fig. 14.15). In the What Type of Chart Do You Want? box, Works highlights the Bar chart type by default and a sample bar chart showing the data you selected in your spreadsheet appears in the Your Chart area. If you include column and row headings in your selection, a legend appears under the sample chart. As explained earlier, based on the cell range you select Works determines how to chart the data.

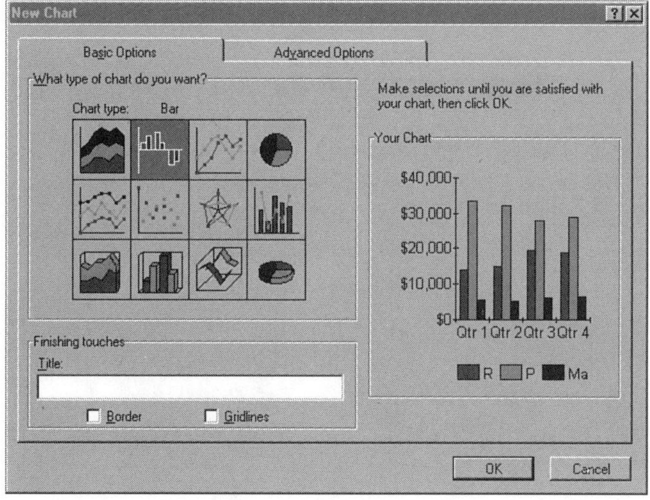

Fig. 14.15
Choose a chart type that will most effectively display the selected information.

The Finishing Touches area enables you to enter a chart title, as well as add a border and gridlines to your chart. If you don't select these options now, you can add a title, border, and gridlines to the chart.

If Works misinterprets the cell range you selected (that is, confuses the x-series range with y-series ranges), you can change any of the settings. In the New Chart dialog box, choose the Advanced Options tab (see fig. 14.16).

▶ See "Enhancing a Chart," p. 311

Based on the cell range you select, Works fills in the options in the How Is Your Spreadsheet Data Organized? area. The following list explains these options:

- The first step asks which way your series go, Across or Down. This refers to the y-series data ranges. If your data items appear in rows, Works chooses the Across option. If your data items appear in columns, Works chooses the Down option.
- The second step, First Column Contains Legend Text or A Category, refers to the purpose of the entries in the first column. If the first column describes data items, Works creates a legend from the entries. If the first column describes categories of data, Works creates category names from the entries.
- The final step, First Row Contains Category Labels or A Value (Y) Series, refers to the purpose of the entries in the first row. If the first row describes categories of data, Works creates category names from the entries. If the first row describes data items, Works creates a legend from the entries.

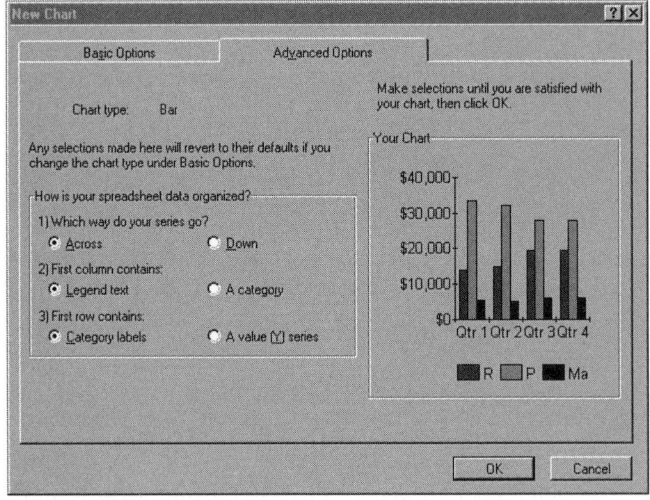

Fig. 14.16 In the Advanced Options tab, you change the way Works charts the data.

To create a new chart, follow these steps:

1. In the spreadsheet, select the range of cells you want to chart. If you want Works to create category labels and a legend, be sure to select row and column headings along with spreadsheet data.

2. Choose Tools, Create New Chart command; or click the New Chart button on the toolbar. The New Chart dialog box appears (refer to fig. 14.15).

3. From the examples in the What Type of Chart Do You Want area, choose a chart type.

4. To add a title to your chart, type the title text in the Title text box.

5. To add a border or gridlines to a chart, select the Border or Gridlines check boxes.

6. (Optional) To change the way Works interprets and charts the selected data, choose the Advanced Options tab (refer to fig. 14.16). Change any of the options in the How Is Your Spreadsheet Data Organized? area.

7. Check the sample chart to make sure that the chart is correct, then click OK. Works displays your chart in a separate window on-screen. Your spreadsheet window, still open, is located under the chart window.

Using the Charting Toolbar

As you learn in Chapter 1, "Introducing Microsoft Works 4.0 for Windows 95," each of the Works programs has a unique toolbar. After you create a chart using spreadsheet data and the chart window is active, the spreadsheet toolbar changes to the charting toolbar shown in figure 14.17.

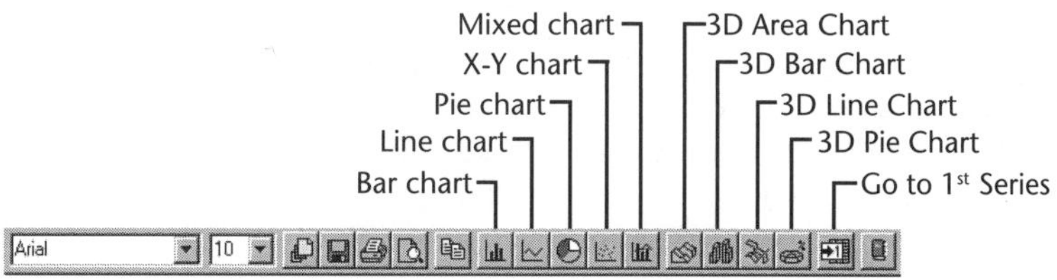

Fig. 14.17
Use buttons on the charting toolbar to speed up your work.

Tip
You can also add buttons to the chart toolbar for area, stacked line, and radar charts. See Chapter 2.

The first seven buttons and the last button on the toolbar are familiar: Font, Point Size, Save, Print, Address Book, and so on. The remaining 10 buttons let you choose a 2D or 3D chart type, or switch you back to the spreadsheet window with the first set of data, called a data series, highlighted. Clicking a chart type button displays a dialog box that shows the variations for a particular chart type. When you select a variation from the dialog box, Works switches the current chart to the chart type you select.

To switch quickly back to the spreadsheet window and highlight the cells that represent the first series, click the Go to 1st Series button on the toolbar. You learn more about changing chart types in Chapter 15, "Editing and Enhancing a Chart."

Managing Charts

After you create one or more charts, you need to know how to name and save the charts you want to keep, delete the charts you don't want, and recall a chart when you want to use it again. These topics are described in the following sections. You also learn how to duplicate a chart.

Troubleshooting

Category labels weren't included in my chart when I created it. What did I do wrong?

When you select the range of cells to chart, you must include the cells that contain category labels for them to be included in the chart. In a cell range that contains more columns than rows, category labels usually appear in the first row. To add category labels to an existing chart, refer to the section "Changing X and Y Series Cell Ranges" in Chapter 15, "Editing and Enhancing a Chart."

The x and y ranges in my chart were plotted exactly the opposite of what I expected; row headings were translated to x-axis categories and values in columns were used to plot data points. What did I do wrong?

You didn't do anything wrong; the range of cells you selected had more rows than columns, so Works placed the row headings on the x-axis. You can reverse the way Works plots the chart without re-creating it. Change the cell ranges that define the x series and y series. Refer to the section "Changing X and Y Series Cell Ranges" in Chapter 15, "Editing and Enhancing a Chart."

Saving a Chart

Because charts are tied to spreadsheet data, charts save with the spreadsheet to which they belong; they don't save as separate files. After you create a chart, it is treated just like new or edited data in the spreadsheet. When you choose File, Save or File, Save As, Works saves the chart along with any changes to the spreadsheet itself.

Naming a Chart

As you learned earlier in this chapter, you can create up to eight charts per spreadsheet in Works. The first chart you create is named Chart1. Subsequent charts you create are named Chart2, Chart3, and so on, through Chart8. You can use these chart names that Works assigns, or you can assign more meaningful names to your charts, such as 1993 Income Sources. Works displays chart names in the title bar of a chart window, on the Window drop-down menu when a chart is open, and in the Charts dialog box when you choose View, Chart.

Follow these steps to rename a chart:

1. From either the spreadsheet or chart window, choose Tools, Rename Chart. The Rename Chart dialog box appears.
2. All existing charts for the current spreadsheet are shown in the Select a Chart list box. Highlight the name of the chart you want to rename.
3. In the Type a Name Below text box, type a new name of no more than 15 characters. The name can include spaces if you like.
4. Click the Rename or OK button.
5. Repeat steps 2 through 4 to rename additional charts.
6. When you finish renaming charts, choose OK.

Deleting a Chart

Because Works can store only eight charts with a spreadsheet, it's important to delete charts that you no longer use or need. Perhaps you use the Chart feature to help analyze data, and find you create several charts before you settle on the charts that accurately and effectively describe your data. To continue creating charts, you first need to delete a few of the charts. When you try to create a chart in a spreadsheet that already has eight charts, Works tells you to delete a chart to make room for another.

To delete a chart, follow these steps:

1. From either the spreadsheet or chart window, choose Tools, Delete Chart. The Delete Chart dialog box appears.
2. All existing charts for the current spreadsheet are shown in the Select a Chart list box. Highlight the name of the chart you want to delete.

3. Click the Delete or OK button.

4. Repeat steps 2 and 3 to delete additional charts.

5. When you finish deleting charts, choose OK.

When you delete a chart, Works displays a warning that says you cannot undo this deletion if you proceed. You can change your mind by choosing the Cancel button.

Duplicating a Chart

When you create a variety of charts using the same or similar data, it's often easier to duplicate an existing chart rather than to create a new chart from scratch. For example, suppose you want to create a chart that depicts expenses for 1993, but you want a bar chart as well as a line chart. The data series, titles, and legend are the same for both charts, so it's quicker to duplicate the first chart and then change the chart type.

After you duplicate a chart, you can change any of the data, titles, or other features, if necessary. When you duplicate a chart, Works assigns the new chart the next available chart name. So, if you have already created three charts, and then you duplicate one of them, Works automatically names the new chart Chart4.

Use the following steps to duplicate a chart:

1. From either the spreadsheet or chart window, choose Tools, Duplicate Chart. The Duplicate Chart dialog box appears.

2. All existing charts for the current spreadsheet are shown in the Select a Chart list box. Highlight the name of the chart you want to duplicate.

3. In the Type a Name Below text box, type a name of no more than 15 characters for the duplicate chart. The name can include spaces if you like.

4. Click the Duplicate or OK button.

5. Repeat steps 2 through 4 to duplicate additional charts.

6. When you finish duplicating charts, choose OK.

Viewing a Saved Chart

To view a saved chart, you must open the spreadsheet to which the chart belongs. Then choose View, Chart, which displays the Charts dialog box. All saved charts that belong to the current spreadsheet are shown in the Select a Chart list box. Highlight the chart you want to recall and choose OK. Works opens the chart in its own window on top of the spreadsheet window.

Switching Between a Spreadsheet and a Chart

As you work with your spreadsheet and create new charts, you might find it helpful to switch back and forth between the chart window and the spreadsheet window. If the two windows are not maximized, you should be able to see at least a portion of each window on-screen and click the window you want. If you cannot see the window you want on-screen, and therefore cannot click it, use either the View menu or the Window menu to choose a new active window.

To switch back to the spreadsheet window from a chart window, choose View, Spreadsheet. Or you can choose Window and then choose the spreadsheet's file name in the list at the bottom of the menu. If you want to return to the first y-series in the spreadsheet, you can click the Go to 1st Series button on the toolbar (refer to fig. 14.17).

To switch back to a chart window from a spreadsheet window, choose Window and then choose the chart name from the bottom of the menu. On the Window menu, all open charts are listed with the spreadsheet name first, followed by the chart name, such as INCMSTMT.WKS - Chart1. To switch to a different chart window (one that is not currently open), choose View, Chart, or click the New Chart button on the toolbar. When the New Chart dialog box appears, highlight the chart you want and press Enter. All additional chart windows you open are added to the list at the bottom of the Window menu.

Tip
If you want to see all the open charts at once, choose Window, Tile.

Setting a Preferred Chart Type

If you don't select a chart type in the New Chart dialog box, Works always defaults to creating a bar chart. If you seldom use bar charts or most often create a different type of chart, you can change the default chart type by following these steps:

1. Create a new chart of the type you want to use as a default.

2. When the new chart appears on-screen in its own window, choose Format, Set Default Chart. Works sets the current chart type as the preferred chart type.

Tip
If you frequently switch from a chart to the spreadsheet, you can add the Spreadsheet button to your toolbar. Refer to Chapter 2 for instructions on customizing your toolbar.

The next time you create a new chart, the chart type you specified as the default chart is highlighted in the New Chart dialog box. You can redefine the preferred chart type at any time using the preceding steps.

Printing a Chart

Before printing a chart, you should review the current page and print settings shown in the Page Setup dialog box. (Choose File, Page Setup to display the Page Setup dialog box.) In this dialog box, you specify the page, header, and footer margins; the source, size, and orientation for the paper you are printing on; page numbering and footnote options; and other standard settings for your particular printer. When all page settings are correct, it's a good idea to preview a chart as a final check before printing. In the following sections, you learn how to specify page settings in the Page Setup dialog box.

Setting Margins

Page margins are the white space that surrounds the text on the printed page. To set page margins for a chart, you use the Page Setup dialog box shown in figure 14.18. (Notice that Page Setup is a tabbed dialog box. In the figure, the Margins tab is selected and the default margin settings are displayed.) Unless you change margin settings, the Page Setup dialog box shows the default margins that Works uses: 1 inch for top and bottom margins, and 1.25 inches for left and right margins. The Sample area displays a graphical representation of these settings. For some charts, you might want to change the default margin settings in order to fit a larger chart on a page.

To change margin settings, follow these steps:

1. Choose File, Page Setup command. The Page Setup dialog box appears.
2. In the dialog box, choose the Margins tab (see fig. 14.18).
3. In the appropriate margin boxes, type the settings you want to use in inches. Type a decimal fraction for fractions of an inch (such as 1.25 for 1 1/4 inches). The Sample area of the dialog box reflects the settings you choose.
4. When all margin settings are correct, choose OK.

Note

If you commonly work with centimeters or another unit of measure rather than inches, you can change the Works default units setting. Choose Tools, Options to display the Options dialog box. Select the General tab and in the Units box, choose a unit of measure, and then choose OK. Notice that the unit of measure you choose applies to *all* tools in Works.

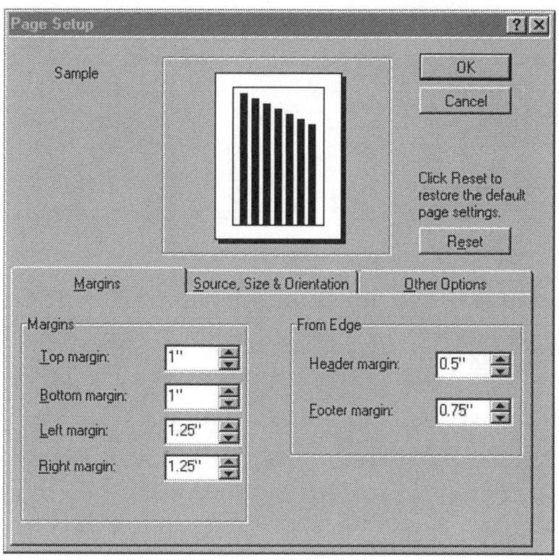

Fig. 14.18
The Page Setup dialog box displays margin settings for the current chart.

Setting Paper Source, Size, and Orientation

Before printing a chart, you must specify in Works which paper source to use, the size of the paper you're printing on, and the direction you want the print to appear on the page. To change the paper source, paper size, and print orientation, you use the Source, Size & Orientation tab of the Page Setup dialog box (see fig. 14.19). The page in the Sample area reflects the current paper size and orientation settings.

Depending on the type of printer you use, you can choose the correct paper source (such as the default paper tray, second paper tray, envelope feeder) from the Paper Source drop-down list.

The Paper Size drop-down list offers a variety of standard paper and envelope sizes. Choose a size from the list or enter the correct size in the Width and Height boxes.

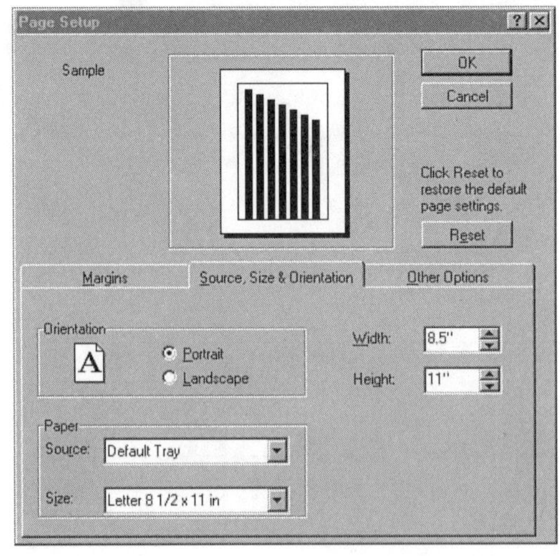

Fig. 14.19
The Page Setup dialog box displays paper source, size, and orientation settings for the current chart.

Paper orientation refers to the direction the paper is facing before it is printed on. Most documents printed on standard 8 1/2 X 11-inch paper are printed in *portrait* orientation, using the 11-inch dimension as the *height* of the paper. For documents that are printed in landscape orientation, the paper is rotated 90 degrees so that the 8 1/2-inch dimension is used as the height of the paper. (The paper is not actually rotated in your printer; your printer simply prints the image "sideways.")

Tip
Because the natural orientation of most chart types is landscape, printing the chart using landscape orientation makes for an attractive presentation that maintains the original chart proportions. The printed chart can be much larger without distortion in landscape orientation, making fine details easier to read.

The default orientation is Portrait; to print in landscape mode, select the Landscape option. For many charts, you will prefer to use landscape orientation. The illustration of the paper in the Sample area of the dialog box rotates. Notice, also, for the paper size you specify, the settings in the Width and Height boxes automatically reverse.

To change source, size, and orientation settings, follow these steps:

1. Choose File, Page Setup. The Page Setup dialog box appears.
2. In the dialog box, choose the Source, Size, and Orientation tab so the dialog box resembles figure 14.19.
3. Choose a paper source from the Paper Source drop-down list box.
4. Choose a paper size from the Paper Size drop-down list box, or specify a custom size in the Width and Height text boxes.

5. Choose a paper orientation by clicking either the Portrait or Landscape option button.

   The Sample area of the dialog box reflects the settings you choose.

6. When all settings are correct, choose OK.

Setting Other Page Options

The third tab in the Page Setup dialog box is Other Options (see fig. 14.20). Use the settings on this tab to specify the first page number and how you want a chart to be printed—that is, screen size or full page size.

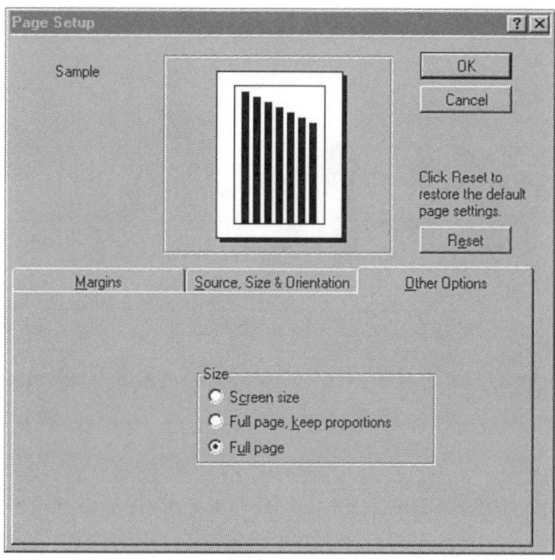

Fig. 14.20
The Other Options tab displays miscellaneous page settings.

When you choose the Screen Size option, Works prints a chart as closely as possible to the size that is displayed on-screen. You can also choose to print a chart using the full page, and maintain the correct proportions. Or, you can print a chart using the full page but ignoring the correct proportions. When you choose this last option, Works stretches the chart to fill as much of the page as possible.

Previewing a Chart

One of the most important steps you can take before printing any document is to *preview* it. Previewing enables you to see on-screen how your chart will look on the printed page. When you use the preview screen, Works displays a full-page view of your chart. This gives you a chance to see how the chart fills the page, how the proportions look, and to check the page orientation.

To preview a chart, choose File, Print Preview, or click the Preview button on the toolbar. The current chart appears in a preview screen like the one shown in figure 14.21.

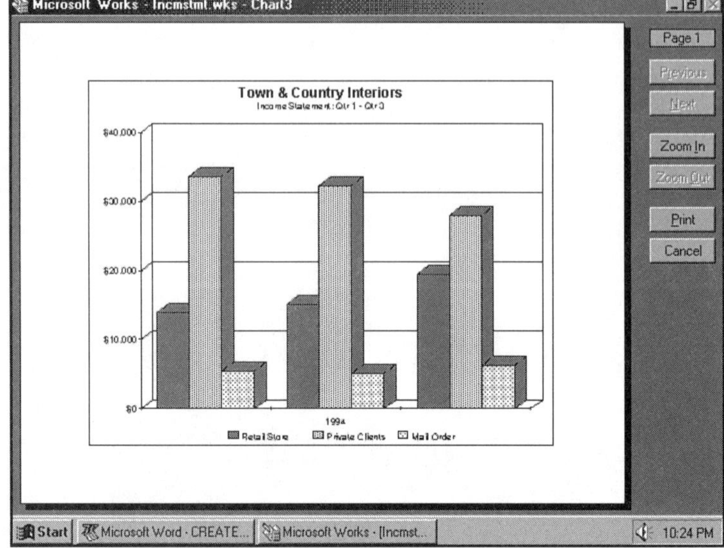

Fig. 14.21
Previewing a chart shows you how it will appear when printed.

The actual text and numbers displayed in the preview screen can be difficult to read because it is reduced, but reading the text isn't the important consideration here—checking the layout is. If you think you spot a problem, however, you can zero in on a particular location. Notice that the mouse pointer changes to a magnifying glass when it is pointing anywhere on the page. Click the left mouse button once anywhere on the page to zoom on the spreadsheet, or click the Zoom In button. If you need to magnify the spreadsheet further, click the left mouse button once more anywhere on the page, or click the Zoom In button again. Use the scroll bars, if necessary, to view a part of the spreadsheet that isn't visible. To zoom back out, click a third time anywhere on the page, or click the Zoom Out button.

When you're ready to print a chart, you can print directly from the preview screen by clicking the Print button. This button displays the Print dialog box, described in the next section.

Sending the Chart to the Printer

You use the Print dialog box shown in figure 14.22 to specify the number of copies you want to print. The currently selected printer is shown in the Name drop-down list box. If the printer is not correct, click the arrow button to display the list of installed printers and choose the one you want.

> **Note**
>
> Because charts include various shades of gray and might use curved lines, high quality graphics printing is important. Use the options available by choosing the Properties button to change the print quality, select the highest dots-per-inch resolution, darken or lighten the printed result, switch between raster and vector graphics, and change the dithering. The output of every printer model is a bit different; try adjusting the settings until you are satisfied with the results.

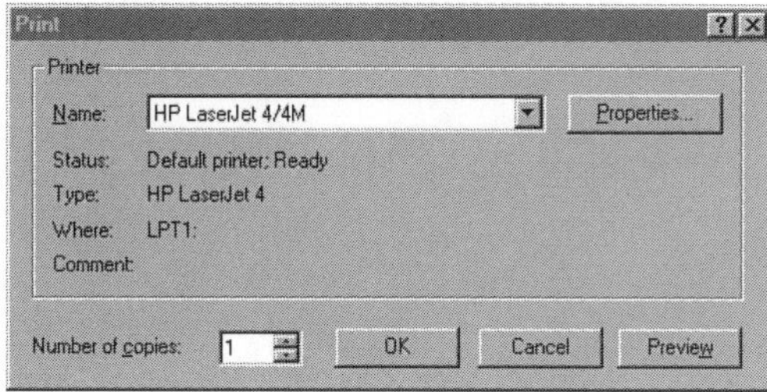

Fig. 14.22
Change the printer properties and set the number of copies in the Print dialog box.

Tip
From the Preview screen, you can just click Print to print the chart. This alternative skips the Print dialog box, but if the chart hasn't been closed since it was last printed, the previous Print settings, such as number of copies, are used.

To print a chart, follow these steps:

1. To display the chart you want to print, select View, Chart and then choose the desired chart.
2. Choose File, Page Setup to specify print margins, paper source, size, orientation, and other print settings.
3. To preview the chart, choose File, Print Preview; or click the Preview button on the toolbar.
4. Choose File, Print. The Print dialog box shown in figure 14.22 appears.
5. Choose the appropriate print settings, and then choose OK. ❖

Chapter 15

Editing and Enhancing a Chart

by Judy Petersen

After you have created a basic chart, you might want to change the data the chart represents or switch to a different chart type. You also might want to make a chart more attractive by experimenting with different fonts and colors, or adding titles, a legend, borders, gridlines, patterns, and so on. You can make these kinds of changes at any time and as often as you like.

In this chapter, you learn about the following:

- Choosing a different chart type
- Adding titles, subtitles, and axis titles
- Adding borders and gridlines
- Choosing a font, size, color, and style for text
- Creating a chart legend
- Specifying various x- and y-axes settings

Editing a Chart

After you create a chart, you sometimes realize that you selected the wrong cell range to chart or that you want to change some of the data in the spreadsheet. Or perhaps you want to experiment with a different chart type. These changes all are editing changes you can do at any time. The following sections describe these tasks in more detail.

Changing the Chart Type

When you first begin working with charts, experimenting with different chart types is a good idea. The more you work with charts, the more familiar you become with the unique features of each chart type. You also want to find the chart type that best conveys the message of the numbers you're charting. Obviously, some chart types are more appropriate than others, depending on the data you're charting and the data you want to emphasize.

> **Note**
>
> Charts are more than a way to jazz up your presentations; charting your data is a powerful analytical tool. Try several chart types and study the results, looking for trends and relationships that are less obvious when you look only at columns and rows of numbers.

You learn in Chapter 14, "Creating Charts," that Works automatically creates a bar chart unless you specify a different chart type in the New Chart dialog box. You also learn that every chart type offers several chart variations from which to choose. After you create a standard bar chart, you might decide to use a variation of the bar chart or a different type of chart altogether.

To see a sample of the chart variations, choose Format, Chart Type or click one of the chart buttons on the charting toolbar. (Note that the Chart Type command appears on the Format menu only when the active window contains a chart.) With the bar chart selected in the Basic Types tab of the Chart Type dialog box, the Variations tab shows examples of the bar chart variations (see fig. 15.1). Each of the six bar chart variations is slightly different, as the following list shows:

- The first variation is the standard bar chart that Works creates automatically.
- The second variation stacks the bars on top of one another, illustrating the combined total of data items.
- The third variation also stacks the bars but shows each value as a percentage of the whole (100%).
- The fourth variation is identical to the first except horizontal gridlines are added.

- The fifth variation adds data labels to each bar and shows only a single data series, also called a 1-series chart.
- The sixth bar chart variation displays a 1-series, and varies the color of each bar.

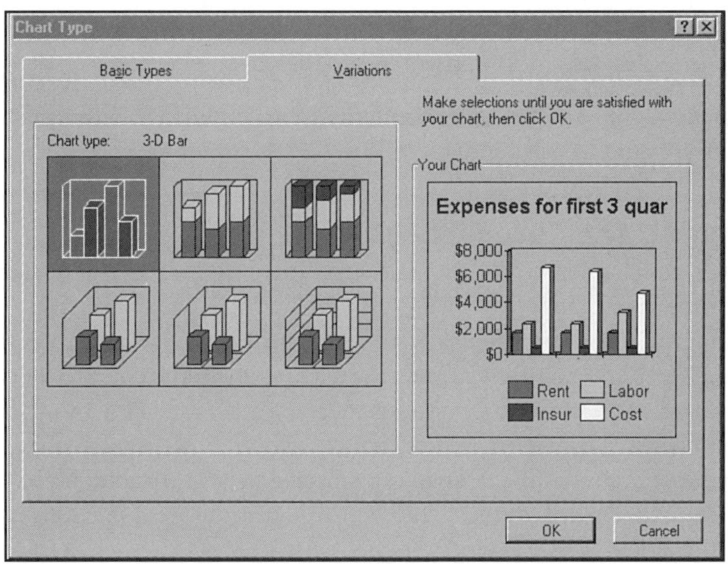

Fig. 15.1
Works offers six bar chart variations in the Variations tab of the Chart Type dialog box.

Each type of chart offers variations similar to those just described for the bar chart. Most charts offer variations that add data labels and gridlines. Some variations are unique, appropriate to the particular chart type. For instance, pie chart variations include exploded slices, and 3D area and bar charts enable you to show the x- and y-axes in 3D.

To change the chart type of an existing chart, you display the chart in the active window and then select a new variation or chart type from the Chart Type dialog box. In most cases, the new chart type does not affect the x- and y-series cell ranges you originally selected. The exception to this rule is when you change from a chart that depicts multiple y-series ranges (such as a bar chart) to a chart that depicts only one y-series range (such as a pie chart). In this case, Works charts only the first y-series you selected. To adjust x- or y-series cell ranges, see the "Changing X- and Y-Series Cell Ranges" section in this chapter.

Tip
You can add buttons to the charting toolbar for area, stacked line, and radar charts. To customize the toolbar, refer to Chapter 2.

To select a new chart type or a variation of the same chart, follow these steps:

1. In the active window, display the chart you want to change.

2. Choose Format, Chart Type to display the Chart Type dialog box.

3. Select the basic type of chart you want to switch to, then choose the Variations tab. Works displays the dialog box showing the available chart variations for the basic type you selected.

4. Choose the variation you want to use, then choose OK. Works redisplays your chart using the new variation or chart type you selected.

Changing the Spreadsheet Data

After you create a chart, you can make changes to the data in the spreadsheet at any time. The changes you make in individual cells are automatically reflected in the chart. For instance, if you change one value from $2,345 to $2,298, Works automatically adjusts the data points in the chart to reflect the changed entry. If you change a row heading from Mail Order to Catalog, Works changes the reference in the chart legend. If, however, you change the *type* of entry in a cell (for example, from a value to a row heading), you must adjust the x- and y-series ranges the chart uses because Works no longer charts the ranges the same way.

Recall from Chapter 14, "Creating Charts," that Works determines x- and y-series ranges based on the shape of the cell range you select. If the range includes more columns than rows, columns become x-series ranges (categories) and rows become y-series ranges (data items). If you insert a new row or column in a spreadsheet that would add a category to a chart, Works automatically includes the new cells in the x-series range and adds the new category to all the spreadsheet's existing charts. Likewise, if you delete a row or column that represents a category in a chart, Works automatically deletes the category from the chart.

The rule is not the same, however, for data items. If you insert a new row or column that would add a data item to a chart, Works does not automatically add the new data as a y-series; you must add the new y-series range and adjust the existing y-series ranges, if necessary. The reason Works *does not* automatically add new y-series ranges is so you can control the order in which y-series ranges appear in a chart.

Changing X- and Y-Series Cell Ranges

As discussed in the preceding section, because Works automatically determines x- and y-series ranges from the shape of the cells you select, you sometimes might need to adjust the x- or y-series ranges, or both series ranges. In addition to the case mentioned earlier where you add data to a spreadsheet, perhaps in another case you originally selected the wrong cell range. This situation also requires you to alter series ranges.

Before you change a range reference, check your spreadsheet and make note of the new ranges you want to define. Then define a new range by choosing Edit, Series, which displays the Edit Series dialog box shown in figure 15.2.

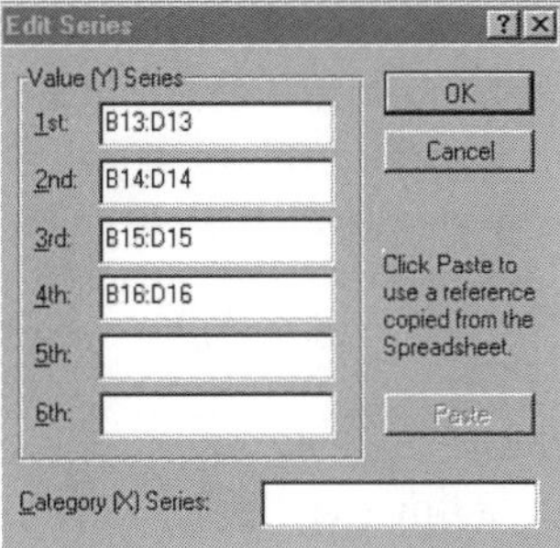

Fig. 15.2
The Edit Series dialog box displays existing x- and y-series cell ranges.

Use the following steps to add or change existing series ranges:

1. In the active window, display the chart for which you want to change series ranges.
2. Choose Edit, Series to display the Edit Series dialog box shown in figure 15.2. The Value (Y) Series area lists y-series cell ranges from 1st to 6th. The Category (X) Series box lists the x-series cell range.
3. To add a range or adjust existing y-series ranges, type the correct cell range in the 1st, 2nd, 3rd, 4th, 5th, or 6th boxes.

> **Note**
>
> To quickly enter new cell references, select the last series and press Cut (Ctrl+X). Move up to the next series and press Paste (Ctrl+V). Repeat this process to move each reference down one series until you reach the box for the new series and enter the cell references.

4. To adjust the x-series range, type the correct cell reference in the Category (X) Series box.

5. When you have entered the new ranges correctly, choose OK. Works redisplays your chart reflecting the new series ranges you specified.

Changing Mixed Line and Bar Charts

The combination chart type is a powerful tool when you are charting data of different types. When you chart two value series, Works displays the first series as a bar and the second series as a line. You can chart more than two series in a combination chart. Perhaps you want to chart the monthly sales of several regional offices compared to the Dow Jones stock average for the month. Typically, the months occupy the first column of the spreadsheet, the next columns contain the monthly sales results for each office, and a final column contains the Dow Jones values. If you select all the columns to chart, Works charts the first series as a bar and the rest as lines.

To change the series for the other offices to bars, display the chart on-screen, then choose Format, Mixed Line and Bar. In the Format Mixed Line and Bar dialog box that appears, choose the Bar option for every series except the series you want to display as a line (see fig. 15.3). In the figure, Line is chosen for the 3rd value.

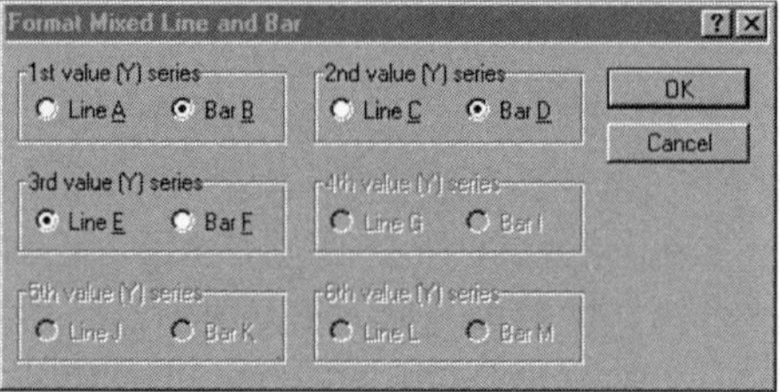

Fig. 15.3
In the Format Mixed Line and Bar dialog box, choose whether to display each series in the chart as a bar or line.

Troubleshooting

When I switched my chart type from a bar chart to a line chart, the data labels, colors, and patterns I added to my bar chart disappeared. Why?

When switching from one chart type to another, try to make the switch before enhancing the chart. When you switch to a new chart type, Works erases all previous enhancements such as colors, patterns, gridlines, data labels, and so on. You can return to the original chart, however, by immediately choosing Edit, Undo or pressing Ctrl+Z.

When I switched my bar chart to a pie chart, Works charted the wrong data series in the pie chart. Why does this happen, and how can I solve this problem?

When you switch from a chart that displays multiple y-series ranges (such as a bar chart) to a chart that displays only one y-series range (such as a pie chart), Works charts the first y-series in the new chart and ignores the remaining y-series ranges. If the new chart doesn't show the correct data, the correct data is not defined as the first y-series range. In the Edit Series dialog box, type the correct range reference in the first box and then choose OK.

Enhancing a Chart

Chapter 14, "Creating Charts," introduced you to the wide variety of chart types Works offers. Figures 14.1 through 14.12 showed many of the enhancements you can add to a chart, such as titles, borders, gridlines, colors, and patterns. Enhancements constitute anything you can add to or remove from a chart to improve its appearance or make a chart more readable. The following sections describe in detail how to add and remove enhancements.

Adding a Title, Subtitle, and Axis Title

When you create a new chart using the New Chart dialog box, you can specify a chart title at that time. If you don't specify a title when you create a new chart, you can add a title to an existing chart by choosing Edit, Titles, which displays the Edit Titles dialog box shown in figure 15.4. You also use this dialog box to specify a chart subtitle and horizontal and vertical axes titles.

Works centers a chart title at the top of a chart. If you add a subtitle, Works centers it just beneath the chart title. When you add a title such as Dollars to the vertical axis, the title appears alongside the scale. A title for the horizontal axis appears just below the axis and above the legend, if the chart includes one. Some chart types enable you to add a right vertical axis to a chart. When you use a chart of this type, you can add a title to the right vertical axis as well.

To add titles to a chart, use the following steps:

1. In the active window, display the chart to which you want to add titles.
2. Choose Edit, Titles. The Edit Titles dialog box shown in figure 15.4 opens.

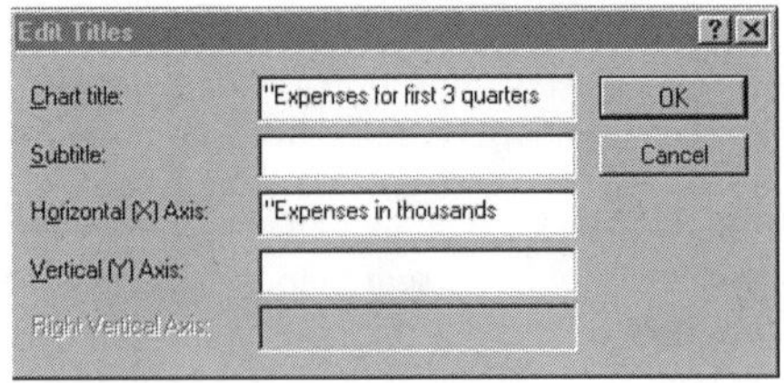

Fig. 15.4
Use the Edit Titles dialog box to add a title, subtitle, and axis title to a chart.

3. Type text for the titles in the appropriate text boxes.

4. Choose OK. Works returns to your chart and inserts the titles you specify.

To remove a title from a chart, open the Edit Titles dialog box and clear the text box that contains the title you want to remove. When you return to the chart, the title is gone.

Adding Borders, Gridlines, Droplines, and 3D Effects

Tip
If you use chart borders frequently, you can add a Border button to the charting toolbar. Refer to Chapter 2 for instructions on customizing the toolbar.

The New Chart dialog box enables you to add a border to a chart when you create it. If you choose not to add a border at the time you create a new chart, you can add a border later to an existing chart. First, display the chart in the active window, then choose Format, Border. Works shrinks the chart slightly and adds a border that surrounds all chart elements. A check mark appears next to the Border command. To remove a chart's border, choose Format, Border again to remove the check mark.

Gridlines help your eye follow the scale across a chart or the category markings on the x-axis of a chart. Gridlines also help you pinpoint exact values depicted in a chart. If you add gridlines to a new chart using the New Chart dialog box, Works automatically adds both horizontal and vertical gridlines. However, if you wait until after you create a chart to add gridlines, you have the freedom to add horizontal or vertical gridlines separately.

To add gridlines to an existing chart, use the following steps:

1. In the active window, display the chart to which you want to add gridlines.

2. To add horizontal gridlines, choose Format, Horizontal (X) Axis.

3. In the Format Horizontal Axis dialog box that appears, select the Show Gridlines check box, then choose OK.

4. To add vertical gridlines, repeat steps 2 and 3, choosing the Vertical (Y) Axis command rather than the Horizontal (X) Axis command.

When you create a 2D area or 3D area chart, consider adding droplines to the chart. *Droplines* are vertical lines that extend from data points to the x-axis to help emphasize the data points along the x-axis for each of the data items in the chart. In figure 15.5, droplines make the data points for each of the income sources much easier to distinguish from month to month.

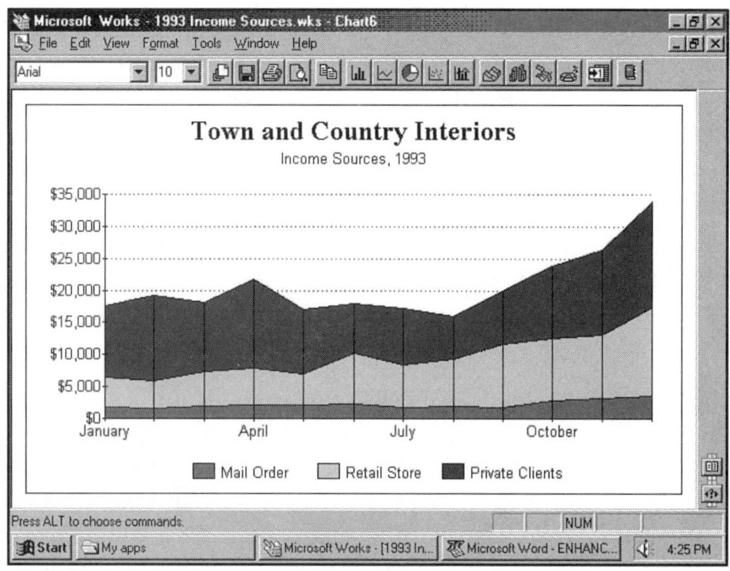

Fig. 15.5
In area charts, you can add droplines that extend from data points to the x-axis.

To add droplines to an area or 3D area chart, display the chart in the active window, then choose Format, Horizontal (X) Axis. In the dialog box, select the Show Droplines check box and then choose OK. To remove droplines from a chart, remove the check mark from the Show Droplines check box in the Format Horizontal Axis dialog box.

Note

Droplines usually stand out better on the printed chart than on your computer monitor. However, your printer and the colors in the chart might cause the droplines to be less visible. To make droplines easier to see, edit the chart to select lighter colors for the data items. See the section "Choosing Colors, Patterns, and Markers," later in this chapter.

Tip
You can rotate a 3D bar chart five degrees at a time by pressing Ctrl and any arrow key. Press Ctrl+Home to return the chart to its original position.

The Format menu includes a handy command, 3D, that enables you to change a 2D chart into a 3D chart instantly. When you choose this command, Works switches the area, bar, line, or pie chart displayed in the current window to a 3D version of the same chart and retains the current chart variation. The 3D command saves you the trouble of choosing the correct variation of a 3D chart from a dialog box. To switch back to a 2D version of the same chart variation, choose Format, 3D again to remove the check mark.

Choosing a Character Font, Size, Color, and Style

In the word processor and spreadsheet sections of this book, you learn how to use the Format Font and Style dialog box to change the font, size, color, and style of text. Recall that *font* refers to the unique design of characters, *size* refers to the point size of characters, *color* refers to the color of text displayed on-screen, and *style* refers to special features such as bold, underline, italic, and strikethrough. These characteristics collectively are called *text format*. To change the text format for a chart, you use the same Format Font and Style dialog box you use in the word processor and spreadsheet tools.

In a chart, you can change the text format of the title independently of the subtitle, axis titles, legend text, data labels, and other text in a chart. However, changing the format of any text other than the title or subtitle affects *all* other text. The Format Font and Style dialog box for a chart title is shown in figure 15.6. Notice, the name in the dialog box specifically states `Format Font and Style - Title`. When you change the text format for a subtitle in a chart, the title in the dialog box reads `Format Font and Style - Subtitle` but the options in the dialog box are identical. The Sample area of the dialog box displays sample text using the settings you choose. Remember to check this area to preview your choices before closing the dialog box.

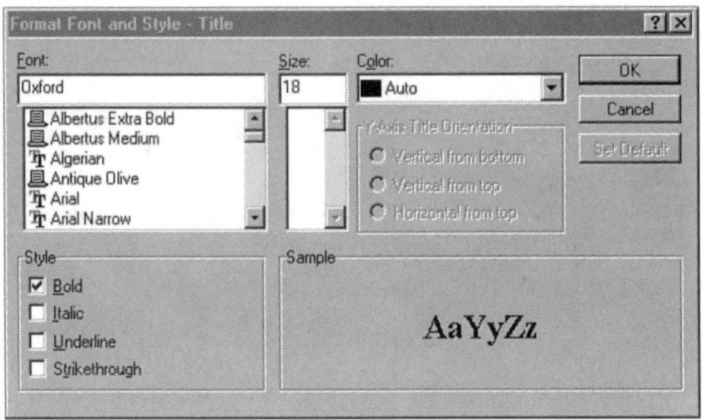

Fig. 15.6
Use the Format Font and Style dialog box to change font, size, color, and style of text in a chart.

To change the text format of a chart's title, use the following steps:

1. Click the chart title; Works highlights the title by surrounding it with a box with handles.

2. Choose Format, Font and Style. The Format Font and Style - Title dialog box opens.

3. In the Font box, select a font for the title.

4. In the Size box, select a point size for the title.

5. In the Color box, select a screen-display color for the title text.

6. In the Style area, choose the Bold, Italic, Underline, or Strikethrough options to add these features to the title.

7. When all settings are correct, choose OK. Works reformats the title using the settings you specified.

To change the format of the subtitle or axis titles, click the subtitle or axis title, then follow steps 2 through 7. To change the format of all text other than the chart title, subtitle, and axis titles, click any other part of the chart, then choose Format, Font and Style and follow steps 2 through 7. Works displays the Format Font and Style - Tick Labels, Data Labels, etc. dialog box, which includes settings identical to the other Format Font and Style dialog boxes.

Tip
To quickly access a Format Font and Style dialog box, click the right mouse button on the title or subtitle to display the context menu. Choose the Font and Style command.

Choosing Colors, Patterns, and Markers

When you create a new chart, Works automatically assigns colors to the bars, lines, areas, and pie slices that depict spreadsheet data. For the y-series data ranges 1 through 6, Works uses red, green, blue, yellow, cyan, and magenta as the default colors. Dark shades of these colors and shades of gray, black, and white are also available.

When a chart is printed, the colors you see on-screen are translated to shades of gray. Sometimes this translation results in bars or slices that do not contrast sufficiently from other bars or slices. Using a pattern rather than a color provides excellent contrast. *Patterns* are designs that appear inside bars, areas, and slices of a pie, or the line style used in a line chart. You can choose diagonal or vertical lines, or you might prefer a crosshatch pattern. When you create a line chart, you can change the pattern for the lines to dashed, dotted, or dot-dash rather than solid lines. By default, Works does not use patterns in the charts it creates, but you can assign patterns to selected y-series ranges in a chart if you want. Figure 15.7 shows an example of pattern style used in a pie chart.

Caution

If you use two or more patterns in a chart (particularly cross-hatching), check the results carefully. Adjacent patterns can appear to flicker, a phenomenon called Moiré distortion.

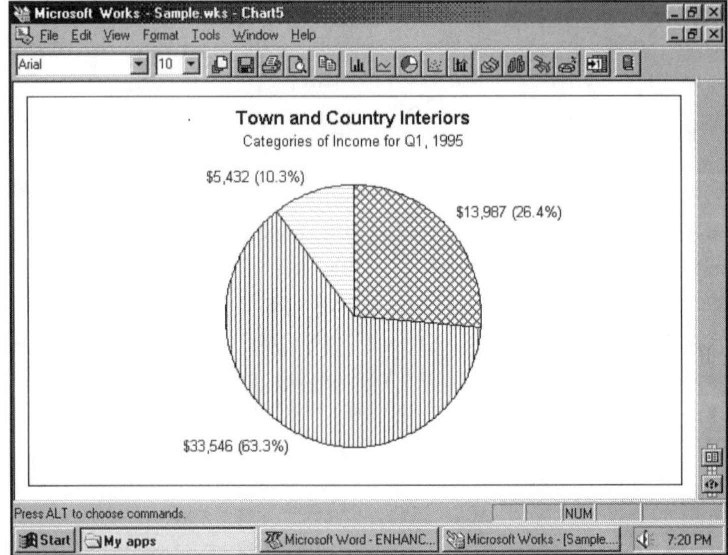

Fig. 15.7
Various pattern styles appear in the slices of this pie chart.

Tip
If you change patterns and colors in a chart frequently, you can add a Patterns and Colors button to the charting toolbar. Refer to Chapter 2 for instructions on customizing the toolbar.

When you create a line chart or an x-y scatter chart, Works uses *data markers* for each data item. Data markers pinpoint the locations in the chart that represent actual values from the spreadsheet. The default data marker is a filled circle, but you can change the style of the data markers for each y-series range, just as you can change colors and patterns used in bars, lines, areas, and pie slices. Data marker styles include a filled circle, filled box, filled diamond, asterisk, hollow circle, hollow box, hollow diamond, dot, or dash.

To change the color, pattern, or data markers used in a chart, you choose Format, Shading and Color, which displays the Format Shading and Color dialog box shown in figure 15.8. In the Series area, you choose the y-series for which you want to make changes, and then scroll through the lists in each of the Colors, Patterns, and Markers boxes to make specific choices. (Note that the Markers box is available only for line and x-y scatter charts.) The patterns available in the Patterns list box vary depending on the type of chart you are using.

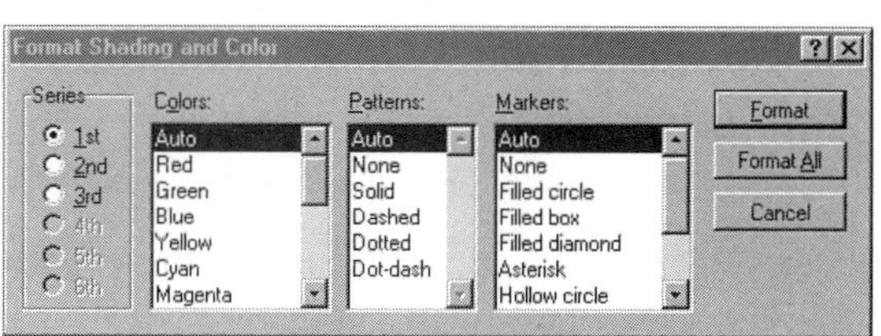

Fig. 15.8
Here you can customize the colors, patterns, and markers in your charts.

The Format button changes the color, pattern, and marker for the y-series currently selected. The Format All button changes *all* y-series ranges to the selected color, pattern, and marker choices.

To change colors, patterns, or markers in an existing chart, use the following steps:

1. In the active window, display the chart you want to change.
2. Choose Format, Shading and Color to display the dialog box shown in figure 15.8.
3. In the Series area, select one y-series range.
4. In the Colors, Patterns, and Markers list boxes, highlight the options you want to use.
5. To assign the current choices to the selected y-series range, click the Format button. Or to assign the current choices to all y-series ranges, choose the Format All button.

Note

When you choose the Format or Format All button to apply a selected color, pattern, or marker, you can see the change behind the Format Shading and Color dialog box. Drag the dialog box by the title bar so you can check the result to see if it is satisfactory before closing the dialog box.

6. Repeat steps 3, 4, and 5 to select a color, pattern, or marker for other y-series ranges.

7. When all settings are correct, choose the Close button. Works returns to your chart and assigns the colors, patterns, and markers you specified.

Adding a Chart Legend

Tip
You can display the Edit Legend/Series Labels dialog box instantly if you add the Edit Legend/Series Labels button to the charting toolbar. (See Chapter 2.)

When you create a new chart using the New Chart dialog box, Works automatically creates a chart legend for you if your cell selection includes row and column headings. If you don't include row and column headings in your original cell selection, you can add a legend to an existing chart later.

To add a legend, choose Edit, Legend/Series Labels, which displays the dialog box shown in figure 15.9. Use this box to specify which cells contain the data for the legend. In the Series Labels section, you enter the cell address for the label of each y-series data range. For instance, suppose that your first y-series range in cells A3:E3 is mail-order income and cell A3 contains the entry `Mail Order`. To use this entry in the chart legend, you enter A3 in the 1st Value Series box.

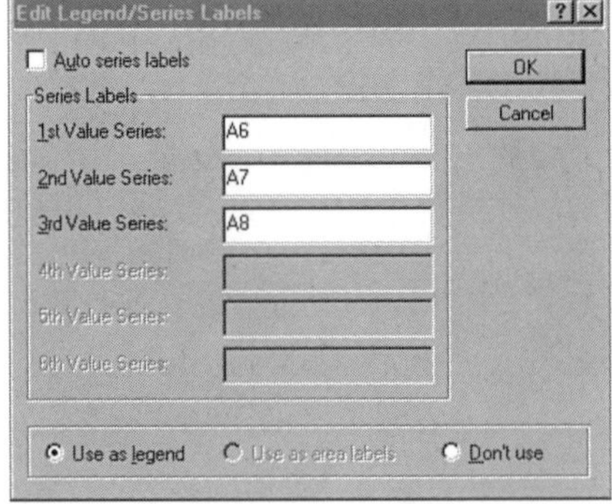

Fig. 15.9
Use the Edit Legend/Series Labels dialog box to add a legend to an existing chart.

Follow these steps to add a legend to an existing chart:

1. In the spreadsheet, note the cell range that contains the descriptions for each y-series range.
2. Display the chart for which you want to add a legend.
3. Choose Edit, Legend/Series Labels. The Edit Legend/Series Labels dialog box shown in figure 15.9 opens.
4. In the 1st Value Series box, type the cell reference for the description of the first y-series data range.

5. Repeat step 4 for all y-series ranges, entering references in the 2nd and 3rd Value Series boxes, and so on.

6. Choose the Use as Legend option button, then choose OK. Works adds a legend to your chart.

Tip

If text is more descriptive than the labels used in the spreadsheet, type the text in each Value Series box.

Note

If you select the Auto Series Labels check box in the Edit Legend/Series Labels dialog box, Works creates a legend using `Series 1`, `Series 2`, `Series 3`, and so on as the legend text for the y-series ranges in your chart. Use this option only when you did not include y-series cells in the original selection for your chart.

After you add a legend to a chart, you can turn off the legend display easily by deleting the contents of each Value Series in the Edit Legend/Series Labels dialog box.

Adding Data Labels

If showing precise values is important, you might want to enhance your chart with *data labels*. Data labels show the exact values used to plot a y-series range in a chart. Works inserts the labels at the top of each bar in a bar chart, next to the points plotted in a line or area chart, or to the side of each slice in a pie chart.

An example is shown in figure 15.10. In the figure, you clearly can see that expenses for Qtr1, Qtr2, Qtr3, and Qtr4, respectively, are `$34,097`, `$31,717`, `$38,378`, and `$40,203`, but the exact values might be difficult to determine without the use of data labels.

You can add data labels for all y-series ranges in a chart or just to selected y-series ranges. Notice in figure 15.10 that data labels were added to the expense data points but not the income bars. Use data labels sparingly; they can make a dense chart look cluttered. Data labels are not available for 3D charts.

To add data labels to a chart, you choose Edit, Data Labels, which displays the dialog box shown in figure 15.11. In each of the Value (Y) Series boxes, you type the cell reference from the spreadsheet containing the values. If you are adding data labels for only one y-series range, you can select and copy (using the Copy command on the Edit menu) the correct cell range in the spreadsheet, then choose the Paste button in the Edit Data Labels dialog box. When you choose the Paste button, Works automatically inserts the cell reference you copied from the spreadsheet.

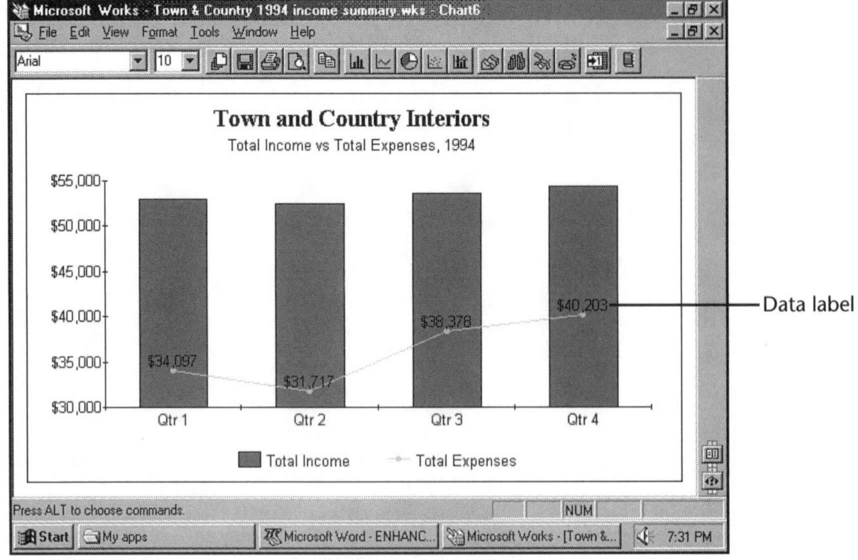

Fig. 15.10
Data labels pinpoint exact expense amounts for Qtr1, Qtr2, Qtr3, and Qtr4.

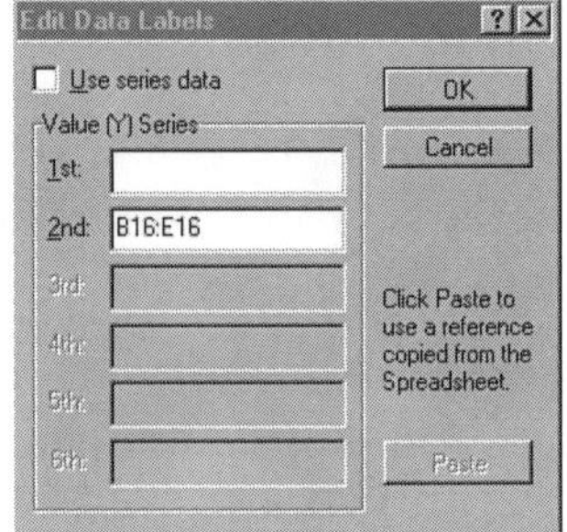

Fig. 15.11
Use the Edit Data Labels dialog box to add data labels to a chart. Note that a range reference was used to add the four labels in figure 15.10.

To add data labels to selected y-series ranges in a chart, use the following steps:

1. In the spreadsheet, note the cells that contain the values you want to use as data labels for y-series ranges. If you are adding data labels to a single y-series range, you can select the cell range then choose Edit, Copy.

2. Display the chart for which you want to add data labels.

3. Choose Edit, Data Labels. The Edit Data Labels dialog box shown in figure 15.11 opens.

4. Click the Value (Y) Series box (1st, 2nd, 3rd, and so on) for which you want to add data labels. If you copied a cell range from the spreadsheet in step 1, choose the Paste button to automatically insert the correct range. Otherwise, type the correct cell range in the Value (Y) Series box, or select the Use Series Data check box.
5. Type the correct cell range in all other Value (Y) Series boxes for which you want to add data labels.
6. When you have entered all ranges correctly, choose the OK button. Works returns to your chart and adds data labels.

Troubleshooting

I changed the colors, patterns, and markers used in my chart, and now I want to change them back to the default settings Works uses. I can't undo the changes I made, because I have used other commands since I made these changes.

Display your chart again and then recall the Format Shading and Color dialog box by choosing Format, Shading and Color. In the Colors, Patterns, and Markers boxes, select the Auto setting, then choose the Format All button. Works restores the default colors, patterns, and markers to your chart.

When I checked the Auto Series Labels in the Edit Legend/Series Labels dialog box, Works used `Series 1`*,* `Series 2`*,* `Series 3`*, and so on as data labels in my chart. Why didn't it use the actual labels from the spreadsheet?*

To use the actual labels, you must include the cells that contain the labels in your original range of cells to chart. If labels aren't included in that range, Works doesn't know what they are and uses Series 1, Series 2, and Series 3 instead. You can change the auto labels to the actual labels by entering the correct cell addresses in the Value Series areas of the Edit Legend/Series Labels dialog box.

Specifying Various X- and Y-Axes Settings

Earlier in this chapter, you learned how to add gridlines to a chart's axes. Works lets you control other aspects of a chart's axes as well. These options are described in the following sections.

Specifying Horizontal X-Axis Settings

Works enables you to control the label frequency used on the x-axis or remove the x-axis entirely from a chart. *Label frequency* refers to the intervals along the x-axis where labels appear. In figure 15.12, some of the month labels are so long that they overlap and cause the x-axis to look cluttered. This chart uses a label frequency of 1; that is, Works labels each month.

To improve the appearance of this chart and still print category labels, you can change the label frequency so a label prints for every other month or every third month. A small number creates more frequent labels; a large number creates less frequent labels. For example, a label frequency of 2 prints a label every other month; a label frequency of 6 prints a label every sixth month. In figure 15.13, the label frequency is 3, so January, April, July, and October labels are well-spaced. Each label is quite readable, and the x-axis displays tick marks for the intermediate months.

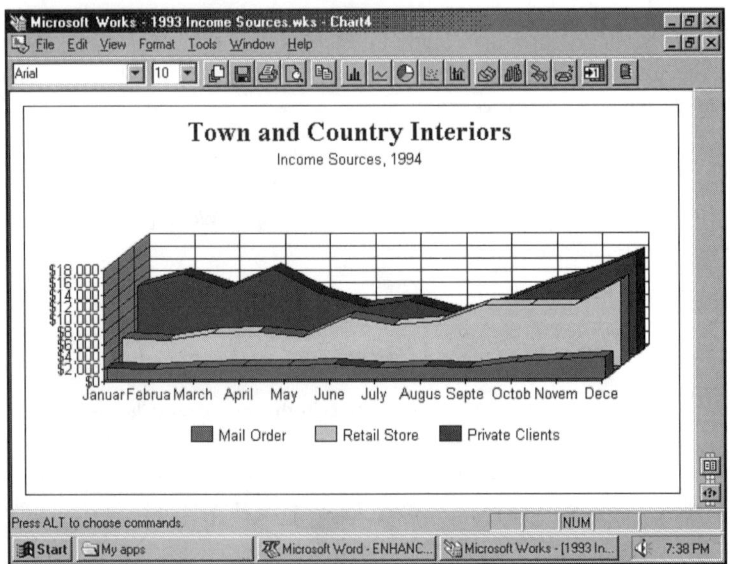

Fig. 15.12 Category labels that overlap clutter the x-axis and are difficult to read.

To control horizontal axis settings, you use the Format Horizontal Axis dialog box shown in figure 15.14. This dialog box is the same box you use to add gridlines and droplines to a chart. Notice the third setting in this dialog box enables you to remove the x-axis entirely from a chart.

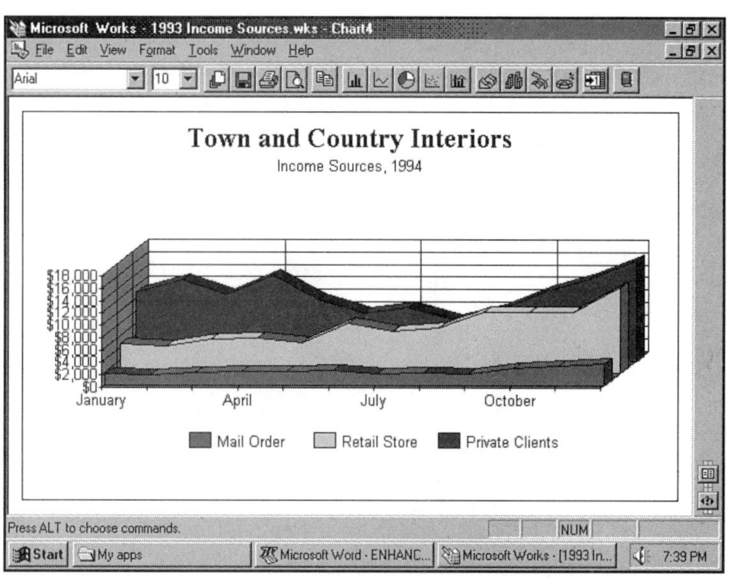

Fig. 15.13
A label frequency of 3 prints labels every third month.

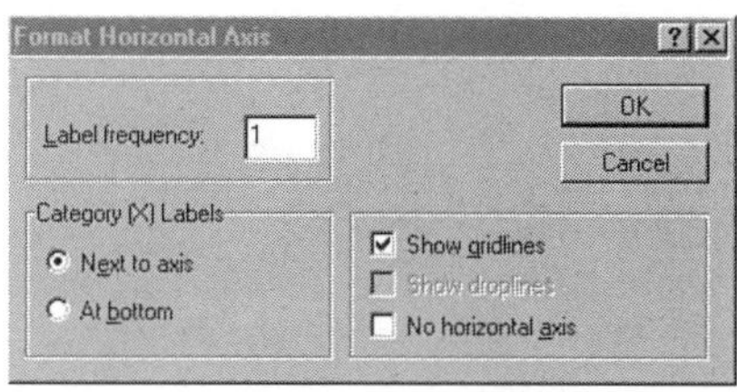

Fig. 15.14
Use the Format Horizontal Axis dialog box to specify x-axis settings.

To specify horizontal axis settings, use these steps:

1. In the active window, display the chart you want to change.
2. Choose Format, Horizontal (X) Axis, which displays the Format Horizontal Axis dialog box shown in figure 15.14.
3. To remove the horizontal axis for the displayed chart, select the No Horizontal Axis check box.
4. To change the label frequency of the x-axis, type a number in the Label Frequency text box.
5. Choose OK.

Specifying Vertical Y-Axis Settings

Just as you can specify horizontal axis settings, you can specify vertical axis settings. Choose Format, Vertical (Y) Axis, which displays the dialog box shown in figure 15.15. On the left side of the dialog box, you specify the markings and measurements to use on the y-axis scale (Minimum, Maximum, and Interval).

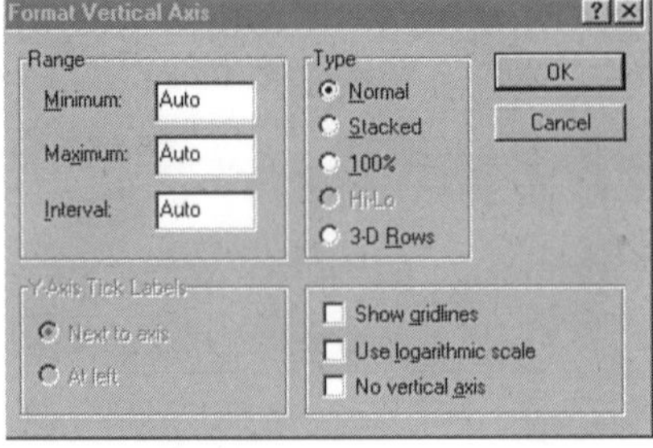

Fig. 15.15 Use the Format Vertical Axis dialog box to specify y-axis settings.

Figures 15.16 and 15.17 illustrate how you can change the y-axis scale. In figure 15.16, Works uses Auto as the setting in the Minimum, Maximum, and Interval boxes. Auto means that Works determines the best scale to use based on the data you selected to chart. For this chart, Works uses 0 as the minimum, 100 as the maximum, and 10 as the interval.

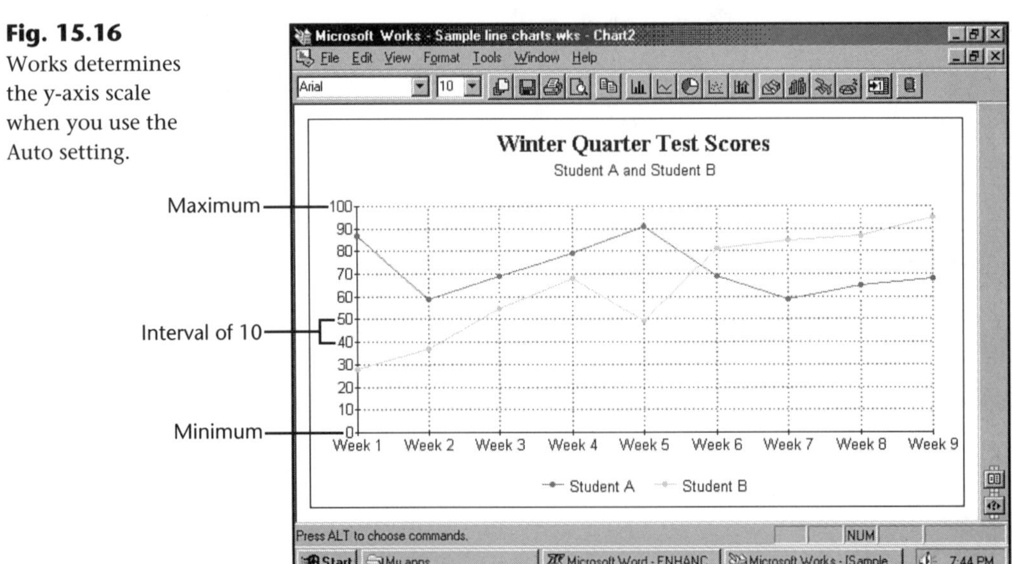

Fig. 15.16 Works determines the y-axis scale when you use the Auto setting.

If you examine the spreadsheet for this chart, you find that Student A's test scores range from 59 to 91, and Student B's test scores range from 28 to 95. If you wanted the chart to show scores more precisely, you could change the minimum to 25, the maximum to 95, and the interval to 5. An example of this scale is shown in figure 15.17.

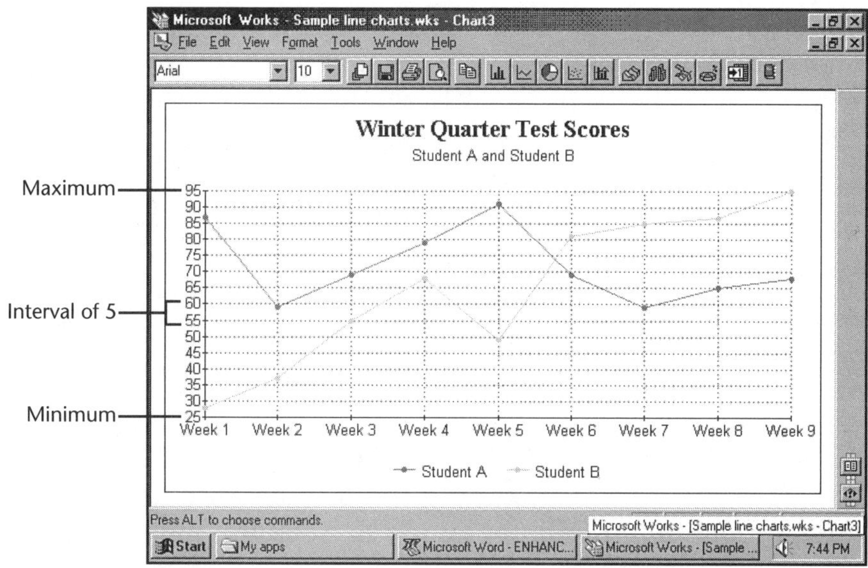

Fig. 15.17 Customized maximum, minimum, and interval settings on the y-axis.

The Format Vertical Axis dialog box also enables you to choose the type of axis to use in a chart (refer to fig. 15.15). Normal is the setting Works chooses by default. For a line chart, you could use a scale that stacks y-series ranges, a 100% scale, or a Hi-Lo scale (commonly used for charting stock performance). Note that the options in the Type box are different depending on the type of chart you are using.

Suppose that the data shown in figures 15.16 and 15.17 reflected Student C's test scores on quizzes and exams rather than the test scores for Student A and Student B. To chart Student C's cumulative performance over the nine-week period, you would choose the Stacked option from the Type box. A stacked scale produces a very different type of chart, as shown in figure 15.18.

The check boxes in the Format Vertical Axis dialog box enable you to show or hide gridlines, show or hide the y-axis, or use a logarithmic scale.

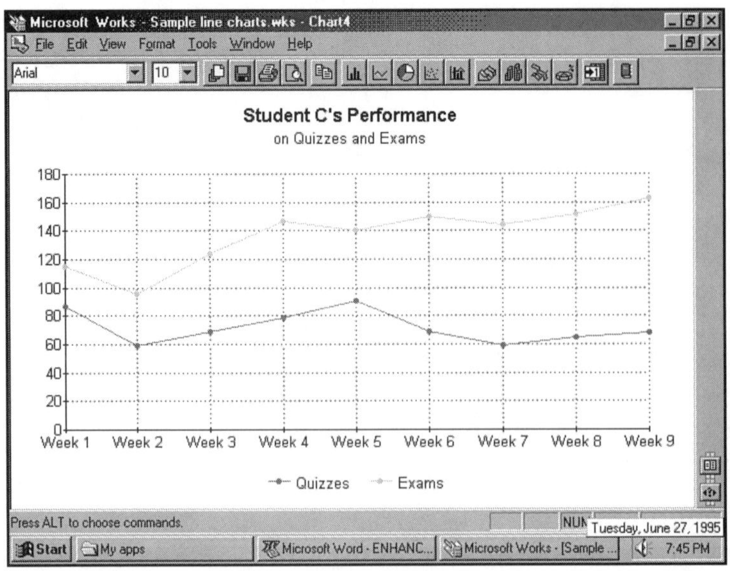

Fig. 15.18
A stacked scale stacks y-series ranges to show cumulative values.

Note

When you use a logarithmic scale, the interval you specify in the Interval box is the factor by which numbers are multiplied to determine the scale for the y-axis. For example, if you specify 10 as the interval, the y-axis scale is 10, 100, 1000, 10000, and so on. Using a logarithmic scale works best when the values you are plotting are very large.

To change any of the vertical axis settings in the Format Vertical Axis dialog box, use the following steps:

1. In the active window, display the chart for which you want to change axis settings.

2. Choose Format, Vertical (Y) Axis to open the Format Vertical Axis dialog box shown in figure 15.15.

3. To change the y-axis scale, type values in the Minimum, Maximum, and Interval boxes.

4. To use a scale type other than Normal, choose an option in the Type area.

5. To show gridlines, select the Show Gridlines check box.

6. To hide the vertical axis, select the No Vertical Axis check box.

7. To use a logarithmic scale, check the Use Logarithmic Scale check box.

8. When all settings are correct, choose OK.

Using Two Vertical (Y) Axes

You might add a second vertical (y) axis to any 2D chart. Using two vertical axes, you can chart two or more series that are measured differently. Figure 15.19 shows a combination chart in which the first series (Sales in Thousands) is represented by bars and the second series (Average Monthly Temperature) is represented by a line. Similarly, a second vertical (y) axis can facilitate comparing monthly changes in data such as the Dow Jones average and interest rate percent, or manufacturing output in dollars and the unemployment rate.

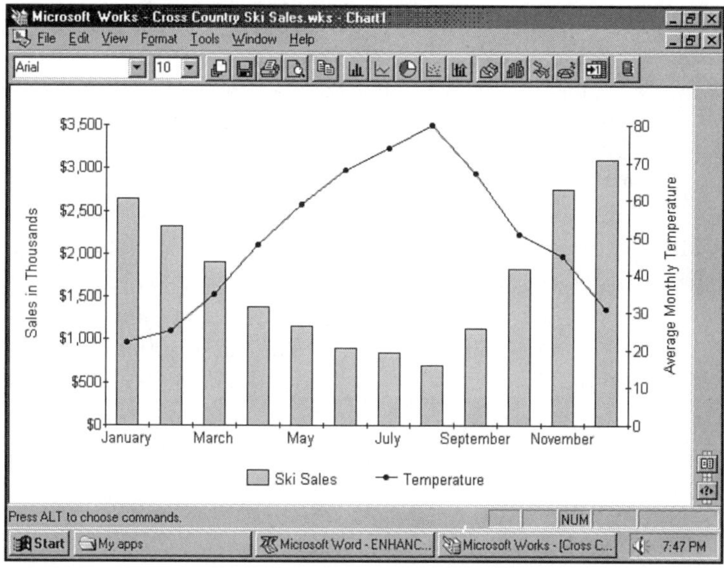

Fig. 15.19
The left vertical axis uses a currency scale and the right vertical axis is formatted for temperature.

To add a second vertical (y) axis to a chart, follow these steps:

1. In the active window, display the chart for which you want to change axis settings.

2. Choose Format, Two Vertical (Y) Axis to open the Format Two Vertical Axes dialog box shown in figure 15.20.

3. In Format Two Vertical Axes dialog box, indicate for the 1st and the 2nd value series which is the left axis and which the right. To create a chart like the one in figure 15.19 where temperature is the 2nd series, choose Right D in the 2nd series box.

4. When all settings are correct, choose OK.

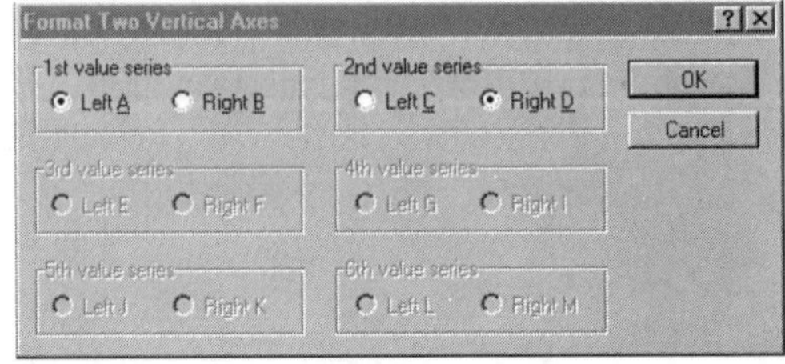

Fig. 15.20 In the Format Two Vertical Axes dialog box, choose one series for the left vertical axis and the other series for the right axis.

When you choose Right D in step 3, Works scales the vertical axis that is added according to the values in the 2nd series—temperature in this example.

It is not necessary for both vertical axes to be scaled differently. The two vertical axes can be identical. For example, when a chart is crowded with detail or the width is much greater than the height, the viewer might have difficulty determining the value of the data points at the right side of the chart. Adding gridlines is an attractive solution for simple charts, and it is the only solution for 3D charts. With some charts, gridlines add clutter rather than clarity. A better solution is to add a vertical axis on the right end of the chart.

To create a vertical axis on the right that is a duplicate of the one on the left, follow these steps:

1. Choose Right D for the 2nd series.
2. Now you need to format the second vertical axis. Choose Format, Right Vertical (Y) Axis to display the Format Right Vertical Axis dialog box.
3. Type values in the Minimum, Maximum, and Interval boxes that match the values displayed on the left vertical axis.
4. When all settings are correct, choose OK. ❖

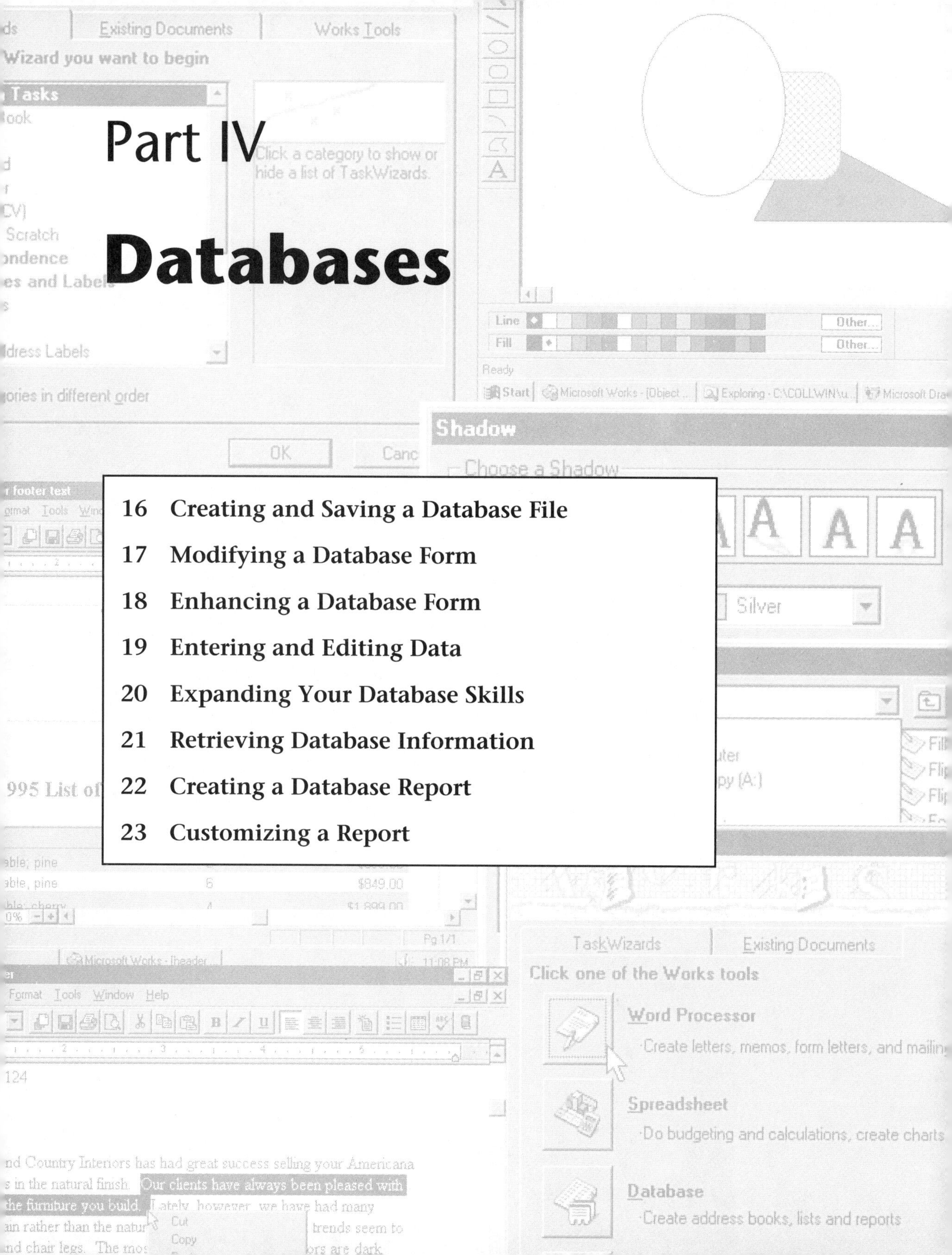

Part IV

Databases

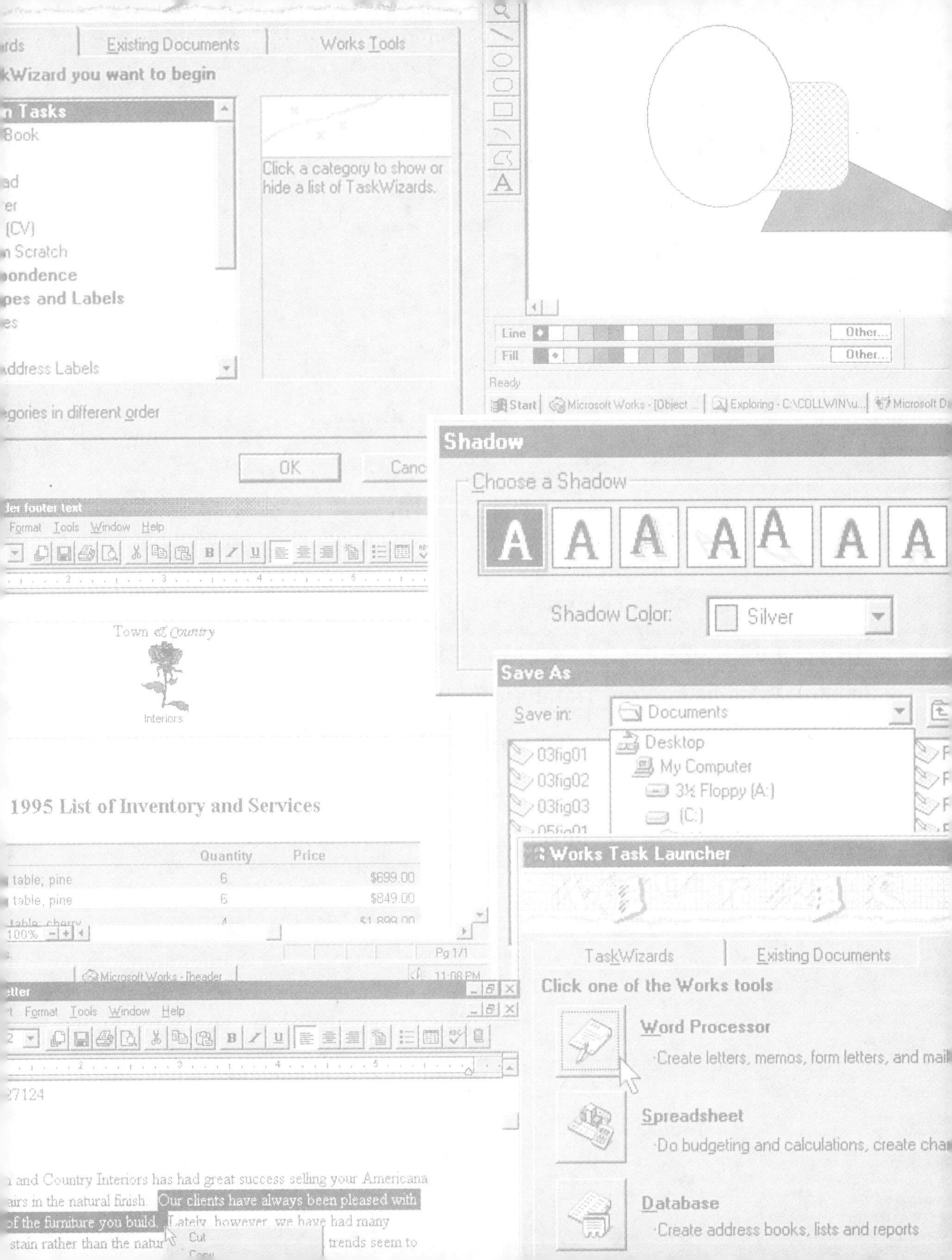

Existing Documents
Works Tools
kWizard you want to begin
n Tasks
Book
(CV)
n Scratch
Click a category to show or hide a list of TaskWizards.
ddress Labels
gories in different order
OK
Line
Fill
Other...
Other...
Ready
Start
Microsoft Works - [Object ...
Exploring - C:\COLLWIN\u...
Shadow
Choose a Shadow
A A A A A A A
Shadow Color:
Silver
Format Tools Window Help
Town & Country
Interiors
1995 List of Inventory and Services
Quantity
Price
table; pine
6
$699.00
table, pine
6
$849.00
100%
Pg 1/1
Microsoft Works - [header...
11:08 PM
Save As
Save in:
Documents
Desktop
My Computer
3½ Floppy (A:)
(C:)
03fig01
03fig02
03fig03
Works Task Launcher
TaskWizards
Existing Documents
Click one of the Works tools
Word Processor
·Create letters, memos, form letters, and mail
Spreadsheet
·Do budgeting and calculations, create char
Database
·Create address books, lists and reports
27124
n and Country Interiors has had great success selling your Americana
airs in the natural finish. Our clients have always been pleased with
of the furniture you build. Lately, however, we have had many
stain rather than the natur
trends seem to
Cut

Chapter 16

Creating and Saving a Database File

by Faithe Wempen

With the Microsoft Works for Windows 95 Database module, you can store many common types of information, such as mailing lists, inventories, employee data, sales contact information, and fundraising records. You can even store spreadsheets and graphic images.

Works makes creating a database easy. Unlike many other programs, Works performs most of the chores involved in designing a database form and printing reports. With the supplied database *TaskWizards*, you can even select a predesigned database application and choose a variety of appearance and design options.

This chapter deals with the first steps of using a database file. You learn about these topics:

- Planning a new database
- Creating a database file
- Naming and saving database files
- Using Form and List views
- Understanding the Database window and toolbar

Understanding a Database

In its simplest form, a *database* is like a traditional file card system. In a file card drawer, you store file cards, each of which contains the same type of information: names and addresses, for example, or a videotape collection, or business equipment records, or pledge information for a school jogathon. In the Works Database, each file card is called a *record*.

Each record (card) in the database (file drawer) holds information about just one item: one name and address, one videotape, one item of business equipment, etc.

In each record, you list relevant information about the item. For example, a personnel record might list an employee's name, address, city, state, ZIP code, and birth date. A videotape record might list the videotape title, category (action, adventure, comedy), length, cost, purchase date, and so on.

Each type of information in a record is called a *field*. Figure 16.1 shows a sample record from a Works database that contains information about business clients.

Fig. 16.1
A sample record from a Works client database, displayed in Form view.

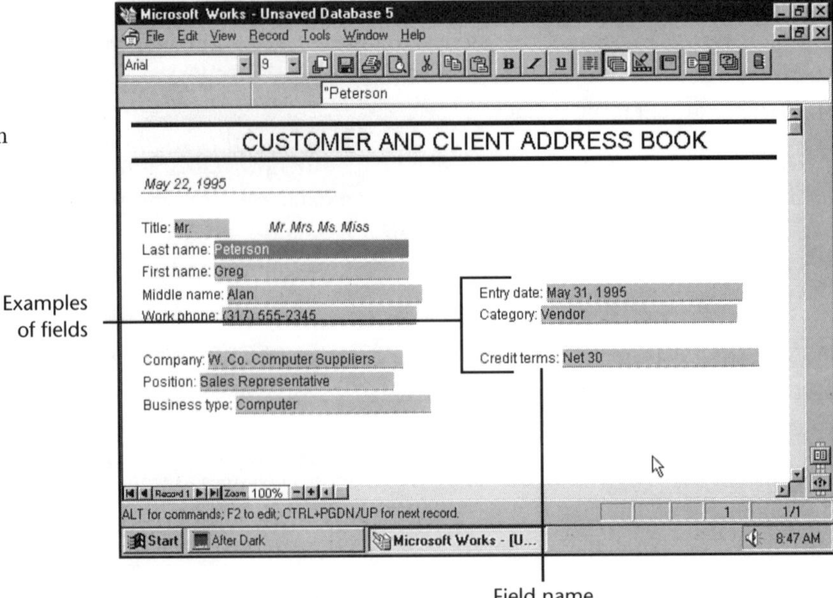

Figure 16.1 shows one record in the Customer and Client Address Book. Notice the fields in the record: `Title`, `Last name`, `First name`, and so on.

The data screen you see in figure 16.1, corresponding to a card in a file card drawer, is called a database *form*. Laying out a database form is very much like typing in the Works word processor. (The Works word processor is covered in

Chapters 4 through 9.) You can change a database form at any time, even after you add records to the database.

Planning a Database

In Works, you can change database forms at any time, even after you add information to a database. For example, you may discover that a better arrangement of fields would enable you to enter data more efficiently. However, adding or combining fields may require hours of retyping or reformatting. For example, imagine that you have created a database of names and addresses. The database form contains the following fields:

```
Last Name:

First Name:

Address 1:

Address 2:
```

A sample record looks like this:

```
Last Name: Anderson

First Name: Donna

Address 1: 234 West Harris

Address 2: Seattle, WA 98112
```

After creating your database form, you enter 250 records. Then you decide to do a bulk mailing. The U.S. Postal Service may require you to sort your labels in ZIP code order. But Works is unable to sort your records because the `Address 2` field combines the city, state, and ZIP code. With separate fields, you can sort records based on the city, state, or ZIP code.

You're faced with a real dilemma. The brochure needs to be mailed immediately, but before you can print labels, you need to create new fields for the city, state, and ZIP information, and retype that information for all 250 records.

Clearly, you would have been ahead to create separate fields initially:

```
Last Name:

First Name:

Address:

City:

State:

ZIP:
```

Planning your database form on paper beforehand is highly advisable, especially if you're not going to use a TaskWizard (see "Starting a New Database with a TaskWizard" later in this chapter). When planning database forms, consider the following factors:

- *Which fields are always filled and which fields are seldom filled?* Entering data goes more efficiently if you don't need to press the Tab key to skip over seldom-used fields. You may want to group the most often-used fields together, at the top of the form.

- *Will you use the database to print mail-merge letters?* If so, you may want to include `Greeting` and `Title` fields. For example, you may want to address Donna Anderson as *Mrs. Anderson*, Susan Caran as *Ms. Caran*, Don Ritchie as *Don*, and Dr. Carl Ekman as *Dr. Ekman*. Including a `Greeting` field allows you to format mail-merged letters appropriately. A `Title` field enables you to include the addressee's title: *Vice-President*, *Chairman of the Board*, and so on.

- *Do you have fields you're not sure you will ever use?* Include them! Typing the information now may be somewhat inconvenient, but it's much less frustrating than adding the field later.

▶ See "Annotating Documents Using Note-It," p. 527

- *Will other people use the database to add and retrieve information?* Be sure to include labels or Note-Its to guide the user through the database form. For example, you may add a Note-It that advises: `Fill in the part number only if the part is in stock!`

After thinking about all these questions, and any others that might contribute to your database, make a list of the fields you think you'll need. It may be that you need two separate databases to store your information—don't overlook that possibility either. You should have a very clear picture of the database you want to create before you go any further.

Starting a New Database File

This section shows you the basic steps for designing a new Works database. The steps take you through the creation of a no-frills model, which you can dress up later if you like. Chapter 17, "Modifying a Database Form," describes how to make changes to your form, and Chapter 18, "Enhancing a Database Form," explains how to dress up a form's appearance.

Creating a New Database with a TaskWizard

Works comes with several pre-formatted databases that cover almost all the situations a casual user might encounter—an address book, a client list, a home inventory, and so on. If you don't have a very specific layout in mind for your database form, or if your needs are fairly simple (such as "I want a generic address book"), you are best off using a TaskWizard to create what you want. After you create the basic design with a TaskWizard, you can modify it to fine-tune it for your needs.

◄ See "Using TaskWizards," p. 56

Creating a database with a TaskWizard is the same as creating any other document type with a TaskWizard. Follow these steps:

1. Choose File, New. The Works Task Launcher appears.
2. Click the TaskWizard you want. Some TaskWizards are in folders; click the folder to open the list of TaskWizards.
3. Click OK. The TaskWizard begins.
4. Follow the directions in the TaskWizard screens to create the type of database you want.

Creating a New Database from Scratch

To create a new database from scratch, you first should design the database form on paper, as discussed earlier in this chapter. Then follow these steps:

1. Choose File, New. The Works Task Launcher appears.
2. Choose the Works Tools tab.
3. Choose the Database button. The Create Database dialog box opens, as shown in figure 16.2. The first field is named `Field 1` by default.

Note

The first time you click the Database button, you see the First Time Help dialog box. Just click the button labeled To Create a New Database, and then proceed with step 3.

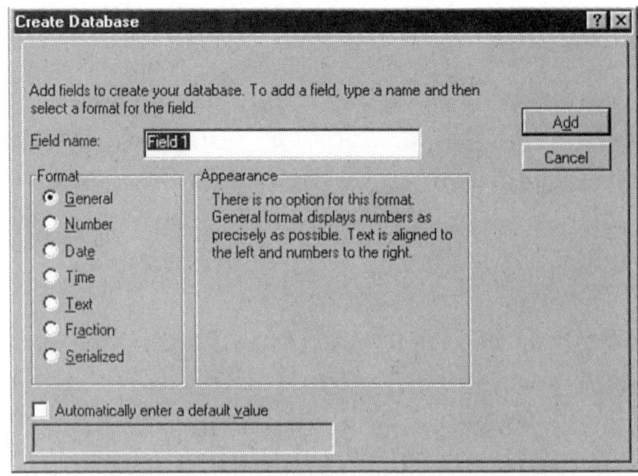

Fig. 16.2
In the Create Database dialog box, Works leads you through the process of creating the database fields.

4. Type a new name to replace the default in the Field Name box. You may use spaces in the name.

5. Select a format for this field:

   - *General*—A generic format. Choose General if you aren't sure what kind of data you'll be entering in the field. General is the default. Numbers are displayed as precisely as possible and aligned to the right; text is aligned to the left.

   - *Number*—A number-only format. Works doesn't let you type any letters or symbols in a `Number` field. Two additional options appear: Appearance and Decimal Places. Select a sample on the Appearance list that resembles how you want the numbers formatted, and choose the number of decimal places in that box. The default number of decimal places is 2, but if you're entering whole numbers, like quantities on hand, set the number to 0.

   - *Date*—A date-only format. Works doesn't let you enter anything but a valid date in this type of field. That means you cannot accidentally enter a date like 21/56/95. Works watches out for these errors. Choose which date format you want from the Appearance list.

   - *Time*—The same as date, but on a daily clock. Works doesn't let you enter invalid times, like 36:14. Choose which time format you want from the Appearance list.

- *Text*—This format enables you to enter any characters, symbols, or numbers. Text format is good for typing ZIP codes, (where you need to enter hyphens sometimes and therefore cannot use Number format), names and addresses, and phone numbers (which, because of the parentheses and hyphens, cannot be Number format either).

- *Fraction*—This format is a bit complicated. It works just like Number format for whole numbers, but it rounds off decimal places to the nearest fractional amount set in the Appearance box. For instance, if you entered 1.123 in a fraction-formatted field with $^1/_2$ Appearance, it would appear as 1. But if 1/8 were set as the Appearance, the number would appear as 1 $^1/_8$.

Note

You can select the Do Not Reduce check box to make sure Works does not round off fractions to a lower number. This is helpful, for example, if you're measuring lumber for projects where a little bit over is okay—but a little bit under is not.

- *Serialized*—A handy format for automatically numbering records, this format increments its value each time you enter a new record. For instance, in the first record, Works automatically enters a 1. In the second record, Works enters a 2, and so on. In the Next value box, you can control what number appears next, and in the Increment box, you can control how much the number increases with each record.

6. Click Add to add the field to your database.

7. Repeat steps 4 through 6 to add more fields as needed.

8. Click Done when you're finished adding fields. Your new database appears in List view, as shown in figure 16.3.

   The field names you entered appear as column headings. You will enter a record in each row as you begin to fill the database, as described in Chapter 19, "Entering and Editing Data." At this point, you can save your work, as explained in the following section.

Tip
To change the view of the database, see "Selecting the Database View," later in this chapter.

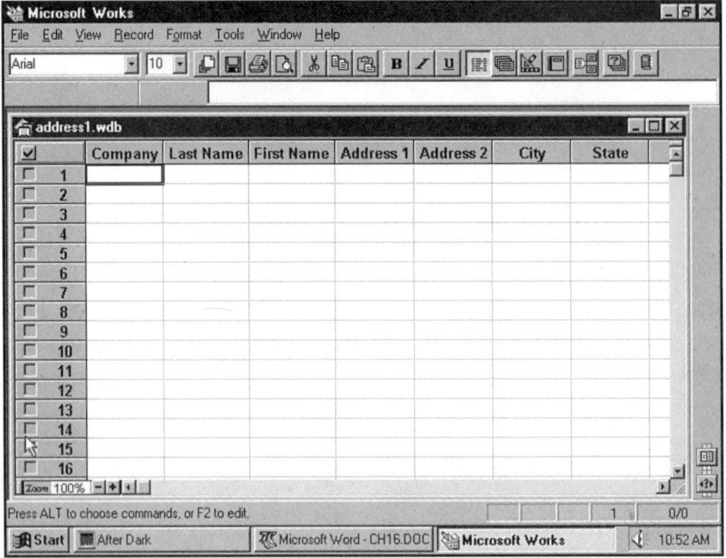

Fig. 16.3
The fields you created appear as column headings in the new database.

> **Troubleshooting**
>
> *What's the difference between Text and General formats?*
>
> The difference is subtle. Both formats display symbols, numbers, and letters the same way. But General displays numbers as concisely as possible, and Text displays the number exactly as you entered it. For instance, the number 6.000 appears exactly like that in Text format, but it appears as 6 in General format.

Saving a Database File

After entering or editing records in a database file, you need to save the new information on disk. Until you save your changes, they are held in your computer's memory and can be lost if power is interrupted or if you accidentally turn the computer off.

To save the database, choose File, Save or File, Save As. You can also press Ctrl+S or click the Save toolbar button. Works displays the Save As dialog box (see fig. 16.4).

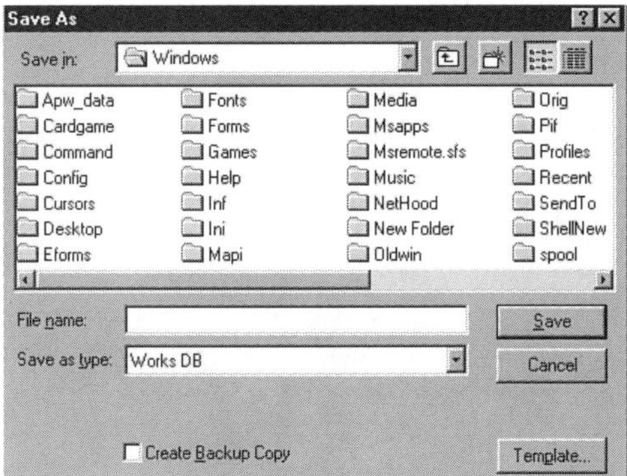

Fig. 16.4
Save your database the first time using the Save As dialog box.

In the Save As dialog box, type a name for the database in the File Name text box. Change folders and/or drives if needed. Then choose OK. Works saves the database and automatically assigns the file extension WDB (for *Works Database*).

◄ See "Naming and Saving Documents," p. 48

If you have already saved a file, saving it again is easy. Just choose File, Save; click the Save button in the toolbar; or press Ctrl+S. Works doesn't ask for a name or location, because it already knows them.

To save a file in a different location, or under a new name, choose File, Save As. You see the original Save As dialog box that you worked with in the preceding section. Type a new name for the file in the same directory, or choose a new drive or directory.

Troubleshooting

Why does the Save button do different things at different times?

The Save button always tries to do the same thing—save the file under its existing name. However, sometimes it can't—like when a file doesn't yet have a name. In this case, the Save As dialog box appears when you click the Save button, so you can input a name.

Opening an Existing Database File

After you create a database and save it on your computer's hard disk, you can exit Works and do something else. Then later, when you need the database again, you open it. (To learn how to save a file, see the previous section, "Saving a Database File.")

You can open a database file in two ways, as the following sections describe.

Opening a Database from the Works Task Launcher

The easiest way to open a database file is to use the Works Task Launcher. This feature works from inside any Works application or from the main Works window; it lists the most recently used Works documents. Follow these steps:

Tip
Instead of using File, New in step 1, you can just click the Task Launcher button on the toolbar.

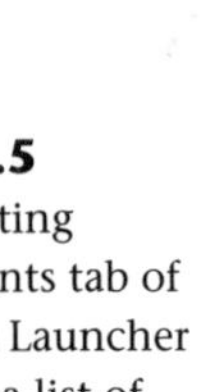

1. If the Works Task Launcher is not already displayed on-screen, choose File, New. (Note that you use the New command, not the Open command, for this method.)

2. Choose the Existing Documents tab. The most recently opened Works documents appear on the list (see fig. 16.5).

   The list might display any file types, including database, spreadsheet, or word processor files. The database files will end in WDB, for Works Database.

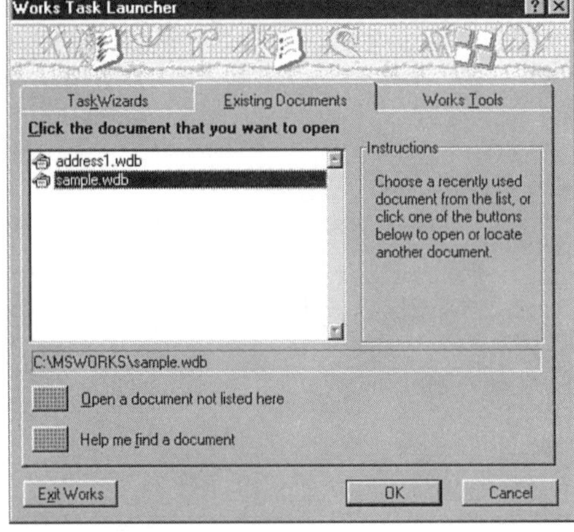

Fig. 16.5
The Existing Documents tab of the Task Launcher displays a list of the most recently used files.

Tip
To learn how to change the default folders where files are stored, see Chapter 3.

3. If you see the file you want to open, highlight the file and then click OK.

4. If you don't see the file you want on the list, do one of the following:

◄ See "Opening an Existing Document," p. 83

   - If you know where the file is stored (in another folder or on another drive), click the button labeled Open a Document Not Listed Here, which opens the Open dialog box (see fig. 16.6).

Select the folder and drive, and double-click the file to open it, or highlight the file and click the Open button.

Fig. 16.6
Find files in other folders and drives with the Open dialog box.

- If you aren't sure where the file is, click the button labeled Help Me Find a Document, and use the Windows Find feature to locate the file.

Opening Files with the Open Command

The second way to open a database file is to choose File, Open from within the Database screen. The advantage to this method is that it's quick—the disadvantage is that if you keep your files in several different folders, you'll have to wade through the various folders on your hard disk to find the one you want. Follow these steps:

1. Choose File, Open. The Open dialog box appears.
2. The default folder that opens is Documents. If the file you want to open is there, just double-click it (or click once and then click Open).
3. If the file you want to open is not there, change to a different drive or folder to locate it, then open it as in step 2.

Selecting the Database View

The Works database gives you four ways to view or print your data:

- Form view shows each record one at a time on-screen (see fig. 16.7). This view looks like a fill-in-the-blanks form that you might fill out on paper.
- Form Design view is just like Form view, except you use it to change how the form looks rather than to browse records.

- List view looks like a spreadsheet (see fig. 16.8). It displays the fields in columns and the records in rows beneath them.
- Report view enables you to view and print reports.

▶ See "Printing Reports," p. 465

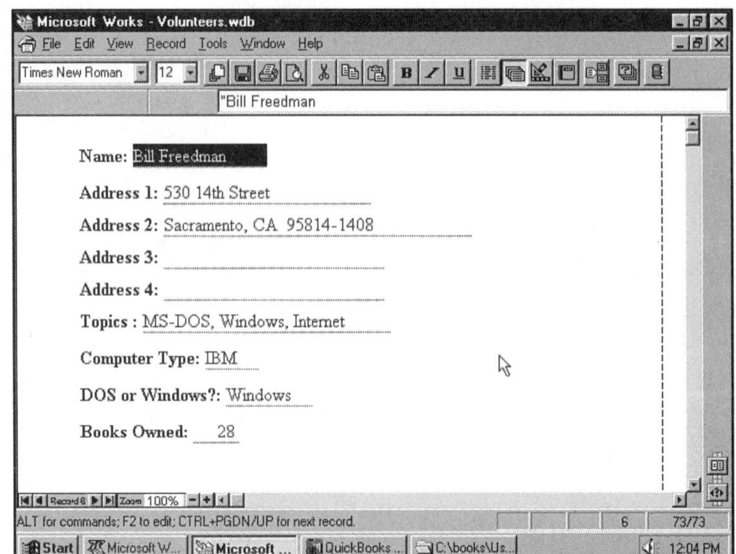

Fig. 16.7
A database in Form view shows a clear view of only one record.

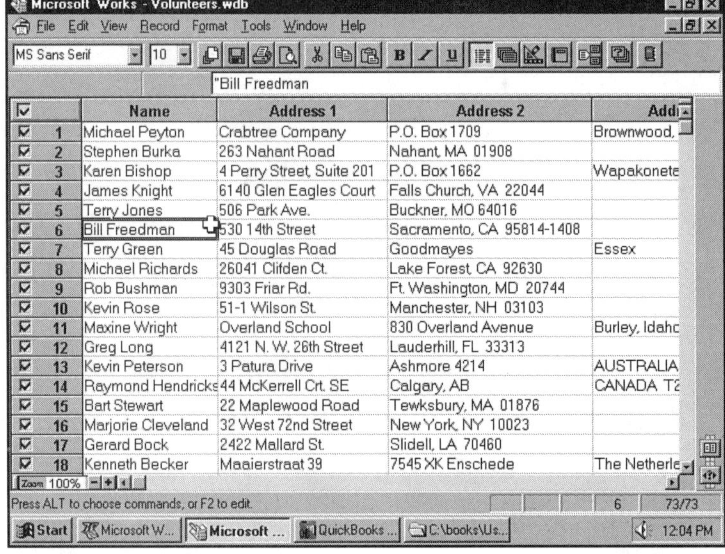

Fig. 16.8
A database in List view shows many records at one time.

As you work with your database, you will want to switch frequently between Form and List view. To do so, press F9 (for Form view) or Shift+F9 (for List view); or choose the Form or List command from the View menu; or click the Form view or List view button on the toolbar.

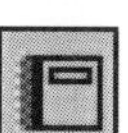

In Report view, you set up the criteria for a report you want to view or print (see fig. 16.9). You cannot switch to Report view unless you have created a report for this database. (Choose Tools, ReportCreator to start a report.) If you try to switch to Report view with no report created, the ReportCreator will start automatically. If you have created a report, you can switch to Report view by choosing View, Report or by clicking the Report button on the toolbar. See Chapter 22, "Creating a Database Report," for more information.

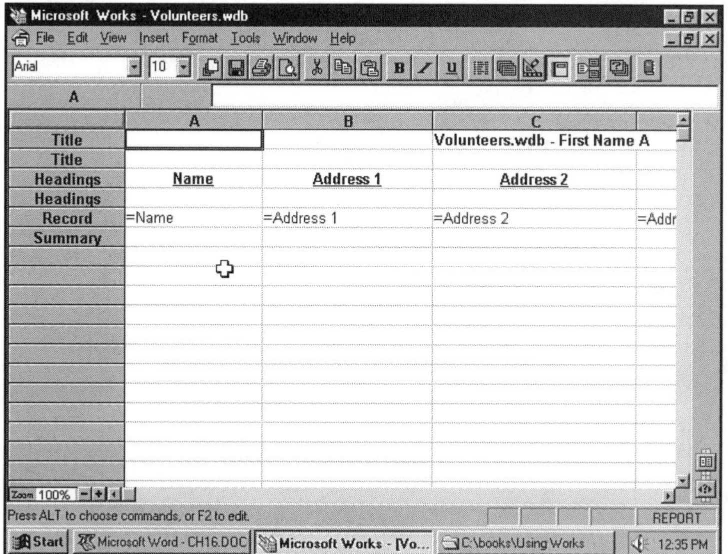

Fig. 16.9
Report view is a specialized view that you use to modify your report definition.

Troubleshooting

I have more than one report! How do I choose which one I want to see in Report view?

If you go into Report view by clicking the Report view button on the toolbar, Works opens the most recent report you worked with.

To switch to a different report, you choose View, Report. If more than one report is available, a dialog box appears from which you can select the report you want.

Reviewing the Database Window

Now that you know how to switch among the views, take a look at List view, Form view, and the toolbar, so you can understand the screen elements as you work in the upcoming chapters.

Working in List View

Figure 16.10 shows the Works Database window in List view, with each element labeled. Just like in a spreadsheet, a cell is located at the intersection of a row and column. The content of the active cell appears in the formula bar.

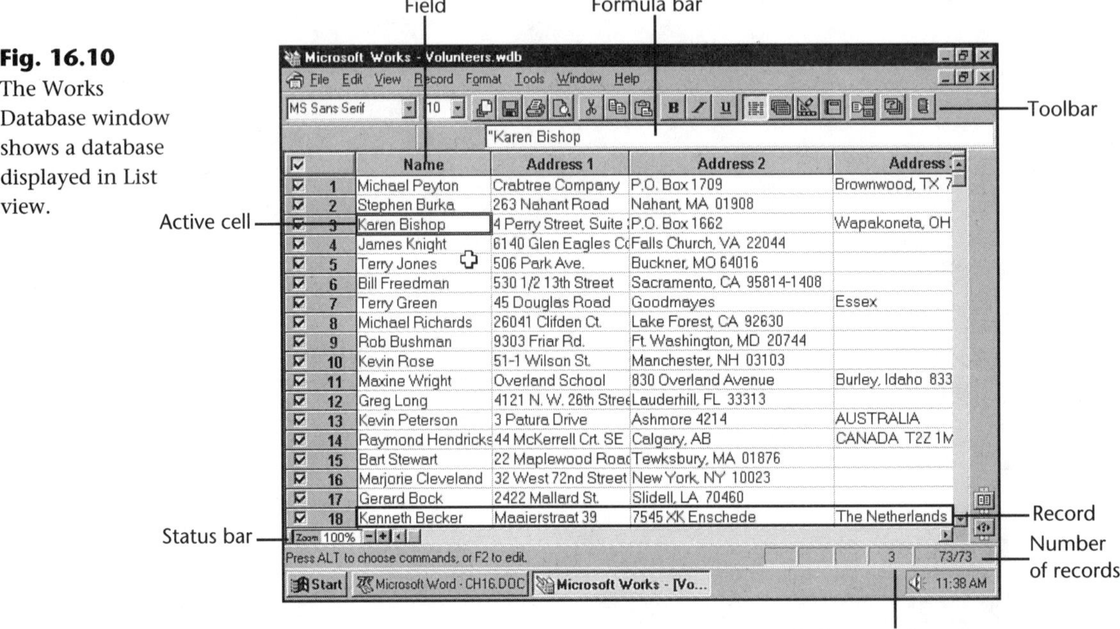

Fig. 16.10 The Works Database window shows a database displayed in List view.

Notice in figure 16.10 that the formula bar displays the contents of the selected field, preceded by double quotation marks: `"Karen Bishop`. If you select more than one field, the formula bar displays the contents of the first field in the selection. To select multiple fields, hold down the Shift key and click each field.

▶ See "Working with Filters," p. 440

Notice also in figure 16.10 that the status bar in List view displays the number of records—73—and the number of the active record—3. The number 73 is repeated, as in 73/73, to indicate that all 73 records are shown on the list. If you use the Filter function to display just five database records, the status line indicates 5/73, meaning that five records of 73 total records are displayed.

Moving around in a database in List view is identical to moving around in a spreadsheet. You can use the arrow keys to move from field to field, or click the field where you want to move.

► See "Moving Around the Spreadsheet," p. 183

Working in Form Design View

Form view is fairly simple. It contains many of the same elements as List view, including the toolbar, the formula bar, and the status bar. Each field is listed with the values for a single record. You can move among records by clicking the arrow buttons in the bottom-left corner of the screen (see fig. 16.11). You can also move by pressing the arrow keys or the Tab key on your keyboard.

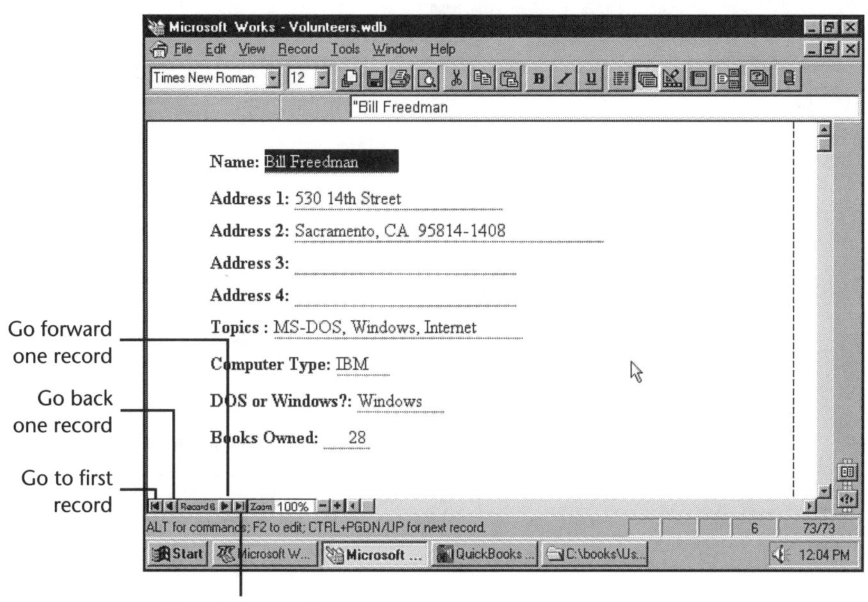

Fig. 16.11
In Form view, you move from record to record by clicking the arrow buttons.

Using the Database Toolbar

The toolbar is the same in all views, and very similar to the toolbars found in the other Works components. With the toolbar, you can perform common procedures with a simple mouse click. Toolbar buttons can format text, insert new records, and cut, copy, or move data, for example. You can even customize the toolbar to add buttons for the commands you use most frequently.

◄ See "Customizing the Toolbars," p. 33

Tip
If you prefer not to use the toolbar, you can turn it off. This creates a little more space on your screen, so you can see more records at one time in List view. Choose View, Toolbar to remove the check mark beside the Toolbar command.

Note

To turn off display of toolbar button messages, choose Tools, Customize Toolbar and deselect the Enable ToolTips check box. If you turn off display of button messages, Works still displays a button description in the status bar when you place the mouse pointer on a toolbar button.

Table 16.1 shows the buttons on the default database toolbar and their functions.

▶ See "Changing the Appearance of Text," p. 377

▶ See "Entering and Editing Data," p. 391

Table 16.1 The Default Toolbar Buttons

Button	Description
Times New Roman	Clicking the down arrow displays a list of available fonts.
12	Clicking the down arrow displays a list of standard font sizes available for the currently selected font. If the font is proportionally spaced, you can specify a different size by typing it in the Font Size box.
	Displays the Works Task Launcher.
	Saves the file displayed in the active Database window. When you save a file for the first time, clicking the Save button displays the Save As dialog box.
	Prints the file displayed in the active Database window. See Chapter 20, "Expanding Your Database Skills," for more information on printing your database records.
	Displays the Print Preview screen.
	Cuts selected text.
	Copies selected text.

Button	Description
	Pastes selected text.
B	Boldfaces selected text.
	Italicizes selected text.
U	Underlines selected text.
	Switches to List view.
	Switches to Form view.
	Switches to Form Design view.
	Switches to Report view.
	Inserts a new record. See Chapter 17, "Modifying a Database Form," for more information.
	Opens the Filter dialog box, where you can create or apply a filter.
	Opens the database that you have defined as your address book.

► See "Working with Filters," p. 440

Troubleshooting

Address book? What address book? I didn't define one of those.

Works thinks that everyone should have an address book. If you haven't defined an address book yet and you click the Address Book button, Works asks if you want to run the Address Book TaskWizard to create one. After you have done so, whenever you click the Address Book button, that database automatically opens.

Chapter 17

Modifying a Database Form

by Faithe Wempen

In Chapter 16, "Creating and Saving a Database File," you learned how to start a new database file. When you start a new database file, Works automatically creates a form.

Seldom do you design a database form perfectly from the outset. This chapter helps you make changes to your database form. Specifically, this chapter covers these topics:

- Adding new fields to a database form
- Editing and deleting fields
- Moving fields around
- Formatting data in fields

Reviewing the Parts of a Database Form

When you create a new database, you create the fields that make up the database form. Each field has two parts: the *field name* (which tells you what information to enter in that field) and the *field entry* (the area where you enter that record's data). Figure 17.1 shows a simple database form, much like one you may have created in Chapter 16. This figure has a record already entered in it, for example purposes. You learn how to enter records in Chapter 19, "Entering and Editing Data."

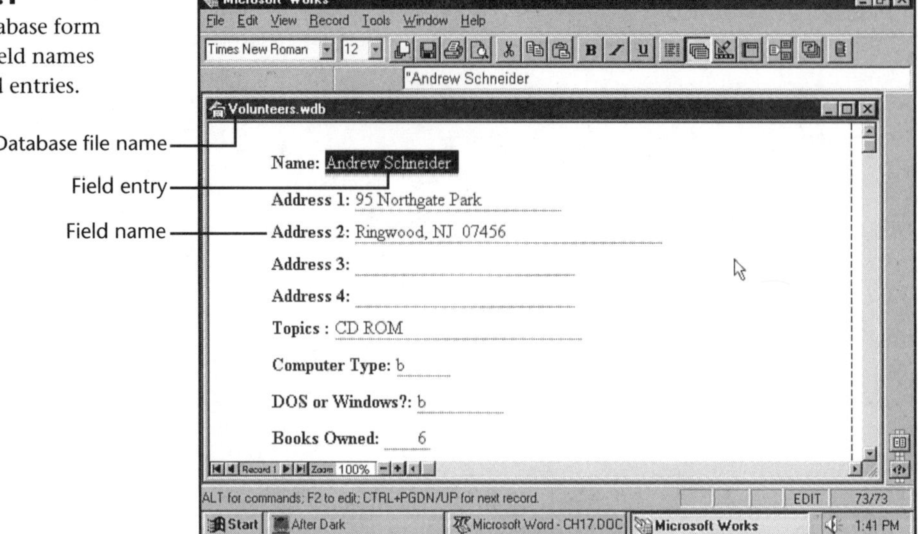

Fig. 17.1
This database form shows field names and field entries.

◄ See "Selecting the Database View," p. 343

Figure 17.1 shows a record in a database called VOLUNTEERS.WDB. Notice that the database file name appears in the Form view title bar. The figure shows the record for Andrew Schneider and includes data entry fields for `Name`, `Address` (4 lines), `Topics`, `Computer Type`, and so on. You can create very basic Works database forms that contain only data entry fields, like this one, or you can customize your forms with clip art, lines, fonts, and labels. Learn how to dress up a form in Chapter 18, "Enhancing a Database Form."

Understanding Form Design View

You do most form-editing work in Form Design view, a new feature in Works for Windows 95. Form Design view looks just like Form view, except dotted lines surround each field and each graphic, indicating that you can change them (see fig. 17.2).

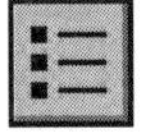

To enter Form Design view, click the Form Design button in the toolbar or choose View, Form Design (or press Ctrl+F9).

When you click a field in Form Design view, you select the field. The part of the field you clicked (field name or field entry area) is black, and sizing handles appear around that area. Sizing handles are little black squares in the corners of a selected area. You learn how to use sizing handles to resize a field later in this chapter. You can select the field name and the field entry area separately, because you can format them separately, as you also learn later in this chapter.

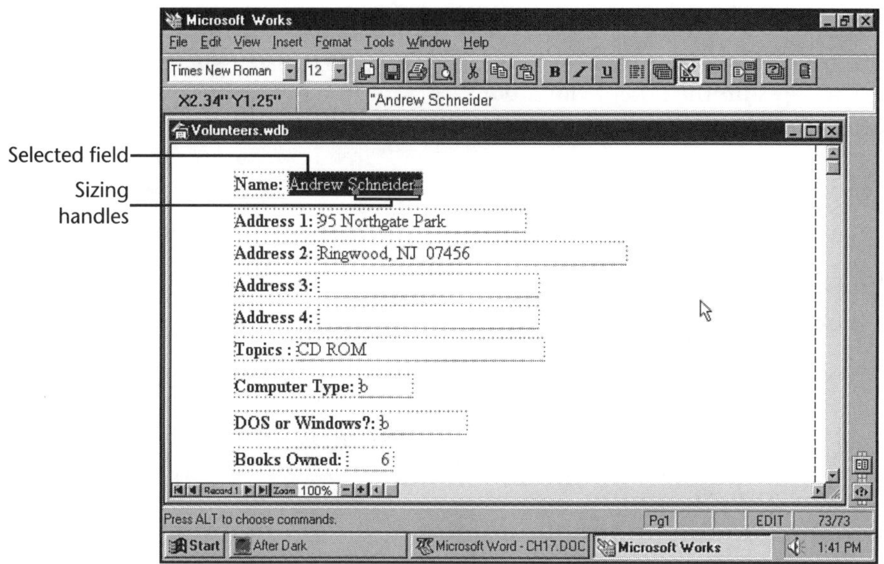

Fig. 17.2
Form Design view enables you to change almost every aspect of a database form.

Notice the difference in the menu bar between figure 17.1 (in Form view) and figure 17.2 (in Form Design view). In Form Design view, the Record menu is gone because you aren't working with a particular record. In its place are two other menus: Insert and Format. You will be using these menus extensively in the rest of this chapter.

Adding Fields

If you planned your database carefully before you created it, you should not need to add many fields to your database after you create it. But perhaps you have forgotten a less-obvious field you need, such as Client Number or Fax. No problem—you can easily add a field to the database.

◄ See "Planning A Database," p. 335

> **Note**
>
> If you have already entered records into your database, and you add a new field, this field appears blank in all the records. You need to go back and enter data into the new field for each record.

► See "Entering and Editing Data," p. 391

You can add a field from either Form Design view or List view. A field added in either view shows up in all views, not just the one in which you added it.

Adding a Field in Form Design View

When you add a field in Form Design view, you can put it anywhere on the form. (You can shift the other fields around later to make room for it; see "Moving Fields" later in this chapter.)

To add a field to your form, follow these steps:

1. Click the Form Design button or choose View, Form Design to enter Form Design view.

2. Click where you want to position the new field.

3. Choose Insert, Field. The Insert Field dialog box appears (see fig. 17.3).

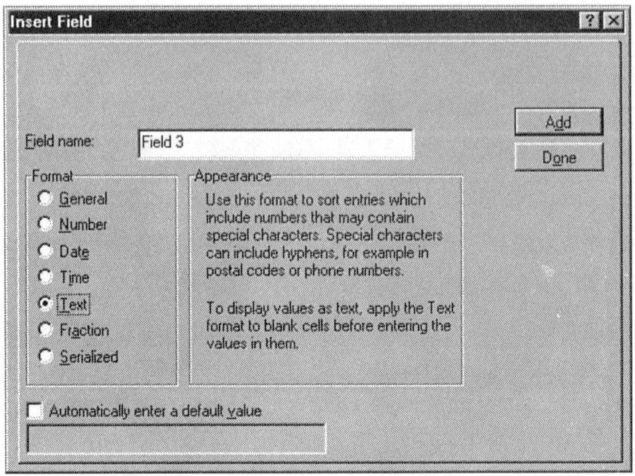

Fig. 17.3
Enter information about the new field in the Insert Field dialog box.

Tip
Instead of using steps 3 and 4, you can simply type the new field name followed by a colon directly onto the form.

4. Type a field name. For instance, if you want to add an optional 5th address line to the form in figure 17.2, type **Address 5**.

5. Choose a field type from the Format list. The appearance options for that field type appear under Appearance when you click a field type. (Some types have no appearance attributes; in those cases, the Appearance area is empty.)

6. If any options are listed under Appearance, select the ones you want.

7. Click OK.

Note

When you add a field, the *tab order* changes automatically based on where you positioned the new field. As you press Tab to move from field to field, you always move from top to bottom on the form. If two fields are side-by-side, the left field is selected first, then the field to the right. If you want a different tab order, see the section "Changing Tab Order" later in this chapter.

When you switch to List view, the added field appears at the end of the database (the right-most column). You can change that position; see "Moving Fields in List View" later in the chapter.

Adding a Field in List View

In List view, you can add new fields to any position, not just to the end of the database.

To add a field in List view, follow these steps:

1. If you're not already in List view, click the List View button on the toolbar or choose View, List.
2. Select the field name next to where you want the new field inserted. (You can place the new field on either side of the selected field.)
3. Choose Record, Insert Field. From the submenu that appears, choose 1 Before (to place the new field to the left of the selected one) or 2 After (to place the new field to the right).
4. The Insert Field dialog box appears, just like the one you used when you first created the fields (refer to fig. 17.3). Type a name in the Field Name box.
5. Select a field type from the Format list.
6. If any appearance options appear in the Appearance area, select the ones you want.
7. Choose the Add button.
8. Repeat steps 4 through 7 to insert another field, or click Done.

When you add a field in List view and then switch to Form view, the new field appears at the bottom of the Form. You can move the field anywhere on the form; see "Moving Fields in Form Design View" later in this chapter.

Moving Fields

After creating a database, you may decide that you want the fields to appear in a different order on-screen. You can rearrange the way the fields appear in Form or List view, or even set up two columns of fields in Form view, so you can see more fields at one time.

Note

The rearranging you do in one view does not affect the other views. For instance, the changes you make in Form Design view affect only Form view, not List view, and vice versa.

Moving Fields in Form Design View

You can easily move fields around in Form Design view. Just click the field you want to move (click the field name or field entry part—it doesn't matter which, for this action). The word `DRAG` appears below your mouse pointer when you point at the selected field.

To move the selected field, just drag it to any new location on-screen. If you want several fields to appear side-by-side, just drag them into position—you can have as many columns of fields across a form as you like (well, as many as will fit on screen, anyway.)

If you want to move many fields at one time, you can save time by holding down the Ctrl key while you click each field, or by drawing a *lasso* around them to select them. (Just click at one corner of the block, then drag to the other corner, to lasso a block.) Then drag the selected fields as a group. This method is especially helpful if you have created a new field that you want to insert in the middle of a group of existing fields. For example, in figure 17.4, all the fields below `Address 4` are dragged down a bit to make room for moving the `Address 5` field into place.

Tip
You can undo a move by choosing Edit, Undo immediately after you move.

Another way to reposition a field (or several) is to use the Position Selection command:

1. If you're not already in Form Design view, click the Form Design button or choose View, Form Design.

2. Select the field(s) you want to move.

3. Choose Edit, Position Selection. The mouse pointer becomes an arrow with the word `DRAG` under it.

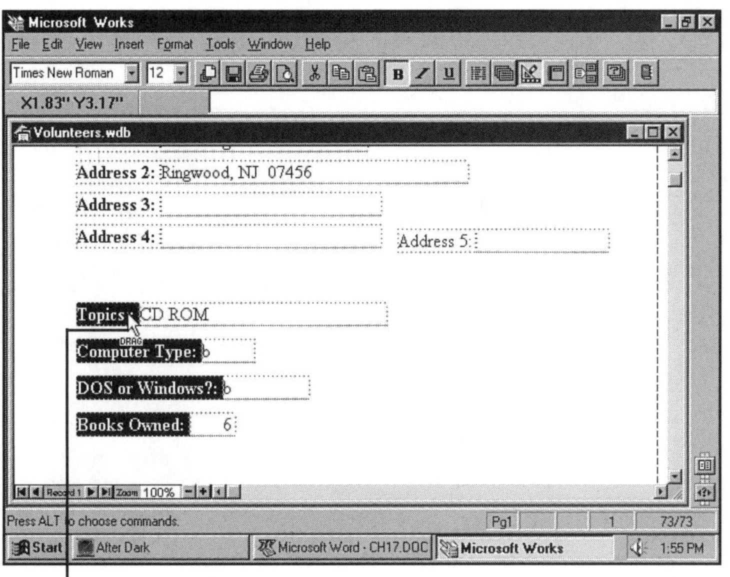

Fig. 17.4
You can select a single field or multiple fields then drag the selection to a new position on-screen.

4. Use the arrow keys or the mouse to move the field to the new position. You don't need to hold down the mouse button.

5. Press Enter when the field is repositioned.

> **Troubleshooting**
>
> *I want to position a field in a precise place, but it keeps shifting!*
>
> You're experiencing the Snap To Grid feature at work. An invisible grid exists in Form Design view, with lines .08" apart. Whenever you move a field, it aligns with one of those invisible grid lines. This feature is meant to keep your screen tidy, but if it annoys you, turn it off by choosing Format, Snap To Grid.

Moving Fields in List View

In List view, each field is represented by a column. To move a field, just point at the column heading (the field name) until the word MOVE appears. Then drag it to a new position. As you drag, thick lines appear between columns to show where the column will be inserted (see fig. 17.5). Release the mouse button when the thick line appears between the two columns where you want to move the field.

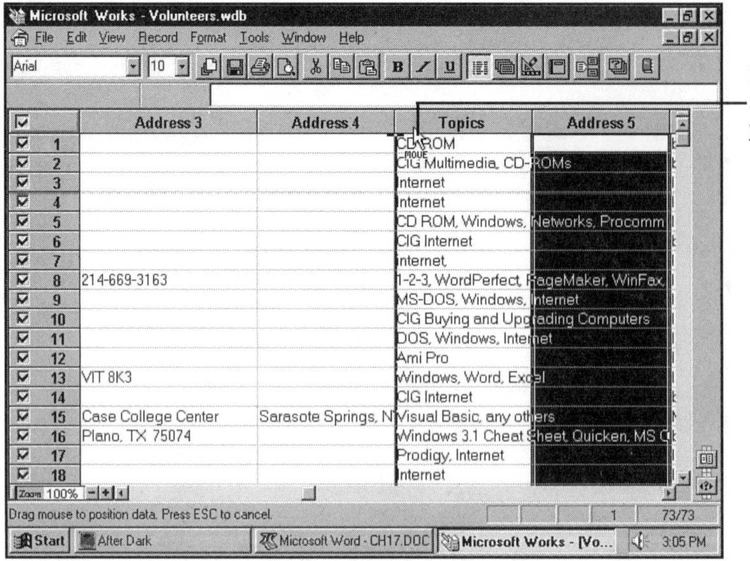

Fig. 17.5
Just move a column heading to rearrange fields in List view.

Mouse pointer shows that you're moving

Another way to move a field in List view is with the Clipboard. (You learn how to cut and paste with the Works Clipboard in Chapter 5.) Follow these steps:

1. If you're not already in List view, click the List View button on the toolbar or choose View, List.

2. Select the field (column) you want to move.

3. Choose Edit, Cut or click the Cut button. Works asks if you want to permanently delete this information.

4. Click OK. You aren't really permanently deleting your field, so don't panic. You're just cutting the column to the Clipboard.

5. Select the column to the left of the position where you want to move the column you cut.

6. Choose Edit, Paste or click the Paste button.

Troubleshooting

I can't drag a field to the last (rightmost) position in List view.

This problem is a limitation of Works, but you can get around it easily enough. Just drag the field to the next-to-rightmost spot and then drag the rightmost field one place to the left.

I can't drag a field to a spot that's not visible on-screen.

Again, this is another limitation of Works. Suppose that you want to drag a field 10 places to the left. Obviously, you can't see the ultimate destination on-screen when you first start to drag. But you can make stopovers along the way. Drag the field to the leftmost position you can see, then use the scroll bar to move the display a few places further to the left, and drag the field some more. Repeat until you get to the final location.

This dragging-by-stages method works fine but is a bit time-consuming. A better way to move a field long distances in List view is with the cut-and-paste method.

Changing Tab Order

With some database programs (such as Microsoft Access), when you rearrange or add fields, the tab order doesn't change. That means when you press Tab to move from field to field, the highlight moves according to the original order of the fields, not the order in which they currently appear on-screen. What a pain! In such programs, you need to adjust the tab order just to get the Tab key working in a logical manner again.

In Works, tab order changes automatically when you rearrange fields. The tab order always goes from top to bottom and right to left. Figure 17.6 shows the tab order Works would use for a sample form.

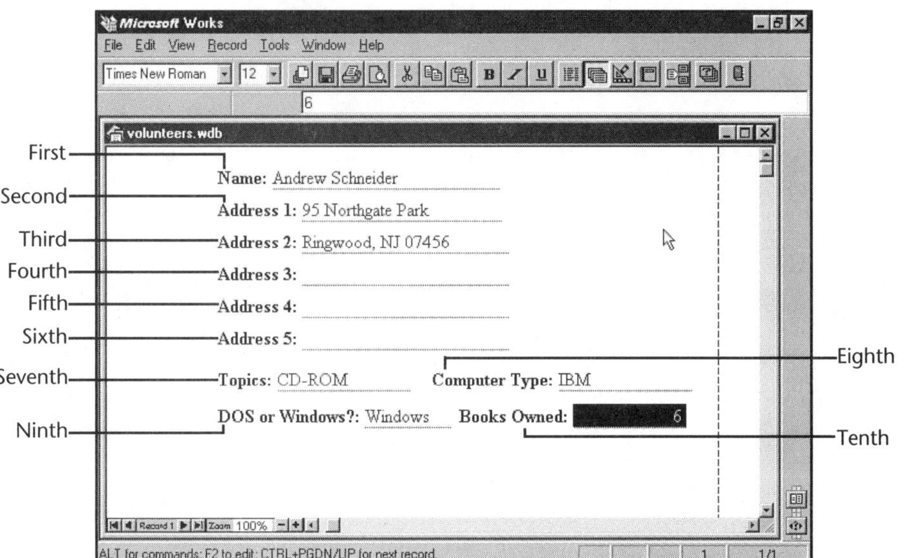

Fig. 17.6
Tab order runs from top to bottom and right to left.

You aren't stuck with the obvious tab order that Works provides. Entering data in a different order may be easier. For instance, you could put `Address 5` last on the tab order, because the vast majority of addresses will not have anything to enter in that field. Here's how to change the tab order:

1. If you're not already in Form Design view, click the Form Design button or choose View, Form Design.
2. Choose Format, Tab Order. The Format Tab Order dialog box appears (see fig. 17.7), with your fields listed.

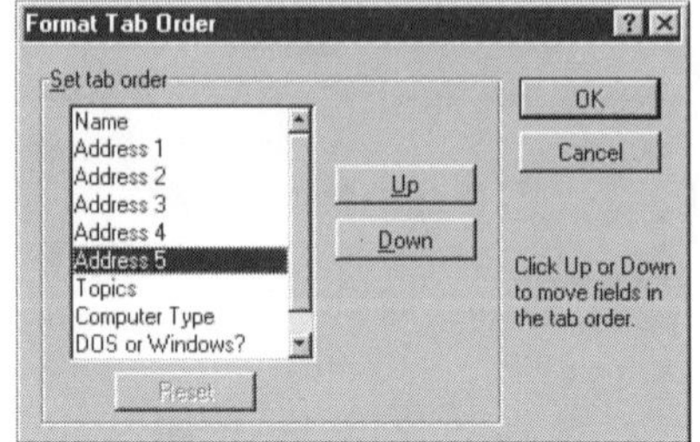

Fig. 17.7
Change the tab order from the normal top-to-bottom with this dialog box.

3. Select the field you want to move in the tab order.
4. Choose the Up or Down button to move the field in the order.
5. When you're satisfied with the field's position, repeat steps 3 and 4 to change another position, or click OK to finish.

Now press Tab repeatedly to move through your fields. The new tab order is in effect.

Deleting a Field

► See "Clearing Data from a Field," p. 394

In Works, you can *clear* a field or you can *delete* a field. Clearing a field removes only the data in the field. Deleting removes the field, the field's name, and all the data and formatting. You can clear a field for a single record, or for all records in the database, but a deletion automatically applies to the entire database.

No matter the view in which you delete a field, all views are affected. Any fields you delete in List view also are deleted in Form Design view, and vice-versa. The deleted fields are completely removed from the database.

Note

To reverse a clear or delete, before you perform any other actions, choose Edit, Undo. The only deletion you cannot undo is deleting a field from Form Design view.

Deleting a Field in Form Design View

It's better to delete fields from List view rather than Form Design view, because you can undo your deletion in List view if you make a mistake. But you can delete a field in Form Design view if you want by following these steps:

1. If you're not already in Form Design view, click the Form Design button or choose View, Form Design.
2. Highlight the field name you want to delete.
3. Choose Edit, Delete Selection or press the Delete key.

   Works prompts you to confirm the deletion and warns that you cannot undo this operation (see fig. 17.8).
4. Choose OK to confirm the deletion. Works deletes the field and all its data from the record.

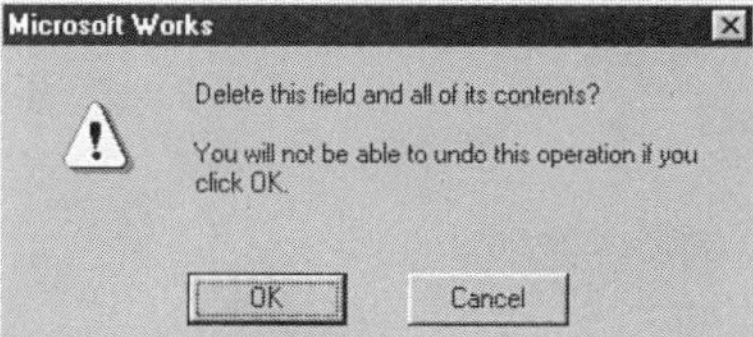

Fig. 17.8
Make sure you really want to delete the field from every record in this database.

Troubleshooting

When I try to delete a field, I can't. Works tells me I can't delete a protected field.

If Works won't delete a field, the field is probably protected. For example, databases that you create with TaskWizards contain protected fields. To unprotect a field, choose Format, Protection, and then deselect the Protect Form check box and choose OK.

Deleting a Field in List View

Follow these steps to delete a field in List view:

1. If you're not already in List view, click the List View button on the toolbar or choose View, List.

2. Highlight the field you want to delete by clicking its name.

   You can delete several adjacent fields at one time. To select the fields, click the first field and drag to the last field name in the series; or hold down the Shift key and click the first and last fields in the series.

3. Choose Record, Delete Field.

4. When asked to confirm, click OK.

Troubleshooting

Oops! I deleted a field by mistake. How do I get the field back?

To undo the deletion, choose Undo Delete Field from the Edit menu; or press Ctrl+Z. You must undo the deletion before you choose another command or delete another field, record, or data.

Changing Field Width

You can type over 2,000 characters in a Works Database field, regardless of the field's length on the database form. Works enables you to type data in a field even if the data is longer than the field. If the field is a text field, the long text scrolls past the right end of the field and becomes invisible. If the field is a number or date field, Works replaces the long number or date with number symbols: #####. (To find out how to format number and date fields, see "Formatting Numbers in Fields" later in this chapter.)

Note

You set field sizes separately in Form Design and List views. For example, a field can be 10 characters wide in Form Design view and 125 characters wide and 3 lines long in List view.

If you need to see long data on-screen, you can change the size of a field. You use different commands to change field size in Form Design and List views.

Changing Field Width in Form Design View

In Form Design view, you see the field name and field entry side-by-side. When you change field size, what you're really changing is the size of the field entry area, where you enter the text in each field.

The easiest way to resize a field is with the mouse. Follow these steps to change the size of a field in Form Design view using the mouse:

1. If you're not already in Form Design view, click the Form Design button or choose View, Form Design.

2. Select the field entry you want to resize. (In this case, it's important to select the field entry, not the field name.)

   When you select the field entry, it turns black, and sizing handles appear around it (see fig. 17.9).

3. Move the mouse pointer onto one of the field sizing handles at the right edge of the field until the pointer changes to a box with an arrow labeled `RESIZE`.

4. Drag the field to the size you want. Drag horizontally to change the field width, or drag diagonally or vertically to change height.

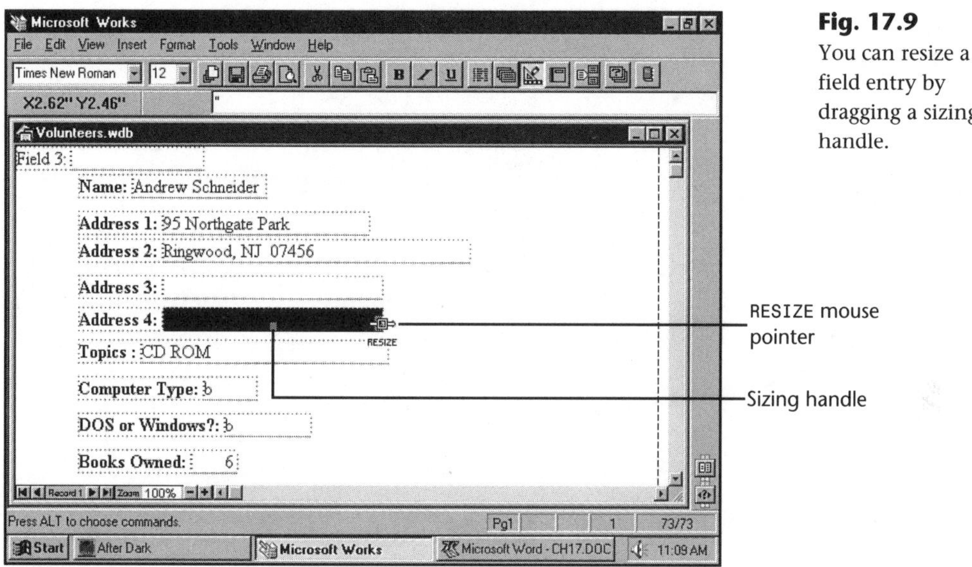

Fig. 17.9
You can resize a field entry by dragging a sizing handle.

You also can resize a field through the menu system if you prefer. This method works well for people who prefer to use the keyboard rather than the mouse:

1. If you're not already in Form Design view, click the Form Design button or choose View, Form Design.

2. Select the field you want to resize.

3. Choose Format, Field Size. The Format Field Size dialog box appears (see fig. 17.10).

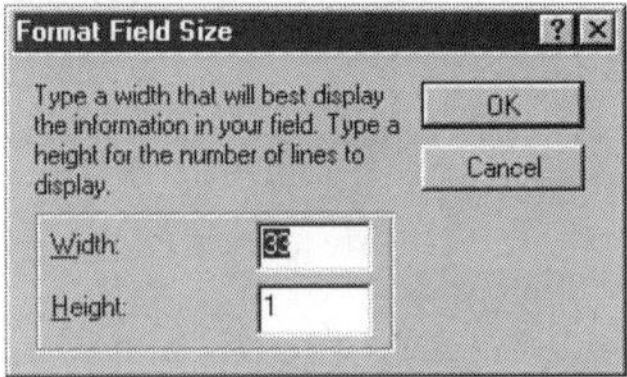

Fig. 17.10
You can resize a field very precisely with the Format Field Size dialog box.

4. Type a Width between 1 and 325 characters.

5. Type a Height between 1 and 325 lines.

6. Choose OK to return to the Database window.

Changing Field Width in List View

In List view, Works displays fields in columns. All the columns start out the same width, but you can easily resize them in a number of ways. The easiest way is to simply drag the columns:

1. Position your mouse pointer to the right of the column heading for the column you want to resize. The mouse pointer changes to read ADJUST (see fig. 17.11).

2. Drag the column divider to the left or right to increase or decrease the width of the column. All the columns to the right of the line you're dragging move to compensate.

Another, more precise way to resize a column in List view is to use the Field Width dialog box:

1. Select the column heading for the field whose width you want to change.

2. Choose Format, Field Width to open the Field Width dialog box, shown in figure 17.12.

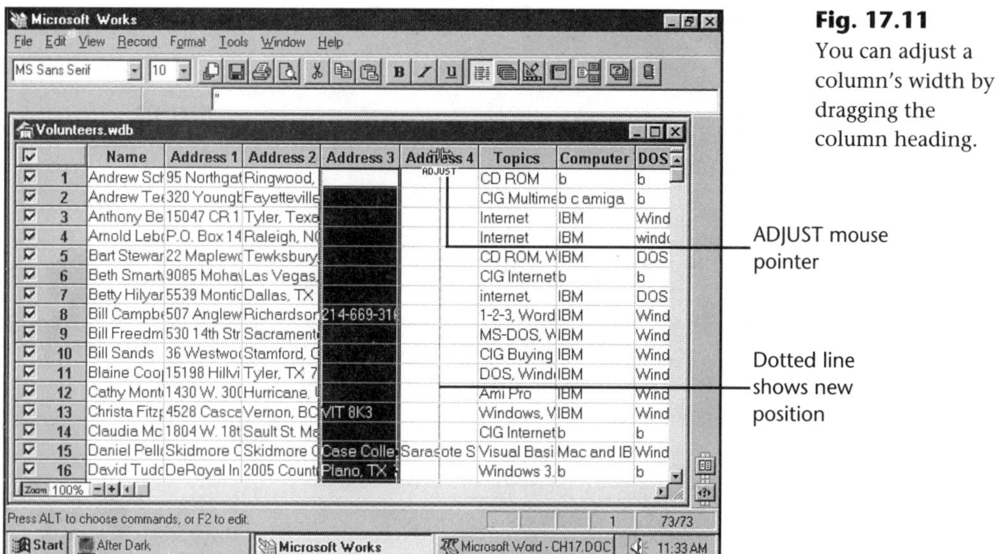

Fig. 17.11
You can adjust a column's width by dragging the column heading.

3. Take one of the following steps:

   - Type an exact width in the Column Width box.
   - To create a field wide enough to display the longest data currently in the field, choose Best Fit.
   - To reset the field to its standard width (usually 10), click Standard.

4. Choose OK.

Fig. 17.12
Set a precise field width with the Field Width dialog box.

Note

Field width in List view can be 0 to 79 characters. If you set width to 0, you hide the field. The field width changes you make in List view do not affect Form Design view.

► See "Hiding Fields and Records," p. 404

Note

Best Fit is only useful after you enter records in a database. If you haven't entered any records in your database yet, Best Fit does nothing.

Tip
If you have a field that contains a lot of text, consider turning on Text Wrap instead of widening the field to make it all fit. See the section "Aligning Text in Fields" later in this chapter.

Changing Record Height

Record height is the vertical space taken up by a record (a field entry in Form Design view, or a row in List view.) Because record height means different things in the different views, the procedures for changing record height are different.

Changing Record Height in Form Design View

You already know how to resize a field entry horizontally—that is, change its width. You can change a field's height in exactly the same way—just select the field and drag a different sizing handle. To resize vertically only, drag the handle at the bottom. To resize vertically and horizontally at one time, drag a corner handle.

Changing Record Height in List View

In List view, Works displays records in rows. Each record (row) can have a unique height; it doesn't need to match the height of other records.

► See "Changing the Font and Size," p. 378

By default, Works sets record height to one line at the size of the largest font used in the line. For example, if the largest font size used in the record is 24 points, the record height is made tall enough in List view to accommodate the 24-point font.

You can set record height easily in List view by dragging the bottom edge of the record number box to the height you want. This method works just like resizing the field. Follow these steps:

1. Select the row number for the row you want to resize.
2. Position the mouse pointer directly under that row number.
3. Drag the row up or down to increase or decrease height (see fig. 17.13). You can hide a record completely by setting the Height to 0, the same as you can hide a row in a spreadsheet.

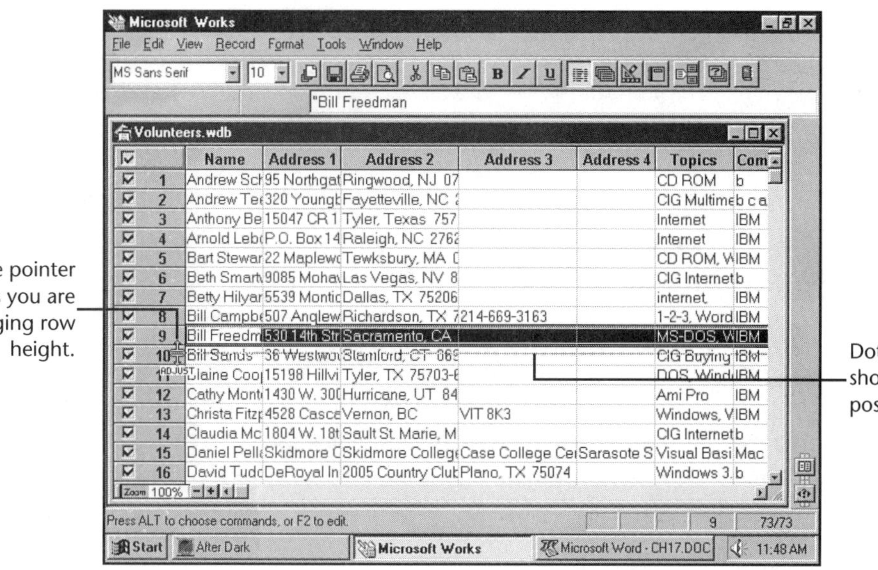

Fig. 17.13
You can drag row height with the mouse pointer quickly and easily.

Again, you may use a more precise method, although it takes a bit more time:

1. Select the record whose height you want to adjust.
2. Choose Format, Record Height. The Format Record Height dialog box appears (see fig. 17.14).
3. Take one of the following steps:
   - Type a new Row Height.
   - Click the Best Fit button to change the height to fit the data in the record.
   - Click Standard to return the record height to the default.
4. Choose OK.

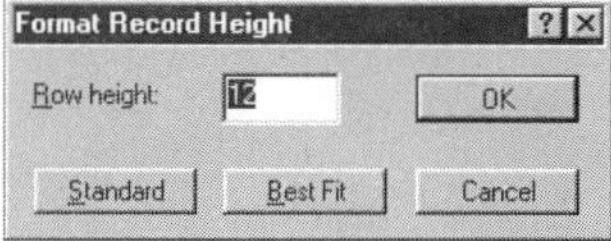

Fig. 17.14
Adjust the record height precisely using the Format Record Height dialog box.

Changing a Field Name

You can change a field name at any time. For example, you may want to change a field's name if you discover that it doesn't accurately describe the field's contents and creates confusion for other users.

No matter which view you use to change a field name, the name change appears in all views. So you can make a name change in Form Design view, then switch to List view to see the change there.

Changing a Field Name in Form Design View

To change a field name in Form Design view:

1. If you're not already in Form Design view, click the Form Design button or choose View, Form Design.

2. Select the field name you want to change. Make sure you select the field name, not the field entry.

3. Type the new field name.

   Remember, field names may contain up to 15 characters, may not begin with a single quotation mark ('), and must be followed by a colon.

4. Press Enter.

Changing a Field Name in List View

To change a field name in List view, follow these steps:

1. Select the column heading for the field whose name you want to change.

2. Choose Format, Field.

3. Type a new name in the Field Name box.

   Field names can contain up to 15 characters, and cannot begin with a single quotation mark (').

4. Click OK.

Aligning Text in Fields

▶ See "Using Dates and Times," p. 428

So far in this chapter, you have learned to create standard text fields. Works automatically formats standard text fields with flush-left alignment for text and flush-right alignment for dates and numbers.

The default formatting works well for most text data, such as names and addresses, comments, descriptions, and so on. But certain types of information may require special alignment. Works is very flexible—you can align any field to the left, right, or center horizontally. In List view, you also can align text vertically to the top, bottom, or center.

The following sections show you how to format text fields in Form Design and List views. Later in this chapter, you learn how to align numbers.

> **Note**
>
> Unlike in the previous version of Works, horizontal alignment changes made in one view now affect other views. For instance, if you change a text field's alignment to right in List view, it also will be right-aligned in Form Design view. Vertical alignment is a feature of List view only and does not affect Form Design view.

These horizontal alignment options are available in both Form Design and List views:

- *General*. Aligns text entries to the left and numbers and dates to the right.
- *Left*. Aligns all entries to the left, including numbers and dates.
- *Right*. Aligns all entries to the right, including numbers and dates.
- *Center*. Places entries in the center of the field, including numbers and dates.
- *Wrap Text*. Wraps text to another line, increasing the record height, if the field width is too small to display all the contents. This option is available only in List view and does not affect Form Design view.
- *Slide to Left*. Fields align left when printed, regardless of how they're set on-screen. This option is available only in Form Design view and does not affect printing in List view.

> **Note**
>
> Works can wrap text fields but does not wrap dates, times, numbers, or other values.

In List view, you also have some vertical alignment options for fields. These options don't make much difference if you stick with the default field heights (one line of text), but if you increase the height of a field, you can clearly see the difference in vertical alignment. (You learned how to change the field height earlier in this chapter.) You have these options:

- *Top*. Aligns text with the top of the field.
- *Center*. Centers text vertically in the field.
- *Bottom*. Aligns text with the bottom of the field.

Bottom is the default vertical alignment for all fields, regardless of type.

Figure 17.15 shows some fields in List view formatted with the various alignment options, so you can see the differences.

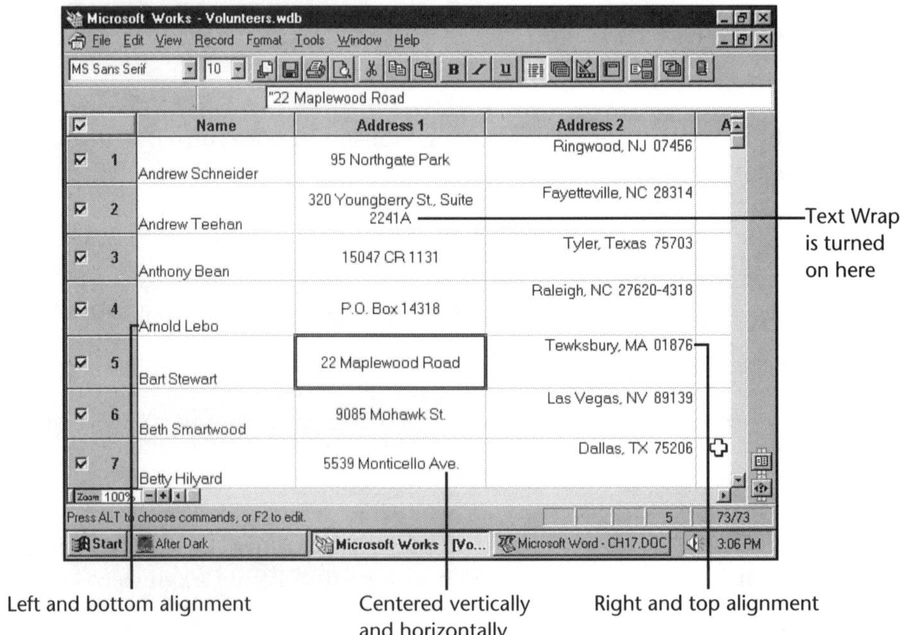

Fig. 17.15 You can align text both vertically and horizontally in fields.

Aligning Text in Form Design View

To change field alignment in Form Design view, follow these steps:

1. If you're not already in Form Design view, click the Form Design button or choose View, Form Design.
2. Select the field or fields you want to align.
3. Choose Format, Alignment.

   The Alignment tab of the Format dialog box appears. It looks much the same as figure 17.16 (in the following section), but it doesn't have the

Vertical alignment options, and the Wrap Text check box is replaced by the Slide to Left check box.

4. Choose a Horizontal alignment: General, Left, Right, or Center.

5. If you want to eliminate extra spaces between fields when you print the database, choose the Slide to Left check box.

6. Click OK.

▶ See "Printing Database Records," p. 412

Aligning Text in List View

Alignment changes made in List view also affect Form Design view alignment.

Follow these steps:

1. If you're not already in List view, click the List View button or choose View, List.

2. Select the field name.

3. Choose Format, Alignment.

   The Alignment tab of the Format dialog box appears, as shown in figure 17.16.

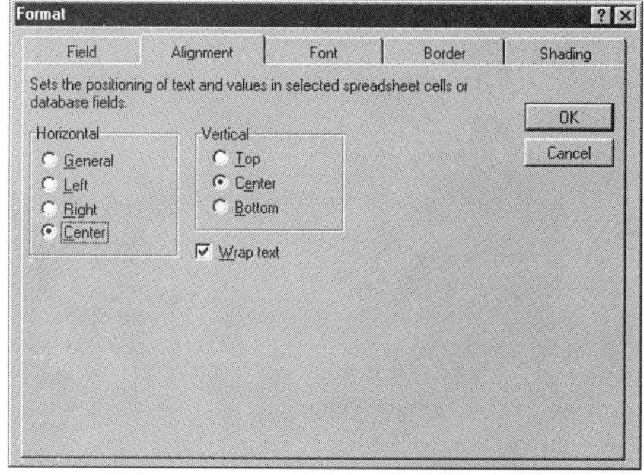

Fig. 17.16 Change text alignment in the Format dialog box.

4. Select a Horizontal option: General, Left, Right, or Center.

5. Select a Vertical option: Top, Center, or Bottom.

6. If you want, choose the Wrap Text check box.

7. Click OK.

Formatting Numbers in Fields

Works can display numbers in a wide variety of formatting options. For example, you can tell Works to format currency amounts with zero or two decimal places, and you can have negative amounts displayed on-screen in red. Works offers formatting options for percentages, fractions, true/false fields, and many other field types.

Depending on the type of data you enter in a field, formatting the field appropriately may be important. For example, if you type a percentage amount such as 75% in a field that has the default number format, works formats the percentage as 0.75, which may not be the effect you want.

When you first create a field, unless you specifically chose a number format, Works automatically formats it as a General field. That means numbers are aligned to the right, with no special symbols, as precisely as possible. That look may not always be what you want.

Follow these steps to change the way Works formats field numbers in Form or List view:

1. Select the field you want to format.
2. Choose Format, Field, and click the Field tab.

   Works displays the Format dialog box, with the field formatting options.

3. Choose Number from the Format list. A list of number formats appears in an Appearance list (see fig. 17.17).

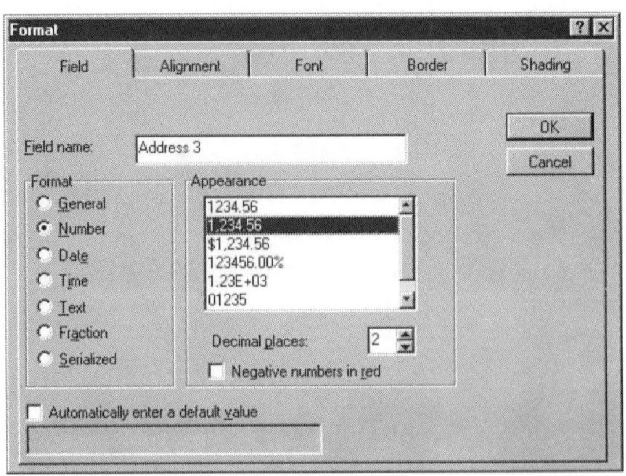

Fig. 17.17
The Appearance list shows a variety of number formats.

4. Choose a number format from the Appearance list.
5. Select a number of decimal places to show in the Decimal Places box.
6. If the Negative Numbers in Red check box is available, and you want that feature, select the check box.
7. Click OK.

Notice that the Format dialog box has a check box labeled Automatically Enter a Default Value. If you almost always enter the same value in a field for every record, select this check box, then type that value in the text box beneath it. For instance, if 90 percent of your clients come from Illinois, you might want to enter IL as the default value in your State field.

Note

You may use other formats for numbers besides Number, such as Date, Time, Fraction, and Serialized. See the full descriptions of these formats in the section "Creating New Databases From Scratch" in Chapter 16, "Creating and Saving a Database File."

Displaying or Hiding Database Elements

To make the Works database work best for you, you can make adjustments that affect how fields and records appear on-screen.

Displaying or Hiding Field Entry Lines in Form Design View

In Form view, Works automatically displays a line under each field's data entry area to help you see how long the field is. This line appears on printouts as well as on-screen.

You can turn off the display of field lines in Form view. For example, you may want to turn off field lines to print forms you have designed as formal invitations. To turn off field lines, use these steps:

1. If you're not already in Form Design view, click the Form Design button or choose View, Form Design.
2. Choose View, Field Lines.

You can repeat these steps to turn on field lines again later.

Displaying or Hiding Field Names in Form Design View

Usually, you want field names to appear in Form view, so you can see what fields you're entering data into. But if you want to display or print the database so that only the data appears, you can turn off the display of field names using these steps:

1. If you're not already in Form Design view, click the Form Design button or choose View, Form Design.
2. Select each field for which you want to hide the field name. (Hold down the Ctrl key while you click each one.)
3. Choose Format, Show Field Name.

Repeat this procedure to turn the field names back on again.

Displaying or Hiding Gridlines in List View

In List view, Works separates fields and records with gridlines. Turning gridlines off may make reading records across the screen more difficult. But if you prefer this effect, you can turn off gridlines by choosing View, Gridlines. Repeat this procedure to turn gridlines back on again.❖

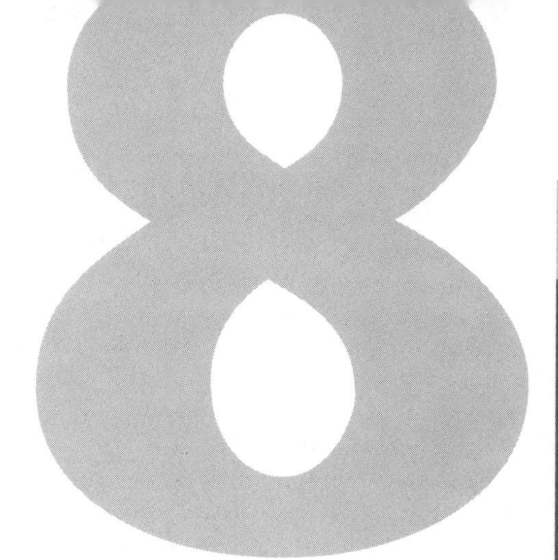

IV

Databases

Chapter 18

Enhancing a Database Form

by Faithe Wempen

In Chapter 16, you created a simple database, and in Chapter 17, you learned how to make structural changes. This chapter discusses ways to make your forms more visually attractive.

In the last two lessons, you switched frequently between List view and Form Design view, learning to make changes in both views. In this chapter, you work mostly with Form Design view to make changes that affect Form view.

This chapter shows you how to perform the following tasks:

- Enhance a database form with labels and descriptive text
- Use different fonts and text sizes for visual variety
- Use rectangles, borders, colors, and shading to set off areas of a form
- Add drawings and pictures to lend visual appeal and guide users

Note

Remember that you enter Form view by clicking the Form View button on the toolbar or choosing View, Form Design.

Creating Field Labels and Text

In Form Design view, you can insert descriptive text and labels to guide the user around a form and provide other useful information.

For example, if you have two databases that use identical name-and-address forms, you easily may forget which database you are working in. Placing a descriptive label at the top of each form saves the user from having to check the title bar to find out which database is active. You also can use labels to provide useful information, such as how to format phone numbers (see fig. 18.1).

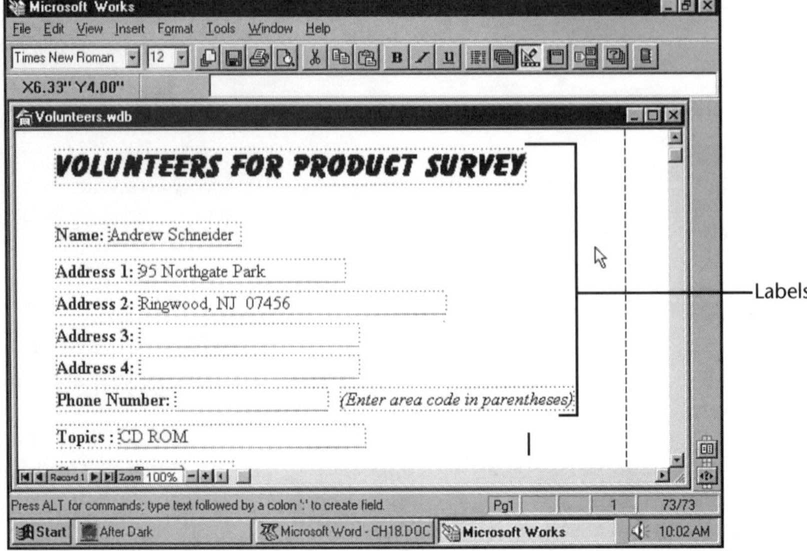

Fig. 18.1
Labels can identify the database and tell other users how to format data.

To create a label in a database form, follow these steps:

1. Move the cursor to the position where you want to place the label.
2. Type the label's text, using any fonts and character enhancements. (See the section "Changing the Appearance of Text" later in this chapter.)
3. Press Enter.

If the label is not positioned exactly where you want it, you can move the label, as the next section describes.

> **Note**
>
> Unlike field names, labels don't end with a colon. If you want to create a label that ends with a colon, begin the label with a double-quotation mark (") and end with a colon(:). The double-quotation mark doesn't appear on the form. If you don't type it, Works interprets the label as a field name.

Moving a Label

To move a label with the mouse, click and drag the label to the new position on the form. This procedure is just like moving a field.

◄ See "Moving Fields in Form Design View," p. 356

You also can move a label with the keyboard, although the process is more laborious. Follow these steps:

1. Select the label.
2. Choose Edit, Position Selection.
3. Move the label with the arrow keys. (You can move with the mouse if you prefer.)
4. Press Enter.

Works places the label in the new position.

Deleting a Label

You may need to remove labels when you redesign a form or you discover that you don't need the label. Follow these steps:

1. Select the label.
2. Press the Delete key; or choose Edit, Delete Selection.

Works removes the label immediately. To undo a deletion, before you make another deletion, choose Edit, Undo Delete Selection or press Ctrl+Z.

Changing the Appearance of Text

You can use different fonts in the Works Database Form and List views to create a decorative effect, to make text stand out on the page, or to fit more information on-screen. A *font* is a particular style of lettering. Windows 95 comes with several fonts, including Times New Roman, Arial, and Courier. Each of these fonts is scalable, which means you can use it in any size, from very tiny (8 points) to large (48 points or more). You also can apply attributes to a font, like bold or italic, to further change its look.

On a database form, you can type labels, field names, and field contents in different fonts, with different colors and styles. You even can use the Works WordArt utility to create special effects with text. (See "Using Microsoft Draw, ClipArt, WordArt, and Note-It" later in this chapter.)

Changing the Font and Size

You can set the font for a label or field in one of two ways. The first way is to select the font before you create it; the other way is to highlight existing text then select the font.

You can select a font from the toolbar if you have a mouse. This method is the quickest way to change the font. Follow these steps:

1. If you're formatting existing text (a field or label), select it. To select multiple elements, hold down Ctrl as you click them.

   or

   If you're going to type new text, position the cursor where you want to begin typing.

2. Open the Font Name drop-down list on the toolbar by clicking the down-pointing arrow next to the font name (see fig. 18.2).

Fig. 18.2
Works shows each font on the Font Name list as it appears in the database.

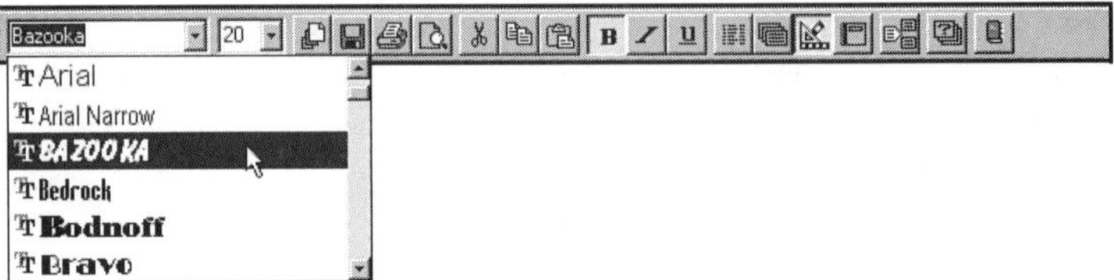

3. Click the font you want to apply.

   Works changes the highlighted text to the font you selected or enables you to begin typing with the new font.

4. To change the font size, open the Font Size drop-down list, right next to the Font Name (see fig. 18.3). Then type a new size or click a size on the drop-down list.

   Works adjusts the highlighted text to the selected font size or enables you to begin typing in the new size.

Tip
You can also change the font and size by right-clicking the selected text and selecting Font and Style from the shortcut menu if you prefer.

To reverse your changes, before choosing another format command or deleting text, choose Edit, Undo Format or press Ctrl+Z.

If you prefer, you also may select a font with the Format, Font and Style command. In this dialog box, you don't get to see a font as it will appear in the database unless you select it (so it appears in the Sample area). This is unlike the list of fonts that appears on the toolbar, which shows all the fonts as they will appear. However, you do get the extra control of being able to set the color and the style in this same step. (Color and style are covered in the following two sections.)

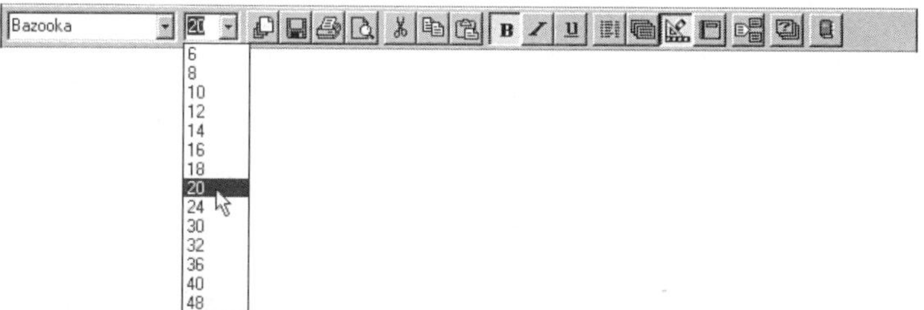

Fig. 18.3
Choose a size from the Font Size drop-down list.

Follow these steps to select a font using menu commands:

1. Highlight the field names or labels you want to change.

   or

   Position the cursor where you want to begin typing with the new font.

2. Choose Format, Font and Style.

   Works displays the Format Font and Style dialog box (see fig. 18.4).

3. Click a font name from the Font list.

4. Click a font size from the Size list or type a number in the Size text box.

5. Choose OK.

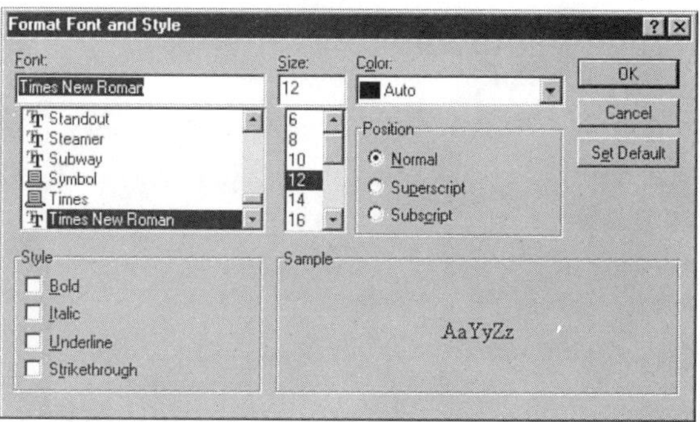

Fig. 18.4
Select your font and size in the Format Font and Style dialog box.

Choosing a Font Color

Works can display fonts in color on color monitors. Using color is a good way to set off labels and field names on-screen. With a supported color printer, color fonts also print in color. If your printer doesn't support color, these fonts print in black.

To change the color of a field entry label, or field name, follow these steps:

1. Highlight the text you want to change.

   or

   Position the cursor where you want to begin typing in color.

2. Choose Format, Font and Style.

   Works displays the Format Font and Style dialog box (refer to fig. 18.4).

3. Open the Color drop-down list.

4. Select a color from the list, then choose OK.

   Works returns to the Form view window and applies the color to the highlighted text.

Troubleshooting

I used several colors of fonts, but when I print on my black-and-white printer, some of the text vanishes. Why?

Black-and-white printers force Works to make a choice—is it black or is it white? Dark-colored fonts will be black, and light-colored fonts will be white—that is, invisible. If you're printing on a black-and-white printer, it's best to confine yourself to dark colors in your database or report.

Choosing a Font Style

A *style* is a special attribute that modifies a font, such as bold, italic, or underlined. You can use the Format Font and Style dialog box, as shown in figure 18.4, but using the toolbar or keyboard is much quicker.

Follow these steps to use the toolbar:

1. Highlight the text you want to change.

   or

   Position the cursor where you want to begin typing with the character enhancement.

2. On the toolbar, click the Bold, Italic, or Underline button.

or

Press Ctrl+B for bold, Ctrl+I for italic, Ctrl+U for underline, or Ctrl+space bar for plain text.

To remove an enhancement, click the toolbar button again. For example, to remove bold, click the Bold button. To quickly remove all attributes, press Ctrl+space bar.

To use the Format dialog box, follow these steps:

1. Highlight the text you want to change.

   or

   Position the cursor where you want to begin typing with the character enhancement.

2. Choose Format, Font and Style.

   Works displays the Format Font and Style dialog box (again see fig. 18.4.)

3. Click the check boxes for the styles you want to apply: Bold, Italic, Underline, and/or Strikethrough.

4. Click OK.

Changing the Default Font

If you find yourself constantly changing the font or size of everything you type, you may want to change the default font to a font you use more often. The default font is the font that Works uses if you don't specifically choose a different one.

Follow these steps to change the default font:

1. Choose Format, Font and Style. The Format Font and Style dialog box appears, as shown in figure 18.4.

2. Select a Font, Size, Color, and Style, as you learned in earlier sections.

3. Click the Set Default button, then choose OK.

4. When Works prompts you to confirm the new default, choose Yes to return to the database window.

Works uses the new default font and style for all future database form documents. Changing the default font does not change any fonts you have used in existing documents, however.

Using Rectangles, Borders, Colors, and Shading

You can enhance your database input forms with rectangles, borders, colors, and shading. For example, you may want to highlight a message to the user by placing the message in a shaded, colored rectangle.

Note

The rectangles, borders, colors, and shading you apply in Form Design view affect only Form view.

Creating Rectangles

Rectangles are very useful for organizing database forms so the user can find labels and data entry areas quickly. For example, you may want to set apart two separate areas on a database form—one area for a customer's name, address, and customer identification number, and the other area for the customer's credit information.

Use these steps to create a rectangle in Form view:

1. Position the cursor where you want the rectangle.
2. Choose Insert, Rectangle.

Works inserts a standard, square, gray-edged rectangle at the insertion point (see fig. 18.5). The shape may not be exactly what you want, but you're not done yet. The next step is to move and size the rectangle.

Moving and Sizing Rectangles

After inserting a rectangle, you can change its size or move the rectangle anywhere on the form.

Moving a Rectangle

To move a rectangle with the mouse, follow these steps:

1. If you don't see sizing handles on the rectangle, click the rectangle to make them appear (refer to fig. 18.5).

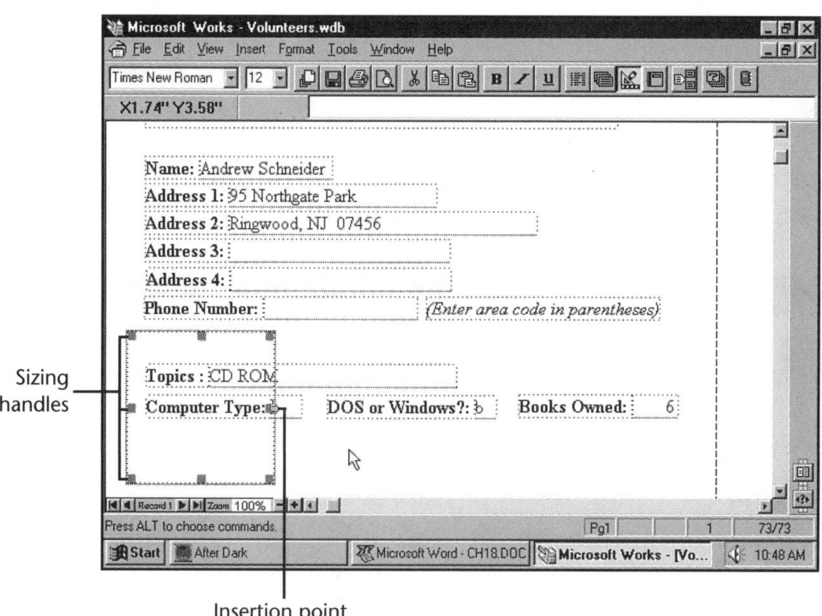

Fig. 18.5
When you first create a rectangle, Works inserts a rectangle at the insertion point.

2. Move the mouse cursor onto the rectangle until the word `DRAG` appears under the arrow.

3. Drag the rectangle to the new location.

If you prefer, you can use menu commands to move the rectangle. With this method, you can do the actual moving with the keyboard or the mouse. Follow these steps:

1. Select the rectangle.

2. Choose Edit, Position Selection.

   The mouse cursor becomes a double arrow with the word `DRAG`.

3. Use the arrow keys or mouse to move the rectangle to a new position.

4. Press Enter or click the left mouse button to drop the rectangle in the new location.

Resizing a Rectangle

Follow these steps to resize a rectangle:

1. Click the rectangle. Works displays sizing handles around the object (refer to fig. 18.5).

2. Move the mouse cursor onto a resizing handle. The cursor becomes a box and double arrow labeled RESIZE.

3. Drag the handles to the new size.

Figure 18.6 shows a rectangle that was created, moved, and resized around a group of fields.

Fig. 18.6
You can move and resize a rectangle to neatly contain a group of fields.

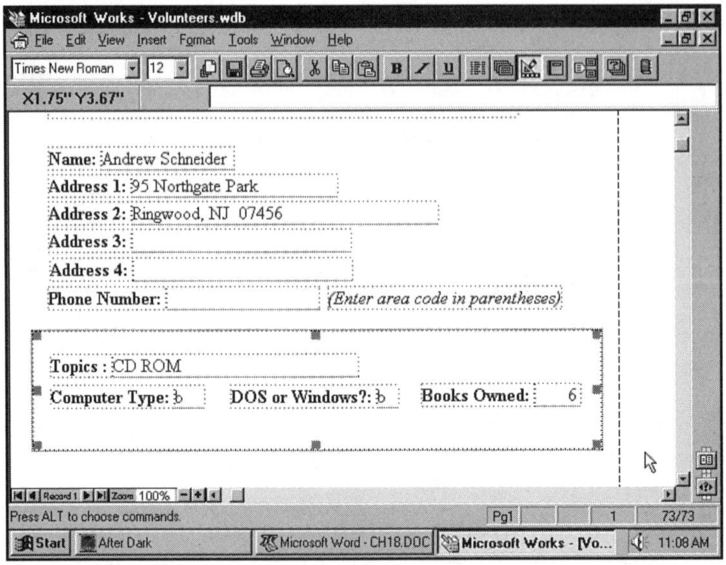

Note

The *Snap to Grid* feature makes positioning objects easier. It automatically aligns objects with the nearest invisible vertical and horizontal gridlines, .08" apart. With Snap to Grid turned off, you can position objects more precisely, in increments of a hundredth inch (.01"). To turn Snap to Grid on or off, choose Format, Snap to Grid.

Troubleshooting

I can't select the fields that are inside the rectangle.

When you put a border around a group of fields, you can't select those fields anymore in Form Design view, because when you click them, Works thinks you're clicking the rectangle itself. You can drag the rectangle out of the way temporarily or use the Send to Back command, which you learn about later in this chapter.

Creating a Border

After you create a rectangle and position it where you want it, you may want to dress it up with a border. The black line that forms the rectangle is rather plain, but if you apply a border to the rectangle, you can choose from several line thicknesses and designs.

You also can apply borders to individual field names and/or field entries, without creating the rectangle. Figure 18.7 shows a border applied to the rectangle from figure 18.6, and borders also are applied to several fields.

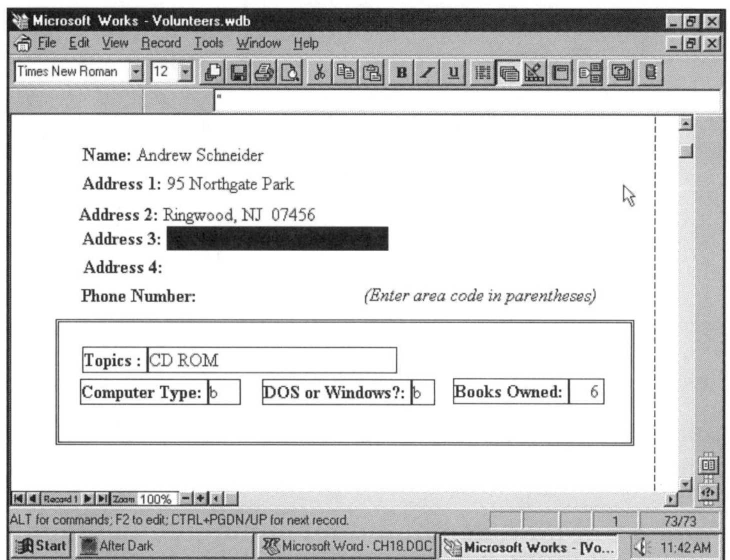

Fig. 18.7
You can apply borders to rectangles, to the fields themselves, or to both.

Follow these steps to create borders:

1. Select the object you want to format with a border. It can be a rectangle, a field—anything.

   To select more than one object, hold down Ctrl and click each object.

2. Choose Format, Border.

   Works displays the Border tab of the Format dialog box (see fig. 18.8).

3. From the Line Style list box, select a style for the border.

4. To change the border's color, select a color from the Color drop-down list box.

5. Choose OK. Works adds the border to any elements you selected.

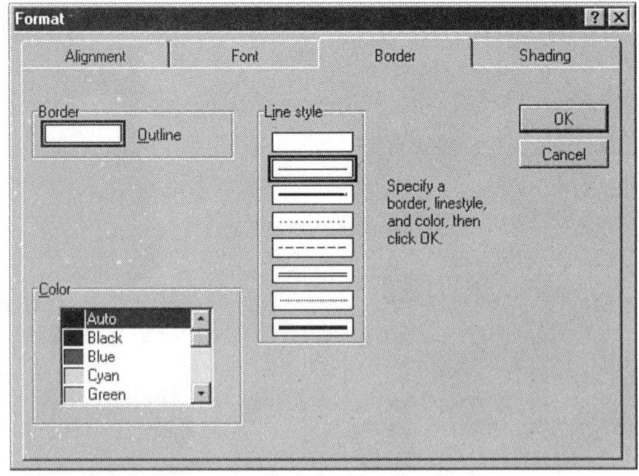

Fig. 18.8
You can specify a border style on the Border tab of the Format dialog box.

Deleting a Border

You easily can remove a border if you decide the border is unnecessary or unattractive. Follow these steps:

1. Click the bordered object to select it.

   To select more than one object, hold down Ctrl and click each object.

2. Choose Format menu, Border.
3. In the Line Style list box, select the empty line style.
4. Choose OK.

Works removes the border from the elements you selected.

Using Bring to Front and Send to Back

When you create an object such as a rectangle or drawing, Works places it on top of any other existing objects. For example, in figure 18.7, the rectangle was placed around the fields first, then the borders were added around the fields. But the rectangle is on top, so you need to select it and send it to the back so you can work with the fields.

Follow these steps to bring an object to the front or send it to the back:

1. Select the object.
2. Choose Format, Send to Back.

   or

   Choose Format, Bring to Front.

You now can select the front object by clicking it or moving the cursor onto the object with the arrow keys.

Using Color and Shading

Earlier in this chapter, you learned to apply color to fonts and borders. In this section, you learn to add color and shading to labels, field entries, and field names, or to an entire database form. Follow these steps:

1. Select the element you want to format with color and/or shading. To select more than one object, hold down Ctrl and click each object.

   or

   To add color and/or shading to an entire database form, do not select any objects.

2. Choose Format, Shading.

   Works displays the Shading tab of the Format dialog box (see fig. 18.9).

3. Select a pattern from the Pattern list, or select None for no pattern.

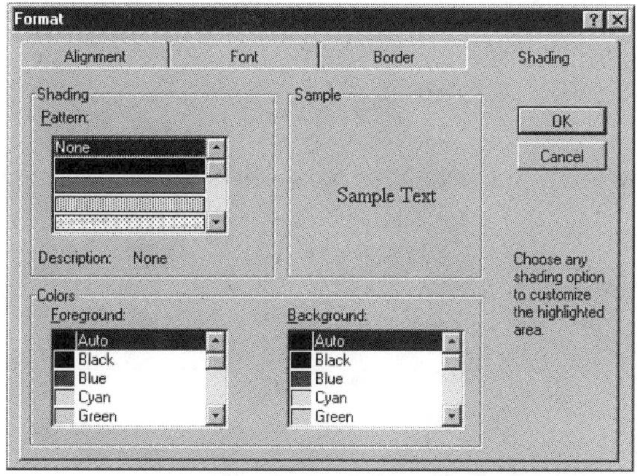

Fig. 18.9
Add color and/or shading to a form using the Shading tab of the Format dialog box.

4. Choose a foreground color from the Foreground list.

5. Choose a background color from the Background list.

   Works displays your choices of pattern and colors in the Sample area.

6. Choose OK.

Works applies the pattern and colors to the objects you selected or to the entire form if you did not select any objects.

Tip

After selecting an object, click the right mouse button to bring up a formatting menu. You can quickly apply attributes to labels and rectangles using this feature.

Note

The foreground color applies to the lines in the pattern. The background color applies to the spaces between the lines in the pattern. If you select a solid pattern, only the foreground color appears.

Figure 18.10 shows a yellow and cyan pattern for the rectangle. Then the fields in the rectangle were formatted with a white-on-white solid pattern, so they would stand out.

You can remove color and shading from a rectangle, form, or other object. Follow these steps:

1. Select the objects from which you want to remove color and shading.

   or

   To remove color and shading from the entire form, don't select any objects.

2. Choose Format, Shading.

3. From the Pattern list in the Format dialog box, select None.

4. Choose OK.

Works removes color and shading from the selected objects or the entire form.

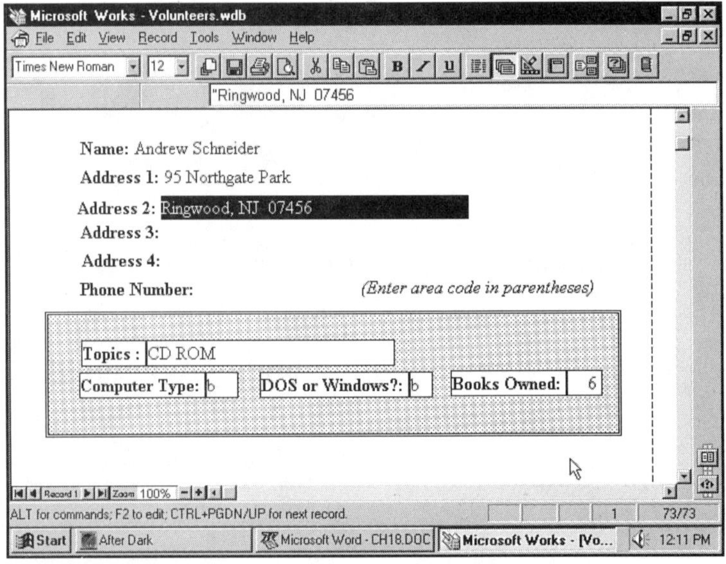

Fig. 18.10
Adding patterns to the rectangle behind these fields makes them really stand out.

Using Microsoft Draw, ClipArt, WordArt, and Note-It

You can make your Works Database forms more visually attractive by enhancing them with drawings from the Works ClipArt library, with pictures from other sources, or with WordArt and Note-Its. These features can provide visual clues to the purpose of a form or a specific area of a form. For example, you might have a graphic of two people shaking hands on a form that your salespeople fill out when working with a customer. To learn how to use these options, see Chapter 24, "Using Microsoft Draw and ClipArt," and Chapter 25, "Using WordArt and Note-It."

The following steps briefly review the procedure for inserting ClipArt, WordArt, or a Note-It note:

1. Position the cursor where you want to insert the ClipArt, WordArt, or Note-It note.
2. Choose Insert, ClipArt, WordArt, or Note-It.
3. Follow the steps in the appropriate sections of Chapter 14, "Creating Charts," for inserting a drawing, WordArt, or Note-It note.❖

Chapter 19

Entering and Editing Data

by Faithe Wempen

In Chapters 16, 17, and 18, you learn how to create and customize database forms. When your form is ready to go, you can start entering data into it.

In this chapter, you learn about the following topics:

- Entering data in database fields
- Editing data in a field
- Adding new records to a database
- Copying and moving data between fields
- Copying and moving fields and records
- Hiding fields and records

Entering Information in a Works Database

◄ See "Starting a New Database File," p. 337

◄ See "Reviewing the Database Window," p. 346

You can get data into a Works Database in two ways. One way is to import the data from another program; for information about this method, see Chapter 26, "Using the Works Tools Together."

The other, more common way to get information into a Works Database is to type the information in the fields you created. This chapter describes the details of using this method.

You can type information in fields using Form view or List view. Which method is better? If you're used to filling out paper forms, you may prefer

Form view. A form appears on-screen, where you enter all the data for a single record. Then you save that record and move to the next "page," which is another blank form.

If you're used to keeping track of information on a spreadsheet, List view may be more familiar. The fields are in columns, and the records are rows that intersect the columns. Entering information in List view is helpful if you are entering data for one field in many records; you can move quickly down through that field's column, filling in the information.

Entering Data

Typing information in a Works Database is easy. You use the following steps in Form or List view:

1. Highlight the field.

   To highlight a field in Form view, click the field (the data entry area, not the field name). In List view, click the field entry area (the intersection of row and column) where you want the information to appear. You can move from field to field by pressing the Tab or arrow keys on your keyboard if you prefer. Figure 19.1 shows a database record with the `Name` field highlighted.

2. Type the data.

3. Move to the next field by clicking the next field, pressing Tab, or using the arrow keys. You can move to the previous field by clicking it, using the arrow keys, or pressing Shift+Tab.

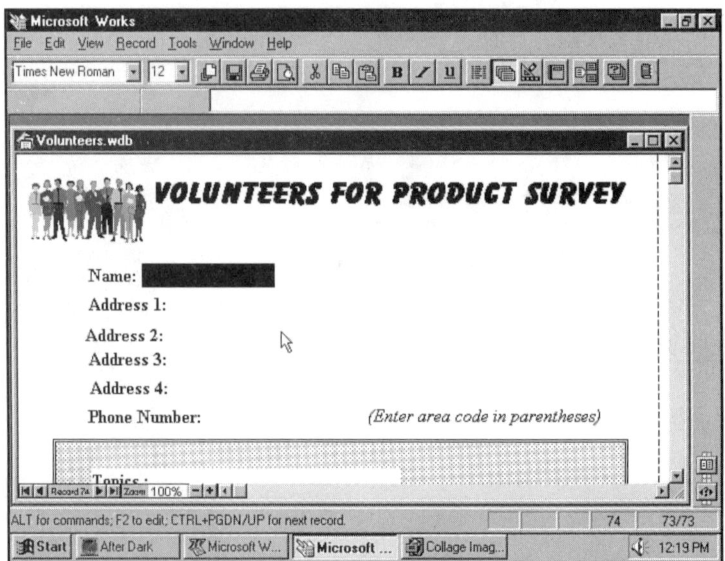

Fig. 19.1
A blank database record in Form view with the `Name` field highlighted.

Editing Data in a Field

After you type data in a Works Database, you can make changes to the information in a field using Form view or List view. Changes made in one view affect the other, because all views are simply different vantage points of the same data.

You can replace all the data in a field or edit the existing data. To replace the information in a field, follow these steps:

1. Highlight the field entry area (not the field name).

2. Type the new entry.

   When you type the first character of the new entry, Works deletes the old entry and begins inserting your new keystrokes.

3. After you finish typing the new entry, press Enter or click the Enter box on the formula bar. (The Enter box is the check mark at the left end of the data entry area on the formula bar, as shown in figure 19.2.) You can also press an arrow key or the Tab key to move to another field and enter the data.

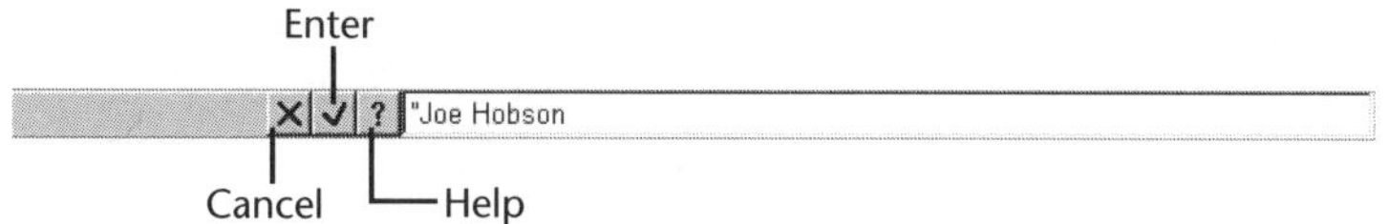

Fig. 19.2
The formula bar has buttons you can use to enter or cancel an edit.

Tip
If you want to enter or change data in another field, you can skip step 3 and just move to the next field.

If you prefer, you can make changes to an existing field entry, without wiping out all the data. Use these steps:

1. Highlight the field.

2. Click the formula bar or press F2 to enter Edit mode.

   Works moves the cursor into the data entry area of the formula bar.

3. Use the editing keys to edit the entry. Table 19.1 shows the keystrokes and mouse actions you can use to edit information in a Works Database field.

4. Press Enter or click the Enter box.

Table 19.1 Data Editing Keystrokes and Mouse Actions

Action	Mouse	Keyboard
Move to beginning of line	Click beginning of line	Home
Move to end of line	Click end of line	End
Left one character	Click left one character	Left arrow
Right one character	Click right one character	Right arrow
Move insertion point	Click to correct position	Arrow keys
Highlight characters	Drag mouse pointer	Shift+arrow keys
Delete highlighted characters	N/A	Delete or Backspace

Clearing Data from a Field

In the preceding section, you learned how to edit information in a field and replace field data. But what if you want to clear the field entirely? To remove all information from a field, follow these steps:

Tip
To reverse the effect of choosing Edit, Clear, choose Edit, Undo or press Ctrl+Z before you choose another command.

1. In Form view or List view, highlight the field or fields you want to clear. (Highlighting multiple fields is described later in the section "Copying and Moving Data in a Field.")

2. Choose Edit, Clear or press the Delete or Backspace key.

   Works clears the field entry. If you previously applied formatting commands to the field (for example, right alignment), Works retains the formatting.

Creating a New Record

The easiest way to create a new record is to add it to the end of the database. In Form view, when you're in the last field of the last record, pressing Tab takes you to the first field of a blank form, ready to fill out.

Another way of moving to a blank form in Form view is to click the Go to End button in the bottom left corner of the screen. A blank form appears, ready for your input.

In List view, you can begin typing a new record simply by moving to the row below the last existing record and typing your new record there.

Inserting a New Record Between Existing Records

If you want your records in a particular order, you can insert a record between two existing records.

In List view, you can insert a new record anywhere in a database by following these steps:

1. Highlight the record *below* the row where you want to insert the new record.

2. Choose Record, Insert Record.

   Works inserts a new record above the highlighted row.

Tip
To add more than one record at one time in List view, highlight the same number of existing records as the number of new records you want to add, then choose Record, Insert Record.

To insert a new record anywhere in a database in Form view, follow these steps:

1. Display the record that the new record should precede. (The new record will be inserted *before* the record you display.)

2. Choose Record, Insert Record.

   or

   Click the Insert Record toolbar button.

   Works inserts a new, blank record and places the insertion point in the first field.

Deleting Records

You can remove records quickly in Form or List view. You can either cut them (such as move them to the Clipboard, to paste somewhere else if you choose) or delete them entirely (with no option to paste).

> **Note**
>
> When you delete a record, Works renumbers all remaining records.

Follow these steps to cut a record to the Clipboard in Form view:

1. Display the record you want to cut.

2. Choose Edit, Cut Record.

3. (Optional) To paste the record somewhere else, display the record before which the cut record should be pasted, then choose Edit, Paste Record.

Follow these steps to cut a record to the Clipboard in List view:

Tip
An easy way to highlight the entire record is to click the record number.

1. Highlight the entire record you want to cut.
2. Choose Edit, Cut.
3. (Optional) To paste the record somewhere else, highlight the entire record before which the cut record should be pasted, then choose Edit, Paste.

You also can delete the record if you prefer, leaving no trace of it. Follow these steps to delete a record in Form or List view:

1. Highlight any part of the record you want to delete. You can select several records to delete at once.
2. Choose Record, Delete Record.

Tip
To restore a record you deleted in Form or List view, before you choose other program commands, choose Edit, Undo Delete Record; or press Ctrl+Z.

Works deletes the record immediately, without asking for confirmation.

Using Formulas To Enter Data in Fields

Just like in a spreadsheet, Works enables you to perform math calculations on numbers in database fields. When Works performs the calculation you specify, it inserts the result in the field that contains the formula. For example, figure 19.3 shows a database form with a calculated field.

Notice in figure 19.3 that the field named `Total Amt. Due` is highlighted and the formula used to calculate the amount due appears in the formula bar:

```
=Current Balance+(Current Balance*0.02*Past Due)
```

▶ See "Using Formulas and Functions," p. 430

As the figure shows, when you type the `Current Balance` and the `Past Due` amounts, Works automatically inserts the result of the formula in the `Total Amt. Due` field.

When you enter a formula into a field, the formula is automatically copied to the same field in every other record. You can create your formula in Form view or List view (but not Form Design view).

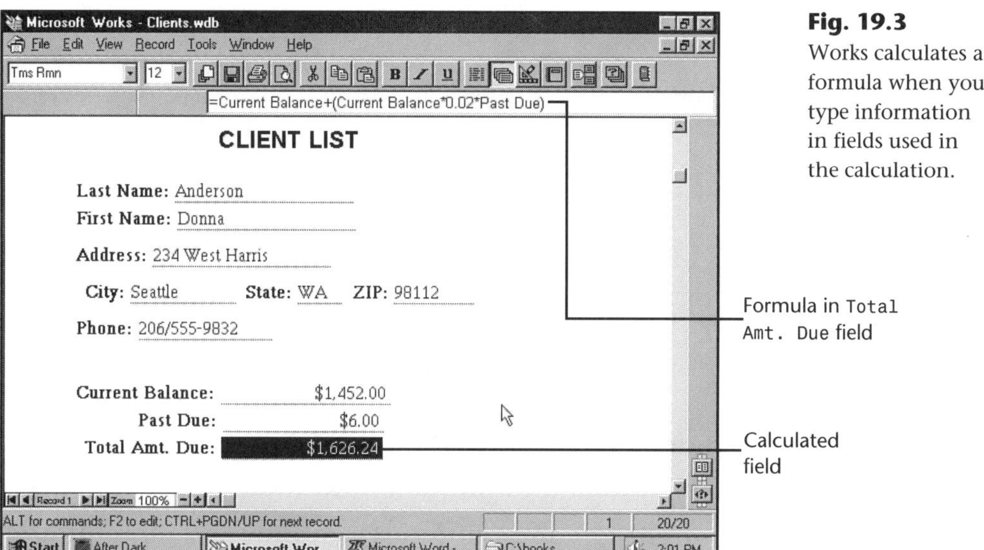

Fig. 19.3
Works calculates a formula when you type information in fields used in the calculation.

Follow these steps to enter a formula:

1. Highlight the field where you want to create a formula.
2. Type an equal sign (=), and then type the formula.

   As you type, the formula appears in the field and in the formula bar.
3. Press Enter. (You can also press Tab or an arrow key if you prefer.)

   Works calculates the formula and inserts the results in the field. After you create a formula, Works calculates the formula in the field for each record you display.

Clearing Formulas

When you clear a formula from a field, you are clearing it not only from the displayed record, but from all other records in the database. For this reason, the steps to clear a formula from a field are different from the steps to clear a regular field entry.

To clear a formula from a field in Form or List view, follow these steps:

1. Highlight the field in Form view or the field name in List view.
2. Choose Edit, Clear Formula.

   Works removes the formula from that field in all the records in the database.

Filling in a Numeric Series

In List view, Works can automatically enter a series of numbers or dates into adjacent records. For example, you can tell Works to insert a series of dates seven days apart into adjacent records for the period 1/1/95 to 12/31/96. This procedure is very useful for numbering invoices, parts lists, and so on.

To number or date several records sequentially, follow these steps:

1. In List view, type a starting date or number in the first field of the series.

2. Highlight the fields in which you want to insert the series of dates or numbers, including the field containing the starting number or date.

3. Choose Edit, Fill Series.

   Works displays the Fill Series dialog box (see fig. 19.4).

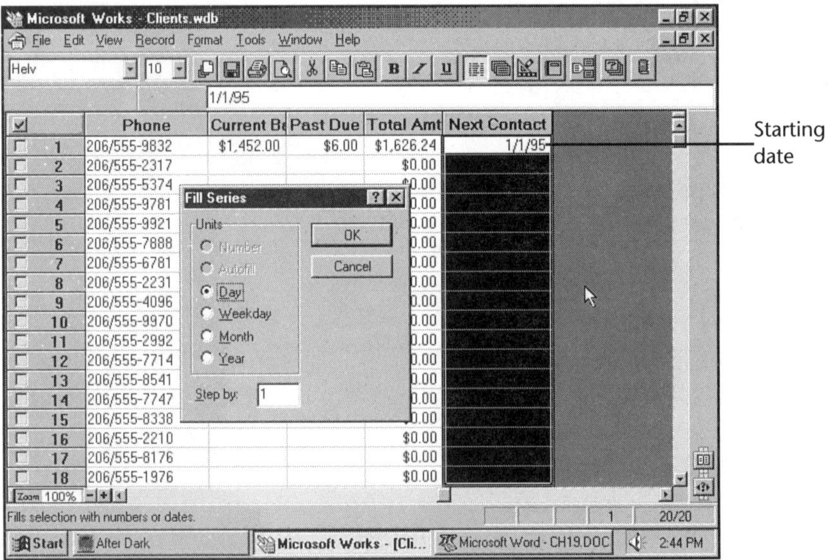

Fig. 19.4 Use the Fill Series dialog box to insert a series of numbers, dates, weekdays, months, or years.

4. Choose a unit: Number, Day, Weekday, Month, or Year.

5. Type a numeric or date interval in the Step By text box.

   For example, if you want to number a series of records in intervals of 7, type 7 in the Step By text box. To number the adjacent records in descending order, type a negative number.

6. Choose OK. Works fills in the numbers or dates.

Figure 19.5 shows the results of specifying dates in the Next Contact field for every seven days.

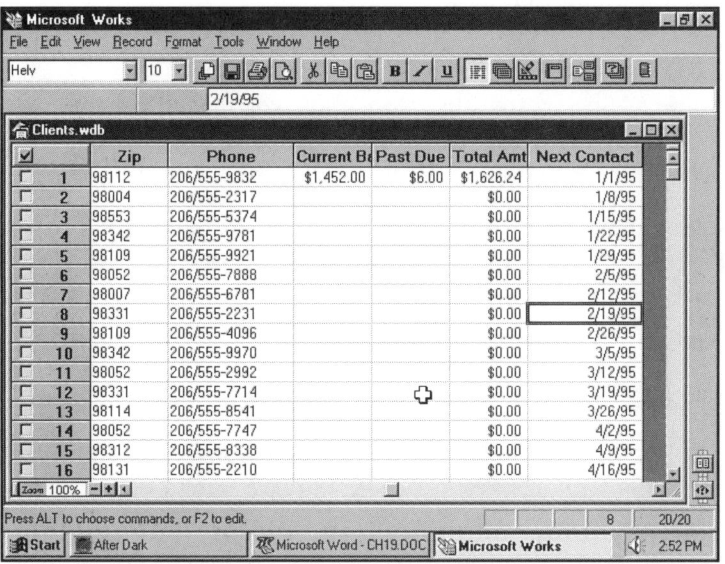

Fig. 19.5
The Fill Series feature can automatically insert dates or numbers in fields.

> **Troubleshooting**
>
> *I want to set up unique serialized numbers in a field, like invoice or receipt numbers. Is Fill Series a good way to do that?*
>
> It's not the best way. A better way to ensure that the serialized numbers entered in a field are unique is to set the field type to Serialized. (Choose Format, Field, then click Serialized.) Enter the starting number and increment, then click OK. As you enter each record, the value in this field will be automatically entered according to your specifications.

Copying and Moving Data

You can copy and move information to another location in a Works Database, or you can copy and move database information to another Works application. Copying leaves the original information and inserts a copy at a new location. Moving deletes the original information and inserts it at a new location.

For example, you can copy data from one record to another, or you can copy an entire record into a Works Word Processor document. To find out how to copy and move information between applications, see Chapter 26, "Using the Works Tools Together." The following sections describe copying and moving information within the database.

Copying and Moving Data in a Field

Before you can copy or move the information, you must highlight it. To highlight a field's contents in Form or List view, click the field data entry area or move the highlight into the field using the Tab or arrow keys.

You also can highlight more than one field and copy or move the contents of the highlighted fields in one step, if you're in Form Design or List view. To highlight more than one field with the mouse in Form Design view, hold down the Ctrl key and click each field. (This Ctrl key method does not work in List view.) To highlight a series of fields in List view, click the first field, then hold down Shift and click the last field in the series.

In List view, you can highlight the contents of multiple fields and copy or paste them into multiple fields elsewhere, but be careful. Copying or moving information into fields that already contain data may produce undesirable results. You also can copy or move an entire record into a new record, as described later in "Copying and Moving Records."

To copy or move the field contents you have highlighted, follow these steps:

1. To copy the information in a field, highlight the information, and then choose Edit, Copy; or press Ctrl+C; or click the Copy toolbar button.

   To move the information, choose Edit, Cut; press Ctrl+X; or click the Cut toolbar button.

2. Highlight the field where you want to insert the cut or copied information.

3. Choose Edit, Paste; or press Ctrl+V; or click the Paste toolbar button.

Works inserts the copied or cut information into the highlighted field, replacing any existing field contents.

Note

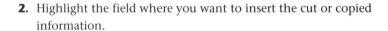

Moving records may leave empty records behind. You should delete these blank records to avoid undesirable results when printing the database. (Use the Record, Delete Record command.)

Using Drag-and-Drop to Copy and Move Data

You can move database information quickly with the mouse using the *drag-and-drop* method. From Form view, you can drag-and-drop data among fields in a single record; from List view, you can drag-and-drop between records as well.

To use drag-and-drop, first highlight the information you want to move or copy. For example, in List view, click a record number to highlight the entire record. Or click the field name to highlight an entire field.

To move the selected information, move the mouse cursor onto one of the borders of the selection. In List view, the mouse cursor displays the word DRAG (see fig. 19.6). In Form view, it doesn't display anything special at this point.

The mouse pointer shows DRAG

Fig. 19.6 When you move the cursor onto the border of a selection in List view, the cursor displays the word DRAG.

You then click the mouse button and drag the selection to a new location. While you drag, the mouse cursor displays the word MOVE. If you hold down Ctrl while you drag, Works copies the selection and the mouse cursor displays the word COPY.

When you release the mouse button, Works inserts the moved or copied information. If you move field contents vertically, Works inserts the field contents in the record(s) above the record that contains the mouse cursor. If you move field contents horizontally, Works inserts the selection in the field to the left of the field that contains the mouse cursor.

Tip
To undo a drag-and-drop operation, before you perform any other actions, choose Edit, Undo Drag and Drop; or press Ctrl+Z.

To cancel a drag-and-drop operation after you begin dragging a selection, press Esc. Works restores the highlight at the original location.

Copying and Moving Fields and Records

In the preceding sections, you learned to copy and move information in fields. You also can copy and move entire fields and records. For example, you may want to place several records next to each other in List view so you can view them without scrolling.

Copying and Moving Fields

Works enables you to copy and move fields while you design a database or later, after you have entered information in your database. Moving fields is especially useful. For example, you may discover that you always enter information in certain fields but seldom enter information in other fields. By placing the most-used fields adjacent to each other, you can enter data without having to move over seldom-used fields.

Follow these steps to move a field's position in List view:

1. Highlight the field you want to move.
2. Choose Edit, Cut; or click the Cut toolbar button; or press Ctrl+X.

3. A dialog box appears asking if you want to permanently delete this information. Click OK to continue.

4. Highlight the field before which you want to insert the cut field.
5. Choose Edit, Paste; or click the Paste toolbar button; or press Ctrl+V.

You also can drag-and-drop entire fields in List view. Just highlight the field name then drag the field to the right or left to change its position.

Copying and Moving Records

You can copy or move an entire Works Database record. Moving records is useful when you want to group two or more records together so you can scroll quickly between them in Form view or view them together in List view. Copying a record is useful when you want to create a new record with very minor changes to an existing record.

Form view has special commands for cutting and copying records. To copy or move a record in Form view, follow these steps:

1. Display the record you want to copy or move.
2. To copy the record, choose Edit, Copy Record; or press Ctrl+Shift+C.

   or

   To move the record, choose Edit, Cut Record; or press Ctrl+Shift+X.

   > **Note**
   >
   > Press Ctrl+C to copy a single field; press Ctrl+Shift+C to copy an entire record.

3. Display the record before which you want to insert the copied or cut record.
4. Choose Edit, Paste Record; or press Ctrl+V.

   Works inserts the copied or cut record before the displayed record.

To copy or move a record in List view, it's a little different. (Notice the different shortcut keys in step 2, for example.) Follow these steps:

1. Highlight the record(s) you want to copy or move.

   To highlight a record in List view, click its record (row) number; or move the highlight into the record and choose Edit, Select Record. To highlight more than one adjacent record, drag across the record numbers.

2. To copy the record, choose Edit, Copy; or press Ctrl+C.

   or

   To move the record, choose Edit, Cut; or press Ctrl+X.

3. Highlight the record before which you want to copy or move the record.
4. Choose Edit, Paste; or press Ctrl+V.

Works inserts the copied or moved record before the displayed record.

You also can drag-and-drop records the same way you can drag-and-drop fields in List view. Just highlight the entire record and then point at it so the word `DRAG` appears. Drag the record to its new position. Hold down the Ctrl key as you drag to copy rather than move.

Troubleshooting

I am trying to copy a record in Form view and insert the copy immediately so that Works places it next to the original, but it doesn't work. What am I doing wrong?

You cannot copy the displayed record and immediately insert a copy next to the original. (This problem appears to be an oversight on the part of the Works programmers.) You must paste the copy at a location not adjacent to the original, and then cut and paste the record next to the original record.

I sometimes begin copying information with drag-and-drop, and then change my mind and decide to move the information instead. Is there a way to do that?

To toggle between copying and moving the selection, before you release the mouse button, press or release the Ctrl key.

Hiding Fields and Records

When you display a database on-screen in Form or List view, Works shows you the fields, field labels, and any other elements such as lines or drawings. In List view, you can hide fields to keep other people from reading the information in the field, to temporarily display fewer fields on-screen, or to display fields together.

In Form view, hiding field names is useful when you want to display the contents of several fields together. For example, you can display the contents of the `First Name` and `Last Name` fields together on one line, without their field labels. Also, if field names on a form are not helpful, you can hide or replace them.

You also can hide entire records in Form or List view. You then can print only the records that appear. This step is very useful when you want to print selected records that you cannot retrieve using a database query.

Hiding Field Names in Form View

Figure 19.7 shows the result of hiding the field names for the name, address, and phone, and arranging them to form natural-looking address lines like you might find in an address book.

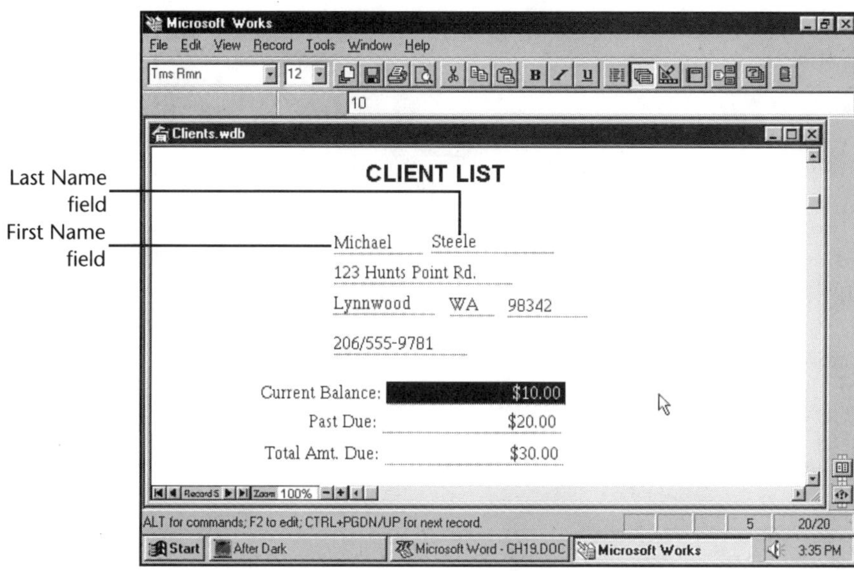

Fig. 19.7
To create a cleaner form, you can hide the field names for the fields whose content is obvious.

To hide field names in Form view, use the following steps:

1. Enter Form Design view.
2. Highlight the field name you want to hide.
3. Choose Format, Show Field Name to remove the check mark beside that command.

Works hides the field name. Show Field Name is a toggle. To turn field names back on, repeat steps 2 and 3.

◄ See "Moving Fields," p. 356

After you have hidden the field names, drag the fields around on the form to rearrange them as you want.

Hiding Fields in List View

Hiding a field in List view is easy. With the mouse, you drag the right border of the field's name to the left until the field disappears. It works just like in a spreadsheet.

To hide a field with the keyboard, follow these steps:

1. Highlight the field you want to hide.
2. Choose Format, Field Width.

   Works displays the Field Width dialog box (see fig. 19.8).

3. Type **0** in the Column Width text box then choose OK. Works hides the field.

Fig. 19.8
Use the Field Width dialog box to hide a field.

To display a hidden field again, follow these steps:

1. Choose Edit, Go To; or press F5.

   Works displays the Go To dialog box (see fig. 19.9).

2. In the Select A Field list box, select the hidden field you want to display.

3. Choose OK.

   Works highlights the field but doesn't display it on-screen.

4. Choose Format, Field Width.

5. In the Field Width dialog box, type the field width you want in the Column Width text box. Or click the Standard or Best Fit buttons. Then choose OK.

   Works redisplays the field.

◀ See "Changing Field Width in List View," p. 364

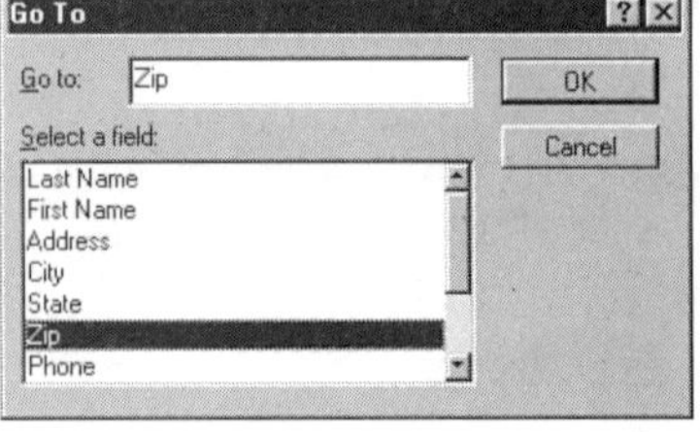

Fig. 19.9
Use the Go To dialog box to redisplay a hidden field.

Hiding Records

In Chapter 21, you learn how to create a query to narrow down a list of records to match certain criteria, such as Amount Due, Birth Date, or other quantifiable data. Hiding records is useful when you want to print selected records that don't meet the standard Works Database query criteria. For example, if you want to hide certain records based on some criteria that's not listed, such as the records of everyone who's related to your secretary. Or you might want to hide certain records for confidentiality. Whatever the reason, you can hide records by following these steps:

To hide a record, follow these steps:

1. In Form view, display the record you want to hide.

   or

   In List view, highlight the record(s) you want to hide.

2. Choose Record, Hide Record.

   Works hides the selected record(s).

To redisplay hidden records, choose Record, Show, 1. All Records. Works displays all the hidden records.❖

Tip
After you hide records, you still can tell your total number of records, displayed and hidden. For example, if 16 records appear out of a total of 25 records, the record count indicator at the right end of the status bar shows 16/25.

Chapter 20

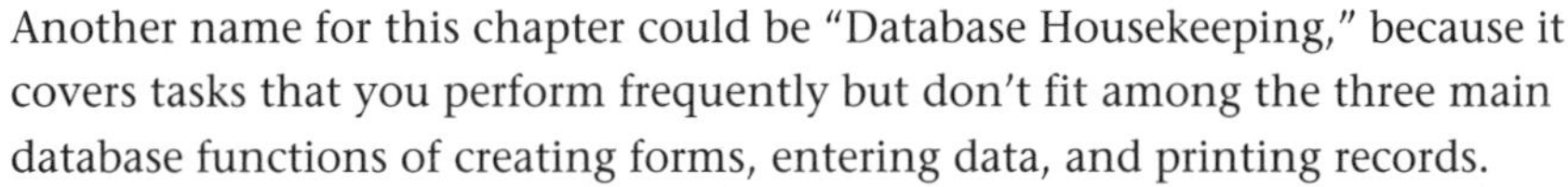

Expanding Your Database Skills

by Faithe Wempen

Another name for this chapter could be "Database Housekeeping," because it covers tasks that you perform frequently but don't fit among the three main database functions of creating forms, entering data, and printing records.

This chapter explains how to use the Works Database sort feature. Now that you have learned how to create database forms and enter data, you may find that you sometimes need to arrange the information in alphabetical or numerical order according to the data stored in a field. For example, the U.S. Postal Service may require you to sort address labels in ZIP code order for a bulk mailing.

You also learn about these topics, which help make your database more useful:

- Printing database records
- Using dates and times in database fields
- Using formulas and functions
- Protecting your data and form designs

Sorting Database Records

The *sort* function arranges the records in a database in alphabetical, numerical, or date or time order, by any field you like. You can even pick up to three fields, for more precise sorting.

For instance, if you choose three fields to sort by (like `Region`, `Last Name`, and `First Name`), Works sorts by each field in turn. First, the database is sorted by the first field you chose (`Region`). Then, all the records that have identical entries for the first field are sorted by the second field you chose (`Last Name`). Finally, all the records with identical entries for the first and second fields are sorted according to the third field (`First Name`).

Figure 20.1 shows a database in List view sorted by `Region`, `Last Name`, and `First Name`. Notice that the South region has two people with the same last name of Jones. These records were sorted by `First Name`, because their entries for both `Region` and `Last Name` were identical.

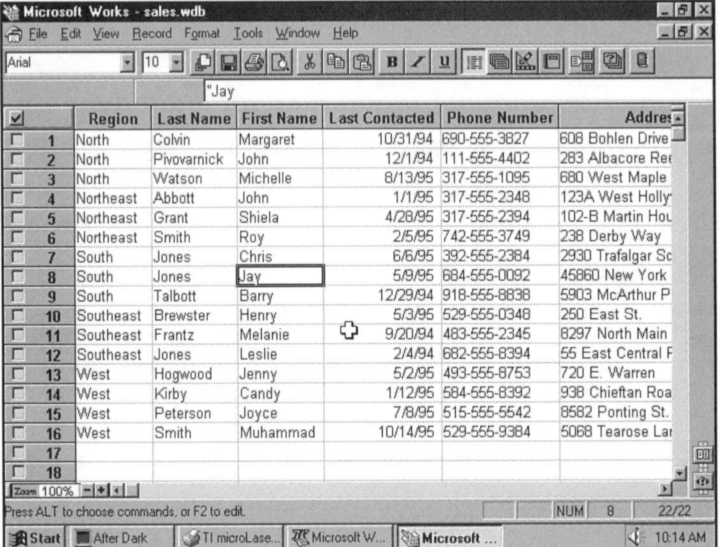

	Region	Last Name	First Name	Last Contacted	Phone Number	Addres
1	North	Colvin	Margaret	10/31/94	690-555-3827	608 Bohlen Drive
2	North	Pivovarnick	John	12/1/94	111-555-4402	283 Albacore Ree
3	North	Watson	Michelle	8/13/95	317-555-1095	680 West Maple
4	Northeast	Abbott	John	1/1/95	317-555-2348	123A West Holly
5	Northeast	Grant	Shiela	4/28/95	317-555-2394	102-B Martin Hou
6	Northeast	Smith	Roy	2/5/95	742-555-3749	238 Derby Way
7	South	Jones	Chris	6/6/95	392-555-2384	2930 Trafalgar Sc
8	South	Jones	Jay	5/9/95	684-555-0092	45860 New York
9	South	Talbott	Barry	12/29/94	918-555-8838	5903 McArthur P
10	Southeast	Brewster	Henry	5/3/95	529-555-0348	250 East St.
11	Southeast	Frantz	Melanie	9/20/94	483-555-2345	8297 North Main
12	Southeast	Jones	Leslie	2/4/94	682-555-8394	55 East Central F
13	West	Hogwood	Jenny	5/2/95	493-555-8753	720 E. Warren
14	West	Kirby	Candy	1/12/95	584-555-8392	938 Chieftan Roa
15	West	Peterson	Joyce	7/8/95	515-555-5542	8582 Ponting St.
16	West	Smith	Muhammad	10/14/95	529-555-9384	5068 Tearose Lar
17						
18						

Fig. 20.1 This database is sorted first by `Region`, then by `Last Name`, then by `First Name`.

To sort a database, follow these steps:

1. With the database displayed in Form Design view or List view, choose Record, Sort Records.

   Works displays the Sort Records dialog box (see fig. 20.2).

2. From the Sort By drop-down list, select the name of the field to sort by.

3. Choose Ascending or Descending to sort the database records by that field in ascending or descending order.

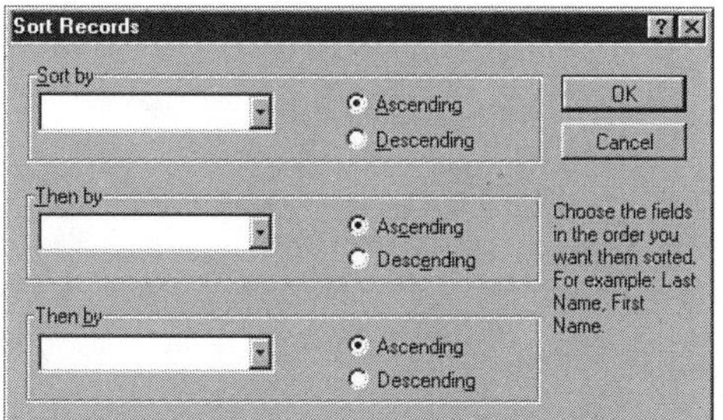

Fig. 20.2
Use the Sort Records dialog box to sort up to three fields at a time.

Note

Works sorts text without regard for capitalization.

4. Optionally, select the names of up to two more fields to sort by in the Then By boxes, selecting Ascending or Descending for each.

5. Choose OK.

   Works sorts your records on-screen according to the criteria you specified.

Tip
To undo a sort, choose Edit, Undo Sort; or press Ctrl+Z. You must choose Undo Sort before you choose any other program commands.

You can repeat a sort quickly within the same Works session by using the same sort criteria. For example, you can re-sort a database after adding new records in unsorted order. To repeat a sort, follow these steps:

1. Choose Record, Sort Records.

   Works displays the Sort Records dialog box with the sort options you chose previously.

2. Choose OK.

Works resorts the database using the same sort criteria.

Troubleshooting

I'm planning a database and would like to create a field that will hold mixed information: dates, text, and numbers. But I want to be able to sort the field. Is that possible?

(continues)

(continued)

Works can create orderly lists from this kind of mixed information, because Works automatically groups mixed data in the following order: text, time, number, date. For example, if you specify an ascending sort, all the text entries appear first in the sorted list (sorted in ascending order), followed by all the time entries, and so on. In a descending sort, Works groups mixed data in the reverse order: date, number, time, text.

I would like to sort my database on more than three fields, but the standard sort procedure doesn't allow that.

Sort the database twice, using the three *least* important criteria first. For example, suppose you want to sort a database on five fields: `Amount Due`, `Credit Rating`, `Last Name`, `First Name`, `ZIP`. `Amount Due` is the most important sort field, followed by `Credit Rating`. Sort the database first on `Last Name`, `First Name`, and `ZIP`. Then sort the database again and specify `Amount Due` in the Sort By text box and `Credit Rating` in the first Then By text box.

Printing Database Records

◄ See "Printing a Document," p. 74

Regardless of the kinds of databases you create, you will almost certainly want to print some of the information stored in the database from time to time. Printing database information uses similar steps to printing with the Works word processor. Before you can create printed database documents, you must know how to set up header and footer margins; the source, size, and orientation of the paper you are using; page numbering and footnote options; and other standard settings for your particular printer. For more information, see Chapter 8, "Adding Headers, Footers, Footnotes, and Bookmarks to a Document."

While setting page parameters, you can preview the printed results, just as you can preview a word processor document. In the following sections, you learn how to specify page settings.

Note

The settings you choose in the Page Setup dialog box affect only the current document.

Setting Margins

Page margins are the white space that surrounds the text on the printed page. To set page margins, follow these steps:

1. Choose File, Page Setup.

   Works displays the Page Setup dialog box (see fig. 20.3).

2. In the appropriate margin boxes on the Margins tab, type the settings you want to use.

3. When all margin settings are correct, choose OK.

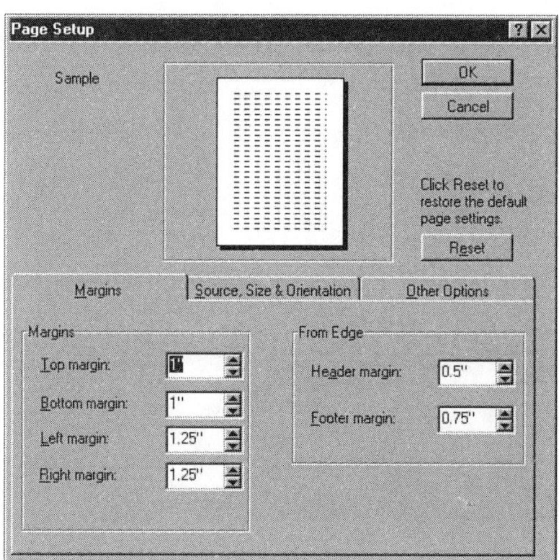

Fig. 20.3
Use the Page Setup dialog box to get ready to print your database records in Form or List view.

Works automatically reformats your database form or list using the new margin settings.

Note

In Form Design view, page breaks are shown on-screen. For example, if you set a top margin of 6 inches and the database form now extends onto a second page, Works inserts a page break at the corresponding point of the form in the Form Design view screen. In List view, your changes are not reflected in the Works database window. You must use Print Preview to view the effects of your changes. (See "Previewing a Document" later in this chapter.)

If you decide to include a header or footer in your document, you can change the header and footer margins in the From Edge section of the Page Setup dialog box. (See "Creating Headers and Footers" later in this chapter.)

Note

If you commonly work with centimeters or another unit of measure other than inches, you can change the Works default units setting. Choose Tools, Options, and click the General tab. In the Units section, choose a unit of measure and then click OK. The unit of measure you choose applies to *all* tools in Works.

Setting Paper Source, Size, and Orientation

Before you can print your database, you must tell Works which paper source to use, the size of the paper you are using, and the direction you want the print to appear on the page. To change the paper source, paper size, and print orientation, you use the Page Setup dialog box, but this time you display the Source, Size & Orientation tab, shown in figure 20.4. The page in the Sample area reflects the current paper size and orientation settings.

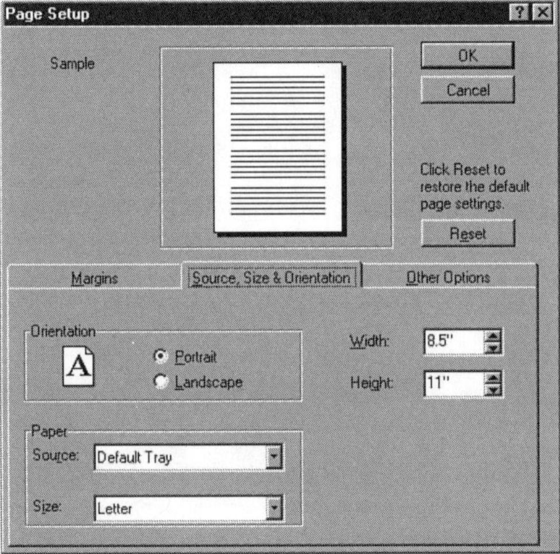

Fig. 20.4
Select settings for the current document in the Source, Size & Orientation tab.

If you have more than one paper tray or feeder, you can choose among them from the Source drop-down list. The Size list offers a variety of standard paper and envelope sizes. Choose a size from the Size list or type the correct size in the Width and Height boxes.

To change source, size, and orientation settings, follow these steps:

1. Choose File, Page Setup. The Page Setup dialog box appears.
2. Choose the Source, Size & Orientation tab. The options in figure 20.4 appear.
3. Select a paper source from the Source drop-down list.
4. Select a paper size from the Size drop-down list, or specify a custom size in the Width and Height boxes.
5. Select a paper orientation by clicking the Portrait or Landscape option button. The Sample area of the dialog box reflects the settings you choose.
6. When all settings are correct, choose OK.

Setting Other Page Options

The third tab in the Page Setup dialog box is Other Options. Its contents change depending on which view you're in when you select it. Figure 20.5 shows the tab from Form Design view, and figure 20.6 shows it from List view.

When in Form Design view, you use the Other Options tab to specify these items: the page number that should appear on the first page of the document, whether you want field lines printed and page breaks inserted, and whether you want Works to print the entire form, including the labels, or the field entries only.

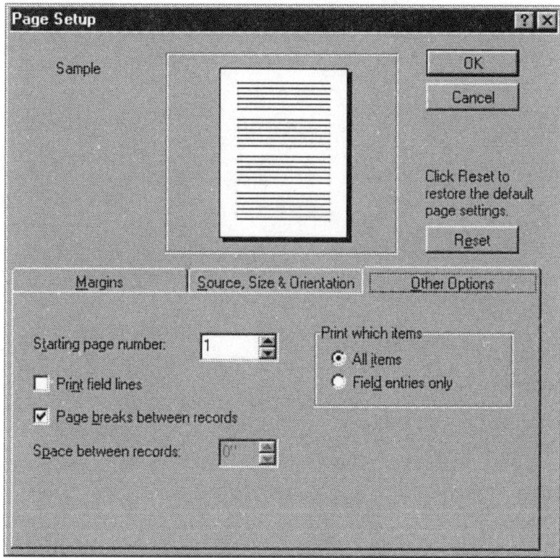

Fig. 20.5
This shows settings for printing first page number, field lines, page breaks, and printing of entire form or field entries.

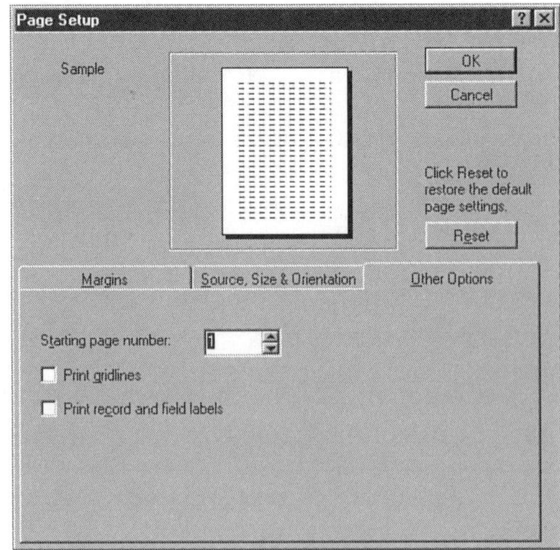

Fig. 20.6
The Other Options tab in List view displays settings for printing first page number, gridlines, and record and field labels.

With a database displayed in List view, you use the Other Options tab to number the first page and to tell Works whether to print gridlines and labels for records and fields. With these items checked, Works prints the database just as it appears on-screen. Gridlines separate the field contents, field labels appear at the top of the field columns, and record labels appear at the left of record rows.

Previewing a Document

One of the most important steps you can take before printing database information is to *preview* it. Previewing enables you to see on-screen how your document will look on the printed page. When you preview a document, Works displays a full-page view, one page at a time, of the document. You can make sure that margins are the appropriate size, line spacing is appropriate, page breaks are correct, header and footer text is positioned correctly, inserted objects appear in the proper locations, and so on. All these elements appear on the preview screen.

To preview a document, choose File, Print Preview or click the Print Preview button on the toolbar. The current database appears in a preview screen like the one shown in figure 20.7.

The actual text displayed in the preview screen can be difficult to read because it is reduced, but reading the text isn't the important consideration here; checking the document's layout is.

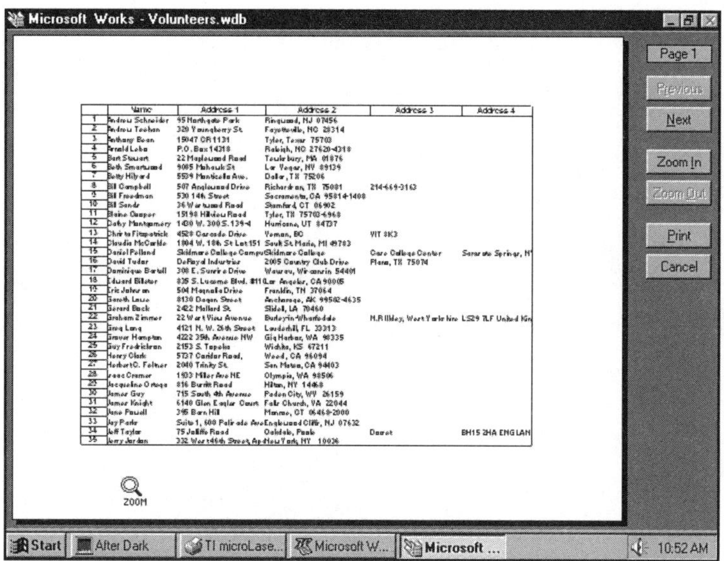

Fig. 20.7
This Print Preview screen shows a database formatted for printing in landscape mode with field names and record labels displayed.

If you think you spot a problem in the layout, you can zero in on a particular location. Notice that the mouse pointer changes to a magnifying glass when you point it anywhere on the page. To magnify an area, point to the area you want to enlarge and click it; or click the Zoom In button. Works magnifies the area. To magnify the area further, click the Zoom In button again. To return to the full-page view, click the document you're viewing or choose Zoom Out. You can scroll the zoomed display with the horizontal and vertical scroll bars that appear.

If your document is longer than one page, display the page you want to preview by clicking the Previous or Next button, or use the Page Up and Page Down keys on the keyboard. When you're ready to print the document, you can print directly from the preview screen by clicking the Print button. This button displays the Print dialog box. You learn how to use the Print dialog box in the next section.

Printing a Database

For a quick printout, just click the Print button on the toolbar, and all pages of the current view print using default options.

If you want to change any of the defaults or specify a different printer, you need to go the longer route, through the Print dialog box. To display the Print dialog box, choose File, Print.

The Print dialog box is slightly different when opened from different views. Figure 20.8 shows the Print dialog box when you're working in List view, and figure 20.9 shows it from Form Design view.

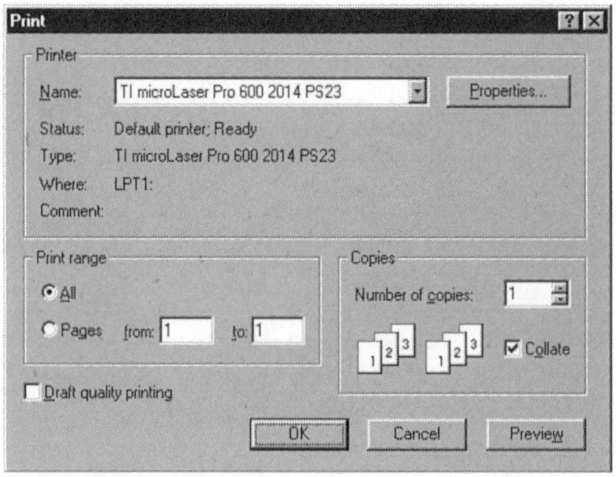

Fig. 20.8
The Print dialog box from List view.

Fig. 20.9
The Print dialog box from Form Design view.

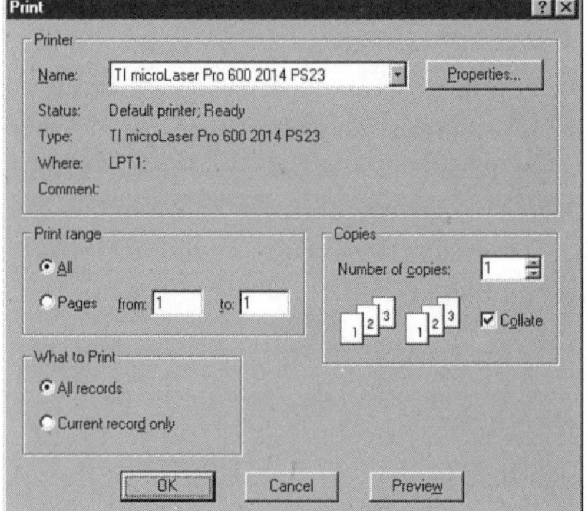

You use the Print dialog box to specify which printer to use, the number of copies you want to print, the pages you want to print, the quality of printing you want to use (in List view), and whether to print all records or just the current one (in Form Design view).

Notice that a Preview command button is available in the Print dialog box. If you forget to preview a document before choosing the Print command on the File menu, you can choose the Preview button in the Print dialog box. Table 20.1 describes the options in the Print dialog box.

Table 20.1 Options in the Print Dialog Box

Option	Description
Name	Select the printer you want to use from this drop-down list, if you have more than one printer.
Properties	Click this command button to open a dialog box where you can set properties for the selected printer, such as paper type and graphics handling. The available settings vary depending on the printer.
Print Range: All or Pages	The default setting is to print all pages of the current document. To print selected pages, choose the Pages option button and then type the first page to print in the From box and the last page to print in the To box.
Number of Copies	The default setting is 1; to print more than one copy of the current document, select a number greater than 1.
Collate	Select this check box if you are printing multiple copies and want to collate each copy. Otherwise, Works prints all copies of each page together.
Draft Quality Printing	This option is available in List view only. If your printer is capable of printing at draft quality, choose this setting to print more quickly but at a lower print quality.
What to Print: All Records or Current Only	This command is available in Form Design view Record Records is the default, which prints every record in the database. Current Record Only prints only the record that's displayed on-screen when you issue the Print command.

Printing a Single Record

If you want to print a single record, you must do it from Form Design view; you cannot use List view. Follow these steps:

1. Display the record you want to print in Form Design view.
2. Choose File, Print.
3. Choose Current Record Only.
4. Choose OK.

   Works prints the displayed record.

Tip
You can print a blank record to use as a paper form to manually copy data. Press Ctrl+End in Form Design view to display a blank record, then proceed with steps 1 through 4.

Printing an Entire Database

To print an entire database, you can use Form Design view or List view. If you print in List view, the printout is much more compact; if you print in Form Design view, each record appears on its own page (unless you specify otherwise, as you learn to do later in this section).

Follow these steps to print an entire database:

1. Open the database you want to print.
2. If needed, choose File, Page Setup to specify print margins, paper source, size, orientation, and other print settings.
3. Preview the database using File, Print Preview or by clicking the Print Preview toolbar button.
4. Choose File, Print.

   Works displays the Print dialog box (refer to fig. 20.8 or 20.9, depending on your view).
5. If you're printing from Form Design view, make sure the All Records option is selected.
6. Choose any other print options you like (such as number of copies), then click OK.

Tip
You can hide records that you don't want to print in List view. See "Hiding Records" in Chapter 19, "Entering and Editing Data."

You can print more than one record on a page in Form Design view, to save paper and produce a more compact printout. To print several records on one page, follow these steps:

1. In Form Design view, choose File, Page Setup.
2. Click the Other Options tab (refer to fig. 20.5).
3. Deselect the Page Breaks Between Records check box.
4. In the Space Between Records box, type the space you want Works to insert between records on the page, in inches, or click the up or down arrow to change the spacing.
5. Choose OK.

When you print the database, Works prints the records continuously, without inserting a page break between records.

Removing Extra Space between Fields

When you print a database, Works inserts a sufficient space in the printout for the entire length of each field. For example, if field entries are formatted flush left, Works adds space to the right of the entry in the printout; or if a field entry is formatted flush right, Works adds space to the left of the entry in the printout.

You can tell Works to eliminate extra space from fields when it prints a database. This step can be useful for printing addresses. For example, you can tell Works to eliminate extra space from the fields `City`, `State`, and `ZIP`. With field labels hidden, Works prints the field contents on the same line, with no extra spaces between field contents. To achieve this effect, you use the Slide to Left command.

To slide a field to the left in Form Design view, follow these steps:

1. Highlight the field or label you want to slide to the left.
2. Choose Format, Alignment.
3. Select the Slide to Left check box.
4. Choose OK.

To preview the effect of using the Slide to Left command, choose File, Print Preview; or click the Print Preview toolbar button.

Using Page Breaks

As you learned earlier in this chapter, you can eliminate the mandatory page break between each record when printing in Form Design view, so that Works runs as many records as it can on each page. This method is good for saving paper, but sometimes the pages break awkwardly, leaving half a record dangling between pages. To solve this problem, you can insert manual page breaks exactly where you want them.

Determining your own page breaks may be useful for other purposes. For example, you may want to print the name and address section of a single database form on one page, and the credit account status on a separate page.

> **Note**
>
> Page breaks that you insert in Form Design view do not affect the way Works prints in List view, and vice versa. In List view, Works automatically prints as many records as it can fit within the current margins of each page. But you can insert vertical and horizontal page breaks in List view, as described later in this section.

To insert a page break in Form Design view, follow these steps:

1. Move the insertion point to where you want to insert a page break.
2. Choose Format, Insert Page Break.

Works inserts a page break above the insertion point. The page break appears as a single line across the form.

Follow these steps to delete a page break in Form Design view:

1. Move the insertion point immediately beneath the page break.
2. Choose Format, Delete Page Break.

You also can use page breaks in List view to break the page wherever you want it. In List view, you have a choice of horizontal or vertical page breaks, because a database in List view often can span multiple pages in width as well as length.

To insert a page break in List view, follow these steps:

1. Highlight any field in the record below which you want a horizontal page break.

   or

   Highlight any field entry in the field to the right of where you want a vertical page break.

2. Choose Format, Insert Page Break.

   The Insert Page Break dialog box appears (see fig. 20.10).

3. Choose Record to insert a horizontal page break, or Field to insert a vertical one.
4. Choose OK.

Works inserts a dashed page break line above the record or to the left of the field.

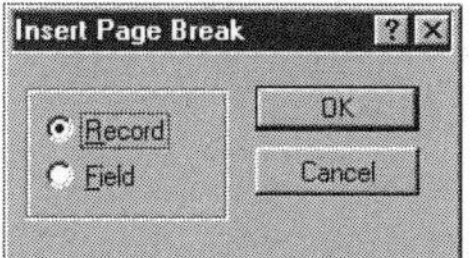

Fig. 20.10
Choose which type of page break you want: horizontal (Record) or vertical (Field).

You can insert page breaks in List view *without* using the Insert Page Break dialog box:

1. To insert a horizontal page break, highlight the entire record below which you want the page break.

   or

   To insert a vertical page break, highlight the entire field to the right of where you want the page break.

2. Choose Format, Insert Page Break.

   Works inserts a page break above the record or to the left of the selected field.

To delete a page break in List view, follow these steps:

1. Highlight the record below or the field to the right of the page break.

2. Choose Format, Delete Page Break.

   Works removes the page break.

Displaying Forms as They Will Be Printed

The spacing that Works uses to display a form on-screen may be slightly different from the spacing used to print the form. Normally, the differences are slight and do not cause problems. In rare cases, however, you may need to view the spacing exactly as a form will be printed (for example, if you intend to print database forms on preprinted paper forms).

To display a form as it will appear when printed, use these steps:

1. Switch to Form Design view by choosing View, Form Design or clicking the Form Design button on the toolbar.

2. Choose View, Format For Printer.

Works displays the form on-screen and uses the same letter spacing that it will use to print the form with the currently selected printer.

Creating Headers and Footers

When you print a database, having descriptive text at the top or bottom of each printed page can be useful. For example, when you drop a big stack of printed database forms, it's easier to pick them up if you have page numbers printed on each form.

Follow these steps to create a header or footer:

1. Choose View, Headers and Footers.

   Works displays the View Headers and Footers dialog box (see fig. 20.11).

2. Type the header and/or footer text in the Header and Footer boxes.

3. To tell Works not to print a header or footer on page 1 of the printout, select No Header on First Page and/or No Footer on First Page.

4. Choose OK.

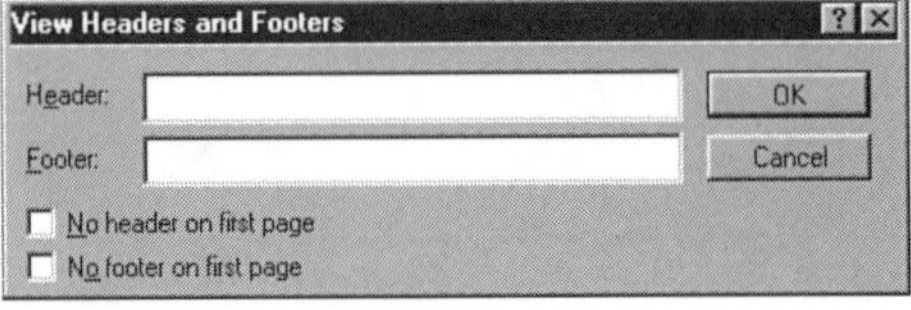

Fig. 20.11
Use the View Headers and Footers dialog box to add text to the top and bottom of each printed database page.

When you print the database, Works adds the header or footer at the top or bottom of the printout.

Note

Works doesn't display headers and footers on-screen. To preview the text and position of headers and footers, use File, Print Preview; or click the Print Preview toolbar button.

Using Special Header/Footer Codes and Page Numbers

Works can automatically print the page number, file name, date, or time in a header or footer. Works also can format text in a header or footer flush left, flush right, or centered. For example, you may want to print the author's name flush left in a header, the database name centered, and the current date flush right.

To print page numbers and such, and format header/footer text, you type special codes in the Header or Footer text box in the View Headers and Footers dialog box.

You can use the following special codes, in either upper- or lowercase:

Purpose	Code
Page number	&p
File name	&f
Current date	&d
Date in long format	&n
Current time	&t
Print an ampersand character	&&
Left align the characters that follow	&l
Right align the characters that follow	&r
Center the characters that follow	&c

To insert a page number and specify the page number position, follow these steps:

1. Choose View, Headers and Footers.
2. Type one or more of the following codes immediately before the header/footer text, and then choose OK.

Page Number Position	Code
Centered at top of page	&c&p in the Header box

(continues)

Page Number Position	Code
Centered at bottom of page	&c&p in the Footer box
Flush right at top of page	&r&p in the Header box
Flush left at top of page	&l&p in the Header box
Flush right at bottom of page	&r&p in the Footer box
Flush left at bottom of page	&l&p in the Footer box

Figure 20.12 shows two database records displayed in the Print Preview, formatted with the following header:

```
&lACCOUNTING DEPT.&cClients Database&r&d
```

Fig. 20.12
A database printout formatted with header alignment and date codes.

Changing the Starting Page Number

When you print database records, you may need to number your pages starting with a number other than one. For example, you may want to insert a database printout in the middle of a word processing report.

To set a new page number, follow these steps:

1. Choose File, Page Setup.

2. Choose the Other Options tab (refer to fig. 20.5 if you're in Form Design view, or to fig. 20.6 if you're in List view).

3. In the Starting Page Number box, type a new page number for the first page.

4. Choose OK.

Works begins numbering the pages of the database with the number you specified.

Changing Header and Footer Margins

Headers and footers are placed outside the regular margins, and they don't affect the margin settings for the rest of the printout. After previewing or printing your database, you may discover that the header or footer is too close or too far from the rest of the printout, or from the top or bottom of the page.

To change header and footer margins, use these steps:

1. Choose File, Page Setup.

2. Choose the Margins tab (refer to fig. 20.3).

3. In the Header Margin and Footer Margin boxes, type the new margin settings.

4. Choose OK.

Note

Notice that when you are setting header and footer margins, Works does not reflect your settings in the Sample area.

Removing Headers and Footers

When you create a header or footer and then decide to print the database without a header or footer, follow these steps to delete the header and/or footer from the database:

1. Choose View, Headers and Footers.

2. Highlight any text in the Header or Footer box and press Delete or Backspace.

3. Choose OK.

Troubleshooting

When I create a two-line header, it prints immediately above the top line of text. Is there a way to insert extra space between the header and the body text?

In the Margins tab of the Page Setup dialog box, check that the Top Margin and Bottom Margin are large enough to accommodate a header and/or footer. For example, for a Footer Margin of 1.5 inches, the Bottom Margin must be larger than 1.5 inches.

Using Dates and Times

With the Works database, you can store four kinds of data: text, numbers, dates, and times. When you type a date or time in a field using a date or time format that Works recognizes, Works automatically interprets the field as a date or time field when you sort the field or use it in a formula.

Note

The Works database can accept dates in the range January 1, 1900, to June 3, 2079. Dates and times outside this range are interpreted as text. You can verify the format by examining the formula toolbar. If you enter a date that is outside the range specified, a quotation mark precedes the date and signifies it is text and not a date.

Entering Dates and Times

To type a date or time in a Works database field, follow these steps:

◄ See "Formatting Numbers in Fields," p. 372

1. Type the date or time in a format that Works can recognize.
2. Click the Enter box in the formula bar; or press Enter.

Works converts the date to the default date format, MM/DD/YY, and aligns it flush-right in the field. For example, if you type November 30, 1996, Works reformats the date as 11/30/96.

Changing the Date Format

You can change the format Works applies when it accepts a date in a field by following these steps:

◄ See "Formatting Numbers in Fields," p. 372

1. From List or Form Design view, highlight the field or data you want to change.

2. Choose Format, Field.

   Works displays the Format dialog box.

3. Choose Date or Time.

   Works displays the available formats in the Appearance list box.

4. Choose a format from the Appearance list.

5. Choose OK.

Works applies the new format to the field.

Tip
To save keystrokes when entering dates in a date field for the current year, type only the month and day. Works automatically inserts the year. For example, when you type 11/1 during 1995, Works inserts 11/1/95.

Entering the Current Date or Time

To enter the current date or time in a field, follow these steps:

1. Highlight the field where you want to insert the date or time.

2. To insert today's date, press Ctrl+; (semicolon).

   or

   To insert the time, press Ctrl+Shift+; (semicolon).

3. Press Enter.

Tip
To enter dates and times in international formats, you must change the country selection in the International dialog box of the Windows Control Panel.

Note

The current date and time are only as accurate as your computer's clock. When you enter a date and time with the shortcut keys as described in the preceding steps, the date and time *do not change* automatically the next time you open the file.

Troubleshooting

I formatted a field with a time format, but Works changes the format when I enter data. What's happening?

To retain the date or time format for a field, don't enter text or numeric data in the field, because Works changes the data type to match the most recently entered data. Formulas then interpret the field's data as text or numeric.

(continues)

(continued)

Works is suddenly displaying some sort of cryptic code in a date field. How can I restore the dates?

Works uses numeric codes to interpret numeric and date fields. If you change the format of a field that contains dates or times, Works displays the numeric code for the date in the field. For example, if a field contains the date 11/1/94 and you format the field as a percentage, Works displays `3463900.00%`. To restore the date, switch back to the date format.

Using Formulas and Functions

You learned how to type a math formula in a field in Chapter 19, "Entering and Editing Data." This section gives more detailed information for using formulas and functions.

You can use a formula to perform a math calculation and insert the results in a field, or to insert a "most likely" data entry in a field. For example, you can multiply the `Price` field and the `Quantity` field and insert the results in the `Amount` field. Or you can use a formula to insert Seattle in the `City` field. This formula would be useful if you expect most of the entries in the `City` field to be Seattle.

Using a Formula to Perform a Calculation

When you type a formula in a database field in Form Design view or List view, Works automatically inserts the formula in that field for all records in the database. When you display a new record and enter data in fields that the formula uses, Works automatically enters the results in the field that contains the formula. You don't need to re-enter the formula for each new record.

Caution

Entering a formula in any record replaces any existing data in the other records with the new calculated value.

When you display a new, blank record and begin entering data, you don't see the formula in the field; but when you highlight the field, Works displays the formula in the formula bar.

Note

Formulas can refer to any number of fields, but a formula can refer only to fields in the same form and database.

Follow these steps to enter a formula in a field in Form Design view or List view:

1. Highlight the field where you want to type the formula.
2. Type an = (equal sign) followed by the formula.
3. Press Enter.

For example, you might type **=price*quantity** in a field named `Amount`, where `Price` and `Quantity` are fields in the same database form. When you type new data in the `Price` and `Quantity` fields, Works automatically calculates the formula and inserts the results in the `Amount` field. If you don't type anything in the `Price` and `Quantity` fields, Works inserts zero in the `Amount` field.

Tip

To perform math calculations on a field in more than one record, use a database report. For example, you can use a report to calculate the sum of all the entries in the `Amount` field in a database, (see Chapter 22).

Using a Formula to Enter Most Likely Data

You can use a formula to type the most likely data in a field. For example, if you know that most of the entries in the `City` and `State` fields will be Seattle and WA, you can use a formula to insert these words in the fields automatically. If the city and state are different (for example, Portland and OR), you can simply type over the data that the formula proposes.

Follow these steps to create a formula that inserts most likely data:

1. Highlight the field where you want to insert the formula.
2. Type = (equal sign) followed by the most likely data in quotation marks.

   For example, in the `City` field, type **="Seattle"**, and in the `State` field, type **="WA"**.
3. Press Enter.

   Works inserts the most likely data in each record of the database.

Note

You must enclose proposed *text* data in double quotes, as shown. You don't need to enclose numbers, dates, or times in double quotes, however.

Using Functions

Works contains 77 built-in mathematical formulas that you can apply to the field entries in a database. These built-in formulas are called *functions*.

Functions perform calculations or enter data without requiring you to type complex formulas or long text. For example, you can use the `AVG` (average) function to calculate the average of the contents of the fields `Distance1`, `Distance2`, and `Distance3`. In the field where you want Works to insert the average, type **`=AVG(Distance1,Distance2,Distance3)`**. When you enter data in the distance fields, Works calculates the average and inserts the results in the field where you typed the formula with the `AVG` function.

Note

Unfortunately, you cannot browse a list of the available functions from within the database. However, you can see the functions from a spreadsheet by choosing Tools, EasyCalc. For more information, see Chapter 11, "Working with Formulas and Functions."

To enter a formula that uses a function, follow these steps:

1. Highlight the field where you want to type a formula.
2. Type = (equal sign) followed by the function you want to use.

   For example, type **=avg**. You may use uppercase or lowercase letters when you type function names.
3. In parentheses, type the names of the fields you want the function to use, separated by commas.

   Your line should look something like this:

   =avg(Distance1,Distance2,Distance3)
4. Press Enter.

Protecting Your Data

If the Works Database has one fault, it's that users can too easily make accidental or deliberate changes to a form design. For example, if you use the mouse to move around in a form, you can accidentally drag a field label to a new location. With the keyboard, you also can quite easily delete part or all of a field label.

You can prevent yourself and others from making unwanted changes by protecting fields and field entries.

Protecting Fields

You can protect any field, or all fields, from changes. When field protection is on, no one can change, delete, clear, or change the tab order in the protected fields. (You still can copy and sort protected fields.) You cannot protect a single record—protection works by entire field only.

You can protect fields in List or Form Design view. The procedure is the same for both. To protect a field, use these steps:

Tip
To quickly protect all fields, select an entire record, then choose Format, Protection. Select the Protect Field check box and choose OK.

1. Highlight the field(s) you want to protect.
2. Choose Format, Protection.

   The Format Protection dialog box appears (see fig. 20.13).
3. Select the Protect Field check box to protect the field(s), or deselect the check box to leave the field(s) unprotected.
4. Choose OK.

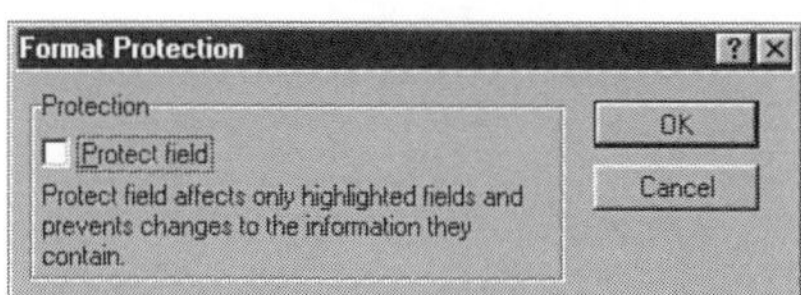

Fig. 20.13
The Format Protection dialog box enables you to turn field protection on or off.

Chapter 21

Retrieving Database Information

by Faithe Wempen

The preceding chapters on the Works database have explained how to create forms and enter information in a database. But after you build a database and store information, how do you get the information out again? Suppose, for example, that you want to print a list of all the people in your database who have birthdays in December, or all the distributors who stock left-threaded brass bolts with square heads. In this chapter, you learn how to retrieve information from a database.

Specifically, this chapter covers these topics:

- Performing basic find and replace operations
- Creating basic database filters
- Editing, saving, and deleting filters
- Creating advanced filters by using selection criteria

Understanding Works Searches

When you're searching a database with the Find or Replace commands, a filter, or any other Works search tool, you can search for specific text, like *Smith* or *5/5/94*. The text you search for doesn't need to be the only thing in that field entry; a search for *Smith* could find *Joe Smith* and *Karen Smithburg.*

If you don't know exactly what you're looking for, or you are looking for a range, you can use *wild cards* to assist you. Wild cards are symbols that stand for any character or group of characters. Works recognizes two wild cards: an asterisk (*), which represents any number of characters, and a question mark (?), which represents any single character.

Because Works' normal mode of searching is to find any record that contains the text you're searching for, you don't need to use wild cards at the beginning or end of a search string. For instance, searching for *Smith* is the same as searching for *Smith** or **Smith*. All three requests would find *Smith*, *Blacksmith*, and *Smithsonian*.

Wild cards are uniquely useful in some cases—like when you know the first and last part of a search string but not the middle. For instance, *Peters?n* finds both *Peterson* and *Petersen*, and *12/??/95* finds all dates in December 1995.

Using the Find Command

Tip
If you want to search several records in your database using the Find command, you may find it easier to find all records at one time, as explained in the next section.

The easiest way to locate information in a database is with the Find command. The Find command has two purposes: it can help you move quickly among the occurrences of a phrase or number in your database, or it can display a list of all the records in your database that contain that phrase or number.

Using Find to Move Quickly to a Record

Use Find when you simply want to locate a record that contains a search term. For example, you might want to move quickly to the first record in the database where the last name is Smith, and then skip to the next Smith entry, and so on, until you have seen all the Smiths.

You can use Find from List or Form Design view. Follow these steps:

Tip
You can add a toolbar button that displays the Find dialog box. Choose Tools, Customize Toolbar, and select Edit from the Categories list. Drag the button with binoculars onto the toolbar, then choose OK.

1. To search only certain fields, highlight those fields. If you don't make a selection, Works searches all fields.

2. Choose Edit, Find.

   Works displays the Find dialog box (see fig. 21.1).

3. In the Find What text box, type the characters you want to search for.

   For example, to find the first record with *east* in it, type **east**.

4. Choose OK.

   Works moves to the first field entry that contains the search string.

5. (Optional) To move to the next occurrence of that string in the database, press Shift+F4.

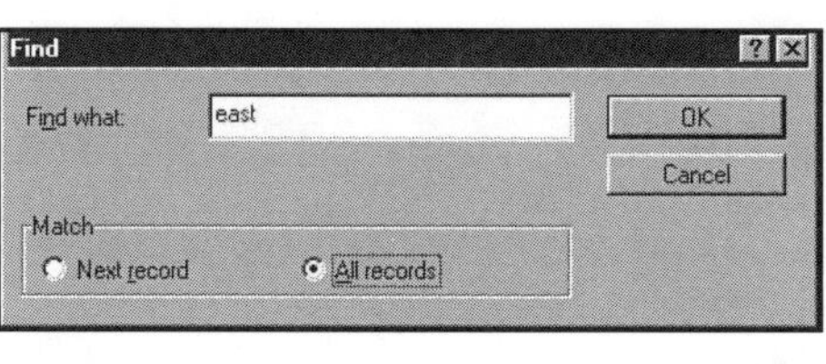

Fig. 21.1
Use the Find dialog box to search for records that match the search term.

Using Find to Narrow the Records Displayed

The other use of the Find command is to whittle down a large list of records (in List view) to a list of only records that contain what you're searching for. For example, you could look for records where a field named `Region` contains *east*.

◄ See "Reviewing the Database Window," p. 346

You can use Find in either List or Form Design view. If you use List view, the records that match the criteria appear in a list; if you use Form Design view, you can page through the found records with the usual navigation buttons.

To filter out the unwanted records with Find, follow these steps:

1. To search only certain fields, highlight those fields. If you don't make a selection, Works searches all fields.
2. Choose Edit, Find. Works displays the Find dialog box (refer to fig. 21.1).
3. In the Find What text box, type the characters you want to search for.
4. Click the All Records option button.
5. Choose OK.

Works retrieves all the records that contain the search string. Figure 21.2 shows a database in List view after selecting the `Region` field then searching for *east*. Notice that Works retrieved all the records where `Region` contained the letters *east*, including Northeast and Southeast.

After performing a search, you can display all the records that Works did *not* select by choosing Record, Show, 4 Hidden Records. Works displays the records that *do not* contain the search term (see fig. 21.3). When you're finished viewing the subset of records, you can return to viewing all records by choosing Record, Show, 1 All Records.

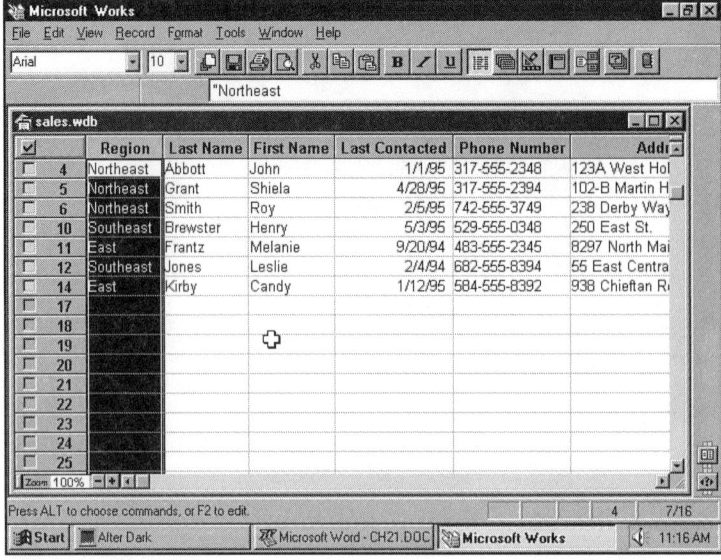

Fig. 21.2
The result of searching for "east" with All Records selected.

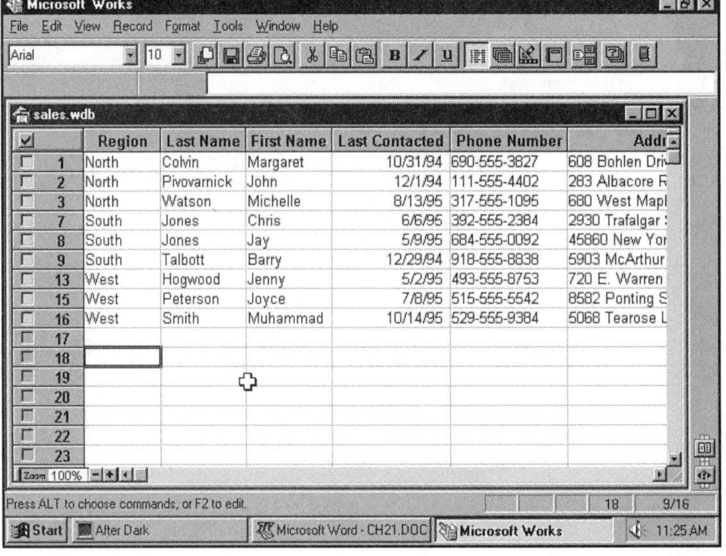

Fig. 21.3
When you choose Record, Show, 4 Hidden Records, Works displays the records that do not contain the search term "east."

Using the Replace Command

Works not only can locate records that contain a search term, it can automatically replace the search term with an entry that you specify. For example, it can replace Northeast with East in all records where the `Region` field contains Northeast. Follow these steps to find and replace text or numeric values in List view:

Tip

Find and Replace are not case-sensitive. For example, if you type **EAST**, you will find EAST, East, and east.

1. If you're not already in List view, switch to it.

> **Note**
>
> Remember, you can switch to List view by choosing View, List, by clicking the List view button on the toolbar, or by pressing Shift+F9.

2. If you want to replace a string only in a certain field, highlight that field's entire column.

   If you don't highlight a field, Works performs the replacement in all fields where it finds the specified text.

3. Choose Edit, Replace. Works displays the Replace dialog box (see fig. 21.4).

Fig. 21.4
Use the Replace dialog box to automatically change the contents of a field.

4. In the Find What box, type the field entry you want to find and replace.

   As with the Find command, you can use wild-card characters, as described earlier in the section "Using the Find Command." In figure 21.4, a wild card is used to replace all words that end in east, such as Northeast and Southeast.

5. In the Replace With box, type the characters with which you want Works to replace the found item.

   In figure 21.4, the word East replaces the found text.

Note

You cannot use wild-card characters in the Replace With box. If you use a wild-card character like *, Works will actually search for and replace that character.

6. Choose Records or Fields.

   If you choose Records, Works replaces the search term moving from left to right through one record at a time. If you choose Fields, Works replaces the search term moving from top to bottom one field at a time.

Note

If you're fairly sure that what you're looking for is in the current field, choose Fields in step 6. If you're fairly sure that what you're looking for is in a nearby record, choose Records. If you have no idea, it doesn't matter which you pick.

Tip

To replace a search term with nothing (to delete the search term), type the search term in the Find What box, but leave the Replace With box empty. To clear all fields, enter a * (wild card) in the Find What box and leave the Replace With box empty. This clears all fields specified.

7. To locate the next occurrence of the Find What term, choose Find Next. Choose Replace to perform the replacement for that record, and choose Find Next again.

   or

   To automatically find and replace throughout the database without stopping, choose Replace All.

8. When you finish replacing, choose Close. (If you selected Replace All, it closes automatically.)

Caution

Be careful when using the Replace command. You cannot undo a replacement.

Working with Filters

As you learned earlier in this chapter, you can use Find to perform simple searches—for example, to find a person's birthday. Sometimes, however, Find isn't sufficiently powerful, like when you need to look at the records where the `Purchase Date` is greater than or equal to 12/15/94, the `Amount Due` is more than $100, and the `City` is Seattle.

For times like these, you need a *filter*. A filter works like a Find in that it narrows down the group of records to match certain criteria, but a filter is more powerful and feature-rich. When you perform a filter, Works searches all the records in the database. Just as with Find, Works displays the records that match the filter and hides the records that do not match.

Note

A filter looks in all records in the database, not just the ones that are displayed. If you have performed a Find operation, some of the records are displayed and some are hidden. This situation makes no difference to a filter—it checks all records, even the hidden ones.

With a Find operation, you can search only for certain characters (along with wild cards) contained in fields. With a filter, you can use a wide range of search criteria to retrieve records. Here are a few examples:

- *Exact matches.* You can retrieve only the records where the purchase amount is exactly $97.57.
- *Partial matches.* You can retrieve records where the `Component` field contains the letters *switch*, as in *switches*, *switching*, and *switcher*.
- *Greater than or less than.* You can select records where the ZIP code is greater than 98000 but less than 99000.
- *By range criteria.* You can select records where the `Birthdate` field is between 1/1/42 and 1/1/50.
- *By more than one field entry.* You can retrieve records where the `Product` field contains *crusher*, and the `Sales Territory` field contains *Southeast Florida*.
- *By non-matches.* You can select records for people who have not purchased an Acme Juice-O-Matic.

Works' filter feature provides powerful search tools. You can even filter your database using calculations. For example, you can find the records where `Current Date` minus `Purchase Date` is greater than 90 days.

You have two options to create a filter: Easy Filter and Filter Using Formula. The Easy Filter is much easier, as the name implies. This chapter focuses mainly on working with the Easy Filter, although the Filter Using Formula feature is explained at the end of the chapter.

Creating a Filter

In an Easy Filter, you specify which fields to compare and how you want them compared. Figures 21.5 and 21.6 show a database in List view before and after using a filter to retrieve all records where the ZIP code is greater than 40000 and the `Last Name` field entry begins with a letter that comes after M in the alphabet.

	Last Name	First Name	Address	City	State	ZIP
1	Colvin	Margaret	608 Bohlen Drive	Sault St. Mai	MI	49783
2	Pivovarnick	John	283 Albacore Reef	Anchorage	AK	99502
3	Watson	Michelle	680 West Maple	Wausau	WI	54401
4	Abbott	John	123A West Hollywoo	Ringwood	NJ	77456
5	Grant	Shiela	102-B Martin House	Tewksbury	MA	71876
6	Smith	Roy	238 Derby Way	Stamford	CT	36902
7	Jones	Chris	2930 Trafalgar Squar	Tyler	TX	75703
8	Jones	Jay	45860 New York Ave	Dallas	TX	75206
9	Talbott	Barry	5903 McArthur Park	Richardson	TX	75081
10	Brewster	Henry	East St.	Fayetteville	NC	28314
11	Frantz	Melanie	8297 North Main	Franklin	TN	37064
12	Jones	Leslie	55 East Central Plac	Raleigh	NC	27620-4318
13	Hogwood	Jenny	720 E. Warren	Los Angeles	CA	90005
14	Kirby	Candy	938 Chieftan Road	Las Vegas	NV	89139
15	Peterson	Joyce	8582 Ponting St.	Hurricane	UT	84737
16	Smith	Muhammad	5068 Tearose Lane	Sacramento	CA	15814-1408

Fig. 21.5
The database before applying the filter.

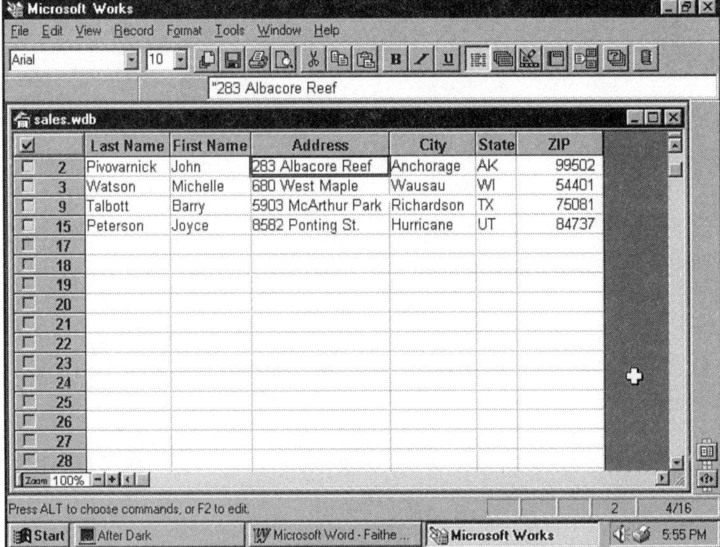

	Last Name	First Name	Address	City	State	ZIP
2	Pivovarnick	John	283 Albacore Reef	Anchorage	AK	99502
3	Watson	Michelle	680 West Maple	Wausau	WI	54401
9	Talbott	Barry	5903 McArthur Park	Richardson	TX	75081
15	Peterson	Joyce	8582 Ponting St.	Hurricane	UT	84737
17						
18						
19						
20						
21						
22						
23						
24						
25						
26						
27						
28						

Fig. 21.6
The database after applying the filter.

Note

When you apply a filter, you can view the results in List view, Form view, or Print Preview.

Follow these steps to create a new filter:

1. Choose Tools, Filters or click the Filters button on the toolbar.

   If you have never used filters before in Works, you'll see the First-Time Help dialog box. Click To Create and apply a new filter.

   If you have not created a filter before in this database, Works displays the Filter Name dialog box, as shown in figure 21.7. Works suggests the name Filter 1.

Tip
You probably want to type a more descriptive name than Filter 1 so it is easier to remember.

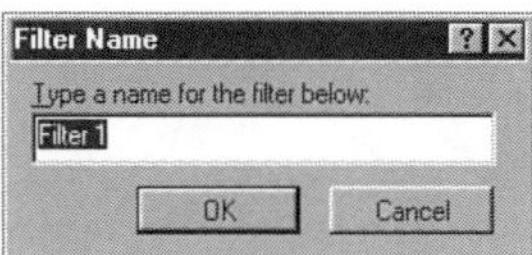

Fig. 21.7
Use the Filter Name dialog box to choose a name for your filter.

2. Type a new name for the filter, if you want, then click OK. The name can be up to 15 characters long.

   The Filter dialog box appears (see fig. 21.8).

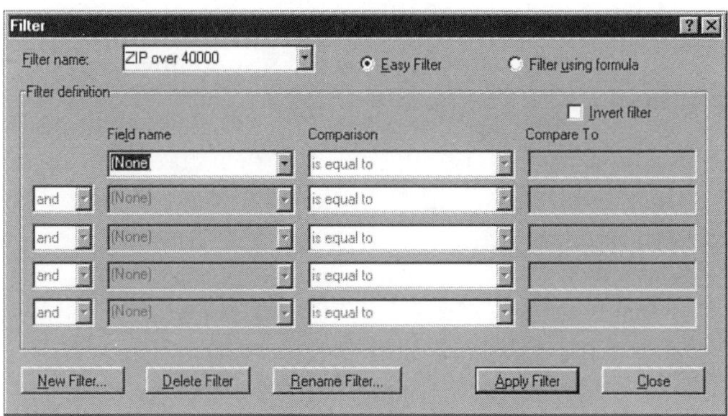

Fig. 21.8
In the Filter dialog box, you choose the criteria for your filter.

3. In the first drop-down list box under the Field Name heading, select the field you want to use for the first filter criterion.

For the ZIP code example given earlier in this section, you would select the `ZIP` field.

4. In the first drop-down list box under the Comparison heading, select the way you want the field content compared.

   For ZIP codes greater than 40000, you would choose Is Greater Than. See table 21.1 for examples of how each comparison works.

5. In the first text box under the Compare To heading, type the value you want the field's contents compared to.

   For the ZIP code example, you would type 40000. Figure 21.9 shows entries indicated in steps 3 through 5.

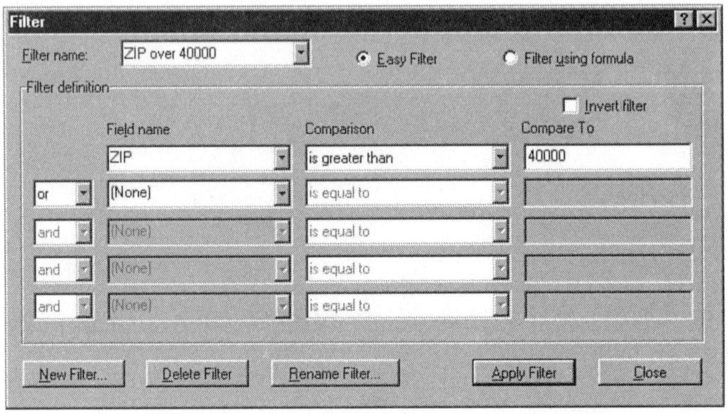

Fig. 21.9
This example shows how to filter ZIP codes that are greater than 40000.

6. (Optional) To add another filter sentence, choose *and* or *or* from the drop-down list on the far left side of the second line, and then repeat steps 3 through 5 for that line.

   If you choose *or*, the filter finds records for which either line of your filter is true. If you chose *and*, the filter identifies only the records for which both lines are true.

7. (Optional) To display only the records for which your filter does *not* apply, click the Invert Filter check box.

8. When you are finished entering filter lines, click the Apply Filter button.

Works displays the records that match your filter, if there were any. If not, a message appears telling you that there aren't any.

Table 21.1 Comparison Choices in the Filter Dialog Box

Comparison	Meaning
Is equal to	Contains only the specified text. *Smith* would not find *Joe Smith* or *Smithsonian* and 7 would not find 70 or 77.
Is not equal to	Does not contain only the specified text. The field may contain the specified text plus some other text, or it may not contain the specified text at all.
Is less than	Is a smaller number or earlier first letter in the alphabet than the specified text.
Is greater than	Is a larger number or later first letter in the alphabet than the specified text.
Is less than or equal to	Same as Is less than, except exact matches count, too.
Is greater than or equal to	Same as Is greater than, except exact matches count, too.
Contains	Contains the specified text, either as part or a whole of the contents. *Smith* would find *Smith*, *Joe Smith*, and *Smithsonian* and 7 would find 70, 77, and 873.
Does not contain	Does not contain the specified text anywhere in the field.
Is blank	The field is completely empty.
Is not blank	The field contains something (could be anything).
Begins with	The first character(s) in the field entry match the specified text.
Does not begin with	The first character(s) in the field entry do not match the specified text.
Ends with	The last character(s) in the field entry match the specified text.

To redisplay all the records after filtering them, choose Record, Show, 1 All Records.

After you have applied a filter, the Filter Name dialog box does not automatically appear when you choose Tools, Filters. Instead, the Filters dialog box appears with the last filter you used still showing. You can reapply the filter by clicking the Apply Filter button again.

To create another new filter, follow these steps:

1. Choose Tools, Filters. The Filters dialog box reappears, with your previous filter showing (refer to fig. 21.9).
2. Choose the New Filter button. The Filter Name dialog box appears over the Filter dialog box (refer to fig. 21.7).
3. Repeat the procedure for creating a new filter, which is explained in the preceding set of steps.

After you have more than one filter created, you can apply any of them whenever you choose. Just choose Tools, Filters, select the filter from the Filter Name drop-down list, then click the Apply Filter button.

Hiding a Filtered Record

After you have used your filter, you may want to exclude a few of the records that matched the criteria before you act on the group of records. For example, if you used a filter to retrieve the names of people on your mailing list who have birthdays in June, you may want to exclude a few names for people to whom you do not want to send a birthday card. To hide an individual record, follow these steps:

1. In List view, highlight the record(s) you want to hide.

   or

   In Form Design view, display the record you want to hide.
2. Choose Record, Hide Record.

To redisplay all records later, when you're finished working with the group, choose Record, Show, 1 All Records.

Renaming Filters

When you create a filter, the first thing Works asks for is a name for it. If you use the names that Works automatically assigns—Filter 1, Filter 2, Filter 3, and so on—you may want to rename the filter later to something more helpful.

Follow these steps to name (or rename) a filter:

1. Choose Tools, Filters or click the Filters button on the toolbar. The Filter dialog box appears (refer to fig. 21.9).

2. Select the filter you want to rename from the Filter Name drop-down list.

3. Choose the Rename Filter button. The Filter Name dialog box reappears (refer to fig. 21.7).

4. Type a new name, up to 15 characters.

5. Click OK. Works renames the filter.

6. Click Close.

Deleting Filters

Works automatically saves every filter you create. If you don't intend to use a filter later, you can delete it. A Works database can have a maximum of eight filters, so you may need to delete an existing filter before Works enables you to create a new one.

Follow these steps to delete a filter:

1. Choose Tools, Filters or click the Filters button on the toolbar. Works displays the Filter dialog box.

2. From the Filter Name drop-down list, select the filter you want to delete.

3. Click the Delete Filter button.

4. Choose Close.

> **Caution**
>
> You cannot restore a deleted filter with the Undo command.

Creating Advanced Filters

With the Filter dialog box's Easy Filter settings—the ones you have been working with so far in this chapter—you can perform almost all the filters you may ever need. However, sometimes you may need to create a filter with more than five criteria (you have only five lines to enter criteria in the Filter dialog box). Or you may need to use a mathematical formula in a filter. In such cases, you must choose the Filter Using Formula option rather than Easy Filter in the Filter dialog box.

Figure 21.10 shows how the Filter dialog box changes when you select the Filter Using Formula option button. Before switching to Filter Using Formula view, I entered the following criteria:

> `ZIP` is greater than 40000
>
> and `Last Name` is less than E
>
> or `Last Name` is greater than or equal to P

Then I switched to Filter Using Formula view. As you can see in figure 21.10, Works has translated the criteria I entered in Easy Filter view into a more sophisticated code.

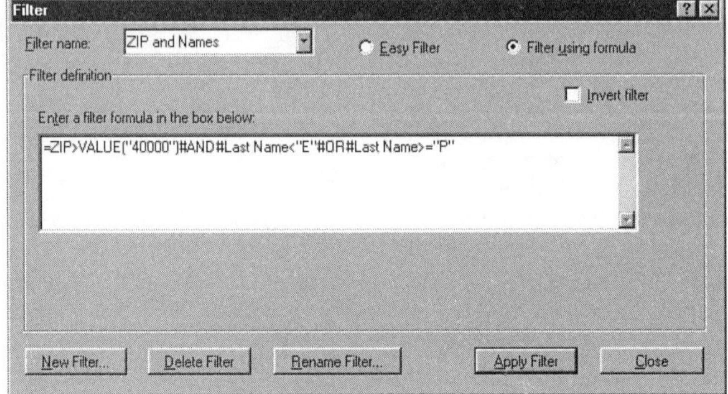

Fig. 21.10
The Filter Using Formula option can make even a simple filter look complex.

Each filter instruction in the code defines the text or values you want Works to look for. The following table shows how Works translated each line of the filter into a formula:

Easy Filter View	Filter Using Formula View
`ZIP` is greater than 40000 and `Last Name` is less than E or `Last Name` is greater than or equal to P	`=ZIP>VALUE("40000")` `#AND#Last Name<"E"` `#OR#Last Name>="P"`

The rules for writing formulas are fairly straightforward:

- Begin each formula with an equal sign.
- When including a number to compare to, format it like this: `VALUE("`*`number`*`")`

- When including text to compare to, format it like this: `"text"`
- Separate each criterion with `#AND#` or `#OR#` operators, encased in # marks as shown.
- Use operator symbols to indicate what kind of comparison you want to do. See table 21.2 for a list of the operators you can use.

Table 21.2 Operator Symbols to Use in Filter Formulas

Comparison in Easy Filter View	Formula Operator in Filter Using Formula View
Is equal to	=
Is not equal to	<>
Is less than	<
Is greater than	>
Is less than or equal to	<=
Is greater than or equal to	>=
Contains	"**text*"
Does not contain	<>"**text*"
Is blank	""
Is not blank	<>""
Begins with	"*text**"
Does not begin with	<>"*text**"
Ends with	"**text*"

Just like in a mathematical formula, you can group conditions in parentheses. For example, in the following instruction, the `OR` operator applies to all the conditions enclosed in parentheses:

```
=Name="Johnson"#OR#(Age>30#AND#Sex="M")
```

This filter retrieves records for people who are named Johnson or are male and over 30 years old.

If you place the parentheses differently, the filter will find different records. For example:

```
=Name=("Johnson"#OR#Age>30)#AND#Sex="M"
```

would find males who are either named Johnson or are over 30.

Creating Filters Based on More than Five Criteria

Works enables you to create filters easily using up to five criteria, as described earlier in this chapter. You can create filters with more than five criteria, but you cannot use the Easy Filter view of the Filter dialog box. Instead, you must type the filter in the Filter Using Formula view.

Follow these steps to create a filter based on more than five criteria:

1. Choose Tools, Filters or click the Filters button on the toolbar. Works displays the Filter dialog box.
2. If you want to create a new filter, choose the New Filter button, type a name, and click OK.
3. Type the first five criteria in Easy Filter view.
4. Click the Filter Using Formula option button to switch to Formula view.
5. Type the additional filter criteria into the formula, using the operators in table 21.2.
6. Choose the Apply Filter button. Works applies the filter formula.

When you are finished, save your filter for future use. When you open the filter later, all criteria are there, not just the first five that appear in the Easy Filter window.

Filtering Records Using Math

In Filter Using Formula view, Works enables you to use math calculations in a retrieval. This method is useful when you need to create a comparison by adding, subtracting, multiplying, dividing, or exponentiating one or more fields. You can use the math operators shown in table 21.3.

Table 21.3 Math Operators for Filter Formulas

Operator	Example	Purpose
+ (addition)	`=(Premium+Principal) >500`	Selects records where premium plus principal is greater than $500
– (subtraction)	`=(PastDue-DueDate)>30`	Selects records where the past due date less the due date is greater than 30
* (multiplication)	`=(Cost*Qty)<1000`	Selects records where cost times quantity is less than $1000
/ (division)	`=(Pledge/Miles)>25`	Selects records where pledge per mile is greater than $25
^ (exponentiation)	`=side^2<200`	Selects records where the area of a square is less than 200

Filtering Records Using Functions

Works functions are built-in conditions that save you the trouble of typing complex formulas in a filter. Functions are most famous for their use in spreadsheets, but they also work in databases. (See Chapter 11, "Working with Formulas and Functions," for more information.)

Almost any function you can use in a spreadsheet, or in a database field, can be used in a filter. The following examples show filters that use functions:

> `=DateDue-NOW( )>30`. This filter selects records where the due date is more than 30 days from today's date.
>
> `=PI( )*diameter>400`. This filter selects records where the circumference of a circle is greater than 400.

Note

Notice in the examples that some functions require you to include empty parentheses after the function name, even though no function parameters are specified. One example is PI( ). Refer to the EasyCalc feature in the Spreadsheet portion of Works for information on certain functions.

Tip
You don't need to include the current year when you type a date filter. If you type only the month and day, Works assumes that the year is the current year.

Using Dates in Filters

As you have already seen in earlier parts of this chapter, you can filter by date using the Find feature or using an Easy Filter. But you also can use dates in a filter formula using these operators: is equal to, is greater than, is less than, and is not equal to.

When you use a date in a filter, you must enclose it in single quotation marks: '4/15/96'.

The following examples show dates used in filters:

`DateDue-'5/15/96'>90`. This filter selects records where the due date falls more than 90 days after May 15, 1996.

`>='1/1/96'#AND#<='7/1/96'`. This filter selects records where a date falls in the first six months of 1996.

`=AmtDue>500#AND#(Now( )-DateDue)>90`. This filter selects records where the amount due is more than $500 and payment is more than 90 days overdue.

Troubleshooting

When I apply a filter, Works retrieves records that weren't displayed in List view before I applied it. What's the problem?

You previously applied a filter or chose the Record, Hide Records command to hide some of the records in the database. When you apply a filter to a database with hidden records, Works searches the entire database, including the hidden records, and displays all the matching records it finds.

You cannot perform a filter on only non-hidden records, but you can hide selected records after you apply a filter. See "Hiding Fields and Records" in Chapter 19, "Entering and Editing Data."

I would like to save a filter that retrieves records saved no earlier than 30 days before today's date. How can I do that?

Use the built-in Works `NOW` function. For example, the following statement retrieves records where the date entered in the `Date` field is no earlier than 30 days before today's date: `=(NOW( )-Date)<=30`.

Chapter 22

Creating a Database Report

by Faithe Wempen

After you enter information in a database, you occasionally need to review what you entered. As the preceding chapters explain, Works gives you several ways to look at your stored data. You can display the database in Form or List view and scroll between records. You can use the Find or Filter commands to locate specific records. You can print the information in your database, or display it with Print Preview. Or you can create a report, as described in this chapter.

The primary purpose of a report is to produce printed output. A report enables you to organize and format database information before you print. For example, you might want to print your database of addresses, so you can carry it in your briefcase. You could print directly from Form view, but with a report, you can format the printout specifically for your needs.

In this chapter, you learn how to do the following:

- Create and save a basic Works Database report
- Review your report in Print Preview
- Review your report in Report view
- Rename, delete, and copy reports
- Print your report with or without records

Understanding Reports

When you print or display database records using the methods described in the previous chapters, you have little control over how Works formats the retrieved information. Works simply displays or prints the records as they appear in Form or List view. With a report, you can tell Works to print or display only the fields you want, and you can tell Works to calculate and print report statistics, such as a count of the records in the database or an average value for various groups. You can add titles, headers, and footers to a report. Figure 22.1 shows a simple report displayed in Print Preview, where the average sales for each sales region is displayed.

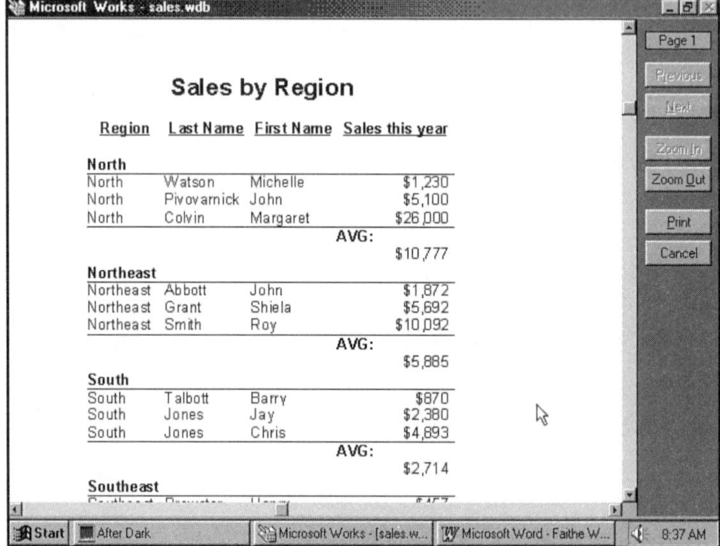

Fig. 22.1
In this report, the records are grouped by region, and then the sales to date for each region are averaged.

After you create a report that displays information the way you want, you can save the report and use it again later. You can save up to eight reports for each Works Database.

Works enables you to create reports in two ways:

- You can create almost any report with the Tools, ReportCreator command.

- You can fine-tune a report and use advanced report features not available in ReportCreator, in Report view.

ReportCreator walks you through a series of dialog boxes in which you specify your reporting preferences, such as which fields to include in what order, what title to give your report, how to group records, and what statistics to display. You learn to use ReportCreator in this chapter.

After you have created a report, you can enhance it by adding more titles and notes, changing the fonts, changing alignment and number formats, and more. These changes are discussed in Chapter 23, "Customizing a Report."

Creating a Works Report

Note

In previous versions of Works, you had to apply filters and sort the records before you ran your report, because the Report feature did not sort or filter. Works 4.0, however, has incorporated the filter and sort features, so you don't need to do them beforehand.

When you create a report with ReportCreator, you use dialog boxes to specify the options and settings you want in the report. After you create a report, you can preview or print it.

Follow these steps to create a report with ReportCreator:

1. Display the database for which you want to create a report.

2. Choose Tools, ReportCreator. Works displays the Report Name dialog box, as shown in figure 22.2. (If this is your first time creating a report, you will see the First-Time Help dialog box. Click OK to move past it.)

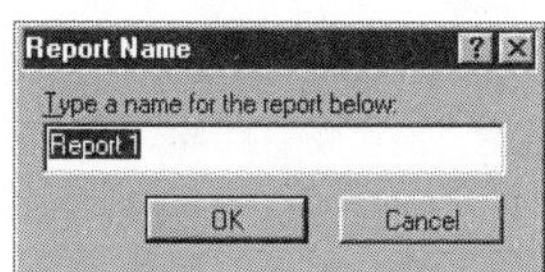

Fig. 22.2 Use the Report Name dialog box to give a name to your Works Database report.

3. If you want, replace the default name (probably Report 1) with a more descriptive name and click OK.

   The ReportCreator dialog box appears, with the Title tab showing (see fig. 22.3).

4. If you want, replace the text in the Report Title field with the text you want to appear at the top of the report.

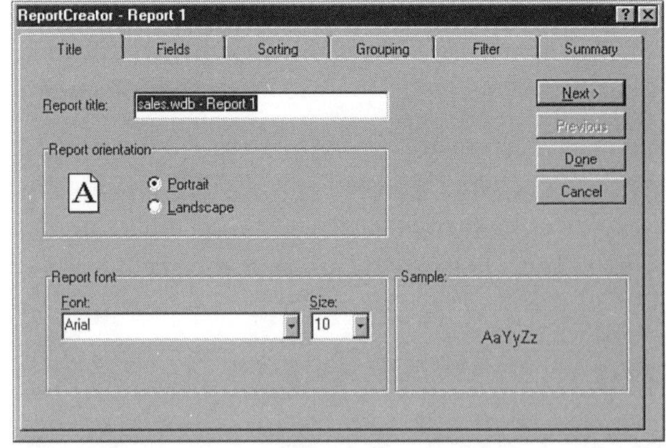

Fig. 22.3
The first tab you encounter in the ReportCreator dialog box asks for a report title to appear on-screen.

By default, the report title is the database name, a dash, and the report name you specified in step 3. The default title is a bit awkward, so you probably want to replace it.

5. Click an orientation button to choose a page layout: Portrait or Landscape.

6. Choose a default font and font size for the report from the Font and Size drop-down lists. Your choices are shown in the Sample area.

   Works uses the font you choose to format *all* text in the report, but you have the opportunity to change the font for titles and headings when you customize the report, as explained in Chapter 23.

7. Click the Next button to continue. Works displays the Fields tab, as shown in figure 22.4.

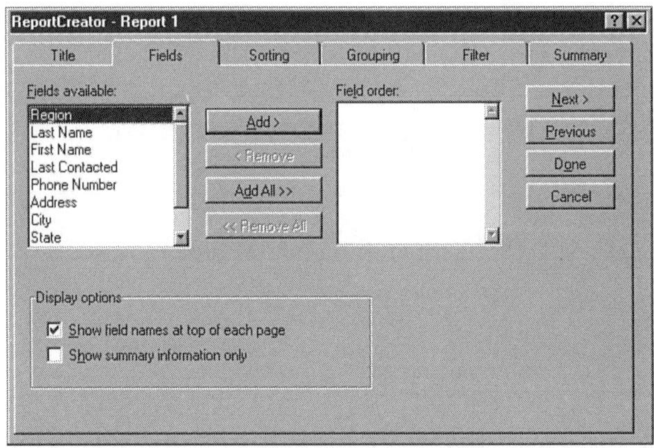

Fig. 22.4
Choose the fields you want to include on the Fields tab.

8. In the Fields Available list, highlight the first field you want to include in the report.

   Works prints the first field in the left-most column of the printout, so make sure you select them in the order that you want them to appear on the report, from left to right.

9. Click the Add button.

   or

   To add all the fields, in the order they are listed in the Fields Available box, click the Add All button.

10. Repeat steps 8 and 9 to add other fields.

Note

If you make a mistake and need to remove a field you have added, highlight it in the Field Order list and click the Remove button. To remove all the fields and start over, choose Remove All. You can double-click a field to add or remove it.

11. Select or deselect either of the Display Options check boxes:

    Show Field Names at Top of Each Page—if selected, and your report runs more than one page, the field names are repeated on each page.

    Show Summary Information Only—if selected, your report shows only the summary of the groups you select in later steps. The report does not show individual records.

◄ See "Sorting Database Records," p. 409

12. Click Next. Works displays the Sorting tab, as shown in figure 22.5. Now you specify in what order your records will appear.

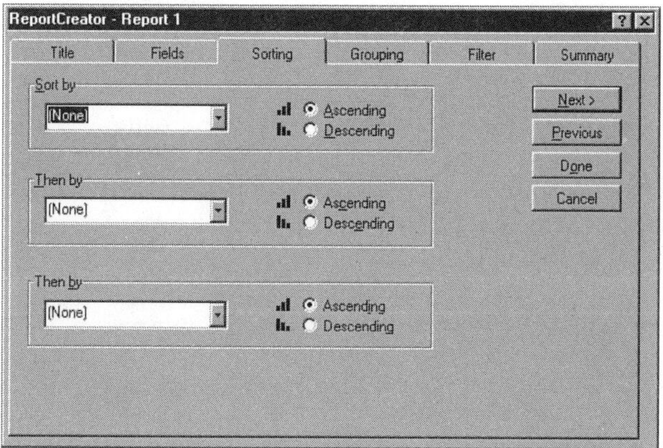

Fig. 22.5
Use the Sorting tab to specify in what order the records will appear on the report.

13. If you want your records sorted, choose the field to sort by from the Sort By drop-down list, and click the Ascending or Descending button.

14. If you want to sort by additional fields, choose them from one or both of the Then By drop-down lists.

15. Click Next to move on to the next tab. The Grouping tab appears, as shown in figure 22.6.

> **Note**
>
> If you did not choose any fields to sort by, all the options on the Grouping tab will be unavailable, and you can skip to step 17.

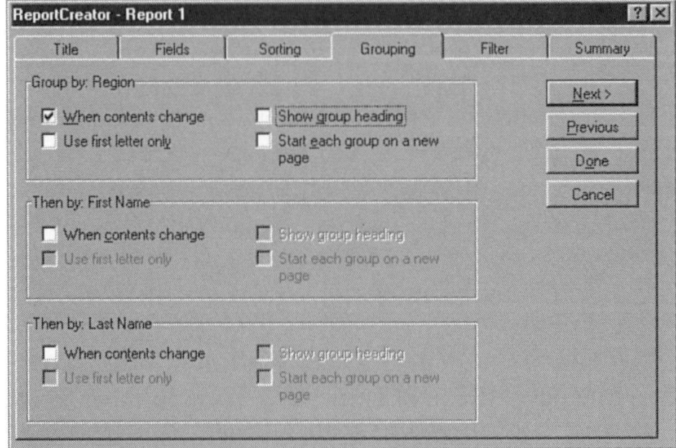

Fig. 22.6
Use the Grouping tab to choose how to display your sorted records.

16. For each of the fields you chose to sort by on the preceding tab, the following options appear. Select the options you want.

    When Contents Change—This check box tells Works to insert a blank line whenever the field by which you're sorting is different from the previous record. For instance, if you're sorting by Region, Works displays a blank line after the last record from the North region, before it starts the first record from the Northeast region. If you don't select this check box, none of the remaining check boxes will be available.

    Show Group Heading—When you select this check box, the field name appears above the blank line that the When Contents Change check box inserts.

Use First Letter Only—If you are sorting by a field that does not contain any identical entries, you may find it more useful to group by the first letter of the field entry only—for instance, all the last names that begin with A grouped together. Selecting this check box groups by first letter, instead of identical field entries.

Start Each Group on a New Page—By default, Works prints each group separated by a blank line. If you prefer to have each group on a separate page, select this check box.

◄ See "Working with Filters," p. 440

17. Click Next to move to the Filter tab. The Filter tab appears, as shown in figure 22.7.

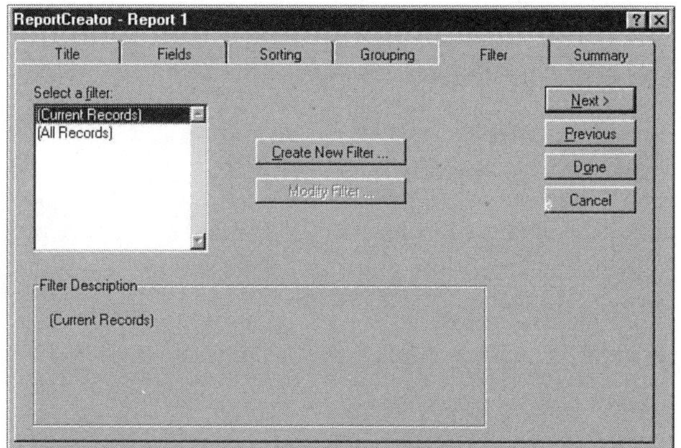

Fig. 22.7
Use the Filter tab to specify which records to include in the report.

18. The Select a Filter list contains all the filters you have created so far for this database, plus two other entries: [Current Records] and [All Records]. Take one of these steps:

- Select Current Records to use all records that were displayed at the time you began the ReportCreator process.
- Select All Records to use every record in the database.
- Select a filter you have already created.

Click the Create New Filter button to access the Filters dialog box (described in detail in Chapter 21) and create a new filter now.

19. Click Next to continue. The Summary tab appears (see fig. 22.8).

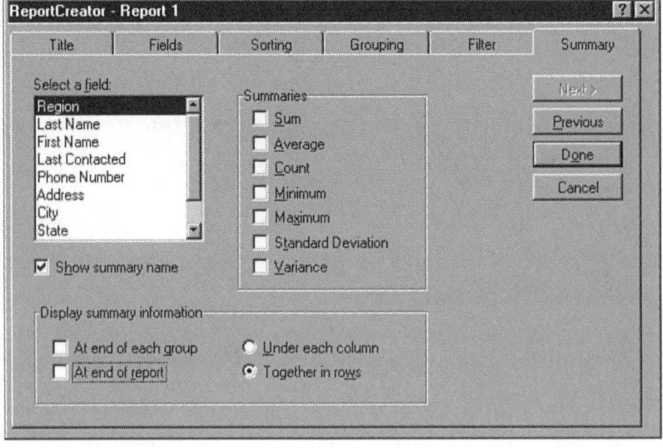

Fig. 22.8
On the Summary tab, you choose what kinds of calculations you want to use to summarize the data.

20. Choose the field to summarize from the Select a Field list.

21. Select one or more check boxes from the Summaries section to indicate which calculations to perform.

For example, to add the contents of all the records in the group, choose Sum. To print the smallest value, choose Minimum, or to print the largest value, choose Maximum.

> **Note**
>
> Most of the Summaries options do not work on text fields—only fields that contain numbers. Count is the exception; this calculation counts the number of records in that group.

22. Select any of the following options to further customize the way the summary will appear:

Show Summary Name—this option is selected by default. If you deselect this option, the descriptive label for the summary type you choose under Summaries will not appear on the report. For example, if you choose Average, you get the average, but no label appears to tell you it's an average rather than a sum.

At End of Each Group—selecting this check box summarizes each group individually.

At End of Report—selecting this check box summarizes the report as a whole.

Under Each Column or *Together in Rows*—choose one of these options to indicate where you want the summaries to appear.

23. Click the Done button. Works asks if you want to Preview or Modify your definition. Click Preview, and the report appears, as shown in figure 22.9. (This figure shows the report zoomed in so you can see it more clearly; for this magnification level, click the report twice.) If you choose Modify, the report definition appears on-screen so you can make changes to it.

You can summarize at the end of each group, at the end of the report, or in both places. For example, you might want to sum at the end of each month to show the monthly sales figures, and then sum at the end of the year for a grand total.

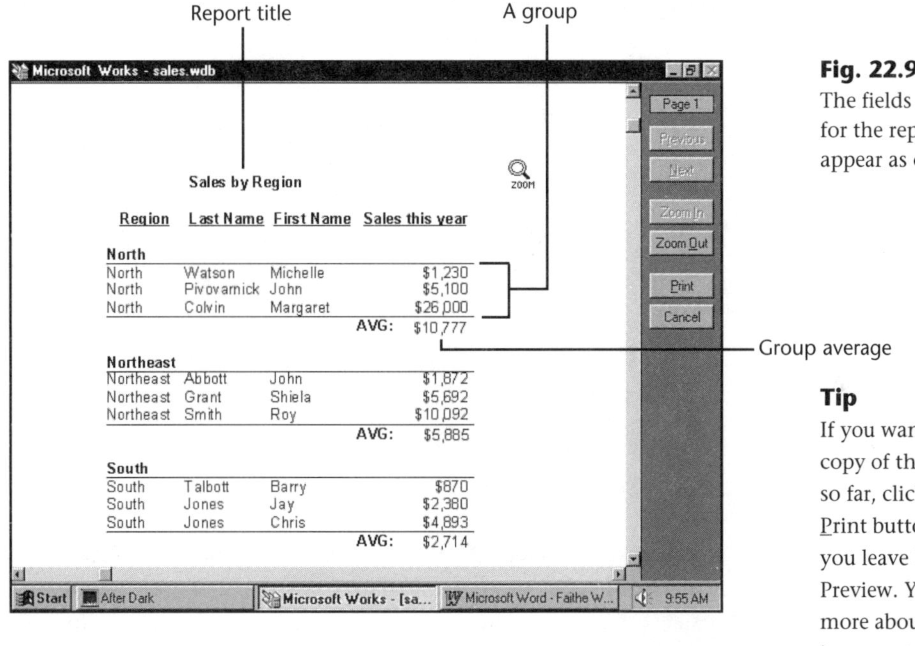

Fig. 22.9
The fields chosen for the report appear as columns.

Tip
If you want a hard copy of the report so far, click the Print button before you leave Print Preview. You learn more about printing reports later in this chapter.

After you create a report, Works saves it automatically with the database. You don't need to worry about losing the report if you switch out of Print Preview.

To close Print Preview, click the Cancel button. Works takes you to Report view, which may seem a little foreign to you at first. You learn about Report view in the next section.

◄ See "Selecting the Database View," p. 343

From here, you can move freely between Report, List, Form, and Form Design views in the normal way: choose one of these views from the View menu or click the appropriate button on the toolbar.

To re-enter Print Preview for your report, switch to Report view, then click the Print Preview button on the toolbar or choose File, Print Preview.

If you have created more than one report, you can choose which report you want to view with the following steps:

1. Choose View, Report.

   The View Report dialog box appears, listing all the reports associated with the database, as shown in figure 22.10.

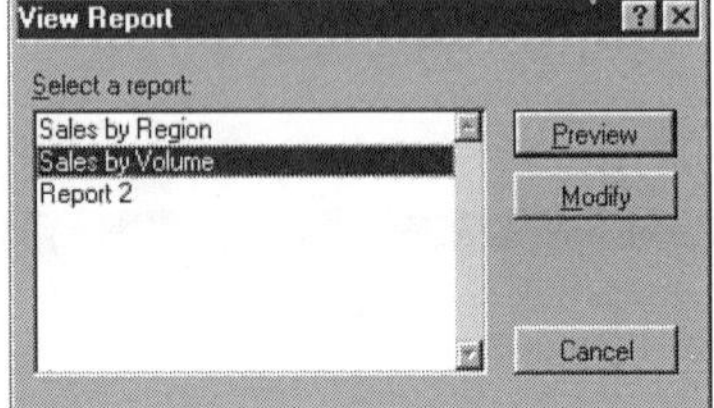

Fig. 22.10
Choose which report you want to work with from the View Report dialog box.

2. Select a report from the list.

3. To go to Print Preview for that report, click Preview.

   or

   To go to Report view for that report, click Modify.

Renaming Reports

When you first create a report, Works automatically names it Report 1, Report 2, Report 3, and so on unless you give it a better name. Obviously, it's much easier to remember the purpose of a report that has a descriptive name. For example, you might name a school jogathon report "Pledge Tally."

If you didn't name your report adequately when you created it, you can rename it later. Follow these steps to rename a report:

1. Choose Tools, Rename Report.

   You can be in any view when you choose this command. Works displays the Rename Report dialog box (see fig. 22.11).

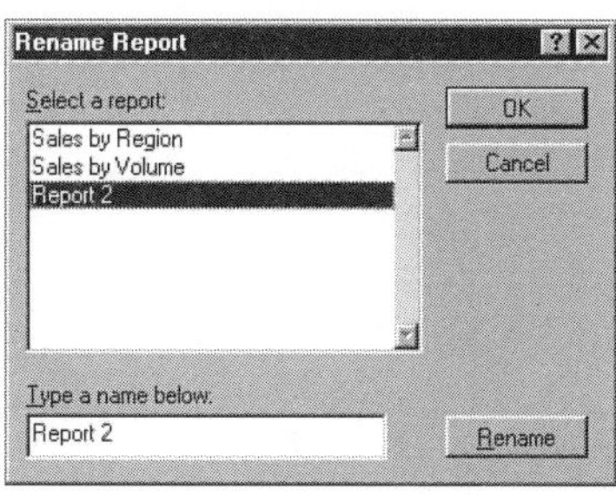

Fig. 22.11
Use the Rename Report dialog box to give your reports different names.

2. In the Select a Report list, select the report you want to rename.
3. In the Type a Name Below text box, type a new name of up to 15 characters.
4. Choose the Rename button.
5. To rename another report, repeat steps 2 through 4.
6. Choose OK.

Deleting a Report

You can delete reports that you no longer need. Each Works Database can have no more than eight reports associated with it, so you may need to delete reports before you can create new ones.

Follow these steps to delete a report:

1. Choose Tools, Delete Report.

   Works displays the Delete Report dialog box (see fig. 22.12).

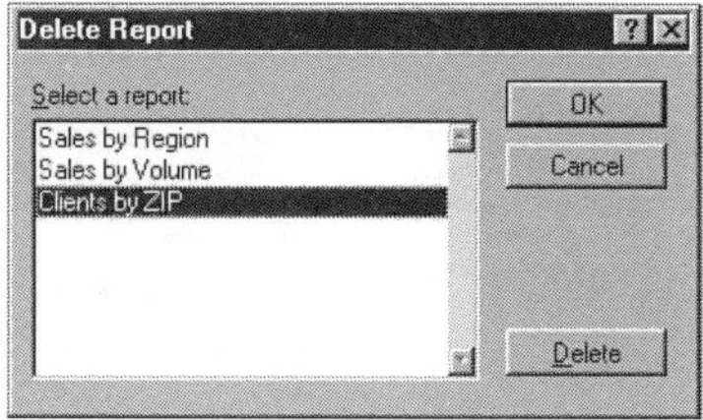

Fig 22.12
Use the Delete Report dialog box to discard reports that are no longer useful.

2. In the Select a Report list box, select the report you want to delete.
3. Choose Delete.
4. To delete other reports, repeat steps 2 and 3.
5. Choose OK.

Caution

Be careful when deleting reports. You cannot restore a deleted report with the Undo command.

Copying a Report

Copying reports is a very useful feature. For example, you can create a complex report and create a slight variation of it by copying and editing it rather than starting over from scratch.

Works calls copying *duplicating* when referring to reports. Follow these steps to duplicate a report:

1. Choose Tools, Duplicate Report.

   Works displays the Duplicate Report dialog box (see fig. 22.13).

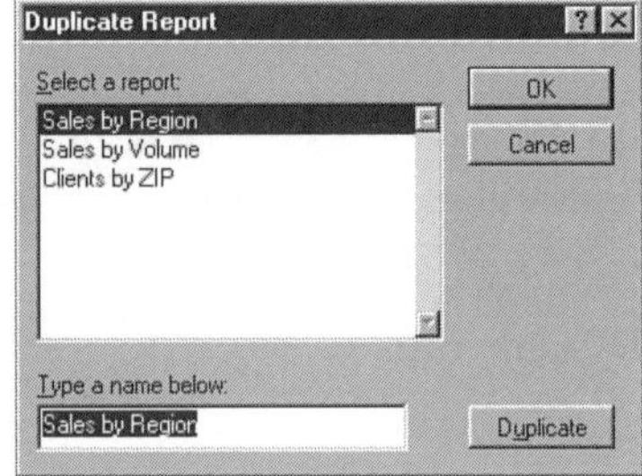

Fig. 22.13
Use the Duplicate Report dialog box to copy a report.

2. In the Select a Report list box, highlight the name of the report you want to copy.
3. In the Type a Name Below text box, type a new name of up to 15 characters for the copy.
4. Choose Duplicate.
5. To copy other reports, repeat steps 2 through 4.
6. Choose OK.

Works includes the copy whenever you display a dialog box with a list of reports for this database.

Troubleshooting

I want to use this copy with a different database, but when I open the other database, the report isn't on the list!

Sorry, but you have just run up against a limitation of Works. You can use a report only in the database in which it was created.

However, you have a couple of workarounds. First, you can make a copy of the entire database, and when you open the copy, all your reports will be available, ready to use with the copy.

Second, depending on how similar the other database is to your original, you may be able to copy a report with the Copy and Paste commands on the Edit menu. In Report view, highlight the parts of the report you want to copy. Then choose Edit, Copy. Now, open the other database, create a blank Report view (as described in Chapter 23), and choose Edit, Paste. The report is pasted into Report view in the new database, but it does not work unless the new database has all the same fields that the report references.

Copying Report Data into Other Programs

One of Works' handy features is that you can include the results from a report in other Works components. For instance, you can import your sales figures from your database directly into your monthly status report in the word processor. To do so, follow these steps:

1. Display the report in Report view.
2. Choose Edit, Copy Report Output.
3. Open the document where you want to place the output.
4. Choose Edit, Paste.

Printing Reports

In Chapter 20, "Expanding Your Database Skills," you learned how to print a Works database. In connection with printing, you learned how to use the Page Setup dialog box to set margins, paper source, size and orientation, and other options.

◄ See "Printing Database Records," p. 412

Printing a Works Database report involves the same steps as printing a database. The only difference between printing reports and databases is that when you choose File, Page Setup from Report view, Works displays a report-specific option in the Other Options tab, as shown in figure 22.14. This option enables you to print reports without records.

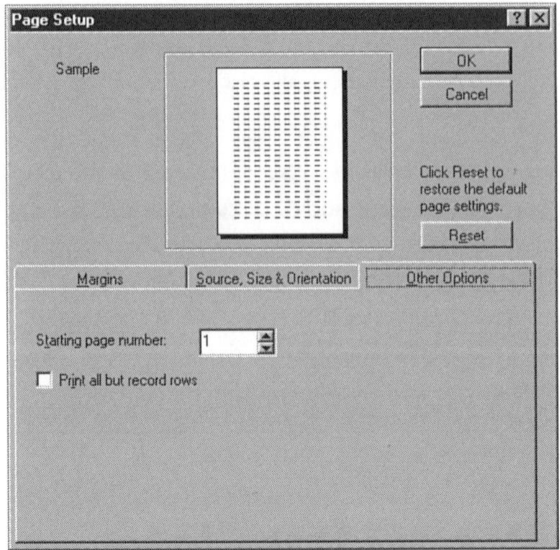

Fig. 22.14
In Report view, you use the Other Options tab to specify whether to print the records.

To print the report without printing any records, just select the Print All but Record Rows check box on the Other Options tab of the Page Setup dialog box. Then you can Print Preview or actually print the report to see how it will look.

Why would you want to print without records? If you are fine-tuning the layout of your report, and you have many records, you don't want to print all the report pages just to see how the report will look. Choosing not to print the records gives you a more compact printout with which to evaluate your report design.

When you choose Print All but Record Rows from the Other Options tab, Works prints only the introductory (Intr) and summary (Summm) row types that you specify in the report definition. To learn about using Intr and Summ, see Chapter 23, "Customizing a Report."❖

Chapter 23

Customizing a Report

by Faithe Wempen

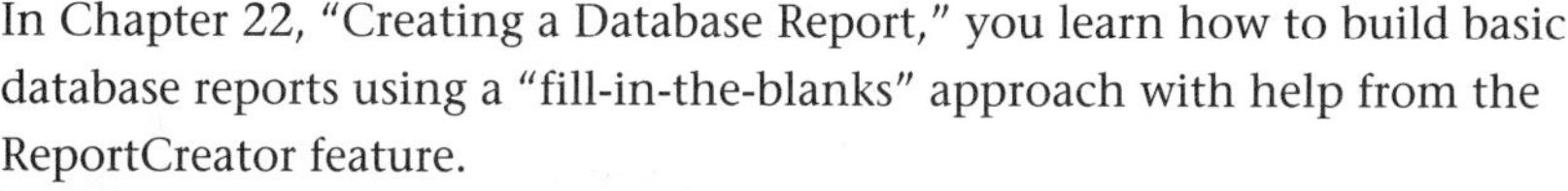

In Chapter 22, "Creating a Database Report," you learn how to build basic database reports using a "fill-in-the-blanks" approach with help from the ReportCreator feature.

ReportCreator reports work fine for most purposes, but they do have limitations. For example, the New Report dialog box enables you to create only a single, centered title for a report. You cannot edit the header rows, or create column breaks.

With Report view, Works provides the means for creating complex reports as well as simple ones, and for dressing up reports to look exactly the way you want.

In this chapter, you learn how to do the following:

- Edit reports in Report view
- Edit a report's sorting, grouping, and filtering functions
- Add and remove rows and columns
- Add new fields to a report
- Use mathematical calculations
- Format a report with fonts, alignment, and more

Creating a New Report in Report View

Because the ReportCreator is so easy and powerful, it's unlikely that you would ever choose to create a new report from scratch in Report view—building your own formulas from the ground up. More likely, you'll want to create a report with ReportCreator, and then modify it in Report view. However, there could be unusual circumstances when you might need a blank report. For example, if you are using Copy and Paste to paste a report definition from one database to another, you might need a blank Report view in the target database, in which to paste the copied report definition.

Follow these steps to display a blank report definition in Report view:

1. Choose Tools, ReportCreator.
2. Type a name for the report, then click OK.
3. In the ReportCreator dialog box, click the Done button.
4. Click the Modify button. Works displays a blank report, with only the default title across the top.

From this blank report, you can enter your own formulas and codes to create the report.

Understanding Report View

◄ See "Creating a Works Report," p. 455

In most cases, you create your report with ReportCreator. Then, if there are changes you want to make, you can make them in Report view.

After you complete the ReportCreator process, you decide whether you want to Preview or Modify the report. If you choose Preview, Works takes you to Print Preview. When you close Print Preview, Report view appears. If you choose Modify, Works takes you directly to Report view. An example of Report view is shown in figure 23.1.

Notice in figure 23.1 that each row of a report definition contains a label. The following list shows the purpose of each type of label:

- *Title.* A title row shows the title, if any, that Works prints at the top of the first page of the report.
- *Headings.* A heading row prints a field name or other text at the top of each column.

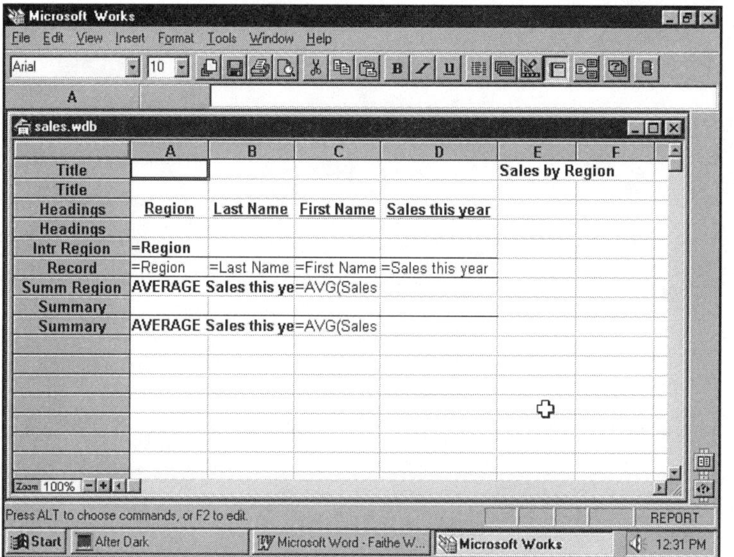

Fig. 23.1
Report view looks a bit like List view. It shows the framework used to create the report that you see in Print Preview.

- *Record.* Record rows indicate which records Works prints in the report. You can use formulas and functions in the Record row to tell Works to print other kinds of data in a column, as described in the section "Performing Arithmetic Calculations" later in this chapter.
- *Intr <fieldname>.* This label tells Works to print a blank row or a heading before each group of records when you sort the report.
- *Summ <fieldname>.* You use this label to tell Works to print a statistical summary after each group of records when the report is sorted.
- *Summary.* The summary label indicates which statistics Works prints at the end of the report.

Figure 23.2 shows a report created with this report definition, in Print Preview. You can see how each of the rows in figure 23.1 translated into the finished report.

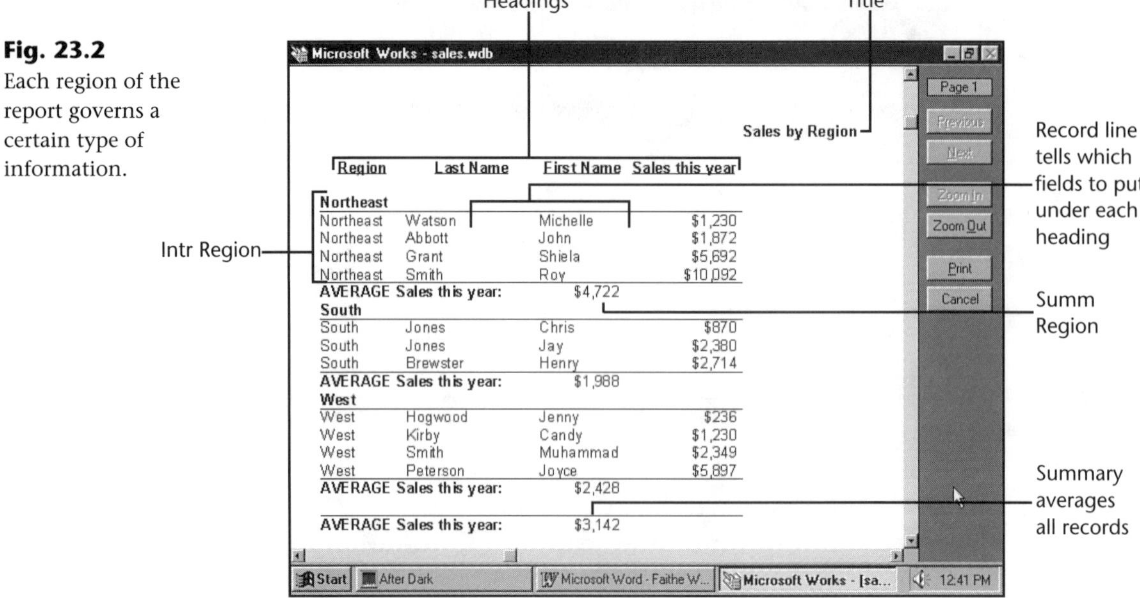

Fig. 23.2
Each region of the report governs a certain type of information.

Editing a Report Definition

After you've been through ReportCreator once for a report, you can't go back to ReportCreator. You must make your edits from that point on in Report view. However, to make it easier for you to change the more complicated parts of a report, like filters and sorting, Works provides some commands on the Tools menu to help you edit certain facets of a report.

Typing Changes in Report View

You must manually do some editing in Report view, as in List view. You highlight the existing entry, and then type over it. For example, you might want to change the column heading Last Name to Client's Name. Changing the heading name does not affect the field being used in the database. You might want to type something into a new row or column you added (see the section "Adding and Removing Rows and Columns" later in this chapter).

There are two kinds of entries in Report view: text (that will print as-is on the report) and instructions (that tell Works to pull certain information from your database and place it on your report). To change a text entry or an instruction, follow these steps:

1. Highlight the text or instruction you want to edit.

2. Click the formula bar; or press F2.

   Works moves the insertion point into the formula bar. (You won't see it if you pressed F2, but it's there.)

3. Edit the entry in the formula bar by using the Works cursor movement and deletion commands for the mouse and keyboard.

Follow these steps to delete an entry:

1. Highlight the text or instructions you want to delete.

   or

   To delete all the information from two or more adjacent rows or columns, highlight the rows or columns.

2. Choose Edit, Clear; or press Delete.

Works deletes the entry, but keeps any formatting intact. For example, if you format an instruction with a font, any new text or instructions you type in the row or column is formatted with the same font.

Editing the Report's Sorting, Grouping, or Filtering

If you change your mind about the sorting, grouping, or filtering options you set when you created your report, you can change them. Follow these steps to redisplay the dialog box that sets sorting, grouping, and filtering:

1. Choose Tools, and select the command for the option you want to edit: Report Sorting, Report Grouping, or Report Filter.

   A Report Settings dialog box appears, with three tabs, one for each of the three commands (see fig. 23.3). The tab for the one you selected appears on top, but you can easily switch among tabs by clicking them.

2. Make any changes to the settings on that tab.

3. If you need to make changes to any of the other tabs, click the tab and do so.

4. Click OK.

◄ See "Sorting Database Records," p. 409

◄ See "Working with Filters," p. 440

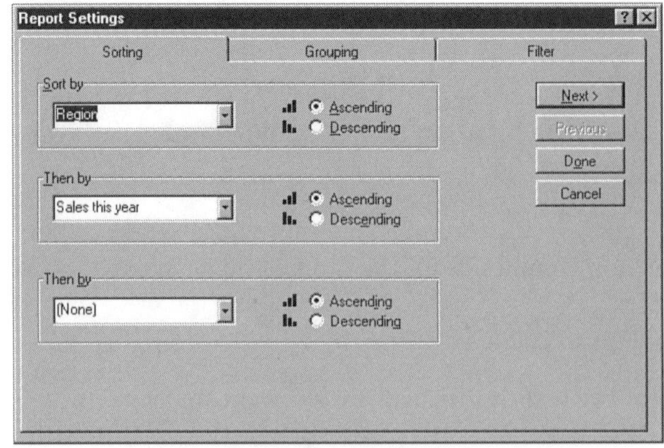

Fig. 23.3
You can make changes to sorting, grouping, and filtering options in the Report Settings dialog box.

Adding and Removing Rows and Columns

You can delete or insert rows and columns to customize your report. For example, an ordinary report has two title rows at the top—one with the ReportCreator-generated title, and one blank one. You might discover that you need three title rows at the top of your report, so you can add a subtitle. Or you might want to add an additional Summary line, in which to add more calculations (explained in the section "Performing Arithmetic" later in this chapter).

To insert a blank row or column, follow these steps:

1. Select the row above which you want to insert a blank row, or select the column to the right of where you want to insert a blank column.

2. Choose Insert, and then choose either Insert Row or Insert Column.

   If you choose Insert Column, Works inserts a column immediately. If you choose Insert Row, Works displays the Insert Row dialog box (see fig. 23.4).

3. Highlight the name of the row type you want to insert. You can insert a row for any of the regions on your report.

4. Choose Insert.

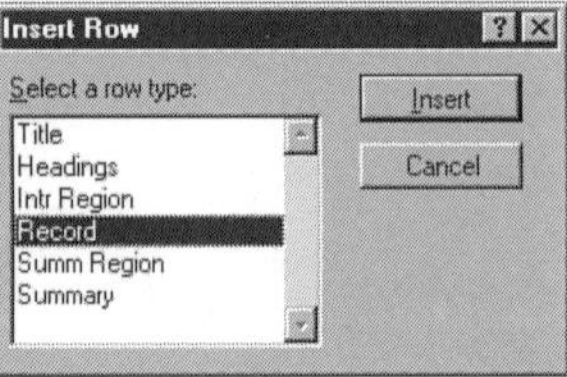

Fig. 23.4
Use the Insert Row dialog box to choose the type of row you want to insert.

Works inserts a new row and automatically places it first among the rows of the same type. For example, if you insert a new Summary row, Works places the new row first among the Summary rows.

To delete a row or column, do the following:

1. Position the insertion point in the row or column you want to delete.
2. Choose Insert, and then choose Delete Row or Delete Column.

   Works deletes the row or column immediately.

Adding New Fields to the Report

If you discover that you left out an important field on your report, you can add it. It's a three-step process: first you insert the new column to hold the field, then you add the heading, and then you add the field name. Follow these steps:

1. If needed, add a new column to hold your new field, as explained in the previous section.

   If you are adding the new field to the right-most end of the report, there are already blank columns there, so you don't need to add a new one.

2. Position the insertion point in the Headings row, in the column where you want to add the new field.

> **Caution**
>
> If you highlight a cell that already contains a heading, Works overwrites the heading when you insert the new field.

3. Choose Insert, Field Name.

   The Insert Field Name dialog box appears, as shown in figure 23.5.

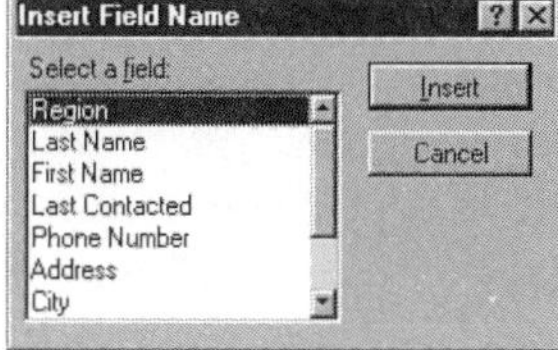

Fig. 23.5
Use the Insert Field Name dialog box to add a heading for your new column.

4. Select a field name from the Select a Field list, then click Insert.

   Works inserts the chosen field name at the insertion point.

5. Position the insertion point in the Record row, in the column where you just added the new heading.

6. Choose Insert, Field Entry.

   The Insert Field Entry dialog box appears, as shown in figure 23.6.

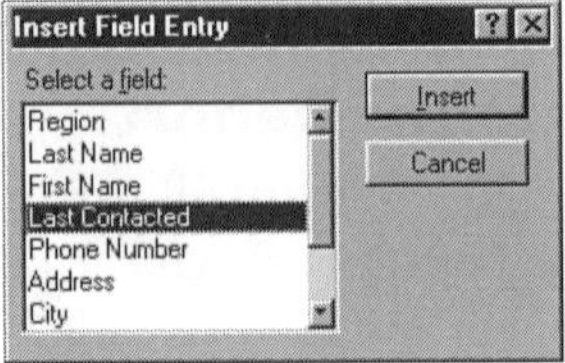

Fig. 23.6
Choose a field on which to report from the Insert Field Entry dialog box.

7. Select a field name from the Select a Field list, then click Insert.

   Works inserts the selected field entry at the insertion point.

8. Click the Print Preview button on the toolbar or choose File, Print Preview to see the new field in your report.

9. When you're done examining the results, click Cancel to return to Report view.

Tip
You don't have to use the Insert Field Entry dialog box to insert field entry instructions; you can simply type them directly in a report definition cell. For example, type **=DATE** to print the Date field.

Note

If a field contains an object such as a drawing, Works does not print the object in the report; instead, it prints `<<object>>`.

Troubleshooting

I added a field, but it's not formatted like all the other fields! It looks out of place.

The ReportCreator formats its reports with some simple formatting, which you can easily duplicate using the formatting skills you'll learn later in this chapter. For instance, the headings are bold and underlined, and there are horizontal rules marking off each group. Don't worry about this formatting now—you'll learn to create even better formatting for your report in the section "Formatting a Report" later in this chapter.

I added a date field, but in Print Preview, instead of the dates appearing, there are strange numbers.

Works stores dates as numeric codes, so it can perform calculations on them. To make your dates appear in a format that you can understand, format that column in Date format. You'll learn to do this in the section "Changing a Number Format" later in this chapter.

Adding a Summary Calculation

When you use ReportCreator, you have the opportunity to summarize fields with calculations, as you learn to do in Chapter 22. You can add more summaries that you might have overlooked from Report view.

Adding a field summary is just like adding a field name and field entry, as you learned in the previous section. Just place your insertion point where you want the summary to be, and then issue the command to open the dialog box that will help you set it up. Follow these steps:

1. If necessary, add a Summ <*fieldname*> row or a Summary row for the calculation. (Refer to the section "Adding and Removing Rows and Columns" earlier in this chapter.)

   Not sure what kind of row to insert the calculation into? Here are some guidelines.

   - For a formula you want Works to apply to a field for each sorted field group, insert a formula in a Summ <*fieldname*> row. (You must have set up sorting and grouping in your report already.)

     Note

     You can set up sorting and grouping when you create your report (see Chapter 22), or you can edit the report to include it, as explained in the section "Editing the Report's Sorting, Grouping, or Filtering" earlier in this chapter.

   - For a formula you want Works to apply to a field for the entire report, place the formula in a Summary row.

2. Position the insertion point in the row and column where you want the summary to appear.

> **Note**
>
> The summary command is self-contained—it does not rely on the column that it's in to determine which field to summarize. Therefore, you can place the command in any column, as long as it's in the correct type of row.

3. Choose Insert, Field Summary.

   The Insert Field Summary dialog box appears (see fig. 23.7).

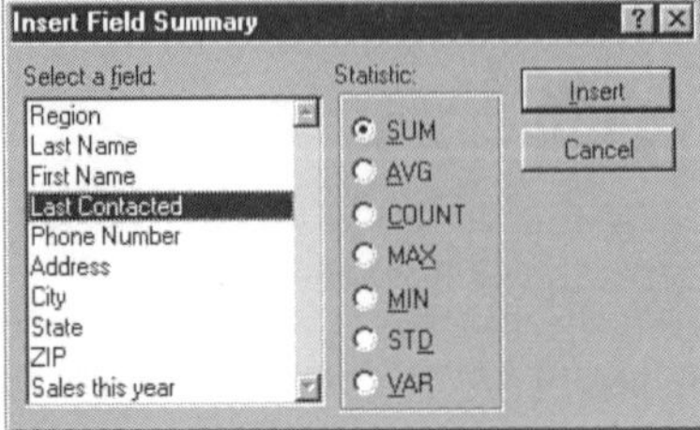

Fig. 23.7
The Insert Field Summary dialog box lets you pick a field and a calculation to perform on its entries.

4. Select the field to be summarized from the Select a Field list.
5. Choose a calculation from among the Statistics listed (see Table 23.1).
6. Click the Insert button.

   Works inserts the formula to perform that calculation at the insertion point.

7. To check your progress, click the Print Preview button on the toolbar or choose File, Print Preview.
8. When you're done looking at the results, click Cancel to return to Report view.

◄ See "Using Formulas and Functions," p. 430

Table 23.1 The Built-In Report Functions

Function	Meaning	Example
SUM	Totals the values in a numeric field	=SUM(Amt. Due)
AVG	Averages the values in a numeric field	=AVG(Pledge94)

Function	Meaning	Example
COUNT	Counts the number of entries in a field	=COUNT(Stock No.)
MAX	Finds the largest value in a numeric field	=MAX(Annual Income)
MIN	Finds the smallest value in a numeric field	=MIN(Diameter)
STD	Calculates the standard deviation for a numeric field	=STD(Acreage)
VAR	Calculates the variance for a numeric field	=VAR(Dept. Sum)

Performing Arithmetic Calculations

You don't have to use the Works built-in functions in a calculated report column. You can calculate column contents by using arithmetic operations on fields. For example, if you plan to contact each customer every 60 days, you could use the following formula to calculate the date to contact the customer again, based on the Last Contacted field: =Last Contacted+60.

Note

How does Works know that 60 means 60 days? The Last Contacted field is formatted as a Date, and dates are automatically calculated by the day in Works. If the field were formatted as some other data type, 60 might mean something else, like 60 minutes or 60 dollars.

You can use the following Works math operators in a report definition:

Operator	Purpose
+	Addition
–	Subtraction
*	Multiplication
/	Division
^	Exponentiation

Follow these steps to insert a mathematical calculation in a report field:

Tip
See the section "Adding and Removing Rows and Columns" earlier in this chapter to learn how to insert a row.

1. If necessary, add a Record row, a Summ <*fieldname*> row, or a Summary row.

   Place a simple calculation that you want to appear with each record in a Record row. Place a calculation that should apply to each group in a Summ <*fieldname*> row. Finally, place a calculation that applies to the entire report in a Summary row.

2. Move the insertion point to the row and column in which you want to insert the calculated field.

3. Type the mathematical formula.

   The formula can include a combination of numbers, math operators, and field names. For example, type **=Last Contact+60**.

4. Press Enter.

Works inserts the formula in the cell. When you preview or print the report, Works displays the results of the mathematical calculation in the field column.

Figures 23.8 and 23.9 show a report definition and previewed report (respectively) that include a Recontact field that contains dates 60 days after the date listed in the Last Contacted field.

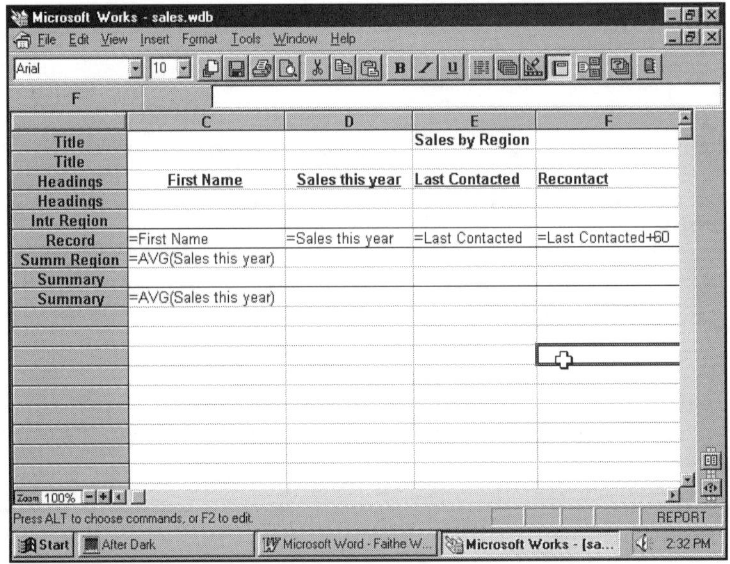

Fig. 23.8
Type a math formula in a report definition cell to print the calculated results in a report column.

Sales by Region

Last Name	First Name	Sales this year	Last Contacted	Recontact
Watson	Michelle	$1,230	8/13/95	10/12/95
Abbott	John	$1,872	1/1/95	3/2/95
Grant	Shiela	$5,692	4/28/95	6/27/95
Smith	Roy	$10,092	2/5/95	4/6/95
Sales this year	$4,722			
Jones	Chris	$870	6/6/95	8/5/95
Jones	Jay	$2,380	5/9/95	7/8/95
Brewster	Henry	$2,714	5/3/95	7/2/95
Sales this year	$1,988			
Hogwood	Jenny	$236	5/2/95	7/1/95
Kirby	Candy	$1,230	1/12/95	3/13/95
Smith	Muhammad	$2,349	10/14/95	12/13/95
Peterson	Joyce	$5,897	7/8/95	9/6/95
Sales this year	$2,428			
Sales this year	$3,142			

Page 1
Previous
Next
Zoom In
Zoom Out
Print
Cancel

Fig. 23.9
When you print a report, Works calculates mathematical formulas and inserts the results in the corresponding columns.

Formatting a Report

After you create your report, you can dress it up with formatting to make it more readable and attractive. For example, you can add titles, headings, and labels, and change column widths, row heights, number formats, alignment, and fonts. You can insert page breaks between sections of the report, and you can change page and margin settings.

Adding Titles and Labels

You can add extra text anywhere in the report, such as additional titles, headings, descriptions, or labels. You can insert additional rows and columns for the new text, or you can type it into existing rows.

There is no special trick to inserting text; just follow these steps.

1. (Optional) Insert a new row or column by choosing Insert, Insert Row or Insert Column.

2. Position the insertion point where you want the new text to appear.

3. Type the text.

Note

If you type a long line of text, it might not fit in the cell; if that happens, you can change the column width, as described in the next section.

Changing Column Width and Row Height

Works displays a report definition using the same column width and row height that it uses to display a database in List view. The default column width is often not wide enough to hold text or formulas without spilling over into adjacent cells. If there is information in the column to the right, Works might hide part of the information you type, as shown in Column B in figure 23.10.

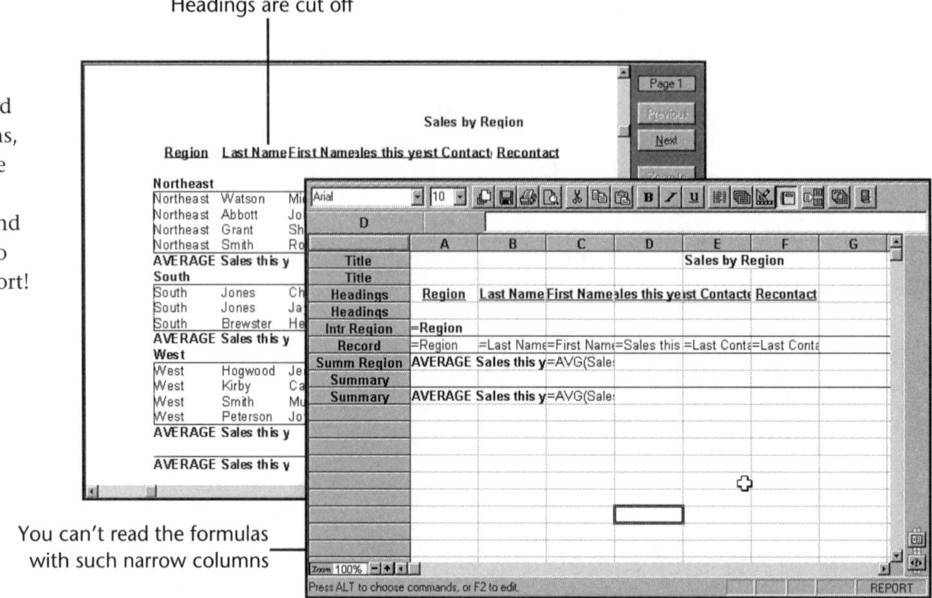

Fig. 23.10
Using standard column widths, it's hard to see your report definition—and even harder to read your report!

> **Caution**
>
> It's okay to widen columns in Report view just so you can see the formulas in them, but be sure to adjust the column widths to the way you want them in the actual report when you're done examining the formulas. If you make a column very wide in Report view so you can see its contents, the column might look unnaturally broad on your printed report.

To change column width or row height in Report view, you can simply drag the right or bottom border for the column or row you want to change. As you drag, the column or row changes.

If you want to set the column width or row height to a specific measurement, or return it to standard measurement, follow these steps:

1. Highlight the column or row you want to change by clicking the column or row label.

   You can select more than one row or column to take care of several at once.

2. Choose Format, Column Width or Row Height.

   The Format Row Height dialog box is shown in figure 23.11; the Format Column Width dialog box looks virtually identical.

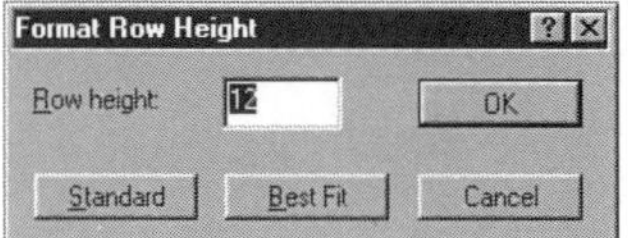

Fig. 23.11 The Format Row Height dialog box and the Format Column Width dialog box have the same settings, and work the same way.

3. Do one of the following:

   - Type a width between 1 and 79 (characters) or a height between 4 and 409 (points).
   - Click the Standard button to return the row or column to the default height or width.
   - When setting Row Height, click the Best Fit button to automatically adjust the row to accommodate the tallest entry. (Best Fit is not available for column width in Report view.)

   Caution

   If you use Best Fit, it adjusts the row based on the formulas in Report view; the setting it chooses might not be appropriate for the printed report.

4. Choose OK.

Tip
Another way to fix a long line is to make it wrap to a second line within its column. See the section "Changing Alignment in a Report" later in this chapter to learn how to do this.

Works adjusts the row height or column width. Figure 23.12 shows the report from figure 23.10, with each column widened enough so the data is not crowded. It looks much nicer!

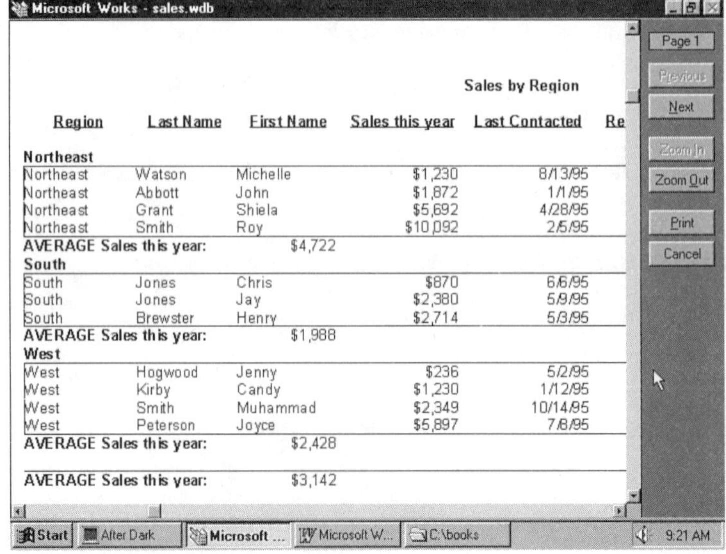

Fig. 23.12
The report is much more attractive when row and column heights and widths are set correctly.

Changing a Number Format

◄ See "Formatting Numbers in Fields," p. 372

In Chapter 17, "Modifying a Database Form," you learn how to change the number format of a field in a database form. For example, you can format currency amounts with dollar signs and two decimal places, and long numbers with comma separators after every third digit.

The number formats you assign to certain fields in Form Design or List view do not automatically translate to Report view. You must format the cell containing that field in Report view with the correct number format for that field. This might seem like an inconvenience, but it serves a practical purpose: flexibility. In Report view, you can format entire rows or columns at once, or you can format individual cells differently.

Follow these steps to change a field's number format in a report:

1. In Report view, highlight the entry or entries you want to format.

   For example, to apply the currency format to the sales figures (=Sales this Year), click the cell that contains that formula, or select the entire column.

Note

You can select a block of cells to format all at once, but you can't select non-contiguous cells in Report view, as you can in the spreadsheet.

2. Choose Format, Number.

   Works displays the Number tab of the Format dialog box, as shown in figure 23.13.

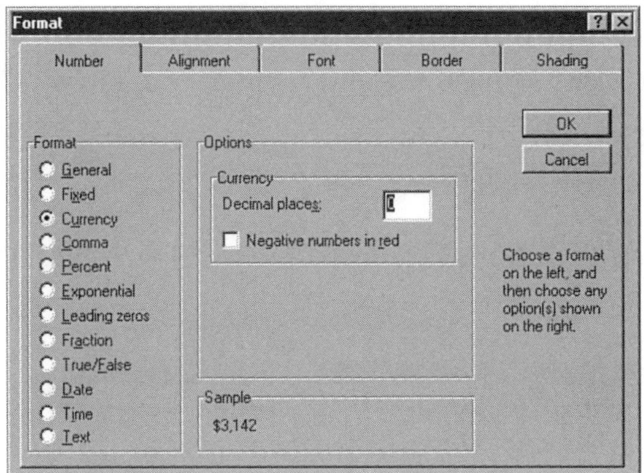

Fig. 23.13
Select a number format from the Number tab of the Format dialog box.

3. Choose the number format you want from the Format list.
4. If any options appear in the Options area, select the ones you want.

◄ See "Creating a New Database from Scratch," p. 337

When you choose a number format that uses decimal places, a box in the Options area of the Format dialog box enables you to set the number of decimal places you want to use (refer to fig. 23.13).

If you consistently find yourself changing this number, you should change the default number that appears in this box. Follow these steps:

1. Choose Tools, Options. The Options dialog box appears.
2. Click the Data Entry tab.
3. Type a new number in the Default number of decimals text box.
4. Choose OK.

Works changes the default number of decimals until you change the default again.

Changing Alignment in a Report

Report columns are sometimes easier to read when Works aligns the column contents flush left, flush right, or centered, depending on the type of data in the column. For example, text is easier to read when formatted flush left, and numbers are easier to read formatted flush right. This is the alignment that Works applies by default, but you can change the alignment for any column in Report view.

You also can have Works wrap long text in the specified column width.

Follow these steps to change the alignment in a row, column, or individual cell:

1. In Report view, highlight the row, column, or cell in which you want to change the alignment.

2. Choose Format, Alignment.

   Works displays the Alignment tab of the Format dialog box (see fig. 23.14).

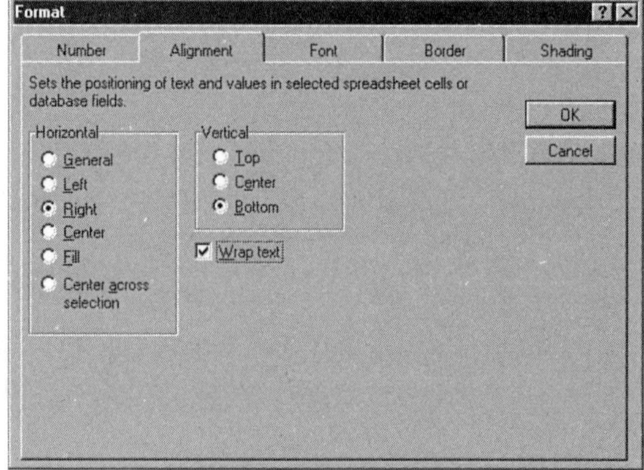

Fig. 23.14
Here you can align text and numbers horizontally and vertically in a cell and wrap long text.

3. Under Horizontal, choose General, Left, Right, Center, Fill, or Center Across Selection.

   General is the default alignment. It aligns text to the left and numbers to the right.

   Use the Fill option to copy a row heading into empty cells to the right or left of the heading. Select the heading and the empty cell or cells, and choose Fill.

Use Center Across Selection to center a title across several columns. To use this, you must have selected the columns in step 1.

4. In the Vertical area, choose Top, Center, or Bottom.

   When you align text vertically, Works moves the text or numbers to the top, bottom, or center of a cell.

5. If you want text that's longer than the column width to wrap to a second line, select the Wrap Text check box.

6. Click OK.

Tip
Works only wraps text. It does not wrap numbers, dates, times, percentages, or other values.

Choosing Fonts and Font Sizes, Styles, and Colors

When you create a report with ReportCreator, you have the opportunity to choose a single font and font size for the report. The resulting report is visually dull.

If you are preparing a report for a formal presentation, you probably want to improve its appearance. One of the best ways to begin "dressing up" your reports is by formatting text with fonts. Figure 23.15 shows the report you've been working with in this chapter, after some font and font size changes. It's much more attractive!

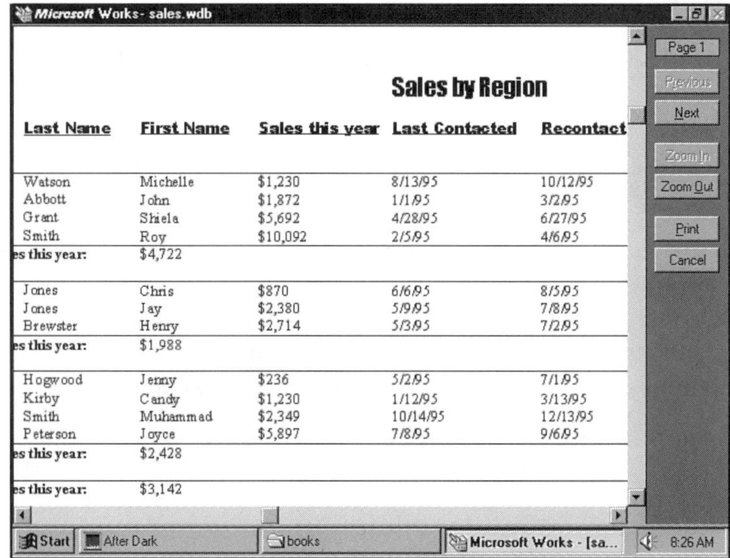

Fig. 23.15
The familiar sales report, dressed up with some different fonts.

◀ See "Changing the Appearance of Text," p. 377

Follow these steps to change the font for information in a report:

1. Highlight the rows, columns, or cells for which you want to change the font.

   For example, move the highlight into the cell that contains the report title.

2. Click the Font Name drop-down arrow on the toolbar (see fig. 23.16) and select a new font from the list.

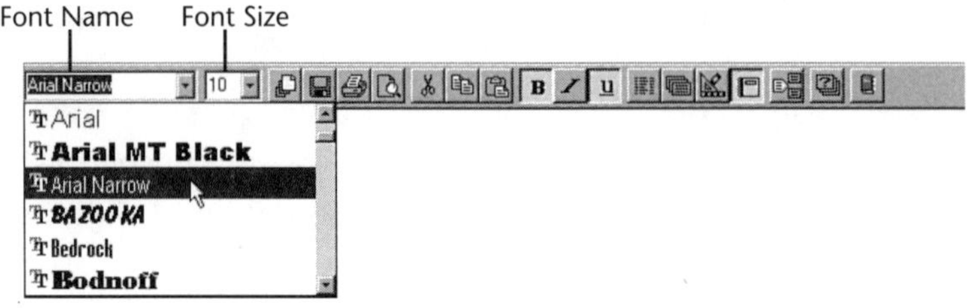

Fig. 23.16
The easiest way to change font and font size is with the drop-down lists on the toolbar.

3. Click the Font Size drop-down arrow and select a size from the list.

There are many more font and text options you can use in reports too:

- To apply bold, italic, or underline, click the appropriate buttons on the toolbar.
- To use colored fonts, choose Format, Font and Style, and choose from the Color drop-down list.
- To use strikethrough, choose Format, Font and Style, and select the Strikethrough check box.

Tip
You can also set the font, font size, bold, italic, and underline attributes by choosing Format, Font and Style.

To change the default font and style that Works uses for all new report definitions, choose Format, Font and Style, choose a Font, Size, Color, and so on, and then click the Set Default button. Works uses the new default font for each new database report, for databases that you design in List view, and for new spreadsheets, until you change the default again. Existing reports and spreadsheets are not changed.

Creating a Page Break in a Report

Page breaks enable you to divide report contents logically. Works' ReportCreator helped you insert some page breaks if you wanted (for instance, between groups), but you might want to insert your own page breaks as well. You can also insert a column page break to have Works print the columns to the right of the page break on a new page.

Tip
You can set a separate default font for database forms and for Works Word Processor documents. To set the default font for database forms, see Chapter 18, "Enhancing a Database Form."

When you create a report that is too wide for the paper you're printing on, Works automatically prints as many columns that will fit on the first page and prints the remaining columns on subsequent pages. You can use a column page break to tell Works which columns to print on each page. For example, you might prefer to print columns 1 through 3 on page 1, columns 4 and 5 on page 2, and columns 6 through 10 on page 3.

Row page breaks work differently, depending on where you insert them. For example, if you insert a page break between two Summ *<fieldname>* rows, Works inserts a page break after it prints each summary group for the field.

◄ See "Creating a Works Report," p. 455

Follow these steps to insert a page break in a report:

1. In Report view, highlight the row below the row where you want to insert a page break.

   or

   Highlight the column to the right of the column where you want to insert a page break.

2. Choose Format, Insert Page Break.

   Works inserts the page break. To see how the page break affects the report, display the report with Print Preview.

3. To remove a page break, place the highlight in the row below or the column to the right of the page break, then choose Format, Delete Page Break.

Note

If you don't select a row or column before you issue the Page Break command, a dialog box appears asking you whether you want a row or column break. Choose one or the other, then click OK.

Creating Report Headers and Footers and Numbering Pages

As with a Works word processor document, you can create headers and footers that print on each page of a report. A report header or footer can contain text such as the report title and author, the page number, the date, and so on.

Follow these steps to create a header or footer:

1. In Report view, choose View, Headers and Footers.

   Works displays the View Headers and Footers dialog box (see fig. 23.17).

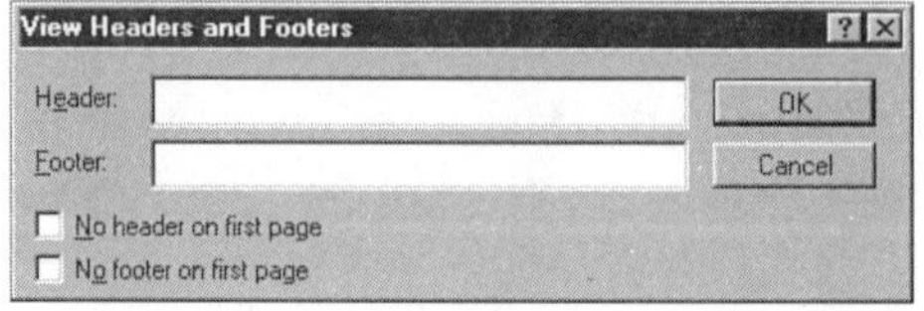

Fig. 23.17
Use the View Headers and Footers dialog box to print a header and/or footer on each report page.

2. In the Header and Footer text boxes, type the text for the header and/or footer, including the date, time, file name, page number, or special characters to align text.

◄ See "Creating Headers and Footers," p. 424

3. Choose No Header On First Page or No Footer On First Page to omit the header or footer from the first page of the report.
4. Choose OK.

You might occasionally have to change the page number that Works uses for the first page of a report. This might be necessary, for example, if you insert the report in a word processor document that someone else has created using a different application. Follow these steps to change the starting page number of the report:

1. From Report view, choose File, Page Setup.
2. Choose the Other Options tab.
3. In the Starting Page Number box, type the page number for the first page of the report.
4. Choose OK.

Works numbers the report beginning with the page number you typed.

To format headers or footers attractively, you can change the header or footer margins. For example, you might want to print a flush-left report title and flush-right page number in a header, and print this information using margins a little bit wider than the body of the report.

Follow these steps to change the header and footer margins:

1. Choose File, Page Setup.
2. Choose the Margins tab.
3. Type new settings in the Header Margin and Footer Margin boxes, or click the arrow buttons to set them.
4. Choose OK.

To remove headers and footers from a report, follow these steps:

1. Choose View, Headers and Footers.
2. Highlight the text in the Header or Footer box and press Delete or Backspace.
3. Choose OK. ❖

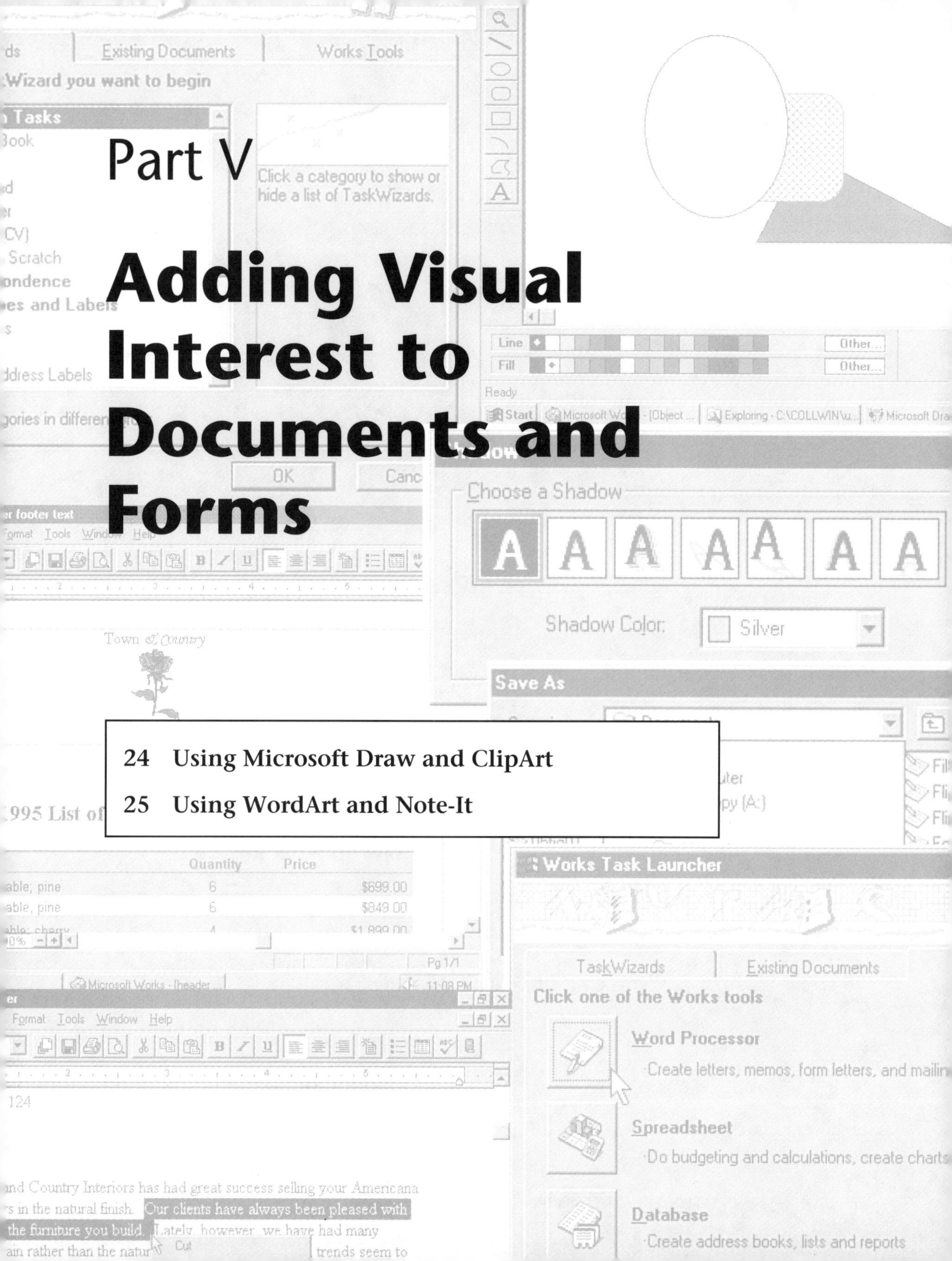

Part V

Adding Visual Interest to Documents and Forms

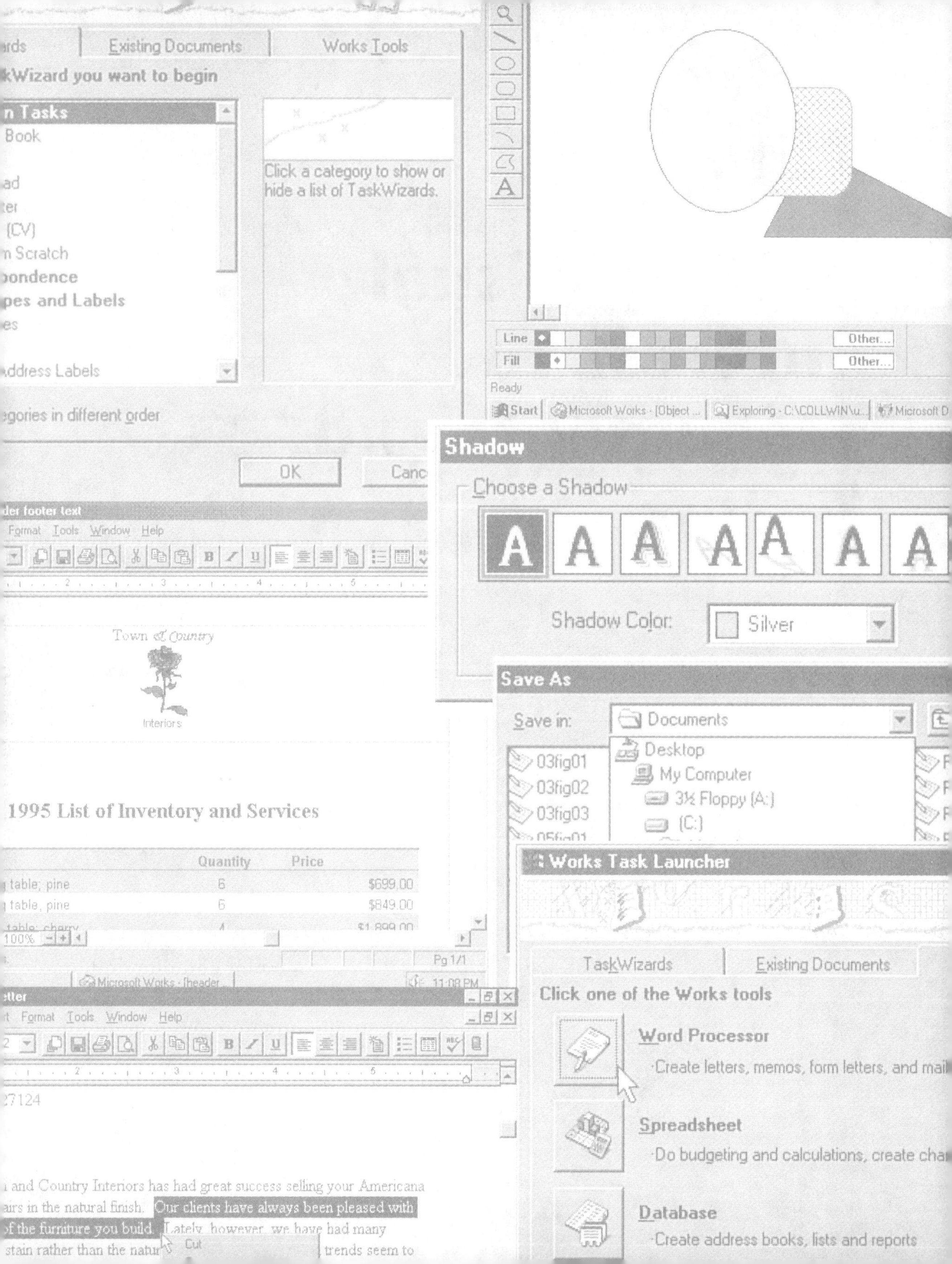

Existing Documents
Works Tools
Click a category to show or hide a list of TaskWizards.
OK
Line
Fill
Other...
Ready
Start
Shadow
Choose a Shadow
Shadow Color:
Silver
Save As
Save in:
Documents
Desktop
My Computer
3½ Floppy (A:)
(C:)
03fig01
03fig02
03fig03
Town & Country
Interiors
1995 List of Inventory and Services
Quantity
Price
Works Task Launcher
TaskWizards
Existing Documents
Click one of the Works tools
Word Processor
Create letters, memos, form letters, and mai
Spreadsheet
Do budgeting and calculations, create cha
Database
Create address books, lists and reports

Chapter 24

Using Microsoft Draw and ClipArt

by Debbie Walkowski

For each of the applications in Works, you have learned how to enhance the appearance of the documents you create by changing fonts and point sizes of text, aligning and formatting text in special ways, adding color, borders, patterns, and so on. But nothing enhances a document more than a picture. Works provides the means for you to include pictures in your word processor documents and database forms using Microsoft Draw or ClipArt.

Chapter 1, "Introducing Microsoft Works 4.0 for Windows 95," explains that Microsoft Draw is a special drawing tool included with Works that enables you to create your own color drawings. The ClipArt Gallery, also included in Works, is a collection of prepared drawings that span a wide variety of categories; you simply select the drawing you want and insert it in your document. Use Microsoft Draw or ClipArt to add humor, draw attention, or illustrate a point in a document or form.

In this chapter, you learn how to do the following:

- Insert drawings in word processor documents and database forms
- Create, save, and change a drawing using Microsoft Draw
- Select a ClipArt drawing to insert
- Size, modify, and delete a ClipArt drawing

Inserting Drawings in Documents and Forms

The word processor and database parts of this book introduce you to working with pictures, or *inserted objects*, as they are called in Works. Specifically, in Chapter 7, "Working with Tables, Columns, and Inserted Objects," and Chapter 17, "Modifying a Database Form," you learn how to work with inserted objects in a word processor document and database form. You learn how to position an object, size it, and format surrounding text. What you don't learn in these chapters is how to create and insert the object itself.

Before you can insert an object from Microsoft Draw or the ClipArt Gallery, you first must open a word processor document or a database form. From either of these types of documents, you have access to Microsoft Draw and ClipArt via the Insert menu, shown in figure 24.1. The bottom portion of the menu includes the ClipArt and Drawing commands. This particular menu is from the word processor application, but the same commands appear on the Insert menu in the database application.

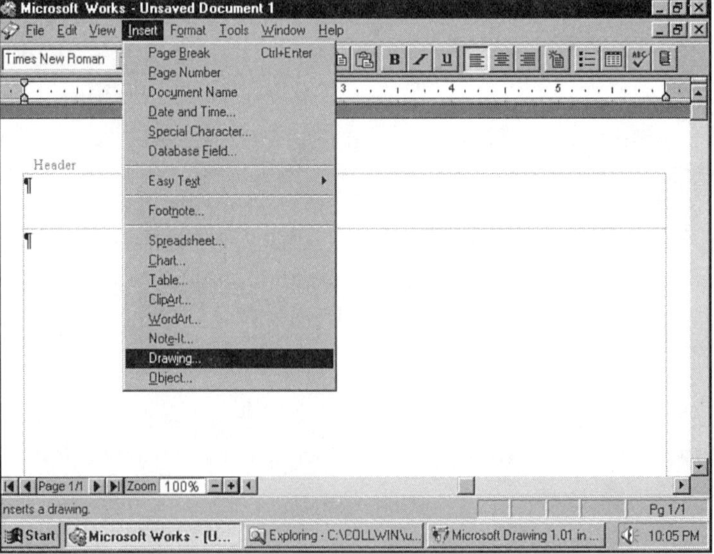

Fig. 24.1
The Insert menu gives you access to Microsoft ClipArt and Draw.

Before inserting an object, you move the highlight or insertion point to the position in your document where you want to insert the object. Then you choose the command you want to use.

When you choose Insert, Drawing, Works starts up Microsoft Draw in a separate window on-screen. You create your drawing, then insert it by returning to your document or database form.

When you choose Insert, ClipArt, Works displays the ClipArt Gallery dialog box from which you select a ClipArt picture to insert. After you select a picture, the ClipArt Gallery dialog box closes and Works copies the ClipArt picture into your document.

Creating and Saving a Drawing

After you display the Microsoft Draw window on-screen, you're ready to create a drawing. Microsoft Draw is a separate application program that has its own set of menus and drawing buttons. In figure 24.2, you see how the window looks on-screen after you choose Insert, Drawing.

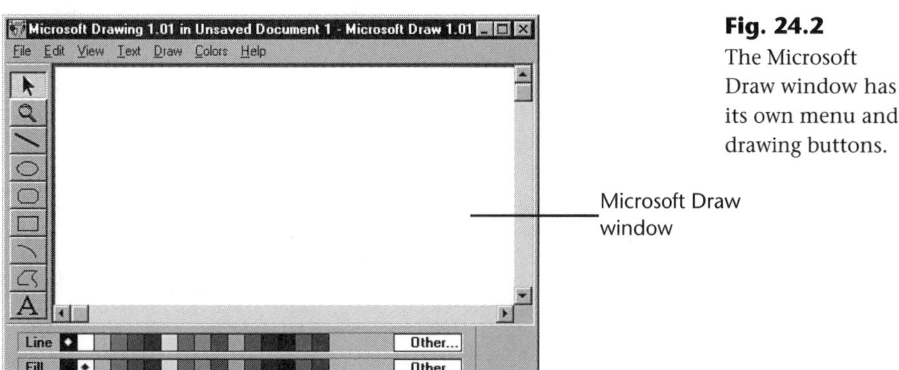

Fig. 24.2
The Microsoft Draw window has its own menu and drawing buttons.

The Draw window appears on top of the document window from which you chose the command—in this case, the word processor document window. The grayed area that appears in the document window acts as a place holder for the drawing you create. This place holder is a reminder to you that Works will place a drawing in your document at this location.

Note

Don't be concerned about the size of the grayed area; at this point it is simply a place holder and not representative of the size of the drawing you create. After you create the drawing, you can size it appropriately for your document.

Using the Drawing Tools

Along the left side of the Microsoft Draw window is a toolbar of drawing buttons (refer to fig. 24.2). You use these buttons to select and draw objects. Techniques for using each button are described in table 24.1.

Table 24.1 Microsoft Draw Drawing Buttons

Button	Purpose
Pointer	Selects objects.
Zoom	Enlarges or reduces your view of an entire drawing. To enlarge, click the Zoom button, then click the drawing repeatedly until it is the size you want. To reduce your view of a drawing, hold down the Shift key, then click the Zoom button repeatedly until the drawing is the size you want.
Line	Click and drag to draw a single straight line. To draw a line at any angle of 45° increments (0°, 45°, 90°, 135°, and so on), hold down the Shift key while dragging the Line button. To draw a line at any angle for which the center point is constrained, hold down the Ctrl key while dragging the Line button.
Oval	Click and drag to draw an ellipse. To draw a circle, hold down the Shift key while dragging this button. To draw a circle constrained to its center point, hold down the Ctrl key while dragging this button.
Rounded rectangle	Click and drag to draw a rectangle with rounded corners. To draw a square with rounded corners, hold down the Shift key while dragging this button. To draw a rectangle with rounded corners for which the center point is constrained, hold down the Ctrl key while dragging this button.
Rectangle	Click and drag to draw a rectangle. To draw a square, hold down the Shift key while dragging this button. To draw a rectangle for which the center point is constrained, hold down the Ctrl key while dragging this button.
Arc	Click and drag to draw a pie-wedge shaped object. To constrain the center point, hold down the Ctrl key while dragging this button. To draw a 45° angle with arc, hold down the Shift key while dragging this button.

Button	Purpose
Freeform	Click and drag to make a freeform drawing.
Text	Click, then type up to 255 letters on a single line of text.

To draw a line, circle/ellipse,rectangle/square, rounded rectangle/square, or arc, follow these steps:

1. Click the drawing button you want to use.
2. Move the crosshair mouse pointer to the location where you want to draw the object.
3. Press the Shift or Ctrl keys as indicated in table 24.1 to draw specialized objects (such as a perfect circle or a 45° line). Click and drag the mouse until you're satisfied with the shape of the object.
4. Release the mouse button. Four frame/resize handles appear at the outer corners of the object. (Two handles appear in the case of a line.)
5. Click any blank area of the drawing area or click the Pointer button to deselect the object.

Using the Freeform button, you can draw open objects or closed polygons, or open or closed freehand drawings. You also can combine straight lines and freehand drawing in one object. Examples are shown in figure 24.3. To draw polygons consisting of straight lines, you click and release the mouse button at each vertex of the polygon. To draw freehand shapes, click the Freeform button, then drag the crosshair mouse pointer, releasing the mouse button where you want the line or shape to end. The Freeform button remains in effect until you complete an object by double-clicking or pressing Enter.

To draw an open or closed polygon, use these steps:

1. Select the Freeform button.
2. Move the crosshair mouse pointer to the location where you want the object to begin.
3. Click the mouse button, then release it.
4. Move the crosshair to the point where you want the first line to end and the connecting line to begin.
5. Click the mouse button, then release it.

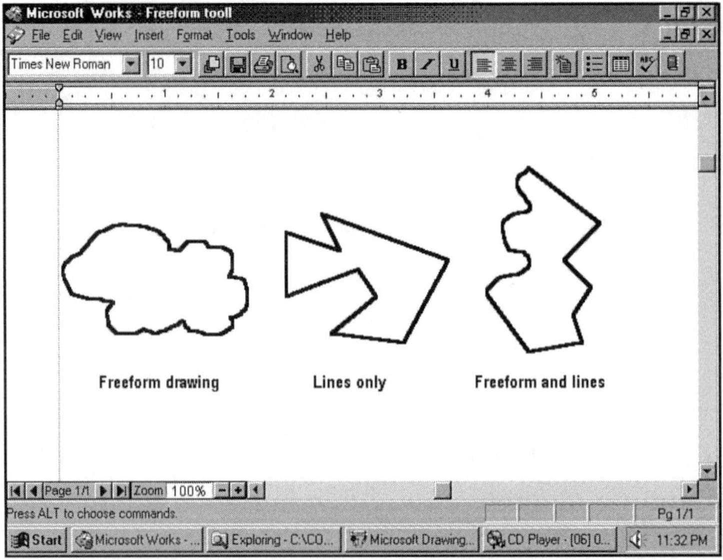

Fig. 24.3
These objects were drawn with the Freeform button.

6. Repeat steps 4 and 5, clicking the mouse button at each vertex.

7. To make the object an open polygon, double-click after you draw the last line or press Enter. To make the object a closed polygon, move the mouse pointer near the point where you began drawing, then click the mouse button. Works draws a straight line connecting the last line to the first.

8. Click the Pointer button or click anywhere in a blank area of the screen to deselect the object.

To draw an open or closed freehand shape, use these steps:

1. Select the Freeform button.

2. Move the crosshair mouse pointer to the location where you want the object to begin.

3. Click and drag the mouse in any direction, drawing the shape you want.

4. To leave the object open, double-click after you finish drawing or press Enter. To close the object, move the mouse pointer near the point where you began drawing, then click the mouse button. Works draws a straight line, connecting the beginning of the shape to the end of the shape.

5. Click the Pointer button or click anywhere in a blank area of the screen to deselect the object.

> **Note**
>
> While drawing freehand shapes, you can pause at any point by releasing the mouse button. Before beginning to draw again, position the crosshair in its location before you paused, then click and drag to continue drawing. To mix straight lines and freehand shapes in the same drawing, alternate between clicking the mouse and dragging the mouse.

Selecting Objects

Before you can make any changes to an object—move, copy, delete, resize, or enhance it—you first must select it. You select an object by clicking the Pointer button, then clicking anywhere on the border of the object. When you select an object, Works displays four black squares that form a rectangle surrounding the object (see fig. 24.4). The black squares, called *frame* or *resize handles,* enable you to adjust the size of the object. The handles also indicate that an object is selected.

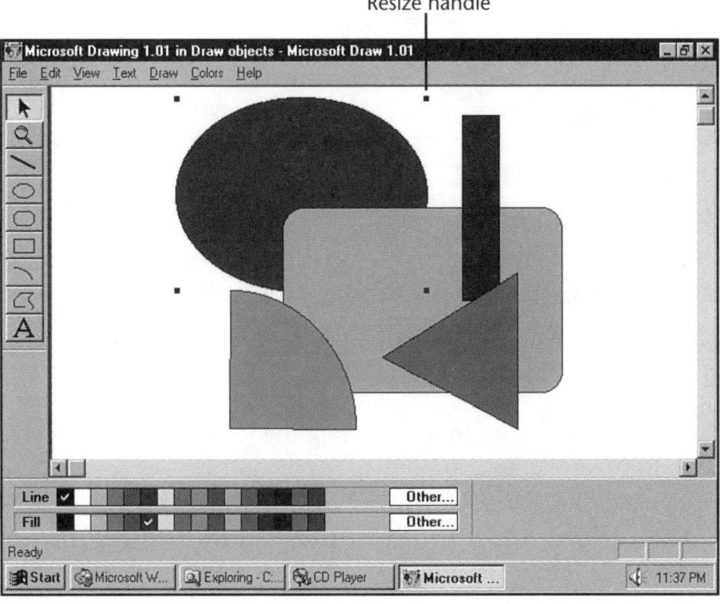

Fig. 24.4
The visible resize handles indicate the ellipse is selected.

Note

When you enter text in a drawing, Works considers text an object. You can select text just like any other type of object.

You can select multiple objects at the same time by holding down the Shift key as you click each object individually. After you have selected all the objects you want to include, release the Shift key. Figure 24.5 shows a group of objects selected.

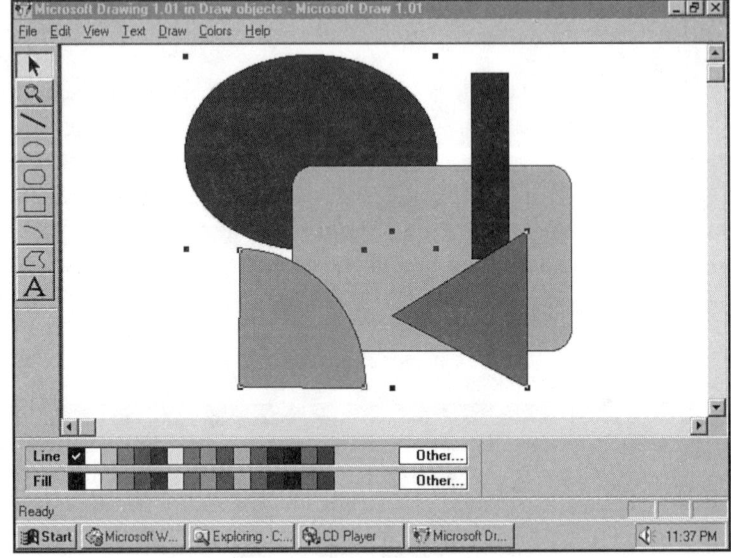

Fig. 24.5
Select multiple objects by holding the Shift key as you click. Here, the ellipse, arc, and triangle are selected.

Tip
When you want to select *all* objects in a drawing, choose Edit, Select All, or press Ctrl+A. This command is particularly useful when you want to clear the current drawing and start over.

Another way to select multiple objects is to draw a selection box around them, as described in the following steps:

1. Select the Pointer button from the toolbar.

2. Click and drag the crosshair pointer from the upper-left corner of the first object to the lower-right corner of the last object you want to include in the selection. As you drag the mouse, a selection box in the form of a dashed rectangle defines the area you cover (see fig. 24.6).

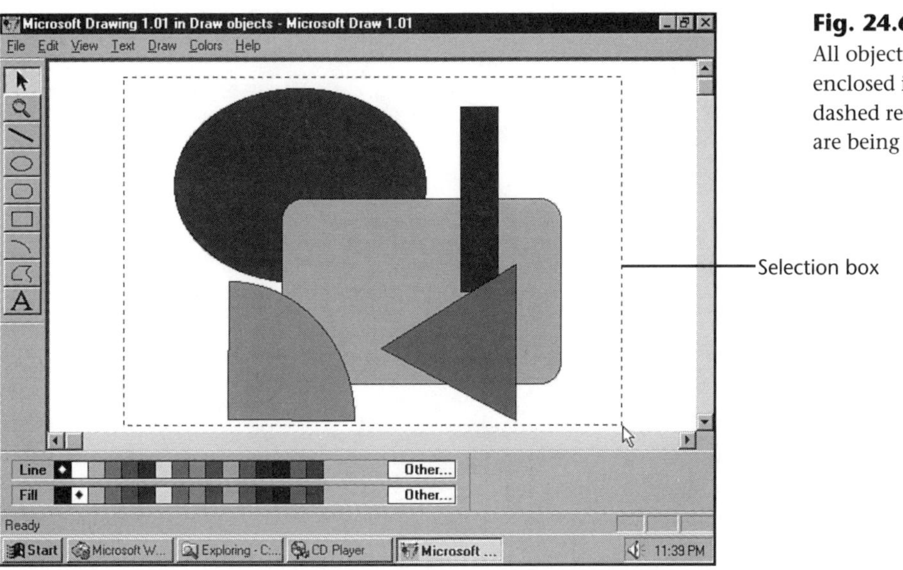

Fig. 24.6
All objects enclosed in the dashed rectangle are being selected.

3. Release the mouse button. Draw selects all objects that you fully enclosed in the selection box. You can add objects to the selection by holding down the Shift key as you click additional objects.

If you select the wrong object, you easily can cancel the selection by clicking any blank part of the drawing area. If you have selected multiple objects and want to remove one object from the selection, hold down the Shift key and click again on the object you want to remove. Works removes only the object you click from the selection.

Tip
To group several objects together and treat them as a single object, select the objects and choose Draw, Group or press Ctrl+G. To ungroup grouped objects, choose Draw, Ungroup or press Ctrl+H.

Using Color in a Drawing

Color is one of the most important aspects of a drawing. Using Draw, you can change the line color or the fill color of objects. In this context, *line* refers to individual lines, the frame or outline of objects, text, and the foreground of a pattern. (You learn about using patterns later in this chapter.) *Fill* refers to the interior portion of a closed object or the background of a pattern. Available colors are shown on the color palette at the bottom of the Draw window (see fig. 24.7). A diamond marker on the palette indicates the default colors Draw uses for line (black) and fill (white). When an object is selected, a check mark indicates the line and fill colors the object uses.

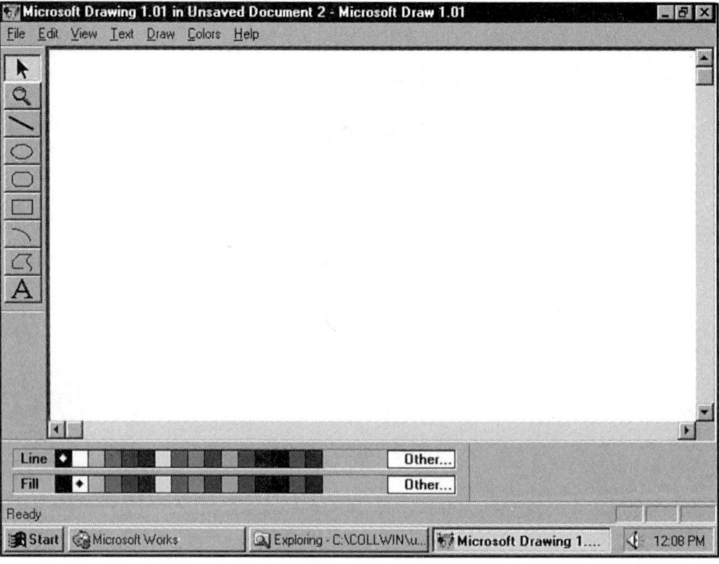

Fig. 24.7
Select a line and fill color for all objects and text in a drawing.

To change the line or fill color of an object, select the object, then click a color in the appropriate palette. A check mark appears on the color you select as long as the object is still selected. When you cancel the selection, the diamond markers return to the color palette, indicating the default colors.

You also can select a line and fill color *before* you draw an object. Click the Pointer button or click any blank area of the drawing palette to make sure no objects are selected. Select the line and fill colors you want to use for all new objects you draw. Diamond markers appear on the colors you select, indicating these colors now are the default colors. Click a drawing button and begin drawing. The new colors you select remain in effect until you select new default colors.

Entering and Editing Text in a Drawing

To add text to a drawing, click the Text button. When you move the mouse pointer into the drawing area, the pointer changes to a vertical bar insertion point. Click the drawing area where you want the text to appear, then begin typing. You can type up to 255 characters on a single line of text (Draw does not wrap text). After you finish entering text, press Enter or click any blank portion of the drawing area to select the text you typed. Click again in any blank portion of the drawing area or click the Pointer button to cancel the selection.

If you create a particularly long text object and realize it contains an error, you can correct the error without retyping the entire entry. To edit the text, select the text object, then choose Edit, Edit Text or press Ctrl+E. When you choose this command, the insertion point is visible at the beginning of the text entry. (You also can double-click the character you want to edit to place the insertion point at that location.) Use the arrow keys to move the insertion point to the character you want to correct. Use the Delete or Backspace keys to erase the error, then retype.

Tip
If the Text button isn't visible in your Draw window (you can't see it in fig. 24.7), resize or expand the window until the Text button is visible.

Note

You can edit text in a drawing at any time; even after you insert the drawing in your document. Just double-click the drawing to recall the Draw window.

The default font and size used when you create a text object is System 12 Bold. You can use the Font dialog box to select a different font, size, and style (see fig. 24.8).

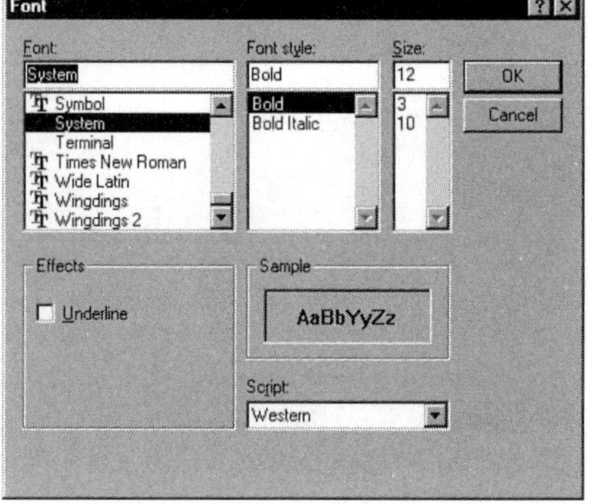

Fig. 24.8
The Font dialog box enables you to change a font, size, and style.

To change the font or size of an existing text object, follow these steps:

1. Select the text for which you want to change the font or size. Works displays the frame/resize handles for the object.

2. Choose Text, Font. The Font dialog box shown in figure 24.8 appears.

3. To change the font, select a font name in the Font list.

4. To change the font style (such as italic, bold, and bold italic), select an option in the Font Style list.

5. To change the size of the font, select a point size in the Size list.

6. To underline text, select the Underline check box.

7. Click OK.

The fonts used in figure 24.9 are Monotype Corsiva, Arial, Desdemona, and Braggadocio. These fonts appear in a variety of point sizes.

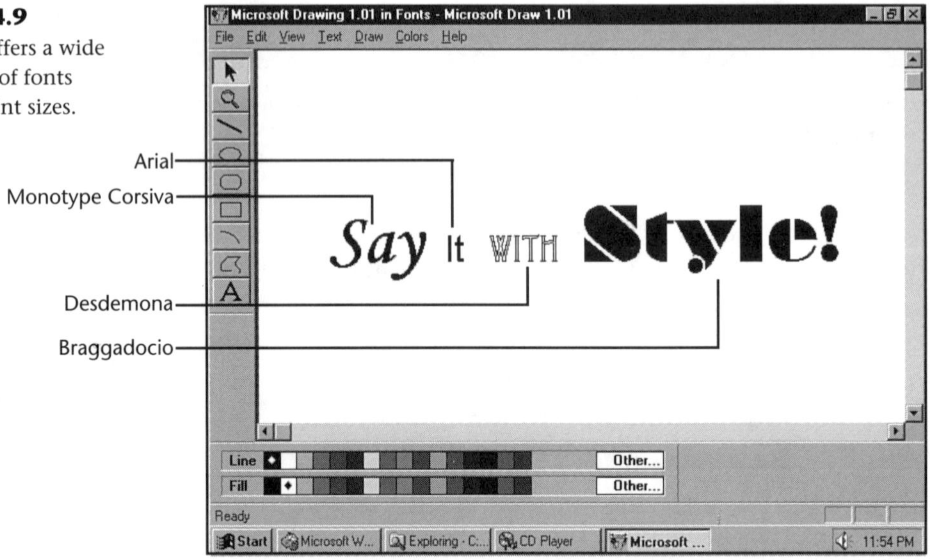

Fig. 24.9
Draw offers a wide variety of fonts and point sizes.

Arial
Monotype Corsiva
Desdemona
Braggadocio

You also can change the default font and size. When you change the default font and size, all new text you type conforms to the font and size you specify until you select a new font and size. To change the default font and size, click the Pointer button or click any blank portion of the drawing area to make sure no objects are selected. Then make your choices using the Text, Font command. Works places a diamond marker next to the font and size you select, indicating they are now the default settings. Now when you enter new text, it appears in the new default font and size.

Saving Your Drawing in Your Document

After you complete your drawing and you are ready to insert it in your document, choose File, Exit and Return. When you choose this command, you are asked if you want to save changes to Microsoft Drawing in your document. Choose Yes, No, or Cancel. When you choose Yes, the Draw window closes and Works automatically inserts the drawing in the database form or word processor document you are using.

If you want, you can insert intermediate versions of a drawing into a database form or word processor document as you are working. This process is called *updating* and ensures that your document includes at least the previous version of your drawing. When creating a complex drawing, updating is an important feature that prevents you from losing your drawing should your equipment fail or a power interruption occur. To update a document at any point, choose File, Update in Draw.

Troubleshooting

I drew a selection box around several objects to select all of them, but some of the objects I included were not selected.

When you draw a selection box using the Pointer button, you must completely enclose all objects you want to select. Any objects that are only partially enclosed in the selection box are not included in the selection.

I changed the fill color of an object to red. Now all new objects I draw are filled with red.

You changed the default fill color instead of changing the color of a single object. To restore the default fill color of white, click the Pointer button to make sure no objects are selected. Then click the white square in the fill color palette. The diamond on the white square indicates white is the default color for all new objects you draw.

When I try to draw any type of object or enter text, nothing shows on-screen except frame/resize handles. What's wrong?

You changed the default line color to white, which matches the default fill color as well as the screen background, so your objects are not visible on-screen. To recover the objects you drew, choose the Edit, Select All command, then change the default line color back to black (or any other color that's visible on a white background).

Editing a Drawing

Just as you can edit text in a document, you can edit an inserted drawing. Editing includes changing the pattern or line style used in an object; copying, moving, and deleting objects; rearranging the order of objects; and sizing, rotating, and flipping objects. To edit a drawing, double-click the drawing in your word processor document or database form. The Microsoft Draw window opens with your drawing displayed.

Changing Your View of a Drawing

Changing your view of a drawing can help you see portions up close, or you can view an entire drawing that is too large to appear on-screen at full size. This feature is called *zoom*. You can use the View menu or the Zoom button on the drawing toolbar to change your view of a drawing. The View menu, shown in figure 24.10, indicates that you can reduce a drawing to 25%, 50%, or 75%. You also can enlarge a drawing to 200%, 400%, or 800%. Just select the percentage you want to use from the View menu. When you want to return to 100%, or full-size view, choose the View, Full Size command.

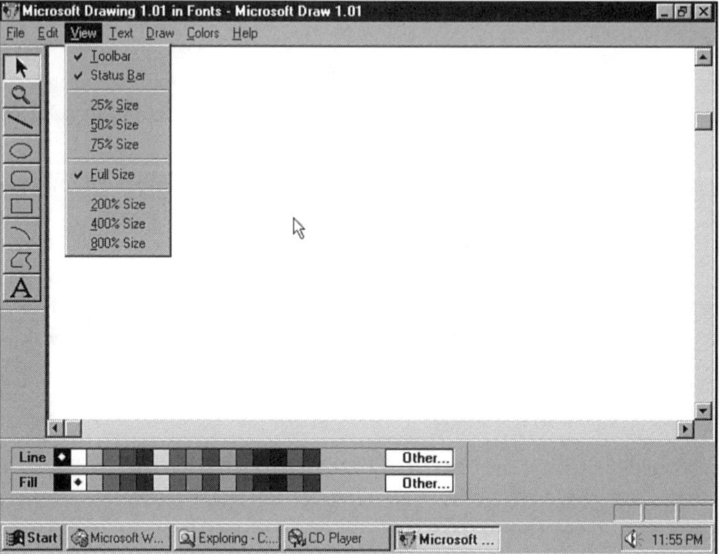

Fig. 24.10
The View menu enables you to enlarge or reduce your view of a drawing.

To change your view of a drawing using the Zoom button, click the button to select it. The mouse pointer changes to a magnifying glass with a + (plus) symbol inside. Click anywhere in the drawing area to zoom to 200%. Click a second time to zoom to 400% or click a third time to zoom to 800%. (800% is the maximum magnification.) To reduce your view, hold down the Shift key while using the Zoom button. The magnifying glass mouse pointer now has a – (minus) symbol inside. Click anywhere in the drawing area until the drawing appears in the size you want.

Note

The zoom feature in Draw does not alter the size of the drawing, only your *view* of the drawing. To learn how to change the actual size of the drawing, see the section "Resizing, Rotating, and Flipping Objects" later in this chapter.

Selecting Line Styles and Patterns

Whenever you draw an object such as a circle or rectangle, an *outline* defines the object. By default, Draw uses a solid line the width of one point to define objects. However, you can increase the line width or change the line style (to dotted, dashed, and so on) using the Draw, Line Style command. The Line Style command displays a submenu that lists line style choices. If you prefer to set a custom line width, choose the Other option and enter a point size in the dialog box that appears. Examples of line styles and point sizes are shown in figure 24.11.

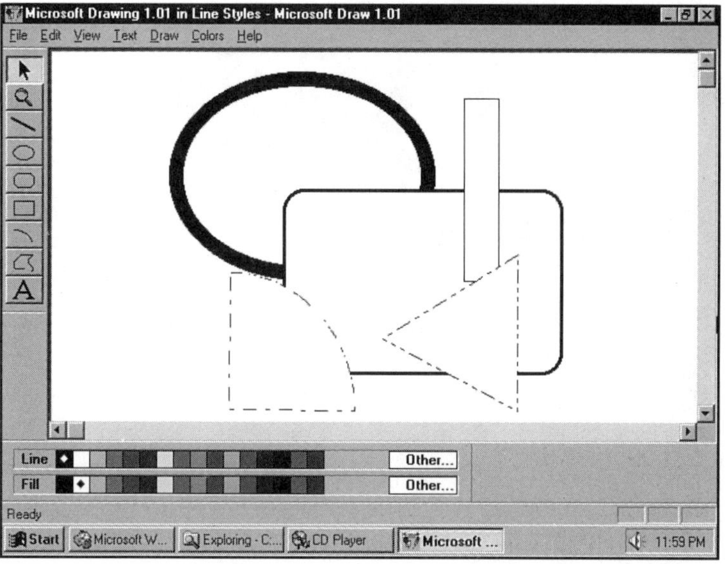

Fig. 24.11
Select a line style to suit your drawing.

As with fonts, sizes, and colors, you can change the line style for an existing object or the default settings for all new objects you create. To change an existing object, first select the object, then select a line style by choosing Draw, Line Style. While the object is selected, a check mark appears next to the line style the object currently uses. To change the default line style, click the Pointer button to make sure no objects in the drawing are selected, then select a new line style. On the Draw, Line Style submenu, diamond markers appear next to the current line style and width choices, indicating the default settings.

Earlier in this chapter, you learned how to fill an object with a color from the color palette. You also can fill an object with a two-color pattern. Available patterns appear when you choose Draw, Pattern. Pattern examples are shown in figure 24.12.

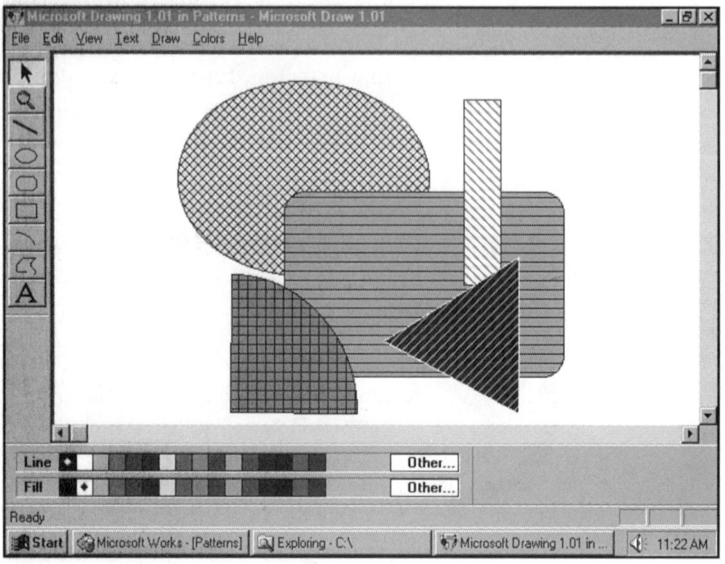

Fig. 24.12
Dress up an object by filling it with a pattern rather than a solid color.

Tip
When you are moving, copying, or deleting a large number of objects, you can select all objects in an area quickly by enclosing them in a selection box. See "Selecting Objects," earlier in this chapter.

To fill an object with a pattern, select the object, then select a pattern style from the Pattern submenu. If you are using the default line and fill colors, Draw makes the pattern background white and the pattern foreground black. To change the colors used in the pattern, select the object, then select line and fill colors from the color palette at the bottom of the Draw window. Draw changes the black and white to the colors you select.

Moving, Copying, and Deleting Objects

In a text document, you frequently move, copy, and delete words, phrases, sentences, and entire paragraphs. In a drawing, moving, copying, and deleting objects are common tasks as well, and you use the same commands and keystrokes you use for text.

To move an object, select it and drag it in any direction to a new location. After you have properly positioned the object, release the mouse button.

To copy an object, select it, then choose Edit, Copy. The keyboard shortcut for the Copy command is Ctrl+C. This command does not remove or change the selected object, but Works places a copy of the object on the Clipboard. To insert a copy of the object, choose Edit, Paste. The keyboard shortcut for the Paste command is Ctrl+V. Draw pastes a copy of the object near the original object. You then can move the object to a new location if you want.

To delete an object, begin by selecting the object, then choose Edit, Clear or press the Delete key. If you think you may want to use the object again later, choose Edit, Cut, which places a copy on the Clipboard.

Caution

When you place an object on the Clipboard using Edit, Cut, it remains there only until you cut another object from your drawing; the second cut object replaces the first. If you want to use the first object, be sure to paste it into your drawing before you cut any other objects.

You can move, copy, and delete more than one object at a time if you want. To move a group of objects, select all objects, then drag them to a new position and release the mouse button. To copy or delete multiple objects, select all objects, then use the Copy or Delete commands on the Edit menu, or use the appropriate keyboard shortcuts.

Rearranging the Order of Objects

If you draw multiple objects in succession and overlap them, each new object you draw appears on top of the previous one, as shown in figure 24.13.

You can change the order in which Works stacks objects by Choosing Edit, Bring to Front and Edit, Send to Back. The Edit, Bring to Front command brings the selected object to the top of the stack; the Edit, Send to Back command sends the selected object to the bottom of the stack. In figure 24.14, objects were rearranged using both of these commands. The keyboard shortcut for the Edit, Bring to Front command is Ctrl+=; the shortcut Ctrl+– sends the selected object to the back.

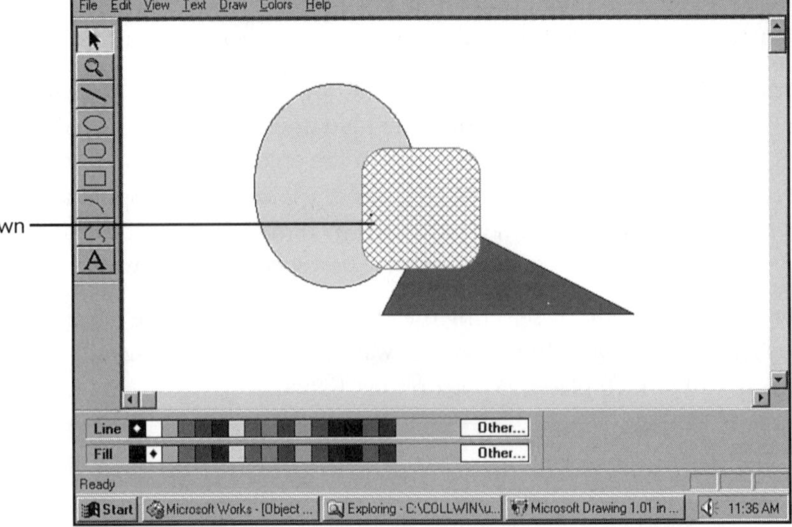

Fig. 24.13
When objects overlap, the most recent object appears on top.

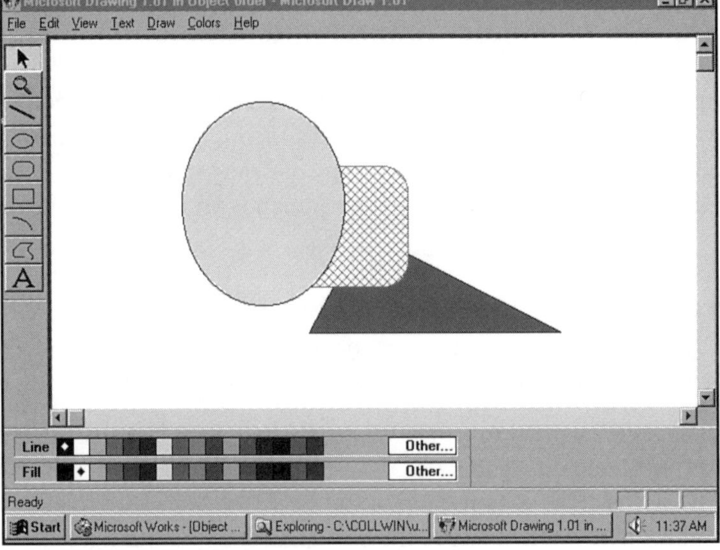

Fig. 24.14
You can restack objects using the Edit, Bring to Front and Edit, Send to Back commands.

Resizing, Rotating, and Flipping Objects

By now you are familiar with the frame/resize handles that appear each time you select an object. Resizing an object is as easy as dragging a resize handle in the direction you want to enlarge or shrink the object. For example, to increase or decrease the width of an object, select the object, then drag any of the resize handles to the left or right. Release the mouse button when the object is the width you want. To increase or decrease the height of an object, select the object, then drag a resize handle up or down. You can change an object's height and width at the same time by dragging a resize handle diagonally.

Microsoft Draw also enables you to rotate an object to the right or left 90°. In effect, *rotating* an object turns an object on its side. An example is shown in figure 24.15.

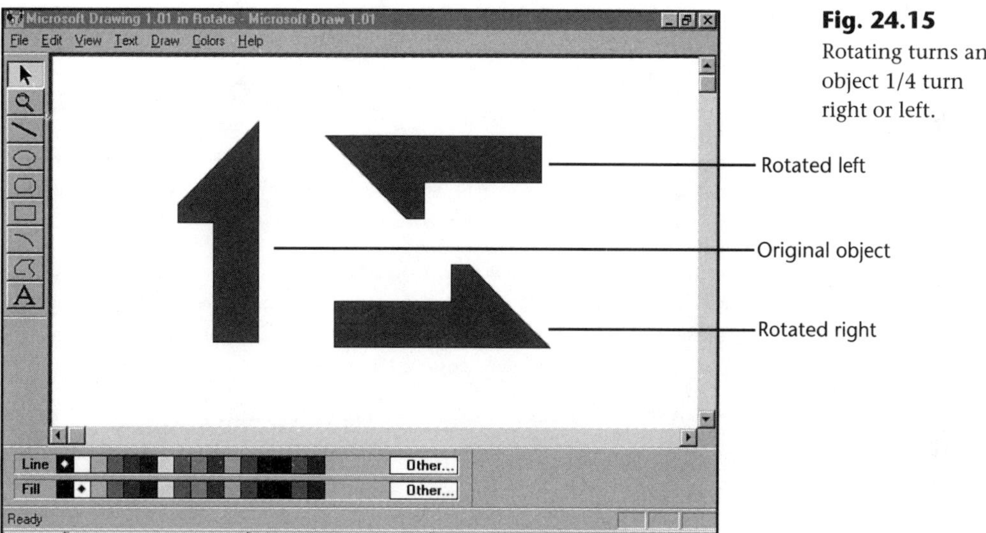

Fig. 24.15
Rotating turns an object 1/4 turn right or left.

To rotate an object to the right or left, select the object, then choose Draw, Rotate/Flip. From the submenu that appears, choose the Rotate Left or Rotate Right command.

Flipping enables you to create a mirror image of an object. You can flip an object vertically to turn it upside down or horizontally to turn it backward. To flip an object, select the object, then choose Draw, Rotate/Flip. From the submenu that appears, choose the Flip Horizontally or Flip Vertically command. An example of flipped objects is shown in figure 24.16.

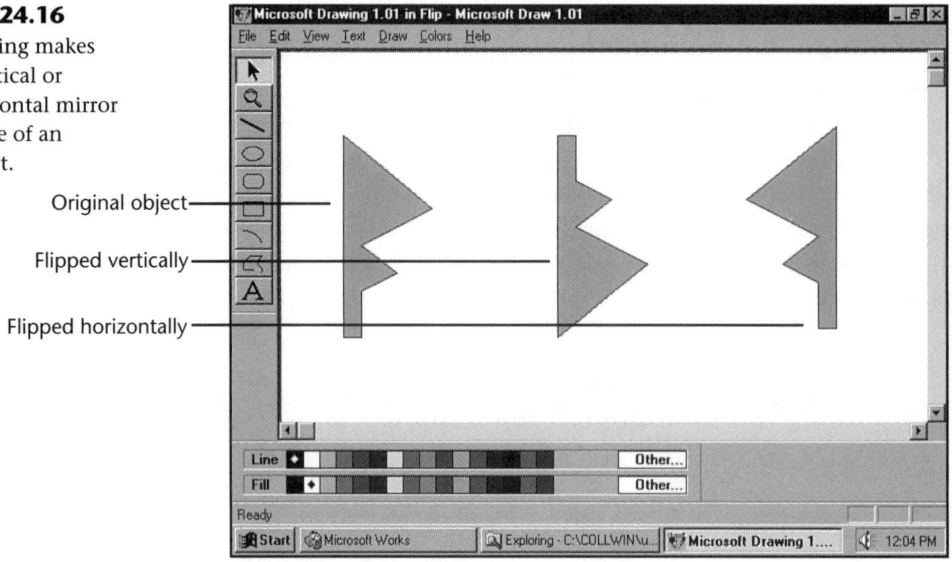

Fig. 24.16
Flipping makes a vertical or horizontal mirror image of an object.

Original object

Flipped vertically

Flipped horizontally

Troubleshooting

When I try to select and copy an object, nothing happens—I don't see the copy of the selected object on-screen, only the original object.

If you are using an enlarged view when you copy an object—especially 400% or 800%—you may not see the copy of the object on-screen because the view is too large. Switch back to full-size view before copying. When you use full-size view, Draw pastes the copy on-screen very close to (often overlapping) the original object.

When I try to move an object, Draw resizes the object instead. Why?

If Draw is resizing your object, you are dragging a resize handle. To move an object, click and drag it all in one step. If the object is already selected, click inside the object and drag it to a new location instead of clicking a handle.

I want to rotate (or flip) several objects as a single unit. Will Draw let me do this?

Yes, but you need to group the objects first. Select all objects you want to group, then choose Draw, Group. Draw encloses all objects within the boundaries of four frame/resize handles. You now can manipulate the objects as a single unit. You can edit the object in any way, including using the Draw, Rotate/Flip command. To separate the objects after you finish, choose Draw, Ungroup.

Using ClipArt

If you lack confidence in your drawing ability, ClipArt is a tremendous option you can use instead of drawing your own pictures. Even for the adept artist, ClipArt can be useful when you are in a hurry. Available directly from within a database form or word processor document, the ClipArt Gallery includes pictures across a wide range of categories. Just select the ClipArt picture you want to use and insert it in your document.

Choosing a ClipArt Picture

To select a ClipArt picture, move the highlight or insertion point in your database form or word processor document to the location where you want to insert a picture. Then choose Insert, ClipArt. Works displays the ClipArt Gallery dialog box shown in figure 24.17.

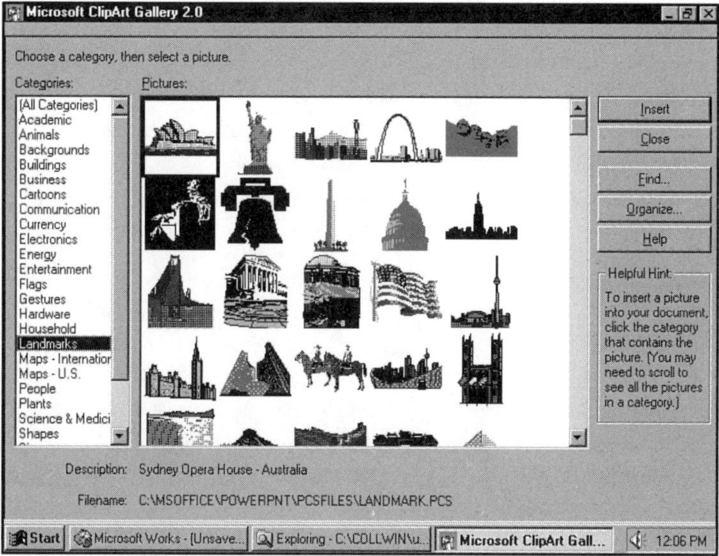

Fig. 24.17
Use the ClipArt Gallery dialog box to insert a ClipArt picture in your document or database form.

> **Note**
>
> Many application programs include ClipArt. Depending on the variety of applications installed on your computer, your screen might display different ClipArt categories than the ones shown in figure 24.17. This is because all applications that include ClipArt files use the common ClipArt Gallery.

On the left side of the dialog box is a list of categories. The area on the right side displays a sample of all ClipArt pictures in the current category. Figure 24.17 shows a selection of ClipArt pictures in the Landmarks category. Use the scroll bar to see a sample of each picture in a category. If you prefer to scroll through the entire selection, you can select the (All Categories) option in the Categories box.

When you find a ClipArt picture you want to use, click the picture to select it, then choose Insert. Works closes the ClipArt Gallery dialog box and returns to your database form or document, pasting a copy of the ClipArt picture at the insertion point.

Sizing and Arranging ClipArt

ClipArt pictures usually are quite large—often too large to view at 100% zoom. Switch to a zoom percentage that allows you to see the borders of the picture, then resize as needed.

Resizing objects, such as ClipArt pictures, is covered in detail in Chapter 7, "Working with Tables, Columns, and Inserted Objects." Refer to that chapter for specific instructions about resizing by using the frame/resize handles or by indicating a specific size in the Picture/Object dialog box. That chapter also discusses how to arrange the text surrounding an inserted object. For help sizing and arranging a ClipArt picture in a database form, refer to Chapter 17, "Modifying a Database Form."

Deleting ClipArt

To delete a ClipArt picture from a database form or word processor document, first select the picture. Then press the Delete key; or click the Cut button on the toolbar; or choose Edit, Cut. In a word processor document, Works automatically reformats the surrounding text. In a database form, surrounding fields remain unchanged. ❖

Using WordArt and Note-It

by Debbie Walkowski

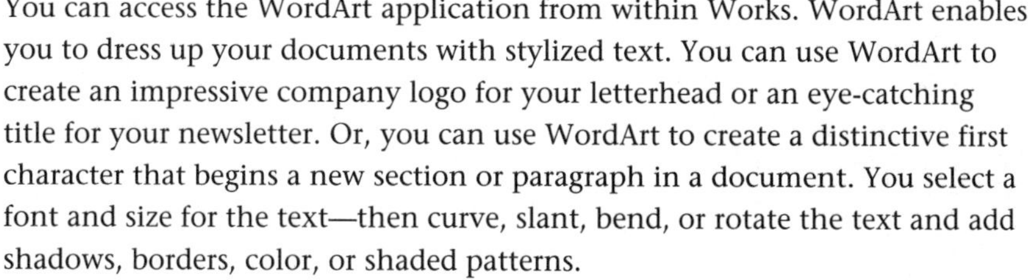

You can access the WordArt application from within Works. WordArt enables you to dress up your documents with stylized text. You can use WordArt to create an impressive company logo for your letterhead or an eye-catching title for your newsletter. Or, you can use WordArt to create a distinctive first character that begins a new section or paragraph in a document. You select a font and size for the text—then curve, slant, bend, or rotate the text and add shadows, borders, color, or shaded patterns.

Note-It is a handy tool that enables you to annotate your documents in a distinctive and unique way by creating pop-up notes. You can access Note-It within Works and use it to add instructions for working with a document, insert a reminder to yourself, include additional information on a particular topic, or include a note to a colleague. Note-It inserts an *icon* (a picture of a notepad, envelope, file folder, or other item) in your document to mark the location of the note. Just double-click the icon to pop up the note.

This chapter covers the following topics:

- Using the WordArt toolbar and menus
- Creating and editing WordArt text
- Adding special effects to WordArt text
- Sizing, moving, and deleting WordArt text

- Creating a note with Note-It
- Reading, editing, and deleting a note

Creating WordArt Text

When you choose Insert, WordArt, Works displays the Enter Your Text Here dialog box shown in figure 25.1. In the dialog box, the sample text, `Your Text Here`, is highlighted. When you begin entering your own text, the sample text disappears. Just above the dialog box is a grayed frame in your document that acts as a place holder for the WordArt you create.

Fig. 25.1
WordArt displays a dialog box and inserts a place holder in your document.

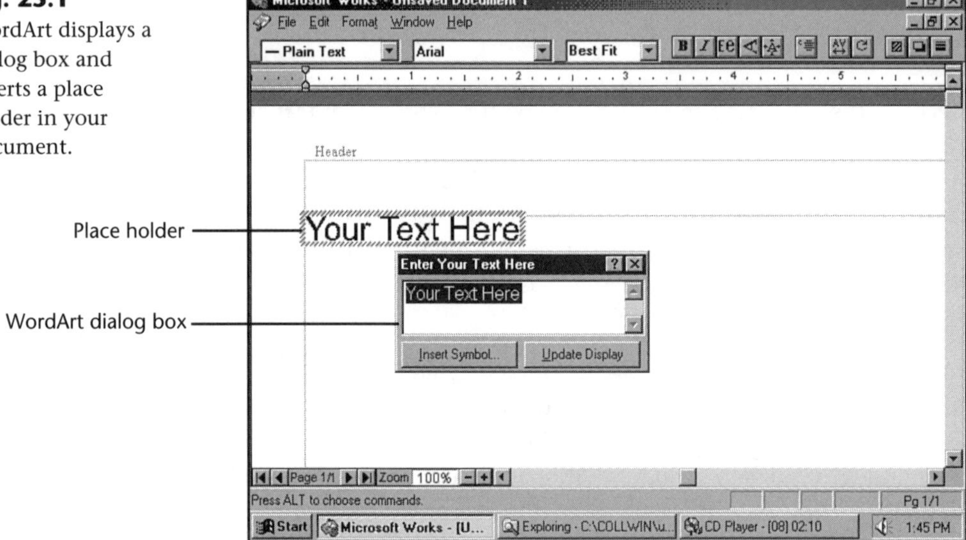

Tip
If the Enter Your Text Here dialog box obstructs your view of the WordArt in your document, drag the title bar to move the dialog box out of the way.

Examining the WordArt Toolbar and Menus

When you choose the Insert, WordArt command, notice that the menus and toolbar in the document window change to reflect WordArt commands. The File and Window menus are identical to those in the Works word processor and database components. The Help menu displays help topics on WordArt only. To change the font, size, shape, or add special effects to your WordArt text, you use the WordArt buttons on the toolbar. (Examples of special effects are shown in this section or later in the chapter.) The following list describes the toolbar buttons (from left to right):

- *Shape.* Click this button to display the Shape drop-down list. After you select a shape, your WordArt text follows the shape. For example, if you select a wave or semicircle, your text bends to form the shape of a wave or semicircle.
- *Font.* Select a font from the list. The available fonts are the same as those found in the word processor and database components.
- *Size.* Select a point size from the list. Choose the Best Fit option if you want Works to select the best point size to fit the WordArt frame.
- *Bold.* Changes the WordArt text to bold. This button toggles the Bold feature on and off.
- *Italic.* Changes the WordArt text to italic. This button toggles the Italic feature on and off.
- *Even Height.* Makes the letters in WordArt—including uppercase and lowercase—all the same height (see fig. 25.2). This button toggles the Even Height feature on and off.

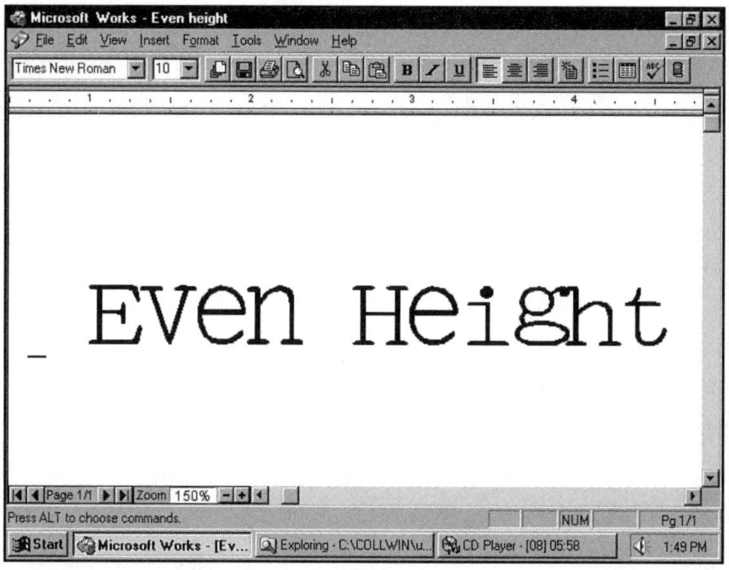

Fig. 25.2 WordArt can display characters at an even height, regardless of capitalization.

- *Flip.* Click this button to turn each letter on its side (see fig. 25.3). This button toggles the Flip feature on and off.

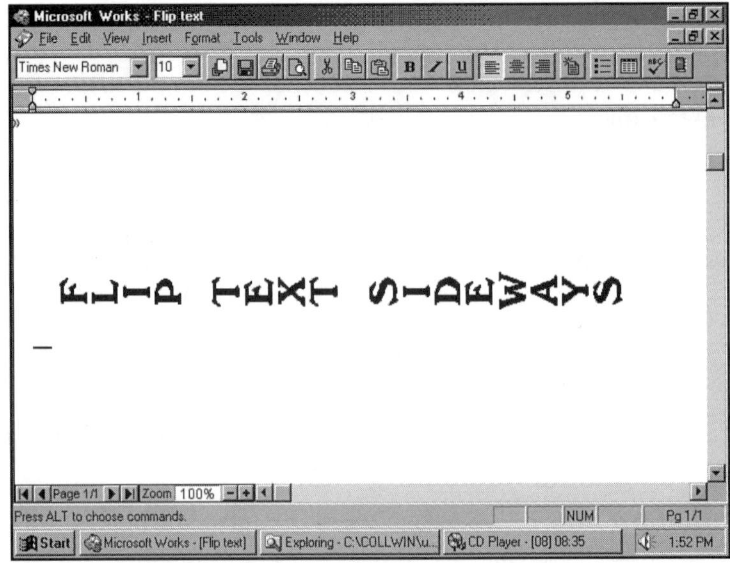

Fig. 25.3
Click the Flip button to turn individual letters on their side.

- *Stretch.* Click this button to make your text fill the WordArt frame horizontally and vertically. This button toggles the Stretch feature on and off. When the feature is off, WordArt text aligns in the center.
- *Align.* Select an alignment style to align the text within the WordArt frame. If you don't select a style, WordArt automatically uses the Center alignment style.
- *Spacing Between Characters.* Displays a dialog box that enables you to control the space between characters in WordArt. You can move characters closer together or farther apart.
- *Rotation.* Displays a dialog box that enables you to rotate text by degrees and adjust the angle or arc of the text.
- *Shading.* Displays the Shading dialog box in which you select a two-color shaded pattern and the foreground and background colors to apply to WordArt characters.
- *Shadow.* Displays a drop-down list of shadow styles for individual characters in your WordArt text (see fig. 25.4). To select a color for the shadow, click the More button to display a Shadow dialog box.

Fig. 25.4
The Shadow drop-down box displays shadow styles.

- *Border*. Displays the Border dialog box in which you select a border style and color. Note that in this context, border refers to a character border, not a frame border. When you select a border style or color, Works borders individual characters.

Creating and Editing WordArt Text

When you're ready to add WordArt to a document or database form, follow these steps:

1. Open the word processor file or database form to which you want to add WordArt text.
2. Place the insertion point at the location where you want to insert the WordArt text.
3. Choose Insert, WordArt. The Enter Your Text Here dialog box opens (refer to fig. 25.1).
4. Type your text in the dialog box. Press Enter if you want to begin a new line.
5. Click the appropriate toolbar buttons to add special effects to the text.
6. After you finish, click in the document where you want to continue working. Works closes the Enter Your Text Here dialog box and displays your WordArt text in your document or database form.
7. To save the WordArt text in your document or database form, choose File, Save or File, Save As, then continue working as usual.

From your database form or word processor document, you can return to the Enter Your Text Here dialog box at any time to change text or special effects of your WordArt text. Just double-click the WordArt text object in your document or database form, or select the WordArt object, then choose Edit, WordArt 2.0 Object, Edit. WordArt starts, and the Enter Your Text Here dialog box reappears. To change the text, click where you want to position the insertion point and then delete or retype existing text. Click the Update Display button to view the changes in your document. To change any special effects, click the appropriate toolbar buttons.

Adding Special Effects to WordArt Text

In the preceding section, you learned about the special effects you can apply to WordArt text. Some special effects—such as font, size, bold, italic, and even height, flip, stretch, and alignment—are self-explanatory. When you click the appropriate button, Works immediately applies the special effect to the WordArt text without displaying a dialog box.

This section describes and illustrates how to apply the special effects that require you to choose options or respond to a dialog box. These effects include shaping, spacing, rotating, shading, shadowing, and bordering. The important thing to remember when working with special effects is to *experiment.* Try different fonts with different effects. Explore how combinations of shapes and other effects change your WordArt—the possibilities are almost limitless. The examples in this section only introduce you to the possibilities.

As you add special effects to WordArt, you might see the Size Change dialog box shown in figure 25.5. This dialog box appears whenever the special effect you are using makes the text too large to fit in the current WordArt frame. Choose Yes to resize the WordArt frame to fit the text. (If you choose No, you can continue working but some of your text may not be visible in the WordArt frame at its current size.)

◀ See "Wrapping Text around Inserted Objects," p. 145

Note

You can resize a WordArt frame in your document at any time, just like you can resize any other type of object.

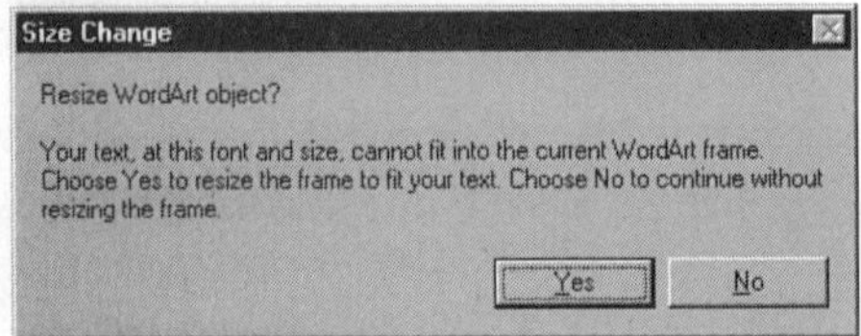

Fig. 25.5 Choose Yes to display your WordArt text accurately.

Wrapping Text in a Shape

Shaping text is one of the most important features of WordArt. Some word processors enable you to shade or shadow text, but few enable you to bend text to a particular shape. After you enter your text in the Enter Your Text Here dialog box, you can apply a shape or an angle. Click the Shape button to display the drop-down list, then click a shape or angle (see fig. 25.6).

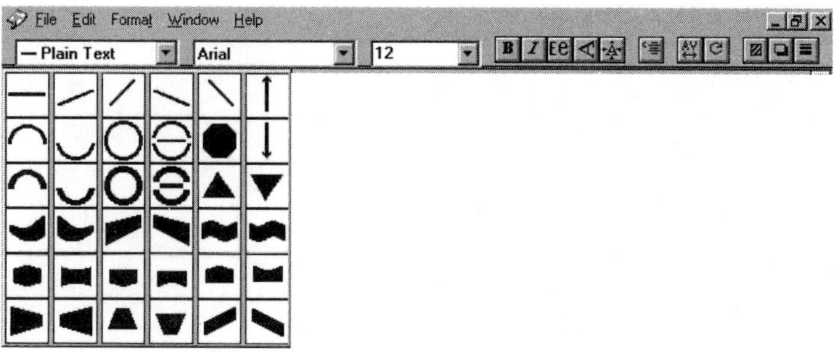

Fig. 25.6
Select a shape or an angle from the Shape drop-down list.

Tip
To display the name of a shape, select a shape from the Shape drop-down list. The name is displayed in the Shape button on the toolbar.

In figure 25.7, you see three examples of WordArt that conform to shapes. The first example uses the Slant Up shape, the second uses the Wave 1 shape, the third uses the Fade Down shape.

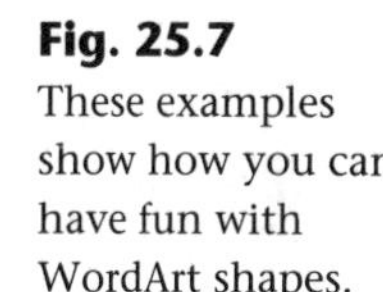

Fig. 25.7
These examples show how you can have fun with WordArt shapes.

Controlling Spacing

You can control the space between characters in WordArt by clicking the Spacing Between Characters button on the toolbar or choosing Format, Spacing Between Characters. Either method opens the Spacing Between Characters dialog box shown in figure 25.8.

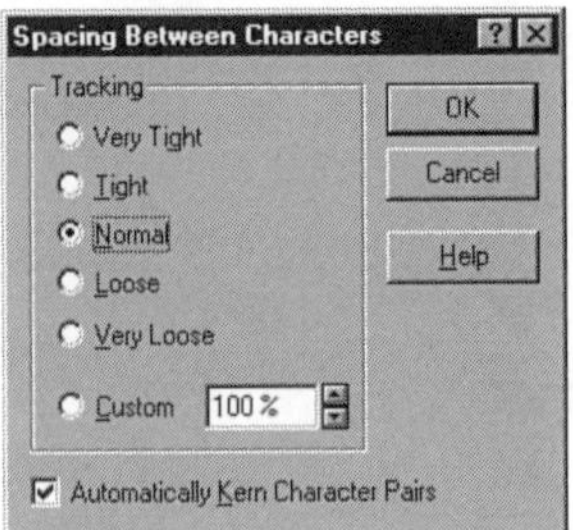

Fig. 25.8
Use the Spacing Between Characters dialog box to specify how tight characters are.

In the dialog box, *tracking* refers to the space between all characters in the WordArt frame. For instance, if you choose the Very Tight option, the characters in your WordArt text move as close together as possible (60 percent of their normal spacing). You can use the Custom option to enter a specific tracking percentage. Figure 25.9 shows examples of tracking percentages.

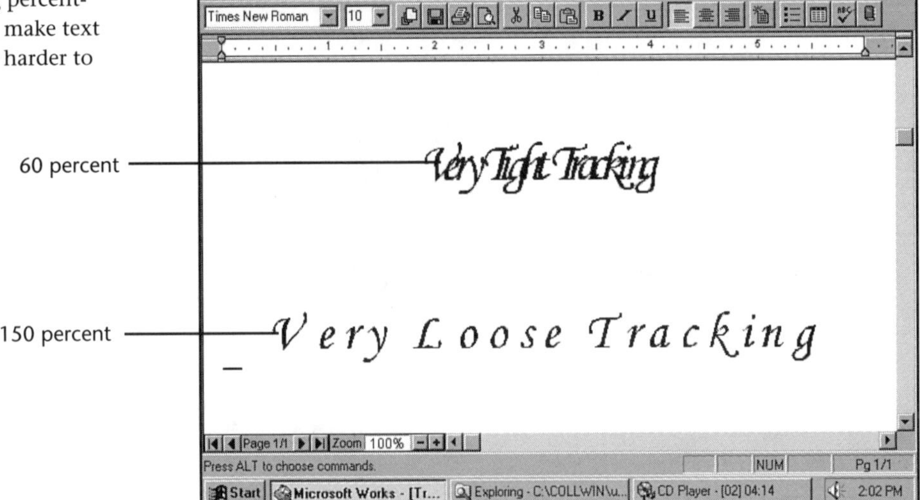

Fig. 25.9
Tracking percentages can make text easier or harder to read.

Kerning refers to the space between pairs of characters. Because of their shapes, certain characters typed next to one another often look like they are spaced too far apart. For instance, when you type the letters **Ti**, the stem on the T can cause a large space between the two characters depending on the font you use. Kerning moves the two characters closer together. To have WordArt automatically kern pairs of characters for you, choose the Automatically Kern Character Pairs check box.

Changing the Rotation, Arc, and Slant of WordArt Text

After you create WordArt text, you can rotate it, change the depth of its arc, or alter its slant. When you rotate WordArt text, you change the way the text revolves (right or left) around its center point. To rotate WordArt text, click the Rotation button on the toolbar or choose Format, Rotation and Effects. Either method opens the Special Effects dialog box shown in figure 25.10. In the Rotation box, click the up arrow to rotate text to the right; click the down arrow to rotate text to the left. Click OK when you're finished.

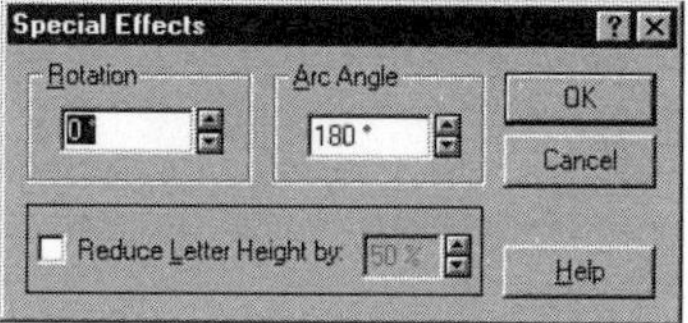

Fig. 25.10
Use the up and down arrows in the Rotation box to change the rotation (+ or – up to 360 degrees) of your WordArt text.

When you apply an arc shape (such as Arch Up) to WordArt text, you can control the depth of the arc. Choose Format, Rotation and Effects to display the Special Effects dialog box. In the Arc Angle box, click the up arrow to make the arc deeper; click the down arrow to make the arc shallower, then click OK. For example, if you applied the Arch Up shape to your text, the Arc Angle box shows that your text is arced at 180 degrees. If you change the setting to 90 degrees, you shallow out the arc to one half of its original depth.

If you applied any shape other than an arc (such as Slant Up, Slant Down, Fade Up, or Fade Down) to your WordArt text, you can alter the slant of the characters. To do this, choose Format, Rotation and Effects to display the Special Effects dialog box shown in figure 25.11. This dialog box is similar to the one shown in figure 25.10, except that the Slider box appears in place of the Arc Angle box. To adjust the slant of characters, click the up or down arrow key in the Slider box, then click OK.

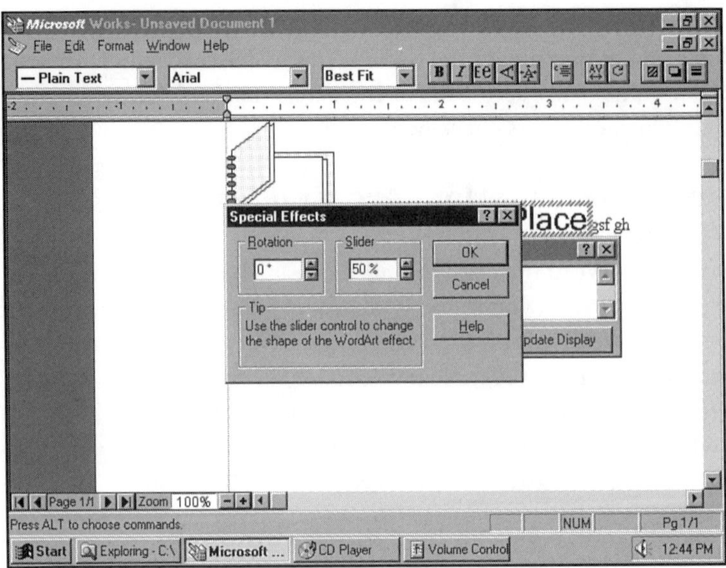

Fig. 25.11
The Slider setting changes the slant of WordArt text.

Experiment with all three of these special effects. In all cases, the shape you apply to the text *before* you add special effects will determine the final results.

Shading WordArt Text

To enhance WordArt text, you can add *shading* to individual characters. When you click the Shading button on the toolbar or choose Format, Shading, the Shading dialog box shown in figure 25.12 opens.

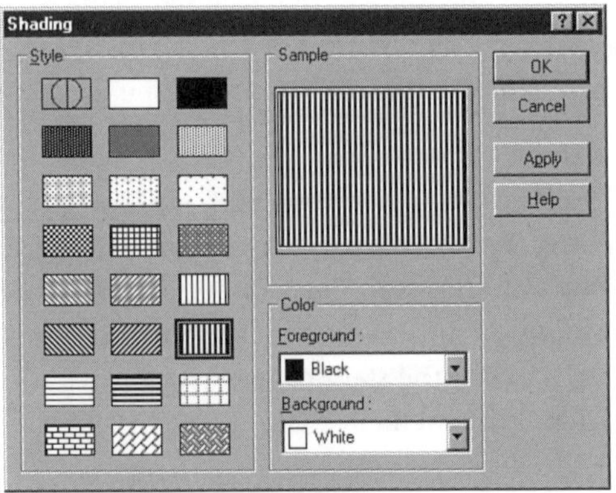

Fig. 25.12
Use the Shading dialog box to apply a shade pattern and color to WordArt.

From the Style box, select a shading style. From the Color box, select Foreground and Background colors. The Sample area displays the choices you make. Choose the Apply button to apply the selected shading to your WordArt. If you aren't satisfied with the way the shading looks, select a different pattern of colors then choose the Apply button again. When you're happy with the results, choose OK to close the Shading dialog box. An example of shaded WordArt is shown in figure 25.13.

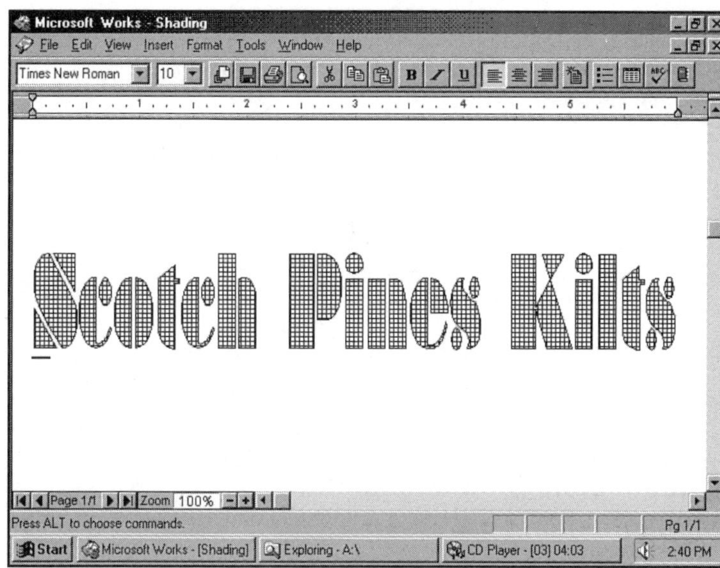

Fig. 25.13
Apply a pattern to dress up your WordArt text.

Shadowing and Bordering WordArt Text

Shadowing is a technique that adds depth to WordArt text by creating the illusion of light cast on the characters. You can select from several different styles of shadows, and you can specify the shadow's color rather than simply using gray.

Choose Format, Shadow to display the Shadow dialog box (see fig. 25.14). You also can display this dialog box by clicking the Shadow toolbar button (which displays a drop-down list of shadow styles), then selecting the More option from the drop-down list. To add a shadow to text, select a shadow style and color, then choose the OK button.

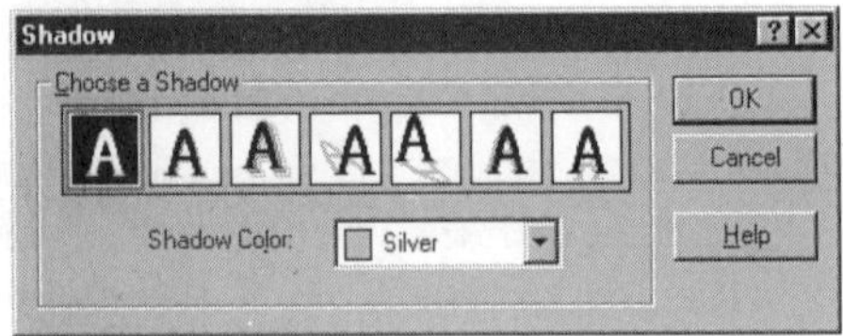

Fig. 25.14
Select a shadow style and color from the Shadow dialog box.

Bordering is a special effect that makes characters stand out by outlining each character individually. To specify the thickness of the border, choose Format, Border. The Border dialog box appears (see fig. 25.15). The default border color is the background color defined in the Shading dialog box. To change the border color, select a color from the Color drop-down list in the Border dialog box. Examples of shadows and borders are shown in figure 25.16.

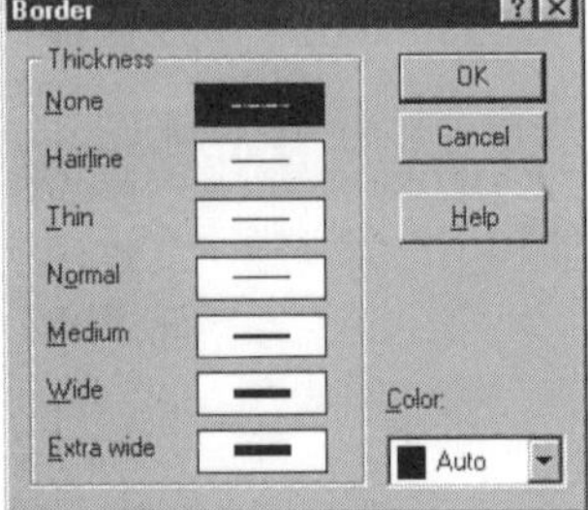

Fig. 25.15
Select a border style and color from the Border dialog box.

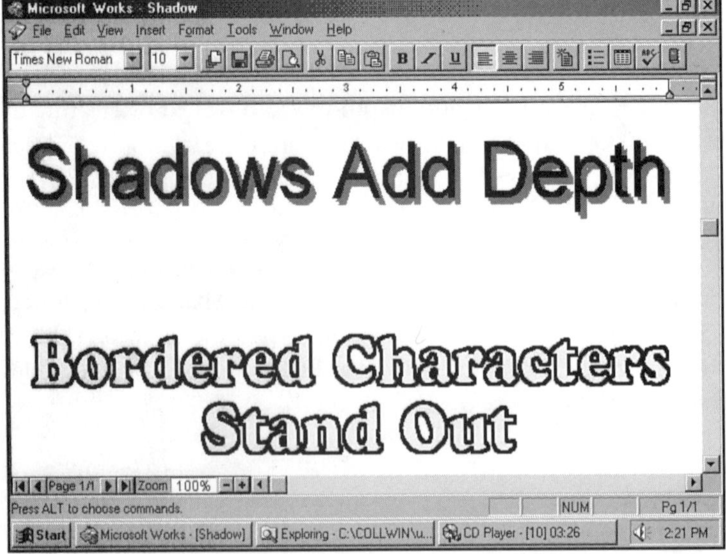

Fig. 25.16
Shadows add depth to WordArt, and borders make characters stand out.

Troubleshooting

How can I change the color of WordArt characters?

Although you don't apply a shade, you use the Shading dialog box to change the color of characters. In the dialog box, select a foreground or background color, then instead of applying a shading pattern, click the solid color in the top row of the Style box (refer to fig. 25.12).

I can't get my text to conform to the Button Pour and Button Curve shapes shown earlier in figure 25.6.

The Button Pour and Button Curve shapes require three lines of text in the Enter Your Text Here dialog box. Type the text you want to appear on the top curve, then press Enter and type the text you want to appear on the middle line. Press Enter again then type the text you want to appear on the bottom curve.

Tip

Works immediately applies shadows and borders to your WordArt characters when you choose options in the dialog boxes. To see how your choices look, move the dialog box out of the way if it obstructs your view.

Sizing and Positioning WordArt Text

When you return to your word processor document or database form, WordArt text appears in the position of the insertion point. You can move or resize WordArt just like you can any other inserted object (such as a Microsoft Draw drawing or ClipArt). Working with inserted objects is discussed in detail in Chapter 7, "Working with Tables, Columns, and Inserted Objects," and Chapter 17, "Modifying a Database Form." Refer to these chapters for specific instructions about moving, copying, and sizing inserted objects.

Deleting WordArt Text

To delete WordArt from a document or database form, click the WordArt object to select it. You can delete the selected object by choosing Edit, Cut; by pressing the Delete key on the keyboard; or by pressing Ctrl+X. If you delete WordArt by mistake, immediately choose Edit, Undo Editing or press Ctrl+Z to restore the WordArt.

Annotating Documents Using Note-It

Documents often contain notes of one sort or another, and the notes are always visible within the text of the document. Using Note-It, you can insert an icon, or picture, in a document rather than the note itself. When you want to read the note, you double-click the icon to pop up the note; otherwise, the note stays hidden.

The Note-It feature is especially useful for including instructions for using a document, inserting a reminder to yourself, or adding a comment for a colleague to read. An example of a note is shown in figure 25.17. In the figure, one note is closed, and the other note is popped up (open).

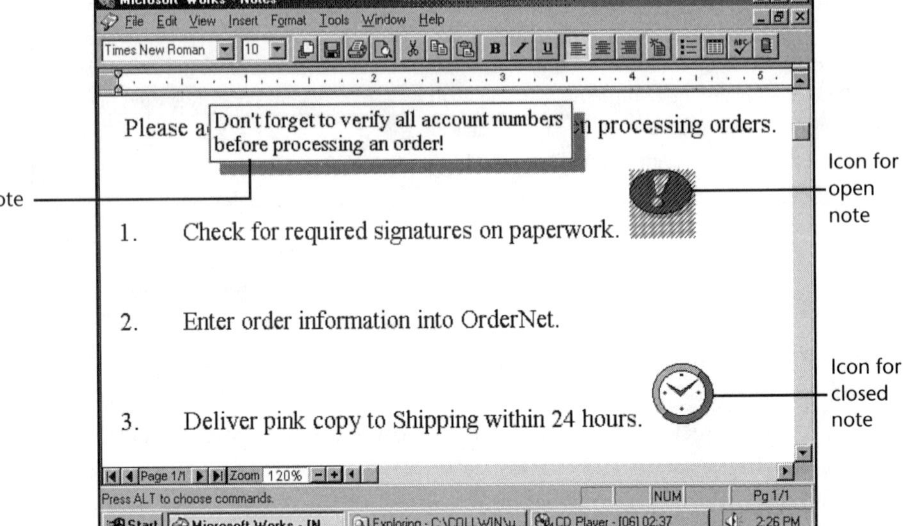

Fig. 25.17
Note-It notes appear as icons in a document until you open the note.

Creating a Note

To create a Note-It note in a document or database form, follow these steps:

1. Choose Insert, Note-It to display the Note-It dialog box shown in figure 25.18.

2. In the Choose a Picture box, select the picture you want to use as your note icon. Be sure to use the scroll bar to view all the icons—many icons are available. Select the picture that best suits your needs, such as the string on the index finger for a Reminder note or the amber traffic light for a Caution note.

3. To add a note caption, enter the text in the Type Your Caption Here box.

4. Enter the text for your note in the Type Your Note Here box.

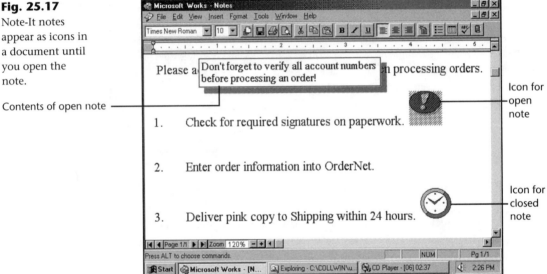

5. Choose Big or Small for the font size of the pop-up note.

6. Choose OK to close the dialog box.

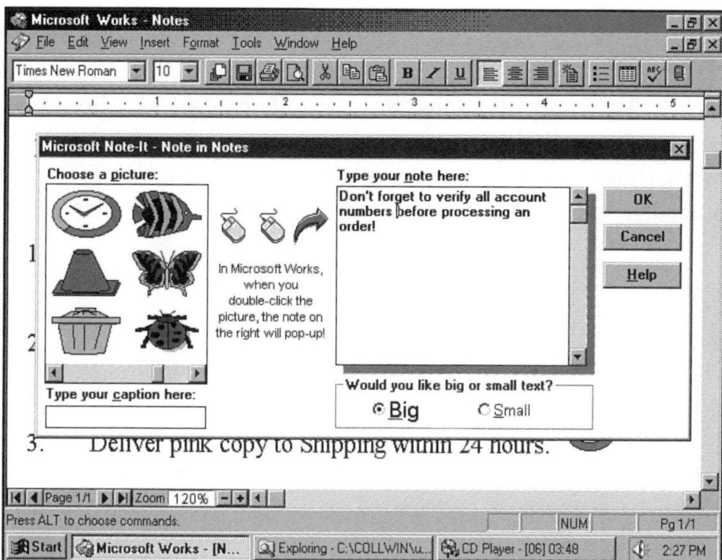

Fig. 25.18
Use the Note-It dialog box to select a note icon and enter the note text.

Reading a Note

To read a note, double-click the note icon in the document. The note icon becomes shaded, and the note text pops up in a small frame near the top of the document window. After you finish reading the note, click anywhere in the document or press Enter to close the note.

Editing a Note

You can edit the text of a note any time by following these steps:

1. Select the Note-It icon.

2. Choose Edit, Microsoft Note-It Object, Edit.

   The Microsoft Note-It dialog box opens. Your note text appears in the Type Your Note Here box, and your caption (if you included one) is shown in the Type Your Caption Here box. The note icon you are using is selected.

3. To edit your note text or caption, click the appropriate box then use the arrow keys to move to the characters you want to change or retype.

4. To change the Note-It icon, select a different picture from the Choose a Picture box.

5. When you're satisfied with the changes, choose OK.

Deleting a Note

You delete a Note-It note the same way you delete WordArt, ClipArt, or a Microsoft Draw drawing. First, select the Note-It icon. Then choose Edit, Cut, or press the Delete key, or press Ctrl+Z. If you delete a Note-It note by mistake, immediately choose Edit, Undo Editing to restore the note.❖

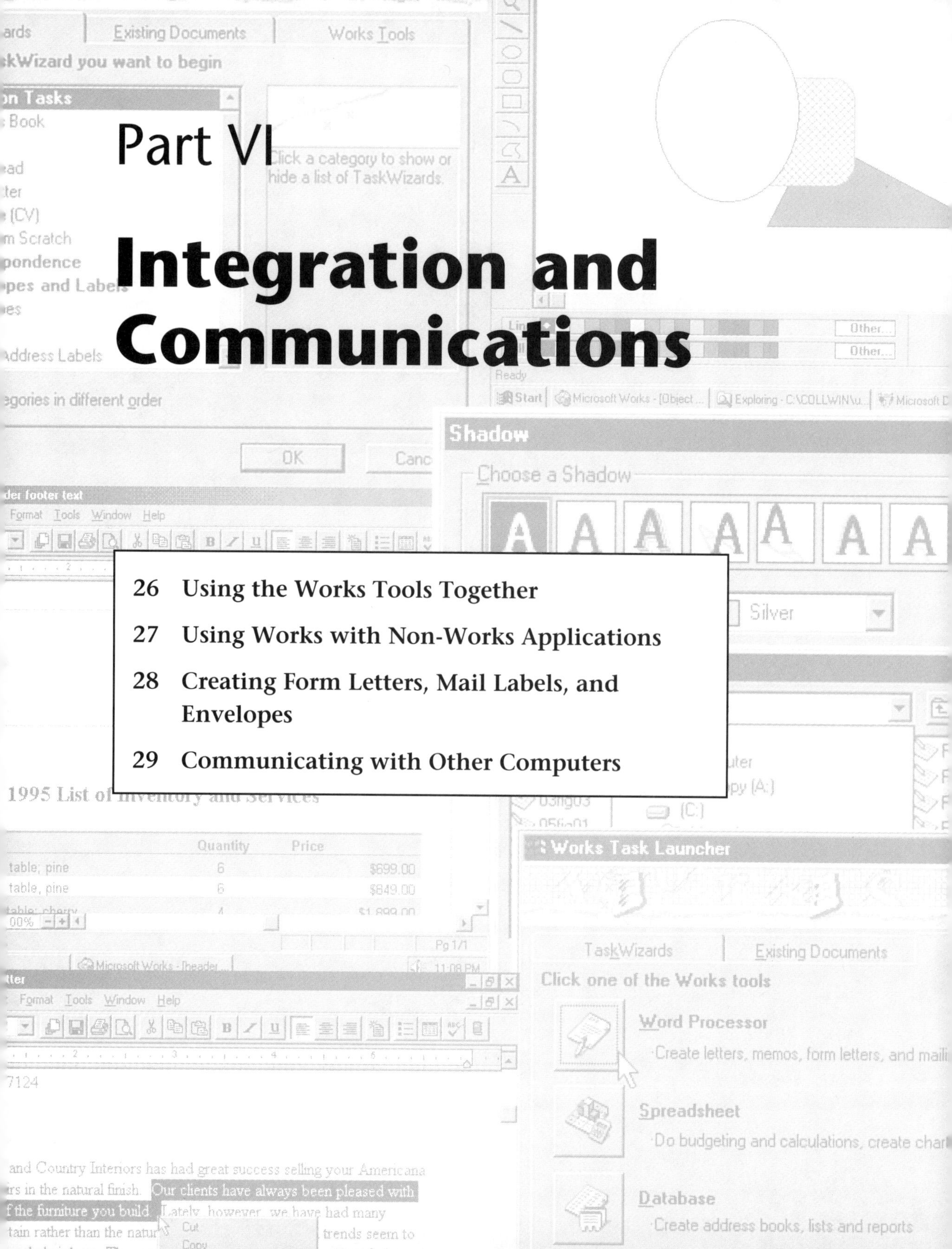

Part VI

Integration and Communications

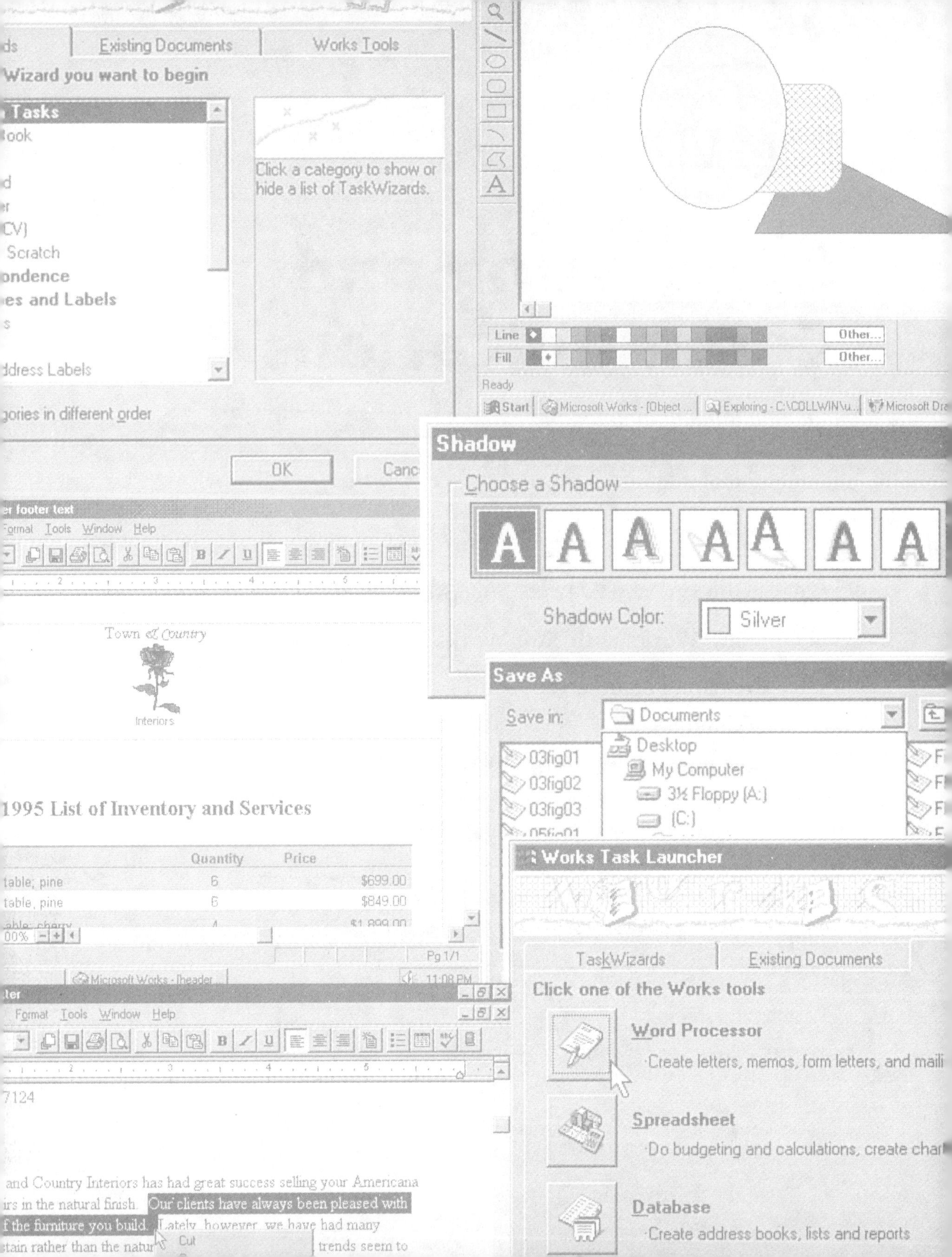

Existing Documents
Works Tools
Wizard you want to begin
Tasks
Scratch
ondence
es and Labels
ddress Labels
Click a category to show or hide a list of TaskWizards.
gories in different order
OK
Line
Fill
Other...
Other...
Ready
Start
Microsoft Works - [Object ...
Exploring - C:\COLLWIN\u...
Microsoft Dra
Shadow
Choose a Shadow
Shadow Color:
Silver
er footer text
Format Tools Window Help
Town & Country
Interiors
1995 List of Inventory and Services
Quantity
Price
table; pine
6
$699.00
table, pine
6
$849.00
Pg 1/1
Microsoft Works - [header
11:08 PM
Save As
Save in:
Documents
Desktop
My Computer
3½ Floppy (A:)
(C:)
03fig01
03fig02
03fig03
Works Task Launcher
TaskWizards
Existing Documents
Click one of the Works tools
Word Processor
Create letters, memos, form letters, and maili
Spreadsheet
Do budgeting and calculations, create char
Database
Create address books, lists and reports
Format Tools Window Help
7124
and Country Interiors has had great success selling your Americana
irs in the natural finish. Our clients have always been pleased with
f the furniture you build. Lately, however, we have had many
stain rather than the natur
Cut
trends seem to

Chapter 26

Using the Works Tools Together

by Kathy Murray

Perhaps the strongest feature of Works is its integration. Each of the Works tools—word processor, spreadsheet, database, and communications—work together seamlessly so you can get more done in less time. When you create a chart using the spreadsheet tool, you can easily use it in the report you're writing in the word processor. You can copy information from a communications file you downloaded into the database report you're preparing by choosing just a few simple commands.

In some cases, you will want to copy information from one file to another; in other cases, you will want to link or embed the information. Maintaining a *link* between the files ensures that the item you place in the document (for example, you might embed a chart in a word processing document) gets updated when the information changes. *Embedding* data enables you to edit the information without leaving your current application. (For more information about linking and embedding information, see the section "Understanding Linking and Embedding," later in this chapter.)

In Chapter 23, "Customizing a Report," you find out about transferring data between Works tools by exporting a report. In the Works database, you can copy a report and insert it into another Works tool document.

Because you use the Works word processor more often to transfer information than the database or spreadsheet, the figures in this chapter are based on word processor documents. However, you should also be aware that you can use exactly the same steps to copy, link, or embed information into a Works database form or report or into a Works spreadsheet.

In this chapter, you learn how to do the following:

- Copy and paste with the Windows Clipboard
- Link with Dynamic Data Exchange (DDE)
- Embed with Object Linking and Embedding (OLE)
- Move and resize objects
- Wrap text around objects

Copying and Moving Information

Copying and pasting is the simplest way to transfer information among the various Works tools. Use this method if you don't expect the transferred information to change, or if you don't need the same information in more than one document. You might, for example, copy and paste product information from a database you created into a proposal you're writing in the word processor. You won't need the information for more than this one document, and it is unlikely to change.

When you copy information, you switch to the source application and highlight the information you want to copy. Choose Edit, Copy to copy the information to the Windows Clipboard. Switch to the destination document and insert the information by choosing Edit, Paste.

◀ See "Moving and Copying Text," p. 90

◀ See "Editing a Document," p. 83

◀ See "Editing Cell Entries," p. 199

◀ See "Creating, Saving, and Printing a Spreadsheet," p. 177

◀ See "Copying and Moving Data," p. 399

Note

If you choose Edit, Cut to cut the information from the source document instead of copying it, Works deletes the original information, effectively moving it instead of copying it.

Moving and copying information between applications is essentially the same as moving and copying in or between documents in the word processor, spreadsheet, or database.

Caution

When you turn on Typing Replaces Selection in the Options dialog box (choose Tools, Options) and you highlight text before copying or moving information, Works replaces the highlighted information when you insert the copied or moved text. To restore the deleted text, immediately choose Edit, Undo Editing or press Ctrl+Z.

Transferring Information with Drag-and-Drop

Works lets you transfer information quickly with the mouse using the *drag-and-drop* method. You can drag-and-drop data from one location to another in the same document, between two documents you create in the same application, or between different applications. You can also use drag-and-drop to link information.

Follow these steps to drag-and-drop:

1. To copy or move information between documents created with the same or different applications, open the documents and arrange them so you can see both documents.
2. In the destination document, move the insertion point to where you want to insert the information.
3. Switch to the source document, and highlight the information you want to copy or move.
4. Then, to copy, move, or link the information using drag-and-drop, position the mouse pointer on the information. When the description beneath the pointer says DRAG, press and hold the mouse button while dragging the information to the destination.

   To link information to another Works document or Windows application, click the highlighted information and hold Ctrl and Shift while you drag it to the new location. In the Works spreadsheet, click the selection border and hold Ctrl and Shift while you drag.

   > **Caution**
   >
   > If the cursor changes to a circle with a diagonal line, you cannot move, copy, or link the information because it is the wrong type or because the application does not support drag-and-drop or linking.

5. Release the mouse button.

   > **Note**
   >
   > To undo a drag-and-drop copy, move, or link, choose Edit, Undo Drag and Drop (or press Ctrl+Z) immediately after you use drag-and-drop. If you copied or moved information to another application, choose Edit, Undo Drag and Drop in the destination document, and then choose Edit, Undo Drag and Drop in the word processor document.

Figure 26.1 shows two documents in the Works document window: a letter named LETTER and a spreadsheet titled INCMSTMT. The figure shows the spreadsheet and document prior to a drag-and-drop. Notice that the entire spreadsheet has been selected using the Edit, Select All command.

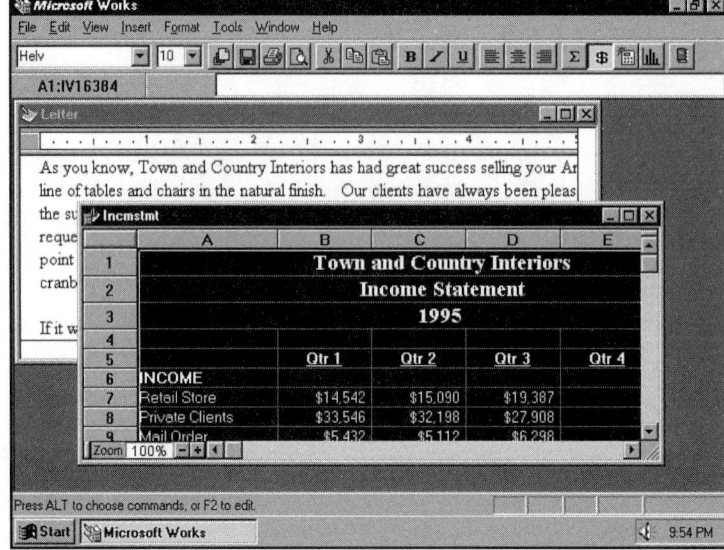

Fig. 26.1
To copy or move information using drag-and-drop, display both documents and highlight the information in the source document.

Figure 26.2 shows the Word processor document after the spreadsheet was copied to the insertion point.

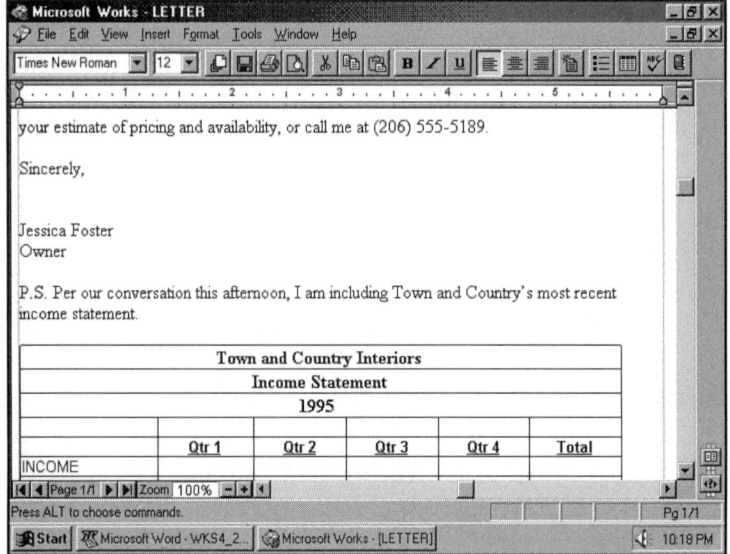

Fig. 26.2
Drag-and-drop enables you to copy the spreadsheet into the document with a simple mouse movement.

Note

The new Easy Text feature inserts text (that you have specified as Easy Text) at any point in your document. This enables you to add a phrase you use often, such as a particular disclaimer or salutation, by entering a single keyword. Then, when you press F3, the text is automatically placed in the document.

◀ See "Creating, Saving, and Printing a Document," p. 65

Transferring Information with the Menus

Sometimes it's easier to use the Copy, Cut, and Paste commands in the Edit menu (or the Copy, Cut, and Paste toolbar buttons) when you want to transfer information in Works. Using drag-and-drop to move several pages of information with the mouse can be less convenient than using these menu commands. If you accidentally click outside the selection or press a key, Works removes the highlight from the selection—and you have to start over.

To copy or move information using the menu commands, follow these steps:

1. Open the source document.
2. Highlight the text or object you want to copy.
3. To copy the selection, choose Edit, Copy; press Ctrl+C; or click the Copy toolbar button.

   or

   To move the selection, choose Edit, Cut; press Ctrl+X; or click the Cut toolbar button.
4. To copy or move the information to another location in the same document, move the insertion point where you want to insert the copy.

   or

   To copy or move to another document, open the destination document and move the insertion point where you want to insert the copy.
5. Choose Edit, Paste; press Ctrl+V; or click the Paste toolbar button. Works inserts the information at the insertion point.
6. To insert another copy, repeat steps 4 and 5.

Figures 26.3 and 26.4 show a word processor document and a database form before and after copying the drawing in the letter into the database form.

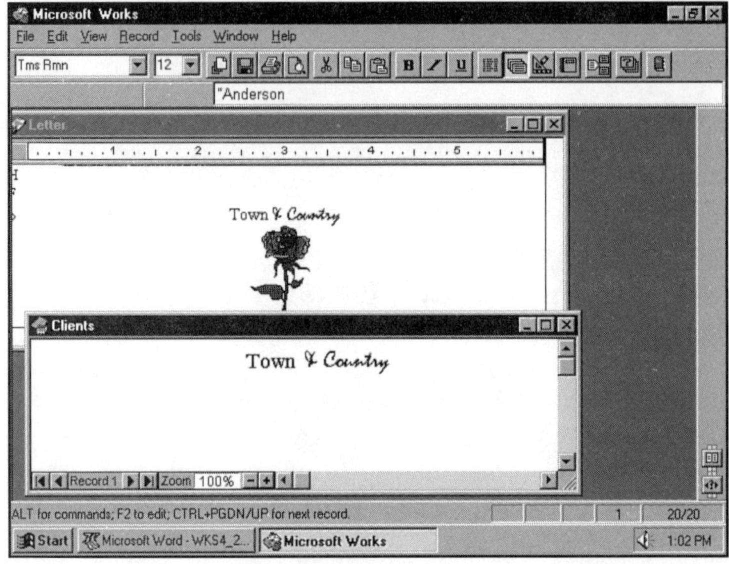

Fig. 26.3
This drawing is ready to be copied from a word processor letter to a database form.

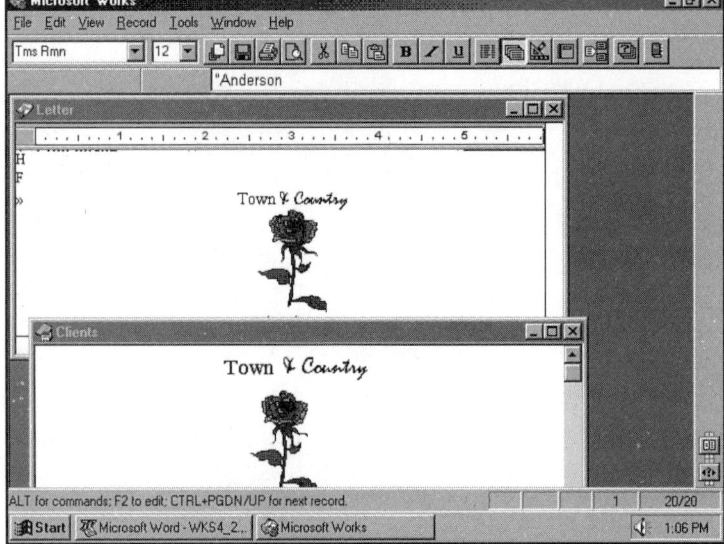

Fig. 26.4
The drawing was copied from the word processor letter to the database form.

Understanding Linking and Embedding

The Copy, Paste, and Cut commands are fine when you need to copy information from here to there. But what happens when you're copying a chart showing stock prices into an annual report you're preparing? If the stock prices change, your report will be outdated before the annual meeting.

Use linking or embedding to transfer information between Works documents when you expect the source of the information to change. With linking, you copy the information and Works automatically updates the information when the source changes. With embedding, you can edit the source information without leaving your document. You can link or embed information into a Works document from any Windows program that supports linking with Dynamic Data Exchange (DDE) or embedding with Object Linking and Embedding (OLE).

The following guidelines help you make the decision to use linking or embedding:

- When you want to transfer information into a Works document and you expect the source information to change or if you need to include the information in several Works documents, use linking. You can then edit the source information, and Windows automatically changes the linked copy.

- If you don't expect to copy the information to other documents, but you do need to edit the information, choose embedding. When you edit embedded information, Windows automatically opens the source application and displays the embedded object, ready for you to edit. When you close the source application, Windows returns you to the Works document screen that contains the object.

Linking Objects

When you want to copy and paste selected information into another document so that it will be updated whenever the source object changes, you create a link between the documents. You do this by choosing Edit, Paste Special.

Figure 26.5 shows a Works spreadsheet that was copied and linked into a word processor document.

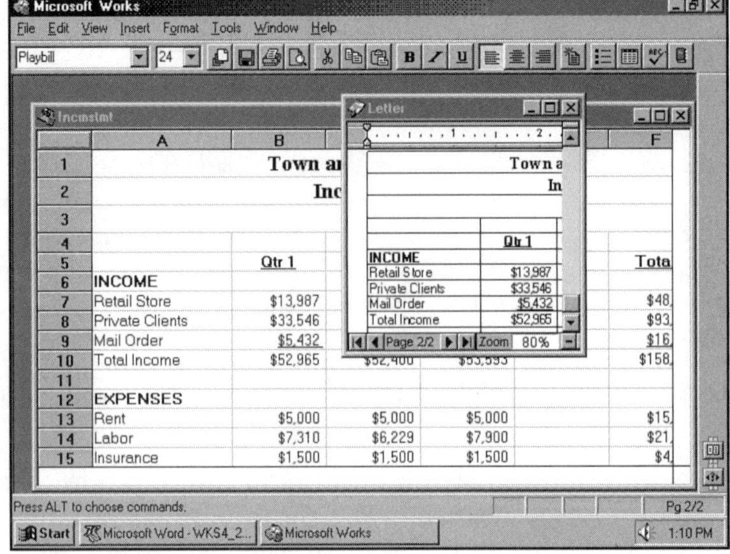

Fig. 26.5 You can easily use information from another file in your current file. This example shows spreadsheet information linked to a document file.

Figure 26.6 shows the same spreadsheet and letter after the amount for Retail Store income in Qtr 1 was changed from $13,987 to $14,542 in the spreadsheet. Notice that Works has automatically changed the number and the column total in the letter as well.

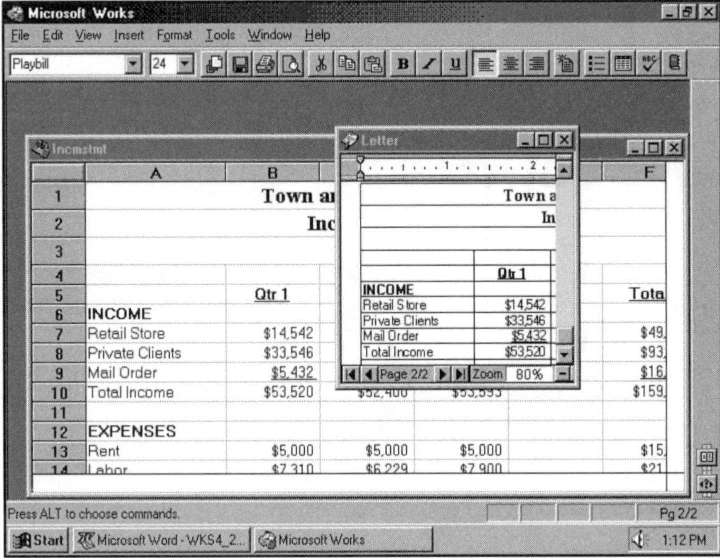

Fig. 26.6 Works updates a linked object, such as a spreadsheet, automatically when you change the source document.

Use the following steps to link information:

1. Open the application that contains the information you want to link, and display the source document.

   Note

   You must name and save the source document before you can link information from it.

2. Highlight the information you want to link.

   For example, highlight a spreadsheet or spreadsheet cell(s), a drawing, a word processor table, or cells in a database displayed in List view.

3. Choose Edit, Copy in the source application. You can also press Ctrl+C or click the Copy toolbar button.

4. Move to the location in the document where you want to insert the linked information.

5. Choose Edit, Paste Special.

   Works displays the Paste Special dialog box (see fig. 26.7). In this figure, the Works 4.0 Sheet or Chart Object option is selected in the As list in the center of the dialog box. This means that Works does not need to paste the link separately because you are pasting information from another Works document. If you were linking information from a document other than one created in Works, you would select Paste Link in the Paste Special dialog box.

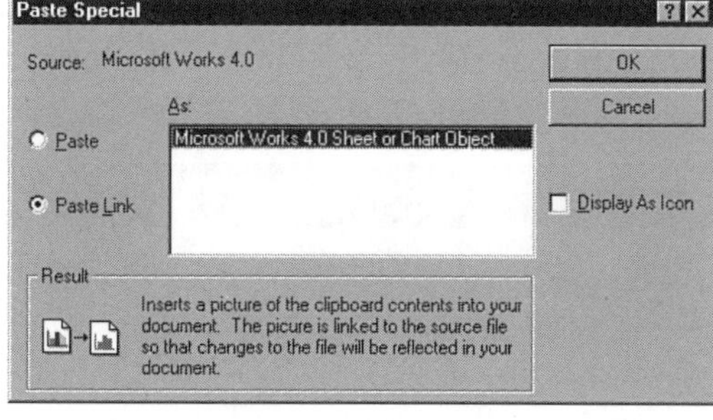

Fig. 26.7
Use the Paste Special dialog box to insert linked information.

> **Note**
>
> If Paste Link is not available, the other application might not be able to create a link or might not support DDE (Dynamic Data Exchange). This also can mean that the source document has not been saved as it must be before you can link it to other files. Consult the other program's documentation to find out more DDE support.

6. Choose OK.

   Works inserts the linked information.

> **Note**
>
> Although Works automatically updates a linked object when the source object changes, you can turn off this feature and update the object manually. For example, you might want to update linked payroll spreadsheet information in a word processor document just once a month, when payroll figures are completed. For more information, see the section "Updating Linked Objects Manually," later in this chapter.

Linking an Entire File

You can also insert not just a portion of information from a source file, but the entire file. For example, you might want to link a standard contract document from the Works word processor into other word processor documents. When you change the standard contract, all the contracts change. Use the following steps to link an entire file:

1. Open the document where you want to insert the information, and choose Insert, Object. Works displays the Insert Object dialog box (see fig. 26.8).

> **Note**
>
> When you select Insert, Object for the first time, the First-time Help dialog box appears. You can choose to take a tour to learn about objects; view a demonstration of how to add clip art, a drawing, or WordArt; or find out how to create and embed an object. To begin one of the demonstrations, click the one you want. To bypass the choices, click OK.

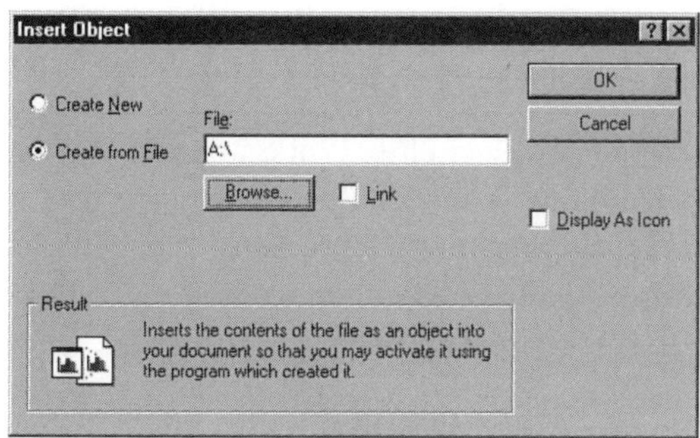

Fig. 26.8
Use the Insert Object dialog box to insert and link an entire file.

2. In the Insert Object dialog box, choose Create from File.
3. In the File text box, enter the name of the file to which you want to link.

   or

   Choose Browse, and use the Browse dialog box to find the file you want. Choose OK to return to the Insert Object dialog box.
4. To have Works display the file as an icon, select the Display As Icon check box.

   Works displays and prints the file as an icon. To display the actual contents of the linked file, do not select Display As icon. (If you select Display As Icon, you can later open the object by double-clicking it.)

Note

When you choose Display As Icon, another button appears at the bottom of the Insert Object dialog box. This button enables you to change the icon used to represent the linked document. Click Change Icon to display the Change Icon dialog box and then select Default or From File to choose an icon other than the current one. You also can use the Label option to change the label that appears beneath the icon when it displays in the document. When you finish selecting a new icon, click OK.

5. Select the Link check box.

   This tells Works that you want to establish a link between the source document and the open document. Any changes you make in the open document reflect in the source document, and changes in the source document appear in the open document. A picture of the file appears in the document so you know that any changes made in the source document will also be made in this linked copy.

If you choose not to select Link, Works assumes you want to embed the file instead of linking it. Embedding a file means that you simply insert the source file into the current document; changes in either file will not affect the other. For more about embedding, see "Embedding an Object," later in this chapter.

6. Choose OK.

   Works runs the application that you used to create the source document, and displays the source document. If you selected Display As Icon, the document appears as an icon in the second document.

7. Make any desired changes to the source document.

8. To return to the destination document, click anywhere in the destination document.

Works inserts the file in your destination document as an icon. Figure 26.9 shows the icon Works inserts when the original contract (the source document) is inserted into another word processor document.

Fig. 26.9 Works displays the linked file as an icon in the new document. To view the contents of the file, double-click the icon.

> **Note**
>
> You can change the source of a linked object. For example, if you link a drawing that you created with Microsoft Draw, you can change the link to a different drawing. Windows then automatically updates the linked object in any destination documents to reflect the new drawing. For more information, see "Reconnecting a Link or Changing the Source of a Link," later in this chapter.

Linking Spreadsheet Information

One of the most popular uses for linking is to display spreadsheets, spreadsheet ranges, and spreadsheet charts in word processor documents. Because this is such a common use of linking, this section gives the exact steps to link a Works spreadsheet worksheet or chart.

Follow these steps to link a Works spreadsheet chart:

1. Open the spreadsheet that contains the chart you want to link.

> **Note**
>
> You must name the range you're using and save the spreadsheet before you can link the chart.

2. Switch to the word processor document and move the insertion point where you want to insert the chart.

3. Choose Insert, Chart.

   Works displays the Insert Chart dialog box (see fig. 26.10).

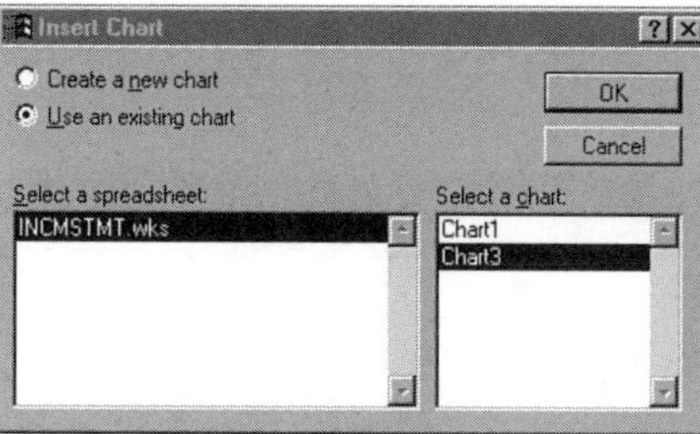

Fig. 26.10
Use the Insert Chart dialog box to select a chart and insert it.

4. Select Use an Existing Chart.

5. From the Select a Spreadsheet list box, select the spreadsheet where you created the chart.

> **Note**
>
> You must open a spreadsheet in step 1 before Works includes it in the Select a Spreadsheet list box.

6. In the Select a Chart list box, highlight the chart you want to insert.

7. Choose OK.

Works inserts the chart in the destination document (see fig. 26.11).

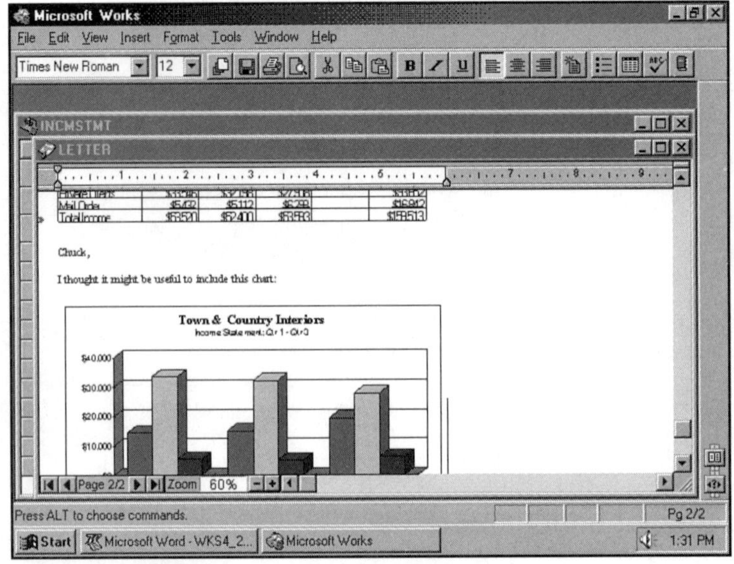

Fig. 26.11
You can insert linked spreadsheet charts and spreadsheet ranges in a Works word processor document.

> **Note**
>
> The document in figure 26.11 is displayed in 75 percent zoom view in order to show more information.

The following steps for linking a spreadsheet range are similar to linking a chart:

1. Open the spreadsheet that contains the range of cells you want to link.

   > **Note**
   >
   > You must save the spreadsheet and name the range of cells before you can link it.

2. In the word processor document, move the insertion point where you want to insert the spreadsheet cells.

3. Choose Insert, Spreadsheet.

   Works displays the Insert Spreadsheet dialog box (see fig. 26.12).

4. Select Use a Range from an Existing Spreadsheet.

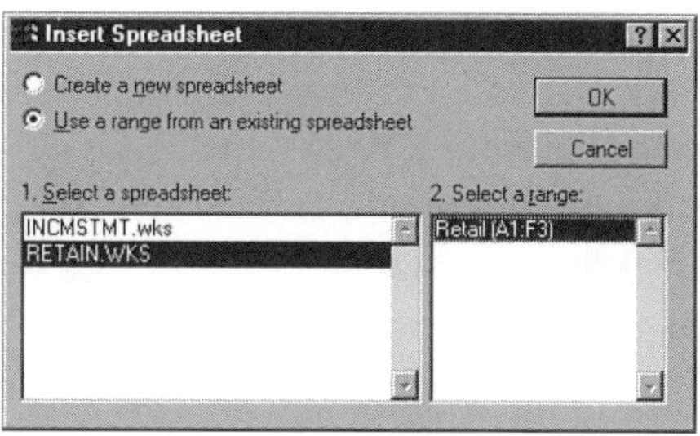

Fig. 26.12 Use the Insert Spreadsheet dialog box to link a range of spreadsheet cells.

5. From the Select a Spreadsheet list box, select the name of the spreadsheet you want to link.

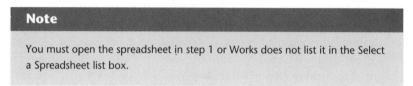

> **Note**
>
> You must open the spreadsheet in step 1 or Works does not list it in the Select a Spreadsheet list box.

6. From the Select a Range list box, select the spreadsheet range you want to link.

7. Choose OK.

Works inserts the spreadsheet range in your document at the insertion point (see fig. 26.13).

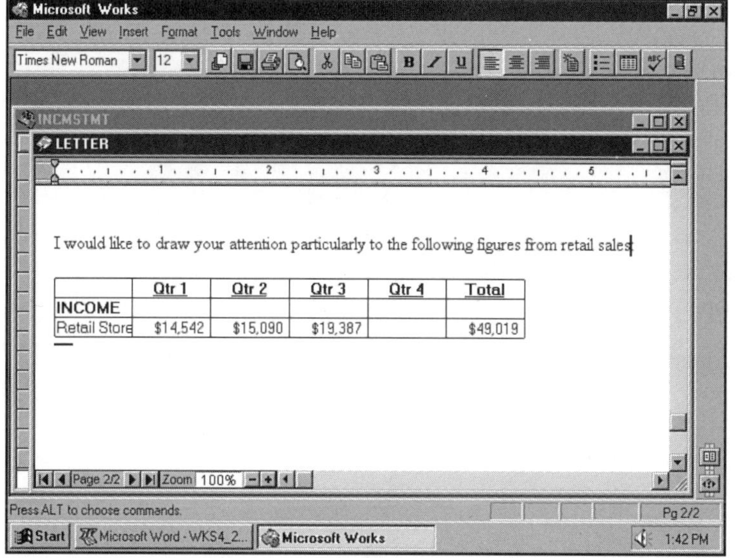

Fig. 26.13 Linking a spreadsheet range gives you a means of showing, in your document, how a particular aspect of a spreadsheet can change over time.

Editing Linked Objects

After you insert linked data in a Works document, you can make changes to the data in the source application. Works then automatically reflects the changes in the destination document, or you can update the link manually at some later time. For example, you might want to wait until you finish a complex series of changes before you take the time to update the link.

Follow these steps to edit linked information:

1. In the destination document, double-click the object you want to edit.

   or

   Use the arrow keys to move the insertion point to the left of the object. Press Shift+right-arrow to select the object. Works displays sizing boxes around the object's borders. Choose Edit, [Object Name] Object. For example, for a linked spreadsheet range, the Edit menu displays Linked Works Sheet or Chart Object. When you move the mouse pointer to that command, a submenu appears. Choose Edit from the submenu (see fig. 26.14).

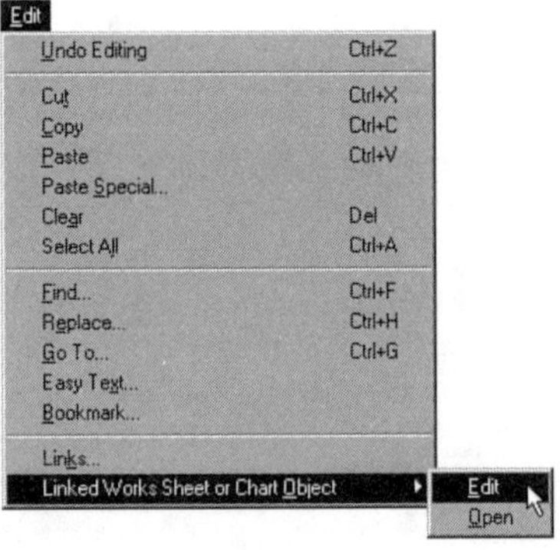

Fig. 26.14
After you add an object to a Works document, you can easily edit it by selecting the object and choosing the appropriate command from the Edit menu.

Tip
To select an object that has text wrapping around it, move the cursor above or below the object, then press the up- or down-arrow.

   Works opens the source application and displays the linked object. For example, if the linked object is a Works spreadsheet cell range, Works opens the spreadsheet and highlights the range.

2. Make any desired changes to the source information.

3. Save the source document.

   or

   If you are editing the object in another Windows application, choose File, Exit.

Works changes the linked information in the destination document. Works also reflects your changes when it updates other occurrences of the linked information in other documents.

Updating Linked Objects Manually

Sometimes, it is convenient to update linked objects manually, instead of letting Works update them each time they change. Works takes a moment to update an object—this can interfere with your work flow, especially if you make frequent changes and switch back and forth between the source and destination documents.

Follow these steps to switch between automatic and manual link updating:

1. Choose Edit, Links. Works displays the Links dialog box (see fig. 26.15).

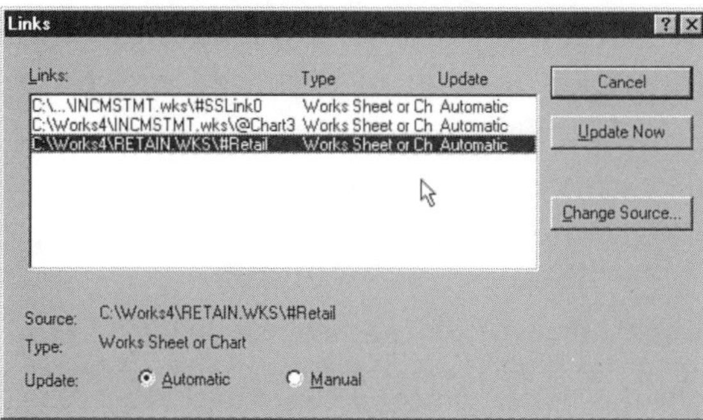

Fig. 26.15 Use the Links dialog box to switch between automatic and manual link updating.

2. In the Links list box, select the link you want to update manually.
3. Select Manual or Automatic as appropriate.

   Works displays Manual or Automatic in the Update column of the Links list box.
4. Choose Cancel.

Works no longer updates the link automatically. To update the link manually, follow these steps:

1. Choose Edit, Links.
2. In the Links dialog box, choose the link you want to update (refer to fig. 26.15).

3. Choose Update Now.

Works reflects any changes you made since the last update.

> **Note**
>
> Works can update all links automatically anytime you open a document that contains links. Works asks whether you want the links updated. Choose Yes to update the links, or choose No to bypass updating and open the document.

Reconnecting a Link or Changing the Source of a Link

When you change the name of a source document, Works breaks any links from that document to other documents. If you want to continue updating the linked data, you must reconnect the link. You can also change the source of a link at any time. For example, you might decide to choose a different spreadsheet chart as the source of a link.

Follow these steps to reconnect or change the source of a link:

1. Choose Edit, Links.

   Works displays the Links dialog box (refer to fig. 26.15).

2. Choose the link whose source you want to change.

3. Choose Change Source.

   Works displays the Change Source dialog box (see fig. 26.16).

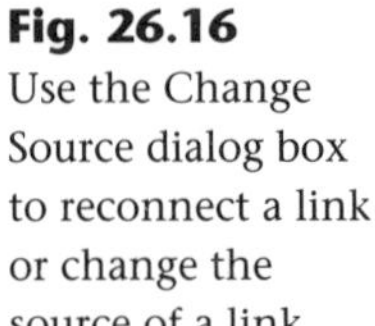

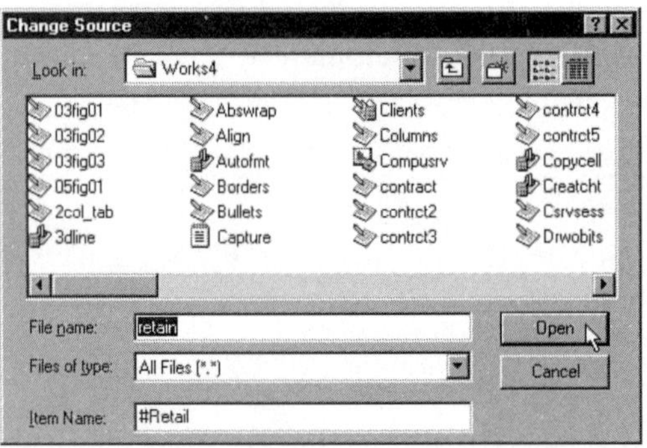

Fig. 26.16
Use the Change Source dialog box to reconnect a link or change the source of a link.

4. In the Look In list box, type the path for the source file or spreadsheet range to which you want to reconnect or change the link.

   or

   Choose a new source from the list of file names.

5. Choose OK.

6. In the Links dialog box, choose Close.

If you have other links to the same source file, Works asks you to confirm that you want to change the source file for all of the linked data.

Embedding

Embedding is different from linking—when you embed an object in a Works file, the information you embed (a chart, a spreadsheet, text, or data) is saved in the file. In contrast, when you link an object to a file, the actual information that creates the object is stored in the original file; only the link is saved in the new file.

Embedding lets you make changes to objects in a Works tool using the source application, without leaving the tool. For example, suppose you embed a drawing you created in Microsoft Draw in a Works word processor document. When you need to make changes to the drawing, you can simply double-click the drawing to open Microsoft Draw and edit the drawing without leaving Works.

Embedding is convenient for sharing documents between users. Both users must have the source application if they want to edit embedded information, but they don't need the source application to view documents that contain embedded objects. With linking, all users must not only have the source application, but they must have the source document and must save the linked source data in subdirectories with the same names as the original user created. To summarize:

- Use linking when the same information changes frequently in several documents.

- Use embedding when you don't need to place information in several documents, and you want to edit the information without leaving a Works tool.

Follow these steps to embed an object:

1. In the Works document, move the insertion point where you want to insert the object.

2. Choose Insert, and then choose the type of object:

   Spreadsheet

   Chart

   Table

   ClipArt

   WordArt

   Note-It

   Drawing

   Object

3. Follow the steps given in the detailed descriptions in the sections that follow for each of the specific object types.

Inserting a Chart

Choosing Insert, Chart displays the Insert Chart dialog box (see fig. 26.17).

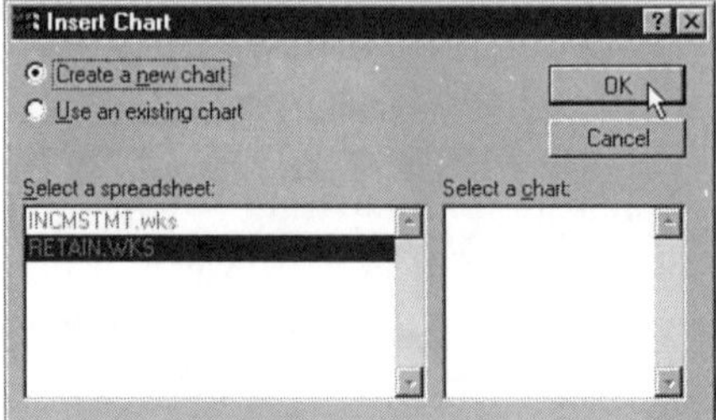

Fig. 26.17
Use the Insert Chart dialog box to insert an existing chart or a new chart.

To insert an existing chart, first make sure the spreadsheet you want to use is open, and then follow these steps:

1. Choose Insert, Chart. The Insert Chart dialog box appears.
2. Choose Use an Existing Chart.
3. Choose a spreadsheet from the Select a Spreadsheet list box or choose a chart from the Select a Chart list box.
4. Choose OK. Works inserts the chart in the document.

To insert a new chart, follow these steps:

1. Choose Insert, Chart. The Insert Chart dialog box appears.
2. Choose Create a New Chart and choose OK.

   Works displays a message saying: `There is no data available yet to create a chart. First type your data in the cells, select the data, and then click the Chart button on the toolbar.`

3. Click OK. Works embeds a blank spreadsheet window in your document at the insertion point (see fig. 26.18).

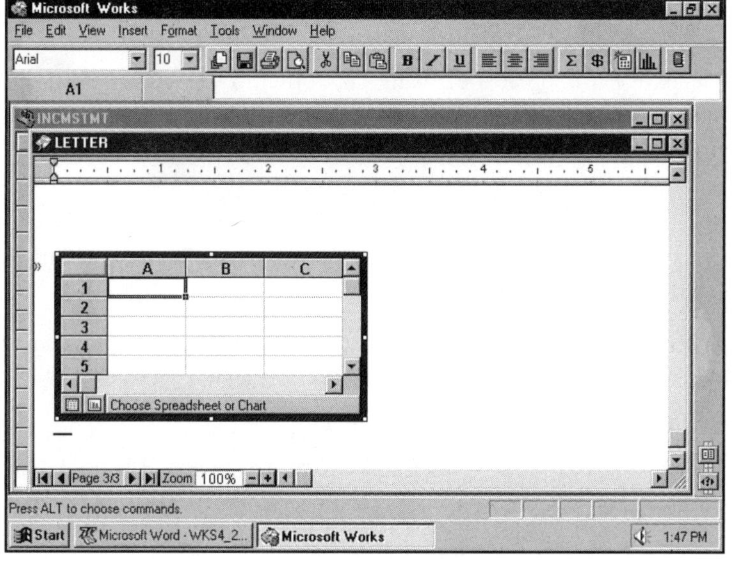

Fig. 26.18
Use the spreadsheet window to insert a new spreadsheet from which Works will create a chart.

Tip
To move the spreadsheet window, click an edge and drag it.

3. Create the new spreadsheet in the embedded spreadsheet.

   Works replaces the current Works tool menu bar with the Spreadsheet menu bar.

4. To embed a spreadsheet from the new data, click the Spreadsheet button.

   or

   To embed a chart from the data, select the cells from which you want to create the chart, and click the Chart button. If you click the Chart button, Works displays the New Chart dialog box. To learn how to use the New Chart dialog box, see Chapter 14, "Creating Charts."

5. To return to the underlying Works tool, exit the New Chart dialog box by choosing OK, after you create your chart. Then click outside the spreadsheet, or press Esc.

Now that the chart is embedded, you can edit it without leaving your Works document. Follow these steps:

1. Double-click the chart.

   Works activates the chart window and replaces the current Works tool's menu bar with a chart menu bar.

2. To change the spreadsheet values on which the chart is based, click the Spreadsheet button in the chart window to display the spreadsheet and make changes.

   or

   To change the chart design, choose Tools, Create New Chart, make any changes in the New Chart dialog box, and choose OK.

3. If you changed spreadsheet values in step 2, highlight the values that you want included in the new version of the chart, and click the Chart button.

4. To return to the underlying Works document, click outside the chart window or press Esc.

Inserting a Spreadsheet or Table

The process for embedding a spreadsheet or table is basically the same as embedding a chart. Choose Insert, Spreadsheet or choose Insert, Table. Follow these general guidelines to determine which one you should choose—and when:

- A spreadsheet is the best choice for organizing and working with financial data
- A table is helpful for displaying textual information in a structured format

When you choose Insert, Spreadsheet, the Insert Spreadsheet dialog box appears. With the exception of the dialog box title, this dialog box is identical to the Insert Chart dialog box. Decide whether to use an existing spreadsheet or begin a new one. If you decided to use an existing spreadsheet, choose the spreadsheet you want to work with from the Select a Spreadsheet list and choose a range from the Select a Range list. Click OK.

When you choose Insert, Table, the Insert Table dialog box appears (see fig. 26.19). Here you can choose the number of rows and columns, as well as the format (a preset table design with a variety of colors, bar styles, and fonts) for the table.

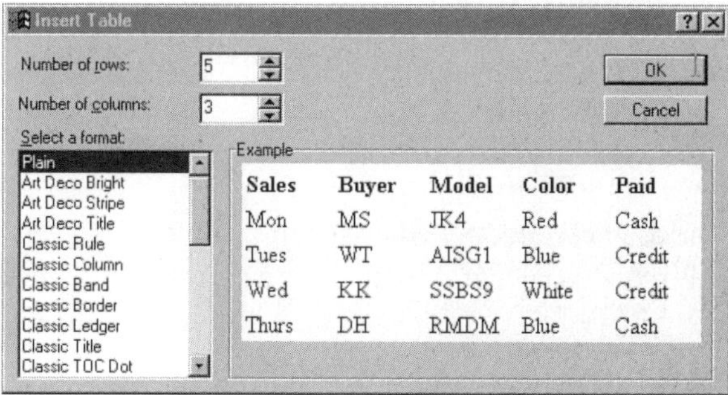

Fig. 26.19 In the Insert Table dialog box, you select the number of columns and rows you want to include in the table. You can also select one of the preset formats.

Inserting ClipArt, WordArt, Note-It, or a Drawing

Other types of objects add to the special look or function of your documents. You might, for example, want to add graphics, enhance text with Word-Art, or add popup notes to your document with Note-It. To add one of these objects to your Works document, choose ClipArt, WordArt, Note-It, or Drawing from the Insert menu to start the tool you want. Follow these steps to embed one of these types of objects:

1. In your Works document, move the insertion point to where you want to insert the object.

2. Choose Insert, and then choose ClipArt, WordArt, Note-It, or Drawing.

   Works starts the corresponding tool. For example, figure 26.20 shows the dialog box that appears when you choose Insert, Note-It. The Note-It feature embeds a note in your Works document that appears when the user double-clicks the small icon in the file. This is handy when you want to leave a note for someone reviewing your report, when someone is learning how to use a spreadsheet you set up, or when you're just sharing access to a common file.

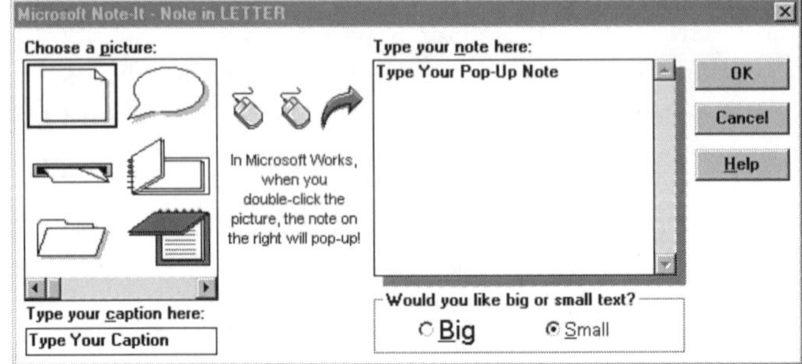

Fig. 26.20 Works embeds its special features—ClipArt, WordArt, Note-It, or Drawing—as soon as you use them in your document.

3. Create or open and select the object you want to embed.

4. To return to the underlying Works document, use one of the following methods:

   - If the application opened a separate window, such as Microsoft Draw, choose File, and then choose Exit, Exit and Return, Quit, or Return. You also can click the Close box in the upper-right corner of the window.

   - If the application replaced the underlying Works tool's menus and toolbar, click outside the object or press Esc.

   - If the application is in a dialog box, as with Note-It, choose OK.

   - If Works asks whether you want to update the object, choose Yes to add your changes or choose No to abandon your changes. If Works asks whether you want to update the document, choose Yes to insert the new version of the object.

Embedding an Object

Depending on the kind of project you're working on, you might need to embed other types of objects as well. You might, for example, want to add a voice-over note to a spreadsheet file or add a video clip of last year's corporate meeting in this year's annual report. You embed both sound files and video clips by choosing Insert, Object. Similarly, if you want to add objects from other applications—such as Microsoft Word, NotePad, or Microsoft Equation—you use this command. (For more information about working with non-Works files, see Chapter 27, "Using Works with Non-Works Applications.")

Follow these steps to create and embed other objects:

1. In your Works document, move the insertion point to where you want to embed the object.

2. Choose Insert, Object. The Insert Object dialog box appears (see fig. 26.21).

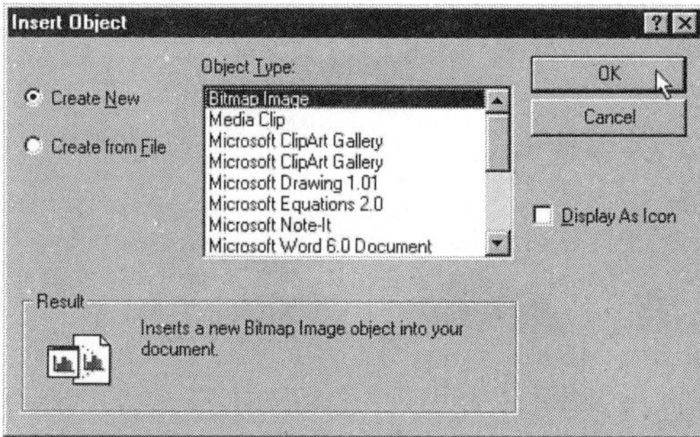

Fig. 26.21
Use the Insert Object dialog box to embed objects that are available with applications that support OLE (Object Linking and Embedding).

3. To create a new object, select Create New.

4. From the Object Type list box, select the type of object you want to embed.

5. Select the Display As Icon check box if you want the object to appear as an icon. (If you select this option, you can double-click the icon when you need to display the object.)

   Do not select this check box if you want the object to display as it is—a drawing, a document, a spreadsheet, or a chart.

6. Click OK.

7. The application you use to create the object appears. Create the object you want to use. Then, depending on the application, use one of the following File menu commands to exit the application and return to your Works document: Exit, Exit and Return, Quit, or Return.

   You also can click the Close box in the upper-right corner of the window to return to your Works document, where the object is placed. If you chose Display As Icon, the object appears as a picture in the file. If you did not choose that option, the object is embedded in the document as it appears in its source document.

Embedding a File

There are occasions when you might want to embed an entire file. For example, if you perform market research, you can show the results in spreadsheet charts. In your Works document, you can embed the spreadsheet file along with its charts. Then, if you are asked how things would look if you showed results quarterly instead of semiannually, you can have the answer in a matter of minutes with a quick double-click on the chart and some simple data modification.

To insert an existing file as an object, follow these steps:

1. Choose Insert, Object to display the Insert Object dialog box.

2. Choose Create from File. Works displays a text box where you can type a file name.

3. In the File text box, type the file name or click the Browse button to locate the file.

4. If you want to link the object instead of embedding it, select the Link check box.

   This creates a link to the file you select, meaning that the actual information that creates the file is stored in the source document rather than being embedded in your current document.

5. Decide whether you want the file to appear as an icon.

   If you want the embedded file to appear in your current document as an icon—so you can display it later by double-clicking it—select the Display As Icon check box.

Caution

To link or embed an existing file, the application that created the file must support OLE (Object Linking and Embedding). To link an existing file, the source application must support DDE (Dynamic Data Exchange).

6. Choose OK. Works starts the application you selected.
7. Create the object you want.
8. Return to your Works document by using one of the following methods:

   If the application opened a separate window, choose File, and then choose Exit, Exit and Return, Quit, or Return.

   If the application replaced the underlying Works tool's menus and toolbar, click outside the object or press Esc.

   If the application is in a dialog box, as with Note-It, choose OK.

Editing an Embedded Object

After embedding an object, you can open the object's source application and make changes without leaving the currently active Works tool. Follow these steps:

1. Double-click the object you want to edit.

   or

   Use the arrow keys to place the insertion point to the immediate left of the object, and press Shift+right arrow. Then choose Edit, [Object Name] Object, Edit. (For example, if you embedded a bitmap image object, the command in the Edit menu will read Bitmap Image Object.)
2. Make the changes.
3. Close the object by using one of the File menu commands, by clicking outside the object, or by clicking OK (if the object is displayed in a dialog box, like Note-It).

Moving and Resizing Objects

After you embed or link an object in a Works document, you can move it or change its size without disturbing the active embedding or linking function.

Moving Objects

The first step in moving an object is selecting it. If you are using the mouse, click the object and the sizing handles appear, indicating that the object is selected. If you are using the keyboard, use the arrow keys to move the insertion point to the immediate left of the object, and then press Shift+right arrow to select the object.

Next, move the object by dragging it (if you're using the mouse), or by cutting and pasting it (if you're using the keyboard). To cut and paste the object using the keyboard, choose Edit, Cut or press Ctrl+X. Next, move the insertion point to where you want to place the object, and choose Edit, Paste or press Ctrl+V.

Resizing Objects

To change an object's size with the mouse, click the object and drag one of the object's sizing handles.

To change an object's size using exact measurements, follow these steps:

1. Click the object or move the insertion point to the immediate left of the object, and press Shift+right arrow.

   Works displays sizing handles around the object.

2. Choose Format, Picture. Works displays the Format Picture dialog box (see fig. 26.22).

   The Size tab is selected automatically. The dialog box shows a number of options that control the size and scale of the selected object.

3. If you want to change the size, enter new dimensions for the object in the Size area for Width and Height.

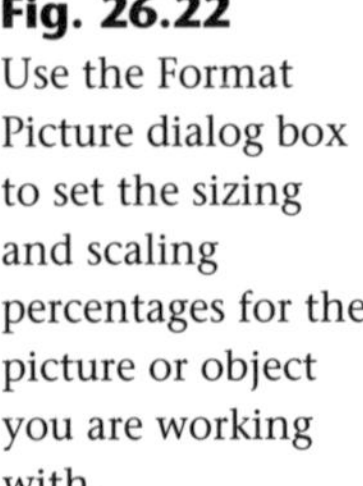

Fig. 26.22
Use the Format Picture dialog box to set the sizing and scaling percentages for the picture or object you are working with.

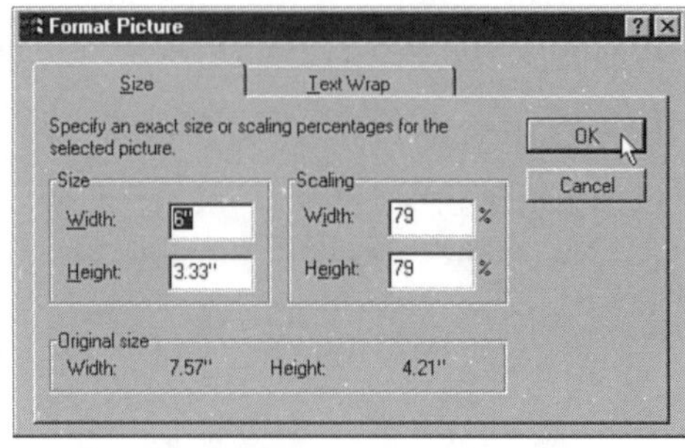

4. If you want to change the scale, enter a new percentage in the Scaling area for Width and Height.

5. Choose OK.

   Works changes the object's size.

> **Note**
>
> The Original Size area at the bottom of the Format Picture dialog box shows you the original dimensions of the object. If you're unhappy with the new size or scale, you can always go back to the drawing board and start again.

Wrapping Text Around an Object

In the previous section, you learned how to change the size and scale settings in the Format Picture dialog box. As you'll notice from figure 26.22, there is another tab in the Format Picture dialog box behind the Size tab—the Text Wrap tab. Figure 26.23 shows the Text Wrap tab of the Format Picture dialog box.

When you place an object in a Works document, you can choose how Works formats text around the object. You have two choices:

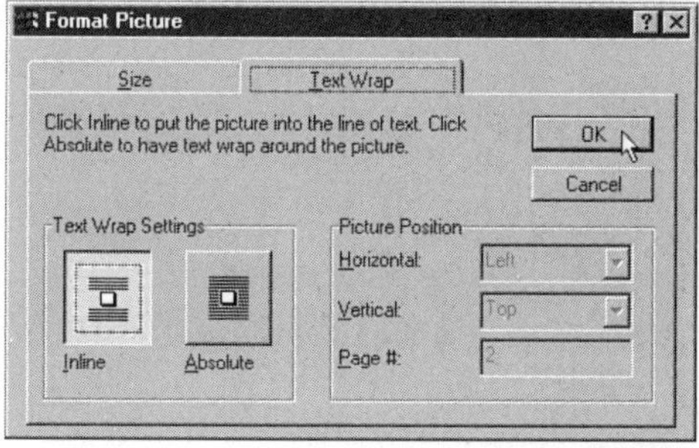

Fig. 26.23
You can place objects so they move with the text when it moves or so they remain in one absolute spot on the page.

- *Inline*. This places the object as though it is in a line of text. When you choose this option, Works automatically adjusts the line height to accommodate the object. If you insert, delete, or move text, Works moves the object just as it would move text.

- *Absolute*. You can specify an exact (absolute) position for the object on the page. Regardless of any changes to the text on the page, Works keeps the object in exactly the same position on the page. Text wraps around the object. The Picture Position settings—Horizontal, Vertical, and Page #—become available when you click the Absolute option.

Follow these steps to tell Works how you want text wrapped around an object:

1. Select the object by clicking it.

   or

   Select the object by moving the insertion point to the immediate left of the object and pressing Shift+right arrow.

2. Choose Format, Picture. The Format Picture dialog box appears.

3. Choose the Text Wrap tab.

4. Works selects Inline by default. To change the text wrap setting, choose Absolute. The icons in the Text Wrap Settings area show what you've selected. Continue to step 5.

   If you choose Inline, choose OK to return to the document.

5. Choose Horizontal, and then either enter the exact distance from the left edge of the page where you want to place the left edge of the object, or click the down-arrow and choose Left, Center, or Right.

6. Choose Vertical, and then either enter the exact distance from the top edge of the page where you want to place the top edge of the object, or click the down-arrow and choose Top, Center, or Bottom.

7. To tell Works to print the object on a specific page, enter a page number in the Page # text box.

8. Choose OK.

Tip
To print an object in a header or footer on each page of the document, specify a Vertical position that places the object in the header or footer area of the page.

If your document does not appear in Page Layout view, Works displays a message and asks whether you want to switch to Page Layout view now. Choose Yes to switch to Page Layout view, or choose No to remain in the current view.

Works positions the object on the page as you specified. ❖

Chapter 27

Using Works with Non-Works Applications

by Kathy Murray

The varied tools in Microsoft Works make it possible for you to accomplish a wide range of tasks without ever leaving the program. The spreadsheet makes working with numbers, functions, and formulas easy. The word processor can take care of anything from a memo to a report to a mass mailing. The database keeps track of all those hard-to-organize small details—making it simple for you to access the data you need instantly. The communications tool links you—literally—to the world, putting you in touch with information resources so vast you can't exhaust them.

Combine all these tools with the fact that they work together seamlessly and that files created in one can be linked, embedded, or copied to the others, and you have a powerful program with the capability to handle just about any small business or home-computing need.

But what was your life like before you began using Microsoft Works? Chances are, if you used a computer at all, you used one program to track client names and addresses, another to balance your checkbook, another to write a simple letter now and then, and another to use your modem. If you were busily creating and working with data in those programs before you had Works, you might be concerned now about using those data files in your Works documents.

Don't worry. This chapter explains the basics of using files you created in other programs.

In this chapter, you learn how to do the following:

- Import files from non-Works applications
- Export files to non-Works applications
- Save files in other formats

The Basics of Importing

In the last chapter, you learned to link and embed objects. Some of the objects you use can be items you create in other Works applications—such as charts, spreadsheets, or documents. Some objects, like drawings, bitmap images, or sound files, you will create in other programs and then import into Works. *Importing* in this sense means simply to bring the file into Works in a usable format.

Suppose, for example, that you have been working on a document in Microsoft Word and you want to use it in Works so you can add spreadsheet information and a chart or two. You can easily import the document into Works and add information from any or all of the other Works tools.

Works can import files you create in any of the following programs:

Word Processing

Works for Windows 3.0 WP
Works for Windows 2.0/Work for DOS WP
Text
Text (DOS)
RTF
Word 2.x for Windows
WordPerfect 5.0
WordPerfect 5.1 for MS-DOS
WordPerfect 5.x for Windows
WordPerfect 5.1 or 5.2 secondary file
WordPerfect 5.0 secondary file
Window Write 3.0
Word for MS-DOS 3.x- 5.x
Word for MS-DOS 6.0
Works 3.0 for Macintosh WP
Works 4.0 for Macintosh WP

Spreadsheet

Works for Windows 3.0 SS
Works for Windows 2.0/Works for DOS SS
Text and Commas
Text and Tabs
Text and Tabs (DOS)
Excel SS

Lotus 1-2-3
Works 3.0 for Macintosh SS
Works 4.0 for Macintosh SS

Database

Works for Windows 3.0 SS
Works for DOS DB
Text and Commas
Text and Tabs
Text and Tabs (DOS)
dBASE III
dBASE IV
Works 3.0 for Macintosh DB
Works 4.0 for Macintosh DB

In addition, Works can open files of the following types:

Works WP (*.wps)
Works SS (*.wks)
Works DB (*wmc)
Backup files (*.b*)
Excel SS (*.xl*)
Text (8txt)
dBASE (*.dbf)
Sylk (*.SYK)
Lotus 1-2-3 (*.wk.)
RTF (*rtf)
Word for Windows 2.x (*.doc)
Word for Windows 6.0 (*.doc)
WordPerfect 5.x (*.doc)
WordPerfect 6.x (*.doc)
Windows Write (*.wri)
Word for DOS 3.x-5.x (*.doc)
Word for MS-DOS 6.0 (*.doc)
Works 3.0 for Macintosh DB (*.db)
Works 4.0 for Macintosh DB (*.db)
Works 3.0 for Macintosh SS (*.ss)
Works 4.0 for Macintosh SS (*.ss)
Works 3.0 for Macintosh WP (*.wp)
Works 4.0 for Macintosh WP (*.wp)

In some cases, you might want to import only selected data and not an entire file. If you were copying information from Quickbooks for Windows, for example, you might not want to use the entire file (which would give you an error anyway); you might want to import only a portion of the data you select. The next section follows this example and shows you how to import data from another Windows program.

Importing Data

There are a variety of ways you can bring data into Microsoft Works. These different methods apply also to many non-Works applications. Generally speaking, any way in which you get already-entered data into Works is a kind of importing. The following tasks fall into the "importing" category:

- Copying and pasting information from another Works file into your current file (covered in Chapter 26, "Using the Works Tools Together.")
- Copying and pasting information from a non-Works program into your Works file.
- Using the commands in the Insert menu to import objects, clip art, spreadsheets, tables, or entire files. (For more information about inserting objects and information in your Works document, see Chapter 26, "Using the Works Tools Together.")
- Opening a non-Works document from within your Works application.

Copying and Pasting Information from Non-Works Applications

Windows 95 makes it easier than ever to run multiple applications, whether you're running only Windows programs or a mixture of DOS and Windows applications. In some cases, you will want to copy information from a non-Works file to paste in your Works document, without using the entire file.

Copying Text from Microsoft Bookshelf

For example, suppose you're using Microsoft Bookshelf (which is a collection of articles and reference materials you can use in your documents) to add items of interest to a report you are writing. Here's the process for copying Bookshelf information into your Works document:

1. Begin with your Works document open on the screen. Position the cursor at the point you want to insert the copied information, as shown in figure 27.1.

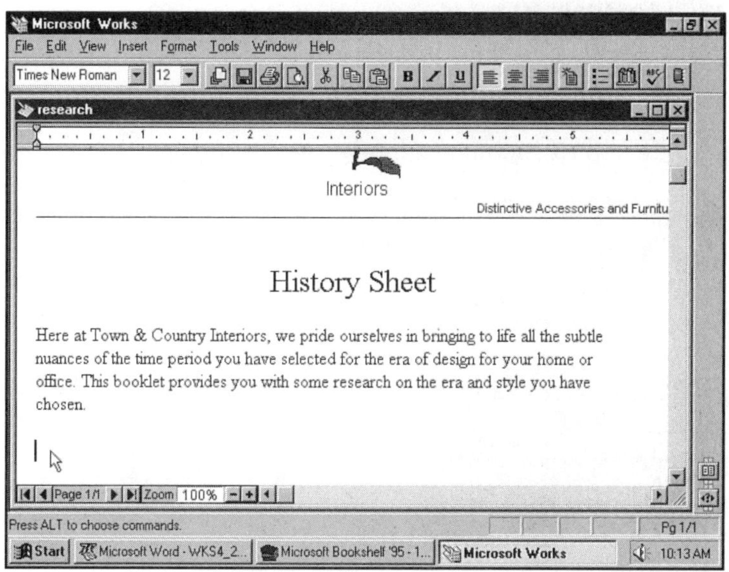

Fig. 27.1
Pasted text or data will appear at the insertion point in your Works document.

2. Start Microsoft Bookshelf. Locate the information you want to use in Bookshelf and highlight it, as figure 27.2 shows.

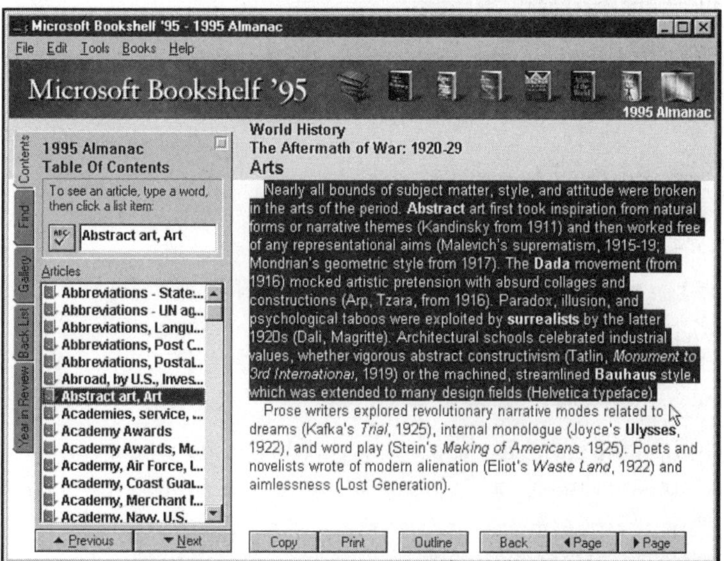

Fig. 27.2
Highlight the information you want to copy.

3. Copy the information following the usual convention for the non-Works program. (Look for a Copy command in the Edit menu.) In Bookshelf's case, click the Copy button at the bottom of the screen. This places a copy of the information on the Windows Clipboard.

4. Display Microsoft Works by clicking the Works button in the taskbar at the bottom of the screen.

5. Choose Edit, Paste; click the Paste toolbar button; or press Ctrl+V to paste the copied information into the document.

The information is then pasted into the document at the cursor position, as shown in figure 27.3. If you pasted the information at the wrong point, choose Edit, Undo to "pick up" the information; then reposition the cursor in the right place and press Ctrl+V to paste.

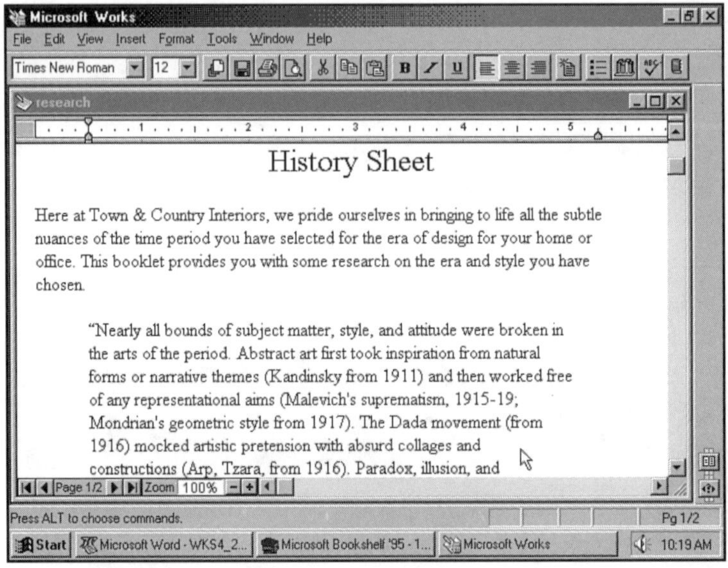

Fig. 27.3
The Bookshelf information adds a special touch to your Works document quickly and easily.

Tip
If the information you are bringing into Works will change and you want the changes to be reflected in your Works document, link the object you're importing to its source document. To find out more about linking, see Chapter 26.

Importing a Range from an Excel Spreadsheet

In another example, you might want to use data you entered in an Excel spreadsheet in your Works spreadsheet file. To use selected information from your Excel spreadsheet, follow these steps:

1. Position the cursor at the point in your Works file where you want the information to appear. (The spreadsheet is used in this example.)

2. Display Excel and highlight the range you want to copy. You might want to do this by tiling the windows, as shown in figure 27.4. In the figure, the Excel spreadsheet is shown on the left and the new Works spreadsheet, into which the information will be pasted, is shown on the right.

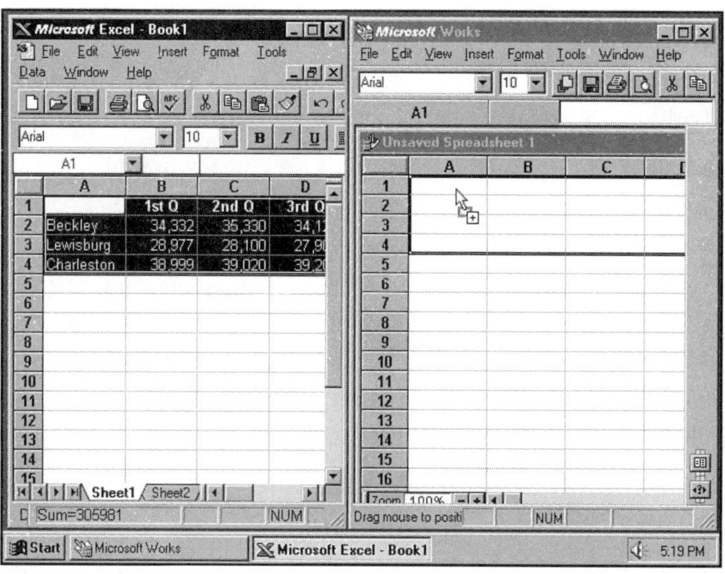

Fig. 27.4
Works is simple to use with other popular programs, which means you don't have to enter the same data twice.

3. Highlight the Excel range and then drag-and-drop it into the waiting Works spreadsheet, as figure 27.4 shows. If you prefer, you can choose Edit, Copy or Edit, Paste to copy the information into Works.

   The information then becomes part of the Works spreadsheet.

> **Troubleshooting**
>
> *The values in my Excel spreadsheet didn't come into my Works spreadsheet correctly.*
>
> If you're trying to drag-and-drop a section from your Excel spreadsheet and you're either getting strange values or errors, take a look at the way you entered information in the original spreadsheet. Are your column labels really labels? (They should have an apostrophe preceding the first character.) Are you attempting to copy a portion of the spreadsheet that needs a formula in another portion of the spreadsheet in order to produce the correct result? In any case, the answer lies in the original application—not in Works, and a little sleuthing should quickly reveal your problem.

Importing an Excel Chart

You've heard the old saying "a picture's worth a thousand words," but have you heard that "a chart sticks where words won't?" If you want to communicate something strongly in as few words as possible, use a chart. If you are attached to charts you created in other programs, you might be able to use them in Microsoft Works as well.

To use an Excel chart in a Works document, follow these steps:

1. Position the cursor at the point in the document where you want to insert the chart.

2. Display the file in Excel that contains the chart you want to use. (Again, you might want to tile the windows so you can see both Excel and Works at the same time.)

3. Click the chart to select it.

4. Drag the chart to the Works window.

   When you release the mouse button, the chart is pasted at the cursor position in your Works document (see fig. 27.5).

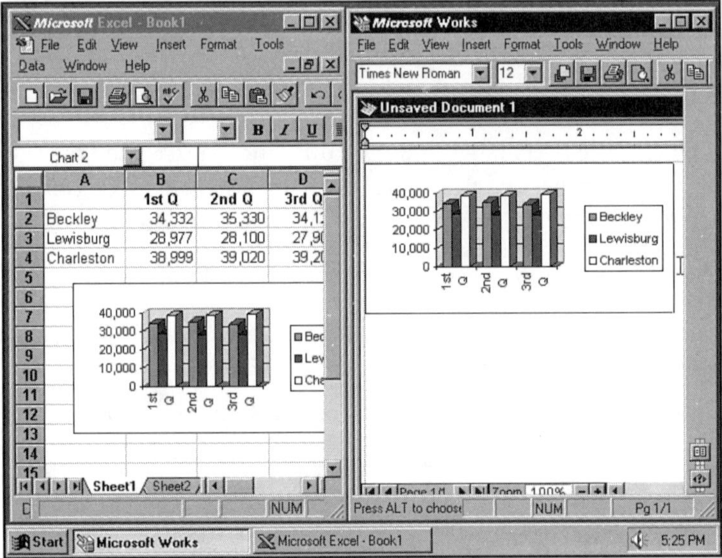

Fig. 27.5
A chart can communicate sometimes complicated relationships in a glance. Use charts to reinforce ideas and projections in your reports and other documents.

> **Troubleshooting**
>
> *The chart takes up too much room on my document page.*
>
> After you insert the chart, click outside the chart area and then click directly on it. Handles appear on the chart, showing that it is selected (see fig. 27.6). You can now position the pointer at a corner or edge of the object and resize it as you would any placed object. Choose File, Print Preview to see how the object looks on the page.

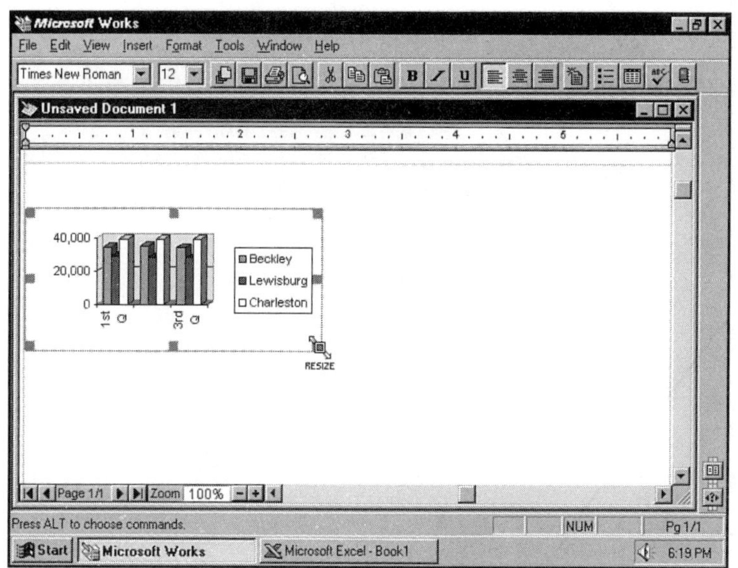

Fig. 27.6
A chart in Works is an object, which means you can click it to select it and then resize or move it as necessary.

Importing a PowerPoint Slide

If you are ever called to produce a presentation—whether it's for your peers, your clients, or your company—you might find yourself working with Microsoft PowerPoint, a powerful presentation graphics program that is part of the Microsoft Office package. One of the benefits of PowerPoint is how easy it is to use. Suppose that you are creating a corporate report in Microsoft Works that will go along with the presentation you will be giving. You can easily use the first page of your presentation as a cover page for your report. Here's how:

1. Open the Microsoft Works document that you plan to use as the annual report.
2. Position the cursor at the point you want to add the cover page.
3. Start PowerPoint and open the necessary presentation file. Display the presentation in Outline view.
4. Highlight the first page, as shown in figure 27.7.
5. Choose Edit, Copy to paste the page on the Windows Clipboard.
6. Select your Works document, and paste the text at the cursor position.

The presentation page appears at the cursor position, as shown in figure 27.8.

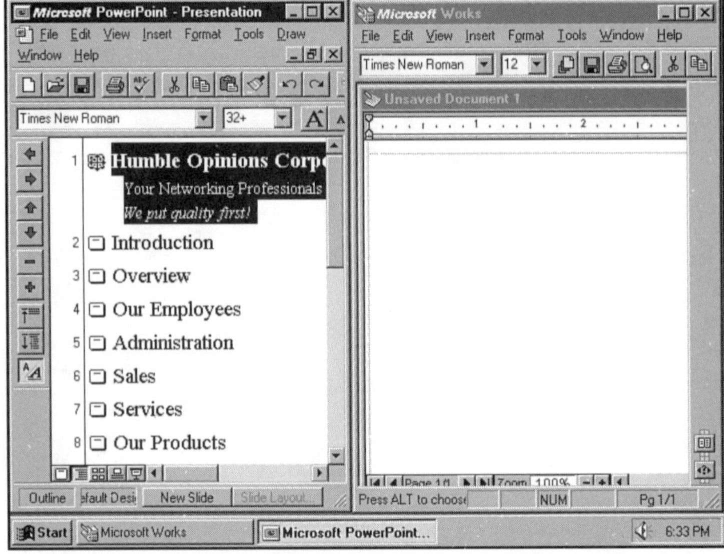

Fig. 27.7
You can easily use a page from your presentation in your Works documents by copying the text you need.

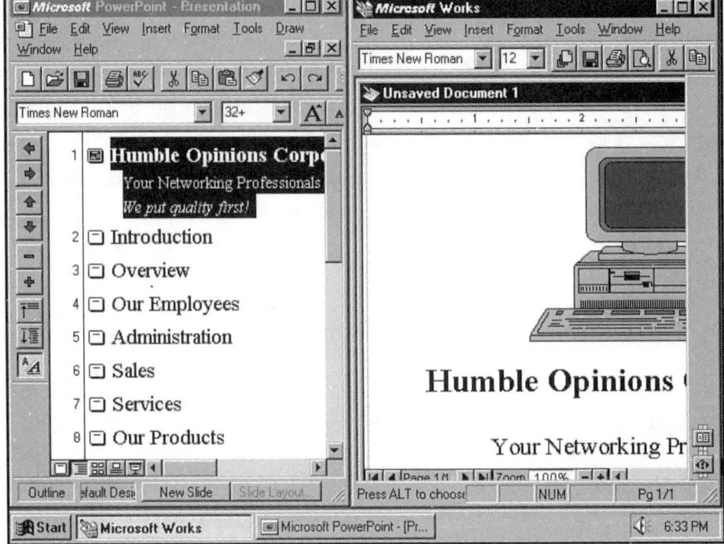

Fig. 27.8
After you copy the presentation page to your Works document, you can resize or reshape it by clicking and dragging one of its borders.

Using a Microsoft Word Outline for Your Works Document

If you have ever agonized over an outline, you'll be glad to know that you can use your already-created Microsoft Word outlines with Microsoft Works.

To use a Word outline in a Works document, follow these steps:

1. Begin with your Works document open and the cursor positioned at the point you want the outline to be inserted.

2. Open the Word document with the outline you want to use.

3. Display the document in Outline view.

4. Highlight the outline and choose Edit, Copy to make a copy of it (this places the copy on the Windows Clipboard).

5. Display your Works document and choose Edit, Paste to paste the outline at the cursor position.

   The outline is then pasted into the document, as figure 27.9 shows. It is treated as an object, which means you can click on it to select and then resize or reshape it as necessary. You also can delete the outline by pressing Delete or Backspace.

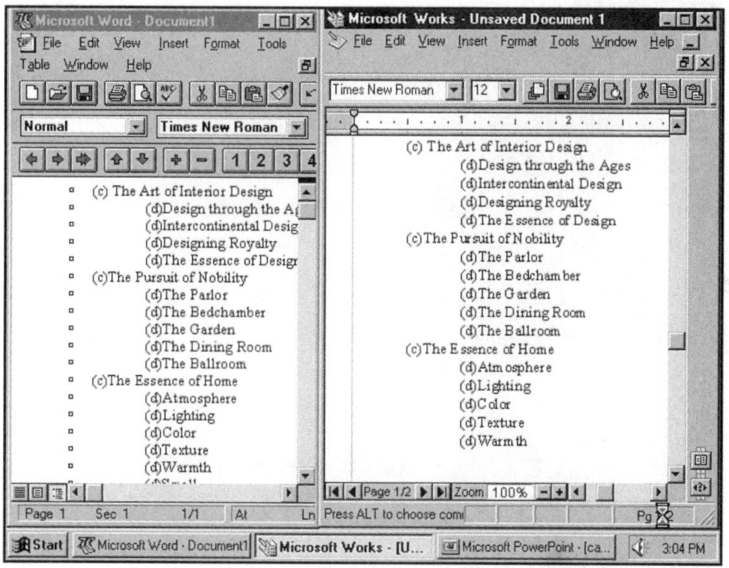

Fig. 27.9
You can include an outline you created in another word processor when you want to add a table of contents page or provide the reader with the overall game plan of your document.

Tip
Before you begin importing data, make sure you have a current backup of important files. Although experiencing a lockup or losing data during this type of procedure is unlikely, it's better to be safe than sorry.

Importing Files

If you ever created files in other programs, you might be hoping you can use that information in your Works files. As mentioned earlier in this chapter, Works supports a number of popular file formats. In this section, you learn to import an entire file into Microsoft Works.

To import a file into Microsoft Works, follow these steps:

1. Choose File, Open.

   The Open dialog box appears, as shown in figure 27.10. The Look In list box shows you the folder Works displays in the List area.

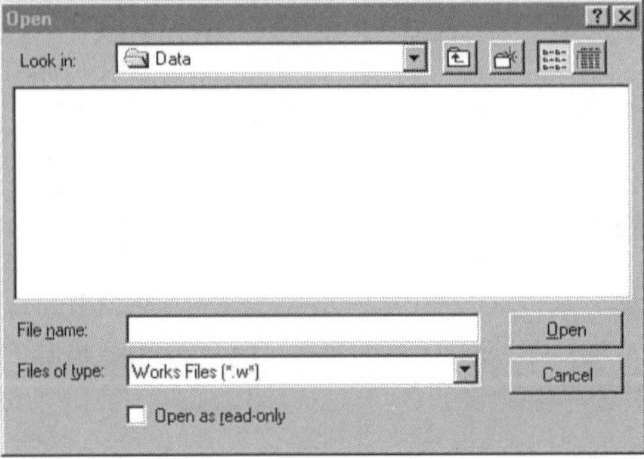

Fig. 27.10 After you locate the files you want to import, you can specify the file type and import the files.

2. To move to a different folder, click the Look In down-arrow and choose the folder you want from the displayed list.

3. When the file you want to import is displayed in the List area, highlight it. The name of the file you select appears in the File Name box.

4. Click the down-arrow to the right of the Files of Type box. A drop-down list of supported file types appears, as shown in figure 27.11.

   If you want to import a file that is not shown as one of Works' supported types, try opening the application in which you created the file and saving that file in a format that Works supports. Most popular programs can save files in a variety of formats.

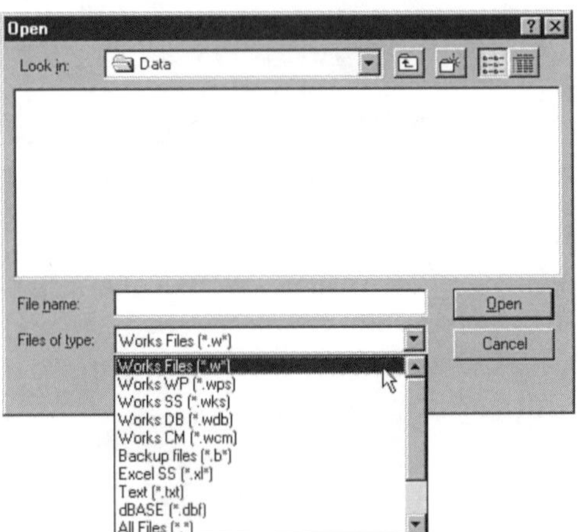

Fig. 27.11 You can double-click the Files of Type selection to begin importing the file you've selected.

5. Click the file type; then click OK.

Works displays the message `Converting:` in the left side of the status bar at the bottom of the screen. When the file has been converted, it appears in the document window.

Tip
If you're unsure what type of file you're importing, click the Details button (furthest to the right at the top of the Open dialog box) to have Works show you the type of the files in the selected folder.

If you are importing a file type not recognized by Works, the Open File As dialog box appears, asking whether you want to open the file as a Text for DOS or Text for Windows file (see fig. 27.12). Choose the option that fits what you're trying to accomplish (in this case, choose Text for Windows) and then select the Works tool you plan to use the file with (here, it's the Word Processor). When the file opens, you might have some "garbage characters" to clean up.

Fig. 27.12
When you import text files in this manner, you might lose formatting such as boldface and italic characters; however, you can easily select the text and format it in Works.

Tip
If a file includes information that might change and you want to keep the file updated, you can create a link between the imported file and the original file so that changes are reflected in both files. For more about linking, see Chapter 26.

Troubleshooting

I don't see the other word processor type I use. Can I still import files?

Although Works doesn't include many of the other popular word processing formats in the Files of Type box (in the Open dialog box), you can still attempt to open files from word processing programs like WordStar and Write. For best results, go into those programs and save the file as a Works format, a Word format, or a Text Only format. This will make the importing easier and give you less formatting to clean up.

What are all these boxes and weird characters?

Those are the formatting characters you need to clean up (see fig. 27.13). Some programs produce a massive amount of garbage characters that "stick" to all the words in the file. Other programs seem to include the character primarily at the beginning and end of the file. (These files are easier to clean up.) In Works, just highlight the characters and delete them by pressing Delete. It can be a time-consuming process, especially if you have a mass of unnecessary formatting characters, but it still saves you the time of retyping the file from scratch.

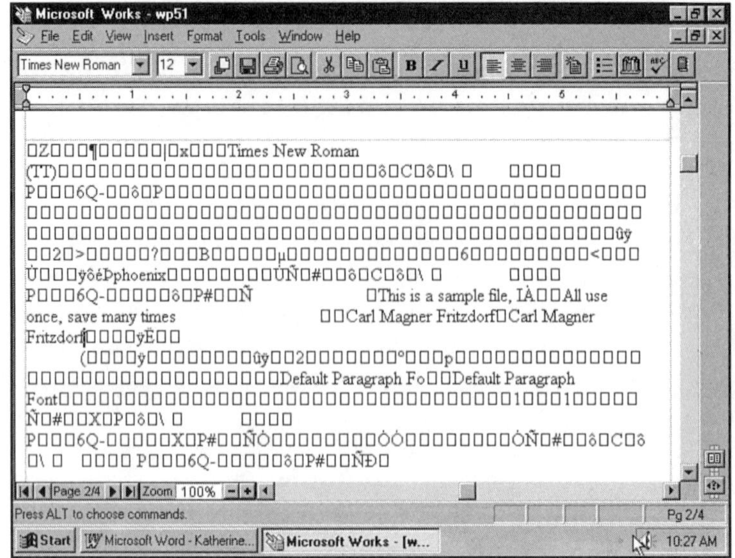

Fig. 27.13 The formatting characters from the other word processor are an unnecessary jumble of screen clutter—just highlight and delete the characters as you would any unneeded text.

Exporting Files to Other Programs

The process of preparing files to be used in other programs—or saving them in other formats—is known as *exporting*. When you export a Works file, the data you entered is kept intact, but the formatting and the internal file codes are changed so the other program can read the file.

Exporting Options

Works enables you to save files in a number of different formats, depending on the tool you are using. You select the format you want to use by choosing it in the Save as Type box in the Save As dialog box (covered in the next section). The choices available to you—the program formats in which you can save the file—depend on which tool you used to create the file.

For example, if you are exporting a word processing document, you can save it in the following formats:

- Works WP
- Works for Windows 3.0 WP
- Works for Windows 2.0/Works for DOS WP
- Works 3.0 and 4.0 for Macintosh WP
- Text
- Text (DOS)

- RTF
- WordPerfect 5.x for Windows
- Word 2.x for Windows
- Windows Write 3.0
- Word for MS-DOS 3.x, 5.x, 6.0, 7.0

If you are exporting a spreadsheet file, your choices are these:

- Works SS
- Works for Windows 3.0 SS
- Works for Windows 2.0/Works for DOS SS
- Text & Commas
- Text & Tabs
- Text & Tabs (DOS)
- Excel SS
- Lotus 1-2-3
- Works 3.0 and 4.0 for Macintosh SS

If you are exporting a database file, you can choose from these formats:

- Works DB
- Works for Windows 3.0 DB
- Works for Windows 2.0 (Works for DOS) DB
- Text & Commas
- Text & Tabs
- Text & Tabs (DOS)
- dBASE III
- dBASE IV
- Works 3.0 and 4.0 for Macintosh DB

The options for exporting a communications document are somewhat more limited:

- CM Settings
- Session data

Exporting a File

When you want to export a file to be used in another program, follow these steps:

1. Display the file you want to export. This example uses a word processing document.

2. Choose File, Save As. The Save As dialog box appears, as shown in figure 27.14.

3. Choose the folder in which you want to save the file.

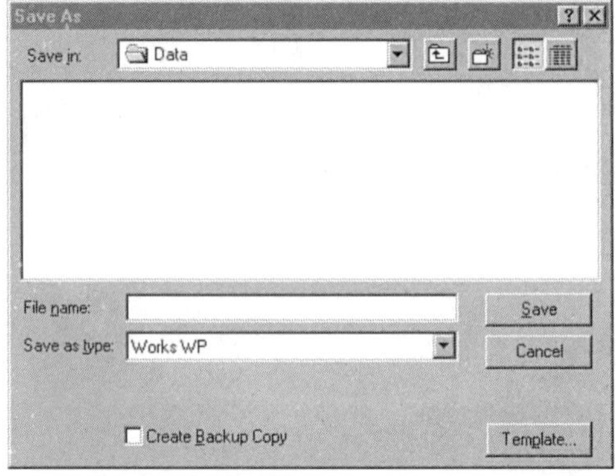

Fig. 27.14
Use the Save As dialog box to save files under a different name or to choose a different type of file format for the saved file.

4. In the File Name box, type a name for the saved file.

5. In the Save as Type box, click the down-arrow. A list of file types appears, as shown in figure 27.15.

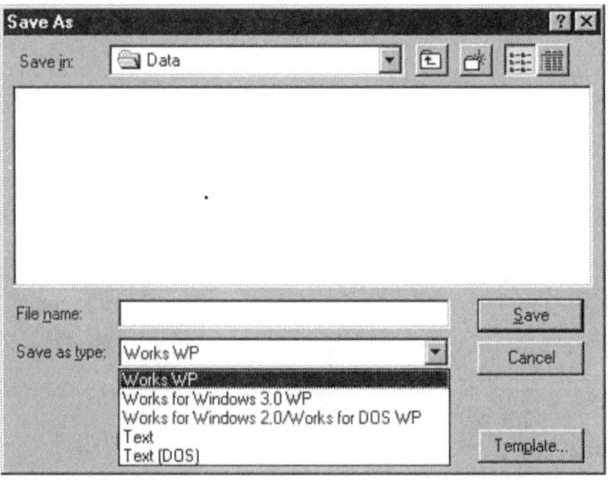

Fig. 27.15
You can choose several different formats in which to export the Works file.

6. Click the format you want for the file; then click OK.

   Works saves the file in the format you selected.❖

Chapter 28

Creating Form Letters, Mail Labels, and Envelopes

by Kathy Murray

If you own and operate a small business or if you're responsible for tracking and organizing client lists and addresses, the Works database is an invaluable tool for keeping your data straight. In addition, the Works word processor makes creating and printing letters and reports easy. You can use the information you create in both these tools—a customer database file from the Works database and a letter from the Works word processor—to create form letters and mailing labels that reduce your work time and increase your productivity.

After you create a database that contains names and addresses, you can create (or adapt) a form letter in the word processor. You can then print the letters, letting Works insert the names and addresses for you. (This process is sometimes called *merge printing* or *mail merge*.) Works inserts in each copy of the form letter the name and address from one record in a database, so you can print literally hundreds of copies of the same letter by choosing a few simple commands. You can also use database tools to sort and select addresses for the form letters, so you print only the letters you want.

Works can use database information to print envelopes and mailing labels, or Works can print a single envelope or label using a name and address in a document displayed on-screen. This chapter describes all of these techniques.

In this chapter, you learn how to do the following:

- Create and print a form letter
- Print mailing labels
- Print envelopes

Creating a Form Letter

Before you can print form letters, you must do two things:

- You must create a Works database that contains the names and addresses you want to print on the form letter.
- You must type the form letter in the word processor and insert codes, called *placeholders*, that tell Works where to print the merged information from the database. For example, you could insert placeholders that tell Works to first print the First Name database field, then the Last Name field, followed by the Company, City, State, ZIP, and Country fields.

Figure 28.1 shows a form letter with placeholders inserted for the name, address, and greeting; figure 28.2 shows a Works database in List view; and figure 28.3 shows several letters printed from the database and form.

Fig. 28.1
Placeholders mark the place where Works will insert data from your database.

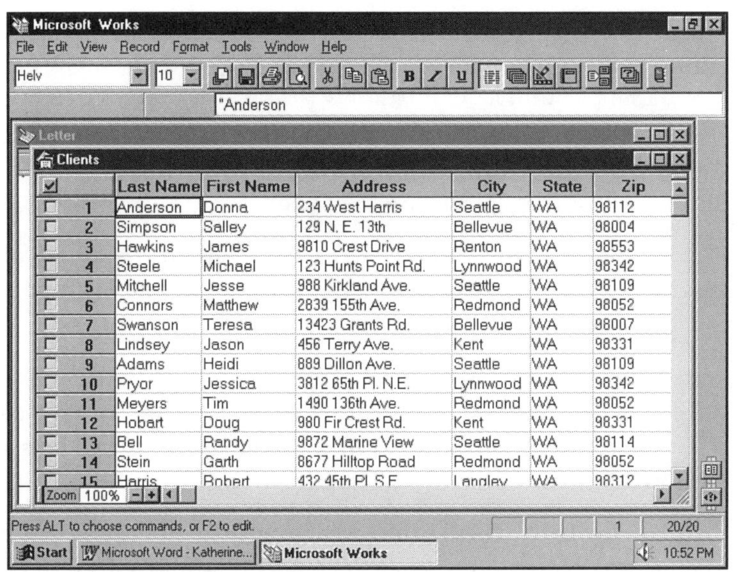

Fig. 28.2
With merge printing, you can make the most of information you already entered, saving you time and trouble.

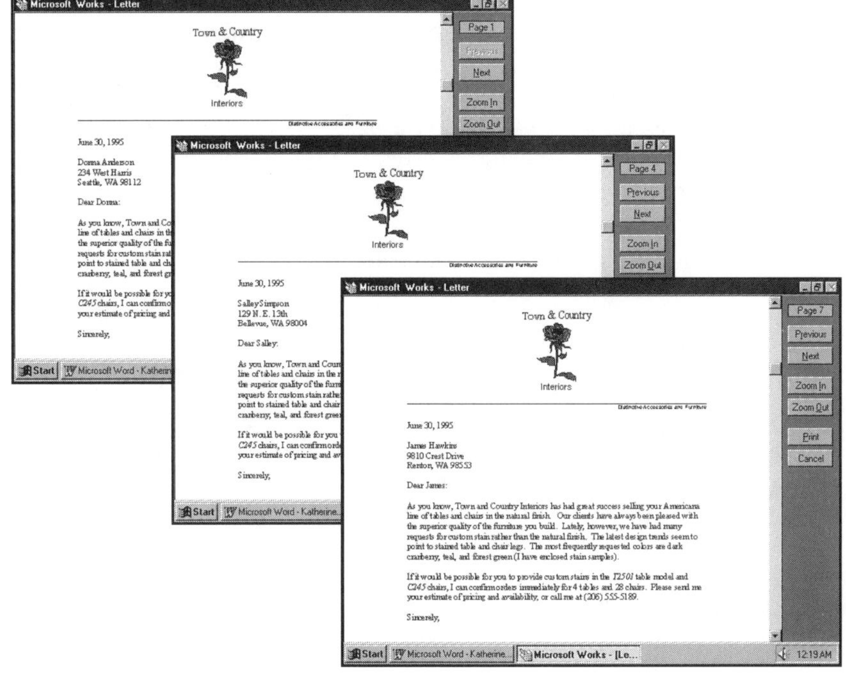

Fig. 28.3
Works helps you "work smarter, not harder" by enabling you to write a letter once and send it to hundreds of people—personalized and professional.

Form Letter Tips

In Chapter 4, you learn to work with the Works word processor. The process for creating a simple form letter is basically the same as that for creating any Works document. In fact, you might find it easiest to modify an existing letter, turning it into a form letter by adding the necessary placeholders. Here are some tips for creating an effective form letter:

- Plan the placeholders you want to use. Do you want First Name and Last Name? Will you include a Title, such as Mr. or Mrs.? Do you need to include Company Name and/or Position?

- Watch punctuation closely. All punctuation needs to appear outside the placeholders so that it will appear printed on the page. For example, be sure to include the comma between City and State so the address appears as expected.

- You can use placeholders in the body of the letter, if necessary. For example, if you have a field named Product in your database and it stores the names of different products your company carries, you might want to include the line "Thank you for your interest in Product" in the body of your letter. This enables you to further customize the letter and speak directly to the reader's experience.

- Try not to give the impression that you're writing a form letter. We all like to receive correspondence written just for us—but few of us enjoy receiving cookie-cutter letters. However, mail merge makes good business sense. Personalize the letters as much as possible by using placeholders tailored to your clients' information.

Creating the Form Letter

Now you're ready to tackle the task of creating the form letter. When you open Works, choose Works Tools and then select the Word Processor. Works opens a blank document in which you can work. Works 4.0 includes a new command in the Tools menu—Form Letters—that walks you through the process.

Start by choosing Tools, Form Letters. The Form Letters dialog box appears as shown in figure 28.4. The Instructions tab explains the steps involved in creating a form letter.

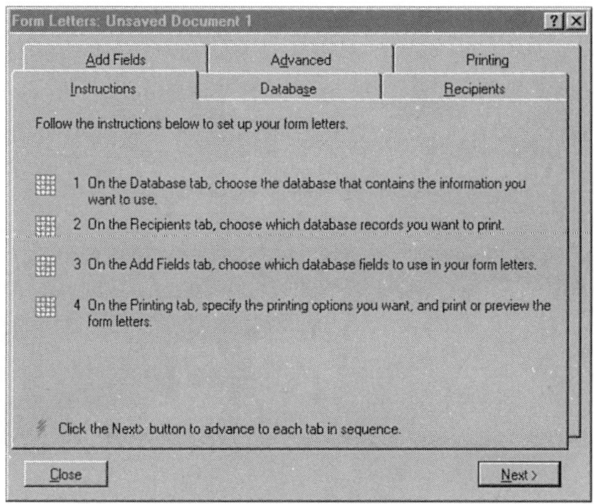

Fig. 28.4
Works leads you through the process of creating a form letter, removing the guesswork and potential errors that are common the first time you try a new procedure.

After you read the Instructions tab, click the Next button to display the tab that describes how to choose a database.

Choosing the Database

Before you get too far into creating a form letter, Works asks you to choose the database file you want to use. The database file you choose is the file that stores the data you will merge with the form letter. You specify the database file in the Database tab of the Form Letters dialog box (see fig. 28.5).

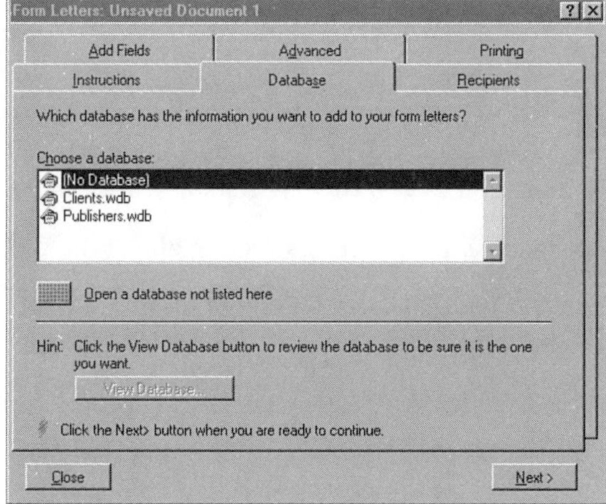

Fig. 28.5
In the Database tab, you choose the database file you want to work with.

Tip
If you don't know which file to use, click a database name in the Choose a Database area and then choose View Database. Works displays the database in its own window and tells you to click the Go Back button when you finish viewing the file.

Click the name of the file you want to use. If you don't see the file you need, click the Open a Database Not Listed Here button. The Open Another File dialog box appears, in which you can search for the file you want. When you select the file you want, choose Next. The Instructions tab appears again, showing that you have completed the first step. Next, you need to decide who you want to include in the printing.

Note

Works can print records from only one database at a time in a form letter. If you print the form letters you want from the current database and then want to use a different database, you can easily change the database you're using. To switch databases, choose the Database tab and select the database you want to use.

Specifying Letter Recipients

Depending on the size of your database, you might not want to send form letters to all the clients in the file. You might, for example, want to send form letters only to all customers who purchased a particular product or to customers in a certain sales region. You use the Recipients tab of the Form Letter dialog box to specify the records you want to use in your merge print. Follow these steps:

1. Click the Recipients tab (see fig. 28.6).

   By default, all records in the database are chosen. This means that when you print, a form letter will print for every record in the database. If you want to use only selected records, you can mark the records you want to create a filter to produce only the records you want to include. For more information about selecting and filtering specific database records, see Chapter 21, "Retrieving Database Information."

2. Choose the Recipients option by selecting one of the following:

   - *All Records in the Database*. This option is selected by default. If you leave it selected, form letters for all records will print.

   - *Current Records Visible in the Database*. This option prints form letters for only those records currently displayed in the database window.

   - *Currently Marked Records in the Database*. This option prints form letters for records currently marked. If you want to return to the database window to mark records before using this option, click the View Database button to display the database file; mark your records; and then click the Go Back button when you're through.

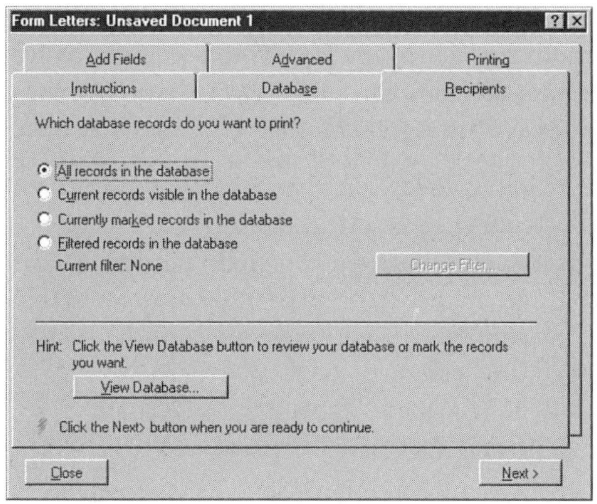

Fig. 28.6
On the Recipients tab, you choose who you want to send the form letters to. You can select the entire database or you can narrow the selected records to a specific group.

- *Filtered Records in the Database*. This option allows you to choose a filter you already created or to create a new filter that will make a subset of the records you want to print.

3. After you make your selection, click Next. The Instructions tab appears again, this time with another step marked off.

Adding Fields

Click the Next button to move to the Instructions tab and click Next again. Works moves you to the next step in the process: adding fields. The Add Fields tab appears, as shown in figure 28.7. Here, you tell Works which fields you want to use in the database to fill in information on the form letter. Typical fields used in form letters are First Name, Last Name, Company Name, Address, City, State, and so on.

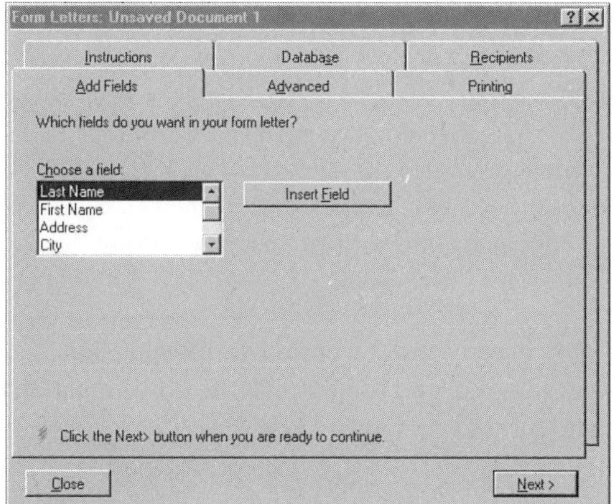

Fig. 28.7
The Add Fields tab shows a list of the available fields in the database you selected. You can choose the ones you want to include on the form letter.

Click a field you want to add and then click the Insert Field button. Works automatically adds the field to the form you're creating. Repeat the step for each field you want to add to the letter: select the field in the Choose a Field list and then click the Insert Field button.

When you finish adding fields, click Next. Again, the Instructions tab appears. The third step is checked off, and printing is all that remains. Before you print the documents, however, you might need to rearrange the way the fields are placed, add some text, or make other changes to the document. The Advanced tab contains the button you need to get back to the letter in the word processing window.

Editing the Form Letter

If you started with a blank word processing document, chose a database, selected your recipients, and then inserted fields, Works just dropped the fields in one at a time in a line across the top of your document. You need to be able to move the fields, write the letter, and include a salutation at the end before you print the document.

To display the letter in a document window, click the Advanced tab and then click the Edit button to return to the document. The names of the fields you selected—the placeholders—are shown in curly braces. You can now edit the document as necessary to position the fields where you want them and add the body text of the letter.

To edit the letter, enter the text as you normally would in a document. You can select and cut any of the field names (make sure you include the curly braces) and move the field names to the proper locations in the letter. Insert paragraph returns, spaces, and punctuation between the field names, if necessary. Figure 28.8 shows the edited document.

Note

You can format the field placeholders using fonts and character enhancements such as italics or boldfacing. You can also copy placeholder chevrons (also called *curly braces*) to insert new placeholders without using the Insert Field dialog box. However, you cannot format placeholders with left and right pointed brackets (<<, >>). Placeholders must be enclosed in chevrons and you must make sure that field names are *exactly* the same (upper- and lowercase, spaces, and so on).

When you're ready to return to the Form Letter dialog box, click Go Back. This returns you to the Advanced tab. Click the Printing tab to display the final screen of the Form Letters dialog box.

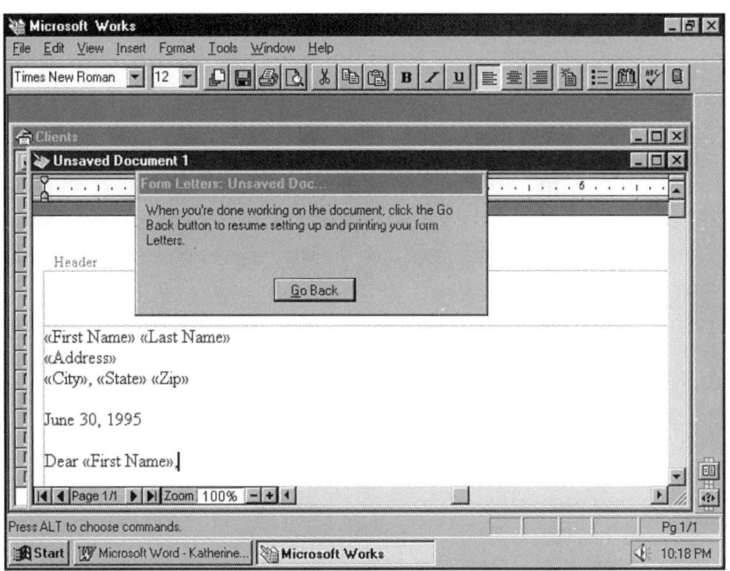

Fig. 28.8 Copy a Name placeholder and paste it elsewhere in the document to personalize the letter.

Previewing and Printing the Form Letters

Now you have come to the final step: printing the form letters. On the Printing tab, shown in figure 28.9, you have all the options you need for previewing and printing the document.

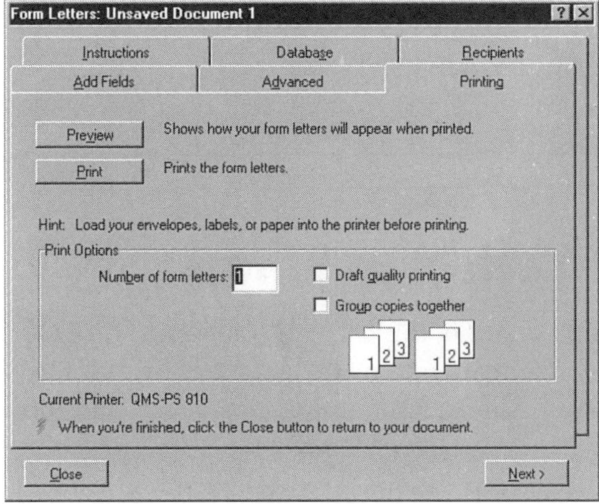

Fig. 28.9 Choose print options in the Printing tab; you can, alternatively, select another tab to make last minute corrections before printing.

To see the form letters before you print them, choose the Preview button. Works asks you whether you want to preview the current records. Click OK. The first form letter appears in Preview mode. You can use Zoom In and

Zoom Out to examine the letter. Click Cancel to return to the Printing tab. Check the punctuation, spacing, and so on in a letter or two to make sure they are right before you print; a little time well spent now will save you time, and paper, in the long run.

Next, check the printing options. Make sure you specify the correct number of copies (the default is 1) and that you select Draft Quality Printing or Group Copies Together, if you need those options. When printing your form letters, group the copies together if there is more than one page in the letter; Works prints pages one, two, and three of the first letter; then pages one, two, and three of the second letter; and so on. Grouping the copies saves you the time and trouble of gathering and collating the printed copies yourself.

Finally, choose Print. Works asks whether you want to print the current records. Click OK. Works tells you the status of the file being sent to the printer.

Troubleshooting

I accidentally added a placeholder to my letter. How can I get rid of it?

Select the placeholder by highlighting it (curly braces and all) and then press the Delete key.

My letter printed with the field names instead of the merged database information. What did I do wrong?

An option in the Print dialog box needs to be checked. To do that, choose File, Print. Select the Print Merge option to place a check mark beside it, and then choose OK to print the letter.

Working with Mailing Labels

In the preceding sections of this chapter, you learned how to print form letters by inserting information from a Works database into a word processor document. In a very similar fashion, you print names and addresses on labels from a database. Printing labels is simpler than printing form letters—Works includes formatting information for printing on most popular mailing label sizes. You can also create your own customized label definitions.

After you select or customize a mailing label definition, you can print a few test labels to ensure that you selected the proper label definition and that the labels are aligned correctly in the printer.

> **Note**
>
> Works deals with labels and envelopes differently; if you choose to create labels in a word processing document, you cannot use that same document for envelopes.

Printing mailing labels involves four steps:

1. Choose the database containing the information you want to print on the labels.
2. In a word processor document, insert placeholders for the database information you want to print on each label. For example, insert placeholders for First Name and Last Name.
3. Choose a preset label size, or customize a label definition.
4. Print the labels. Optionally, you can preview the merge-printed labels and print a few test labels to make sure the labels print correctly.

Creating and Printing the Labels

The first step in printing mailing labels is, of course, creating them. The following process is similar to that of creating a form letter, with a few simple changes:

1. Create the database that contains the information you want to print on the labels.
2. Display the word processor document for which you want to print mailing labels. This can be a new document or one you worked with previously.
3. Choose Tools, Labels. The Labels dialog box appears, asking you to choose whether you want to create labels or multiple copies of one label, as described in the following list:
   - If you want to create many different labels—for example, if you're preparing labels for a large number of form letters—choose Labels.
   - If you want to create many copies of the same label—for example, if you're creating a label for disks or cassette tapes—choose Multiple Copies of One Label.

When you click Labels, the Labels dialog box shown in figure 28.10 appears. Similar to the process for creating form letters, the label printing process involves choosing the database you want to use and specifying the records for which you want to print labels. Additionally, you need to select the size of the labels you're using and the layout of the labels before you print.

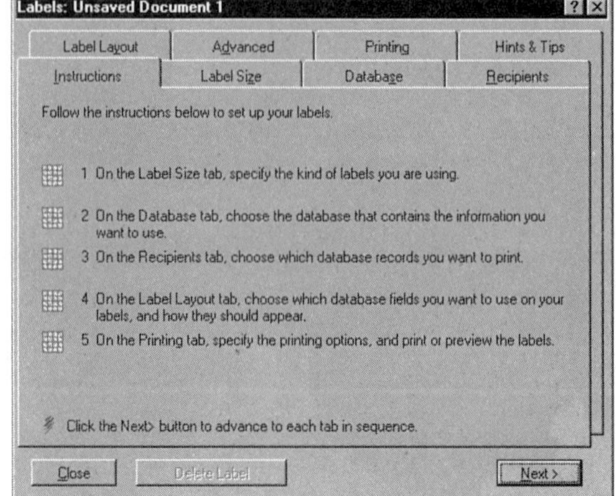

Fig. 28.10 Many of the tabs in the Labels dialog box are the same as those in the Form Letters dialog box: Database, Recipients, Advanced, and Printing.

When you first open the Labels dialog box, you see the Instructions tab. Additionally, each time you click the Next button, the Instructions tab appears again to guide you through the process of creating mailing labels. Click Next and continue to the next step in the process.

In the Labels dialog box, follow these steps to create mailing labels:

1. Click Next. The Label Size page appears (see fig. 28.11). Choose the label from the displayed list of label types or click Custom to enter measurements for your own custom labels. (See "Creating Custom Labels" later in this chapter for detailed instructions on working with custom settings.) After you select the label, click Next. The Instructions tab appears again, showing that you have completed the first step.

2. In the Instructions tab, click Next. The Database tab appears. Choose the name of the database you want to use to print the labels, and click Next. You return to the Instructions tab.

> **Note**
>
> For a more detailed explanation of the steps, see the previous section, "Creating a Form Letter."

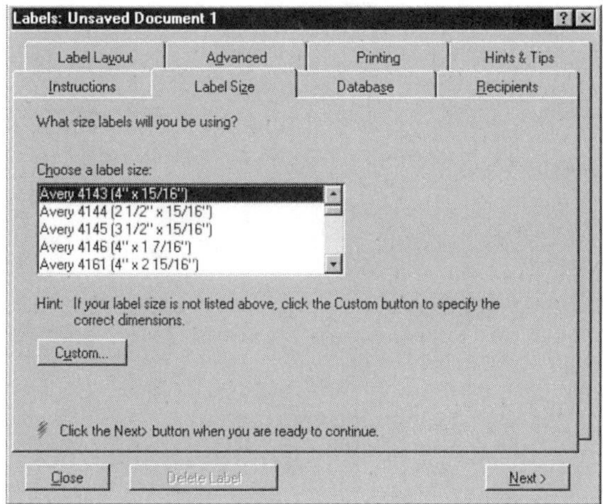

Fig. 28.11
If your label is not an Avery, it might list its compatible Avery size on the back of the label package; otherwise, you'll have to set a Custom label size.

3. Click Next again. This time, the Recipients tab appears. Choose whether you want all records, displayed records, marked records, or filtered records used in the labels. Click Next after you make your selection.

4. Click Next again. The Label Layout tab appears. On this page, you specify the field placeholders and design the format—that is, how you want the placeholders arranged on the label. Simply select the field you want to add and click Add Field. When you want to begin a new line, click New Line. If you want to start over, click Clear All. To add punctuation characters, such as a comma or space, position the cursor where you want the item and type as usual. Figure 28.12 shows the Label Layout tab after adding standard label fields.

   After you finish entering and arranging the field placeholders, click Next. You return to the Instructions tab.

5. Click Next again. The Printing tab appears.

6. First, click Preview to see how the labels will look when printed. Works asks whether you want to see all the records in the database. Click OK. The labels display in Preview mode. Figure 28.13 shows the labels when the view has been enlarged with Zoom In.

Tip
If you want to change the font, size, style, or color of the label text, click the Font button and make your choices.

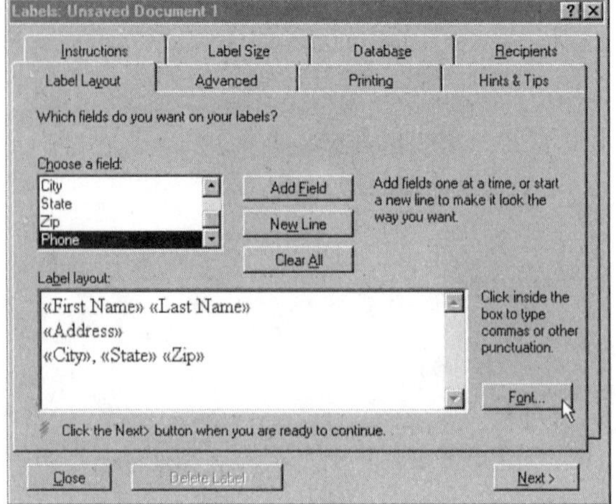

Fig. 28.12
In the Label Layout tab, you add and arrange field placeholders.

Fig. 28.13
If you aren't happy with the way labels appear in Preview mode, you can return to the Labels dialog box and make any necessary changes.

Note

Before the labels display in Preview mode, Works checks the page margins and page settings for your document and compares them to the margins and settings used for printing mailing labels. If the labels are positioned too far out in the margins—in the unprintable area—Works tells you to increase your page margins and preview the labels again.

7. When you're ready to print, click the Test button on the Printing tab to have Works test print the first two rows of labels. This way you can check the alignment and the margins to make sure everything lines up. If you need to make changes, select the Label Size tab and select a different label, or click Custom and modify the Label Size or Page Size settings.

8. Finally, click Print to begin the process of printing the labels. Works tells you how many records are left to print. If you want to stop printing at any time, click Cancel.

Tip
The Hints & Tips tab gives you additional suggestions for working with mailing labels.

Creating Custom Mailing Labels

When you select the Label Size tab in the Labels dialog box, you have the option of choosing a custom label and entering the necessary settings. When creating custom mailing labels, use one of your label sheets as a sample and measure all margins and spaces carefully.

If you want to design a custom label, follow these steps:

1. In the Choose a Label Size list, scroll to the very bottom and click the Custom Label Size option.

2. Click the Custom button to display the Custom Labels dialog box (see fig. 28.14). Use this dialog box to create your own custom labels.

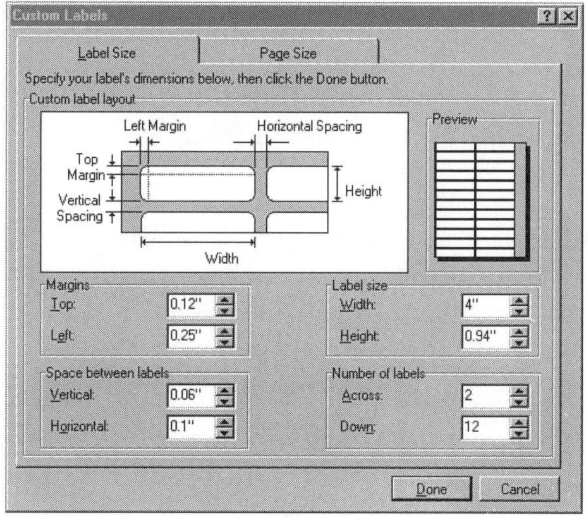

Fig. 28.14
Enter the measurements and settings for the labels you will use.

VI

2. In the Margins area, enter the measurement (in inches) you want to reserve for the Top and Left margins. Carefully measure your label page

from the top edge of the page to the top of the first label to get the top margin and from the left edge of the page to the left edge of the first label to get the left margin size.

3. In the Space Between Labels area, enter the amount of space you want to leave vertically and horizontally between labels in the appropriate boxes.

> **Note**
>
> You can change the settings in the Custom Labels dialog box by clicking in the box so the current entry is highlighted and typing a new number. Or you can click the up- and down-arrows to adjust the displayed value.

4. In the Label Size area, specify the Width and Height of the selected label. Again, carefully measure your label page to get the correct measurements.

5. In the Number of Labels area, type the number of labels you want Works to print on the page, according to your sample page. First, in the Across box, specify the number of labels that will print across the page (the default is 2). Then, in the Down box, specify the number of labels to print down the page.

> **Note**
>
> The diagram in the Label Size page does not reflect your changes; it merely gives guidelines for horizontal and vertical spacing. The Preview box does give you an idea of how your labels fit onto the page.

6. Click the Page Size tab to display page measurement and margin settings. You also choose the orientation here—whether to print the page vertically (in portrait orientation) or horizontally (in landscape orientation). Figure 28.15 shows the Page Size options.

7. When you finish changing settings, click Done. You return to the Label Size tab of the Labels dialog box.

> **Note**
>
> If you specified label dimensions too large for the page, Works warns you of the problem. Choose OK to close the message box and Works highlights the problem area, the top margin, for example. Correct the problem and then choose Done.

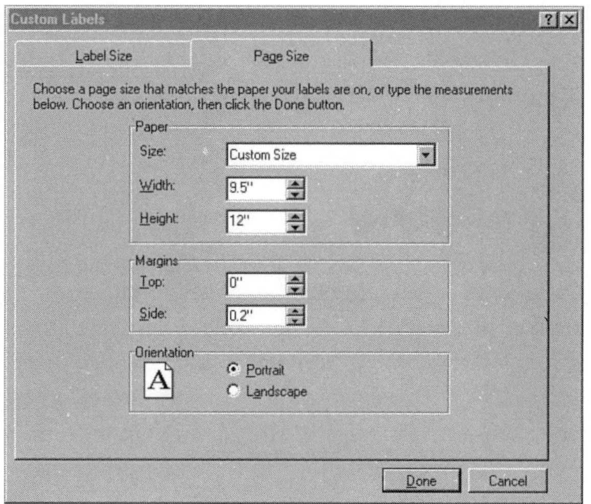

Fig. 28.15
Here you can specify new page settings and change page orientation.

Changing a Label Definition

After you insert a label definition in a word processor document, you might need to change the definition. For example, you might decide to print labels using a different label size. Follow these steps to change the existing label definition:

1. Open the document that contains the label definition.

2. To make simple changes to the field placeholders and any text that prints on the labels, edit the label definition at the top of the document.

3. To choose a different label size, paper size, or to create a custom label definition, choose Tools, Labels. Select the Labels button. Make the desired changes, following the steps given previously in this section. For example, choose a different standard label type, choose different field placeholders, or change the page size. When you finish making changes, click Done.

   Works inserts the new definition at the top of the document, replacing the previous definition.

Finishing Labels

After you print your labels, you need to decide whether to keep or delete the label you created. If you plan to use the label again (if it works, keep it!), save the label by choosing File, Save and entering a name in the File Name box.

If you want to delete a label you no longer need, click the Delete Label button at the bottom of the Labels dialog box. Works asks you whether you want to delete the current label. Click Yes to delete the label; click No to return to the Labels dialog box.

Printing Envelopes

Works makes it easy to print an envelope using an address in a word processor document. You can also print one envelope for each name and address in a Works database. When you tell Works to print a single envelope from a name and address in a document, you can save the envelope definition with the document, making it easy to print the envelope next time. Or, you can save the envelope printing instructions in a different document and print only the envelope later.

Caution

A word processor document can include instructions for printing envelopes or labels, but not both.

Works can print envelopes using your printer's manual feed or envelope bin, or using form-feed, continuous envelopes.

Troubleshooting

My custom labels didn't print right; the names and addresses are in the margins between the labels. What did I do wrong?

When measuring custom labels, it's important to correctly measure the top margin. Check your top margin again and make sure it is correct in the Margins area of the Label Size tab of the Custom Labels dialog box. If the measurement is correct, check to make sure you're feeding your labels into the printer correctly. Often, the bottom margin of the label page is not the same as the top margin.

My labels are not Avery and I don't want to measure out for a custom label. Isn't there anything else I can do?

Yes, first check the label's packaging to see if an Avery number is listed as being compatible. If so, look for that number in the list of label sizes. If there is no Avery number listed, you can measure the label size and see if that size is listed in the label size list box. For example, if your label is $4 \times 1^{7}/_{16}$ inch, try printing a test page with the selected size: Avery 4146. It will most likely work with your label page.

Preparing Envelopes

Works makes the process of creating and printing envelopes easy by mapping it out for you in the Envelopes dialog box. Many of the Envelopes dialog box tabs are similar to those described in the previous two sections; refer to those sections for more information.

Here are the steps for creating envelopes:

1. Open the database you plan to use with the envelopes.

2. Choose Tools, Envelopes. The Envelopes dialog box appears, with the Instructions tab displayed (see fig. 28.16).

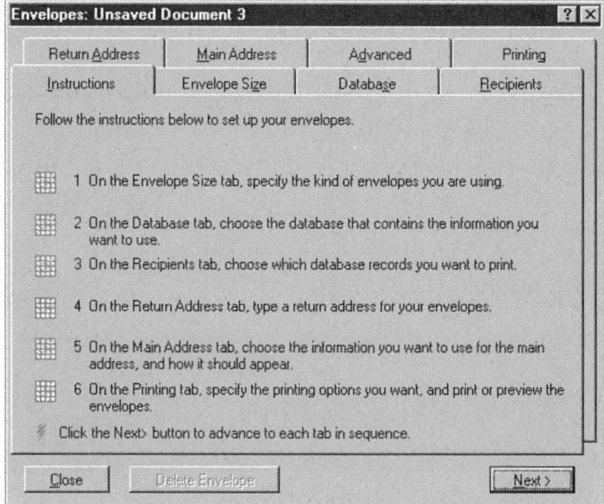

Fig. 28.16
The Instructions tab explains the various steps involved in printing envelopes with Works.

> **Note**
>
> If you've never prepared envelopes before, you'll see the First-time Help dialog box. Choose OK to continue.

3. Click Next. The Envelope Size tab appears. The most common envelope size, 10, is highlighted. If you want to change the size, scroll through the list and choose the size you need. If you have an envelope that is an unusual size, choose the Custom button to display the Custom Envelopes dialog box. Enter the dimensions of the envelope; then click OK to return to the Envelope Size tab. When you're finished selecting the size, click Next.

4. In the Instructions tab, click Next again. The Database tab appears. Click the database file you want to use with the envelopes; then click Next. The Instructions page appears again, with another step checked off.

5. Click Next again. On the Recipients tab, select whether you want all records, only displayed records, marked records, or a subset of filtered records used in the envelope printing process. After you make your choice, click Next.

6. Now you have to specify a return address. Click Next to display the Return Address tab. Type the information you want to use as a return address, and choose the Font button to change the font, size, style, and color if necessary. Click Next.

7. The Instructions tab shows that entering a main address is the next step. Click Next to display the Main Address tab (see fig. 28.17). Add the field placeholders as you want them to appear on the envelope. Choose Add Field to add the field placeholders; click New Line to move the cursor to the next line; and click Clear All if you want to remove the address fields and start again.

   When you finish adding fields, click Next to return to the Instructions tab.

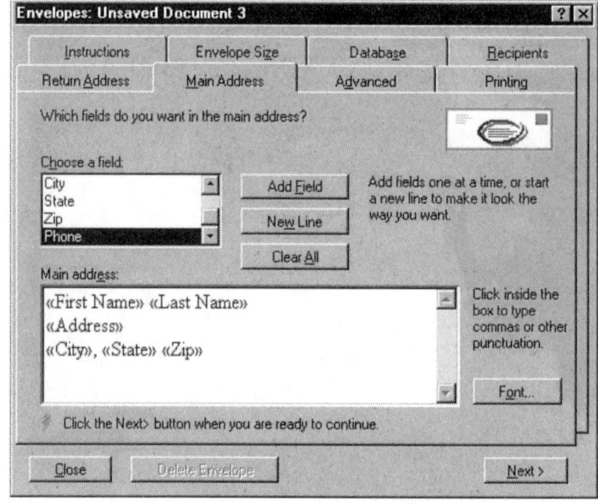

Fig. 28.17
You use the Main Address tab to create the format in which you want the fields printed on your envelopes.

8. If you want to edit the envelope in the document, click the Advanced tab. Choose the Edit button to format text, insert a picture, or otherwise edit the envelope. Choose Go Back when you're done and choose Next.

9. The last step involves previewing and printing the envelopes. Click Next to display the Printing tab. You then have the following options:

   - Preview displays the envelope in full-page view. You can enlarge the view, check the placement of the return and main addresses, and check margin and alignment settings. Figure 28.18 shows an envelope in Preview mode. When you finish previewing, you can begin printing by choosing Print or return to the Printing tab by choosing Cancel.

   - Test prints one envelope so you can see and, if necessary, adjust settings before you print envelopes for all records.

   - Print begins the printing process. Works asks for confirmation before continuing, alerting you that envelopes for all records in the database are going to be printed. Click OK to continue or Cancel to stop printing.

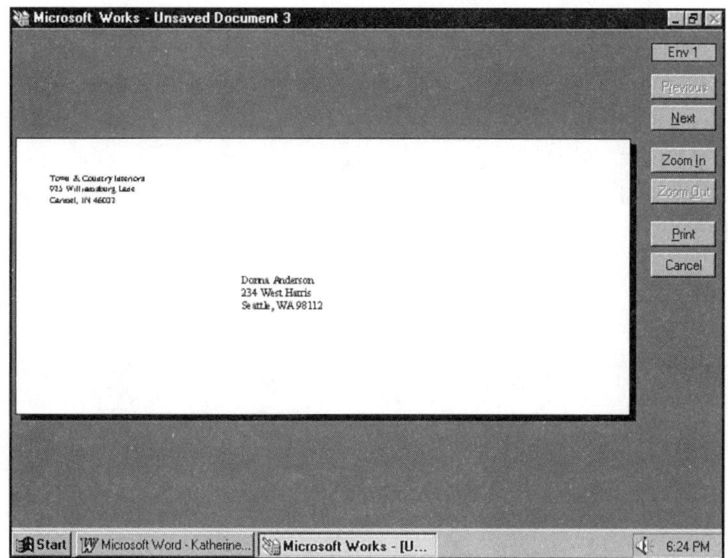

Fig. 28.18
Previewing the envelopes before printing lets you make sure you selected the correct envelope size, margins, and text style.

Note

If you finish a letter and want to print an envelope quickly using the address at the top of the letter, highlight the name and address and then choose Tools, Envelope. Go through the Envelope dialog box tabs, clicking Next. When you get to the Database tab, choose No Database, and Works will use the information you highlighted in the letter. This will appear in the Main Address tab. Click Print in the Printing page to print the envelope. When you save the file, the envelope information will remain with the document as well.

Saving Envelopes

After you print the envelopes, you might want to save the file so you can use it again the next time you need to merge print. First, click Close in the Envelopes dialog box to return to the document window. Then, to save the envelope definition, choose File, Save. The Save dialog box appears. In the File Name box, type the name for the envelope file; then click OK.❖

Chapter 29

Communicating with Other Computers

by Kathy Murray

If your computer system has a modem, you have an "on ramp" to the information superhighway—that elusive and somewhat abstract world of data transmitted through phone lines all over the world. Microsoft Works includes a Communications component, available in the Works Task Launcher, that enables you to connect with other computers, fax modems, MCI mail boxes, as well as online news and information services like CompuServe, Prodigy, and America Online. Today, with the world traveling beyond bulletin boards into Internet cyberspace, you can tap into a virtually unlimited resource potential—all the best libraries and reference points in the world.

After you connect to these other sources—whether it's a computer in the next office or on the other side of the world—you can send and receive messages, read resource information, retrieve files, or send files. On some communications services, you also can play games, be part of an online conference, and shop in an electronic mall.

In this chapter, you learn about the following topics:

- Reviewing communications capabilities
- Understanding communications terminology
- Using the communications menus and toolbar
- Choosing communications settings
- Saving a communications file
- Starting a communications session

- Capturing text
- Sending and receiving files

Putting Communications to Work for You

The Communications component in Works is a software application that enables you to connect your computer to another computer so you can exchange information. You might want to use communications in the following situations:

- You're writing an article on the history of bicycles and need information above and beyond what you have at home. You can access many different reference sources in local library bulletin boards or larger information services like CompuServe. You also can use the Internet to access university libraries all over the world.
- You are working at home and need to send a report to the office but don't have time to mail or even overnight it and the report is too long to fax. You can use Works to transmit the file to the waiting computer or use another electronic service—like CompuServe or America Online—to send the file.
- You need to ask a coworker a question but don't want to begin a lengthy conversation just now. An e-mail note in his mailbox, which he can answer when it's convenient for him, will do the trick.

You can connect to a large computer shared by hundreds of users or to another personal computer. In either case, both computers must be equipped with a modem and communications software.

If you are connecting to another computer—for example, to send a file to another office across town—the other computer does not have to be using Works to receive your file. Microsoft Windows 95 comes with its own communications program, called HyperTerminal, and there are many other communications programs that are popular today. A few of the most popular communications programs include BitWare, Crosstalk, and Procomm for Windows. The program you use to send and receive the information doesn't matter; it's the way in which you send the data—the *transfer protocol* (explained later in this chapter)—that must be the same.

Whether you are connecting to a large computer system at your office, a large computer that runs an online information service like CompuServe, or a colleague's personal computer, the operator of the other computer has complete control over which programs and files you can access on that computer. The other computer must be set to receive the connection or no connection will be made.

When you make the connection to another computer, the communications software in Works provides the tools for you to perform any of the following tasks:

- *Use your computer as a terminal.* The hundreds of users connected to a large computer system access the computer through a *terminal*, which is nothing more than a keyboard and a screen. When you use the Communications component in Works to connect your computer to a large computer, you are using your computer as though it were a terminal directly connected to the large computer. You have access to all programs and files on the computer that you are authorized to use. When you use your computer to connect to a computer information service such as CompuServe, you are using your computer as a terminal. Likewise, when you use your computer to connect to a large computer at your office to read and send e-mail or edit a file, you are using your computer as a terminal. You might use this setup, for example, if you were using a laptop computer and visiting clients; when you need to look something up, you plug the modem into the phone line, dial up your office, and have instant access to all the information on your desktop computer.

- *Send and receive files.* You might want to share some of your computer files with business or academic colleagues who are users on large computer systems or who have personal computers. Using the Communications component in Works, you can send a file stored on a disk, and you can receive a file from a user on another computer and save the file on your computer. Sending and receiving files is different from simply reading e-mail or information from an online information service; the result is a usable file, like those you create on your computer in Works.

- *Capture text.* Sometimes you might want to save on your computer all the information you receive from another computer, even if you are just reading files. For example, if you are gathering the latest stock quotes from Dow Jones for a report you are writing, you can save that information in a file on your computer so you can use it later in a Works document. This technique is called *capturing* text. Works saves the captured text in a file called CAPTURE.TXT or any other file name you specify.

Understanding Communications Terms

Many new users are intimidated by computer communications when they hear terms like *stop bits, parity, protocol,* and *baud.* It's true that computer communications is a topic with terminology all its own. But familiarity with this terminology can help you feel more comfortable with communications and get you started more quickly.

You don't need to understand the intricacies of how computers actually communicate; in fact, with the newest generation of Windows and the resulting upgrades in programs, we are on the brink of "smart" technology that goes through your system and finds out what you have in there, even if you don't know! The time is passing—albeit too slowly for some people—where you need to understand all the technical aspects. But you can benefit by understanding enough about these terms to recognize them and be able to figure out, in a pinch, which settings you need to communicate with another computer. The following list describes some general communications terms. Throughout this chapter you learn additional terms where appropriate.

- *Modem.* A hardware device that converts a computer's digital signals into analog signals used by telephone lines, then converts the signals back again so that computers can "talk" to one another across telephone lines. The word *modem* is actually an abbreviation, short for the phrases that describe what the device does—MOdulates and DEModulates data. You must have a modem connected to your computer to communicate with other computers. Two basic types of modems exist: internal and external. Internal modems are computer cards that plug into a slot inside your computer. External modems are boxes that sit outside your computer. Today, fax modems are popular. They are modems with fax capabilities built right onto the board, enabling you to send files, messages, or faxes right from your PC. For all types of modems, you plug your telephone cord into the modem. Another cord connects your modem to your telephone jack so the modem acts as an intermediary between your phone and your computer.

- *Port.* Put simply, a port is a receptacle in your PC where you can attach another device. You have a printer port, a mouse port, and a graphics port. Depending on your system, you might have a joystick port and a MIDI port. Two basic types of ports exist: a physical connector on the back of your computer or a slot inside your computer. Your printer port is a physical connector on the back of your computer, into which you plug your printer cable. A port inside your computer is used for plugging in computer cards such as internal modems and communications cards. Before using communications, you must know which port is your communications port (usually COM1, COM2, COM3, or COM4). When you install Windows 95 (and also Works 4.0), the software automatically checks to find the port to which your modem is connected.

- *Host computer.* The computer to which you establish a connection via your computer. A host can be a large computer or a personal computer. It's the computer that is "hosting" your visit.

- *Mainframe computer.* A large computer that supports sometimes hundreds of users and can run dozens of programs at one time. Mainframe computers are almost always connected to a computer network, organized so that many users can share the programs and data stored in the mainframe. Whereas each personal computer runs its own version of Windows, the mainframe contains applications and files the users can access.

- *Computer network.* Computers that are connected to one another for the purpose of sharing information are *networked*. Users on one networked computer have immediate access to all other computers on the network. Computers in a network can be physically connected, but most often are connected via direct telephone lines, fiber optic cable, or satellite. Networked computers can be located in a single building, a single city, or they might be hundreds (even thousands) of miles apart from each other.

- *Online information service.* A service available only by computer that provides information on a variety of topics such as news, weather, travel, shopping, educational resources, hobbies, and investments. CompuServe and America Online are two popular online services that provide a wide variety of information. You first get these programs by purchasing them through normal channels, such as software houses or by mail order. You also can call the 1-800 numbers for these services to request a new membership kit. (See Note later in this section.) After you sign up, most online services charge you a set monthly fee, which entitles you to a certain number of hours online. Some services have additional charges, as well as alternative payment plans. If you are interested in checking out an online service, start by contacting one of these companies:

CompuServe	1-800-524-3388
America Online	1-800-827-6364
Prodigy	1-800-PRODIGY

An additional online service comes with Windows 95: The Microsoft Network. To start the network, double-click the Microsoft Network icon on your desktop. If you did not install the service with Windows 95, double-click the Set Up The Microsoft Network icon on the desktop and follow the directions.

Note

One of the newest support features offered by Microsoft is The Microsoft Network (MSN), an online information service that provides support not only for Microsoft products but for hundreds of other products. Additionally, on MSN you can find up-to-date news, Internet access, e-mail, and all the fun, shopping, and resources you can handle. You can take MSN for a test drive by choosing Help, Launch Works Forum.

- *Internet.* Going beyond the online information services, the Internet is truly a global network that connects users in over 80 countries around the world. Use your modem to cruise the information superhighway and you can find worlds of information you didn't know existed. You can connect to the Internet through a local Internet provider, such as a university, library, or commercial service; or you can connect to the Internet through The Microsoft Network, CompuServe, America Online, and other online services.

- *Terminal emulation.* A terminal, also called a *dumb terminal,* is a computer system that consists of only a keyboard and screen—with no "brain" of its own. Instead of a CPU or system unit, the terminal relies on a mainframe or other networked computer to do its processing. Programs and data are stored on the primary system. Some mainframe computers allow only certain types of terminals to connect, so if you want to connect to that computer, your computer must *emulate*—that is, act like—the particular type of terminal the computer recognizes.

- *Transfer protocol.* Two computers use this set of agreed-upon rules when communicating with one another to check for and correct errors during transmission. This procedure is similar, in practical terms, to two people speaking on the phone; they both need to be speaking the same language for them to understand each other. When transferring (sending or receiving) files to or from another computer, you must specify a single protocol that both computers use. (About six standard transfer protocols exist (including xmodem, zmodem, and kermit), but generally, the protocol chosen by default is the correct one for transmission. Chances are, you will not need to change the protocol to transmit and receive files successfully.)

- *Baud rate.* This term describes the speed at which computers transfer data, such as 1200 baud, 2400 baud, or 9600 baud. (The higher the number, the faster the rate.) The baud rate you set must match the baud rate of the computer to which you are connected, and you can only set a baud rate that your modem supports. Most modems support 2400, 9600, or 14,400 baud. Today's fax modems often send and receive data at a rate of 14,400 or 28,800 baud.

- *Parity.* Parity is a setting that some computers use to determine whether characters are being transmitted accurately. Typical settings are even, odd, or none.

- *Data bits.* Data bits define the number of bits used to represent a single character. Typical settings are 7 or 8.

- *Stop bits.* The number of bits used to signal the end of a character. Typical settings are 1 or 2.

- *Handshake.* A protocol that controls the flow of information between two computers. The computers send Continue and Pause signals to one another when they're ready to receive more information and when they need to pause. Both computers must use the same handshake to communicate, or use none at all.

- *ASCII file.* An ASCII (American Standard Code for Information Interchange) file contains only text characters that can be read by almost any software application. ASCII was created so all computers could exchange and share data. All formatting (such as bold, italic, tabs, and so on), however, is stripped out of an ASCII file.

- *Binary file.* A file in a number format readable only by computers. Rather than containing text, each character in the file is represented in its binary code (combinations of zeros and ones).

- *Communications session.* The time during which you are connected to another computer via your telephone line.

Getting Started with Communications

To use the Communications component in Works, begin in the Works Task Launcher. Click the Communications icon to open a new communications file. The Easy Connect dialog box appears, as shown in figure 29.1.

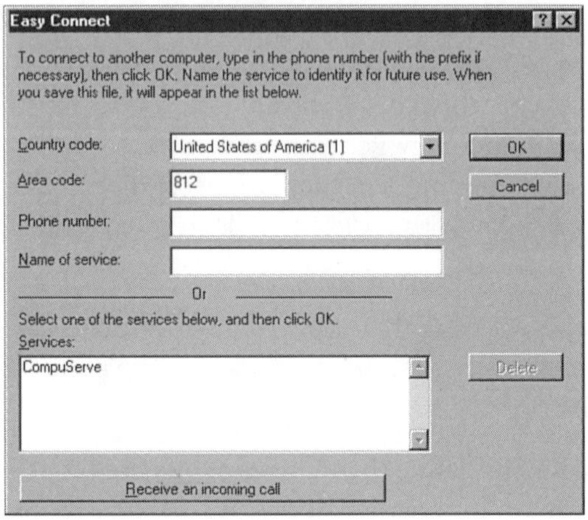

Fig. 29.1
With Easy Connect, you can enter the number and name of computers or services you contact frequently so you can dial up and connect with the click of a button.

Using Easy Connect

The Easy Connect dialog box now appears first in your Works 4.0 communications session. You can enter settings, numbers, and names of often-used services one time and then dial them quickly with the click of a button. In the example shown in figure 29.1, CompuServe has been added and appears in the Services box.

To add a new number in Easy Connect, follow these steps:

1. Choose a Country Code. If you are calling in the United States, you don't need to change this setting. For international calls, click the down arrow to the right of the box and select the country you need from the displayed list.

2. Press Tab to move to the Area Code field or click in the field to select it. Type the area code (parentheses are not necessary) of the computer or service you will be calling.

3. Press Tab to move to the Phone Number field or click in the field to select it. Type the phone number you need your computer to dial. (You don't need to enter *70 to disable call waiting, as some communications programs require; Works enters the number automatically. However, you should enter the number required to get an outside line, such as 8 or 9, if necessary.)

4. Press Tab or click in the Name of Service field. Type the name of the service or system you will be calling.

5. Click OK. The Dial dialog box appears (see fig. 29.2). In this box, you see the number your computer will dial and information related to your modem type. If any of this information is incorrect, you can make corrections by clicking the Modify button and making changes, or by clicking the Location or Device down arrows and selecting the right choice from the displayed list.

6. If you want to dial the service now, click Dial. If you want to postpone the connection, click Cancel.

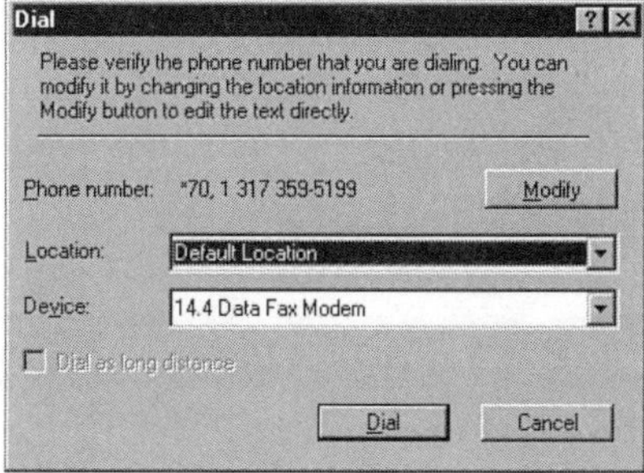

Fig. 29.2
You can edit information and dial the service from the Dial dialog box.

Before you connect to a service or another computer for the first time, however, you might want to become more familiar with the Works Communications screen. As you have seen in all the other Works components, each has a unique menu bar and toolbar.

VI

Examining the Communications Menus

In the Communications component, most of the menus are very different from those in other components because the nature of the application is very different. The emphasis is on communicating with other computers rather than on creating documents, spreadsheets, or databases. As such, the File menu includes the familiar create, open, and save commands, but you don't find any printer, page setup, or print commands. The Edit menu enables you to select, copy, and paste text. On the View menu, you find only one command, Toolbar, which turns on or off the display of the toolbar.

You use the Settings menu to set all of your phone, communications, terminal, transfer, and modem settings before you begin a communications session. Using the Phone menu, you display the Easy Connect dialog box and also dial, pause, and hang up your phone during a communications session. The Tools menu is used primarily for sending and receiving files or text. You also use this menu to customize the Communications toolbar.

The Window menu is similar to the same menu in the other Works components. It enables you to arrange open windows on-screen and switch between open documents. Finally, the Help menu gives you access to online help for communications and any other component in Works.

Examining the Communications Toolbar

The Communications window has its own toolbar. You can customize the toolbar, just like you can in other Works components. For instructions on customizing the toolbar, refer to Chapter 2, "Getting Started with Works for Windows."

The toolbar buttons are described in Table 29.1. To use a button, simply click it. If the button requires that you take some action before clicking the button, Works displays a message telling you what to do.

Table 29.1 Communications Toolbar Buttons

Button	Description
	Displays the Works Task Launcher
	Saves the active communications file
	Copies the selected text to the Clipboard
	Pastes the contents of the Clipboard into the active communications file at the location of the insertion point
	Displays the Communications tab in the Settings dialog box, in which you define communication settings

Button	Description
	Displays the Terminal tab in the Settings dialog box, in which you define terminal settings
	Displays the Phone tab in the Settings dialog box, in which you define phone settings
	Displays the Transfer tab in the Settings dialog box, in which you define transfer settings
8,n,1	Automatically changes your communication settings to 8 data bits, no parity, and 1 stop bit
7,e,1	Automatically changes your communication settings to 7 data bits, even parity, and 1 stop bit
	Displays the Easy Connect dialog box, in which you can enter the phone number and service name of the computer you want to dial
	Dials the current phone number to establish a connection. If you are already connected, clicking this button disconnects your connection.
	Pauses your communications session
	Saves the text you are receiving as a file
	Lets you send an ASCII (text) file to the computer to which you are connected
	Lets you send a binary file to the computer to which you are connected
	Receives a binary file and saves it
	Runs the Address Book TaskWizard so you can create an address book for home or business use

Setting Up Your Computer for Communications

Before you begin to communicate with another computer, you need to know some of the standard communication settings required by the computer to which you are connecting. For example, you must know parity bits, stop bits, data bits, baud rate, handshake, transfer protocol, and terminal emulation settings required by the other computer. You also need to know the phone number to dial to establish the connection.

If you are connecting to an information service such as CompuServe, this information is available in the membership packet you receive. If you are connecting to a large computer at a specific business or organization, the computer's operations staff can provide this information. In all cases, you need to know your user name on the host computer, and in most cases, a password is required.

If you cannot find all the communication settings, don't worry. For some of the setup items, Windows 95 and Works automatically "sense" what type of equipment you're using, what port the item is connected to, and so on. In some cases you can guess which settings to use. For some settings, you have a choice between only two options, so your chances of guessing correctly are fifty-fifty. You know you need to change some settings if the information you see on-screen doesn't make sense or contains a lot of "garbage" characters.

Choosing Phone Settings

Phone settings refer to the phone number of the computer you are dialing and the dialing instructions you want to use. After you specify phone settings, Works can later use the information to automatically redial the phone number and establish a connection to the other computer if the initial Easy Connect attempt is unsuccessful.

To specify phone settings, choose Settings, Phone or click the Phone Settings button on the toolbar. Works displays the Settings dialog box shown in figure 29.3. Notice that the Settings dialog box has several tabs; the Phone tab is selected.

Use the following steps to specify phone settings:

1. Choose Settings, Phone or click the Phone Settings button on the toolbar. The dialog box shown in figure 29.3 appears.

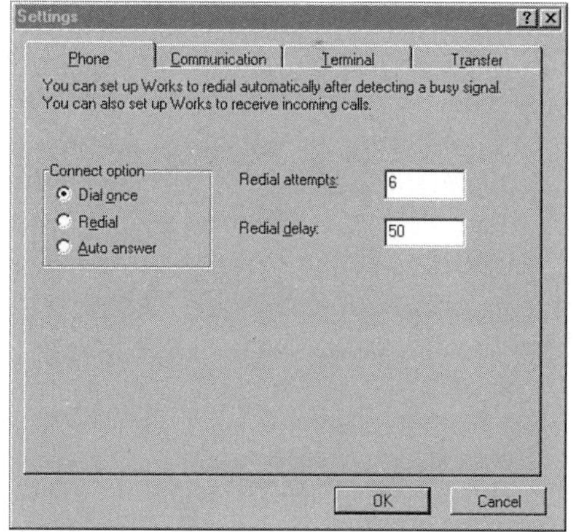

Fig. 29.3
In the Phone tab page of the Settings dialog box, you can choose the number of times a number is dialed if an initial connection is unsuccessful.

2. In the Connect Option box, choose Dial Once, the Redial, or Auto Answer. If you choose Auto Answer, Works automatically answers any incoming calls to your modem.

3. If you choose Redial, set the number of Redial Attempts and the Redial Delay. The redial attempts set the number of times Works redials in an attempt to connect to another computer. The redial delay indicates how many seconds Works should wait between each redial attempt. Using the redial settings are useful for when Works encounters a busy signal or a bad connection.

4. When all settings are correct, choose OK.

Troubleshooting

What causes an unsuccessful dial-up?

Sometimes faulty connections are the culprit—make sure the phone line is plugged securely into your modem and wall outlet. If the line is busy (a common occurrence with small local bulletin boards), you might hear the busy tone transmitted from your computer's speaker.

In other cases, the host computer you're calling might be temporarily out of service, or off-line. Attempt to call back in several minutes after the line has cleared.

If you have an external modem, problems can often be eliminated by turning the modem off and back on.

Choosing Communication Settings

Communication settings define the rules by which your computer communicates with the computer you are connecting to. To set communication settings, choose Settings, Communication or click the Communication button on the toolbar. Works displays the Communication tab in the Settings dialog box, shown in figure 29.4.

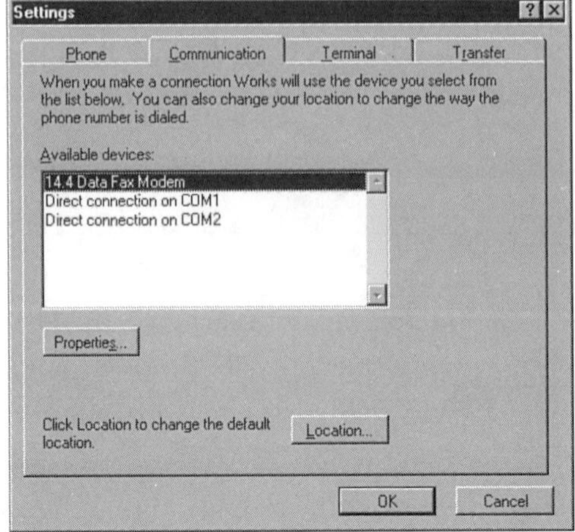

Fig. 29.4
Specify settings for your communications device in the Communication tab page of the Settings dialog box.

The first step in setting up your communications session involves making sure you have the right modem selected. To choose communication settings, follow these steps:

1. Choose Settings, Communication, or click the Communication button on the toolbar, or if the Settings dialog box is already displayed, click the Communication tab. The dialog box shown in figure 29.4 appears.

2. In the Available Devices list, select the device you'll be using to connect with the other computer or service. Choose the modem if you're connecting to another computer over the phone lines; choose a direct connection if your computer is cabled directly to another computer.

3. Click the Properties button. The General tab page appears, showing you some of the basic settings in effect for your modem type, as shown in figure 29.5.

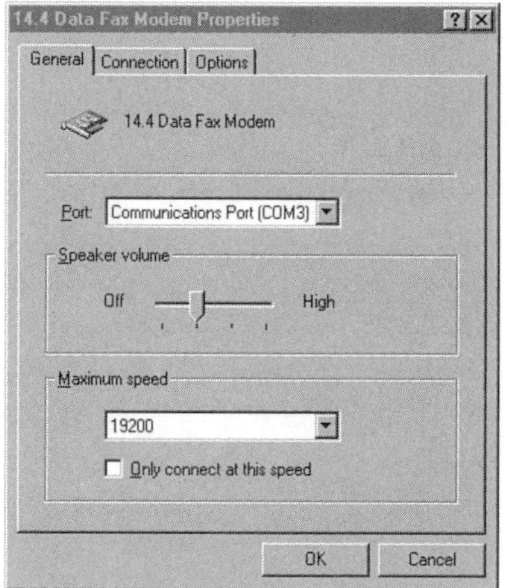

Fig. 29.5
After you select the device you want to use, you can choose the port, speaker volume, and transmission speed in the General tab page.

4. If you need to change the port, click the Port down arrow. From the list, select the port to which your modem is connected.

> **Note**
>
> With the new automated features in Windows 95 that take care of identifying and setting up the necessary drivers for your computer components, the port might already be set correctly by default. Only if you are choosing to use a modem other than your usual one—such as a new external device—should you need to change the port setting.

5. In the Speaker Volume area, you can change the volume by dragging the marker; drag to the right to increase the volume, and drag to the left to decrease the volume.

6. The Maximum Speed setting shows the highest speed at which your modem is capable of operating. You can choose from other settings for those times when you are exchanging information with a slower modem and need to use a slower speed. If you want to make sure that transmissions always happen at a certain rate, click the rate you want and then click the Only Connect at This Speed check box. If you try to connect to a modem with a different speed than the one you selected, you get an error message and a failed connection.

7. Click the Connection tab. You see a dialog box showing the communication settings involving parity, stop bits, and so on (see fig. 29.6).

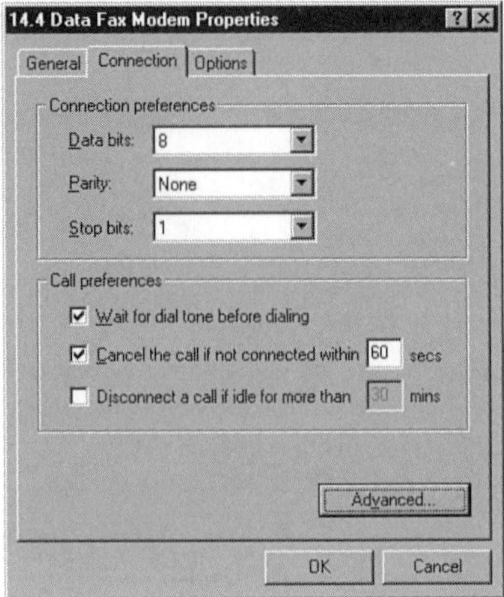

Fig. 29.6
The Connection preferences section contains the preferences for data transfer. For best results, don't change the default settings unless you have a specific reason.

8. Follow these guidelines for making your choices in the Connection tab:

   - Unless a specific communications session (such as using a calling card, cabling directly to another computer, or changing protocol to transmit to another computer) requires that you do so, don't change these settings.

   - If you are unsure whether the communication settings are right for your computer, try connecting to the host first; then change the settings if several communications attempts are unsuccessful.

   - Later, you can change from the default protocol (8,n,1 for *8 bits, no parity, and 1 stop bit*) to another common protocol (7,e,1 for *7 bits, even parity, and 1 stop bit*) by clicking the appropriate button on the toolbar.

9. In the Call Preferences section, choose whether you want the modem to detect a dial tone before proceeding (this option is selected by default). You might check this box, for example, if you have to manually dial the phone. Set your preference for how long you want to wait for a connection before you stop the attempt (60 seconds is the default); and whether you want to set a time-out value that controls when the computer disconnects if no activity is taking place on the line.

Note

Setting a time-out value is a good idea if you set up your computer to receive or retrieve files and then go about your business in another part of your office or home. If you forget to check your computer's progress or get called away unexpectedly, the computer automatically disconnects after the specified period of inactive time. You can save considerably on your phone bill if you must dial long distance to access the computer or service of your choice.

10. In some sessions, you might need to worry about error control and data compression. For most general communications sessions—such as connecting to a service like CompuServe—you don't need to make any changes. You display these settings, shown in figure 29.7, by clicking the Advanced button in the Connection tab page. Use flow control, for example, if your modem is sending data to your computer faster than the computer can read it. Change the modulation type if you're having trouble connecting to another computer using the Standard modulation. Enter additional initialization settings in the Extra Settings text box if your modem requires it. You can check your modem's documentation for more information on any of these advanced connection settings. Make any necessary changes on the Advanced tab page and click OK to return to the Connection tab page.

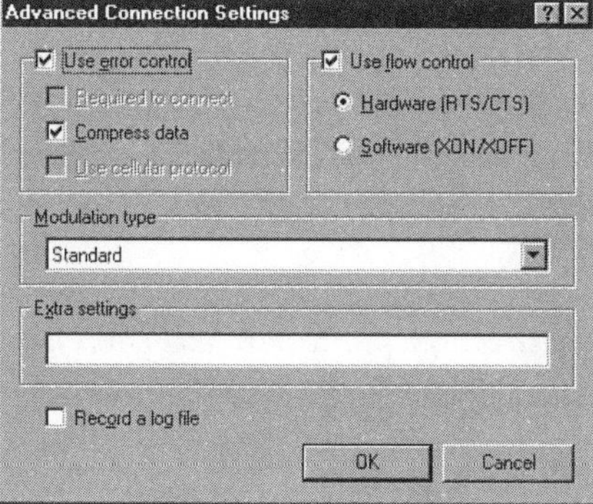

Fig. 29.7 Advanced settings manage the error control of the communications session and the way data is handled by the hardware and software.

VI

11. In the Modem Properties dialog box, click the Options tab. The Options tab, shown in figure 29.8, shows the final set of communication settings you need to review.

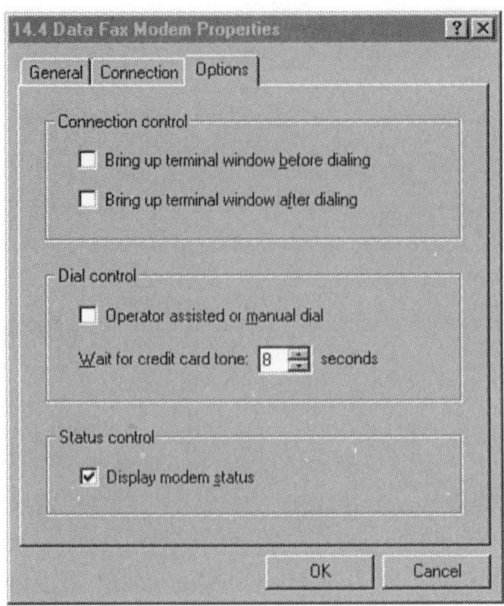

Fig. 29.8
The Options tab page includes a few more specialized choices about dialing, such as whether to dial manually or have the computer do it.

12. In the Options tab page, you choose the following items:

- Whether the terminal window—a screen on which you enter and receive communications information during a session—is displayed before or after you dial. You might display the window before you dial, for example, if you need to type a command directly to your modem before you make a connection.
- Whether you want to dial manually (or have a telephone operator make the call) and then log on after the connection has been made by clicking Connect. (You also can specify how many seconds you want to wait for the credit card tone before connecting.)
- Whether Works displays the status of the call in a message box on-screen.

When you're finished with the Options tab page, you have completed the Communication settings tab. Click OK to return to the Settings dialog box.

Choosing Terminal Settings

Terminal settings determine how your computer displays on-screen the information it receives from another computer. To set terminal settings, you use the Terminal tab in the Settings dialog box (see fig. 29.9).

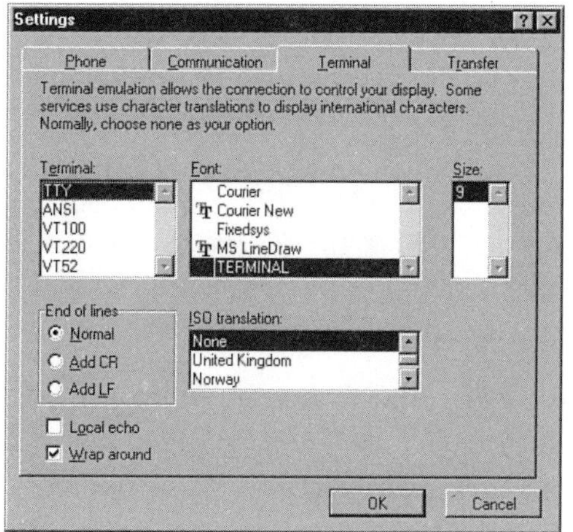

Fig. 29.9
Use Terminal settings to emulate a data terminal for communication with other terminals, such as UNIX.

To set terminal settings, follow these steps:

1. Choose Settings, Terminal; or click the Terminal Settings button on the toolbar; or click the Terminal tab in the open Settings dialog box. The dialog box shown in figure 29.9 appears.

2. From the Terminal list, select a terminal emulation. This is the type of terminal emulation required by the computer to which you are connecting.

3. Choose the Font you want displayed on your screen from the displayed list.

4. Select the Size of the text as you want it to appear.

5. In the End of Lines box, choose Normal, Add CR, or Add LF. In most cases, you can use the Normal setting. If some of the lines of text you are receiving don't begin at the left margin, choose the Add CR option to add a carriage return at the end of each line. If lines of text are overwriting each other, choose the Add LF option to move each new line of text to the next line.

6. If you are connecting to an information service that transmits in a foreign language, select the appropriate language from the ISO translation list. Otherwise, use the default None setting.

7. If you want to use Local Echo or Wrap Around, select these check boxes.

Local Echo is a setting that causes the characters you type to the host computer to "echo" back on your screen. Use this option when the characters you type don't appear on-screen. Turn this option off if you see two of every character.

The Wrap Around option adds a carriage return and line feed to the end of each line on your screen. Turn this option on if characters are over-writing one another at the end of each line or are disappearing beyond the right edge of the screen.

8. When all terminal settings are correct, choose OK.

Choosing Transfer Settings

If you are transferring files (sending or receiving) during your communications session, you need to specify transfer settings. Sending and receiving files is different from reading or capturing information from an online information service. Sending and receiving means actually sending a file stored on a disk to the host computer and vice versa. For instance, a salesperson in a branch office might send a business plan to the regional office for review.

To specify transfer settings, you use the Transfer tab page in the Settings dialog box (see fig. 29.10).

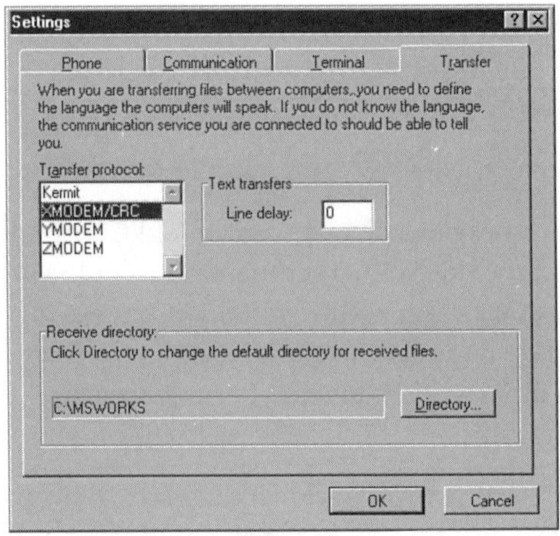

Fig. 29.10
Change transfer protocols to enable communication between your computer and another computer.

Follow these steps to specify transfer settings:

1. Choose Settings, Transfer; or click the Transfer button on the toolbar; or click the Transfer tab in the Settings dialog box. The Transfer tab page in the Settings dialog box appears, as shown in figure 29.10.

2. From the Transfer Protocol list, select the protocol that both computers use to transfer files.

3. If you are sending an ASCII (text) file that the receiving computer cannot receive as quickly as you can send it, type a number representing tenths of a second in the Line Delay box. For example, type **6** to have Works pause six-tenths of a second after each line of text it sends.

4. To specify a default directory or folder (other than the one shown) in which to save files you receive, click the Directory button. Then choose a directory from the dialog box that appears and click OK.

5. When all transfer settings are correct, choose OK.

Choosing Modem Settings

Earlier in this chapter, you learned that Windows 95 automatically checks to determine what kind of modem you have installed in your computer and where the device is located. If you ever need to add or remove a modem or change these basic Works settings, choose Settings, Modem to display the Modems Properties dialog box (see fig. 29.11).

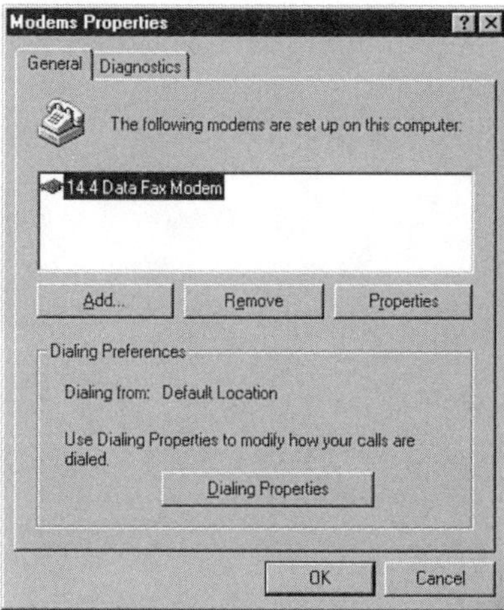

Fig. 29.11
The Modems Properties dialog box tells you what kind of modem you have installed and enables you to add and remove modems.

VI

If you want to add another modem to your setup, click the Add button. A modem installation process walks you through the steps of adding a new modem to your system. To remove a modem you no longer need, click Remove.

Caution

Don't remove a modem unless you're sure you don't need it. Works automatically removes the modem without asking for confirmation or any further action from you.

Tip
If you accidentally remove a modem you need, don't panic. You can use Add to have Works search your system and locate the appropriate device.

If you click Properties, Works displays the General tab page and the Communication tab of the modem's Properties dialog box, enabling you to choose the port, speaker volume, and transfer speed.

Clicking the Dialing Properties button opens the My Locations page, shown in figure 29.12.

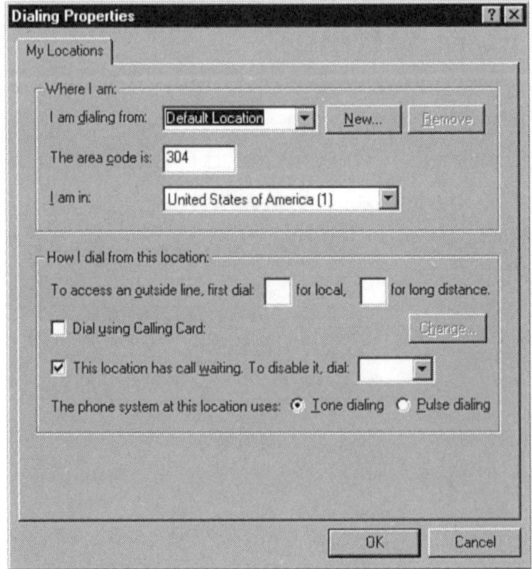

Fig. 29.12
Setting the modem's dialing properties affects all programs—Windows 95 Fax, HyperTerminal, Works Communications, and so on—within Windows.

To change dialing properties, follow these steps:

1. In the Where I Am area of the My Locations tab, make changes in the following options:

   - *I Am Dialing From.* Use the default location in most cases. Choose New and enter a name describing another location; for example, if you are traveling with your computer and modem. Select the new location from the drop-down list to enter new settings or select Default Location to edit those settings.

   - *The Area Code Is.* Enter the area code for the location.

   - *I Am In.* Select the country from which you will call at the new location.

2. In the How I Dial From This Location area, make changes to the following options:

   - *To Access an Outside Line, First Dial.* Enter the number necessary to dial for outside access in the local text box and/or the long distance text box.

   - *Dial Using Calling Card.* Check this option if you want to make your calls using a calling card. Choose the Change button to enter the provider and calling card number.

   - *This Location Has Call Waiting. To Disable it, Dial.* Enter the number the modem must dial to disable call waiting.

   - *Tone Dialing/Pulse Dialing.* Select the type of dialing your phone system uses.

3. Choose OK to close the Dialing Properties dialog box and accept your changes.

Troubleshooting

I sent a text file to a friend but when she received the file, some of the text was missing.

Your friend's computer was not receiving the file as quickly as Works was sending it. Try sending the file again but specify a delay in the Transfer tab page of the Settings dialog box (refer to fig. 29.10).

Saving a Communications File

With the exception of transfer settings, all the settings you just read about in the preceding section are required before you can connect to another computer. (Transfer settings are required only if you are sending or receiving files.) If you regularly connect to several different online information services, or perhaps a mainframe computer at your office, the communication settings for each computer are likely to be slightly different.

So you can avoid having to reset communication settings each time you connect to a different host computer, Works automatically creates a file in which your communication settings are saved. When you first enter information in the Easy Connect dialog box (which appears when you start Communications), the name of the service you enter becomes the name of the file. The name of the file is shown in the upper-left corner of the window. For example, figure 29.13 shows the Easy Connect dialog box in which the name of the current file is entered.

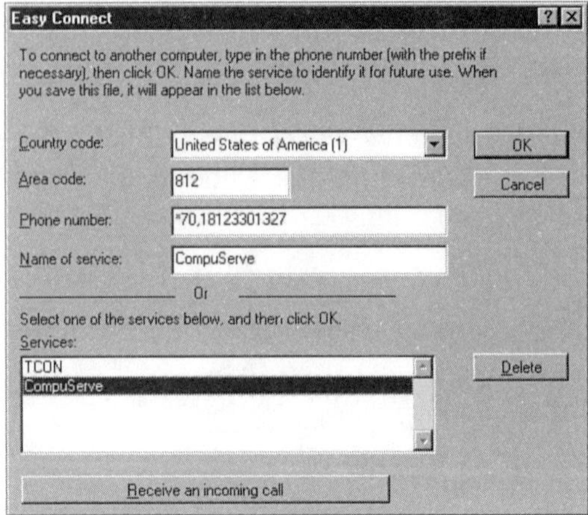

Fig. 29.13
The name of the service you select (or enter) in the Easy Connect dialog box is the name of the file storing the communication settings.

If you bypassed the Easy Connect dialog box without entering the name or information for the service with which you plan to connect, Works names the file UNSAVED COMMUNICATION 1 (or 2, 3, and so on).

Whether Works has named the file for you or not, you need to save the file when you finish making changes. Choose the File, Save command to have Works update the file. If the file is unnamed, Works displays the Save As dialog box so you can enter a name for the communications file. When you want to connect to a specific computer, just retrieve the communications file using the File, Open command.

Starting a Communications Session

When you start a communications session, Works automatically connects you to the host computer you specify. In the case of a mainframe computer system, the host computer prompts you for your user name and password after the telephone connection is established. This is called *logging in* to a computer. After your login information is accepted, the host computer displays its own menu. From this point on, you must use the commands the host computer recognizes to navigate the programs and files available to you on that computer. To log off the host computer, you must use the correct exit command (such as Logout, Quit, Exit, or Off) the host computer recognizes.

If you are connecting to a personal computer, your access to programs and files on that computer is dependent upon the operator of that computer and the communications software his or her computer is running. In some cases, a password might be required.

When you are ready to connect to another computer, follow these steps:

1. Begin the communications session by clicking Communications in the Works Task Launcher.

2. In the Easy Connect dialog box, click the name of the computer or service you want to connect with from the Services list.

3. Click OK. The Dial dialog box appears.

4. Click Dial. You hear your computer dialing the remote computer or service. (How loudly you hear the tones depends on how you have the volume set in the Speaker Volume area of the Communications settings.) Figure 29.14 shows the status message that appears while Works makes the connection.

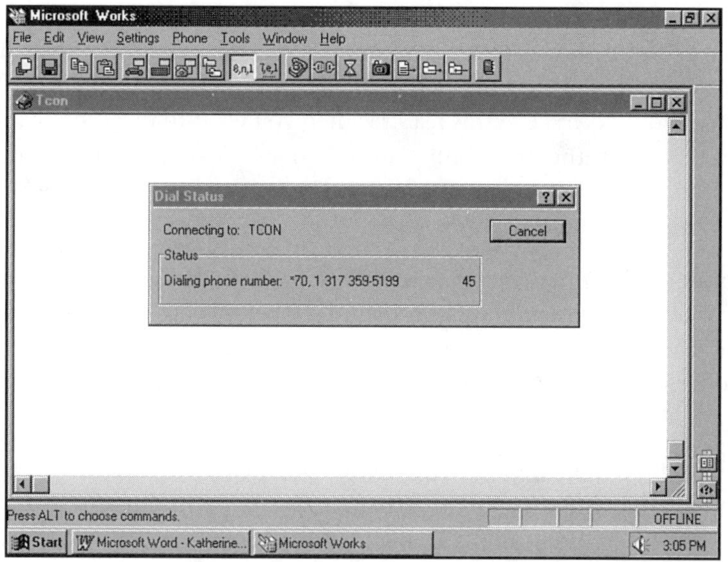

Fig. 29.14
Works shows you the status of the connection as it makes the call.

5. When your computer connects to the remote computer, you begin to see text scroll onto the screen, and the message in the lower-right corner says `ONLINE`. Figure 29.15 shows a connection to a remote computer.

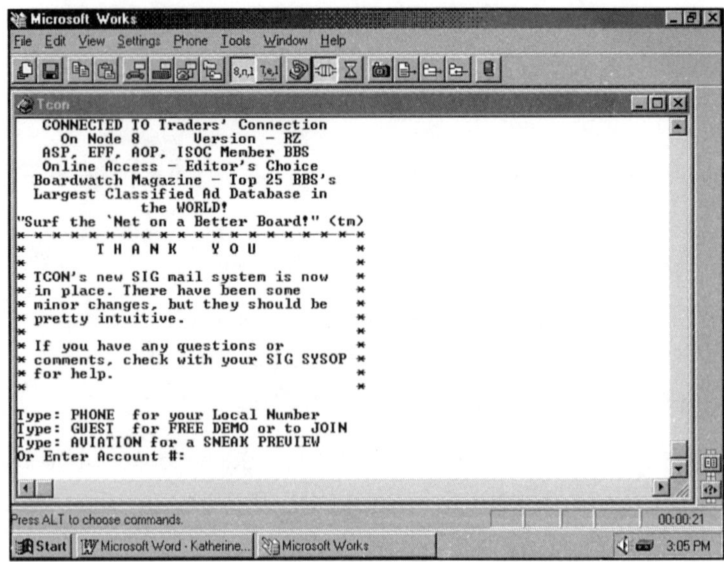

Fig. 29.15
After you connect to the host computer, the message in the bottom right corner of the communications window tells you that you are now `ONLINE`.

Capturing Text

When you capture text during a communications session, Works saves all information that you receive in a file called CAPTURE.TXT or any other file name that you specify. Use this feature when you want to incorporate information that you gather from online information services or other computers into Works documents, or when you want an accurate record of what occurred during a communications session.

To capture text, choose Tools, Capture Text; or click the Capture Text button on the toolbar. You can choose this command before you establish a connection or at any time during a communications session. At whatever point you choose the command, Works begins recording the information received on your computer.

When you choose the Capture Text command or click the Capture Text button on the toolbar, the button is depressed. To stop capturing text at any time during a communications session, choose Tools, End Capture Text or click the Capture Text button again to turn the feature off.

Follow these steps to have Works capture text for you:

1. Choose Tools, Capture Text, or click the Capture Text button on the toolbar. The Capture Text dialog box shown in figure 29.16 appears.

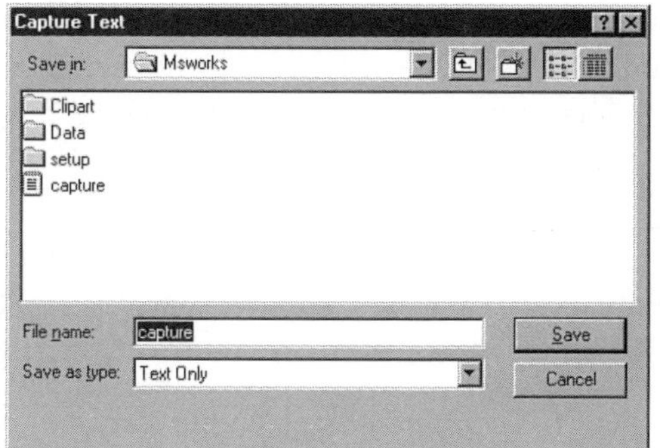

Fig. 29.16
In the Capture Text dialog box, you can type a name for the file that will record the text you capture from the service or host computer.

2. In the File Name box, type the name of the file you want to use, or use the default CAPTURE.TXT file name.
3. To save the file in a folder other than C:\MSWORKS (as shown in figure 29.16), select a different folder.
4. To save the file on a different disk drive, select the Save In down arrow and choose the drive you want.
5. When all settings are correct, choose Save. To remind you that you are capturing text, Works highlights the Capture Text button on the toolbar. After you establish a connection to another computer, the CAPT indicator appears on the status bar in the communications window.
6. To stop capturing text, click the Capture Text button on the toolbar; or choose Tools, End Capture Text. The Capture Text button is no longer highlighted and the CAPT indicator is removed from the status bar.

Sending and Receiving Files

Sending and receiving files is a common task when using the Communications component in Works. The following sections describe the required settings and procedures for sending and receiving files.

Sending Files

Most files you create on your computer are either *binary* files or *text* files. A binary file contains special formatting (such as tabs, bold or centered text, and dollar signs and commas used to display numbers in a spreadsheet). Works files with a file type of WPS, WKS, WDB, or WCM are binary files because they contain special formatting. Most files you create using other software programs are also binary files, because they usually contain formatting.

When you want to send a binary file to another computer, you use the Tools, Send File command, or click the Send Binary File button on the toolbar. The other computer automatically saves the file on disk when it receives the file.

To send a binary file to another computer, follow these steps:

1. Make sure your phone, communications, terminal, transfer, and modem settings are correct for the computer to which you are connecting. You must use the same transfer protocol that the other computer uses.

2. Connect to the other computer using Phone, Easy Connect or Phone, Dial; or click the Easy Connect or Dial button on the toolbar.

3. After connecting to the remote computer, choose Tools, Send File; or click the Send Binary File button on the toolbar. Works displays the Send File dialog box shown in figure 29.17.

4. In the dialog box, select the correct disk drive, folder, and file name for the file you want to send, and then choose OK. Works begins transmitting the file. (You don't see the file on-screen.) During the transfer, Works displays a message indicating the status of the transfer.

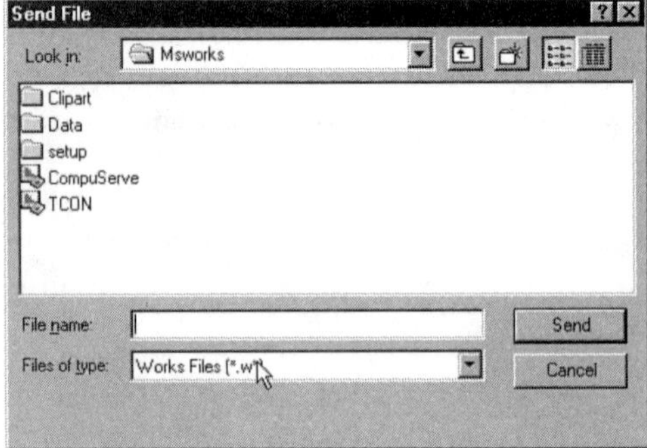

Fig. 29.17
You choose the file you want to send to the remote computer or service in the Send File dialog box.

You can cancel transmission of a binary file at any time by pressing Esc. key. Works displays a message asking you to confirm that you want to cancel the transmission. Choose OK.

In contrast to binary files, text files—or ASCII files, as they are often called—contain no formatting, and the file type is usually TXT.

To send a text file to another computer, follow these steps:

1. Make sure your phone, communications, terminal, transfer, and modem settings are correct for the computer to which you are connecting. You must use the same transfer protocol that the other computer uses.

2. Connect to the other computer using the Phone, Easy Connect or Phone, Dial command; or click the Easy Connect or Dial button on the toolbar.

3. Choose Tools, Send Text; or click the Send Text button on the toolbar. Works displays the Send Text dialog box shown in figure 29.18.

4. In the dialog box, select the correct disk drive, folder, and file name for the file you want to send, and then choose OK. Works begins transmitting the file. (You don't see the file on-screen.) During the transfer, Works displays a message indicating the status of the transfer.

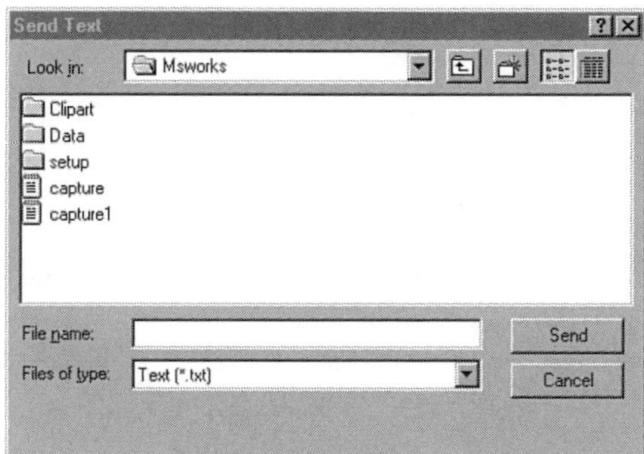

Fig. 29.18
When you are sending an ASCII text file, you choose the file to send to the remote computer in the Send Text dialog box.

Just as when you send a binary file, you can cancel sending a text file at any time by pressing Esc. Works displays a message asking you to confirm that you want to cancel the transmission. Choose OK.

Sending Text

Sometimes you don't want to send an entire file to another computer; you just want to send text. For instance, you might want to send a few pages of a document to a colleague on another computer. To do so, you use the Copy and Paste commands in Works. If the text is formatted, the formatting is not sent to the other computer; only the text transfers.

To send text by copying it, follow these steps:

1. In Works, open the file that contains the text you want to send.

2. Create a new communications file or use the saved file for the computer to which you are connecting. Choose Phone, Easy Connect.

3. Make sure your phone, communications, terminal, transfer, and modem settings are correct for the computer to which you are connecting.

4. Connect to the other computer using the Easy Connect or Dial command on the Phone menu.

5. Using the Window menu, switch to the Works file that contains the text you want to send.

6. In the file, highlight the text you want to send, then choose the Edit, Copy command; or click the Copy button on the toolbar.

7. Switch back to your communications document window.

8. Choose Edit, Paste Text. Works automatically sends the pasted text to the other computer. If the document contains any special formatting, it is not sent; only the text of the document transfers.

Receiving Files

You can receive a binary or a text file from another computer just as easily as you can send one. The other computer must use the same transfer protocol you are using in Works, and you must notify someone at the host computer when you are ready to receive the file.

Follow these steps to receive a file:

1. Make sure your phone, communications, terminal, transfer, and modem settings are correct for the computer to which you are connecting. You must use the same transfer protocol that the other computer uses.

2. Connect to the other computer using the Easy Connect or Dial command from the Phone menu.

3. Contact the other computer user who is sending you the file to let him or her know you are ready to receive a file. If you are receiving a file from an information service, choose the file, then choose the menu option and press the key sequence that enables you to transfer the file to your computer.

4. Choose Tools, Receive File; or click the Receive Binary File button on the toolbar. Works displays the Receive File dialog box shown in figure 29.19.

5. If you are using the xmodem protocol, type a file name in the File Name text box. If you are using any other protocol, Works saves the file with the same file name used on the other computer. Choose OK. Works begins transmitting the file. (You don't see the file on-screen.) During the transfer, Works displays a message indicating the status of the transfer.

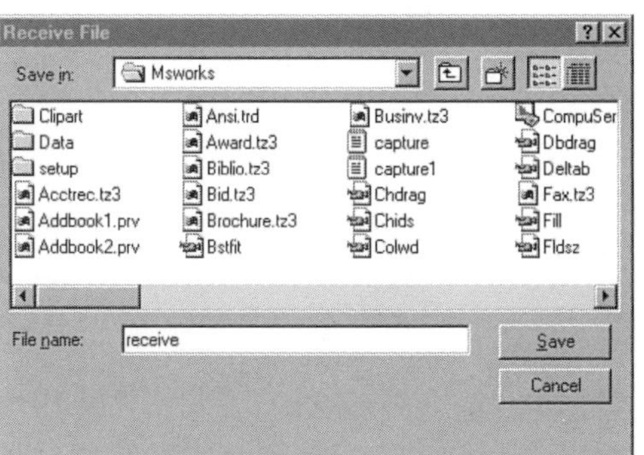

Fig. 29.19
Receive a file from the remote computer or service in the Receive File dialog box.

At any point during the transfer, you can cancel receiving a file by pressing Esc. Works displays a message asking you to confirm that you want to cancel the transmission. Choose OK.

Ending a Communications Session

The final step in your communications session involves disconnecting. After you have finished exploring services, receiving files, or sending messages, you disconnect by choosing Phone, Hang Up or clicking the Hangup button on the toolbar. If you are connected to an online service or BBS, you should first log off before hanging up. Works displays a dialog box asking whether you want to disconnect (see fig. 29.20). Click Yes to hang up, or Cancel to keep your connection and continue working with the remote computer or service.

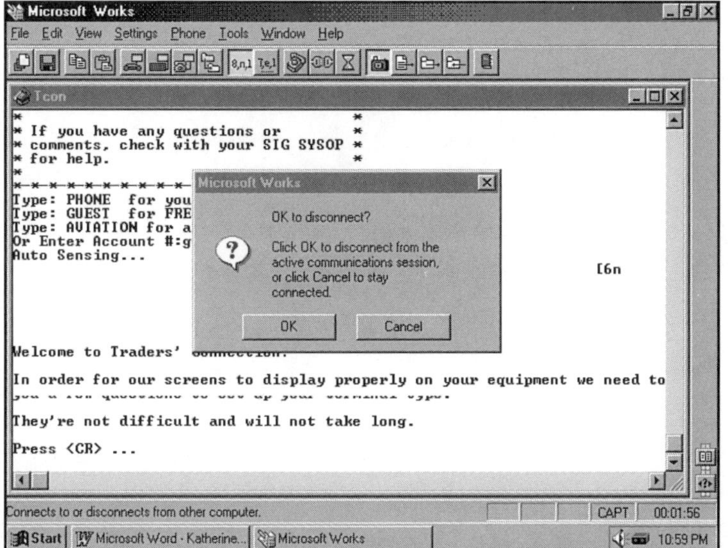

Fig. 29.20
Works asks whether you want to disconnect before the connection is terminated.

Appendix

Works for Windows Functions

This appendix lists all the functions included in Microsoft Works for Windows. The functions appear in alphabetical order, showing the function name, syntax, usage, and an example. Each function consists of a function name and *arguments*. The arguments represent the numbers or text on which the function operates. The *syntax* refers to the order in which the arguments must appear and the placement of parentheses. The PMT function shown below illustrates the elements of a typical function and its syntax. Enter each function exactly as the syntax shows.

=PMT(Principal,Rate,Term)

1. The equal sign signifies the beginning of a formula.
2. PMT is the function name.
3. Principal, Rate, Term are three separate arguments.
4. Parentheses enclose the arguments.

ABS

Syntax: `ABS(x)`

Usage: Returns the absolute value of x, which can be a value or a reference to a cell that contains a number.

Example: `=ABS(12)` returns `12`.

ACOS

Syntax: `ACOS(x)`

Usage: Returns the arccosine of x, which is the angle whose cosine is x. The value of ACOS is returned in radians. x must be in the range from –1 through 1.

Example: `=ACOS(.05)` returns `1.6208172`.

AND

Syntax: `AND(logical1,logical2,…)`

Usage: This function returns 1 (TRUE) if all arguments (logical1, logical2, and so on) are true and returns 0 (FALSE) if one or more arguments are false. You can include up to 14 arguments (logical1...logical14). Arguments themselves must be logical values or must reference cells that contain logical values.

Example: The function `=AND(3*5=15, 20/4=5)` returns TRUE because both arguments are true.

ASIN

Syntax: `ASIN(x)`

Usage: Returns the arcsine of x, which is the angle whose sine is x. The value of ASIN is returned in radians. x must range from –1 through 1.

Example: `=ASIN(-.3)*180/PI()` returns –30 degrees.

ATAN

Syntax: `ATAN(x)`

Usage: Returns the arctangent of x, which is the angle whose tangent is x. The value of ATAN is returned in radians.

Example: `=ATAN(3)*180/PI()` returns `71.565051` degrees.

ATAN2

Syntax: `ATAN2(x coordinate,y coordinate)`

Usage: This function computes the angle for which the tangent is defined by the x and y coordinates. One of the arguments must be a number other than zero.

Example: `=ATAN2(A5,B5)` where A5 is 1.87092 and B5 is 1.24531, returns the value of `0.5872733`.

AVG

Syntax: `AVG(RangeReference0,RangeReference1,...)`

Usage: Calculates the average of the values specified in RangeReference. The value of RangeReference can be a number, a cell reference, a range reference, or a formula. Blank cells in a cell reference are considered to be 0. Blank cells in a range reference are ignored, and all text references are treated as 0.

Example: `=AVG(20,31,A5:A8)` where cells A5:A8 contain the values 12, 4, 22, and 32 returns the value `20.166667`.

CHOOSE

Syntax: `CHOOSE(Choice,Option0,Option1,...)`

Usage: This function uses the value of *Choice* to select an Option from the list of arguments. For example, if Choice is 2, CHOOSE returns the value of the third argument, *Option2*. If Choice is 0 or is greater than the number of options available in the list of arguments, the function returns the error value ERR.

Example: `=CHOOSE(C20,12,24,19)` returns the value of `24` if C20 holds the value of 1.

COLS

Syntax: `COLS(RangeReference)`

Usage: Calculates the number of columns within RangeReference.

Example: If the range B12:G25 is named Sales, the function `=COLS(Sales)` returns `6`.

COS

Syntax: `COS(x)`

Usage: This function calculates the cosine of x when x is an angle measured in radians.

Example: `=COS(0.785)` returns `0.7073883`.

COUNT

Syntax: `COUNT(RangeReference0,RangeReference1,...)`

Usage: Counts the number of cells in RangeReference. COUNT adds 1 for every cell in RangeReference that holds a number, formula, text, ERR, and N/A. RangeReference can be numbers, cell references, range references, or formulas. When using range references, blank cells are ignored. With cell references, blank cells add 1 to the count.

Example: When the values in cells F4:F8 are 1, 5, (blank), (blank), and 4, the function `=COUNT(F4:F8)` returns `3`.

CTERM

Syntax: `CTERM(Rate,FutureValue,PresentValue)`

Usage: Calculates the number of periods required for an initial investment (PresentValue) earning a fixed rate per compounding period (Rate) to grow to a future value (FutureValue). The Rate is the interest rate for a single compounding period, so if the interest rate is nine percent annually, divide the rate by 12 to find the monthly rate.

Example: You put $12,000 into an investment account that has an annual interest rate of nine percent and interest is compounded monthly. Use this function to determine how long it takes to double your investment.

`=CTERM(9.0%/12,24000,12000)` returns `92.76` periods (almost eight years).

DATE

Syntax: `DATE(Year,Month,Day)`

Usage: This function calculates the serial number for the day specified by the Year, Month, and Day arguments. Serial numbers are integers ranging from 1 to 65534 that represent all the dates from January 1, 1900 to June 3, 2079.

The value for Year must be a number ranging from 0 (1900) to 179 (2079), the value for Month must be a number from 1 to 12, and the number for Day must be a number from 1 to 31. If you enter a value outside of these ranges, DATE adjusts the value to the correct date. If Year, Month, and Day are not a valid date in the Works range of dates, ERR is returned.

Example: `=DATE(93,3,28)` returns the serial number `34056` representing the date March 28, 1993.

DAY

Syntax: `DAY(DateNumber)`

Usage: This function returns the day of the date when DateNumber is a serial number or is an integer ranging from 1 to 31.

Example: `=DAY(34056)` returns `28`, the day of the date represented by the serial number 34056.

DDB

Syntax: `DDB(Cost,Salvage,Life,Period)`

Usage: Calculates the depreciation amount in a specific period using the double-declining balance method. Cost is the amount paid for the asset; Salvage is the value of the asset at the end of its working life. Life refers to the number of time periods (usually years) that you intend to use the asset. Period is the specific time period for which you want to find the depreciation amount.

Example: If you purchase capital equipment for $25,000 that has a usable life of 10 years and a salvage value of $3,000, the function returns $2,048, the depreciation amount for the fifth year, based on the function `=DDB(25000,3000,10,5)`.

ERR

Syntax: `ERR()`

Usage: Returns the error value ERR. Use this function to force a cell to display ERR whenever a specified condition exists or to disallow unacceptable values in a cell.

Example: If you want cell C12 to contain values higher than zero, you could use the function `=(IF(C12<=0,ERR(),C12))` to display ERR if the value in C12 is 0 or less. If the value is greater than zero, the function displays the actual value in C12.

EXACT

Syntax: `EXACT(TextValue0,TextValue1)`

Usage: This function compares two text values and returns 1 (TRUE) if TextValue0 and TextValue1 are exact matches and 0 (FALSE) if they are not exact matches. The function is case-sensitive; for example, Sales and SALES are not exact matches.

Example: If cell C3 contains Sales and cell D12 contains SALES, the function `=EXACT(C3,D12)` returns `0` (FALSE).

EXP

Syntax: `EXP(x)`

Usage: Returns e raised to the power of x (where e is 2.718282...). Use the exponentiation operator (^) to compute the powers of other bases. EXP is the inverse of LN.

Example: `=EXP(3)` returns `20.085537`.

FALSE

Syntax: `FALSE()`

Usage: The FALSE ( ) function returns the value 0, the Boolean value for false. Use this function to check for errors.

Example: The function `FALSE()` returns `0`.

FIND

Syntax: `FIND(FindText,SearchText,Offset)`

Example: Use this function to find one string of text in another. The function returns the number of the character at which the FindText begins. This function differentiates between uppercase and lowercase letters.

The FindText argument is the text you want to find; SearchText is the text that contains the text you want to find. Both the FindText and SearchText arguments can be a cell reference that contains text, or the text itself, enclosed in quotation marks. The Offset argument is the character where you want to start the search. To start at the beginning, make this argument 0.

Example: If cell B3 contains the value "Profit and Loss Statement" the function `=FIND("Loss",B3,0)` returns `11`.

FV

Syntax: `FV(Payment,Rate,Term)`

Usage: Calculates the future value of an ordinary annuity of equal payments, earning a fixed interest rate per term, compounded over several terms. The assumption is that the first payment occurs at the end of the first period.

Example: If you deposit $2,000 in your savings account every year for 8 years, how much money is in the account at the end of 8 years if the interest rate of 8.55 is compounded annually?

`=FV(2000,8.55%,8)` returns `21700.499`, or $21,700.50.

HLOOKUP

Syntax: `HLOOKUP(LookupValue,RangeReference,RowNumber)`

Usage: The function HLOOKUP (horizontal lookup) searches the top row of the specified RangeReference until it finds the number that matches LookupValue. It then moves down that column by the number of rows specified in the RowNumber argument. The entry found in that cell is the value returned.

The error value ERR is displayed if RowNumber is negative or is greater than or equal to the number of rows in RangeReference.

Example: `=HLOOKUP(36.1,B3:E19,3)`.

HOUR

Syntax: `HOUR(TimeNumber)`

Usage: Returns the number for the hour of the time represented by TimeNumber. HOUR returns an integer from 0 through 23. TimeNumber can be a number like 8:21:33 or 0.3483, the serial number for the same time.

Example: `=HOUR('8:21:33')` returns `8`.

IF

Syntax: `IF(Condition,ValueIfTrue,ValueIfFalse)`

Usage: This function determines whether the value specified in Condition is true or false and then returns either ValueIfTrue or ValueIfFalse.

Example: If C24 contains the value $123.88, and D24 contains the value $329.99, the function `=IF(C24>D24,C24,0)` returns `0` because the condition is false.

INDEX

Syntax: `INDEX(RangeReference,Column,Row)`

Usage: This function finds the data contained in a specified cell. In the RangeReference, the function returns the value in the cell at the intersection of the specified Column and Row.

If either Column or Row is negative or is greater than or equal to the number of rows or columns in RangeReference, Works returns the error value ERR.

Example: If you enter **INDEX(C2:F5,3,2)**, Works returns the value in cell F4 (three columns to the right of C2 and two rows below C2).

INT

Syntax: `INT(x)`

Usage: This function returns the integer for x by deleting the digits to the right of the decimal point.

Example: `=INT(32.87891)` returns `32`.

IRR

Syntax: `IRR(Guess,RangeReference)`

Usage: This function finds the internal rate of return for the cash flow series specified in RangeReference. The internal rate of return is the interest rate received for an investment of payments and received income by you. The Guess argument is the interest rate you guess to be close to the interest rate found by the IRR function.

Example: Suppose you put $1,000 into an investment and expect your income from the investment in years 2 through 6 to be $500, $600, $700, –$1,000, and $400. (These figures appear in cells A5:F5, with cell A5 showing –$1,000 because that is the amount you invested.) You expect the yield over the 6 years to be about 12 percent. Using these figures, the IRR function below finds the actual internal rate of return to be 0.1309899, or 13.10 percent.

`=IRR(.12,A5:F5)` returns `0.1309899`.

ISERR

Syntax: `ISERR(x)`

Usage: This function allows you to test if the value in the referenced cell is the error value ERR. The function returns the logical value 1 (TRUE) if x is the error value ERR; otherwise, the function returns the logical value 0 (FALSE).

Example: If C19 contains the error value ERR, the function `=ISERR(C19)` returns `1`.

ISNA

Syntax: `ISNA(x)`

Usage: This function allows you to test if a value in the referenced cell is the error value `N/A`. The function returns the logical value 1 (TRUE) if x is the value `N/A`; otherwise, the function returns the logical value 0 (FALSE).

Example: If C19 contains the value N/A, the function `=ISNA(C19)` returns `1`.

LEFT

Syntax: `LEFT(TextValue,Length)`

Usage: This function returns the left-most character or characters in the text string specified as TextValue. Length specifies how many characters you want the function to return.

Example: If cell C21 holds the text value "Figures based on 1992 data," the function `=LEFT(C21,3)` returns `Fig`.

LENGTH

Syntax: LENGTH(TextValue)

Usage: This function returns the number of characters in the string of text specified in the TextValue argument.

Example: If cell C21 holds the text value "Figures based on 1992 data," the function =LENGTH(C21) returns 26.

LN

Syntax: LN(x)

Usage: This function returns the natural logarithm of x. Natural logarithms are based on the mathematical constant e, 2.71828.... The value for x must be a positive integer.

Example: =LN(85) returns 4.4426513.

LOG

Syntax: LOG(x)

Usage: The LOG function returns the base 10 logarithm of x, which must be a positive number.

Example: =LOG(25) returns 1.39794.

LOWER

Syntax: LOWER(TextValue)

Usage: This function converts all uppercase letters in TextValue to lowercase.

Example: If cell B3 contains the text value "Sales Forecast," the function =LOWER(B3) returns sales forecast.

MAX

Syntax: MAX(RangeReference0,RangeReference1,...)

Usage: The MAX function returns the largest number contained in RangeReference. The RangeReference may be numbers, cell references, range references, or formulas. When RangeReference refers to a single cell, a blank cell is treated as 0. When RangeReference refers to a range, blank cells are ignored. In each type of reference, text is treated as 0.

Example: With values of 23, 26, 98, 87, and 38 in cells D12 through D16, the function =MAX(D12:D16) returns 98.

MID

Syntax: `MID(TextValue,Offset,Length)`

Usage: The MID function returns a specific number of characters (Length) from a text string (TextValue), starting with the number you specify (Offset).

Example: If cell B2 contains the value Quarterly Report, the function `=MID(B2,10,6)` returns `Report`.

MIN

Syntax: `MIN(RangeReference0,RangeReference1,…)`

Usage: The MIN function returns the smallest number contained in RangeReference. The RangeReference arguments can be numbers, cell references, range references, or formulas. In cell references, blank cells are treated as 0. In range references, blank cells are ignored. In each type of reference, text is treated as 0.

Example: With values of 23, 26, 98, 87, and 38 in cells D12 through D16, the function `=MIN(D12:D16)` returns `23`.

MINUTE

Syntax: `MINUTE(TimeNumber)`

Usage: This function returns the number for the minute represented by TimeNumber, an integer ranging from 0 through 59. TimeNumber can be a number like 8:21:33 or 0.3483, the serial number for the same time.

Example: `=MINUTE('12:32:33')` returns `32`.

MOD

Syntax: `MOD(Numerator,Denominator)`

Usage: This function returns the remainder (modulus) of after the numerator is divided by the denominator. MOD returns an ERR value if Denominator is equal to 0.

Example: `=MOD(13,3)` returns `1`.

MONTH

Syntax: `MONTH(DateNumber)`

Usage: Returns the number for the month represented by DateNumber. The DateNumber is a serial number, an integer ranging from 1 to 31, or a cell reference.

Example: =MONTH(34056) returns 3, the month of the date represented by the serial number 34056.

N

Syntax: N(RangeReference)

Usage: This function returns the entry in the first cell in RangeReference as a value. If the cell contains text, the value 0 (zero) is returned.

Example: If cells C3:E3 contain the entries =D3-E3, 300, and 100, the function =N(C3:E3) returns 200.

NA

Syntax: NA()

Usage: Returns the numeric value of N/A, which indicates that information is not available. Use NA( ) as a placeholder for empty cells to avoid including empty cells in calculations.

Example: NA()

NOT

Syntax: NOT(Logical)

Usage: This function reverses the value of the argument you specify in Logical. The Logical argument is a value or expression that can be evaluated as TRUE or FALSE. If FALSE, NOT returns 1 for TRUE. If TRUE, NOT returns 0 for FALSE.

Example: =NOT(3*5=15) returns 0 (FALSE).

NOW

Syntax: NOW()

Usage: The NOW function returns the date and time number for the current date and time. This value is updated each time the spreadsheet is recalculated. The integer portion of NOW( ) is the date number, and the decimal fraction is the time number.

Use the Date or Time format in the Number dialog box to display the actual date or time. (The Number dialog box appears when you choose Format, Number.)

Example: If the current date is November 8, 1992 and the current time is 5:20 p.m., the function =NOW() returns 33915.7238.

NPV

Syntax: `NPV(Rate,RangeReference)`

Usage: The NPV function returns the net present value of an investment based on a series of cash flows (RangeReference) and a discount rate (Rate). The net present value of an investment is the value today of a series of payments you make in the future (negative values) and income you receive in the future (positive values). The Rate argument is the rate of discount over the length of one period. The RangeReference argument must refer to a single cell or to a portion of a single row or column; the range cannot be more than one row or column.

The NPV function operates on the assumption that payments occur at the end of periods of equal length. If the payments occur at the beginning of the period, you must modify the formula as shown in the examples below.

Example: Suppose you are considering an investment where you pay $8,000 and receive income of $3,000, $4,000, and $5,000 in subsequent years. The values –8000 (negative because you are paying this amount), 3000, 4000, and 5000 appear in cells D10:G10. You assume a discount rate of 10 percent per year.

If the payment of $8,000 occurs at the end of the first period, the function `=NPV(10%,D10:G10)` returns the result of `1626.9381`, or $1,626.94, the net present value of the investment.

Suppose that the payment of the $8,000 occurs at the beginning rather than the end of the first period, and you expect to receive income of $3,000, $4,000, and $5,000 in years 1, 2, and 3. You don't include the –8,000 in the RangeReference because it occurs at the beginning of the first period. Instead, you add the –8000 to the calculation. In this case, the function `=NPV(10%,E10:G10)+D10` returns `1789.6319`, or $1,789.63, the net present value of the investment.

OR

Syntax: `OR(logical0,logical1,…)`

Usage: The OR function returns 1 (TRUE) if one or more of the arguments is true and returns 0 (FALSE) if all of the arguments are false.

Example: `=OR(1+1=1,1+2=2,1+3=2)` returns `0` for FALSE because all arguments are false.

PI

Syntax: `PI()`

Usage: Returns the number 3.14159..., an approximation of the mathematical constant pi.

Example: When you use PI( ) in a formula, Works inserts 3.14159... in the formula. The formula `=1+PI()` returns `4.14159`.

PMT

Syntax: `PMT(Principal,Rate,Term)`

Usage: The PMT function calculates the periodic payment for a loan or an investment. The Principal is the amount of the loan or investment; the Rate is the fixed interest rate that compounds over a given Term. In the PMT function, Works assumes that payments occur at the end of equal periods.

Example: If you want to borrow $15,000 to pay for a car over a 48-month period at 9 percent interest per year, the function `=PMT(15000,9%/12,48)` returns `373.27564`, or $373.28, the amount of the monthly payment. Note that the 9 percent interest rate is divided by 12 because the interest is compounded monthly.

PROPER

Syntax: `PROPER(TextValue)`

Usage: This function capitalizes the first letter in a text string. When the text string contains characters other than letters (such as a comma or blank space), the letter that follows the character is also capitalized.

Example: `=PROPER("foreign sales by quarter")` returns `Foreign Sales By Quarter`.

PV

Syntax: `PV(Payment,Rate,Term)`

Usage: The PV function returns the present value of an annuity of equal payments that earns a fixed interest Rate compounding over the term of the annuity. Works assumes that the first payment is made at the end of the first period.

Example: Suppose you were to receive $10,000 every year for the next five years. You expect the annual inflation rate over the next five years to be 9 percent. The function `=PV(10000,9%,5)` returns `38896.513`, or $38,896.51, the present value of the $50,000 annuity.

RAND

Syntax: `RAND()`

Usage: This function returns a random number in the range from 0 to 1 but not including 1. A random number is generated every time the spreadsheet is recalculated.

Example: `=RAND()`

RATE

Syntax: `RATE(FutureValue,PresentValue,Term)`

Usage: The RATE function calculates the fixed interest rate per compounding period needed for an investment at present value to grow to a future value over the term.

Example: You purchase a business property for $350,000 and expect to sell it for $750,000 after 5 years. The annual rate of return for this investment is `.1646586`, or 16.47 percent based on the formula `=RATE(750000,350000,5)`.

REPEAT

Syntax: `REPEAT(TextValue,Count)`

Usage: Use the REPEAT function to repeat a text string the number of times you specify.

Example: If cell C1 contains the value "Important!" the function `=REPEAT(C1,5)` returns `Important! Important! Important! Important! Important!`.

REPLACE

Syntax: `REPLACE(OldText,Offset,Length,NewText)`

Usage: The REPLACE function replaces a text string you specify (OldText) with a new text string (NewText). You specify the number of characters to replace (Length) and the character at which to begin replacing text (Offset). The first character in OldText is zero. Enclose OldText and NewText arguments in quotation marks.

Example: The function `=REPLACE("1,2,3,4,5,6,7,8",1,13,"…")` returns `1…8`.

RIGHT

Syntax: `RIGHT(TextValue,Length)`

Usage: The RIGHT function returns the rightmost character in the specified TextValue. Use the Length argument to specify how many characters to return.

Example: If cell F19 contains the value "Based on 1992 Data," the function `=RIGHT(F19,4)` returns the value `Data`.

ROUND

Syntax: `ROUND(x,NumberOfPlaces)`

Usage: This function rounds x to the specified number of places either to the left or right of the decimal point. When NumberOfPlaces is a positive number, x is rounded to the right of the decimal point. When NumberOfPlaces is a negative number, x is rounded to the left of the decimal point. When NumberOfPlaces is zero, x is rounded to the nearest integer. NumberOfPlaces can range from –14 to 14.

Example: `=ROUND(36312.12,-3)` returns `36000`.

ROWS

Syntax: `ROWS(RangeReference)`

Usage: Returns the number of rows in RangeReference.

Example: `=ROWS(C9:F20)` returns `12`.

S

Syntax: `S(RangeReference)`

Usage: The S function returns the text entry in the first cell in the specified cell range. If the first cell is blank, Works returns an empty cell.

Example: If cells A1:B4 contain the strings "First," "Second," "Third," and "Fourth," the function `=S(A1:B4)` returns `First`.

SECOND

Syntax: `SECOND(TimeNumber)`

Usage: This function returns the number for the seconds represented in TimeNumber, an integer ranging from 0 through 59. TimeNumber can be a number like 8:21:33 or 0.3483, the serial number for the same time.

Example: `=SECOND('09:32:14')` returns `14`.

SIN

Syntax: `SIN(x)`

Usage: Returns the sine of the angle of x when x is expressed in radians. When x is expressed in degrees, multiply it by PI( )/180.

Example: `SIN(45*PI()/180)` returns `0.7071068`.

SLN

Syntax: `SLN(Cost,Salvage,Life)`

Usage: The SLN function uses the straight-line depreciation method to calculate the amount of depreciation for one period. Cost is the amount you paid for an asset; Salvage is the amount you expect to obtain when you sell the asset at the end of its life; Life is the number of periods you expect to use the asset.

Example: A computer system that costs $325,000 is expected to have a useful life of 8 years and a salvage value of $20,000. The depreciation for one year is `38125`, or $38,125 based on the function `=SLN(325000,20000,8)`.

SQRT

Syntax: `SQRT(x)`

Usage: Returns the square root of x. If x is negative, the function returns the error value ERR.

Example: `=SQRT(144)` returns `12`.

STD

Syntax: `STD(RangeReference0,RangeReference1,…)`

Usage: The STD function returns an estimate for the standard deviation of a population based on the numbers supplied as RangeReference. The values in RangeReference may be numbers, cell references, range references, or formulas. Blank cells are ignored in range references. Blank cells are treated as 0 in cell references. Text is treated as 0 in any of the references.

Example: If cells B3:B8 contain the values 1321, 1431, 1992, 1762, 1283, and 1298 the formula `STD(B3:B8)` returns the standard deviation of `268.99`.

STRING

Syntax: `STRING(x,DecimalPlaces)`

Usage: The STRING function converts the value of x to a text entry and adds the number of decimal places you specify.

Example: If cell D29 contains the value 492, the function `=STRING(D29,2)` returns `492.00`.

SUM

Syntax: `SUM(RangeReference0,RangeReference1,…)`

Usage: The SUM function calculates the total of all values in RangeReference. The values in RangeReference may be numbers, cell references, range references, or formulas. Blank cells are ignored in range references. Blank cells are treated as 0 in cell references.

Example: When the cells B2, D3, D4, and D5 contain the values 10, 20, 30, and 40, respectively, the function `=SUM(B2,D3:D5)` returns `100`.

SYD

Syntax: `SYD(Cost,Salvage,Life,Period)`

Usage: The SYD function calculates depreciation for a specific period using the sum-of-the-year's-digits depreciation method. Cost is the amount you paid for the asset, Salvage is the amount you expect to get when you sell the asset at the end of its life, Life is the number of periods (usually measured in years) you expect to use the asset, and Period is the period of time for which you want to find the depreciation amount.

Example: A computer system that costs $325,000 is expected to have a useful life of 8 years and a salvage value of $20,000. The depreciation for year 8 is `8472.222222`, or $8,472.22 based on the function `=SYD(325000,20000,8,8)`.

TAN

Syntax: `TAN(x)`

Usage: Returns the tangent of the angle of x when x is expressed in radians. When x is expressed in degrees, multiply it by PI( )/180.

Example: `=TAN(45*PI()/180)` returns `1`.

TERM

Syntax: `TERM(Payment,Rate,FutureValue)`

Usage: The TERM function calculates the number of compounding periods necessary for a series of equal payments earning a fixed interest rate per period to grow to a future value.

Example: You contribute $150 each month to your child's college fund account. You earn 11 3/4 percent interest, compounded monthly. To find out how long it takes to save $15,000 use the function `=TERM(150,11.75%/12,15000)`, which returns `70.06087355`, or 70.06 months, approximately 5.8 years.

TIME

Syntax: `TIME(Hour,Minute,Second)`

Usage: The TIME function returns a serial number for the time specified by the Hour, Minute, and Second arguments. Hour is a number ranging from 0 through 23. Minute and Second are numbers ranging from 0 through 59. If either Minute or Second is outside the specified range of 0 through 59, TIME adjusts the number to the correct time.

Example: `=TIME(8,45,15)` returns `.3647569`, the serial number for 8:45:15 a.m.

TRIM

Syntax: `TRIM(TextValue)`

Usage: This function removes all spaces from the specified text entry except for single spaces between words.

Example: If cell B3 contains the title "1993   Quarterly   Forecast," the function `=TRIM(B3)` returns `1993 Quarterly Forecast`.

TRUE

Syntax: `TRUE()`

Usage: The TRUE function returns the logical value 1 (TRUE). Use TRUE( ) rather than 1 to create more readable logical formulas.

Example: If cell C3 holds the value 45, the function `=IF(45-10=35,TRUE(),FALSE())` returns `1`.

UPPER

Syntax: `UPPER(TextValue)`

Usage: This function converts all lowercase letters in TextValue to uppercase.

Example: If cell B3 contains the text value "sales forecast," the function `=UPPER(B3)` returns the value `SALES FORECAST`.

VALUE

Syntax: `VALUE(TextValue)`

Usage: The VALUE function converts a number entered as a text entry into a value. A number entry must be a value in order to be used in mathematical calculations.

Example: If cell D19 contains the time 8:55 a.m. entered as text, the function `=VALUE(D19)` converts the entry to the value `0.3715278`, the serial number for the time of 8:55 a.m.

VAR

Syntax: `VAR(RangeReference0,RangeReference1,...)`

Usage: The VAR function calculates the variance among the numbers specified in RangeReference. RangeReference may be numbers, range references, cell references, or formulas. Blank cells are ignored in range references. Blank cells are treated as 0 in cell references. Text is always treated as 0.

Example: If cells B3:B8 contain the values 1200, 1220, 1201, 1218, 1230, and 1211, the formula `VAR(B3:B8)` returns `113.22`.

VLOOKUP

Syntax: `VLOOKUP(LookupValue,RangeReference,ColumnNumber)`

Usage: VLOOKUP searches the leftmost column in RangeReference until it finds the number that matches LookupValue. VLOOKUP then moves across that row by the number of columns specified in the ColumnNumber argument. The entry found in that cell is the value returned.

The error value ERR is displayed if ColumnNumber is negative or is greater than or equal to the number of columns in RangeReference.

Example: `=VLOOKUP(1992,B3:F19,3)`

YEAR

Syntax: `YEAR(DateNumber)`

Usage: Returns the number for the year represented by DateNumber. The DateNumber is a serial number, an integer ranging from 1 to 31, or a cell reference.

Example: `=YEAR(34056)` returns `93`, the year of the date represented by the serial number 34056. ❖

Index

Symbols

A

D

E

F

G

H

I-J

M

N

O

P-Q

R

S

T

U

X-Z

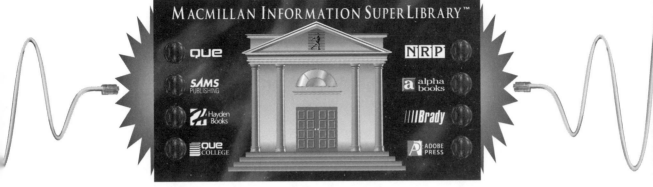

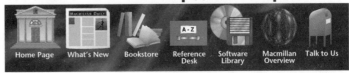

Complete and Return this Card for a *FREE* Computer Book Catalog

Thank you for purchasing this book! You have purchased a superior computer book written expressly for your needs. To continue to provide the kind of up-to-date, pertinent coverage you've come to expect from us, we need to hear from you. Please take a minute to complete and return this self-addressed, postage-paid form. In return, we'll send you a free catalog of all our computer books on topics ranging from word processing to programming and the internet.

Mr. ☐ Mrs. ☐ Ms. ☐ Dr. ☐

Name (first) ☐☐☐☐☐☐☐☐☐☐☐ (M.I.) ☐ (last) ☐☐☐☐☐☐☐☐☐☐☐☐☐☐☐

Address ☐☐☐☐☐☐☐☐☐☐☐☐☐☐☐☐☐☐☐☐☐☐☐☐☐☐☐☐☐☐☐☐☐☐☐

☐☐☐☐☐☐☐☐☐☐☐☐☐☐☐☐☐☐☐☐☐☐☐☐☐☐☐☐☐☐☐☐☐☐☐

City ☐☐☐☐☐☐☐☐☐☐☐☐☐☐☐ State ☐☐ Zip ☐☐☐☐☐ ☐☐☐☐

Phone ☐☐☐ ☐☐☐ ☐☐☐☐ Fax ☐☐☐ ☐☐☐ ☐☐☐☐

Company Name ☐☐☐☐☐☐☐☐☐☐☐☐☐☐☐☐☐☐☐☐☐☐☐☐☐☐☐☐☐☐☐☐☐☐

E-mail address ☐☐☐☐☐☐☐☐☐☐☐☐☐☐☐☐☐☐☐☐☐☐☐☐☐☐☐☐☐☐☐☐☐☐

1. Please check at least (3) influencing factors for purchasing this book.

- Front or back cover information on book .... ☐
- Special approach to the content .... ☐
- Completeness of content .... ☐
- Author's reputation .... ☐
- Publisher's reputation .... ☐
- Book cover design or layout .... ☐
- Index or table of contents of book .... ☐
- Price of book .... ☐
- Special effects, graphics, illustrations .... ☐
- Other (Please specify): ________________ ☐

2. How did you first learn about this book?

- Saw in Macmillan Computer Publishing catalog .... ☐
- Recommended by store personnel .... ☐
- Saw the book on bookshelf at store .... ☐
- Recommended by a friend .... ☐
- Received advertisement in the mail .... ☐
- Saw an advertisement in: ________________ ☐
- Read book review in: ________________ ☐
- Other (Please specify): ________________ ☐

3. How many computer books have you purchased in the last six months?

- This book only .... ☐
- 3 to 5 books .... ☐
- 2 books .... ☐
- More than 5 .... ☐

4. Where did you purchase this book?

- Bookstore .... ☐
- Computer Store .... ☐
- Consumer Electronics Store .... ☐
- Department Store .... ☐
- Office Club .... ☐
- Warehouse Club .... ☐
- Mail Order .... ☐
- Direct from Publisher .... ☐
- Internet site .... ☐
- Other (Please specify): ________________ ☐

5. How long have you been using a computer?

- ☐ Less than 6 months
- ☐ 6 months to a year
- ☐ 1 to 3 years
- ☐ More than 3 years

6. What is your level of experience with personal computers and with the subject of this book?

	With PCs	With subject of book
New	☐	☐
Casual	☐	☐
Accomplished	☐	☐
Expert	☐	☐

Source Code ISBN:

. Which of the following best describes your job title?

- Administrative Assistant ☐
- Coordinator ☐
- Manager/Supervisor ☐
- Director ☐
- Vice President ☐
- President/CEO/COO ☐
- Lawyer/Doctor/Medical Professional ☐
- Teacher/Educator/Trainer ☐
- Engineer/Technician ☐
- Consultant ☐
- Not employed/Student/Retired ☐
- Other (Please specify): ________________ ☐

8. Which of the following best describes the area of the company your job title falls under?

- Accounting ☐
- Engineering ☐
- Manufacturing ☐
- Operations ☐
- Marketing ☐
- Sales ☐
- Other (Please specify): ________________ ☐

9. What is your age?

- Under 20 ☐
- 21-29 ☐
- 30-39 ☐
- 40-49 ☐
- 50-59 ☐
- 60-over ☐

10. Are you:

- Male ☐
- Female ☐

11. Which computer publications do you read regularly? (Please list)

____

____

____

____

____

____

____

____

Comments: ____

____

____

Fold here and scotch-tape to mail.

BUSINESS REPLY MAIL

FIRST-CLASS MAIL PERMIT NO. 9918 INDIANAPOLIS IN

POSTAGE WILL BE PAID BY THE ADDRESSEE

ATTN MARKETING
MACMILLAN COMPUTER PUBLISHING
MACMILLAN PUBLISHING USA
201 W 103RD ST
INDIANAPOLIS IN 46209-9042

ON
NECE
IF MAIL
IN THE
UNITED STATE